BUDDHIST SAINTS IN INDIA

BUDDHIST SAINTS IN INDIA

A Study in Buddhist Values and Orientations

REGINALD A. RAY

OXFORD UNIVERSITY PRESS
New York Oxford

Oxford University Press

Oxford New York
Athens Auckland Bangkok Bogotá Buenos Aires Calcutta
Cape Town Chennai Dar es Salaam Delhi Florence Hong Kong Istanbul
Karachi Kuala Lumpur Madrid Melbourne Mexico City Mumbai
Nairobi Paris São Paulo Singapore Taipei Tokyo Toronto Warsaw

and associated companies in
Berlin Ibadan

First published in 1994 by Oxford University Press, Inc.
198 Madison Avenue, New York, New York 10016

First issued as an Oxford University Press paperback, 1999

Library of Congress Cataloging-in-Publication Data
Ray, Reginald A.
Buddhist saints in India : a study in Buddhist values and orientations
Reginald A. Ray.
p. cm. Includes bibliographical references and index.
ISBN 0–19–507202-2
ISBN 0–19–513483-4 (Pbk.)
1. Buddhist saints. I. Title.
BQ4285.R39 1994 294.3'61—dc20 91-27999

3 5 7 9 8 6 4 2

Printed in the United States of America
on acid-free paper

For Lee

PREFACE

Buddhism, it may be said, finds religious authority not only in texts and institutions, but also in enlightened people. Certainly, those understood as realized have occupied an important if not always well defined place within the early and developed tradition. The following pages will argue that the Buddhist saints have in fact a relatively clear role to play within historical Buddhist tradition, and also one that places them much more at the center of the tradition than has been recognized, either by contemporary scholarship or, sometimes, even by Buddhism itself.

This book raises some basic questions: Who are the Buddhist saints? How have they been understood by their devotees and detractors? What have been their characteristic historical roles in India? In response to these questions, this study offers a definition of the Buddhist saint as such and identifies the major types that existed in India. It also acquaints the reader with the legends surrounding some of the more important and representative individual saints. Further, it introduces the field of the Buddhist saints in India, providing a survey of some of the more significant scholarly studies on the subject. Finally, it gives an overview of some of the more important methodological, structural, and historical issues involved in any attempt to understand these figures.

Indian Buddhism exhibits a number of major periods of formation, including those of the genesis of Buddhism itself, and also of later movements such as the Mahāyāna. This study is particularly concerned with those saints who were important—especially but not only—in these formative periods. These were people who, to find freedom, chose to abandon the world and retreat into the wilds, the "forest" (Skt., *araṇya;* P., *arañña*) in the Indian terminology. These "forest saints" are particularly worthy of our attention not only because they represent the first Buddhist saints, but also because classical Buddhism owes so much to them. They stand at the beginning of many of the most important trends within Indian Buddhism. They articulated a specific ideal of complete renunciation of which later Buddhists were well aware and to which they could return at moments of personal and collective crisis. And the normativeness of the ideal they represented was enduring. Even when, in particular times and places, the specific type of the forest saint defined in these pages was modified or substantially transformed, even when the physical wilds themselves were left behind, the terminology and imagery definitive of the early saints of the forest tended to remain in force.

In its historical method, this book is frankly an experiment. Usually when the history of Indian Buddhism is written, settled monasticism provides the central reference point in terms of which that history is cast. This study takes the different starting point of the forest saint. It asks how the history of Indian Buddhism looks when considered from the viewpoint of this contrasting standard. The success of this approach may be judged by the extent to which it can make sense of certain kinds of evidence surrounding the Buddhist saints for which no fully satisfying explanation has yet been offered, and can yield a more coherent view of certain periods of Indian Buddhist history than those now put forward.

Although the central character in the following study is the forest saint, also entering into the discussion are the classical ideals of the settled monastic and the layperson. In this book, however, monastics and the laity are not viewed in their own rights, but are rather seen in terms of what I shall call "forest values and orientations." Sometimes, for reasons to be discussed, the view provided is not particularly complimentary. I ask the reader to remember that critiques of non-forest ideals are sometimes important parts of the expression of forest Buddhism. At the same time, I would be seriously misunderstood if it is thought that I, as the author, am trying to say that these nonforest types are finally reducible to or should be judged strictly in terms of the views of certain forest texts. The primary intention of this study is to clarify the voice of forest Buddhism in India; in so doing, it abstains from trying to do full justice to other Buddhist types. Maybe, in the end, we can best understand Indian Buddhism (or any religion, for that matter) not by arriving at some supposedly balanced and objective overview, but rather by hearing clearly the different voices that have spoken—without being too put off by contrary perspectives or trying too hard to resolve contradictions. The presumption of this, at least, lies at the basis of this study.

We in the West—perhaps I should say in the modern, increasingly secularized world as a whole—live with what is, when taken in the context of world religions, a remarkably devalued idea of human nature. We seem no longer to believe that human nature is perfectible or that genuine saints are possible. Such a view has, obviously, profound impacts on the way people think about and engage in (or do not engage in) the spiritual life. In my view, prevailing interpretations of Buddhism which, as we shall see, reduce the saints to peripheral actors in the tradition represents another, if perhaps more sophisticated, expression of this same modern devaluation. Buddhism may be seen essentially as an ethical system, an elegant philosophy, a practical psychology, a technique for dealing with mental distress, a cultural tradition, or a force of civilization. Rarely, however, is it seen primarily as a tradition that produces and celebrates genuine saints. Yet, at least in my reading, this is finally what Buddhism essentially is, and as long as this fact is not recognized, the specific genius of Buddhism is missed, a genius with the potential to provide a healthy challenge to our increasingly scientific, materialistic, and consumeristic view of human nature.

Boulder, Colorado R. A. R.
September 1993

ACKNOWLEDGMENTS

I would like to express my indebtedness to a number of people who generously assisted me during the course of this study: Frank Reynolds, who read several drafts of the manuscript and provided helpful suggestions and encouragement at various points along the way; John Strong, who saw the manuscript in an early draft several years ago and subsequently acted as an important resource person for me; Jan Nattier, who gave this study a close and critical reading; Charles Prebish, who critiqued sections dealing with *vinaya;* Gregory Schopen for invaluable bibliographic help; Dan Getz, who kindly fielded my Sinological questions; Lama Ugyen Shenpen for help in locating Tibetan material; and John Rockwell and Jules Levinson, each of whom provided helpful suggestions. I want especially to thank Judith Simmer-Brown, my long-standing friend and colleague in the Buddhist Studies Department at Naropa Institute, who read several chapters and engaged in a lively dialogue with me as the ideas of this study took shape. Thanks also to Charles Long for his constant challenge to look "behind the scenes," not only of religion, but of the scholarship that seeks to understand it, and for his specific support of this project; and to the late Mircea Eliade and Joseph M. Kitagawa, for their personal examples and their encouragement. I want to thank my colleagues Bob Lester and David Carrasco of the University of Colorado for their support during the time this study was in progress. My appreciation goes to the Buddhist Studies students of the Naropa Institute and to the students of Religious Studies at the University of Colorado, where many of the ideas of this study were first tested. I also want to thank Virginia Boucher and her staff in the Interlibrary Loan Department at the University of Colorado for an exemplary success rate in procuring the resources needed for my research. Particular thanks go to the National Endowment for the Humanities for providing a fellowship underwriting the initial stages of my research; to Martha Bonzi for underwriting a semester of release time during the writing; to Lex Hixon, member of the Board of Trustees of the Naropa Institute, for generous grants facilitating the completion and publication of this book; and to Naropa Institute and its former presidents Judith Lief and Barbara Dilley for moral support and sabbatical grants, which helped me bring this study to completion. Thanks to L. S. Summer for her assistance; and special appreciation to Beverly Armstrong for her very substantial editorial contributions to this project. I owe a particular debt to the Ven. Chögyam Trungpa (1939–1987), who initially encouraged me to carry through a study of the Buddhist saints, of which this is the first part, and who suggested the initial questions and perspectives that led me into this fascinating territory. Finally, I want to express my appreciation to my wife, Lee, whose insight, warmth, and good sense have provided an important precondition for this study.

CONTENTS

CONVENTIONS

Pāli and Sanskrit terms are romanized following generally accepted practice. Tibetan is rendered according to the Wylie method and Chinese according to the Wade-Giles system. In the interests of stylistic consistency and to avoid creating unnecessary confusion for the nonspecialist reader, the Sanskrit versions of terms are used, generally also including cases where Pāli and Tibetan texts are being discussed. There are a few exceptions, of which the reader will be advised in the notes, in which the preference for Sanskrit is suspended, particularly in sections where Pāli texts alone are treated. In cases where it is important for the reader to know both the Sanskrit and Pāli of a term, both are given at first occurrence. Italicized foreign terms, unless otherwise noted, are Sanskrit.

Sanskrit words now commonly appearing in English are not italicized. The class names of the major types of Buddhist saints discussed in this book are not italicized, as all but one (the pratyekabuddha) now occur in English. Sanskrit terms, whether naturalized or italicized, are given in standard spelling with diacritics. Occasional exceptions are terms and place names that have become familiar in English in a different form (e.g., brahmin as opposed to *brāhmaṇa*).

Sanskrit and Pāli texts are referred to in their standard editions. Tibetan texts are generally referred to according to the Peking edition of the Tibetan *Tripiṭaka,* with exceptions noted. References to Chinese texts are to the Taishô *Tripiṭaka,* exceptions again noted. For the reader's convenience, citations to Buddhist texts are followed by references to European-language translations, where these exist. Original texts are usually cited by volume and page number of the edition (sometimes including line numbers when specific terms are in question), followed by volume and page number of the translation.

This book contains a great number of references, and citations to text editions and translations are particularly frequent. To help the reader keep track of which texts are being referred to, textual citations are generally given in the body of the text rather than in the notes. In order to minimize visual cluttering, I have adopted several conventions. First, I have generally used abbreviations for text titles and also for translators or translations when they are frequently cited. All of these are given in the list of abbreviations. Second, when a text is frequently cited, I have sometimes adopted a reference form for the original that may also be used to locate the passage in translation. This has been possible particularly in the cases of texts entirely or mostly in verse in which verses contain the same numbering in text edition and standard translation (for example, the *Theragāthā, Therīgāthā, Suttanipāta,* and *Dhammapada*). All such reference forms are explained in the notes. Finally, when the same source is cited consecutively in a single paragraph, after the first reference, only the page number is given. Unless otherwise specified, when quoting from Buddhist texts, I follow existing translations. Quotations from French and German works represent my own translations unless otherwise noted.

ABBREVIATIONS

Primary Texts

Aa	*Aśokāvadāna*
Ak	*Abhidharmakośa*
Als	*Avalokita Sūtra*
Als-1	*Avalokana Sūtra*
An	*Aṅguttaranikāya*
An-c	*Aṅguttaranikāya* commentary
Ap	*Apadāna*
Ara	*Aśokarājāvadāna (A yü wang chuan)*
Ars	*Aśokarāja Sūtra (A yü wang ching)*
As	*Avadānaśataka*
Asp	*Aṣṭasāhasrikāprajñāpāramitā Sūtra*
Bbh	*Bodhisattvabhūmi*
Bc	*Buddhacarita*
Bca	*Bodhicaryāvatāra*
Cd	*Cullaniddesa*
Cp	*Candrapradīpa Sūtra (Srs* as quoted in *Ss)*
Csp	*Caturaśītisiddhapravṛtti*
Css	*Cūḷasuññata Sutta*
Cv	*Cullavagga*
Da	*Divyāvadāna*
Dbs	*Daśabhūmika Sūtra*
Dgn	*Dhutaguṇanirdeśa (Vimuktimārgadhutaguṇanirdeśa)*
Dhs	*Dharmasaṃgraha*
Dn	*Dīghanikāya*
Dp	*Dhammapada*
Dp-c	*Dhammapada* commentary *(Dhammapada-aṭṭhakathā)*
Gbs	*Gilgit Buddhist Manuscripts*
Gms	*Gilgit Manuscripts*
Is	*Isigili Sutta*
Iv	*Itivuttaka*
J	*Jātaka*
Jm	*Jātakamālā*
Kbdd	*bka'.babs.bdun.ldan*
Kn	*Khuddakanikāya*
Kp	*Kāśyapaparivarta*

Ks	*Khaggavisāṇa Sutta*
Las	*Laṅkāvatāra Sūtra*
Lv	*Lalitavistara*
Mgb	*Mi.la'i.mgur.'bum*
Mmk	*Mañjuśrīmūlakalpa*
Mn	*Majjhimanikāya*
Mp	*Milindapañha*
Mpds	*Mahāpadāna Sutta*
Mpps	*Mahāprajñāpāramitā Śāstra (Ta chih tu lun)*
Mps	*Mahāparinirvāṇa Sūtra* (without reference to version)
Mps-p	*Mahāparinibbāna Sutta* (Pāli version of *Mps*)
Mrp	*Manorathapūraṇī* (commentary on the *Aṅguttaranikāya*)
Mss	*Mahāsuññata Sutta*
Mv	*Mahāvastu*
Mvy	*Mahāvyutpatti*
Na	*Nandimitrāvadāna* (in Chin.)
Nk	*Nidānakathā*
Pb	*Pratyekabuddhabhūmi*
Pds	*Pradakṣiṇā Sūtra*
Psp	*Pañcaviṃśatisāhasrikāprajñāpāramitā Sūtra*
Rgs	*Ratnaguṇasaṃcayagāthā*
Rk	*Ratnakūṭa Sūtra* (as quoted in *Ss*)
Rps	*Rāṣṭrapālaparipṛcchā Sūtra*
Rps-m	*Rāṣṭrapālaparipṛcchā Sūtra* (minor) (in Tib.)
Rps-s	*Rāṣṭrapālaparipṛcchā Sūtra* (as quoted in *Ss*)
Rr	*Ratnarāśi Sūtra* (as quoted in *Ss*)
Sds	*Śrīmālādevīsiṃhanāda Sūtra*
Sn	*Suttanipāta*
Sn-c	*Suttanipāta* commentary *(Paramattha–jotikā,* II)
Sns	*Saṃdhinirmocana Sūtra*
Sp	*Sāratthappakāsinī*
Sps	*Saddharmapuṇḍarīka Sūtra*
Srs	*Samādhirāja Sūtra*
Ss	*Śikṣāsamuccaya*
Sv	*Sukhāvatīvyūha Sūtra*
Svs	smaller *Sukhāvatīvyūha Sūtra*
Syn	*Saṃyuttanikāya*
Ta	*Theragāthā*
Ta-c	*Paramatthadīpanī* (*Theragāthā-aṭṭhakathā, Theragāthā* commentary)
Tcj	*Tā.ra.nā.tha'i.rgya.gar.chos.'byung*
Ti	*Therīgāthā*
Ti-c	*Paramatthadīpanī* (*Therīgāthā-vaṇṇanā, Therīgāthā* commentary)
Ud	*Udāna*
Up	*Ugraparipṛcchā Sūtra* (as quoted in Ss)
Vcp	*Vajracchedikāprajñāpāramitā Sūtra*
Vmm	*Vimuttimagga*

Vms	*vinaya* of the Mūlasarvāstivādins (Skt., in *Gms*)
Vns	*Vimalakīrtinirdeśa Sūtra*
V-p	*vinaya* (Pāli)
Vsm	Visuddhimagga
V-t	*vinaya* (Tibetan)

Miscellaneous Abbreviations

B.	Beal 1869
BHSD	*Buddhist Hybrid Sanskrit Dictionary* (Edgerton 1970)
BR.	Bendall and Rouse 1922
Bg.	Burlingame 1921
Bp.	Bapat 1964
C.	Cowell 1895–1913
C.R.	C.A.F. Rhys Davids
Cg.	Chang 1962
Chin.	Chinese
Ch.	Chavannes 1910–35
Cz.	Conze 1973b
D.	Derge edition of the Tibetan *Tripiṭaka*
E.	Ensink 1952
ER	*Encyclopedia of Religion* (Eliade 1987)
ERE	*Encyclopedia of Religion and Ethics* (Hastings 1908–26)
Eh.	Ehara, Soma Thera, and Kheminda Thera 1961
Eng.	English
F.	Feer 1891
H.	Horner 1938–66
Hn.	Horner 1954–59
IIR	Indo-Iranian Reprints
Jns.	Jones 1949–56
K.	Kloppenborg 1974
Kn.	Kern 1884
L.	Lamotte 1935
Lm.	Lamotte 1958
LC.	Lévi and Chavannes 1916
N.	Ñyāṇamoli 1976
Nr.	Norman 1985
P.	Pāli
Pk.	Peking edition of the Tibetan *Tripiṭaka*
Pkt.	Prakrit
pr.	prose
Prz.	Przyluski 1923
PTSD	*The Pali Text Society's Pali-English Dictionary* (Rhys Davids and Stede 1921–25)
R.	Rockhill 1884
Rb.	Robinson 1979

RW.	C.A.F. Rhys Davids and Woodward 1917–30
S.	Speyer 1895
SED	*Sanskrit-English Dictionary* (Monier-Williams 1899)
Skt.	Sanskrit
St.	Strong 1983
Sz.	Suzuki 1932
T.	Taishô *Tripiṭaka*
T.R.	T. W. Rhys Davids
TED	*Tibetan-English Dictionary* (Das 1970)
TSD	*Tibetan-Sanskrit Dictionary* (Chandra 1986)
Tib.	Tibetan
W.	Wiltshire 1990
Wd.	Woodward 1935
WH.	Woodward and Hare 1932–36
Wts.	Watters 1904–5

BUDDHIST SAINTS IN INDIA

INTRODUCTION

Modern buddhology has long recognized that Indian Buddhism shows a particular predilection for its saints, who are many and various.[1] In fact, one cannot examine any piece of Buddhist evidence without coming across one or another of these figures, typically associated as they are with the important texts, places, events, lineages, teachings, practices, schools, and movements of Indian Buddhism. The Buddhist saints, at least within the traditional perspective, are an unfailing source of illumination and creativity, and whatever is good may ultimately be traced to them. It is, then, an ironic fact that modern scholarship has paid relatively little attention to the Buddhist saints.

There seem to be two reasons for this neglect: the place of the saints in the Buddhist texts themselves and certain modern scholarly presuppositions concerning the saints. Although in what follows each of these factors will be explored in detail, some initial comment will be useful.

In spite of the fact that Buddhist saints do appear throughout the evidence, in the scenario described by most Indian Buddhist texts—and particularly those best known in the West—the saints simply do not stand out. Rather, they are part of the assumed background and context, in relation to which the history of the dharma (P., *dhamma*) unfolds. Often enough, Buddhist texts focus their attention upon other matters, such as doctrinal exposition, philosophical or psychological analysis, refutation of false theories, clarification of the conventions and procedures of Buddhist monastic life, and so on. When the saints do occupy the foreground, typically they are either seen to have lived in a remote bygone era or understood as significant because they embody a state in the far distant future to which contemporary Buddhists may aspire.

There is another reason why the saints have not been given more attention in modern scholarship, namely, certain attitudes and beliefs that scholarly interpreters take for granted in treating the Indian evidence. Though appearing in the texts, the saints do not impress because scholars of Buddhism have learned to see them as not significant. Or, perhaps more accurately, we have learned to see them as not having specific, important, and recognizable roles within Indian Buddhist history. Even where prominent in the texts, they are not clearly seen, either because we tend to bypass just that evidence where they appear or because, when we do examine such evidence, our questions and interests are elsewhere and we look past them.

This second reason for the saints' invisibility can be illuminated by the psychoanalytic metaphor. When scholars took up the study of Buddhism in the nineteenth century, for specific historical and cultural reasons that I shall touch upon, they typically became enamored of certain trends within Buddhism. In this process, they ''repressed'' the figure of the Buddhist saint. Although visible in much of the evidence that was studied, the saints' full presence was not consciously acknowledged and their kind of Buddhism was, to a large extent, excluded from the conscious viewpoint of early buddhologists. This repression, the effects of which are still visible today, resulted—I shall argue—in a one-sided view of Buddhism, one in which arguments were constructed to work around the saints and make sense of phenomena deriving directly from them by reference to other factors. This scholarly repression, then, calls for a redressing of the balance, for a reintegration into buddhological consciousness of the important and powerful but repressed force represented by the Buddhist saints.

The metaphor is worth extending. It may be argued that the Buddhist saints cannot be studied as a distinct phenomenon because in the evidence they are so tied in with virtually every level and trend of Indian Buddhism. But the web of Indian Buddhism in which they are imbedded is far from seamless. In fact, the precise way in which the Buddhist saints are placed within the various kinds of evidence almost always invites reflection. There are often tensions, oppositions, and contradictions without any immediately obvious explanation. As in psychoanalysis, so in the study of history, an exploration of such anomalies can provide considerable insight into formative processes, and this insight, in turn, can tell us much about subsequent history. The result is a more integrated and satisfying understanding of the phenomena under consideration. It is toward such a reintegrative process that the present study aims.

This kind of reintegration will show, on the one hand, that the saints have had a considerable historical importance, have been central actors within Indian Buddhism during its major periods, and have played crucial if as yet largely unappreciated roles in certain epoch-making events and developments of Indian Buddhist history. On the other hand, it will show that they stand much closer to the core nature and intentions of Indian Buddhism than has been previously recognized. To continue the psychoanalytic metaphor, the reintegration proposed here has considerable implications that will require, among other things, a reorientation of the conscious viewpoint of scholars regarding not only the Buddhist saints but also the way in which we conceptualize the very nature and structure of Buddhism in India.

The present work originated as a consequence of study of the Tantric Buddhist saints or siddhas in which I have been engaged for a number of years. Uncertain as to how, or even whether, this type of saint was connected with more conventional Indian Buddhist ideals, I began to examine the other kinds of Buddhist saints in the Indian evidence. At the beginning of this process, it did not occur to me that it would be possible to arrive at a general type of ''Buddhist saint'' within the Indian evidence, nor did I even frame this issue as being interesting or important. However, as the work proceeded, it gradually became clear that the various types and categories of the Indian Buddhist saints seemed to have some important things in common. Moreover, interestingly enough, I began to see that these continuities had not really been discussed by writers dealing with the saints. More interesting still, it began to appear that what they *did* say about the saints often contradicted what I was actually finding in the texts. It furthermore appeared that much of what was said about the saints was being said, not to shed light upon the saints themselves, but for other reasons. The saints, it appeared, were being used to construct an overall picture of Indian Buddhism, but one in which, ironically, they were given little essential role to play. It seemed to me that the Indian Buddhist saints needed to be examined in their own right. Finally, I suspected that if they were more fully recognized, they might reveal some important things about Indian Buddhist history and the scholarship that seeks to understand it. These—they can only be called initial impressions—formed the original inspiration behind the present study.

It is one thing to have impressions such as these and another to try to explore them in detail, think them through, and write them up both to clarify one's own understanding and to make them comprehensible to others. Among what are undoubtedly many possible approaches, I selected one with the following principal themes.

1. It was obvious that the various figures functioning as realized beings in the Indian Buddhist evidence are invariably understood to exemplify one or another major type of saint, including: (1) the buddha ("enlightened one"), initiator of Buddhist tradition in any era, the prime exemplar of which is Śākyamuni Buddha; (2) the pratyekabuddha (P., *paccekabuddha*) ("enlightened by oneself"), a solitary saint who lives in remote regions and meditates; (3) the arhant (P., *arahant*) ("worthy [of offerings]"), enlightened disciple of a buddha or later saint within Nikāya Buddhism;[2] (4) the bodhisattva (P., *bodhisatta*) ("enlightenment-being"), who aspires to the realization of a buddha and whose special charisma derives from his aspiration to this supreme enlightenment; and (5) the siddha ("perfected one"), the enlightened ideal of the Vajrayāna. It became clear that each of these to some extent requires separate and specific treatment.[3]

2. Although these five types of saint are in many ways quite different from one another and often represent quite disparate traditions, it is insufficient to treat them as altogether separate. In fact, functioning as one or another variation on the Buddhist theme of enlightenment, they not surprisingly also possess certain things in common. What *is* surprising is that in many cases these continuities are rather more extensive and specific than one might at first suspect. This fact suggests the utility of framing these continuities in a single, overarching type, "the Buddhist saint." As we shall see, once framed, this general type, in its basic structure, reveals itself to be relatively consistent from one geographical region to another, across the lines of traditions, and at widely differing time periods.

3. The siddha needs to be excluded from this overarching type, at least for the time being, for two reasons. First, the siddha is, among the Buddhist saints, a particularly distinct type, considerably more removed from the other types of saint than these latter are from one another. Second, the Tantric saint is bound up with sufficiently difficult historical and hermeneutical problems so as to place this type outside the reach of the present, general study. Thus I leave aside the siddha and in this book deal with the first four types: the buddha, pratyekabuddha, arhant, and bodhisattva.

4. This typological approach was chosen not simply for reasons of clarity and convenience. In addition, to a significant extent, it reflects the character of the saints as evidenced in the Indian Buddhist texts. Generally, specific saints tend to approximate the traditional types: if a particular person is understood to be a Buddhist saint, and moreover a particular type of Buddhist saint, certain kinds of things are expected of him or her. The type and subtypes identified in what follows, then, are not purely scholarly creations, but are—more or less—reflective of the thinking of Indian Buddhists about their saints. Often, these types are implicit and taken for granted in the evidence; sometimes—particularly at moments of confusion and crisis—they become the explicit subjects of debate.[4]

This means that in studying the Buddhist saints, one is to a large extent dealing with relatively stable, stereotypical ideas about where saints come from, who they are, and what they do. In the evidence, moreover, it is these ideas that are of paramount interest to the Buddhist hagiographers, more or less at the expense of much appetite for individual—"historical," we should say—idiosyncrasy. This should not be surprising, for, as Oldenberg observed long ago, "India is, above all, the land of types and one should not seek [in accounts of the saints] individuality."[5] In Indian Buddhism, then, if one knows the commonly held expectations, one has taken a large step toward understanding its saints.[6]

5. The emphasis on types discloses a fundamental structure in the way Indian Buddhism understands its saints: one attains sainthood through the process of divesting oneself of the personal and individual. Lest this emphasis on the collective be misread, however, this does not mean that the journey to sainthood is not understood as a personal—indeed, intimate—one; for, to the Indian mind, it most certainly is. It also does not mean that the saints do not—in a certain way—take their own personal history seriously, for they do. And finally, it does not mean that the great saints are entirely lacking in historical uniqueness. In fact, the whole question of the relation of the impersonal to the personal in Indian, and particularly Buddhist, religious life has yet to be adequately understood in the modern West. It is almost as if we moderns feel that to be a complete individual, one must sacrifice collective patterns of identity, and that by approximating such collective patterns, one sacrifices one's individuality. The Buddhist saints present a different alternative altogether, and some appreciation of this alternative, which I attempt to develop in this study, is essential to a correct reading of who they are.

6. The emphasis on types is not without its difficulties for the scholarly interpreter. Although religious India tends to orient itself by types, there remains the challenge of getting the types straight and of accurately discerning their specific historical roles and relations. For example, when Indian Buddhists think about their saints in terms of a given type, such as an arhant, they are not always thinking of the same pattern. In addition, where the same pattern is in question, interpretations may vary. Finally, even when certain typical variations on subtypes and their interpretations can be identified, one still finds many examples that run counter to type, that can be clarified only through reference to history, and in which individual, textual, institutional, sectarian, and similar considerations come into play. Attention to divergencies and exceptions, then, must form an essential part of any attempt to understand the saints of Indian Buddhism.

This work relies particularly upon two intersecting and complementary traditions of modern scholarship: buddhology, encompassing the work of scholars approaching the study of Buddhism from a variety of angles and in terms of its many cultural traditions; and the history of religions, including both its general attention to religious history and structure and its specific examination of the ideals (myth, symbol, and rite) and the actuals (social, political, and economic contexts) of religious life. The mutual stimulation and fructification of these two fields has generated a sizable and valuable collection of works touching in one way or another upon the Buddhist saints, including text editions, translations, and secondary sources pertinent both to the various Indian Buddhist saintly types and to the Buddha, his realized disciples, and later saints.[7] Although these works touch upon nearly every important aspect of the Buddhist saints, taken as a whole and in the context of the present discussion, they remain incomplete in two respects. First, they usually do not take the Buddhist saints as their primary datum and methodological center. Second, they generally remain isolated, making little connection with one another. The result is that questions concerning the nature of the Buddhist saints and their implications for an understanding of Indian Buddhist history as a whole have not been explored. What has been missing so far is, in short, a sustained attempt to assemble the various pieces of the puzzle of the Buddhist saints into a coherent picture.

The present work again takes up several of the fundamental questions that have played an important role in defining and enlivening Buddhist studies throughout its brief history. For example, is Buddhism more accurately defined as a religious tradition or an ethico-philosophical system? The latter characterization prevails today—perhaps because it is particularly compatible with a modern, secular orientation—and so Buddhism is most often seen as a rational, ethical, and philosophical system. By contrast, the interpretation that defines Buddhism as primarily religious emphasizes its superhuman, supernatural, mythic, and cultic dimensions—all of which are fully accessible only to the eye of faith.

The debate over the nonreligious as opposed to the religious character of Buddhism is as old as the field of Buddhist studies itself.[8] No one, of course, has attempted to argue that historical Buddhism is either without ethico-philosophical or without religious trends. Over the past century or so, the debate has focused rather on what Buddhism may have been in its earliest or at least its most essential manifestations.[9] This debate, particularly in its initial stages, is now a bit hard to follow because proponents on both sides used evidence and arguments now discredited, and because of the occasionally outlandish extremes to which they were prone to carry their points.[10] Nevertheless, although the debate no longer occupies center stage in the study of Buddhism, it does continue and remains important in setting the parameters of the discussion of the character of Buddhism as a tradition.[11] This study, given the subject matter of the Buddhist saints as well as my own interests and training, focuses on the more religious dimensions of Indian Buddhism. Nevertheless, as will be seen, the question of the religious versus the ethico-philosophical nature of Indian Buddhism is more fruitfully discussed when it is not framed as a set of either/or alternatives but rather explored as the complex dialectic of two trends.

This study also raises the related question of the kind of evidence that is most useful in attempting to understand Indian Buddhism. In his magnum opus, *Borobuḍur* (1935), Paul Mus suggests that the type of evidence one chooses to examine significantly affects the conclusions one reaches about Buddhism. In this regard, Mus criticizes the prevailing buddhological emphasis on explicit philosophical evidence and the resultant view of Buddhism as essentially philosophical. Mus points out that philosophy is a specialized domain of Indian Buddhism. It is, in fact, far more incidental to historical Buddhism than has been recognized and does not reflect the actual priorities of the Indian tradition, wherein visual art, hagiography, and ritual, expressed largely in the idiom of symbolism,[12] tend to be more central and definitive.[13] For Mus, it is such concrete expressions, reflecting the exigencies of Buddhist religious life, that are primary. They, in turn, give birth to the relatively ancillary phenomena of the variety of highly refined and sophisticated conceptual abstractions that make up scholastic tradition.[14] According to Mus, if one wants to understand Buddhist philosophy, one may follow modern buddhology and study philosophical texts. But if one wants to understand Buddhism as a whole, one must take a different and much more comprehensive view of the evidence of the tradition.

Mus, in his search for Indian Buddhism, took the Buddhist monument of the stūpa (P., *thūpa*) as his focus and his organizing principle. The present study, in its attempt to understand Indian Buddhism, takes the Buddhist saints as its central cipher. In addition, it follows in the Musian legacy by examining a kind of evidence that, like the stūpa, is not essentially philosophical (although like the stūpa it certainly has profound and far-reaching philosophical implications)—namely, Buddhist hagiography, as found in independent texts, sections of texts, and the background particularly of much historical writing and discussions of discipline (e.g., the *vinaya*). As in the case of the stūpa prior to Mus, hagiography has generally been considered by modern buddhology to be of secondary importance, particularly when compared with more scholastic texts.[15] Yet hagiography is particularly interesting and revealing because here one finds a Buddhism that is alive and in evolution, and also relatively unself-conscious. The more scholastic Buddhist texts typically argue for certain views of doctrine, discipline, or history. Such concerns are not entirely absent from hagiography, but in hagiography one more often finds Buddhists disclosing their deep-seated beliefs and values.[16] In addition, as Migot has pointed out,[17] successive generations of learned compilers and editors have tended to tamper less with hagiography than with other genres of texts,[18] and thus it can often provide particularly effective access to early patterns of Buddhist experience and understanding.[19]

This study raises another, related question, that of the relation of Buddhism to its non-Buddhist, Indian religious environment. In earlier buddhology, there was a lively debate between those who held that the Buddha definitively separated himself from his Hindu religious context[20] and those who held that the Buddha and his teachings are best understood as expressions of that Hindu world.[21] Modern buddhology, perhaps influenced by the preferences of Buddhist tradition itself, has tended to prefer the first of these two alternatives, sometimes even taking it as axiomatic that Indian Buddhism must in some essential and fundamental way be different from its non-Buddhist context. It is significant that this position is not independent of the view one takes of the basic character of Buddhism and of the evidence most definitive of the tradition. The view of Buddhism as distinct from its environment is closely linked with the assumption that real Buddhism is given in its philosophical expressions (here Buddhism argues strenuously for its separate identity) and that its more purely religious dimensions are epiphenomenal, perhaps even non-Buddhist (here Buddhism participates freely and without complaint in pan-Indian patterns of religiosity). In fact, as we shall see, a preference for philosophical evidence tends to bring to light and emphasize differences among the different Buddhist orientations and, even more starkly, Buddhism's disjunction from the non-Buddhist schools, both orthodox and nonorthodox. By way of contrast, examining the kinds of evidence more closely reflecting the religious life as lived (myths, symbols, and rituals) tends to bring to light continuities not only among the various Buddhist schools but also among the Buddhist and non-Buddhist religious worlds.

Finally, this study considers the question of whether anything can be known about the teaching of the Buddha or the earliest Buddhist community. In the early days of Buddhist studies, there was the hope, sometimes even the presumption, that something definitive could in fact be known about Buddhist origins. In this fascinating chapter of Western intellectual history, scholars, with a remarkable engagement and fervor, developed a variety of often quite different and even dramatically opposed reconstructions of this hypothesized "original Buddhism." The variety of reconstructions itself reflects just how uncertain and unstable is the evidence of earliest Buddhism. In the past half century or so, particularly with the increasing recognition of the complex history of the early communities and texts, it has come to be widely agreed that nothing definitive can be known about the Buddha himself or the Buddhism he founded.

In what follows, I certainly have no intention of disputing this well-founded scepticism, at least with respect to what can be known in the way of historical details of Śākyamuni Buddha's person and life or the specific teachings and practices that he taught. At the same time, however, I find that the current agnosticism concerning Buddhism's early days is unnecessarily extreme. I shall in fact suggest that through a recasting of the question, a way may be opened for a search, not for specific biographical traits or doctrines, but rather for the general character and shape of the early tradition and community. The evidence leads to a reasonable reconstruction, and this in turn permits some informative questions to be asked and some provocative hypotheses to be developed.

The questions mentioned here—whether Indian Buddhism is essentially ethico-philosophical or religious, what kind of evidence should be used to understand it, whether the tradition is best seen as a separation from or continuation of its non-Buddhist environment, and what may have constituted the earliest tradition—are as large and provocative as the field of Buddhist studies itself. In this work, I propose a variety of perspectives on these questions and sometimes suggest some possible answers. At the same time, it must be admitted that it is probably the questions themselves rather than any possible answers to them that, in the final analysis, reveal the most about Indian Buddhism. It may also be that in the two alternatives—attempting to provide definitive answers to the large questions (as earlier scholars tried to do) and abandoning these questions as unanswerable (the prevailing trend)—students of Buddhism have missed a third and much more interesting and promising alternative. This is to acknowledge the essential importance of the large questions to our understanding of Buddhism and therefore the ongoing need to reflect upon and debate them, but to carry out that reflection and debate with an appreciation that they likely will remain beyond the reach of our individual or collective minds to resolve in any final sense.

Notes

1. This introduction contains a general orientation to this study in the main body of the text and a discussion of bibliographic and other more technical matters in the notes.

2. That is, the sects *(nikāya)* of the "eighteen schools," what is usually but infelicitously termed "pre-Mahāyāna" (there is uncertainty as to when the Mahāyāna originated and what, within these schools, historically precedes the Mahāyāna) or "Hīnayāna Buddhism" (a term of Mahāyānist deprecation, at best referring to a very limited number of phenomena within the historical Nikāya schools).

3. As we shall see, each of these types in turn has its subtypes. For example, buddhas include not only Śākyamuni Buddha but also buddhas of the past and future and, in the Mahāyāna, celestial buddhas presently presiding over different buddha fields *(buddhakṣetra)* throughout space. The pratyekabuddhas, or "solitary buddhas," are found, according to tradition, as one or the other of two major subtypes, living alone or in groups. To the type of the arhant belong saints of two, three, five, or more subtypes. The bodhisattvas likewise include beings of different sorts: those who are human and those who have transcended the human sphere; those who live in cities, those who live in forests, and monastics. And the siddhas also include a variety of types of Tantric saint, including wandering yogins, monks, and laypeople.

4. The intention behind this study is to identify what Joachim Wach defined as "ideal types"(see 1951)—in the present context, the Buddhist saint or one of the subtypes (buddha, pratyekabuddha, etc.). These forms are not inert phenomena but rather formulations of identity that were, presumably, taken on by certain people and, at the same time, experienced and understood as such by ancient Indian society.

One may seek ideal types on a potentially infinite number of levels of generality. For example, this study seeks, on the most general level, the ideal type of the Buddhist saint, more specifically of buddhas, pratyekabuddhas, arhants, and bodhisattvas, and more specifically still, of subcategories of these types of saint. Any given ideal type, such as those dealt with here, are arrived at through a dialectical interaction of three levels of analysis. First, one identifies and analyzes the various images of the saint in question in the texts. Second, one seeks to interpret the significance of what one finds. Third, one attempts to arrive at a valid picture of the saint, focusing on that inner logic and meaning that defines the saint as a type.

a. From an examination of the evidence one compiles an inventory of elements of the saint, a kind of statistical picture detailing the features that are contained by all, most, some, or only a few saints of the type one is seeking. This picture reveals no more than how the texts explicitly represent the type.

b. In the second level of analysis, one attempts to put together the various images of the type into a coherent picture. This level requires arriving at an understanding of the *significance* of the members of the inventory of images. At this level, one must address the question of the impact of the history and viewpoint of the original hagiographers and their communities, as well as of the successive generations of hagiographers and communities, upon the content of the text. At this level, one needs to pay special attention to questions arising from the appearance of discrepancies and contradictions in one's inventory, both within one text and across the lines of traditions. To what extent are discrepancies within one text or among several texts due to basic differences in the understanding of the type and to what extent are they due to more external factors of the text's history?

c. Finally, one attempts to arrive at a valid picture of the Buddhist saint. The saint is an ideal with a particular inherent logic and meaning, which can be seen both by devotees and detractors as well as by more removed observers such as ourselves. Those in the communities and contexts behind the texts about the saint have some idea—though not necessarily always the same one—of what a saint is and what it means to be one. It is an understanding of this ideal, as it makes sense to ancient Indians, that we seek.

Wach observed that, in seeking the ideal type, one sometimes finds a difference between the statistical appearance of the type in the evidence and the ideal type to which one finally comes in one's analysis. Most often, it will turn out that the essential character and meaning of a given type of saint is revealed by those images of the saint that are most frequent. However, sometimes the statistically infrequent example throws into bold relief some essential element of the structure of the ideal type, thus shedding light on the coherence of the type as a whole.

5. Oldenberg 1934, 156–57, quoted by Migot 1954, 409. Migot adds, "what is striking is [the saints'] lack of personality; each one is stereotypical . . . [and] depersonalized" (1954, 409).

6. The focus on the general means that the treatment of the specific classes of saints or the individual saints will need to be strictly selective. There are, of course, often marked differences among various textual expressions of any type of saint, and in what follows many of these will be noted. However, it will be argued, such differences presuppose and occur within fidelity to the overall type and subtypes of the "Buddhist saint." Moreover, at this stage of our understanding of the saints, concern for the specificity of the saints appropriately defers to a concern for what is generally the case. In spite of what is lost through such an approach, much is to be gained, for it enables us to identify, among the saints, broad and distinctive patterns within Indian Buddhist history, to examine some of their variations, and to begin to develop some hypotheses about their impacts on the history of Indian Buddhism.

7. The following bibliographic summary is no more than selective and representative and also leaves aside the Tantric saints. Specific page references are provided in the following chapters and so are not included here. For additional references, see the following chapters. If one deems Śākyamuni himself to be a Buddhist saint (for some researchers, as we shall see, Buddha Śākyamuni must in some important respects be excluded from the idea of a Buddhist saint), one must initially mention the examination of Buddha Śākyamuni that, taking its lead from the late-nineteenth-century quest for the historical Jesus, is reflected in ever more accurate translations of key texts (e.g., T. W. Rhys Davids 1880; Rockhill 1884; Foucaux 1884–92; Johnston 1936, 1937; Jones 1949–56); and increasingly detailed and sophisticated secondary studies (e.g., Oldenberg 1881; Senart 1882; Thomas 1927; Foucher 1949; Lamotte 1947–48; Bareau 1963, 1970–71, 1975, 1979, etc.). Beyond this, beginning toward the end of the nineteenth century, one finds an initial though small trickle of interest in the other saints. This is exemplified first in the editing of a number of texts containing accounts of Buddhist saints (see the "Texts" section of the bibliography for examples); second, in the translations of several works giving evidence of the Buddhist saints (e.g., Cowell 1895–1913; Watters 1904–5; Beal 1869, 1884; Feer 1891; C.A.F. Rhys Davids 1909, 1913; Chavannes 1910–35; third, in the historical works of buddholo-

gists that refer in their course to the saints (e.g., Burnouf, La Vallée Poussin, Przyluski, etc.); and fourth, in the works of a few scholars who have explicitly devoted attention to specific topics connected with the Buddhist saints (e.g., Feer 1881; Kumagusu 1899; Maung Kin 1903; Duroiselle 1904). Nevertheless, these early studies generally remained isolated notices, largely unappreciated and peripheral to the major direction of buddhology as a whole.

During the past three-quarters of a century or so, the Buddhist saints have continued to be the subject of some attention, in text editions, translations, sections of books, dictionaries and encyclopedias, articles, and, lately, a few monographs focusing on the saints. During this period a considerable range of areas and topics within the field of the Buddhist saints has engaged the attention of scholars, as indicated by the following summary.

a. Introductory surveys of saints and sainthood in Buddhism (e.g., Schmidt 1947; Lamotte 1958, 765–75; Bareau 1972; Spae 1979).

b. General discussions of saints in early Buddhism (e.g., Schayer 1935; Falk 1943; Lamotte 1958).

c. The translation of texts particularly pertinent to the Buddhist saints (e.g., Burlingame 1921; Przyluski 1923; Horner 1938–66; Jones 1949–56; Hofinger 1954; Ensink 1952; Lamotte 1962; Ehara, Soma Thera, and Kheminda Thera 1961; Norman 1969, 1971).

d. Specific saints (e.g., Buddha [as above in this note]; Śāriputra [Migot 1954; Nyanaponika 1966]; Gavāṃpati [Przyluski 1926–28; Lévy 1957; Bareau 1958]; Piṇḍolabhāradvāja [Strong 1979]; Upagupta [Strong 1992]; Devadatta [Mukherjee 1966; Bareau 1988–89]; Nāgārjuna [Walleser 1922; Jan 1970]). Lamotte, in 1944–80 and, to a lesser extent, 1962, mentions a number of Buddhist saints and typically offers a wealth of bibliographical and other information on them. Couture (1988, 33) has provided a useful list of references to Lamotte's discussion of thirty-four of the more important of these saints. Material in Lamotte's two works particularly relevant to the present study is cited in subsequent chapters.

e. Groups of saints (e.g., Lévi and Chavannes 1916; De Visser 1922–23; Bareau 1959].

f. Dogmatic and scholastic conceptions of the different types of "pre-Tantric" saints, including buddhas (e.g., Vogel 1954; Gombrich 1980; Harvey 1983); pratyekabuddhas (e.g., La Vallée Poussin 1908–27; Kloppenborg 1974; Norman 1983; Wiltshire 1990); arhants (e.g., Horner 1936; Bareau 1957; Katz 1980; Bond 1984); and bodhisattvas (e.g., Dayal 1932; Gomez 1977; Basham 1981).

g. Specific codes and traditions reflective of the Buddhist saints (e.g., Bapat 1937a, 1937b, 1964; Filliozat 1963; Khantipalo 1965; Jaini 1970; Keyes 1982; Carrithers 1983; Tambiah 1984).

h. Symbolism of Buddhist saints (e.g., Mus 1935; Bareau 1969).

i. Cults of living saints (e.g., Keyes 1982; Carrithers 1983; Tambiah 1984).

j. Cults of saints "passed beyond" in stūpas, images, etc. (e.g., Combaz 1932–36; Mus 1935; Bénisti 1960; Bareau 1962, 1974, 1975, 1980, etc.; Dallapiccola 1980).

k. The nature of Buddhist hagiography as such (e.g., Bareau 1963 and 1970–71; Tambiah 1984; Migot 1954).

l. Buddhist saints as actors within the sociological world of Buddhism, as identified by anthropologists (e.g., Carrithers 1983; Tambiah 1984; Bunnag 1973).

m. Bibliographical works, including summaries of primary literature on the saints as well as secondary studies (e.g., Lamotte 1944–80; Reynolds 1981, 260–93; Couture 1988).

8. See Guy Welbon's discussion of this issue (1968, 194–295).

9. Some early buddhologists, among them Stcherbatsky (e.g., 1923) and T. W. Rhys Davids (e.g., 1877), held that the Buddha originally taught and that Buddhism most essentially is an ethical and/or philosophical teaching in which the mythic and cultic are secondary. This interpretation sees the Buddha as a human being who cultivated his own person through certain disciplines, won a state of moral and intellectual purity, and taught the sober path he had followed to others. Other early buddhologists, among them La Vallée Poussin (e.g., 1898, 44–47), C.A.F. Rhys Davids (e.g., 1931, 1ff.), Keith (e.g., 1923, 61–68), and Schayer (e.g., 1935), have emphasized the more strictly religious elements in

defining the Buddha's teaching and the essence of Buddhism. Trends in the interpretation of Buddhism as a religion have included notions that, from the earliest times, the master himself was seen as an embodiment of ultimate reality, endowed with a supernatural and mythical character, who possessed magical and miraculous powers, elicited the fervent devotion and cultic response of his disciples, and taught others the same mystical goal that he himself embodied (Welbon 1968, 194–295).

10. For example, those favoring the ethico-philosophical character of Buddhism sometimes affirmed also its nihilism. Stcherbatsky, for example, speaks of the final Buddhist attainment as "a blank" (1923, 50). Those holding for the religious character of Buddhism have sometimes fallen prey to essentialism. C.A.F. Rhys Davids, for example, felt that the Buddha originally taught an *ātman* ("eternal self") doctrine and in this respect did not differ from his Hindu environment (see Murti's discussion [1960, 20ff.]).

11. In more recent times, for example, variants of the ethico-philosophical interpretation have been advanced by scholars such as Lamotte (e.g., 1958, 708 and 712–73) and Bareau (e.g., 1980), while versions of the religious interpretation have been put forward by scholars such as Mus (e.g., 1935) and Snellgrove (e.g., 1973). It is intriguing that the final reading given Buddhism by proponents on either side of the issue has not changed very much in the interim.

12. Mus developed a sophisticated description of the dynamics of religious symbolism, dealing with the genesis of symbols; their development, elaboration, devaluation, fragmentation into parts; assimilation to or combination with other symbols; retention, alteration, or inversion of meaning; and so on (see Victoria Urubshurow's useful summary, 1988). As we shall see, an appreciation of dynamics such as these is essential to a proper understanding of the Buddhist saints.

13. Schopen points out that although nontextual (archaeological) and textual evidence of Buddhism has presented itself from the beginning of Buddhist studies, Western buddhology has exhibited "an overriding textual orientation" (1991, 4), which Schopen finds in buddhology early (e.g., Burnouf) and contemporary (e.g., de Jong). Schopen points out that texts—and, moreover, the kind of texts favored by buddhologists—tend to articulate abstract ideals rather than concrete religious practices. They show "what a small atypical part of the Buddhist community wanted that community to believe or practice" (3). Unfortunately, however, buddhology has tended to take these abstract ideals as if they reflected actual practice. The end result has been that the overriding textual orientation of Western buddhology has led to a picture of Buddhism that has no reliable relation to actual Buddhist practice (see Schopen 1991).

14. Mus argues that Buddhism is more—and more essentially—a praxis than a philosophical enterprise. This suggests that those phenomena standing closest to praxis—symbolism and ritual as they are expressed in art and legend (or hagiography)—are extremely valuable indicators of Buddhism as such. Mus cites Foucher's comment that at a certain point in Indian Buddhist history, the thinkers and the sculptors parted ways, with the sculptors moving ahead of the thinkers. Then Mus remarks, "In reality, it is the collective imagination and cultic practice that anticipate the creation of theoretical forms. And art and legend have but the benefit of reflecting more immediately this natural process" (1935, 1:70).

15. Although Mus's preferred form of evidence is iconography, he frequently mentions the intimate relation of iconography and hagiography and the close proximity of both to the religious life of noninstitutionalized Buddhism in India (e.g., 1935, 1:72).

16. See Hofinger's remarks in his *Le Congres du Lac Anavatapta* (1954, 15–23). Hofinger's characterization of the character and contents of the *Sthavirāvadāna* applies well to Buddhist hagiography as a genre.

17. See Migot's comments (1954, 533). While in the saints we cannot always be confident of encountering historical individuals, at least in our modern Western sense of the term, we do meet with another type of historical individuality, namely, that of traditions, movements, and trends. The Buddhist saints have become noteworthy to Buddhist authors because they exhibit in their lives and characters the personalities of specific Indian Buddhist aspirations, ideas, and communities. As Migot observed four decades ago, "This particular character of [saintly] persons, though inconvenient for the writing of personal biographies, is perhaps an advantage if one wishes . . . to seek behind the 'type' the tendency of the group which he represents and the place of this group in the history of Buddhist doctrines and sects" (1954, 409). As we shall see, the Buddhist saints can become invaluably revealing lenses through which various broad patterns of Indian Buddhist life may be viewed.

18. Migot notes that the hagiography of the Buddha provides an exception to this rule. There are other important exceptions, a number of which will be noted in the discussion of individual saints.

19. It should be noted that the written evidence of Buddhism is notoriously difficult to date with any precision. Manuscripts can, of course, be dated, but this does not tell us when a given text was written down for the first time nor when it may have been first assembled as a discrete (perhaps oral) entity. More important, it does not tell us when the different sections of the text or the material contained therein originated. The texts and portions of texts that concern themselves with saints add special difficulties to the dating process because, as we shall see, although Buddhist texts not infrequently contain hagiographical material, this is often presupposed by the text as its assumed background. This background is generally very hard to place or date. For the immediate goals of this study, fortunately, a close dating of material within texts or of texts themselves is not a primary desideratum, since what is sought here is a pattern, some of its exemplifications, and its implications. At the same time, the distinguishing of types and subtypes of saints sometimes brings to light developmental trends among the saints, and these in turn can suggest significant temporal patterns and sequences.

20. E.g., Oldenberg, T. W. Rhys Davids.

21. E.g., La Vallée Poussin (1927, 259), C.A.F. Rhys Davids, Senart (1882, 255), Schayer.

1

The Buddhist Saints and the Two-Tiered Model of Buddhism

The relative lack of scholarly attention given to the Buddhist saints cannot be explained by an absence of data, for these figures are many and are documented throughout Indian Buddhist history. The primary reason for this neglect, it seems, has to do with a prevailing interpretation given to these figures and, more fundamentally, of Buddhism itself, an interpretation referred to in this study as the "two-tiered model of Buddhism." [1] Any discussion of the Buddhist saints must be preceded by the identification of this model and an assessment of its impact on any attempt to understand the saints.

The Two-Tiered Model

Buddhist Tradition

Modern scholarship typically understands Buddhism itself to articulate and promote a particular norm or ideal, the two-tiered model of Buddhism. This ideal, though derived chiefly from Theravādin evidence, is thought to have general applicability to Indian Buddhism.[2] Although primarily defining the structure of Buddhist community, the two-tiered model is, as we shall see, much more than that and in fact offers an all-inclusive interpretation of Buddhism as such, in its various dimensions. As defined in various important texts, this ideal takes shape as a structure composed up of two normative lifestyles, that of the monk *(bhikṣu)* occupying the upper tier and that of the layperson (Skt. and P., *upāsaka* [m.], *upāsikā* [f.]) occupying the lower.[3] Both of these lifestyles, we are told, were instituted by the Buddha himself and have provided the primary elements of the Buddhist community throughout its Indian history.[4]

The monk follows the highest teachings of the Buddha, having renounced the world and directed his activity toward the gaining of nirvāṇa (P., *nibbāna*).[5] To achieve this aim, he engages in two important pursuits: the cultivation of pure behavior through adherence to the *vinaya* and the study of texts—in the Theravādin formulation, the development of scriptural expertise (P., *pariyatti*), sometimes known as the "vocation of texts and scholarship" (P., *ganthadhura*).[6] As a result of these two preoccupations of cultivating behavioral purity and studying texts,[7] the monk becomes endowed with innumerable virtues and is a worthy object of veneration and donations.

The first major preoccupation of the monk has traditionally been the cultivation of *śīla* (P., *sīla*) (behavioral purity). Although intentionality plays an important role in Buddhist ethics (Gombrich 1984b, 91; Sadatissa 1970, 7–8 and passim), in the case of the monk, *śīla* is defined primarily as compliance with external, behavioral criteria. As Gombrich remarks, for the Buddhist monks, "*śīla* here refers to *conduct becoming to the role of a monk;* in a word, *decorum*" (emphasis in original; 1984, 94).[8] The exact requirements of this monastic etiquette are given in the *vinaya,* which outlines behavioral norms for both individuals and the community of monks as a whole. The *prātimokṣa* (P., *pāṭimokkha*) (and its elaboration in the *Sūtravibhañga* [P., *Suttavibhañga*]) articulates a code of 218 or more rules to be followed by each monk (or nun),[9] and the *Karmavācanā* (P., *Kammavācā*) (and its elaboration in the *Skandhaka* [P., *Khandhaka*]) establishes the structures and procedures governing communal life.[10] The *vinaya* stands at the center of monastic life, not only because it provides the rules for individual and collective action, but also because it serves to guarantee the behavioral purity of the monks. The *poṣadha* (P., *uposatha*) ritual performed fortnightly at monasteries, at which the *prātimokṣa* is recited, for example, certifies compliance with the *prātimokṣa* by each member of the community and thus the sanctity of the monastic *saṃgha* as a whole.

The monk's behavioral purity is, in turn, a central component in his relationship with the laity. The immediate goal of lay Buddhists is not nirvāṇa, but rather the accumulation of merit *(puṇya),* by which they aspire to happiness in this life and a good rebirth in the hereafter. Lay Buddhists gain merit through good actions, and central among these is the making of donations to the monastic *saṃgha* (Bunnag 1973, 30). However, the degree of merit gained by donations is dependent upon the level of sanctity of the recipient (Lamotte 1958, 79–80; Conze 1980, 39). The more blameless the behavior of the monk to whom donations are made, the more merit gained by the donor.[11] Thus it is a matter of considerable concern among the laity that the recipients of their donations be paragons of virtue, again understood as complying with the regulations of the *prātimokṣa* and larger *vinaya.* Weber saw this quite clearly in remarking that "the fellowship [monastic *saṃgha*] appears above all to have served the concerns of status decorum, of the monks' deportment lest their charisma be compromised in the eyes of the worldly" (1958, 214). Levy similarly observes in reference to contemporary Buddhism in Southeast Asia, "you have to have seen the jealous and suspicious surveillance which the parishioners keep over their bonzes, in order to understand the personal importance that they attach to the good conduct of the latter" (1968, 100). This "surveillance" undoubtedly put considerable pressure on the monks to excel in their observance of the *prātimokṣa* for, as Bunnag observes, "the man who earns the disapproval of the laity may well forfeit their continuing material support'' (1973, 31).

The second major preoccupation of Buddhist monks, study of the scriptures, has involved the memorization, preservation, and study of those texts (first oral, later written) most important to the various monastic traditions.[12] That such scholarship has been not only a central monastic preoccupation but also an essential and defining feature of the monastic type of Buddhism was again clearly seen by Weber (1958, 206–7). Lamotte has pointed out the extent to which, from the monastic viewpoint, the study and correct understanding of the textual tradition is a sine qua non of authentic Buddhism (1949, 345–46).[13]

Just as the behavioral purity of the monks was of importance for the laity, so was their textual learning. The monks were to memorize, preserve, and study the texts not only to edify themselves and to maintain the integrity of established Buddhism, but also to act as reliable transmitters of the Buddhist teachings to the laity. In fulfillment of this latter purpose, the monks were thus teachers to the laity, instructing them in the authentic dharma and acting as vehicles through which the sacred power of the dharma became available to them. The monk who was learned thus counted for much in the eyes of the laity.[14] So it was that the worthiness of the monk as a recipient of donations was bound up with one or the other, or both, of these two preoccupations of cultivating pure behavior and studying texts.

The preceding discussion raises an important question: to what extent can these two preoccupations be seen to characterize not only Theravādin monasticism, in which it is most clearly present, but also the Indian Buddhist situation as such? Although this question will be explored in more detail below, a few examples may be cited to suggest that the behavioral and scholastic ideals of Theravādin monasticism do indeed have applicability to Indian Buddhist monasticism in general. Let us consider the revealing fact that, when monastic Buddhists wished to criticize other Buddhist monks, it was typically for deficiencies in these two areas. For example, in one version of the Nikāya *Mahāparinirvāṇa Sūtra* (P., *Mahāparinibbāna Sutta*), preserved in Chinese, certain *bhikṣus* are castigated for not observing the precepts and not delighting in the texts (Bareau 1970–71, 1:238). Similarly, when Hsüan-tsang wants to criticize a certain monastery in northwest India, he remarks that its members are ''very defective in their observance of the rules of their Order'' and are ''without definite learning'' (Watters 1904–5, 1:240; see also 2:73–74). And when the Mahāyāna Buddhist monk Śāntideva is threatened with explusion from his monastery, the reasons given are his behavioral laxity (he eats five bowls of rice a day) and his unwillingness (or inability) to participate in textual study and debate (*Csp* 143–45 [Rb., 146–47]).

There is another preoccupation of the ideal monk that, although appearing in the texts, is less commonly found among the past and present priorities of mainline Theravādin monasticism (and other forms of Nikāya monasticism)—namely, the practice of meditation. The classic texts, in fact, articulate an idealized threefold summary of the Buddhist path for monks: pure behavior *(śīla),* meditation *(samādhi),* and scholarly learning/insight (*prajñā;* P., *paññā*)[15] (Lamotte 1958,

46–52). By its very nature, settled monasticism placed more emphasis on *śīla,* as fulfillment of the *vinaya,* and *prajñā,* defined as knowledge based on learning.[16] At the same time, it placed considerably less emphasis on *samādhi.* Thus, although many classical texts—both Buddha-word[17] and commentaries[18]—recommend meditation as a necessary component of the Buddhist path,[19] in monastic tradition, meditation has often remained a primarily theoretical ideal, followed more in the breach than in the observance (Bunnag 1973, 55–58; Maquet 1980). Progress in meditation necessitates intensive and sustained practice, and this, in turn, requires seclusion and absence of distraction. According to the great spokesman of monastic Buddhism, Buddhaghosa, the institution of the settled monastery, along with its characteristic environment, tends to inhibit the practice of meditation owing to its many inhabitants, its noise, the necessary duties of communal life, obligations to the laity, the arrival of visitors, and other interruptions.[20] Buddhaghosa indicates further that the preoccupations of the settled monastery, and most particularly the study of texts, also tend to militate against the practice of meditation[21] (*Vsm* 95–97 [N., 1:96–98]).[22]

As Buddhist texts reiterate, meditation and realization are indissolubly linked (for example, *Dp* 282 [Radhakrishnan 1950, 148]; Nyanaponika 1962, 117): where meditation ceases to be a priority of the renunciant life, realization tends to fall away, quickly coming to be considered no more than a theoretical possibility. The emphasis on *śīla* and textual study in classical Buddhist monasticism, along with a corresponding deemphasis of meditation, led inevitably to a decline of realization as an immediate and practicable goal of settled monastic life and of the Buddhism in which monasticism predominated. As Conze remarks in relation to the ascendency of nonmeditative concerns in the monastic life of the Theravāda, Sarvāstivāda, and the Nikāya schools in general, "the scholars ousted the saints, and erudition took the place of attainment" (1959, 116).[23] As we shall see, the same is reflected in certain Buddhist lamentations, found in texts of various schools, that complain that the Buddha's dharma, once one of meditation and realization, has become a dharma of pure behavior and textual expertise alone. Such a trend is also visible in the Pāli texts where we find evidence that, in Bond's words, the full realization of "arhantship had become a remote norm fairly early," a trend that only became more pronounced as time went on. In the *Visuddhimagga* (late fourth to early fifth centuries C.E.), for example, it has become virtually unrealizable (Bond 1988, 164). In relation to Buddhist monasticism in contemporary Thailand, Bunnag makes an observation that reflects the same view. After noting that according to Buddhist theory, only monks can legitimately aspire to nirvāṇa, she continues:

> However, none of the Thai monks to whom I spoke appeared to consider *nirvāṇa* a relevant goal for which to strive; those who considered that [it was a relevant goal] . . . believed that only after billions of years of tireless effort could they or their contemporaries achieve this state. The majority of monks . . . chose to rationalize their limited spiritual horizons by saying that only the Buddha and a few of his disciples had become enlightened, and that this facility was no longer available. (Bunnag 1973, 19–20)[24]

As mentioned, even if settled monastics did not hold enlightenment as a practicable goal in this life, this did not leave the laity without criteria by which to evaluate the monastics' worthiness as recipients of offerings. Bunnag's observations about present-day Thailand have some validity, as noted, for settled Buddhist monasticism as a type in other times and places: the laity tended to judge the monastics' sanctity primarily in terms, first, of "conformity to the formal stereotype" outlined in the *vinaya* (1973, 34) and, second, of demonstrable mastery of the sacred texts (1973, 53–54). Bunnag further remarks that, in the context of the monastic institutions she studied, "meditation, which was originally intended to represent a more advanced stage in the process of self-purification, is a less highly regarded activity than is the study of the Pāli texts: which is to say that the latter pursuit, being more easily assessed in terms of academic degrees and certificates, is accorded a higher evaluation than [meditation] for success in which the evidence is less tangible" (1973, 54).[25]

Quite different from the lifestyle of the monastics is that of the laity, who represent the second normative lifestyle of Theravāda and of Indian Buddhism in general, as defined in the two-tiered model. According to classical tradition, as summarized by Lamotte (1958, 69–92),[26] those following the lay ideal are principally to observe the five precepts and, in particular, to cultivate devotion and generosity, virtues that may be practiced in two different contexts. On the one hand, the laity are to revere and support materially the monastic *saṃgha;* on the other, they are permitted to venerate stūpas, those monuments enshrining the remains of a buddha or other holy person.[27] In no less important a text than the Nikāya *Mahāparinirvāṇa Sūtra,* the early account of the events surrounding the passing of the Buddha, the cult of the stūpa—so we are told—is depicted as the particular concern of the laity. In the standard English translation from the Pāli and in interpretations based on it, the Buddha advises his monks not to involve themselves in stūpa worship, leaving that pursuit rather to the laity.[28] The monks should, by contrast, concentrate on their own characteristic (and superior) concerns, defined elsewhere in the text (as we shall see in Chapter 11) as following the *vinaya* and maintaining the textual tradition.

Essentially the same depiction of monk and layperson, as defined by this two-tiered religious structure, is found elsewhere in the normative commentarial tradition of the Theravāda. In the *Milindapañha,* for example, King Milinda asks the monk Nāgasena about the respective roles of monk and layperson (162–64 [T.R. 1890–94, 1:229–33]; 242–44 [2:56–59]). Nāgasena presents very much the same picture as the one just given. The *bhikṣu,* the fully ordained monk who adheres to the *prātimokṣa* and follows the textual pursuits of settled monasticism, pursues the highest ideal of Buddhist life, set forth by the Buddha himself (162–64 [1:231–33]; 243 [2:58]). Thus treading the path to arhantship, he is worthy of salutation, respect, and reverence by the laity (162–63 [1:230–31]). The laity, for their part, follow a lesser but still worthy way of life, revering the monk in symbolic and material ways and venerating stūpas. Through the merit earned by these actions, they may hope to ensure good fortune in the present life and a happy rebirth (see, for example, 228–32 [2:31–38]; 240–42 [2:51–56]; and 161 [1:229]). Although advocating the worship of stūpas by the layperson, the *Milindapañha,* in apparent agreement with the *Mahāparinirvāṇa Sūtra,* holds that this is a practice in which the ideal monk should not engage (177–79 [1:246–48]).

The Buddhism of the monk and that of the layperson are thus very different in lifestyle, activities, and goal; nevertheless, there is clearly an intimate connection between the two. The *Itivuttaka* quotes the Buddha as defining their reciprocal relationship:

> [The laypeople] render you great service, O *bhikṣu,* the brāhmins and householders who give you clothing, alms, seats, beds and remedies. And you also render them great service when you teach them the Good Law and the pure life *(brahmacarya).* Thus, through your mutual assistance, it is possible to practise the religious life. . . . By relying one upon the other, householders and those who live the homeless life will cause the good dharma to prosper. (110–11 [Lm., 73])

According to the two-tiered model as expressed in this Buddhist evidence, then, the monastics practice a Buddhism of emulation, whereas the laypeople practice a Buddhism of devotion. That is, the monastics follow a way of life in which they take the Buddha as model, rather than as an object of veneration. The laypeople, by contrast, are to take the Buddha, and his emulators, the monastic *saṃgha,* as objects of their devotion, a devotion shown in a reverential attitude, acts of respect, and material donations.

Recent Scholarship

Contemporary scholarship generally accepts the main outlines of the two-tiered model of Buddhism as articulated in the Theravādin and other evidence and finds it a useful device for understanding the structure and history of Indian Buddhism.[29] Étienne Lamotte, for example, tells us that "one must admit the existence of two distinct and often opposed Buddhisms: that of the religious and that of the layfolk" (Lm., 59). In Lamotte's characterization, on the one hand are the monks, who live in monasteries, adhere to the *vinaya,* maintain the textual tradition, and strive for nirvāṇa. On the other are the laity, who worship and serve the monks, follow basic moral principles, engage in a devotional and cultic Buddhism, and through these activities strive for a better rebirth (for example, 58, 59, 65). The religious life of the laity, in contrast to that of the monks, also includes worship of ancestral deities and participation in local non-Buddhist religious life. Lamotte summarizes: "Both offspring of Śākya, the religious and the lay person represent divergent tendencies which, without conflicting with one another directly, assert themselves with increasing clarity: on the one hand, the ideal of renunciation and of personal sanctity and, on the other, the active virtues and altruistic preoccupations" (59). Particularly important in Lamotte's interpretation are the differing evaluations given to these two different Buddhisms. The Buddhism of the laity is not the one principally advocated by the master, for the Buddha reserved his highest esteem strictly for those who entered the monastic order. The Buddhism of the laity Śākyamuni deems to be inferior and accords it only a qualified approbation (71–72). In fact, it must be admitted that the Buddhism of the layperson is "a sort of compromise between the Buddha Dharma and the superstitions of paganism." This compromise was not without its deleterious effects: "This was the principal cause of the reabsorption of Buddhism into surrounding Hinduism" (75–76).[30]

Among many other contemporary scholars favoring this two-tiered model of Buddhism[31] is S. Dutt, who emphasizes a theme that will be important later in this study, namely, the stūpa as the special and characteristic concern of the laity. Originally, Dutt tells us, there were two different and divergent forms of Buddhism, a "popular Buddhism" and a "monkish Buddhism." Monkish Buddhism emerges directly from the hand of the founder, was practiced by the learned, scholarly elite, and followed the *abhidharma* (P., *abhidhamma*) (Dutt 1957, 144). Popular Buddhism, on the other hand, cannot be deduced from the doctrines preached by the Buddha (178), but develops out of "folk-myth and superstition" (166). Illiterate and expressed in symbol and ritual, its basis is the stūpa, a manifestation of the "crude, bizarre, comical, realistic,—embracing all that folk mind could conceive in its odd intermixture of folk-lore, superstition, fancy as well as piety" (176).[32]

As articulated by modern scholars, Buddhism from its earliest days thus emerges with a relatively clear and consistent two-tiered structure. On the one hand is the Buddhism of the founder, the Buddhism of the monks, marked by renunciation of the world and entry into the monastic *saṃgha,* decorous behavior as defined by compliance with the *vinaya,* the pursuit of the vocation of texts and scholarship, and the goal of nirvāṇa. On the other hand is the Buddhism of the laity, characterized by virtuous behavior and generosity toward monastics as well as by participation in the cults of the stūpa and of local deities. The laity practiced a compromised Buddhism and, in so doing, acted as a kind of buffer between the authentic Buddhism of the monks and the non-Buddhist environment of larger India. In this role, for whatever assistance they may provide the monks, the laypeople are always a potential threat to the maintenance of the purity of the dharma.

Scholars have embraced the two-tiered model of Buddhism not only because it is found in normative textual tradition. Equally important, this model also provides a coherent and thorough explanation of the basic structures of Indian Buddhism and is particularly useful in placing a number of phenomena that do not seem to conform to the notion of a pure, elite, monastic Buddhism. Thus, the monument of the stūpa, so pervasive across the face of India, may be explained as a product of popular Buddhism. The same is true of the liturgical kind of Buddhism associated from an early time with the stūpa but found elsewhere, such as in the cult of the Buddha image. In addition, the presence of magical and miraculous elements in the Buddhism of all periods receives a similar "popular" explanation (Conze 1959, 175–80). Finally, the existence in early Buddhism of a "cult of saints" is understood in the same way as a manifestation of popular Buddhism.

In explanation of this latter, we may again cite Lamotte, who, in the final chapter of his *Histoire,* entitled "La religion bouddhique," summarizes the transformation that he sees to have occurred in the Buddha's teaching, largely as the result of lay pressure, by which Buddhism was transformed from "a philosophical-mystical message as it originally was . . . into a veritable religion'' (Lm., 712–13). As part of this chapter, Lamotte includes a section on the ''Buddhist saints,'' remarking that although Buddhist saints are acknowledged and venerated in Indian Buddhism, the Buddha had clearly expatiated on the ineffability of the realized ones and thus effectively undercut any attempts to develop a cult of saints in Buddhism. Lamotte explains this discrepancy: ''between the theory and the practice, there is a gap,'' and ''nothing could prevent the Buddhists from also having their saints'' (765). Lamotte expands on this point:

> If monks, dedicated to a life of study and meditation, are able to resign themselves to seeing in their founder *no more* [emphasis added] than a sage entered into nirvāṇa, lay followers . . . require a living god, a ''god superior to the gods'' *(devātideva)* who continues his beneficent activity among them, who is able to predict the future, perform wonders, and whose cult *(pūjā)* will be something more than mere recollection *(anusmṛti)*. (714)[33]

The two-tiered model is also attractive to scholars for its ability to explain historical transformation. If Buddhism undergoes change, it may be ascribed to ''popular (that is, strictly speaking, non-Buddhist) elements'' entering by way of the laity. A great many changes in Buddhism can be explained in this way, and Lamotte shows just how universal a principle of historical explanation the two-tiered model can be when he remarks that ''the conflict, not to say rivalry [between the Buddhism of the monk and that of the laity] conditions the entire history of Indian Buddhism'' (Lm., 59). We have already noted one example of change explained by the two-tiered model, namely, the ''disappearance'' of Buddhism from India around the twelfth century C.E.[34] Another frequently cited example is the rise of Mahāyāna Buddhism itself. Lamotte, for instance, says that ''the formation of the Mahāyāna in the heart of the [monastic] community constituted the triumph of the humanity of the laity over the rigorism of the *bhikṣu*'' (59), and ''the arrival of the Mahāyāna constituted the triumph of lay aspirations'' (89).[35] Similarly, the rise of Pure Land Buddhism in East Asia is likewise often tied to the emergence into dominance of trends in Buddhism from the popular sphere, as is the entire phenomenon of the cult of Maitreya (785). Finally, the origin of Vajrayāna Buddhism is likewise ascribed to lay influences.[36]

The preceding should suggest that the two-tiered model of Buddhism purports to provide an all-embracing and sufficient explanation of Buddhist life in whatever manifestation, where there are only two options available to the would-be Buddhist: to become a monk living in the settled monastery and following the *prātimokṣa* or to become a layperson and to follow the lesser path. No other option is admitted. Further, the two-tiered model has a virtually unlimited field of operation, something shown in a curious dynamic in the way the model works. Whereas the monastic ideal is given a relatively clear and careful definition based on certain normative texts, the lay ideal tends to be defined as whatever does not fit into the ideal of the monk. In this way, the two-tiered model can function in a manner that is both all-inclusive and also difficult to challenge: whatever does not correspond to the normative monastic ideal is automatically relegated to the category of popular Buddhism.[37]

Some Ideological Features of the Two-Tiered Model

The two-tiered model is thus proposed as a hermeneutic for interpreting Indian Buddhism as a whole, including the Buddhist saints. The obvious question arises of the extent to which the model is really adequate to perform its intended function. Of course, in light of the cited Buddhist texts and the interpretations of many modern scholars, the legitimacy of this hermeneutic seems so obvious as to need no justification. However, this model presents a picture that is, in some crucial respects, distorted. Because it is through the two-tiered model that Buddhists and modern interpreters are accustomed to viewing the saints, any understanding of them must involve an exploration both of the model and of the Buddhist saints. The remaining pages of this chapter consider the first issue, while the following chapters address the second.

The Development of Settled Monasticism and the Two-Tiered Model

Max Weber, some of whose insights into early Buddhism have yet to be fully appreciated, suggests a model of the development of early Buddhism that may act as a starting point for the present discussion. According to Weber, the charismatic figure of the Buddha, as fully realized saint, stood at the center of the earliest Buddhist tradition, surrounded by a circle of close disciples as well as a larger group of devoted lay followers. The Buddha thus functioned, in Weber's terms, as a "charismatic personality."[38] Through his meditation and subsequent awakening, the Buddha had come into knowledge of reality itself and, by virtue of that, possessed ultimate wisdom and compassion. The unprecedented nature of the Buddha's discovery meant that it was not naturally accessible to others, and he was therefore "set apart from ordinary men, and treated as endowed with supernatural . . . powers or qualities" (Weber 1968b, 48). However, others might gain access to the ultimate mystery in and through their relationship with the Buddha, to the extent that they recognized his charisma and submitted themselves to him as devotees (49). Weber remarks that "psychologically this 'recognition' is a matter of complete personal devotion" (49). Among the three types of human authority delineated by Weber—those resting on rational, traditional, and charismatic grounds—the authority of the Buddha clearly rested on charisma. In this sense, it was based on "devotion to [his] specific and exceptional sanctity, heroism or exemplary character" (46).[39]

The disciples of the Buddha were characterized by a number of features identified by Weber as typical of members of groups surrounding charismatic figures. For one thing, the recruitment of followers initially occurred chiefly through response to the Buddha's charisma, rather than through his (or his followers') fulfillment of more external criteria such as wealth, social class, title, technical ability, or learning. This goes along with the fact that, in Weber's words, "charisma can only be 'awakened' and 'tested'; it cannot be learned or taught" (Weber 1968b, 58). The subsequent relationship of followers to the Buddha was primarily personal, emotional, and intimate, rather than based on traditional or rationalized structures and procedures (50). In the operation of the earliest community, decisions were arrived at through the Buddha's own response to situations rather than by reference to preexisting codes and patterns. In this kind of situation, Weber tells us, "formally concrete judgments are newly created from case to case and are originally regarded as divine judgments" (51). These judgments are not carried out by administrative organs. "In their place are agents who have been provided with charismatic authority by their chief or who possess charisma of their own" (51).

The community of renunciants surrounding the Buddha lived by the relatively unpredictable means of voluntary gifts obtained by alms-seeking, rather than by regularized means of economic support (Weber 1968b, 51).[40] In this practice, earliest Buddhism fits with other charismatic movements, which are, at least from the viewpoint of more rational considerations, an "antieconomic force" (53) and "foreign to economic considerations" (51). For Weber, the disavowal of predictable, regularized economic maintenance as a priority is an essential part of the Buddha's charisma. His power is not of saṃsāra, and the web of alliances, agreements, and concessions necessary to economic stability are not his concern. In all these ways, the charismatic authority of the Buddha, as of similar leaders, is specifically "outside the realm of every-day routine and the profane sphere" (52). "In this respect, it is sharply opposed both to rational, and particularly bureaucratic authority, and to traditional authority. . . . Both rational and traditional authority are specifically forms of every-day routine control of actions; while the charismatic type is the direct antithesis of this" (51). According to Weber, for some time after the Buddha's passing, this form of organization continued, with the Buddha's disciples functioning as charismatic masters for their disciples, just as the Buddha had for them.

However, soon a marked change took place within the Buddhist community, and Buddhist renunciants began to develop modes of organization, operation, and teaching that were unprecedented in Buddhism up to that point. According to Weber, this change involved a shift in type of authority, from one based on charisma to one based on tradition, whereby the community came to be managed primarily through reference to a given set of traditional structures, rules, and procedures. This change represented, Weber tells us, a fundamental transformation: charisma, the antithesis of routine, was "routinized." Charisma, "outside the realm of every-day routine," was converted into tradition, a form of "every-day routine control of action" (Weber 1968b, 51). Charisma, based on the present and its perceived spiritual exigencies, gave way to tradition, which takes as its primary normative reference point the past.

What were the motivations for this kind of shift among the early Buddhists? With Buddhism as a primary example, Weber points to a number of factors that are typically involved in such transformations away from charismatic authority in religions (1968b, 54ff.). For one thing, the followers have an interest in the continuation of their movement, and they seek to make it something rational, stable, and reliable. They also tend to develop definitive forms and codified procedures to preserve what they have received. Thus "they have an interest in continuing [their movement] in such a way that both from an ideal and a material point of view, their own status is put on a stable every-day basis'' (54). In so doing, ''the great majority of disciples and followers will in the long run 'make their living' out of their 'calling' in a material sense'' (58–59). Thus it is that ''routinization of charisma also takes the form of the appropriation of powers of control and of economic advantages by the followers or disciples, and of regulation of the recruitment of these groups'' (58). This shift from charismatic authority to traditional authority, in early Buddhism as in other similar religious movements, also involves several other factors. The personal charisma of the master as the basis of recruitment is gone, and now ''the followers or disciples . . . set up norms for recruitment, in particular involving training or tests of eligibility'' (58). In addition, the antieconomic character of the charismatic movement is altered so that it is ''adapted to some form of fiscal organization to provide for the needs of the group and hence to the economic conditions necessary for raising taxes and contributions'' (60). In addition, the distinction between laity and clergy (in the case of Buddhism, the monastic) becomes important: ''When a charismatic movement develops in the direction of praebendal provision, the 'laity' become differentiated from the 'clergy'; that is, the participating members of the charismatic administrative staff which has now become routinized.'' ''This process,'' Weber points out, ''is very conspicuous in Buddhism'' (60).[41]

Particularly important in the shift from charismatic to routinized authority is the development of an administrative structure. This structure, in monastic Buddhism, possesses some of the characteristics of Weber's ''bureaucracy.'' It implies a fixed jurisdictional area, namely, the community of monks[42] living in the monastery, which is ''ordered by rules, laws or administrative regulations'' (Weber 1968c, 66–67). It also implies an official hierarchy based on a ''firmly ordered system of super- and subordination'' (67) and a staff, possessing technical training, to manage the institution. Written documents (or, in the early Buddhist case, memorized texts) play a central role, in turn implying a system of scribes (or specialists in memorization) and scholars to transmit and interpret them. Finally, such an administration ''follows general rules which are more or less stable, more or less exhaustive, and which can be learned. Knowledge of these rules represents a special technical learning which the officials possess'' (69). Although, as we shall see, Weber's analysis needs correction on several important points, his account of early Buddhist history is important in suggesting something of the fundamental and far-reaching nature of the transformation that led from the earliest, wandering form of the Buddhist community to classical Buddhist monasticism.[43]

Further insight into the shift in early Buddhism from an originally wandering to a primarily settled, monastic form of community has been provided by scholars studying the early *vinaya*. Erich Frauwallner, for example, has attempted to identify the earliest textual expression of monastic Buddhism, the *Old Skandhaka*, which he has reconstructed from surviving *vinaya*s of the various traditions and from other related early sources (1956). Basing his work partly on that of Louis Finot, Frauwallner believes that he has been able to reconstruct an original work, standing at the very beginnings of Buddhist literature and providing the earliest evidence of Buddhist monasticism.[44] According to Frauwallner, the *Old Skandhaka* was a *vinaya* work, created by earliest monastic tradition before it underwent division into different schools. The later monastic schools preserved different portions of the *Old Skandhaka* in their *vinaya*s and other texts, and it is from these remains, Frauwallner says, that the parent document can be reconstructed. According to Frauwallner, "the core of the work [the original *Old Skandhaka*] [was] the exposition of the Buddhist monastic rules." This urtext was, however, considerably more inclusive than the classical *vinaya*s of the Nikāya schools. Around an essential core of monastic rules, it contained a life of the Buddha, including the earliest version of the *Mahāparinirvāṇa Sūtra* and a history of the early communities. In this material, which Frauwallner dates to the fourth century B.C.E.,[45] one finds a relatively clear and consistent expression of settled monasticism, as it was just then in the process of consolidation. The "text" and the "author" hypothesized by Frauwallner represent a grand justification of monastic Buddhism, in which an overview of Buddhist history is presented, with the character and legitimacy of the monastic institution providing the central raison d'être of the work. Thus the *Old Skandhaka* is at once an expression of classical monasticism in its formative stages and a major force in the process of consolidation.

In Frauwallner's *Old Skandhaka,* we can see in the settled monasticism of the fourth century B.C.E. a very different kind of Buddhism from that of the original wandering community. For one thing, Buddhism is clearly departing from the original peripatetic ideal, and the *Old Skandhaka* views the settled monastery as the norm. The monastery is, moreover, a complex institution, with provision for various bureaucratic functions, including administrative positions responsible for the distribution of clothes, food, and medicine; for the assignment of sleeping places to newcomers; and for the allotment of the works and duties necessary to ongoing monastic life.[46] The *Old Skandhaka* is not only articulating but also justifying its brand of Buddhism. In the fourth century B.C.E. the developing institution of settled monasticism represented an innovation that needed to legitimize itself vis à vis the older and more traditional Buddhist (and non-Buddhist) renunciant style of homeless wandering. This must have been no easy task, and the survival and success of those early monks would have been inseparably bound up with their ability to articulate effectively the normativity of their tradition. In this process, the *Old Skandhaka* had a crucial role to play by presenting an interpretation of Buddhist history in which its own kind of Buddhism is seen not only as authentic but as the one originally intended by the founder and the measure against which other forms are to be judged.

In the *Old Skandhaka,* we thus find settled monasticism in the very midst of a conversation with the older, wandering form, which it wants partly to ignore, partly to refute, and partly to subordinate to its own kind of Buddhism. Against the ideal of wandering mendicancy, the *Old Skandhaka* manages to insist on the normativity of its own settled monastic form in two ways. First, it accepts in principle the major forms of the earlier wandering ideal but then adds so many exceptions that it emasculates the ideal. Second, through its various perspectives and regulations, it goes one step further and makes the wandering life no longer possible, at least for those following the (now) normative life of settled monasticism.[47] These perspectives and regulations are illustrated by the new role played by the ancient ideal of the so-called four *niśraya*s (P., *nissaya*)—to take only food given as alms, to wear only rags, to live only under trees, and to employ as medicine only the urine of oxen—which defined a normative style of life for wandering Buddhist renunciants in earlier times (Frauwallner 1956, 74). In the *Old Skandhaka,* the danger is admitted that one may seek entry into the monastic life out of a desire for a comfortable and secure existence. In the Pāli version of the incident found in the *Mahāvagga* (*V*-p 1:57–58 [H., 4:74–75]), a certain brahmin sees a succession of sumptuous meals arranged for the disciples of the Buddha and, impressed by the fare, joins the order. However, when the succession of meals concludes and all must wander afresh for alms, the brahmin becomes disenchanted and resentful and threatens to leave the order. This is reported to the Buddha, and, when he confronts the monk, the monk admits he joined the order for the sake of his belly. In order to hinder such behavior in the future, in Frauwallner's words, "the Buddha prescribes that at the ordination the four . . . [*niśrayas*] should be communicated to the applicant. . . . This communication should be made after the ordination" (1956, 74). This regulation only makes sense if we suppose that the way of life described by the four *niśraya*s does not have normative force for the monks of the *Old Skandhaka.*[48] To be sure, renunciant life outside of the monastery is not excluded by the *Old Skandhaka.* For example, monks living in the forest are mentioned, but now they appear as an exception (58). In addition, they are under the authority of the *vinaya,* and rules are given for the monastic regulation of their behavior (124–25).

The *Old Skandhaka* moves away from the ancient wandering life in other ways as well. Those who belong to a specific monastic group or *saṃgha* are strictly differentiated from those who do not,[49] and these latter are forbidden to take part in official acts of the *saṃgha* or in the communally central event of the *poṣadha* service (Frauwallner 1956, 38). In addition, the *poṣadha* is not only a privilege of all monks but a duty, and no monk shall avoid this gathering (79). Thus, "the Buddha . . . prescribes that a community procedure should settle the limits of the common dwelling zone, *inside which all monks must come to the same confession ceremony*"[50] (80; emphasis added). Furthermore, a monk is forbidden to go to a monastery that has no monks except in sufficient numbers to perform the *poṣadha* (39). In these and other ways, then, the *Old Skandhaka* promotes an ideal that excludes those who would follow the ancient Buddhist ideal of unrestricted wandering.

There is another way in which the *Old Skandhaka* appears to depart from the earlier wandering ideal—namely, in its devaluation of meditation. In many early texts, meditation in the forest is presented as a central value and concomitant of the wandering life. The *Old Skandhaka* does not encourage the life of meditation and instead puts forward as priorities settled monastic values, including the behavioral purity of monk and monastic community (Frauwallner 1956, 80) and, by implication, the proper maintenance of textual tradition (see later in this chapter and Chapter 11). A possible instance of the *Old Skandhaka*'s devaluation of meditation is provided in the *Mahāvagga* in its explanation of the inception of the *pravāraṇā* (P., *pavāraṇā*), or ceremony at the end of the rains retreat. In the passage in question, we are told that a certain group of monks decided to pass their rains retreat in complete silence. This, of course, is harmonious with a meditative preoccupation during the three months; as we shall see, the practice of "holy silence" sometimes accompanies other practices carried out by Buddhists engaging in intensive meditation. In the *Mahāvagga,* however, the reason given for this silence is that the renunciants in question wished to avoid conflicts with one another. The Buddha, disapproving of this kind of behavior, instituted the *pravāraṇā,* wherein monks asked pardon of each other in public. Thus the Buddha provided a way to maintain harmony that, in effect, criticizes and does away with the practice of silence during the retreat (Olivelle 1974, 39). Such a development suggests a communal context in which the practice of silence was no longer felt to be important and was, in fact, seen as in some way counterproductive to the community's larger aims.

The *Old Skandhaka* departs from the earliest Buddhist ideal in another way, crucial in the present context: it is no longer the charismatic leader who stands at the center of the tradition, but the routinized monastic institution itself. Thus the younger monk must have an older monk as teacher, but their relationship is strictly subordinated to and regulated by the monastic *saṃgha.* A monk may not take a disciple until he has been ordained for ten years, obviously militating in various ways against the spontaneous relationship of disciple and charismatic teacher (Frauwallner 1956, 72). Of particular interest, only fully ordained monks of long standing may be teachers, that is, those who have already established themselves as reliable representatives of monastic tradition. In addition, under various conditions the disciple may be assigned another teacher, thus denying the unique and lifelong bond of disciple and master so clearly exemplified in the Buddha's relation with his own disciples. Thus we read, "subordination under a master shall last only five years" (73). The occasion for this rule is revealing. The story is told that one day the Buddha makes a journey but is accompanied only by a few junior monks because the other monks *"do not wish to leave their masters"* (72; emphasis added). Such devotion to one's personal master is seen as blameworthy by the Buddha as depicted in the *Old Skandhaka.*[51]

In the *Old Skandhaka,* settled monasticism wants to deny the charismatic master as the ultimate reference point for the disciple and for the community of renunciants. But what might be its reason for doing so? Here Weber's insights seem pertinent: the charismatic master, with uncertain loyalty to past ways of doing things, who embodies the unpredictability of the realized saint, represents a potential threat to the ordered organization and operation of the monastic institution.[52] As Weber remarks, the "community of monks clearly did not wish to permit either spiritual succession or, in general, the aristocracy of charisma to gain ascendency in their midst" (1958, 224). Thus classical monasticism replaced hierarchy based on spiritual charisma with a hierarchy based on seniority and bureaucratic function (224).

In the *Old Skandhaka,* it is no longer the individual master but rather the community of monks that has the power to confer full ordination. The texts depict the Buddha's own disciples as coming to him and receiving *bhikṣu* ordination from him as an individual teacher and their spiritual master. Subsequently, the Buddha is shown giving the authority to ordain to his own disciples, such that they can confer ordination on others (Frauwallner 1956, 73). However, according to the *Old Skandhaka,* a person can no longer take the *bhikṣu* ordination from an individual monk, for now there must be at least ten fully ordained monks present for an ordination to be valid. This, in effect, means that an individual monk, however senior and however realized, is debarred from giving ordination to others. In essence, it thus becomes only the collective community of monks that has the power to confer ordination and so control admission into the order (73). The shift of authority away from the freely wandering reununciant is complete. Such a one no longer has the ability to induct a disciple into the full renunciant life, at least in so far as this is conceived in the *vinaya.*

We have seen that, according to the two-tiered model, as propounded in the *Mahāparinirvāṇa Sūtra,* the laity's kind of Buddhism is regarded as different from and inferior to that of the monks. However, in the *Old Skandhaka,* this low estimation casts an interesting shadow in a certain deference, perhaps by way of compensation, paid by monks to laity. As we shall see, in the early and later texts dealing with forest renunciation, one is jealous of protecting one's independence and of maintaining some distance from the laity. In the *Old Skandhaka,* by contrast, there is a tendency for monks to be careful to adapt themselves in so far as possible to the demands and expectations of the laity. Thus the reason that the Buddha first orders his disciples to keep the rains retreat is that the laity wish it (Frauwallner 1956, 82). In the Theravādin *vinaya,* in fact, we find the Buddha instituting the *prātimokṣa* recitation because the layman, King Bimbisāra, has asked him to do so (*V*-p 1:101–2 [H., 4:130–31]). Further, in the *Old Skandhaka,* the monks are told that they should keep the rains retreat in one place. However, a monk may abandon the retreat to accept an invitation of a layperson to receive gifts, although he may not be gone more than seven days. The commitment that a monk makes to a layperson to remain in the retreat in one place cannot be lightly contravened, and if a monk does leave, it is considered an offense and is only not so under certain conditions (Frauwallner 1956, 83). We saw previously how the *Mahāparinirvāṇa Sūtra* (in Frauwallner's view, originally part of the *Old Skandhaka*) appears to devalue stūpa worship and sets the laity on a lower spiritual level than the monk. We have just seen how the more strictly *vinaya* section of the *Old Skandhaka* accomplishes the same kind of devaluation in relation to the ideal of wandering mendicancy. Now it may be observed that these devaluations taken together are nothing other than the two-tiered model of Buddhism, which the *Old Skandhaka* is developing in order to accomplish its central purpose of establishing the authenticity and normativity of its own, settled monastic kind of Buddhism. Thus in its earliest Buddhist rendition,[53] the two-tiered model of Buddhism is ideological in character and part of the attempt of one kind of Buddhism to assert its own special normativity at the expense of others.[54]

It is interesting that the question of the unique normativity of settled monasticism versus peripatetic forms is not solved for all parties concerned at the hypothesized time of the composition of the *Old Skandhaka.* In the *Milindapañha,* written around the beginning of the common era, the issue is evidently not settled, and we see the proponents of the settled monastery still engaged in strenuously asserting the normativity of their own way of life. In chapter 5 of the text, King Milinda puts forward various "dilemmas" that puzzle him. The very first dilemma is the apparent contradiction between the wandering ideal and the ideal of settled monastic life. Citing a venerable passage from the *Suttanipāta,* the king remarks, "Venerable Nāgasena, the Blessed One said: 'In friendship of the world anxiety is born, / In household life distraction's dust springs up, / The state set free from home and friendship's ties, / That, and that only, is the recluse's aim' " (211 [T.R. 1890–94, 2:1]). The king then cites a passage from the *vinaya* that appears to advance a different ideal: "But on the other hand he said: 'Let therefore the wise man, / Regarding his own weal, / Have pleasant dwelling-places built, / And lodge there learned men' " (211 [2:2]). Then the king poses the obvious question: "Now, venerable Nāgasena, if the former of these two passages was really spoken by the *tathāgata,* then the second must be wrong. But if the *tathāgata* really said: 'Have pleasant dwelling-places built,' then the former statement must be wrong" (211 [2:2]).

Nāgasena, here speaking as the proponent of settled monastic life, replies that both statements were made by the Buddha and are, therefore, true. The first statement is true in the sense that it represents the appropriate *psychological attitude* of renunciants: they should remain inwardly free from attachment to any thing. The second statement is true because it indicates the actual lifestyle and physical habitation that is appropriate to monks:

> The gift of a dwelling-place *(vihāra)* has been praised and approved, esteemed and highly spoken of [for monks], by all the *buddhas.* And those [the laity] who have made such a gift shall be delivered from rebirth, old age, and death. . . . And again, if there be a common dwelling-place *(vihāra)* the sisters of the Order will have a clearly ascertained place of rendezvous, and those who wish to visit (the brethren of the Order) will find it an easy matter to do so. Whereas if there were no homes for the members of the Order it would be difficult to visit them. (*Mp* 212 [T.R., 1890–94, 2:3])

By his reply, Nāgasena—without actually contradicting canonical tradition—succeeds in affirming that in effect two kinds of Buddhism are legitimate: the superior and preferable one of the settled monastery and its *vinaya*-abiding inhabitants, and the inferior way of the laity. The old ideal of the wandering renunciant, as a legitimate ideal that can actually be followed, is not acknowledged but has—at least in this rendering—disappeared from the scene. Explicit reference to it in the *Suttanipāta* passage is now reinterpreted so that it no longer refers to a normative lifestyle but rather to a mental attitude. Thus if, as we have seen, the *Milindapañha,* like the *Mahāparinirvāṇa Sūtra,* has placed the stūpa in a subordinate position to its own brand of Buddhism, here we see that it has rendered the Buddhism of the wandering mendicant more or less invisible.

In the *Mahāparinirvāṇa Sūtra,* the *Old Skandhaka,* and the *Milindapañha,* then, we seem to find stūpa worship and the wandering life removed from positions of superior normativity, being supplanted by settled monasticism, which is now seen as the most authentic form of Buddhism. At the same time, the laity are placed in a distinctly subordinated status,[55] a status given also to the stūpa and perhaps, when not entirely ignored, to the unaffiliated wandering Buddhist mendicant as well. These texts, then, put forward a two-tiered model of Buddhism as part of their general project of promoting the normativity of their own preferred Buddhist lifestyle. In so doing, they betray the fact that the two-tiered model of Buddhism is not a disinterested reflection of the situation of early Buddhism so much as an ideological construct.[56]

The Vocation of Texts and Scholarship and the Two-Tiered Model

Settled monasticism is typically linked, as noted, with two characteristic preoccupations, the cultivation of behavioral purity, as defined by the *vinaya,* and the development of expertise in the sacred scriptures through the vocation of texts and scholarship. A closer examination of this latter preoccupation is pertinent in the present context for the additional light it sheds on the two-tiered model of Buddhism. The vocation of texts and scholarship initially takes shape in the *Old Skandhaka,* where, Frauwallner tells us, we can see the first systematic expression of this central feature of classical monasticism. Frauwallner shows how the material reflected in the text presupposes an already existing (oral) textual tradition of *vinaya* rules, legends about the Buddha, and *sūtra* (P., *sutta*) summaries of the Buddhist teachings. In addition, the *Old Skandhaka* also presupposes certain attitudes toward "text" in Buddhism. For example, one finds in the *Old Skandhaka* the idea of a definitive collection of existing oral tradition. This is seen implicitly in the very idea of the composition of the text itself, which reflects an intention "to collect in a definitive form the Buddhist monastic rules" (Frauwallner 1956, 65), and also explicitly in the legend of the first council, contained in the *Old Skandhaka,* which asserts the existence of a definitive collection of the scriptures, purportedly recited shortly after the Buddha's passing. These notions of a definitive body of texts in turn presuppose a group of people who have such texts in memory, a system of training whereby these documents are transmitted to others, and the commitment of substantial amounts of time to memorizing and reciting. These factors in turn imply, more or less, an institution, with priorities of the preservation of a substantial textual tradition. This fits in with what Frauwallner tells us about the intentions reflected in the *Old Skandhaka.* Behind the text we clearly have an agent (or agents, according to Bareau 1970–71 and 1979)[57] extremely learned in the textual sense. This agent was "an outstanding specialist of the *vinaya*" (Frauwallner 1956, 65) and, moreover, was knowledgeable in a wide variety of extant Buddhist literature of different types. This monastic agent inhabited a world where "a learned monk was supposed by everybody to know sacred texts handed down in a fixed tradition and was required to recite them in the proper way." This, in turn, presupposes "a well regulated system of transmission, in which the sacred texts were taught and learnt" (149).

Many of the specific ideas, forms, and methods of textual preservation and transmission evidently did not originate with Buddhism but—if Finot, Frauwallner, Gombrich (1990a, 5ff.), and others are correct—were borrowed from Brahmanical tradition. Certainly the form and contents of the *Old Skandhaka* suggest the plausability of such an origin. Brahmanical tradition possesses the idea of a definitive body of texts (the *Vedas*); so does the *Old Skandhaka.* Brahmanical tradition sees its definitive body of texts as legitimizing its unique spiritual authority; this is implied in the presentation of the *Old Skandhaka* as the authoritative teaching of the Buddha on the renunciant life. The *Vedas* imply a learned priestly elite who are custodians of the sacred texts; so does the *Old Skandhaka*. More specifically, as part of their assertion of their authority, the *Vedas* possess a list of teachers.

Frauwallner believes that the list of teachers of the *vinaya* in the *Old Skandhaka* "was created on the pattern of and as a counterpart to the Vedic lists of teachers, in order to bestow on the[ir] own tradition an authority similar to the Vedic one" (1956, 62). Frauwallner believes that this explanation also clarifies the reason for the legendary account of the first council, an account that scholars generally agree cannot be the story of a historical event pure and simple. In attempting to append a list of teachers to their texts, the early monastic Buddhists faced a problem not faced by their Brahmanical priestly counterparts. The authority on which the texts rested was the Buddha himself. "But it was impossible to attribute all his work to the Buddha and to attach to him the teachers' list, because the Buddha had delivered only individual sermons and given individual precepts; and it was impossible to annex a list of teachers to every single one of them" (64). The problem was solved by the account of the first council, placed before the list of teachers (64). Thus the "author" of the *Old Skandhaka* followed the Vedic model in a general way, by this ingenious maneuver, and succeeded in establishing a single, definitive text, and, more specifically, in putting his material "in a form which would make his work the equal of the great Vedic texts" (65). This modeling of Buddhism on Brahmanical tradition will be discussed further in Chapter 12.

The vocation of texts and scholarship, with its fruition in the writing down of Buddhist texts,[58] must, as it rose to prominence, have changed Buddhist tradition in some dramatic and irreversible ways. Once the letter of the Buddhist teachings has been identified, and once those teachings have been committed to definitive form, first orally and then in writing, once this textual material is understood as canonical, it becomes identified as the repository of the authentic Buddhist teachings. Thus there arises the tendency to locate the "authentic teachings" not, as originally, in the understanding of the realized saint, but rather in external and objectified form, in the authoritative texts. Just such a view is articulated in the *Manorathapūraṇī:*

> As long as the *suttanta* exist, as long as the *vinaya* flourishes, so long will the light shine, as at sunrise. . . . Whether or not there is realization *(paṭivedha)* or practice *(paṭipatti),* scholarship *(pariyatti)* is sufficient for the maintenance of the religion. The erudite man, provided that he is learned in the *Tepiṭaka,* fulfills both. . . . That is why, as long as scholarship remains, the religion remains. . . . Whether there may be a hundred or a thousand *[bhikkhus]* adorned with accurate vision, if scholarship is in default, no realization of the noble path is possible. (*Mrp* 1:93 [Lm., 403])

The mode of access to the teaching also undergoes a change. Whereas previously technical expertise had no particular impact on one's ability to receive the highest teachings, now, in order to gain full access to the teachings and especially to be authoritative in them, one must be able to memorize/recite or, later, to read. More than this, one must be able to understand the often literary language of the Buddhist texts as well as to understand their technical vocabulary and arguments. Further, once a certain body of texts is identified as most authoritative, then inevitably one's ability to read and understand the texts, and to be a specialist of them, is bound up with quantity as well as quality: the more texts one knows, the better (see, for example, Watters 1904–5, 1:162).

This entire process implies, of course, a substantial scholarly training. The magnitude of the training also implies that one will have to spend much of one's time in study and recitation, leaving less time for other pursuits, such as meditation. In fact, given the magnitude of the task confronting textual scholars, it is questionable whether they will have any time for meditation at all. Just this point is reflected in an interesting story recounted by Buddhaghosa. It seems that a certain Elder Revata, a textual specialist and reciter of the *Majjhimanikāya,* went to another elder of the same name, a forest renunciant who lived and meditated in the Malaya (the hill country), in order to receive instruction in meditation. The meditation master asked the scholar,

> "How are you in the scriptures, friend?" "I am studying the Majjhima [Nikāya], venerable sir." "The Majjhima is a hard responsibility, friend. When a man is still learning the First Fifty by heart, he is faced with the Middle Fifty; and when he is still learning that by heart, he is faced with the Last Fifty. How can you take up a meditation subject?" "Venerable sir, when I have taken a meditation subject from you, I shall not look at the scriptures again." He took the meditation subject, and doing no recitation for nineteen years, he reached Arhantship in the twentieth year. (*Vsm* 3:51 [N., 96–97])

In addition, this emphasis on texts and scholarship would seem to be an activity biased toward the higher castes, brahmins in particular, with their predisposition toward scriptural pursuits.[59] This bias, of course, sets up a countertrend to Buddhism's theoretical claim that the monastery is open equally to all, irrespective of caste affiliation, and represents an environment where distinctions of caste are not operative.

The preceding suggests that an emphasis on the text in renunciant life, particularly when this becomes a predominant concern, in turn implies a particular socioreligious context, namely, that of the monastery. A more or less stable canon, especially of some size (that is, not one or a few texts, but a sizable collection of texts), calls for an institutional focus. When the texts are oral, such a focus means a place where textual reciters can congregate and where they can recite their texts and can train younger monks. When the texts are written, a settled institution provides a place where the documents can be stored and be made readily available. The evolving monastery could perform both functions. Solitary meditators or wandering ascetics, living in often unsheltered locations and wandering from place to place, on the other hand, are not in a position to make textual study as integral to their Buddhism as can renunciants dwelling in settled monasteries.[60]

Once Buddhism becomes a tradition of a relatively fixed canon that is written down, the monastery's role becomes even more crucial. Owing to the relatively short lifespan of texts in India, a written tradition requires a large number of people whose main activity is the copying of worn-out texts, in addition to specialists who are expert in one or more texts or classes of texts. All these various specialists must be organized, housed, and fed, and this in turn implies a monastic administration of some complexity. The existence of textual specialists and scribes in turn implies considerable economic resources, including both monasteries large and wealthy enough to support such communities of scholars and also wealth to obtain the necessary materials needed for the scholarly work, such as properly gathered and prepared materials to write on, ink, and writing instruments. Such economic needs imply the necessity of establishing close and stable ties with laypeople of wealth and political power. Thus the settled monastery and the preoccupation with texts and particularly collections of texts tend to be interdependent phenomena.

The writing down of texts and monastic institutions are natural allies in another way. As Weber saw, writing recommends itself to those concerned with the consolidation and maintenence of orthodoxy and institutionalized religious authority (1968b, 48ff.). To put pen to paper may seem merely to put oral tradition into writing, but it also concretizes a particular mode of accessibility to, and transmission of, the Buddhist teachings. This, in turn, has important political implications. Oral tradition in Buddhism, when it is not fixed in authoritative texts and a set canon, retains a certain fluidity. But when teachings are fixed in authoritative form, particularly in writing, orthodoxy and standardization can more easily become dominant concerns.

The movement of the text and canon to center stage and the rise to dominance of the monastic institution within which the vocation of texts and scholarship could flourish tended to represent conservative forces within Buddhism. Where the text reigns supreme, the past exists in the present in a concrete and definitive form and may act to check present deviation from past norms. This tended to be true of Buddhist monasticism, in which, as Beyer points out, from the viewpoint of the Buddhist monastery with its texts, its canon, and its specialized scholars, "the creative work had been done; all that was left was to work out the details" (1975a, 239).[61] Thus it was that, typically, the monastic scholars "had been trained not to explore new problems but rather to lay out the parameters of the old" (239).

In this way, the coming to dominance of the canonical text, and particularly the written canonical text, implied in a number of ways a dramatic shift in the understanding of what constituted authentic Buddhism. Now the authentic view was no longer defined primarily by the realization of the master, or by the oral interchange of master and disciple and the integrity of their connection, but by content of the texts. It was no longer simply personal vocation and application to the teacher that opened the gates of dharma, but rather, to some large extent, technical expertise and the ability to satisfy a variety of criteria not necessarily reflective of inner spiritual capacity, inspiration, or development. The definition of the "accomplished one," or the master, also shifted with the emphasis on the text. Previously, the master was simply the one who was realized. Now this person is the *vinaya*-following monastic, who through the settled monastic vocation has direct access to the sacred scriptures as well as the technical and logical abilities to read and master the textual tradition, canonical and commentarial. Where textual Buddhism reigns supreme, the charismatic teacher has been replaced by the learned and decorous scholar.

The pursuit of textual learning, as understood in monastic tradition, thus cannot be separated from certain ideological features. The teachings of the Buddha tend to be identified with those texts preserved in the monastic canon. The maintenance of this scriptural tradition is understood as a primary task of the monk, above and even tending to exclude the practice of meditation. Those who are proficient in texts are to be given the highest respect. Other texts, other pursuits, renunciants with other accomplishments, are implicitly if not explicitly devalued. Thus the vocation of texts and scholarship as understood in settled monasticism represents, in and of itself, a major buttressing factor of the two-tiered model of Buddhism.

Just how far the vocation of books and learning came to be definitive of settled monasticism as such is suggested by the Chinese traveler Hsüan-tsang, who visited India between 629 and 645 C.E. In a general summation of the scholarly life of Indian Buddhist monasteries, he makes the following observations:[62]

> The Brother who expounds orally one treatise (or class of scripture) in the Buddhist Canon, whether *Vinaya, Abhidharma,* or *Sūtra,* is exempted from serving under the Prior; he who expounds two is invested with the outfit of a Superior; he who expounds three has Brethren deputed to assist him; he who expounds four has lay servants assigned to him; he who expounds five rides an elephant; he who expounds six rides an elephant and has a surrounding retinue. . . . The Brethren are often assembled for discussion to test intellectual capacity and bring moral character into prominent distinction, to reject the worthless and advance the intelligent. Those who bring forward . . . fine points in philosophy, and give subtle principles in their proper place, who are ornate in diction and acute in refined distinctions, ride richly caparisoned elephants preceded and followed by a host of attendants. But as for those . . . who have been defeated in discussion, who are deficient in doctrine and redundant in speech . . . the faces of such are promptly daubed with red and white clay, their bodies are covered with dirt, and they are driven out to the wilds or thrown into ditches. (Watters 1904–5, 1:162)

In spite of the undeniable social and scholarly creativity of monastic Buddhism as seen in its great textual tradition, the development of the monastery with its textual preoccupations was not, as already implied, without its drawbacks. Rather than seeing itself as complementary to other kinds of Buddhism—particularly to types of renunciant Buddhism placing more emphasis on wandering freely and on meditation—in at least some cases it came to regard itself as a self-sufficient form of renunciant Buddhism.[63] It was as the expression of such a view that the two-tiered model arose. Because it was monastic Buddhism that was generally charged with the written tradition, and because the texts provide the primary evidence of Indian Buddhism, the voices of other kinds of renunciant Buddhism in the time following the Buddha's *parinirvāṇa* have not been well heard, either by modern scholars or even by later Buddhists themselves.[64] These other kinds of renunciant Buddhism—characterized by elements such as a wandering mode of life, dwelling in the forest, and a preoccupation with meditation—were deemphasized, ignored, or repudiated by the more (at least to us) visible Buddhism of the settled monastery.

Did this mean, however, that these earlier trends ceased to exist? Some scholars have suspected their ongoing, if mostly invisible, presence in India. Frauwallner, for example, remarks that

> the strongly mystical element, which was powerful in Buddhism from its early days and which in the final analysis went back to the Buddha himself, did not simply allow itself to be eliminated. There were always many members of the community for whom meditative experience was the essential thing and who were indifferent to dogmatic scholarship. (1969, 143)

But who were these people? What was their Buddhism like? How did they understand themselves? How did others see them? It is the intent of the following chapters to begin to provide some answers to these questions.

Notes

1. I adopt this terminology from Peter Brown (1981), who uses it in his examination of the rise and function of the cult of saints in Latin Christianity. Schopen (1988, 153ff.) has made reference to the applicability of this model to the Buddhist case. See also Lancaster's different way of relating Brown's two-tiered model to Buddhism (Lancaster 1984).

2. This is not an unreasonable assumption, as the Theravāda along with its classic texts and practices originated in India.

3. The use in this chapter of masculine terms to refer to the settled monastic ("the monk") as presented in the two-tiered model is intentional. This usage follows the tendency of those favoring the two-tiered model to discuss monastics only in terms of the fully ordained man. The nun *(bhikṣuṇī;* P., *bhikkhunī)* represents a special case to be discussed later. Her status as a renunciant would seem to locate her in the upper tier, but because she is a woman and thus theoretically debarred from enlightenment, when she is mentioned, she tends to be linked with the lower. In general, however, as we shall see, she is usually ignored in literature, both Buddhist and scholarly, articulating the two-tiered model. See Ku 1984.

4. For a useful collection of citations of, and quotations from, Buddhist texts describing Buddhist community in terms of this two-tiered model, see Lester 1973, 47–150.

5. Useful summaries of the monastic ideal are given by Lamotte (1958, 58–71), Hirakawa (1966), Lester (1973, 48–56; 83–129), and Bunnag (1973). By far the clearest and textually best grounded summary has been provided by Wijayaratna (1990). See also Gombrich's helpful review of the original French edition (1986).

6. Lit. "burden of books" (*PTSD* 243.1); cf. Tambiah (1984, 53) and Khantipalo (1965, 5–7). In this study, the phrase "vocation of texts and scholarship," which translates the Pāli, will be used more generally to designate the characteristic settled monastic pursuits connected with textual learning.

7. These two primary preoccupations are discussed by S. Dutt (1962, 25ff. and 50ff.), Bunnag (1973, 30ff. and 50ff.), Khantipalo (1979, 91–127), and Tambiah (1984, 53ff.).

8. Gombrich additionally comments that in Buddhaghosa's classic *Visuddhimagga,* the monastic "*śīla* is envisaged as a kind of protective cloak in which the monk is to remain

wrapped, a cloak of decorum . . . [where] certainly we are dealing with externals'' (1984, 93). This is not to deny, of course, that the fulfillment of the requirements of external, decorous behavior may not, at the same time, serve the needs of inner, spiritual development.

9. Depending on which *vinaya* tradition is followed, 218–263 rules for the monk and 279–380 rules for the nun (Prebish 1975b, 50).

10. For a useful summary of the *vinaya* literature, see Prebish (1979a and, more concisely, 1975a, 49–53).

11. A very ancient idea in Indian Buddhism; see, e.g., *Sn* 466–67, 488ff.

12. The fact that so many early texts have survived intact attests to the care and energy devoted to this ''vocation'' by the Buddhist monastic tradition (Gombrich 1990a, 6).

13. Gombrich similarly remarks that ''the first function and duty of the [monastic] *saṃgha* was to preserve the Doctrine and thus preserve Buddhism as such. Preserving the Doctrine meant in effect preserving the scriptures, the Canon, and its commentaries'' (1984a, 77). Perhaps reflecting such textual preoccupations are affirmations in numerous canonical texts that brahmins (with their inherited and socially reinforced tendencies toward scholarship) were particularly prominent in the early monastic community (Gokhale 1965, 391–402; Gombrich 1984b, 91–101).

14. Among textual descriptions of monks embodying this ideal of textual accomplishment, the one given in the *Milindapañha* of Nāgasena, the teacher of King Milinda, is a good example. He was, we read, ''learned, clever, wise, sagacious, and able; a skilful expounder . . . well versed in tradition, master of the three Baskets (*piṭakas*), and erudite in Vedic lore . . . master of all that had been handed down in the schools, and of the various discriminations *(paṭisambhidā)* by which the most abstruse point can be explained. He knew by heart the ninefold divisions of the doctrine of the Buddha to perfection, and was equally skilled in discerning both the spirit and the letter of the Word. Endowed with instantaneous and varied power of repartee, and wealth of language, and beauty of eloquence, he was difficult to equal, and still more difficult to excel, difficult to answer, to repel, or refute . . . mighty in eloquence, a confounder of the followers of other masters, a crusher-out of the followers of adherents of rival doctrines. Honoured and revered by the brethren and sisters of the Order, and its lay adherents of either sex, and by kings and their high officials, he was in abundant receipt of all the requisites of a member of the Order—robes and bowl and lodging, and whatever is needful for the sick—receiving the highest veneration no less than material gifts'' (*Mp* 21 [T.R. 1890–94, 1:34–35]).

15. The term *prajñā* has, of course, a dual meaning in Indian Buddhism signifying both the ultimate insight that constitutes liberation and also relative methods of approaching the ultimate, such as textual learning (Lamotte 1980, 126–27). In reference to relative methods, Vasubandhu classically spells out three *prajñā*s: learning *(śrutamayī),* contemplating *(cintāmayī),* and meditating *(bhāvanāmayī)* (La Vallée Poussin 1971, 6:143–44, 159).

16. For some examples of this understanding of *prajñā,* see Cousins 1984.

17. For example, the *Satipaṭṭhāna Sutta* (*Mn* X and *Dn* XXII [Nyanaponika 1962, 117–35]).

18. For example, Buddhaghosa's *Visuddhimagga* (Nyāṇamoli 1976) and Vasubandhu's *Abhidharmakośa* (La Vallée Poussin 1971).

19. The necessity of meditation is spelled out, for example, in the *Dhammapada,* which remarks that ''there is no wisdom [P., *paññā*] for one without meditation [P., *jhāna;* Skt., *dhyāna*]'' (*Dp* 372 [Radhakrishnan 1950, 174]).

20. In *Vsm,* Buddhaghosa says that a monastery ''that is unfavourable [to meditation] has any one of eighteen faults.'' These include the many disturbances of (1) a big monas-

tery, (2) new construction, (3) reparation, (4) arrival of people day and night because the monastery is on a busy highway; disturbances of people coming to fetch (5) water, (6) edible leaves, (7) flowers, or (8) fruit, because sources of these are nearby; disturbances because (9) the place is one of pilgrimage, where people gather; it is (10) near a town, (11) a place where people gather wood, (12) fields where people dispute, (13) where there are disagreeable persons, (14) a marketplace; it is (15) in a remote area with no faith in the dharma, (16) in a border region in dispute, (17) in a place where there are other disturbances; or (18) it is located where it is not possible to have a spiritual teacher (*Vsm* 118–22 [N., 122–23]; see also Dhammaratana 1964, 46–47). Because, excepting 15 to 18, these are just the kinds of places where town-and-village monasteries tend to be built, it is hard to imagine a settled monastery without any of these "faults."

21. Maquet has provided a summary of the high level of activity required of monks living in settled monasteries in contemporary Sri Lanka, which more or less rules out serious meditation practice (1980, 143–45).

22. The general incompatibility between the settled monastic lifestyle and a lifestyle defined primarily by meditation, pointed to by Buddhaghosa, does not mean that monks invariably had no opportunities whatsoever to meditate. Motivated settled monastics might, in the monastery, fit short periods of meditation into their daily schedules. Those with a desire for more intensive practice also might have the option of separating themselves from the monastery for periods of time in order to meditate in retreat. In addition, the practice of ritual chanting (e.g., in the *poṣadha*), with its potentially contemplative character, formed a more or less important part of the regular liturgical calendar of settled monasteries. Such were the exceptions, however, and meditation was typically not a primary focus of the settled monastic institution as such or of its way of life.

23. Conze believes such a development is reflected in a Sarvāstivādin text that relates "the terrible and sad story of the death of the last *arhant* by the hand of one of the scholars" (1959, 116).

24. This same general pattern is discussed by Maquet 1980, 140–41. See also Peter Masefield's interesting discussion of the origins of this idea (1986, 136–44). On this same issue, see Richard Gombrich 1971, 285 and R. L. Slater 1951, 49.

25. See also Bunnag 1984.

26. See Bareau's useful summary 1972, 460ff.

27. For a more detailed summary of the essential components of the ideal lifestyle of the lay Buddhist, as seen by early normative texts, see references to laity in Barua 1966 and Bunnag 1973.

28. *Mps*-p 5.10. References are to the chapter and section numbers of the Pāli text. The chapter and section numbers of the Rhys Davidses' English translation of the Pāli *Mps* (T.R. and C.R. 1899–1921, 2:71–191) correspond to the chapter and section numbers of the Pāli text. Therefore, no additional references to the English translation need be given. The reader attempting to locate passages in T. W. Rhys Davids's earlier translation of the *Mps* (1881, 1–136) should be alerted that the section numbers of the Pāli and this translation frequently do not correspond. Questions concerning the correct translation and interpretation of 5.10 cited here have recently been raised by Gregory Schopen. For a discussion of this issue, see Chapter 10, pp. 338–39.

29. The present section provides a summary of some of the more important ways in which the two-tiered model has functioned in modern interpretations of Indian Buddhism. Although precluded by the limits of this study, a full understanding of the use of this model by modern scholars of Buddhism would need to examine the question of whether there may be something in Western understandings of religion as such that predisposes Western scholars to favor such a model, irrespective of its applicability in a given religious situation. A

very suggestive discussion of precisely this question has been carried out by Peter Brown (1981, 1–49).

30. See also Lamotte 1984a.

31. For example, Conze (1962b, 270; 1980, 38–39) and Bareau (1979, 56; 1980, 1ff.).

32. Many other examples of the two-tiered model as a dominant hermeneutic in contemporary studies of Buddhism could be cited. See, e.g., Bareau 1979, 56 and 1980, 1ff.; and Pachow 1976.

33. This same interpretation appears elsewhere in Lamotte's scholarly writing. See, for example, Lamotte 1980, 130–32.

34. I set "disappearance" off by quotation marks because, of course, Buddhism did not disappear from India after the twelfth century. It was *monastic Buddhism* that was eliminated (and this not entirely), largely because of Muslim depredations, and even monastic Buddhism maintained itself for some time in certain regions at a greater remove from the centers of Muslim activity (see, e.g., Vasu 1911).

35. See also Lamotte 1984, 90.

36. As in Conze's reading: "In the course of time, the laymen became more and more predominant, and, although the basic terms and concepts of the monastic philosophical tradition were often used to embellish the utterances of the Tantras, Tantric thought itself descends directly from the lay Buddhism which for many centuries ran parallel to monastic Buddhism" (Conze 1962b, 270).

37. See Peter Brown's similar observation in reference to the function of the two-tiered model in the study of Latin Christianity (1981, 1–22).

38. The following discussion draws particularly on Weber's examination of charismatic authority and its "routinization" as outlined in 1968a, b, and c. In these pages, Weber discusses charisma and routinization as general phenomena in the history of religions, with Buddhism as a primary example. The present discussion applies his generalizations to the Buddhist case.

39. Weber (1968a, 46) defines authority on rational grounds as "resting on a belief in the 'legality' of patterns of normative rules and the right of those elevated to authority under such rules to issue commands (legal authority)." In the same place he defines authority on traditional grounds as "resting on an established belief in the sanctity of immemorial traditions and the legitimacy of the status of those exercising authority under them (traditional authority)."

40. Although it is certainly true—and Weber would have admitted it—that during the rainy season, the Buddha's *saṃgha* did settle down and likely enjoyed some regularization in the reception of donations.

41. For the same kind of shift, as it occurred in Jainism, see Tatia 1980.

42. In Buddhist studies, the English terms "monk" and "nun" are typically used to refer to a wide range of Buddhist renunciants, including both the Buddha's earliest disciples (we read about the Buddha's first five disciples as "monks," the first women renunciants as "nuns," and so on) and later representatives of classical monasticism. At the same time, the terms "monk" and "nun" are also generally understood to translate *bhikṣu* and *bhikṣuṇī*, respectively, and these as defined in classical Buddhism each refer to fully ordained monastics following the *prātimokṣa*. Thus it comes about that in using the terms "monk" and "nun," scholars typically make the assumption that the types of the classical *bhikṣu* and *bhikṣuṇī* are adequate models for Buddhist renunciation in its earliest as well as its later periods.

In what follows, I depart from this conventional usage as follows. First, unless explicitly quoting or summarizing someone else, I usually use "monk" and "nun" to refer to *bhikṣu* and *bhikṣuṇī* in the classical sense, i.e., one who: (1) has passed through two ordination ceremonies, that of the novitiate *(pravrajyā;* P., *pabbajā)* and that of full ordination *(upasampadā);* (2) is beholden to the classical *prātimokṣa;* and (3) primarily (if not always) lives or maintains membership in a settled monastery governed by the classical *vinaya.* Second, I use the term "forest renunciant" rather loosely to refer to those renunciants who are *not* representatives primarily of settled monasticism but rather have renounced the world, undergoing some form of *pravrajyā,* and instead live mostly in retreat, in the wilds. In the texts, sometimes *bhikṣu* and *bhikṣuṇī* refer to forest renunciants rather than to classical monastics; in these cases, the term "forest renunciant" translates *bhikṣu* and *bhikṣuṇī.* In this study, the term "forest renunciant" is also used to refer to pratyekabuddhas and bodhisattvas who similarly live in the wilds.

43. On this shift, see Gombrich (1984a, 80–82). See also Mus (1935, 1:47). Victor Turner, examining material quite removed from that of India studied by Weber, has, of course, developed a model with many features similar to Weber's. Thus Turner explicates what he believes to be two basic modalities of human relatedness, which he calls "liminality," on the one hand, and "social structure," on the other. Liminality contains a number of features reminiscent of Weber's charismatic phase: (1) the whole person stands in relation to other whole persons under the genus "human being," rather than as one understood primarily through a socially assigned value; (2) this generates a different kind of community from that of conventional society; (3) this type of community ("communitas") involves intense comradeship and egalitarianism of value; (4) the routinization and utilitarian values of "society" are replaced by affect, immediacy, and spontaneity; (5) this new form of community is intensely creative—new religious formulations are abundantly produced, including myths, symbols, rituals, and philosophical systems; (6) human beings, their relation to nature, society, and culture are reconceived; and (7) the members of this community submit themselves to "ritual elders." Social structure, corresponding to Weber's "routinization of charisma," represents a contrast on each point: (1) people are judged not as human beings but rather in terms of their socially assigned status and value; (2) community is interpreted through heavily institutionalized norms, roles, and status positions; (3) human interaction is strictly defined and limited by this institutionalization; (4) routinization and utilitarian values prevail; (5) there is conservative adherence to the "tried and true" aspects of religious life; (6) the human being's relations to nature, society, and culture are also marked by adherence to the "tried and true"; and (7) the role of ritual elders is delimited by convention. See Turner 1969. See Peter Homans's useful summary of Turner, adapted here, and his interesting application of Turner's theories in a more modern context (1985, 38–42).

44. Frauwallner's work has been the subject of considerable debate within recent Buddhist studies (see Tambiah's summary, 1984, 116–18). In general, Frauwallner has received praise from scholars for his use of surviving *vinaya*s in the attempt to reconstruct their common source. In what follows, we intend to make use of those aspects of Frauwallner's work that have stood the test of time. Most scholars have accepted the major outlines of Frauwallner's hypothesis—namely, that there was a common, parent text lying behind the *vinaya*s of the various schools and that this text can, by a comparison of surviving documents, to some extent be reconstructed. See the approbations of Frauwallner's work in Conze (1967a, 8–9 and 1980, 19), Lamotte (1958, 195), Prebish (1979a, 303), and Bechert (1984, 79). Frauwallner's conclusions cannot be accepted without qualification, for which see Lamotte (1958, 193–97), Prebish (1973, 669–78), and Bechert (1984, 79). Important in this context is the work of Bareau, particularly his analysis of *Mps* (1970–71 and 1979), for specific references to which, see Chapter 10. Bareau argues for a graduated composition of *Mps* over several centuries. This appears to contradict Frauwallner's hypothesis of a single author (or at least of a relatively unified time and place of composi-

tion) for the entire *Old Skandhaka.* However, when Bareau and Frauwallner refer to *Mps,* they mean different things, for Frauwallner means the original core of *Mps* as contained in the *Old Skandhaka,* prior to its elaborate development, whereas Bareau means the finished document as it exists in its various extant forms. As we shall see, Bareau also identifies a core common to the various extant versions of *Mps* and present prior to its diffusion. In this, he has actually confirmed the major outlines of Frauwallner's thesis of a common, original parent text (see the "Conclusion" of Chapter 11). As we shall see, Bareau's analysis has also clearly confirmed the notion of a monastic hand and perspective behind the text.

45. Based on the fact that schools from both sides of the Sthavira-Mahāsāṃghika schism draw on this early *Skandhaka,* thus suggesting to Frauwallner that the text antedates their parting (1956, 54).

46. Frauwallner 1956, 124. Olivelle, working from the Pāli texts, in confirmation of Frauwallner's basic characterization, comments on the basic shift to the settled monastery thus: in the *vinaya,* he tells us, "we see a fully developed monastic style of life with detailed and minute rules governing the entire life and activities of individuals and of communities. These communities, i.e., the particular *saṃgha,* lived settled lives in monasteries" (1974, xiii). Olivelle remarks further that "the text of the *pāṭimokkha* appears to be a compilation rather than an original composition . . . it has all the marks of an artificial composition prepared for a well defined purpose" (1974, 50–51). See Pachow's discussion of the development of the *prātimokṣa,* which he believes occurred over a 250-year period (1955, 7–18).

47. S. Dutt comments on the way in which the nature and organization of early settled monasticism undercut and made impossible the wandering lifestyle (1962, 92).

48. Olivelle remarks on the various ways in which in the *vinaya,* the basic intention of the four *niśraya*s is weakened and rendered ineffective by the addition of a variety of exceptions to each. One no longer wanders abroad but may dwell in a settled monastery year-round, or in a curved house, a building on high foundations, a mansion, or a cave. The begging of food from house to house can be circumvented by various means. Thus, one is allowed a meal for the *saṃgha,* a meal for a special person, an invitation (for a full meal), food given on ticket, food given on a day of the waxing or waning of the moon, on a *poṣadha* day, or on the day after a *poṣadha.* One no longer need wear a robe stitched from rags but may accept robes made of linen, cotton, silk, wool, coarse hemp, or canvas. And a variety of additional "medicines" beyond cow's urine are permissible to the monk, including ghee, fresh butter, oil, honey, and molasses (Olivelle 1974, 58–59).

49. A point emphasized by S. Dutt (1962, 92–93).

50. See Dutt 1970, 50.

51. How interesting that it is the precisely the more senior monks who do not wish to leave their masters and the junior ones who are willing to do so. Would one not expect it to be the other way around, that it is the younger, more dependent monks who would feel anxiety at the prospect of leaving their masters? On the other hand, as so often in Buddhist historical and biographical writing, we may find reflected here a large pattern of historical development: it is perhaps those representing the "old order" who do not wish to leave their masters, whereas it is those representing the younger "new order" who have no difficulty doing so, because their allegiance is now no longer to the individual master but to the monastic institution as such.

52. As we shall see, in Buddhism realized saints presuppose accomplishment in meditation, itself a potentially destabilizing and decentralizing force vis-à-vis institutional Buddhism. This character of meditation was recognized in the conflict that led to the official

devaluation of meditation in favor of scholasticism by institutional Buddhism in Sri Lanka in the first century B.C.E. In Maquet's words, "The assembled monks of Laṅka decided, after a debate, that scholarship is more important than practice and realization of *nibbāna 'for the stability of religion'* " (emphasis added; Maquet 1980, 145).

53. As I shall suggest, the two-tiered model likely was not originated by the *Old Skandhaka* but rather borrowed from other sources.

54. It need not be doubted that economic motivations were an important part of the need felt by the *Old Skandhaka* to legitimize its kind of Buddhism. Thus, according to Weber: "The decisive motive for the propaganda activities was naturally given by the material interests of the monks in the increase of the givers of subsistence, the *upāsaka*" (1958, 229). Foucher makes similar reference to economic competition: "Legend never tired of blackening the reputation of the heterodox sects by showing how they tried to ruin the Buddha's reputation in the eyes of the population and thus starve him as well as his Order. In all fairness to them it must be added that in so doing his adversaries were fighting for their own lives" (1963, 208). See also Jaini's discussion of the same topic (1970, 57). Economic competition no doubt existed, not only between Buddhist renunciants and members of other sects, but also among Buddhist institutions, groups, and individuals. In this regard, Hirakawa believes that monasteries and certain nonmonastic Buddhist institutions forming around stūpas engaged in economic competition with one another (1987, 94).

55. Lay Buddhism is, in at least some respects, implicitly equated with non-Buddhist forms of religiosity: by what they do, laypeople cannot achieve nirvāṇa but only rebirth into a god realm or another human birth—exactly the same goals that, according to Buddhism, the practice of the non-Buddhist religion will achieve. Max Weber clearly saw this low status accorded by the monastic tradition to laypeople, who are debarred from seeking "complete salvation" (1958, 215), as "the highest degree was attained only by the monks" (222). "The laity ('house-dweller') can only practice the 'lower righteousness' . . . unlike the *'reverend' (arhat)* it does not qualify for the decisive works of salvation" (215). In what does the Buddhism of the layperson then consist? "Material support of the holy seekers fell on the laity and ultimately this alone constituted the highest merit and honour available to the *upāsaka* (adorer)" (214). And what may the layperson hope to attain through this practice? "In the best case, one may be reborn into one of the (to be sure transitory) godly paradises scorned by those entering *nirvāṇa*" (215). In sum, "In the parish [monastic] doctrine the status group of the 'house-dwelling people' in a manner somewhat similar to the tolerated infidels in Islam, existed only for the purpose of sustaining by alms the Buddhist disciple [monk]" (214). Gombrich, in a recent examination of some important continuities between Brahmanical attitudes and practices and those of Buddhism, makes a similar point, remarking that in several important respects, "the Buddhist layman is left looking just like a Hindu *karma-mārgin bubhukṣu* [layperson]" (1984b, 101). Weber remarks, "It is, of course, questionable whether Buddha's teaching from the onset was conceived as a 'monk's' religion. Perhaps, better, it is as good as certain that this definitely was not the case. It is clearly an ancient tradition that the Buddha in his lifetime permitted numerous lay persons who were not in his order to reach *nirvāṇa*" (215). Weber then cites early sources in which the layperson's capabilities are generally evaluated in a more positive way. On the belief that the layperson could not achieve arhantship, see Bond 1988, 144.

56. On the presence and function of ideological constructs in religions, see Long (1986, 13–62, and index references to "ideology").

57. For a discussion of this, see Chapter 11.

58. On this, see Kloppenborg (1974, 5). The accounts of the first writings down of Buddhist texts are illustrative. As far as we know, the ancestors of the Theravādins com-

mitted the Pāli canon to writing in the first century B.C.E., in Sri Lanka. Implicated in this event was a controversy that, in the words of Lamotte, "would dominate . . . the entire religious history of Ceylon. The question was to know whether the foundation of the tradition *(sāsana)* resided in the practice of the *dhamma (paṭipatti)* or in textual scholarship *[la science religieuse] (pariyatti)*" (1958, 403). Lamotte remarks that it was, of course, the Dhammakathika party, with its primary allegiance to *pariyatti,* that prevailed in the Sri Lankan case. On this, see also Tambiah (1984, 54) and Rahula (1966, 158). This latter chronicles the rejection of the ascetic-hermit tradition in Buddhism and the victory of those with a town-and-village monastic orientation. For discussion of the shift from oral to written tradition in the Mahāyāna, see Schopen (1975, 159, 168, 179).

59. Bareau remarks that for entry into monastic life, "high caste men, and above all brahmins, were better prepared by their education" (1972, 464–65). We see here a striking congruity between the concerns of the brahmin caste and the concerns of the conservative monastic sects, a theme to which I shall return. This pattern of upper-class literati, owing to their textual abilities, rising to prominence in Buddhist monastic circles is, of course, also found in non-Indian Buddhism (see Robinson 1967, 9).

60. Gombrich (1990b) is thus quite right to remark on the close connection between the institution of settled monasticism and the Buddhist preoccupation with texts and learning: "the preservation of oral literature . . . depends on institutions, on recognized and regular arrangements for training, rehearsal and performance" (21). All of this was provided by the Buddhist monastery: "from the first the institution which performed the function of preserving the Buddhist texts must have been the [monastic] *saṃgha* . . . [O]nly monks and nuns . . . were so organized that they could hand [the texts] on to future generations" (25). Elsewhere, Gombrich remarks, "None of the other religious leaders contemporary with the Buddha seem to have achieved such preservation of their teachings, and this may well reflect the fact that they did not organize settled religious communities like the Buddhist monasteries" (1990a, 6).

61. Beyer is here speaking of the great monastic universities of northern India, but his remarks may be taken, mutatis mutandis, as an accurate assessment of perspectives bound up with the textual preoccupations of classical Buddhist monasticism as such.

62. This characterization is a general one and does not refer to a given sect or region.

63. Bareau remarks that the authors of the *Vinayapiṭaka* lived a long time after the *parinirvāṇa,* at a time when the mode in which renunciants lived had changed a great deal. Now they lived in relative material comfort and security in monasteries, in contrast to the lifestyle of earlier Buddhist renunciants. Moreover, "they judged the conditions of their existence as completely normal and in conformity with the rules set forth by the Buddha, because the *saṃgha* had become little by little habituated to these over the course of time." Thus it was that they were not always able to comprehend those representing the more austere manner of earlier Buddhism and, in fact, could heap criticism and even vilification upon figures representing these values (1988–89, 546).

64. Gombrich has suggested how important were the monastery and monastic outlook in determining what literature was preserved, remarking that "any earlier texts which deviated from or criticized the canonical norms (by which I mean approximately the contents of the *Vinaya Khandhaka* and *Sutta Vibhaṅga* and the Four *Nikāya* of the *Sutta Piṭaka*) [i.e., monastically preserved canonical works] could not survive because they were not included among the texts which the [monastic] *saṃgha* preserved orally" (1990b, 21). Given the fact that it is the monastic *saṃgha* that had the inspiration and wherewithal to preserve Buddhist textual tradition, "any text which is critical of the current teachings or introduces something palpably new [or perceived as new] has no chance of survival" (20–27). The same themes are developed in Gombrich 1984a, especially 77–78.

2

Buddha Śākyamuni as a Saint

The Buddhist saints, though reflecting a variety of types deriving from different times, geographical locales, and traditions, are nevertheless unified by a common and quite detailed conception of what a holy person is. At the outset, it will be useful to summarize the major features of this conception, as a hypothesis to be clarified, amplified, and tested in the following pages. Most simply put, the saint in Buddhism may be understood as a person in whom the ultimate potentiality of every human, indeed sentient, being has been more or less fully realized. In the Indian Buddhist context, such a realization implies three overlapping and mutually interdependent spheres of religious understanding and action: a characteristic life journey made by the individual from an ordinary human status to saintly perfection; a set of traditional disciplines, including forest renunciation and meditation, that are understood to facilitate this transformation; and a societal dimension, wherein the saint may manifest his or her enlightened charisma and others may respond to it through certain cultic behaviors. These phenomena together form a "religious complex" defining saints and making them recognizable as such to others.

Each element of this complex may be further described as follows:

1. *The paradigm of the general type represented by the saint that takes shape in a specific "life story" that is typical of the Buddhist saints.* The saints' lives typically unfold along certain thematic lines and, as realized beings, their "personalities" conform to a certain structure, making up a generalized hagiographic paradigm. This paradigm contains certain standard features in its various manifestations (the Buddhist saint, as such) and also always appears with more specificity because, beyond belonging to the general type, each saint also belongs to one or another subtype (buddha, pratyekabuddha, arhant, or bodhisattva).

2. *The specific ascetic traditions followed by the saints, including their general lifestyle in the forest, the renunciant codes to which they adhere, and the meditation practice that these are understood to facilitate.* As understood by Buddhist tradition, Buddhist saints do not occur haphazardly or for no reason but are rather most typically "produced" by specific kinds of traditions. The Buddhist saints are usually renunciants but are typically not primarily associated with the settled monastery of town and village. Instead, in order to be able to engage in their primary practice, meditation, they follow certain ascetic codes and dwell in

the forest, or *araṇya,* a term that specifies any locale outside of the town and village, that is, separated from centers of human habitation and activity.[1] *Araṇya* has both a literal and a symbolic meaning,[2] indicating a place removed from population centers and also a particular kind of environment that is solitary, uncivilized, and disjunct from human civilization. This makes the forest frightening to ordinary worldly folk but compelling to those who aspire to realization.[3]

3. *The cult of the saint.* Societal and cultic recognition of the saints develops among all segments of the Buddhist population, lay and renunciant, and is oriented both to living saints and, after death, to the stūpa (or its functional equivalent, such as saints' images or relics), which localizes their ongoing presence. The various dimensions of this cult are actualized through a set of ritual behaviors that are partly common to all suppliants and partly specific to certain subgroups.

The identity of Buddhist saints, then, emerges as the intersection of these three elements. People may be acknowledged as saints because they approximate the hagiographical paradigm by which saints are recognized in Buddhism. They have become saints, in the Buddhist understanding, because they have followed certain classical traditions of meditation and forest renunciation. Finally, the forms of the cult of saints provide a vehicle through which the spiritual charisma of the saints becomes acknowledged by and accessible to individuals and to the culture at large. Buddha Śākyamuni, for example, is who he is by virtue of the religious complex of which he is an expression, with these hagiographic, ascetic, and cultic dimensions.

This definition of the Buddhist saint has a variety of implications, many of which will be clarified in the following pages. One implication that needs to be mentioned at the outset, however, concerns the understanding of the term *cult* in relation to the Buddhist saints. Often, the term *cult,* as used in the history of religions, denotes a specific system of religious worship, especially with reference to a particular set of ritualized procedures and ceremonies. Sometimes in this study, I use the term *cult* in this restricted sense. As in the two-tiered model of Buddhism, a cult is further often understood to imply a "popular" level of religious life, that of the laity, in contrast and even opposition to the "elite" level, that of the monks. However, the definition of the Buddhist saint suggested here, with its three convergent and ultimately inseparable elements, does not permit of such a separation between cultic worship and other kinds of religious activities. In this study, the term *cult* is also used in the broader sense to denote any activities through which devotees (both lay and renunciant worshipers as well as close personal disciples) relate themselves to the saint. These include both cultic (in the narrow sense) actions of worship and also those actions by which devotees seek to emulate the saint (such as forest renunciation and meditation), as well as all other actions through which followers articulate their relationships with the saint. The problem of understanding the Buddhist saints thus resolves itself, to a large extent, into the problem of making sense of the religious complex including the paradigm of the Buddhist saints, their ascetic traditions, and their cults. The following pages contain an examination of this complex and its implications. In the present chapter, I identify the paradigm of the Buddhist saint as an overarching type through a thematic analysis of the life of Buddha Śākyamuni, in whom the paradigm is present in a particularly clear and classic form. This paradigm is further clarified in Chapter 3 through an examination of the many men and women saints represented in the *Theragāthā* and *Therīgāthā* of the Pāli canon. Next follows a discussion of some famous Indian Buddhist saints, including, in Chapter 4, some well-known orthodox figures (Mahākāśyapa [P., Mahākassapa], Upagupta [P., Upagutta], and Śāriputra [P., Sāriputta]) and, in Chapter 5, two saints who are the subjects of varying degrees of criticism, Piṇḍolabhāradvāja and Devadatta. In Chapter 6, I summarize evidence of the Indian Buddhist cult of arhants. Chapters 7 and 8 treat the figures of the pratyekabuddha and bodhisattva, respectively. The next two chapters consider two important facets of the Buddhist cult of saints, the ascetic traditions of the forest they typically follow (Chapter 9) and the stūpa, containing their relics, important to the cult of saints at all periods (Chapter 10). The last two chapters and the conclusion are concerned with the place of the Buddhist saints within the larger scope of Indian Buddhist history. Chapter 11 considers some theological doctrines pertinent to the Buddhist saints while Chapter 12 contains a discussion of the general "process of monasticization" in relation to the Buddhist saints. In the conclusion, I suggest an alternative to the two-tiered model of Buddhism as well as some of the ways in which such an alternative might better serve our understanding of the Indian tradition.

Buddha Śākyamuni may be considered as a unique individual who gave birth to a new religion and whose creativity is more or less unprecedented either before or after his great achievement.[4] This view has, in fact, been the one generally taken by modern scholars. However, this approach, though valid in itself, not infrequently leaves aside the important question of the extent to which the figure of Buddha Śākyamuni reflects a more general paradigm. A discussion of the Buddhist saints appropriately begins with an examination of the figure of Buddha Śākyamuni, not only because he is considered the founder of Buddhism and its preeminent saint, but because, in fact, his life exhibits a paradigm of sainthood that, once identified, can be shown to be more or less applicable to other Buddhist saints. In the present chapter, then, I summarize the Buddha's life in terms of its structural and thematic components and, at the same time, set out the general paradigm of the Buddhist saint.

In the canonical and extracanonical Buddhist literature there are numerous fragmentary, partial, and full-length biographies of the Buddha.[5] This raises the crucial question of which text or group of texts may provide the most effective evidential basis for the kind of thematic analysis proposed here. A study of the biographical documents as a group, reflecting as they do widely differing times and periods, would demonstrate the high degree of thematic continuity in the Indian Buddhist lives of the Buddha. However, they would yield too hypothetical a reconstruction, because they could not show us the paradigm in an actual or integral form as it existed at any one time or place. An attempt to identify the earliest images of the Buddha, perhaps by following Bareau in his important studies of Śākyamuni's hagiography (see Bibliography), would reveal the paradigm in a variety of incomplete forms, reflecting historical and geographical diversity, again providing uncertain ground for gaining a view of the integral paradigm. In fact, it would appear that our purposes will best be served by examining a discrete body of evidence, ideally a single text, wherein the paradigm is expressed in full, detailed, and classic form. The evidence should ideally have several characteristics. First, it should be a full treatment of the Buddha's life wherein a complete biographic picture is given. Second, it should, among such full-length lives, be one that is earlier rather than later, standing as close as possible to the beginning of the period during which full-length biographies were written. Third, it should be a mainline, classic biography, both closely reflecting the major themes of the earlier fragmentary lives and being widely accepted and revered by Buddhist tradition. Finally, the biography should be one that emphasizes Buddha Śākyamuni's status as a saint.

Among extant lives, none fulfills these criteria better than the *Buddhacarita,* the extraordinary life of the Buddha written by the first-century C.E. poet Aśvaghoṣa.[6] In this work, the author's central dramatic intention is to present the Buddha as the paradigmatic Buddhist saint, in whom is embodied an authentic humanity and a genuinely divine nature. In fact, the twenty-eight chapters of the *Buddhacarita* are divided in two parts, with fourteen chapters devoted to each side of the balance: chapters 1 to 14 present the Buddha as a man who begins in ignorance, gradually comes to discover the truths of disease, old age, and death, feels compelled to renounce the world, and follows a spiritual quest to enlightenment. Chapters 15 to 28 depict the Buddha as an accomplished being, superhuman in stature, recognized as fully realized by those in his environment, surrounded by miracles and in possession of magical powers, venerated by gods, human beings, and the cosmos as a whole, one who compassionately leads others on the path to liberation.[7] Aśvaghoṣa's emphasis on the Buddha as a saint leads him to treat in an unusually detailed and articulate manner certain themes that are bound up with the Buddhist saints, such as devotion, the guru-disciple relationship, meditation as the focal point of Buddhist praxis, life in the forest, and the veneration of saints. Moreover, Aśvaghoṣa not only treats these themes but also often explains what they mean within the context of the Buddhist religious life of his day.[8] The following, then, takes Aśvaghoṣa's text as the primary vehicle for identifying the traditional, paradigmatic model of Buddha Śākyamuni, with reference to other biographical works where appropriate.

Buddha Śākyamuni's Life as Paradigm

Most of the early *sūtra* accounts of the Buddha's life[9] begin with the events surrounding his renunciation, and it is with these that this analysis appropriately begins. The prior events may be left aside for the time being, because in the majority of cases, texts discussing other Buddhist saints devote relatively little attention to events prior to leaving home.[10]

The Buddha's Life: Prerealization

1. *Crisis in Gautama's life.* In the *Buddhacarita,* the forest (*araṇya* or *vana* [for example, 5.31]) is a central and recurring motif, appearing at moments of transition, when the human actors come to acknowledge the insufficiency of their immediate strategems and projects and abandon themselves to something larger.[11] Thus it is the forest that precipitates a crisis in Gautama's life. As a youth, Gautama has "listened to songs celebrating the forest" (3.1) and, at a certain point, conceives in himself a longing to enter its precincts (3.2). His father Śuddhodana has previously expressed a fear of Gautama's going to the forest, but now, hearing of his son's wish and vainly believing that he can maintain his control even there, he arranges a protected excursion (3.3). In preparation, the king tries to convert the forest into a civilized environment: all the aged, maimed, sick, and wretched are removed (3.3–6). The king's action implicitly acknowledges the power of the forest: it is the region where things appear as they are, without the cosmetic alterations of "civilization." However, the king's efforts prove futile, for the prince, during his sojourn in the forest, sees things that had previously been invisible to him in the court: an old man, a diseased man, and a corpse (3.26–62). Gautama does not pass by these sights as an ordinary person might, taking no notice. Extraordinary being that he is, he now sees that all life—his own included—ends in death, and this new awareness precipitates a profound, intensely personal crisis. Returned from the forest, he is no long able to live as others do and can no longer take pleasure in the ordinary things of life (for example, 4.84–99).

2. *Personal spiritual longing, which translates into a strong sense of religious vocation.* Although Gautama's experiences in the forest leave him with an intense disquietude and a desire for spiritual peace, these feelings have, as yet, no form or direction. In this unresolved frame of mind, he ventures once more into the forest (5.2) and sits down to meditate. A wandering ascetic, called a *śramaṇa* (P., *samaṇa*), soon happens by (5.16–21), and Gautama, deeply impressed with his spiritual charisma, asks who he is. "I am a *śramaṇa,*" comes the reply, "who in fear of birth and death have left home for the sake of salvation. . . . I dwell wherever I happen to be, at the root of a tree or in a deserted temple, or on a mountain hill or in a forest, and I wander without ties" (5.17–19). After saying this, the *śramaṇa* flies up into the sky and disappears, revealing his saintly identity (5.20). Having "seen" the saint,[12] Gautama is "thrilled and amazed" and finds that he has gained an understanding of the dharma (5.21). His meeting with this saint gives shape to Gautama's spiritual longing, for he now desires to emulate the *śramaṇa,* to renounce the world, enter the forest, and seek liberation (5.21–23). This saint, as epigrammatically depicted in Aśvaghoṣa's text, becomes in fact—as we shall presently see—a specific model that Gautama will follow closely, in matters including personal vocation, the desire for liberation, renunciation, a wandering life, realization and its concomitant, magical power, and veneration by the laity (represented here by Gautama). In particular, the *śramaṇa* follows a specific lifestyle that Gautama will take up, with its specific modes of dress (his

characteristic robe), sustenance (begging), and habitation (such as in a forest, at the foot of a tree, on a mountain).

3. *The formal renouncing of the world.* Inspired to follow the saint's example (5.22) and despite his father's opposition, Gautama determines to renounce the world. He summons his groom in the dead of night, has his horse brought, and leaves the palace and the city, vowing not to return until he has attained realization (5.66ff.). Away from the palace, he cuts off his own hair, gives his royal ornaments to his groom, and exchanges his garments for a simple hunter's robe (6.1), in a kind of self-ordination that is not unknown in later Buddhist times.

4. *The taking up of a particular wandering, renunciant lifestyle, defined by specific ascetic modes of dress, sustenance, and dwelling.* Having renounced the world and entered the forest, Gautama will now follow the way of forest renunciation. From this time forth, he is himself a *śramaṇa,* wearing the garb of a mendicant, begging his food from the laity, and dwelling "in the uninhabited forest" *(nirjanavana)* (8.10) in no fixed abode: he either wanders about or dwells beneath a tree (9.8–12; 12.115–19) or in the mountains.[13]

5. *The seeking and finding of a teacher or guru.* It is Gautama's assumption, as depicted in his life, that in order to follow the ascetic path, one must seek out a teacher. In fact, the *śramaṇa* whom he meets in the forest acts as his first teacher, providing the challenge as well as the inspiration by which Gautama is moved to renounce the world. Now he heads off into the forest to find such a one with whom he may study, for, the events of Gautama's life tell us, such are found in the forest. He goes first to the peaceful forest hermitage of the *śramaṇa* Arāḍa Kālāma and respectfully listens to his teaching (12.69), then to the forest retreat of another *śramaṇa,* Udraka Rāmaputra (12.84). However, neither satisfy him, so in each case he eventually proceeds on his way. Nevertheless, his biography stresses his loyalty to these masters, for, after achieving enlightenment, the Buddha thinks first of returning to them to present his discovery.

6. *The formulation of aspirations and taking of vows in connection with the quest.* At various points in his life, Gautama expresses his spiritual intentions in the form of aspirations and vows[14] of various sorts, expressing both his intention to attain enlightenment and also his resolve to do so for the sake of all beings.[15] These various vows are summarized at the time of his enlightenment, when the Buddha recalls that he has made the vow in times past to liberate the world and now finds that vow binding (14.97); and later, when he remarks, "Of yore . . . I vowed thus, that when I had crossed myself, I would bring the world across" (15.7).[16] The importance attributed to vows of this sort is suggested at many points in the *Buddhacarita,* where we learn that vows cannot be lightly broken (9.44; 9.77) and that they are an essential part of the path to liberation (13.1; 13.4; 13.6; 13.59). The vow, it seems, not only binds the would-be saint to the renunciant life but has a numinous power, positive and transformative if respected, damaging and even disastrous if ignored.

7. *The intensive practice of meditation, which makes up the substance of the spiritual quest.* In the *Buddhacarita* the practice of meditation is depicted as Gautama's central spiritual discipline, and from the time that he leaves the world he is shown meditating and counseling others to meditate (see, for example, 10.18). From his viewpoint, as seen in the text, "it is the taming of the mind only that is required" (7.27). It is in meditation that Gautama attains his first glimpse of realization (5.8–15); it is while meditating that he meets the *śramaṇa* who inspires him to leave the world (5.16); meditation forms the substance of the teachings that Gautama receives from Arāḍa and Udraka (12.1ff.); his practice of austerities is clearly bound up with his meditative path (12.95); and, of course, it is through meditation that he completes his journey and attains enlightenment. In Aśvaghoṣa's work, meditation is presented as the core of the Buddhist dharma itself, the way in which people are transformed.

8. *Personal realization of enlightenment.* Gautama sits beneath the pipal (or "*bodhi*") tree in meditation and attains realization. At the moment of this attainment, we are told, he "saw no self anywhere from the summit of existence downwards and came to tranquility . . . the great seer reached the stage which knows no alteration" (14.84–86). He attained the "highest goal of men" (11.59), and, having reached the state of omniscience (14.86), he "stood out before the world as a Buddha" (14.83). Having attained enlightenment, the thought arose in him, "I have obtained this perfect path which was travelled for the sake of the ultimate reality by former families of great seers" (14.85). The Buddha's enlightenment is crucial to his status, with his authority and charisma resting upon this attainment. As he says in the *Buddhacarita,* he does not rely upon others for his achievement but finds the highest truth out for himself (9.73–74): "No teacher have I. . . . I am a Buddha" (15.4–5).

The Buddha's Life: Postrealization

9. *Recognition of the Buddha's enlightenment.* The Buddha's enlightenment is recognized in three ways. First, the cosmos responds to his attainment: the earth quakes, rain falls from a cloudless sky, flowers and fruit drop from trees out of season, miraculous flowers fall from the sky, and the world becomes peaceful (14.87–90). Second, various superhuman beings—gods, seers, siddhas, and others—mark the Buddha's attainment with their offerings and praises (14.87; 14.91; 14.92–93). Third, human beings acknowledge his attainment, including—in addition to a wandering *śramaṇa* who gives him implicit recognition (15.1–15)—the Buddha's first two lay disciples (14.105) and his five former compeers (15.16ff.). This progressively widening recognition of the Buddha's enlightened status is crucial, for it provides the initial link between him, as the fully attained but as yet unknown sage and the suffering world.

10. *Self-declaration of enlightenment.* The Buddha himself declares his attainment among humans. This first occurs when, just after his enlightenment, he is walking to Banaras (Vārāṇasī) to deliver his first discourse and encounters a wandering *śramaṇa,* to whom he announces his buddhahood (15.4–5). This "self-

declaration'' is, from a biographical viewpoint, a logical necessity: as the Buddha alone has reached the pinnacle of existence, he alone can fully validate this achievement. Others who are not his equal may venerate his attainment, but they cannot fully judge it.

11. *Compassion identified as a central component in the Buddha's enlightened personality.* The theme of the Buddha's universal compassion is one that appears frequently in his life. When the bodhisattva is born, he vows to attain enlightenment ''for the good of the world'' (1.15; see 14.97). Aśvaghoṣa tells us that the Buddha was born ''for the sake of the salvation of all creatures'' (1.27 and 13.66). The inseparability of compassion from the Buddha's aspiration and path is likewise continually affirmed in the *Buddhacarita* (1.67–77; 13.61; 14.1ff.; 16.19–20). The theme of compassion is not only prevalent in the life of the Buddha but also necessary to his type as a buddha, for it connects him to humanity and explains the intensity of the cult that surrounds him.

12. *Miraculous phenomena spontaneously surround the Buddha's person.* The cosmos spontaneously responds to the central events of the Buddha's life with earthquakes and various other similar phenomena. This cosmic response occurs most notably at his birth (1.21), enlightenment (14.87), turning the wheel of dharma for the first time (15.58), and *parinirvāṇa* (passing) (26.92). The cosmos also marks other occasions, such as when he relinquishes his span of life at Māra's request (23.71). The *Buddhacarita* and other hagiographies make it clear that the Buddha's life and enlightenment are not matters of purely human concern but rather affect the entire cosmos.

13. *Possession of supernatural powers.* The Buddha, as a result and essential complement of his realization, possesses supernatural powers. As depicted in Aśvaghoṣa's life, these are typically described in terms of the classical set of *abhijñā* (P., *abhiññā*) (superknowledges). Thus, in the description of his enlightenment, the Buddha is credited with the two mundane *abhijñā,* the power to know former births (14.2–6) and the divine eye by which he sees the deaths and rebirths of other beings (14.7–48). Later, he is credited with another of the *abhijñā,* the power to know the minds of others (for example, 16.35; 18.10). The Buddha demonstrates yet another *abhijñā,* the *ṛddhi* (P., *iddhi*) or magical powers, when converting his father (19.1ff.): he flies up into the sky (19.12), touches the sun with his hand (19.13), makes his body into many bodies (19.13; see also 16.35), and so on. He is also credited with the further *ṛddhi*-like power of traveling distances by flight (21.22) and of traveling to other realms, such as that of the *deva*s, to converse with beings there (20.56–58).[17] As depicted in Aśvaghoṣa's text, the Buddha's supernormal powers are used in service of his compassion, chiefly to teach and convert others (for example, 16.34; 19.12; 19.29).[18] The Buddha is superior to humans, but he is also the ideal human being, showing in his life the perfection of their capacities.[19] Similarly, although above the gods, he is also assimilated to them and credited with their powers: for example, he can live a long time, he knows the thoughts of others, he can fly through the air.

14. *The receiving of darśan* (darśana; *P.*, dassana),[20] a physical-spiritual seeing and being seen, whereby the devotee may participate in the Buddha's enlightened charisma. From one viewpoint, the Buddha stands as the embodiment of human nature perfected, the end point more or less far off, toward which devotees may strive. At the same time, he makes that goal immediately available through the phenomenon of darśan, in the *Buddhacarita* a vehicle of a deep and intimate exchange. The Buddha presents himself to be seen by the suppliant, and the suppliant responds by opening himself—in the imagery of the text, opening his eyes wide—and taking in the spiritual energy of the Buddha. Thus darśan is a vehicle of transformation, wherein one is able to participate in the holy charisma of the Buddha.[21] The theme of darśan runs through Aśvaghoṣa's text, from the time of the birth of the buddha-to-be, through his youth and spiritual search (1.19; 1.54; 3.11–14; 7.7; 12.111). When, after the Buddha's enlightenment, he meets the wandering *śramaṇa,* the latter is struck by the Buddha's appearance (15.13), as are the Buddha's five former companions and others who later meet him (15.15ff.; 16.50). When the Buddha is about to die, Subhadra arrives, specifically to see the Buddha—"let him not pass away without my seeing him" (26.1ff.)—and others likewise come to take final darśan of him (for example, 25.65ff.). After the Buddha has passed beyond, Mahākāśyapa comes to see him one last time (27.73ff.). In Aśvaghoṣa's life of the Buddha, it is significant that it is not just the laity who receive darśan from the Buddha but also renunciants, gods, and even animals. For the renunciants in particular, darśan plays a critical role: for the sage Asita, who sees the Buddha just after his birth, for the ascetics in the hermitage, for the Buddha's five former companions, and for Mahākāśyapa, darśan is a vehicle to knowing who the Buddha really is, and in these cases darśan represents a decisive experience. The gods similarly come, at the times of the great events in the Buddha's life, to receive darśan from him (20.58).[22] Darśan thus occupies an important place in Aśvaghoṣa's soteriology. It enables one to know the Buddha, commune with him, and actively participate in his charisma—experiences that rouse those who see him to faith, to spontaneous acts of devotion, and to insight.[23] And darśan inspires some to renounce the world in order to gain for themselves the state that they have experienced through the agency of the Buddha.

15. *A cult with characteristic features that develops around the Buddha.* The relationship of sentient beings to the Buddha is defined through a series of cultic attitudes and actions. The gods, other supernatural beings, renunciants, laity, and the animals all, to one degree or another, participate in the cult of the Buddha. This cult has two major dimensions: veneration of the Buddha as a living saint and worship of the Buddha, after his death, in his stūpa. The general shape of the cult is the same in both cases, and, indeed, it is doubtful whether in the Buddhist context these cases were seen as essentially different or in any fundamental way separable. Thus there is a somewhat informal set of general cultic behaviors that people are to employ in the presence of the living Buddha: one is to rise, greet him respectfully, offer him a seat, circumambulate him and prostrate oneself to him, present water for his feet as well as food and drink, make other offerings such as flowers, hold a parasol over him to shield him from the elements, ask

after his health, make confession, praise him, express one's commitment as a devotee, request teachings, listen respectfully, follow his instructions, and so on. In the cult of the stūpa, as we shall see, very much the same ritual forms are used, although—at least as seen in the texts—in an often more self-conscious and stylized way.

In addition, different kinds of Buddhists, renunciants and the laity, ordinary laypeople and kings, employ characteristic cultic behaviors toward the Buddha. For example, certain cultic behaviors are mentioned as being appropriate for renunciant disciples to show to their masters. When the Buddha arrives among his five former ascetic companions, they rise, approach him with folded hands, take his mantle and begging bowl, show him a proper seat, and provide water for his feet. In so doing, they treat him as, in Aśvaghoṣa's terminology, their guru (15.19–21). Among the laity, there are also some important distinctions, such as the special cultic forms employed by kings. Thus King Śreṇya (Bimbisāra), drawing near to the Buddha, alights from his carriage, discards his royal paraphernalia, including yak tail and fans, leaves behind his retinue, approaches the Buddha on foot, makes obeisance, obtains permission to sit down, and receives teachings (16.51–53). Cultic forms such as these, then, constitute a veritable grammar of devotion. Through them, one is able to articulate one's relationship as suppliant to the Buddha as realized saint, to make an implicit but well-understood request for transmission of his charisma, and to open oneself to receive his teaching and wisdom. In the context of these ritual attitudes and actions, the Buddha—as a living saint and as incarnated in his stūpa—presents himself as an object of veneration and as a source of wisdom, compassion, and power. The cultic actions become a way for the suppliant to make a connection with his charisma. Sometimes, these cultic forms are a prelude to various kinds of verbal teaching and instruction. On the other hand, sometimes they and the exchange they entail are presented as sufficient in and of themselves.

16. *The teaching of others, including not only humans but supernatural beings as well.* The Buddha, after his realization, is depicted primarily as a teacher, and his various activities can be seen as expressive of this function. The Buddha instructs, leads, and enlightens all beings, not only humans of all stations and conditions, including the departed (20.56–58), but also gods,[24] other nonhumans (for example, *yakṣa, nāga*), animals (including in the *Buddhacarita* an elephant [21.54], a parrot, and a starling [21.30]). Although, as we shall presently see, Aśvaghoṣa avoids a rigid dichotomy between renunciants and laity, still, important distinctions remain in the kinds of teachings given to each. In contrast to teachings presented to renunciant disciples, those given to the laity emphasize the virtue of giving. Thus the Buddha gives a long sermon to Anāthapiṇḍada on the importance of making donations before he instructs in *śīla, samādhi,* and *prajñā* (18.1–87). Another important, if relative difference between laity and renunciants has to do with the goals that are put before each. Whereas the goal of enlightenment is preached to both renunciants and laity, the goals of worldly prosperity and the winning of heaven are recommended particularly to the laity (for example, 18.65–68ff.).

17. *The acceptance of close personal disciples and lay followers.* In Aśvaghoṣa's rendering, the Buddha is a guru (1.27) who accepts both close personal disciples and lay followers. On the one hand, the Buddha accepts close personal disciples who are trained by him, receive full transmission, and can attain enlightenment and act as his successors in teaching and training others.[25] On the other, he also accepts a larger "penumbra"[26] of lay followers who come to see him, participate in his cult, and make gifts to him. However, in Aśvaghoṣa's presentation there is no rigid separation between these two categories. On the one hand, the renunciants receive darśan from the Buddha, venerate him with forms of the cult, make gifts to him of what little they have, and in that context participate in his charisma (for example, 18.16). On the other, the Buddha teaches the laity, instructs them not only in the virtue of giving but also in the importance of their observing morality, practicing meditation, and developing insight (see, for example, 18.1–14). Particularly important, Aśvaghoṣa tells us that the laity may freely gain transformative insight and even realization (16.94–95). Sometimes, they remain laypeople after gaining some realization, as in the case of Anāthapiṇḍada (18.16).[27] For Aśvaghoṣa, the really important distinction is internal, not a matter of external lifestyle: he quotes the Buddha as remarking, "He who leaves his home with his body, but not with his mind, and who is still subject to passion, is to be known as a householder, though he live in the forest. He who goes forth with his mind, but not with his body, and who is selfless, is to be known as a forest-dweller, though he abide in his home" (16.11–12).

18. *The absence in the Buddha of scholarly considerations and particularly of textual study.* In the *Buddhacarita,* the Buddha is depicted as a meditator and a guru, not as a scholar or a textual specialist. Doctrine certainly has a role to play in the life of the Buddha in the *Buddhacarita,* but it is presented as a support to the path to liberation. This point is, of course, particularly stressed elsewhere in early Buddhism, for example in the "questions that tend not to edification," wherein knowledge for its own sake is abjured.[28] Learning, the Buddha seems to say, has no virtue in and of itself but must be measured by its ability to lead directly to liberation.[29]

19. *The communication of teachings in an oral form.* Connected with this is the theme of the oral form of the Buddha's teachings: in the *Buddhacarita,* the Buddha presents his teachings in a strictly oral and also extemporaneous fashion. This is perhaps not surprising for a founder such as the Buddha is, but it will be of particular interest and significance as a feature of later Buddhist saints.

20. *The making of conversions.* The Buddha spends much of his teaching career converting various beings, "whether faring on earth or in the sky" (21.36). Those he converts include all those who can recognize him, venerate him, and receive teachings from him, including the gods, other nonhumans, human beings, and animals. Sometimes, those who subsequently become his followers are converted quickly and without obstacle. For example, the instant the great future arhant, Mahākāśyapa, sees the Buddha, he is convinced of the master's realization and sanctity and asks to be accepted as a disciple (17.24–27). Śāriputra and

Maudgalyāyana, similarly, have only to hear the message of the Buddha from another to gain insight (17.16ff.). And Āmrapālī, the courtesan, comes to the Buddha filled with faith and longing (22.16ff.).[30] But many of those who become the Buddha's devotees present initial obstacles to their conversions. The Buddha's five former ascetic friends fully intend to ignore him. An example of more extreme resistance, King Prasenajit, the rapacious, lustful, and aggressive monarch, presents himself to the Buddha for instruction (20.4ff.). And the Licchavis are proud and haughty rulers whose wrath is not easily quelled (23.1ff.).

21. *The defeat of evil beings.* More than this, there are those who will not be converted, such as the non-Buddhist *(tīrthika)* masters who, seeing the veneration the Buddha receives, are jealous and challenge him to a display of his magical powers (20.54–55); or Devadatta or Māra, whose only wish is to bring the Buddha to injury, defeat, and destruction.

22. *Association with the lowborn and disadvantaged.* In Aśvaghoṣa's text, as in other hagiographies of the Buddha, one finds reference to the Buddha's absence of preference for the highborn and his association with the lowborn as well as with those of upper caste. This theme is, of course, implicitly present in the Buddha's teaching of high-caste and low-caste people alike, and in his noncompliance with the extreme preference, customary in India, shown to those of upper caste. It is also present in a more explicit way, as when we are told that the Buddha accepts alms "without distinction" (10.14) and in the incident—more offensive within a traditional Indian context than it would be in a modern secularized one—in which the Buddha will speak first with Āmrapālī—a courtesan and, moreover, a woman—before he will speak with the highborn Licchavis, which angers them greatly (23.59–60).[31] As we shall see, the Buddhist saints not only show association with the lowborn and disadvantaged but sometimes exhibit an active preference for them. The Buddha's association with the lowborn is important to his sainthood because here he reveals his freedom from bondage to social, economic, and political structures. In this, he demonstrates his solidarity with ultimate reality, which does not align itself with such merely relative and social distinctions.

23. *The unconventionality of the Buddha and his critique of social and religious conventions.* In a similar vein, within the Indian context the Buddha is in some respects an unconventional figure, one who does not affirm the values of the established order.[32] In regard to his own tradition, he is one who does not hesitate to place inner meaning ahead of external form, as in his statement (see theme 17) defining the true forest renunciant as one who, living no matter where, has achieved genuine inner renunciation. As we have seen, the Buddha is unconventional in another way: he will contravene social convention in his interactions with others. He puts the prostitute Āmrapālī ahead of the wellborn Licchavis; he does not hesitate to expose the faults of the high and mighty; and he generally puts no ultimate stock in caste status. As we shall see, the later Buddhist saints may also behave similarly or even more unconventionally. With the Buddha and other saints, what is in question is not an attack on conventionality as such, for these holy persons can often appear decorous and pleasing. The Buddha and other saints

show the path to freedom and, theoretically as well as hagiographically, they act in accord or disaccord with convention in furtherance of this end.

24. *The Buddha criticized and even persecuted for his sanctity, unconventionality, or explicit critiques.* The sanctity of the Buddha, the integrity of his message, and his noncompliance with conventional norms sometimes provoke the antipathy of others, in the form of personal attack or persecution from those who doubt him and from those heretic teachers who would defeat him. In Aśvaghoṣa's text, a variety of beings would like to bring defeat to the Buddha. In the *Buddhacarita,* as in the other of the Buddha's lives, it is primarily his cousin Devadatta who most clearly embodies this enmity. Among the nonhumans, Māra is the Buddha's primary enemy and does everything in his power to undermine the master's own path and his teaching of others. The other Buddhist saints will no less suffer the attacks of the vicious. Such attacks are correlative to the integrity of the message and manifestation of the Buddha and other saints. Just as the Buddha attracts the veneration of the worthy, so he draws, so to speak, the antipathy of those who hold dear the happiness of saṃsāra, of personal gratification and worldly power. For those solely intent upon personal aggrandizement, egolessness must be regarded as the ultimate threat and the Buddha as the ultimate enemy.

25. *The danger of the numinous power of the Buddha.* The Buddha counsels his five former companions on the need to address him with an appropriately respectful address. They must do so, not because the Buddha is attached to praise and blame, but for their own good: otherwise they will themselves suffer by reaping evil karmic consequences (15.22). Such is the power of the Buddha's sanctity that one can be protected in his presence only by possessing the right cultic relationship with him. The consequences of failing in this respect are fully realized by Devadatta who, as a result of abandoning devotion to the Buddha and trying to undermine his work and harm him, falls into the lower realms (21.65).

26. *The Buddha as principal reference point of the dharma for his followers.* The Buddha, as founder, is the central authority for the early community and the definer of tradition for his age. In this role, moreover, we may think him to be unique. Nevertheless, as we shall see, this role is taken by other Buddhist saints, who will be assimilated to the Buddha and will play the part of buddha for their generations. This feature is important because it suggests that the authenticity and power of the Buddha and other saints ultimately derives not from their relationship to the received forms of tradition but rather from their direct access, through realization, to reality itself. Such direct access is the ultimate source of their wisdom and provides them with a purchase from which they can fully understand, interpret, and adjudicate the various elements of tradition.

27. *Possession of a body that is supermundane in some way.* The Buddha's physical body is uncommon for its beauty, radiance, golden hue,[33] and charismatic magnetism (for example, 19.46; 20.55). It possesses the thirty-two marks of the great man (24.50). His body transcends the ordinary also in another way, in its resistance to injury and death. For example, the Buddha at one point lodges in a house inhabited by a malevolent *nāga,* who sets the structure on fire. As the

inferno rages around him and the onlookers are distraught at what they suppose to be his end, the Buddha sits in meditation, his body miraculously unharmed[34] (16.21–31). The Buddha's supernatural body is clearly another aspect of his status as superior to humans and gods. The deities, in particular, appear with perfect, glorious bodies and are invulnerable to the things that injure ordinary people, and the Buddha, as their guide, is in full possession of these qualities as well.

28. *Possession of the power of longevity and the capacity to live even to the end of the* kalpa. The theme of the Buddha's powers of longevity is an important one in his hagiographies. In the *Mahāparinirvāṇa Sūtra,* he is credited—by virtue of his being a *tathāgata*—with the power to live to the end of the *kalpa;* he fails to remain only, we are told, because Ānanda lacks the presence of mind to request him to do so (*Mps*-p 3.3–4, 40). In Aśvaghoṣa's text, the story is told in a slightly different manner, but the assumption is, again, of the Buddha's powers of longevity (23.64ff.). The theme of longevity is an important one among the Buddhist saints, and—in their cases as in that of the Buddha—it serves to show that their essential identity as realized beings renders them beyond the power of death. As we shall see, sometimes this is interpreted as a literally physical longevity and sometimes as a longevity that is achieved in some other way. In either case, however, the saint can remain indefinitely available to the suppliant.[35]

29. *Association of the Buddha with millennial expectations.* Millennialism—the belief that the old world order will pass away and be replaced by one in which peace, justice, and abundance will reign—is in Buddhist tradition most often associated with the figure of Maitreya. Although there is no mention of Maitreya in Aśvaghoṣa's text, the future Buddha does play an important role elsewhere in the Buddha's hagiographical tradition.[36] Millennial expectations are at least implicitly present as a potential in the Buddha's life and type, as a consequence of his critique of saṃsāra and his compassion for all beings.[37] Millennial trends in Buddhism represent the logical outcome of the Buddhist belief in the perfectibility of human nature and its wish to realize this both individually and socially. The Buddhist monastery represents, in fact, a community with a quasi-millennial character, providing as it does a clear and well-organized alternative to communities based on samsaric norms. Millennial trends tend to be found also among other Buddhist saints because, they, like the Buddha, put the Buddhist teachings to their most radical test, and their critique of saṃsāra is perhaps the most thoroughgoing.

30. *Anticipation of death.* The Buddha knows when his time has come to pass beyond. In fact, he participates in the setting of the precise time of death when, at Māra's request, he agrees to die three months hence (23.64–66). For the Buddha as a saint who has transcended death, his own demise holds no fear, and his lack of concern in the face of it is a further confirmation of his realized status. The Buddha spends his final days preparing his followers for his demise, giving final darśan and his last teachings. It is significant that the theme of the forest, which has played such an important role in Aśvaghoṣa's text to this point, once again comes to the fore in the Buddha's final instructions to his followers. Aśvaghoṣa thus has the Buddha counseling his disciples henceforward to follow the

forest way of life; to have moderate desires (26.55); to observe exact measure in eating (26.39); to dwell on mountains, in the forest, or in vacant dwellings (26.72); and to "pass the entire day and also the first and last watches of the night in the practice of yoga" (26.42).[38]

31. *Extraordinary death.* As if in final confirmation of his saintly status, the Buddha dies in an extraordinary manner, accepting death as an occurrence the timeliness of which need not be doubted. This attitude is perhaps most fully revealed in the precise way he dies: he enters into meditation, progresses through its various attainments from first to last and back again, then ascends to the fourth *dhyāna,* and dies in that manner, an expression not of defeat but of his spiritual strength and confidence (26.89–92).

32. *Ritual disposition of the body of the Buddha, by cremation.* The Buddha's body is ritually prepared and placed in a special casket. His followers pay him final homage and his body is then ritually cremated, accompanied by various lamentations. The Buddha's status renders his body, even after death, imbued with enlightened charisma, and it is natural that the same degree of ritual attention that surrounded it in life should do so also in death (27.71–114).

33. *The Buddha's remains enshrined in a stūpa.* The Buddha's remains are collected in one urn, then divided into eight portions, and stūpas are built over these as well as over the original urn and the ashes of the cremation site. Later, King Aśoka opens the stūpas and divides the remains among 84,000 stūpas all over India. In Aśvaghoṣa's rendering, these remains of the Buddha, thus enshrined in stūpas, carry his very enlightened essence, and worship of them is considered just as valuable as the worship of the Buddha in life (27.78–79).

34. *The association of the Buddha with one or more sacred places.* These are connected with events of his life and become focal points of cultic activity. The Buddha is associated with various sacred places where he performed important actions. Preeminent among these are the Lumbinī grove where he was born (1.6–11), the *vajra* seat under the *bodhi* tree at Bodh-Gayā where he attained enlightenment (12.119), the Deer Park in Banaras where he turned the wheel of dharma for the first time (15.15), and the grove of the twin *śāla* trees at Kuśinagarī where he passed away (25.52–55). The cultic usage of sacred places such as these is generally not discussed in the *Buddhacarita;* for this we may turn to the *Mahāparinirvāṇa Sūtra* in its Pāli version, which depicts the Buddha telling his followers that the faithful should visit with reverence these four sites (*Mps*-p 5.8). The *Buddhacarita, Mahāparinirvāṇa Sūtra,* and other accounts mention many additional sites associated with the Buddha's life. Aśvaghoṣa, for example, mentions the site on the Ganges where the Buddha is said to have miraculously traveled from one side of the river to the other and which "is famous in the world as a place of pilgrimage" (22.11).[39]

35. *The development of characteristic kinds of texts, in particular sacred biography and the sayings of the Buddha.* What kinds of texts are depicted in the *Buddhacarita* as characteristic of the community at the time of the Buddha's pass-

ing? Aśvaghoṣa's life shows the Buddha as presenting his teachings in an oral and situationally directed manner, likely retaining a memory of what the first Buddhist texts were like.[40]

These thirty-five themes may perhaps be summarized and drawn together in the central problematic that runs through the *Buddhacarita,* seen in Aśvaghoṣa's attempt to articulate a balance between two dimensions—human and superhuman or divine—of Buddha Śākyamuni's person. Thus Aśvaghoṣa makes no mistake about the full, emotional, intelligent humanity of Gautama, and this is affirmed throughout the earlier portions of the text. The divinity of the Buddha is no less real and actual, affirmed from the account of his miraculous birth onwards. Aśvaghoṣa's life asserts this point in particular both explicitly by comparing the Buddha favorably with the gods and implicitly by attributing to him many of their characteristics.[41] For example, the Buddha literally looks the way gods look: he possesses an unearthly beauty, his body is luminous with golden light, he is explicitly said to have the form of the gods, and so on. At several points in the *Buddhacarita,* he is explicitly compared to the deities in appearance and demeanor (for example, 1.63; 7.7), and this is not just a hagiographic convention but a way of thinking.[42] The deities have control over natural phenomena and so, by virtue of his sancity, does the Buddha, surrounded as he is by spontaneous miracles. The deities are not bound by the constraints of a human body, and neither, through his various miraculous powers, is the Buddha. Finally, the deities come to the Buddha to worship him and to hear him, sure signs that the Buddha is not only equal but superior to them.

Aśvaghoṣa insists on the divinity of the Buddha in two other ways, through using, first, particular terms and, second, certain images. For example, he indicates the superhuman identity of the Buddha by the term *siddha* (perfected one). This term appears in both orthodox and heterodox Indian tradition, where it refers to a human being who has attained an apogee of spiritual realization and has, by virtue of that, transcended the ordinary human condition.[43] Using the term in the same way, Aśvaghoṣa makes clear the superhuman identity of the siddha and the Buddha's participation in that identity.[44] Aśvaghoṣa also reveals the divinity of the Buddha through his description of the appearance of the Buddha's eyes. In India, the eyes of humans and the eyes of gods present different aspects. Gods may be recognized by the fact that their eyes are steady and do not blink,[45] while those of humans are full of uncertainty and movement, and are always blinking (for example, 22.39). In many places in the *Buddhacarita,* Aśvaghoṣa depicts the Buddha as one whose eyes are unmoving, like those of a divinity (for example, 14.94; 14.108; 15.3; 1.38; 10.13). In speaking of the humanity and the divinity of the Buddha, it is crucial to note that these are not two natures. For Buddhism, to be a human being is to have the potential of enlightenment and of a divine and supradivine status. To be a Buddha is to be a human being perfected and to manifest that transcendent potential in realized form. In other words, it is because—not in spite—of his humanity that Gautama can become the god above gods, the Buddha.

It may be noted that the various themes of this paradigm are not, logically speaking, random elements but rather fit together in a coherent pattern and tend to imply one another. For example, personal crisis leads to longing for personal transformation which implies a strong sense of spiritual vocation. These elements in turn suggest the need for a separation *(pravrajyā)* from the conventional world and for a journey beyond the boundaries of the known and familiar into the unknown (the forest). This, in turn, leads to the need for a personal guide or teacher who can point the way and for a method—here the practice of meditation—by which this journey can be made. The initiatory separation required for this quest naturally leads to a calling into question of previously held values, both individual and societal. Thus Gautama is led to distance himself from prevailing conventional social and religious institutions, values, and ideas. In spite of friends, companions, and teachers, his quest is and must be essentially a solitary one.

The coherence of Gautama's life continues in the direct and personal realization that he achieves, involving an initiatory death and rebirth. He abandons the old self *(ātman),* characterized by egocentricity, and with new eyes sees humanity, all other sentient life, and the cosmos as a whole in a transformed way. The Buddha's awakening confers on him matchless charisma, recognized by both his renunciant disciples, who seek to emulate him, and the laity, who express their devotion mainly through offerings, praises, and so on. The two categories of suppliants, on the one hand, as well as the saint they supplicate, on the other, necessitate one another. At least in the Buddhist case, one cannot have a saint without those who recognize him and seek to participate, one way or another, in his achievement. There are two avenues to such participation: emulation and adoration, and in the *Buddhacarita* both renunciant disciples and lay disciples engage in both activities, if not always in the same ways. Much the same forms of adoration are used by renunciants and the laity, but emulation, although a central and immediate aim for renunciants, remains a more removed goal for the layperson, perhaps of a future time in this life or even in another lifetime.

The Buddha exhibits his spiritual power and charisma in his life and also in his death. In life, the timeless condition of his realization has been present and manifest in his physical body, and initimately connected with this condition are his supernormal body and powers of longevity. After his passing, the same timeless condition is reflected in the power and charisma present in that condensed bodily form, his relics, which function as the heart of a new body of the Buddha, the stūpa. Thus the cult of the stūpa and the kind of saint that the Buddha represents are not unrelated to one another or arbitrarily linked together. Rather, as we shall see in more detail, they also imply one another and are elements of a coherent and organically unified religious type.

A century ago, Senart pointed out that Buddha Śākyamuni embodies a type that is understood as common to all buddhas, past and future (for example, 1882). Senart's point may be developed: the type represented by Śākyamuni Buddha is more specifically defined by these thirty-five thematic components and the paradigm that they make up. This paradigm, it may further be suggested, defines not only the essential identity of Buddha Śākyamuni, as seen in his earlier and later hagiographies, but that of the Buddhist saints in general, including not only other buddhas but also arhants, pratyekabuddhas, and bodhisattvas. In the following chapters, I examine additional evidence pertinent to the Buddhist saints and attempt to demonstrate the validity of this contention. This is not to insist, however, that the various individual traditions of Buddhism rigidly conform to this or any other model in exact detail, for such is not and could not be the case. Thus, not every figure identified as a Buddhist saint exhibits every element of the paradigm, and, in fact—apart from the Buddha—probably few if any saints show them all. Along the same lines, although the paradigm as outlined does hold as a general presumption about Buddhist saints, the individual thematic elements appear in various guises and undergo different sorts of interpretations and reinterpretations. But in spite of such differences, this paradigm constitutes a coherent ideal guiding Indian Buddhist thinking about saints, and Indian Buddhist saints—mutatis mutandis—tend to approximate it more or less closely.

The Buddhist saints are able, indeed are bound, to approximate the Buddha and one another so closely and consistently because of the particular notion of human individuality that they presuppose. This notion was pointed out in 1935 by Mus in *Borobuḍur,* in which he comments that in India "the son does not receive the property of the father, he assumes his person and it is this that subsidiarily confers on him right to the property, without any real movement of this latter" (12) and "in ancient India, one *does not inherit from one's father, one inherits one's father. One inherits his person*" (emphasis added) (124). What applies between father and son, holds equally for master and disciple. Mus continues, "To say that the disciples of the Buddha are the inheritors of the *dharma,* and to attribute to the Buddha a *dharmakāya,* a body of *dharma,* is one and the same affirmation. This affirmation [derives from] . . . the desire to specify the relationship which the disciples have with him. . . . This has to do with an identity of persons." Mus then remarks on the functional character of this notion: "This is not an ontology, it is a theory of transmission. . . . For to initiate a disciple is to engender him, and to engender is to transmit one's person" (124). This conception, then, provides the ultimate explanation for the convergence of type among the Buddha and other saints: they share the same core of personality, in later tradition explicitly identified as the *dharmakāya.* And in Indian Buddhist experience, when the essence is the same, its appearance within history tends toward a common pattern. As we shall see, at some times more than at others but always undeniably, the Buddhist saints tend to approximate the type and life of their founder.

Some Historical Considerations

The preceding discussion raises an important question: what is the historical status of the image of the Buddha revealed by the thematic analysis of Aśvaghoṣa's text? How closely does this "paradigmatic Buddha" correspond to the actual "Buddha of history"? Already noted is the marked consistency of basic themes in the life of the Buddha in its different renderings. The reader may further recall that the Buddha revealed by Aśvaghoṣa, as seen through the lens of thematic analysis, is at once human and superhuman, imbued with cosmic and mythic dimensions.

Thus the question becomes more specific: to what extent does the human/superhuman Buddha of hagiography correspond with the Buddha of history? It may be suggested here—and this is a point that is gaining increasing acceptance in buddhology today—that in approaching Buddha Śākyamuni, it is invalid and finally impossible to separate, as some have tried to do, the man from the myth. Western and modernist notions of a demythologized individuality standing apart from and independent of symbol, cult, and legend have no relevance for the early Buddhist case. Gautama, in his own time and in subsequent times, was able to be the Buddha precisely because he was understood to embody, in an unprecedented way, the cosmic and transcendent. Far from being incidental to who he was, myth and cult defined his essential person, for his earliest followers as for later Buddhists.

Thus we arrive at the seemingly ironic position of affirming that we likely come closest to the historical Buddha precisely when we take the legendary and cultic idiom of his hagiographical tradition most seriously. In this context, Snellgrove remarks that "the whole process of deliberately abstracting everything of an apparently unhistorical and mythical character, all too often leads away from any semblance of historical truth. This is because the elements that are deliberately abstracted, usually those relating to religious faith and the cult of the Buddha as a higher being, may be older and thus nearer the origins of the religion, than the supposed historical element" (1973, 399).[46]

The legitimacy of this view is suggested by the interesting fact that the basic themes of the portrait of the Buddha found in the *Buddhacarita* are closely paralleled in the Pāli *Suttanipāta,* one of the earliest Buddhist texts (Lamotte 1958, 172–74; Gomez 1976, 139–40).[47] In this early expression of Buddhism, the Buddha is depicted as a forest renunciant who has attained enlightenment (*Sn* 21; 29); his enlightenment is recognized by humans and gods (pr., 18 [Nr., 17–18]; 377ff.; 548ff.); he proclaims his own enlightenment (25; 558); he is compassionate to all beings (155); he possesses miraculous powers (343ff.; 1018ff.); it is a great blessing to receive darśan from him (31; 410–11; 559; 686ff.); a cult surrounds him (467–78), engaged in by both gods (543) and human beings (236–38) and also by animals (379); he teaches his dharma to both gods and humans (258ff.; 543); he accepts both personal disciples and lay followers (91–115); the Buddha's dharma is not one of texts and scholarship: he deplores "the chanting of texts" (81), and he is one who has done away with theses and speculations (538) (although P., *bahusutta;* Skt., *bahuśruta* [learned] appears as a lauditory epithet in the *Suttanipāta* [for example, 316]; at the same time, we are also told that one obtains the essence of learning [P., *suta;* Skt., *śruta*] through meditation [330]); he overcomes evil beings (563); he is sharply critical of those who outwardly appear to be renunciants *(bhikkhus)* but who inwardly are filled with evil and desire for praise and gain (84–90; 274–83); according to the Buddha, saints possess numinous power, and those who attack them will suffer dire consequences (pr., 123ff. [Nr., 111ff.]); among the Buddha's disciples, there is one (Śāriputra) who will assume his position after he is gone and who will "turn the incomparable wheel of *dharma* turned by [him]" (557); the Buddha's body is marvelous: it has a golden hue (548; 551), the Buddha is radiant (539), shining like the sun, and he illumines the entire world with his spiritual charisma (378).[48]

One particular facet of this depiction of Śākyamuni Buddha deserves further comment, namely, his forest character. It has been noted that one of the key themes of Aśvaghoṣa's text is the Buddha's status as a saint of the forest who, even in his public career, continues to espouse the practices and values of forest renunciation. This raises the question of whether this particular and detailed emphasis on the forest in both pre- and postrealization phases of the Buddha's life is a traditional one or a later innovation, perhaps of Aśvaghoṣa himself. This is a crucial question, as Aśvaghoṣa's portrait of the Buddha, with its emphasis on the forest, reveals—as we shall see—considerable variance from the portrait of the *vinaya* (and of the two-tiered model), wherein the Buddha is typically depicted as an urban individual, whose forest episode in his preenlightenment career is relatively brief and isolated and who, after enlightenment, is constantly surrounded by large groups of disciples and devotees, interacting with the rich and powerful, journeying from one great city to another, and teaching a Buddhism defined primarily by communal lifestyles and values.

Although it is not possible in the present context fully to engage this complex issue,[49] it may be observed that the *vinaya* depiction is among the earliest that we have, far earlier than that of Aśvaghoṣa. This fact may seem to settle the question of which type of depiction, forest or urban, is the earlier. However, such a judgment does not necessarily follow from the evidence, as is shown by several vivid and detailed portraits of Śākyamuni Buddha scattered throughout some of the earlier texts of, for instance, the Pāli canon. In this context, the *Suttanipāta* provides particularly interesting evidence.[50] In this text, in contrast to the *vinaya* depictions, Śākyamuni Buddha, both before and after attaining nirvāṇa, is portrayed as essentially a saint of the forest in whom the communal lifestyle and values of settled monasticism play no significant role.[51] Thus we read that Gautama initially determined to become a wanderer, living in the open air (406), begging his food (408), and practicing meditation (425). Meditating in the forest, he encountered Māra (425ff.), defeated him (431ff., 449), and attained enlightenment. A forest lifestyle continues to define the Buddha after his enlightenment, the *Suttanipāta* says, as he wanders about (25), lives in the forest (165), and dwells alone *(eka)* (166), teaching the virtues of seclusion *(viveka)* (822) and being questioned by others on these virtues (915).[52] In fulfillment of his forest character, he dwells with no roof over his head (19) and lives sometimes in specific forest locales (pr., 115 [Nr., 103]) or upon particular mountains (414). In one verse, he is compared to a lion in a mountain cave (416). In his remote habitation, he does not abandon meditation (157, 165), takes little food (165), and is restrained in speech (158–59). Moreover, abiding in the forest, he is available to teach the dharma to others (167). His suppliants, in order to see him and to engage in his cult, know that he dwells in the forest and that they must go there to find him (165). On one occasion, King Bimbisāra must climb Mount Paṇḍava to see the Buddha (414ff.). The dharma that the Buddha preaches to his renunciant disciples is, not surprisingly, one of forest renunciation, in which solitude and meditation are the essence and are not to be abandoned (35–75; 207–21; 226; 257; 503; pr., 111–12 [Nr., 99]; and passim)[53] and in which sleep is seen as an impediment (331–34).[54] Characteristically, in the *Suttanipāta,* terms later particularly indicative of settled monasticism, such as *bhikkhu* and *pāṭimokkha,* reflect a forest way of life.[55] Moreover, the Buddha's principal successor is depicted as a paradigmatic forest saint, dwelling in solitude, wandering from place to place, delighting in meditation, and preaching a dharma of forest renunciation (557; 955–75).

The depiction of the Buddha in the *Suttanipāta* thus closely parallels, indeed exceeds, that of the *Buddhacarita* in its emphasis on the forest life and its values.[56] This parallelism between the *Suttanipāta* and the *Buddhacarita* is important because it suggests that the understanding of the Buddha as an essentially forest personage goes back to an early time in Buddhism and that the "urban Buddha" is not necessarily the earliest one.[57]

The foregoing discussion leads inevitably to the question of the relation of the specific paradigm disclosed by this analysis to the settled monastic ideal of the monk, the historically dominant renunciant ideal in Indian Buddhism. The Pāli *Mahāparinibbāna Sutta* and *Milindapañha,* as suggested, advocate for the monks a relationship to Buddha Śākyamuni—during his life or after his passing—not of worship or veneration, but rather the taking of him as example. In fact, in the classic monastic tradition, as reflected in these texts, taking the Buddha as example is crucial. As Lamotte remarks, monastic tradition sees in this the characteristic mark of its kind of Buddhism, strictly contrasting with that of the laity, for whom the Buddha is not example but object of worship (1958, 63ff.).

However, one cannot help but notice the literal incongruity between the model that the Buddha provides and the type of the monk as that has traditionally been understood in Indian Buddhism. The Buddha entered a life of renunciation out of intense crisis and a strong sense of personal vocation, whereas monks entered the religious life out of the greatest variety of circumstances and motives. As Weber pointed out long ago and as modern anthropologists have confirmed, as often as not, economic, social, and political considerations played a role as important or more important than strictly religious ones.[58] The Buddha took up a life of wandering, wearing a robe obtained by chance, begging his food from door to door, and—apart from the rainy season of forced immobility—never staying long in any one place. This lifestyle stands in marked contrast to the settled and relatively secure and comfortable life of the monk in the monastery. The Buddha sought out a personal teacher and was himself such a teacher to his disciples, whereas monks typically had a variety of teachers, some of whom were assigned, as well as the *saṃgha* itself, acting in various roles of authority in their training. The spiritual quest of Buddha Śākyamuni was focused on the practice of asceticism and meditation, whereas the monk typically anticipated a life defined chiefly by pure behavior and textual study, wherein the practice of meditation is not a natural priority.

As part of their quest, monks, like Gautama, took a series of vows. However, Gautama's vows were oriented to the forest quest for enlightenment through the practice of meditation, whereas the typical vows of the monk concerned the regularized entry into monastic life, the following of the specific *śrāmaṇera* and *prātimokṣa* codes, and submission to the rules and conventions of collective behavior outlined in the *Skandhaka*. Furthermore, the Buddha was understood to have achieved nirvāṇa, whereas for the monks of both Nikāya and Mahāyāna Buddhism, full realization was usually not considered an immediately practicable goal but was one that had significance for the far-removed future. These repudiations of the possibility of a near enlightenment seem naturally to reflect the life of settled monasticism in which preoccupations other than meditation stood to the fore. In addition, the Buddha exemplified considerable unconventionality in relation to his environment, critiquing the established social and religious institutions of his day. The ideal monk, by contrast, was mild and demure, upholding through adherence to the *prātimokṣa* a lifestyle of studied predictability and conventionality, designed to give the laity no cause for offense and to satisfy their desire for worthy recipients of donations necessary to the maximum accumulation of merit.

The Buddha had great spiritual charisma owing to his realization, which he boldly proclaimed, and his possession of miraculous powers, which he freely exhibited. These, we are told, drew the reverence and awe of those who met him, renunciants and laity alike. By contrast, monks, according to the *prātimokṣa,* are strongly dissuaded from speaking of their attainments. A monk who speaks of them, if they turn out to be untrue, is permanently expelled from the monastic *saṃgha.*[59] Even if they are true, a monk is forbidden to speak of them to the laity.[60] Further, monks are, in effect, forbidden to reveal or show magical powers before the laity.[61] Thus monks took the Buddha as an example to follow only in the most general sense. When it came to the particularities of the motivation, spiritual search, and attainments of the Blessed One, it was not the Indian Buddhist monks who closely followed the Buddha's specific example.

What may be the reason for this incongruity? A plausible answer is found in the fact that the Buddha and the Buddhist monk as classically conceived represent two divergent, indeed quite different, religious trends, each having its roots in the sixth century B.C.E. in northeastern India. Playing a key role in this time and place was the figure of the heterodox renunciant, commonly known as *śramaṇa,* one who abandoned conventional society and its ways to follow a religious life.[62] The importance of the *śramaṇa* for the inception of Indian Buddhism has been universally recognized: Gautama was himself a *śramaṇa* and was known as the Mahāśramaṇa (the great *śramaṇa*); his disciples were known as *śramaṇa*s, and many of the features of early Buddhism reflect elements held in common by the various *śramaṇa*s and *śramaṇa* groups.

However, the *śramaṇa*s represented more than one type, a fact that has not been sufficiently acknowledged or integrated into views of early Buddhism. In the texts of Nikāya Buddhism, for example, one finds two quite different depictions of *śramaṇa*s. On the one hand, there are the *śramaṇa* groups, headed by one or another teacher, who move about in large bodies, seem to live an essentially communal existence, are defined by particular life rules, are found in or near towns and villages, and spend much of their time discussing and debating doctrine. On the other hand, are more solitary *śramaṇa*s, who live in seclusion, practice meditation, and strive for liberation. The Buddha and Mahāvīra (founder of

Jainism), prior to their realizations, are perhaps the best known of this latter type of *śramaṇa,* but other examples are found in the evidence reflecting this period.

Romila Thapar, in an important article (1978; see also 1975), contends that these two different types of depiction in fact reflect two quite distinct and different types of heterodox renunciants in sixth century B.C.E. India that she calls the "ascetic" and the "renouncer."[63] The ascetic, corresponding to the more solitary renunciant, undertakes the more radical renunciation of the two, for he has "opted out of society, renounced social mores and cast himself away." He "isolates himself totally and is thus lost to his kin and his society and to other ascetic colleagues" (1978, 64). Moreover, the goal of the ascetic is also the more radical, for ascetics aim at nothing less than the liberating experience of, and union with, ultimate reality. They also follow a distinctive method, namely, the practice of meditation and austerity *(tapas).* Moreover, they live in isolation, in the forest, obtaining food as they can. The ascetics were thus "figures of loneliness working out their salvation each one for himself" (65). Of the two types of *śramaṇa,* the ascetic is the higher ideal, for he aspires after the unsurpassable goal (63–64).

The renouncer, the *śramaṇa* who represents the more collective ideal, is like the ascetic in opting out of conventional society but unlike the ascetic, joins a group of renouncers and lives in an organized order (Thapar 1978, 64). This order constitutes a society that is different from, but parallel to, conventional society and is characterized by particular rules, some of which are typical of *śramaṇa*s in general, some of which are particular to specific groups. These bodies of renouncers typically live in or near towns and villages, again in contrast to the ascetic, who lives in more isolated places (69). Thapar stresses the renouncers' close relationship with conventional society: "The . . . sects of renouncers lived at the edges of towns, drew their recruits mainly from the towns, and were dependent for alms on the householders. . . . It was the towns which provided the renouncers with an audience and . . . with patronage" (70). The groups of renouncers played an important role in the town and village life of ancient India, such that the bigger towns built *kutūhalaśālā*s, halls for discussion, "literally places for exciting curiosity or interest" (69). This, in fact, identifies a chief preoccupation of the renouncer groups: in addition to seeking knowledge, they engaged in discussion and debate (69). This also indicates the close proximity of the renouncers to the laity and explains another important feature of their lives, namely, their teaching of laypeople. The great majority of those quitting the world were renouncers rather than ascetics, for the ascetic "has always been something of a rarity, more frequently described in literature than encountered in reality" (64).[64]

The Buddhist evidence examined in succeeding chapters suggests that Thapar's typology needs fine tuning in several respects. For one thing, Thapar implies that ascetics do not live in community at all, but this is overstating the matter, for—at least in the Buddhist case—community usually does have a role to play in their lives. In addition, she presents these two types as if they were clear and unambiguous, but in fact one finds examples that seem to lie somewhere in between the pure ascetic and renouncer types. Further, Thapar's description implies that these two types are separate from one another, whereas, in fact, there might be movement of renunciants from one group to the other and back. Furthermore, realized ascetics might come out of their seclusion to teach renouncers and could perhaps even act as heads of renouncer orders. Apart from these corrections, however, Thapar's typology is accurate and will prove useful in the present context. The following discussion will refer to Thapar's two renunciant types under designations reflecting their preferred venues. Thapar's ascetic will be called *forest renunciant;* her renouncer, *town-and-village renunciant.*

The two-tiered model, both in many Buddhist texts and in modern scholarship, depicts the Buddha as establishing a community of renunciants based on the model of town-and-village renunciation. In fact, the two-tiered model suggests that the Buddha taught *only* a dharma of town-and-village renunciation and rejected forest renunciation, except as an elective option for a few. However, given (1) the context of the sixth century B.C.E. with its two renunciant options and the spiritual priority of forest renunciation, (2) the explicit value placed on seclusion, meditation, and realization within so much of the early Buddhist literature, and (3) most especially—as we shall see—the clear evidence of important trends of forest renunciation at early and later times within Indian Buddhist history, it would seem difficult to have confidence in the formulation suggested by the two-tiered model.

An alternative view may be constructed, using Thapar's typology, in which the images of the Buddha as a realized forest renunciant are seen as far more important than has been previously recognized. In fact, the Buddha conforms to the type of forest renunciation as defined by Thapar. This suggests the hypothesis—to be explored in the pages that follow—that the Buddha was indeed a saint of the forest whose earliest disciples were forest renunciants and who espoused a dharma essentially of forest renunciation. This is not, of course, to rule out the possibility that town-and-village renunciation figured in some way in the very early tradition.

However, whether and how it may have done so remains unclear. For example, did the Buddha, during his lifetime, present his dharma not only within a forest context but also within a town-and-village context? Did he teach town-and-village renunciation as a viable form of renunciant life? Did he have as disciples not only forest renunciants but also town-and-village renunciants? Did he, then, condone the formation of town-and-village *saṃgha*s among his disciples, thus giving his implicit if not explicit approval to the formation of a Buddhism of town-and-village renunciation as a second renunciant wing alongside the wing of forest renunciation?

The Nikāya evidence and particularly that of the Pāli canon, with its tendency to view town-and-village renunciation as normative, would certainly suggest affirmative answers to these questions. However, as we have seen, this evidence has its own agenda to promote and cannot necessarily be taken at face value. The question of whether town-and-village renunciation was a part of the original dharma preached by the Buddha must remain open and unanswered, at least for the time being.

Be this as it may, town-and-village renunciation soon came to play a central and dominating role within Indian Buddhism. For it was clearly out of a Buddhism of town-and-village renunciation that classical monasticism developed quickly, within at most a few generations of the Buddha's death. Thus the particular concerns for correct behavior, for communal organization, and for close and regularized relations with the laity on the part of town-and-village renunciants found clear expression in the *vinaya,* while the preoccupation of town-and-village renunciation with doctrinal discussion and debate eventually took shape, it may be strongly suspected, in the vocation of texts and scholarship. The foregoing, then, suggests one possible reason for the literal incongruity between the religious type of the Buddha and the type represented by the monk of classical monasticism. These two are so different because they represent two quite distinct, if interconnected, renunciant ideals, the one of the forest, the other of the town and village.[65]

Notes

1. Buddhaghosa, following received tradition, gives the classical definition: " 'Forest', according to the *vinaya* method firstly, is described thus: 'Except the village and its precincts, all is forest' " (*Vsm* 72 [N., 72]; cf. *PTSD* 76, s.v. *arañña*). Thus, as we shall see, a forest-dwelling saint may live in a variety of places, including mountains, deserts, caves, jungles, and even cremation grounds.

2. This symbolic meaning of the word has been present from an early time. The Sanskrit term *araṇya* derives from the Vedic word *araṇa* (remote) (*PTSD* 76, s.v. *arañña). PTSD* comments further that "in the Rig V. *araṇya* still means remoteness (opp. to *amā,* 'at home')." *SED* similarly says that in the *Rig Veda, araṇya* means "a foreign or distant land" (*SED* 86, s.v. *araṇya*) and that *vana* (forest) can have a similar meaning (*SED* 917, s.v. *vana*).

3. As we shall see, in the texts, the forest refers, on the one hand, literally to the dwelling place and life of extreme renunciation of the typical renunciant in more or less isolated retreat and, on the other, figuratively, to a mental place or attitude in which prevail what one may call the values of the forest, such as inner renunciation, satisfaction with little, and a meditative state of mind. In defining this element of the forest saint, the following pages will specify two countertypes. The first is, not surprisingly, that of the ordinary world and its folk, who are addicted to samsaric values. A second countertype is that of settled monastery, adjuct to town or village, wherein dwell monks or nuns in relative (compared to the forest renunciant) safety and security. As in the case of the forest, both ordinary world and monastery, along with their ways of life, are also used in both literal and figurative ways. Literally, of course, they refer to particular habitations with certain definable characteristics. Figuratively, the ordinary world represents a mental realm or attitude of attachment, whereas the monastery represents a realm or attitude of renunciation, but one that can be seen as partial and imperfect. In this construct, the forest represents the domain of the saint, and the monastery represents a place of greater proximity to the world, understood both literally and figuratively.

As we shall see, this dichotomy between forest and settled monastery can be a useful construct. The identification of the Buddhist saint with a forest location and with forest values works relatively well for much of the Indian Buddhist evidence, particularly that representing formative phases of Buddhism itself and of the Mahāyāna. In this evidence, it helps us to gain some fundamental insights concerning Buddhist saints, their place within Indian Buddhism, and their own assessment of their particular way of being Buddhist. At the same time, however, although this model is useful in clarifying certain patterns in

Buddhist history, given the complexity of Buddhist history, it must be applied with care in any given situation (see the Conclusion of this book).

4. See e.g., Robinson and Johnson (1982), in which we are told that Śākyamuni Buddha's claim to his realized status may be incredible to us moderns, but it "was scarcely less preposterous to professional ascetics in the sixth century B.C.E." (25).

5. For useful summaries of the more important of these, see Lamotte 1958, 718–33, Reynolds 1976, and Reynolds and Hallisey 1987.

6. Aśvaghoṣa, *Buddhacarita* (Johnston 1936 and 1937). The Sanskrit original of the *Bc* is extant only for chapters 1–14 (there are also some Sanskrit fragments from central Asia [Lamotte 1958, 726, n. 20]). The entire text survives in Tibetan and Chinese. Weller (1928) has produced a Tibetan edition for chapters 1–17 and a German translation of the same. Beal (1883) has translated the Chinese version into English in its entirety. Johnston's English translation for chapters 1–14 relies on the Sanskrit, with some missing verses supplied using Weller's edition of the Tibetan and his German translation. Johnston's translation of chapters 15–17 relies on Weller's edition of the Tibetan and his German translation, with reference to the Chinese. For the translation of chapters 18–28 Johnston relies on at least two different Tibetan texts, identified as "the India Office copy" and a "rotograph of the red Peking edition." In the present chapter of this study, references to the *Buddhacarita* are to the chapter and verse of Johnston's translation. For those wishing to consult the Sanskrit and/or Tibetan, the following concordance of verses is provided.

Chapters	Sanskrit (Johnston)	Tibetan (Weller)	English (Johnston)
1	—	1–7	1–7
	8–89	8–89	8–89
2–7	Skt., Tib., and Eng. verses correspond		
8	1–53	1–53	1–53
	54	—	54
	55–87	54–86	55–87
(Skt. 54 is missing in Tib. Verse 55 in Skt. corresponds to 54 in Tib. and so on. Eng. follows Skt.)			
9	1–49	1–49	1–49
	—	50	—
	50–82	51–83	50–82
(Tib. 50 is missing in Skt. Skt. 50 corresponds to Tib. 51 and so on. Eng. follows Skt.)			
10–11	Skt., Tib., and Eng. verses correspond		
12	1–59	1–59	1–59
	60	—	60
	61–121	60–120	61–121
(Skt. 60 is missing in Tib. Skt. 61 corresponds to Tib. 60 and so on. Eng. follows Skt.)			
13	1–72	1–72	1–72
	—	73	—
(Tib. 73, not in Skt., is not translated by Johnston.)			
14	1–30	1–30	1–30
	—	31	—
	31	32	31

Chapters	Sanskrit (Johnston)	Tibetan (Weller)	English (Johnston)
		33–71	32–70
		72	—
		73–110	71–108
(Tib. 31 missing in Skt. Skt. 31 corresponds to Tib. 32 and so on. Johnston's Eng. follows Skt. Tib. 33–71 corresponds to Eng. 32–70. Tib. 72 is defective and is not translated by Johnston. Tib. 73–110 corresponds to Eng. 71–108.)			
15–17	Tib. and Eng. verses correspond		

Given some uncertainty concerning the Tibetan texts used by Johnston and the way in which he used them, I have not tried to correlate Johnston's English translation of chapters 18–28 with a specific edition of the Tibetan. These chapters may be found in the Derge edition of *bstan.'gyur, skyes.rab,* vol. ge, chapter 18 beginning at 1029.4; chapter 19 at 1038.3; 20:1044.4; 21:1050.3; 22:1056.1; 23:1060.4; 24:1066.3; 25:1071.2; 26:1077.7; 27:1089.3; and 28:1098.5. The reader may find Johnston's English translation of chapters 1–14 in Johnston 1936 and that of chapters 15–28 in Johnston 1937. These are bound together in Johnston 1984.

7. Each of these two main sections is again divided in half so that *Bc* is composed of four equal parts: (1) birth up to renunciation (chapters 1–7); (2) the spiritual journey to enlightenment (8–14); (3) the teaching mission (15–21); and (4) the final journey and *parinirvāṇa,* followed by the division of relics and building of stūpas (22–28). Warder makes the interesting observation that this fourfold framework corresponds to the four main places of pilgrimage: Kapilavastu, Bodh-Gayā, Banaras, and Kuśinagarī (Warder 1970, 340). Its structure parallels also, of course, that of the lunar month.

8. Of course, the fragmentary and other full-length biographies also discuss the Buddha as a saint. However, among the Buddha's biographies, Aśvaghoṣa's text exemplifies a unique interest in this topic. Aśvaghoṣa reveals himself to be accomplished in treating what is perhaps (at least for us) the central issue in the Buddha's hagiography, namely, the respective roles in his person of the human and the divine. Aśvaghoṣa's fidelity to the human dimension of Buddha Śākyamuni is, of course, in line with his general "theology." As he himself remarks, "All *bodhisattvas* . . . first tasted the flavour of worldly pleasures and then . . . left for the forest" (2.56). In his fidelity to the humanity of the Buddha, Aśvaghoṣa stands in contrast with some of the other well-known biographies of the Buddha. The *Lalitavistara,* for example, quickly loses sight of the humanity of the Buddha in its glorification of him. His life prior to his realization does not provide a real model for human beings, because even here the Buddha is already fully enlightened and is just going through the motions of an as yet unrealized human life.

The *Mahāvastu* exhibits similar tendencies. In the *Introduction to the Jātaka* (or *Nidānakathā*), a Sinhalese compilation, the humanity of the Buddha slips away in another direction. Here the Buddha is depicted in more scaled-down terms in comparison with *Lv,* but the presentation is wooden, and the Buddha, even in his prerealization days, is credited with few genuine human problems or emotions. Aśvaghoṣa's text is not, of course, the only one to make much of the humanity of the Buddha. However, unlike Aśvaghoṣa's work, which emphasizes Gautama's spiritual quest, other works presenting the humanity of the Buddha often take more interest in his social and political role. Thus the biographical sections of the *vinaya,* given in both the Theravādin and Mūlasarvāstivādin canons, for example, tend to view the Buddha in terms of his religiopolitical role as founder of the Buddhist church.

Three other factors make Aśvaghoṣa's work particularly appropriate in the present context. First, he is faithful to existing tradition and is an accurate summarizer of that tradition, as understood at a relatively early time (Johnston 1984, xxxviii; xl). Second, he provides a window into the Buddha's life, not just as it was expressed in a particular text or tradition, but as it was widely understood among Indian Buddhists of his time (xl). Third, Aśvaghoṣa communicates in a uniquely clear and penetrating way, no doubt owing largely to his calling, training, and accomplishment as a poet, enabling him to speak in a way that is intelligent and apt, that avoids clichés, and that embodies the high literary standards of his culture.

9. One important exception is the *Mahāpadāna Sutta* (*Dn* 2:1–54 [T.R. and C.R. 1899–1921, 2:4–41]).

10. At the same time, it should be noted that the events of the Buddha's life preceding the renunciation also play a paradigmatic role in Buddhist hagiography. However, this role is of a different and more limited nature than the postrenunciation events. It is only the most highly regarded Buddhist saints who are honored by having lives that approximate that of the Buddha, even in the events prior to leaving home. See, e.g., Guenther 1963, 7–22.

In Aśvaghoṣa's rendering, some of the more important of these prior events include: Gautama's entry into the womb of Queen Māyā, his mother-to-be, in the form of a white elephant (1.4); his miraculous birth from her side (1.10); the various cosmic miracles that attend his birth (1.16); the glory of the newborn infant's appearance (1.12–13); his taking seven steps to each of the four quarters and declaring this his final birth (1.14–15); the miraculous washing of the babe by the gods (1.16); the participation of various superhuman beings in cultic acts of reverence (1.18–20); the prediction of his destiny as a world emperor *(cakravartin)* or enlightened buddha (1.31–38); the visit of the sage Asita (1.49–80); the princely training of the young Gautama (2.24); his life in the court (2.20ff.); his marriage to Yaśodharā (2.26); and the birth of his son Rāhula (2.46). For a discussion of the Buddha's birth story, see Hara 1980.

It is worth noting that although these hagiographic features generally do not apply to Buddhist saints other than world-redeeming buddhas, they typically are understood to apply to other buddhas and so are not considered idiosyncratic to Śākyamuni Buddha alone. According to *Mpds* (see Lamotte 1958, 721–22), all buddhas, in their final lives, experience the same events; thus the text tells of the former Buddha Vipaśyin, whose life story duplicates the principal themes of Śākyamuni's life, including the major events surrounding his incarnation and birth. (On this issue, see Dayal 1931, 292–93.) These actions are formalized in the standard set of twelve acts that are attributed to Śākyamuni and other buddhas, an example of which is provided by Bu.ston (Obermiller 1931, 7ff.). The *Sthavirāvadāna* similarly remarks that "by virtue of the nature of reality *[dharmatā], buddhabhagavats,* while they live and exist, must without fail accomplish ten actions" (*Gms* 3.1: 163 [Hofinger 1954, 176–77]). The ten actions mentioned in this text, however, differ from the more well known list of twelve. This reveals one aspect of the pronounced tendency toward assimilation to type among the Buddhist saints. Not only, as mentioned, do Buddhist saints in general tend to approximate the general paradigm as outlined, but the members of a given subtype of saints—here the world-redeeming buddhas—tend to be assimilated to their even more specific subclass.

11. Thus, when Queen Māyā, the Buddha's mother-to-be, is about to deliver her holy child, she longs for the solitude of the forest (1.6). The sage Asita, the fully renounced

one, is also linked with the forest: he comes from the forest to the palace to see the new babe and even amidst the sensual attractions of palace life remains unmoved, "deeming himself to be, as it were, in a forest" (1.51).

12. See the treatment of theme 14, p. 52.

13. As we shall see in Chapter 9, it is precisely these three factors of simple dress, sustenance by begging, and living "in the forest" that receive elaboration in the classical Buddhist ascetic code *(dhutaguṇa).*

14. Terms used include *pratijñā* (e.g., 9.44, 11.50), *vrata* (e.g., 12.91), and *niścaya* (e.g., 13.59).

15. Thus, at his birth, he vows that, for the good of all beings, this will be his last existence (1.15), an intention that is repeated to his father, his groom, and others (5.28; 5.78; 7.48; and 9.78–79). On leaving Kapilavastu, he similarly declares that he will not return until he has attained liberation (5.84; 6.14–22). When visited in the forest, he reaffirms his intention to fulfill his vow to attain realization (12.100–101). And seated beneath the *bodhi* tree, he makes a vow to remain there until he has achieved enlightenment (12.119–20).

16. Such ascetic vows are, of course, not restricted to Gautama and were understood by Aśvaghoṣa as a relatively common feature of the wandering life of forest *yogin*s (see, e.g., 9.44; 9.47; 12.91).

17. In other texts, the Buddha regularly travels to other realms not accessible to mortals, such as Lake Anavatapta (Hofinger 1954, 7). By the time of Asañga, the enumeration of the contents of the *abhijñā* and particularly of the *ṛddhi* had come to be more inclusive than the earlier versions. See the "powers" *(prabhāva)* chapter of the *Bodhisattvabhūmi* (40–54).

Other supernormal abilities attributed to the Buddha include his ability to walk and talk at birth (1.14–15); to learn in a few days lessons that would normally take years (2.24); to cross a river in an instant (22.8–9); to leave his footprints in stone (21.24); and to remain unharmed in the midst of a fire (16.27–37).

18. Other saints also possess, by virtue of their enlightenment, powers like the Buddha. Thus Kāśyapa is called "master of magical powers" (16.66) and is depicted as, among other things, flying like a bird in space; standing, sitting, lying down, and walking in the sky; blazing like a fire; and shedding water like a cloud (16.64–68).

19. Thus it is said that he will become either a world emperor *(cakravartin)* or a buddha (1.34), and, in his youth, he is credited with many masteries—physical, intellectual, and social.

20. For the sake of convenience, I employ the Hindi rendering of the term, the form with which readers are most likely to be familiar.

21. On the phenomenon of darśan in Indian religions, see Gonda 1969 and Eck 1981.

22. In Aśvaghoṣa's biography, one may take darśan not only from the Buddha but from any genuine saint. For example, it is when Gautama "sees" the wandering *śramaṇa* that he is inspired to renounce the world. Similarly, he later takes darśan from Arāḍa (12.4). Again, when the renunciant Aśvajit enters Rājagṛha on his alms rounds, he holds "the eyes of a great crowd by his beauty, his tranquility and his demeanour" (17.3). One is also able to take darśan from Kāśyapa (16.69).

23. Quite interesting in this context is the portion of the text immediately preceding this story, coming at the end of Canto 25, where the Buddha explicitly affirms that "salvation does not come from the mere seeing of me" (25.77). The structure and content of this section raise some interesting questions. It is clear that darśan is one of Aśvaghoṣa's favorite themes and that it receives positive treatment everywhere else in the text. Just before this critique of darśan, the Mallas—aware that the Buddha is about to die—have

just remarked on the salvific implications of seeing the Buddha: "Surely men become objects of derision, like those who come away poor from a goldmine, if, having seen the *guru,* the omniscient great seer, in person, they do not win to the higher path." The text then praises the Mallas' words. Immediately following this, the Buddha comments, "So indeed it is the case that salvation does not come from the mere sight of me." This and the next three verses are, in effect, a homily that in its placement, its subject matter, and particularly in its polemical tone appears out of place. This impression is softened by considering the full context of the argument being made at this point in the text. "So indeed is it the case that salvation does not come from the mere sight of me without the strenuous practice in the methods of yoga; he who thoroughly considers this my law is released from the net of suffering, even without the sight of me" (25.77). The practice of yoga (understood here to refer to meditative techniques) is, of course, implied by the cult of saints—as the method by which saints are produced, so to speak—and yoga is a key concern of Aśvaghoṣa. Considering these facts, this critique of the limitations of darśan alone is compatible with the affirmation of darśan occurring throughout the rest of the text. Everyone should participate in darśan, the text seems to say, but those who would renounce the world, emulate the Buddha, and gain release had better do more than that!

24. For an informative analysis of the rich and multifaceted place and function of the "gods" in early Buddhism, see Wagle 1985.

25. As the Buddha says to some of his disciples, "you have passed beyond suffering. . . . It is proper now to help others" (18.16).

26. Adapted from Tambiah 1984.

27. The gods also figure among those who are devoted to the Buddha and may attain the goal (e.g., 18.16).

28. In the well-known "questions which tend not to edification," one is to renounce knowledge that does not lead directly to the winning of salvation (Warren 1886, 117–28). The passages cited by Warren are interesting because they give evidence of two different viewpoints, one of which puts the practical concern for liberation above all others, the second of which places more value on theoretical knowledge.

29. Indeed, in the *Suttanipāta,* the Buddha remarks, "What is obtained by chanting hymns [or verses] is not to be eaten by me. This is, brahmin, not the practice of those who see rightly. The Buddhas refuse what is obtained by chanting hymns [or verses]" (*Sn* 14 [Sadatissa 1985, 9]; see also Norman 1985, 13). Of course, in this passage, the Buddha distinguishes himself from the brahmins who do make their living by textual recitation, but the Buddha here implicitly advances the efficacy of the meditative life and criticizes certain religious behavior, such as textual memorization and recitation, that does not lead directly to the sought-after goal.

30. When Āmrapālī comes to the Buddha for the first time, he remarks, "This your intention is virtuous and your mind is steadfast by purification" (22.41).

31. Foucher emphasizes this theme: " 'Never,' we are told, 'did it occur to him to say, "This man is a noble; this man is a Brāhman; this man is rich; this man is poor; therefore I shall preach to this one in preference to the other." ' " Foucher continues, "As the rain falls from the sky, his word fell on all—young and old, intelligent and obtuse, virtuous and criminal, of humble and of noble parentage—without exception. Even caste, that rigid mold which modern India has not been able to shed, did not exist for the Blessed One" (1963, 193–94).

32. Notwithstanding the tendency of much nineteenth- and early-twentieth-century scholarship to portray him as, in Schopen's words, "a sweetly reasonable Victorian Gentleman" (1990, 181).

33. It is said to shine with golden spendor (19.46).

34. The next morning, he emerges with the docile Nāga curled up in his begging bowl.

35. On this see Ray 1990.

36. In various sources to be examined later, we are told that the dharma will again find its fruition in a future age, when Maitreya will come and will receive the mantle of Buddha Śākyamuni from Mahākāśyapa to inaugurate a new and perfect world order in which the dharma will flourish. For a summary of sources, see Lamotte 1958, 775–89. See also Lancaster 1987.

37. The Buddha's message is addressed at once to the individual and to the collective. On the one hand, his analysis of *duḥkha* points to both the individual's ignorance and thirst, and also the interlocking web of the unenlightened cosmos as a whole, with all its beings and its samsaric values and motivations. On the other hand, it sets out a path to liberation that emphasizes the importance of both individual effort and also community. The *saṃgha* is thus one of the three jewels, and community is essential, not only to the layperson and the monk in the monastery, but also to the "solitary" meditator in the forest.

38. Johnston points out that in its final chapters (22–28), *Bc* closely recapitulates *Mps* (1937, 7). Thus, the final teachings of the Buddha presented in *Bc* include not only the injunction to forest renunciation cited here but also the advocacy of the values of the settled monastery. For example, one is to replace the living saint with the *prātimokṣa*—"When I have gone to the Beyond, you should treat the *prātimokṣa* as your spiritual director *(ācārya),* as your lamp, as your treasure" (26.26)—and one is also to judge all teachings put forward in terms of whether they accord with the *sūtra*s and the *vinaya* (25.38–45), rejecting those that do not. These and other themes characteristic of settled monasticism do not appear elsewhere in the text. In their appearance here, they provide a contrast with the emphasis on the sainthood of the Buddha and of his disciples that is the unifying theme of the rest of Aśvaghoṣa's work.

39. For a discussion of the eight great principal pilgrimage sites, see Foucher 1963, 201–42.

40. The "earliest Buddhist literature," as reconstructed by Frauwallner and others, clearly presupposes both a significant *hagiographical tradition* and *collections of the sayings* of the master. Early texts such as the *Dhammapada* and the *Suttanipāta* (the former with its short, epigrammatic sayings grouped in short sections, the latter with its brief *sutta*s) and archaeology (which reveals a strong hagiographical concern in stūpa remains) appear harmonious with the view that these two types of literature were primary at an early time. These types of literature are also compatible with the early, meditatively preoccupied, wandering community: usually in verse, these were clearly forms of literature that could be held in memory with relative ease and could be transmitted among renunciants whose main preoccupation was meditation. These kinds of texts contrast, of course, with the later, longer, and more complex works and collections of works such as came to predominate in classical Buddhism, texts whose memorization and understanding clearly required a great deal of energy and attention.

41. We have already seen several ways in which the Buddha has been implicitly assimilated to the gods, such as in the attribution to him of supernormal abilities and the association with his person of various spontaneous and miraculous occurrences, e.g., earthquakes and rain. As we have also seen, this kind of assimilation to the status of a deity is not something unique to the Buddha, for the other Buddhist saints also have powers and attract miracles. One particularly interesting example in the *Buddhacarita* of this sort of assimilation occurs when the Buddha asks Kāśyapa to display miraculous phenomena and the saint responds by performing various feats, including blazing like a fire and emitting water "like a cloud" (16.64–67). Then, we are told, "as he took great strides, blazing

and shedding water, he appeared like a cloud pouring forth rain and brilliant with flashes of lightning'' (16.68). As part of his expression of enlightened appearance, then, Kāśyapa appears in the form of a thunderstorm. Przyluski describes an analogous phenomenon (1926–28, 239–58) in his examination of the saint Gavāṃpati, who similarly appears in the form of a thunderstorm; Przyluski concludes that this saint is essentially a god of the storm who has come to be regarded as a saint. To Przyluski's remarks, it may be added that the association of the Buddhist saints with rain and storm is not atypical, particularly through their frequent connection with and power over the *nāga*s, who control rain and storm. One is also reminded here of the power frequently ascribed to Buddhist saints of emitting fire from the upper part of their bodies and water from their lower (formalized in Asañga's well-known list of ''powers'' [*Bbh* 45]). For some other examples of Buddhist saints with close connections to rain and storm, see I-liang 1945, 241ff.

42. The Pāli texts, for example, regularly show the gods regarding the Buddha as an equal or superior (Wagle 1985, 60).

43. In Jainism, siddhas are those liberated souls who dwell in an assembly in the uppermost realm of the cosmos (Caillat 1987, 512). They are human beings who have attained perfection and who have, by virtue of that, gained a superhuman status. The term is also found in the *Rāmāyana,* where it similarly refers to a human being who has attained perfection and thereby gained superhuman qualities (*SED,* 1215). The term appears with a similar meaning in the *Mahābhārata* (Narasimhan 1965, 230). The term is also well known from a considerably later time as designating the enlightened ideal of Indian Tantric Buddhism (Ray 1987).

44. The term *siddha* is used in several different contexts in the *Bc.* The superhuman identity of the siddha is made clear in the *Bc* account of the Buddha's achievement of enlightenment: the earth quaked and ''the quarters shone bright with crowds of siddhas'' (14.87). In other passages, Gautama's own status as a siddha is affirmed. For example, Aśvaghoṣa tells us that when Gautama left his groom Chanda, he ''preceeded to the hermitage, overpowering it with his beauty, as if he were a siddha'' (7.1). Again, when he tames the *nāga* and emerges unharmed from the inferno, he is himself simply called ''siddha'' (16.27). Finally, one of the Buddha's names is Sarvārthasiddha (19.43).

45. Diana Eck remarks, ''One of the ways in which the gods can be recognized when they move among people on this earth is by their unblinking eyes. Their gaze and their watchfulness [are] uninterrupted'' (1981, 7).

46. On the earliness of the mythic and cultic dimensions of Śākyamuni, see also Snellgrove 1969 and 1970, 75.

47. References to verses of *Sn* do not include separate references to the translation, as the verses in the Pāli text and the English translation of Norman are identically numbered. References to the prose follow the format ''pr.'' for prose, page number in the Pāli text, and page number of English translation.

48. Significantly, the *Suttanipāta* shows little interest in the magical powers of the Buddha (or other saints) or in the miraculous response of the cosmos to them. This is, as we shall see, typical of texts that, like the *Suttanipāta,* reflect the forest life, in contrast to those that are primarily concerned with the cults of such saints.

49. In order to do so, one would need to survey images of the Buddha not only in the various *vinaya*s and related texts (as has Bareau [1963 and 1972]) but also in the full range of Nikāya Buddhist texts extant in Sanskrit, Tibetan, and Chinese. The results would then need to be analyzed, in so far as possible, in terms of the different kinds of communities that retained them.

50. The references to the Buddha are scattered throughout the *Sn* and are particularly

concentrated in the *Hemavata Sutta* (153–80), the *Pabbajjā Sutta* (405–24), the *Padhāna Sutta* (425–49), and the *Nālaka Sutta* (679–723). Lamotte remarks that the latter three are archaic in style but indicates his own suspicions that they represent a Pāli adaptation of fragments borrowed from Northern tradition (1958, 731). Whether this be the case or not, the material they contain is thematically consistent with images of the Buddha occurring elsewhere in the *Sn*.

51. Later sections of *Sn* contain what may be references to settled monasticism; see e.g., the *Ratana Sutta* (222–38).

52. Or "detachment" (Norman's preference). *Sn* occasionally depicts the Buddha among great crowds of *bhikkhus* (1250 in the *Sela Sutta* [pr., 102ff. (Nr., 94ff.)]), but this is the exception.

53. The text occasionally has the Buddha living near a village; for example, we are told that he can be found in villages, on the tops of mountains, or in the Jeta Grove in the *ārāma* of Anāthapiṇḍada (P., Anāthapiṇḍika) (pr., 46 [Nr., 44]).

54. Foregoing sleep is, of course, an important practice of forest renunciation in Buddhism and is associated with one of the twelve- (or thirteen-) member ascetic code of the *dhutaguṇas* (see Chapter 9).

55. In *Sn,* the term *bhikkhu* generally indicates a renunciant of the forest, and in the *Tuvaṭaka Sutta,* where the ideal *bhikkhu* is discussed, he is described as a forest renunciant (915–34). Similarly, the term *pāṭimokkha,* which in the Pāli canon usually implies settled monasticism, appears in *Sn* in a forest context (340). For a discussion of this term see Chapter 3, n. 20.

56. For the similar image of Mahāvīra as a forest renunciant both before and after realization, see Tatia 1980, 322–66.

57. The image of the Buddha as a saint dwelling in the forest, even after his enlightenment, also appears in more developed tradition. Lamotte, for example, calls our attention to the legend according to which, while Buddha Śākyamuni was staying at Kauśāmbī, there occurred a schism over a minor detail of discipline that he was not able to resolve. The Buddha then "withdrew for some time into the Pārileyyaka forest where he lived in the company of wild animals" (1958, 22).

Most scholars, of course, have tended to take the depictions of the Buddha as an essentially urban figure at face value and without question. Edward Conze, for example, remarks that "most of the Buddha's public activity took place in cities and that helps to account for the intellectual character of his teaching, the 'urbanity' of his utterances and the rational quality of his ideas" (Conze 1980, 12). Conze is quite right to link the more rational and intellectual dimensions of Buddhism with an urban environment, the environment of established, settled monasticism, but it would seem an unjustifiable leap to conclude that this also represents the original context of the Buddha and style of his Buddhism.

58. At any given point in Buddhist history, many of those living in monasteries entered at ages sufficiently young that any personal sense of spiritual vocation must be highly doubted. Parents and relatives have, in their turn, typically regarded the monastic vocation as a status-producing one. When the monastic vocation has been entered upon in some maturity of age, one may often have mixed motives as well. For the socially disadvantaged, entry into the monastery might reflect hope of greater opportunities, economic and social as well as religious. Prospective monks, whatever their previous situations, might have the expection of improvement of their standing, relatively reliable sustenance, and a roof over their heads. See Spiro 1982, 321–50, for a discussion of this issue in the Burmese context.

To say this, of course, is not to deny the possibility of deeply personal commitment but rather to point to the relative heterogeneity of motivations and factors behind a given monastic renunciant's entry into the order. This is also not to deny that mixed motives existed for forest renunciants as well. However, for these latter there is typically so much less to be gained in the way of material security, comfort, or social confirmation that such "worldly" motives are less likely to have been primary.

59. Prebish 1975b, 52–53. The *pārājika* rule forbidding a monk to claim any attainments under threat of permanent expulsion, unless he actually possesses them, would certainly discourage any such talk lest he be put to the test by hostile judges.

60. Prebish 1975b, 74–75.

61. See the discussion of Lévi and Chavannes of this restriction in several different *vinayas* (1916, 94–108).

62. Other terms are also used to designate these individuals, e.g., *parivrājaka* and *bhikṣu*. For discussions of the *śramaṇa* as a religious figure in the sixth century B.C.E., cf. S. Dutt 1962, 30–56 and 1984, 35ff.; and Jaini 1970. For a useful summary of some of the most important ideas associated with the prominent *śramaṇa* and Brahmanical schools in the time of early Buddhism, see Collins 1982, 29–64.

63. Thapar's analysis also includes discussion of orthodox renunciants.

64. Both the existence of town-and-village Buddhist renunciants in the early days of Buddhism and tensions that seem to have existed between them and forest renunciants are reflected in certain criticisms of doctrinal and textual preoccupations made from the point of view of the forest renunciant in the oldest section of *Sn,* likely predating settled monasticism. Like other sections of *Sn* but more strongly, the *Aṭṭhakavagga* propounds a solitary, meditative ideal of the forest, while critiquing an ideal that is more collective in orientation, in which there is an emphasis on doctrinal study, advocacy of particular views, denigration of other doctrines and views as inferior, and preoccupation with doctrinal debate. In this kind of Buddhism, "desirous of debate, plunging into the assembly, they reciprocally regard one another as fools . . . they cause a dispute, desirous of praise, saying [they are] experts" (*Sn* 825; cf., e.g., 796–803 and 824–34). *Sn* counsels the good forest *bhikkhu* to avoid this kind of renunciant life. One may presume that these repeated admonitions are necessary both because such practices existed in the environment of *Sn* and also because some Buddhist *bhikkhus* (perhaps many) had succumbed to them. See Luis Gomez's discussion of a number of these passages (1976). One typical passage from the *Nandamāṇavapucchā Sutta* of the *Aṭṭhakavagga* defines the *muni* (the forest renunciant): " 'People say, "There are sages *(muni)* in the world," ' said the Venerable Nanda. 'How do they [say] this? Do they say that one possessed of knowledge is a sage, or truly one possessed of a [particular] way of life? The experts do not say that one is a sage in this world because of view [P., *diṭṭhi;* Skt., *dṛṣṭi*], or learning [P., *suti;* Skt., *śruti*] or knowledge [P., *ñāṇa;* Skt., *jñāna*], Nanda. I call them sages who wander without association, without affliction, without desire' " (1077–78).

65. It is not only the original historical status of town-and-village renunciation that remains unclear but also its evolution within the Buddhist context. At this point in this study, it is not possible nor is it necessary to address the issue of the precise timing or the specific phases according to which settled monasticism took shape. It may simply be acknowledged that several stages would undoubtedly need to be distinguished, after the still-peripatetic life of town-and-village renunciation had been left behind, leading eventually to the development of the classical system of settled monasticism as reflected in the final forms of the various extant *vinayas*. At the same time, it would appear that these various stages, whatever they may have been, do reflect a particular type of renunciant Buddhism. Moreover, this type of renunciant Buddhism, at least in its ideal form, stands in consider-

able contrast to the type represented by that of forest renunciation. For this reason, in what follows, except in instances when I am able to make more precise distinctions, I shall consider the group of the various stages beginning with town-and-village renunciation and leading eventually to the classical monastic system as belonging to a single type, that of monasticism.

3

Saints of the *Theragāthā* and *Therīgāthā*

In the preceding chapter, it was proposed that certain fundamental themes, arranged according to a particular logic, make up the paradigm provided by Buddha Śākyamuni. It was also suggested that this paradigm was in more general use as a presupposition in Indian Buddhism, identifying not just the Buddha but also others understood as Buddhist saints. As a first step in the testing of this hypothesis, the present chapter contains an analysis of two works, the Pāli *Theragāthā* and *Therīgāthā,* which provide a relatively complete definition of the Buddhist saint, this time as arhant. The *Theragāthā* and *Therīgāthā,* books 6 and 7 of the *Khuddakanikāya* in the *Suttapiṭaka* of the Pāli canon,[1] contain the songs of some 240 men and women saints who lived during and after the time of the Buddha.[2] Like other of the more ancient texts in the *Khuddakanikāya*—for example, the *Suttanipāta,*[3] *Dhammapada,*[4] *Udāna,* and *Itivuttaka*—the *Theragāthā* and *Therīgāthā* show us saints who live primarily in the forest and practice forest renunciation.[5] In contrast to these other texts, however, in the *Theragāthā* and *Therīgāthā* these forest saints provide the primary focus of discussion.[6]

Winternitz examined these songs and noticed that their contents are at variance with much of the rest of the Pāli canon, particularly in their concern for mythological themes and supernatural beings. Possibly with a version of the two-tiered model of Buddhism in mind, he concluded that the songs reflect a degradation of normative monasticism and must therefore be relatively late, dating at least after the time of Aśoka (1933, 110). Norman, however, points out that concerns for mythology and supernatural beings existed in earliest Buddhist times (1969, xxvii). He also tells us that in these songs there is mention of ordination at the age of seven, something generally forbidden in the *vinaya,* suggesting that at least some of the material in the texts dates from a time *prior* to the classical formation of the *vinaya* rules. Norman's doctrinal, metrical, and linguistic analyses confirm this judgment and lead him to conclude that the contents of both texts were composed over an extended period, from the end of the sixth century B.C.E. to the middle of the third century B.C.E. (1969, xxix, and 1971, xxxi). This dating, from the lifetime of the Buddha to the reign of King Aśoka, would place the *Theragāthā* and *Therīgāthā* among the earliest Buddhist texts, with portions of them representing a particularly ancient stratum of Buddhist literature. As we shall see, Norman's judgment, pushing the contents of at least some of the songs of the two texts back to the early premonastic days of Buddhism, makes sense. We shall also see that some of the songs clearly postdate the rise to dominance of settled monasticism and give evidence of a time when the forest traditions reflected in the texts were struggling, without great success, to coexist with it.

The content of the individual songs in the two texts shows both a certain standardized format and some variation of content.[7] For example, there is a relatively consistent hagiographical frame to the songs, typically including the name of the saint to whom they are attributed and a declaration of the realization of the saintly author. Beyond this, the content of the songs tends to be of two sorts: either it is primarily hagiographical, telling a specific story of the liberation of a particular saint, or it is mainly doctrinal, expounding some set of principles or practices, with no clearly apparent connection with the life of the particular saint to whom it is ascribed. Some songs are strictly doctrinal, others are hagiographical, but most contain elements of both.

When the hagiographical elements of the songs in the *Theragāthā* and *Therīgāthā* are analyzed, one finds that certain features are standard. Assembled into a whole, these features provide a relatively clear and consistent picture of the Buddhist saint—cutting across gender lines—that is evidently presupposed by the traditions of which these texts are expressions. In the following pages, these typical themes are identified and arranged according to the composite picture that they form. These themes reflect a model similar to the paradigm discussed in the previous chapter.

Prerealization

1. *Crisis in the prospective saint's life.* The lives of the elders often begin with a personal crisis. Most typically, this crisis precipitates the recognition of suffering *(dukkha)*[8] as a fundamental fact of life, seen in the reality of disease, old age, and death. This, of course, recalls Buddha Śākyamuni's similar recognition prior to his leaving home. The crisis leading to renunciation may be brought on by a specific situation, such as the death of a loved one (*Ta* 213–23),[9] which leads to a realization of the inevitability of one's own old age and death (*Ti* 252–70). As another example of such a crisis, the brahmin Aṅgulimāla, "well born on both sides," turns to stealing from others and harming them, which precipitates renunciation (*Ta* 866–91). Others leave the world because their ordinary lives have become intolerable (*Ta* 620–21, 863). Sometimes there is reference to other religious practices in which the renunciant was previously engaged, which proved unsatisfactory: ritual bathing (*Ta* 345–49), the burning of sacrificial fires (*Ta* 341), and the tending of fires in the wood (*Ta* 219). Uruveḷakassapa, for example, was an ascetic with matted hair *(jaṭila)* (*Ta* 377), and Jambuka performed extreme austerities (*Ta* 283–84). Among the women, the precipitating crisis is often associated with home and family. Thus, a number of *bhikkhunīs* remark on the unsatisfactory nature of marriage (for example, *Ta* 23–24). For others, family life is marred by the death of a child (*Ti* 51–53, 131, 133). Another is a widow, without children or relatives (*Ti* 122ff.). Occasionally, women have not yet entered into

family life and simply experience a strong desire to renounce the world (*Ti* 448–522). Other women have completely bypassed marriage and family, such as a successful prostitute who one day awakens to a sense of disgust for her physical body (*Ti* 25–26). In the case of the women, particularly interesting is the theme of insanity as precipitating a break with the conventional world. The woman renunciant Vāsiṭṭhī tells us of insanity that began presumably with the death of a son: "Afflicted by grief for my son, with mind deranged, out of my senses, naked, and with dishevelled hair, I wandered here and there. I dwelt on rubbish heaps, in a [cremation ground], and on highways; I wandered for three years, consigned to hunger and thirst" (*Ti* 133–34).

2. *Personal spiritual longing, which translates into a strong sense of religious vocation.* Personal crisis leads to spiritual longing and a desire to abandon the world (*Ta* 136). Subhā, the smith's daughter, hears the dharma and "long[s] only for renunciation" (*Ti* 338; see *Ta* 167). Pārāpariya yearns for a rule *(ānupubba),* a vow *(vata),* and a practice whereby he may develop himself and not harm others (*Ta* 727). Tāḷapuṭa sings a song of longing for the forest *(vana)* (*Ta* 1091ff.). Not all those with this kind of desire are layfolk. Sīvaka, evidently already a Buddhist renunciant with a preceptor, dwells in the village but yearns for the forest (*Ta* 14). Telakāni is a renunciant who has practiced for some time without a teacher and longs for a competent teacher to guide him (*Ta* 747ff.).

3. *The formal renouncing of the world.* The actual renouncing of the world represents a turning point in the life of each would-be saint. One woman remarks, "Giving up my house, having gone forth *[pabbajitvā],* giving up son, cattle, and what was dear, giving up desire and hatred, and having discarded ignorance, plucking out craving *[taṇhā]* root and all, I have become stilled, quenched *[nibbuta]*" (*Ti* 18). Often leaving the world is occasioned by meeting an enlightened teacher. Mahāpanthaka says that when he saw a realized teacher, he was inspired to abandon "children and wife and money and grain" and "went forth into the houseless state" (*Ta* 510–12). Similarly, a number of thieves, through encountering the enlightened one Adhimutta as their potential victim, leave the world and take up the religious life (*Ta* 705–25). Isidāsī, mistreated and finally cast out by her husband, to whom she has been devoted, suffers deep sorrows until one day a woman renunciant comes to her father's house (*Ti* 400–426). Having paid homage to this *therī* and given her food and drink, she declares, "Noble lady, I wish to go forth" (*Ti* 427–29).

Sometimes, the inspiration for renunciation comes simply from hearing the Buddhist teachings and seeing their validity. The smith's daughter Subhā says that one day she heard the dharma and gained insight into the four noble truths. Turning from sense-pleasures and longing for renunciation, she abandons "the group of relatives, the slaves, and servants, the rich fields and villages, and delightful and pleasant possessions . . . no small wealth" and leaves the world (*Ti* 338–39). Significantly, the songs make clear that the saints do not renounce the world lightly or out of a desire to better their situations. Thus Tāḷapuṭa, seeming to fend off potential criticism, remarks, "I did not go forth because of bad luck, nor from shamelessness, nor because of mere whim, nor because of banishment, nor because of my livelihood,'' but out of a desire for liberation (*Ta* 1124).

The leaving of the world is depicted as taking place at almost any age, even, as mentioned, as young as 7, as in the cases of Sumana (*Ta* 429), Bhadda (*Ta* 479), and Sopāka (*Ta* 486), and as old as 120, as in the case of Dhammasava's father (*Ta* 108). The renunciants usually take up the renunciant life under a master who utters the ancient formula of ordination, as in Bhadda's case: ''Then the teacher . . . , rising up from his solitary meditation, said to me, 'Come, Bhadda *[ehi bhadda]'*; that was my ordination *[upasampadā]*'' (*Ta* 478, 870). Similarly, Sunīta takes ordination *(upasampadā)* with the words ''come, bhikkhu *[ehi bhikkhu]*'' (*Ta* 624–25; see also *Ti* 108). As these passages suggest, the prospective renunciants are generally ordained under a teacher, but this is not invariable. Some stories depict cases of self-ordination, as in the story of the princess Sumedhā, who, having said to her father, '' 'This very day, father, I shall renounce [the world]' . . . having cut her black, thick, soft hair with a knife, having closed the palace [door], entered on the first meditation'' (*Ti* 478–80).

Particularly interesting is the consistent image of a simple one-step ordination by which one becomes a *bhikkhu,* rather than the two-leveled ordination that prevailed in the classical monastic system.[10] It is also interesting that the term for this ordination is *upasampadā,* the same term that, in classical monasticism, is used only for the second, full ordination, which one may take only after the novitiate and by which one becomes obliged to follow the rules of the classical *pāṭimokkha.* That the *Theragāthā* and *Therīgāthā* use *upasampadā* in such a different way suggests that this is an older meaning of the term and perhaps also that such a meaning existed in forest traditions that were contemporaneous with but quite separate from those of settled monasticism. Also significant are the meanings of the terms *bhikkhu* (and *bhikkhunī*) in the *Theragāthā* and *Therīgāthā,* where they serve to designate forest renunciants who have passed through the one-step ordination and not, as in classical monasticism, those who have taken the full ordination (compare, for example, *Ta* 870) and thereby accepted the way of life implied by the *pāṭimokkha.*[11]

4. *The taking up of a particular wandering, renunciant lifestyle, defined by specific ascetic modes of dress, sustenance, and dwelling.* Although the *Theragāthā* and *Therīgāthā* explicitly refer to the *dhutaguṇas*—as in Mahākassapa's (Skt., Mahākāśyapa) remark, ''I am outstanding in the [*dhutaguṇas*]''[12] (*Ta* 1087)[13]—such explicit references are rare (see also *Ta* 1120 and *Ti* 401).[14] However, it is clear that the *dhutaguṇa*-type practices, in either classical or some other form, define the lifestyle of the forest renunciants of the *Theragāthā* and *Therīgāthā* (for example, *Ta* 1120).

WANDERING. Having left the world and become a renunciant in the Buddha's tradition, the elders wander abroad, the women as well as the men (*Ti* 17, 20, 92). With no fixed abode, they ''go to different countries, wandering unrestrained'' (*Ta* 37). Referring to the geographical and temporal expanse of her peregrinations, a *bhikkhunī* tells us, ''Aṅga, and Magadha, Vajjī, Kāsī, and Kosala have been wandered over [by me]. For 55 years without debt I have enjoyed the alms of the kingdoms'' (*Ti* 110).

DWELLING IN THE FOREST. The wandering renunciant takes up residence in the forest, that is, in remote and uninhabited regions, for ''forests *[araññа]* are delightful, where [ordinary] people find no delight. [Only] those rid of desire will delight there'' (*Ta* 992). The specific places where the forest renunciants dwell include mountains *(giri)* (*Ta* 115), mountain peaks *(nagamuddha)* (*Ta* 544), mountain crests *(kūṭa)* (*Ta* 1135), mountain clefts *(nagavivara)* (*Ta* 41), caves *(leṇa)*[15] (*Ta* 309, 545, 1135), woods *(vana)* (*Ta* 545), hillsides *(sānu)* (*Ta* 23), the bases of trees (*rukkhamūla;* Skt., *vṛkṣamūla*) (*Ta* 217, 467, 998), and so on. Sometimes, the renunciant takes up residence in the cremation grounds (*Ta* 6, 315, 393, 599, 854). Occasionally, he or she lives in a small hut *(kuṭī* or *kuṭikā),* and the frequent association of such huts with rain and storm suggests that it was during the rainy season that these were typically used (for example, *Ta* 1, 51, 52, 53, 54, 55, 56, 59, 60, 325–29, 487). An indication of the variety of places in which a renunciant might live and meditate during his or her career is given in several of the songs, such as Saṃkicca's, in which he remarks, ''I have dwelt in woods, caves, and grottoes, in solitary lodgings, in a place frequented by beasts of prey'' (*Ta* 600–601).

ROBE AND APPEARANCE. The garments of the renunciant are typically made from rags, which have been collected ''from rubbish heaps, cremation grounds, and streets'' (*Ta* 578) and stitched together (*Ti* 1, 16). Anuruddha, for example, ''sifted, took, washed, dyed, and wore the rags from a rubbish heap'' (*Ta* 896).[16] Generally, the renunciants of the *Theragāthā* and *Therīgāthā* are tonsured, and both laity and matted-hair ascetics are depicted as having head and beard shaved (*Ta* 377, 512). The *bhikkhunī*s similarly have shaved heads as marks of their way of renunciation (for example, *Ti* 32, 75).

SEEKING ALMS. When the renunciants seek alms, they come from their forest haunts to where the laity live (*Ta* 1054), receiving ''left-over scraps . . . as food'' (*Ta* 1057). Their food is ''cooked a little here, a little there, in this family or that'' (*Ta* 248). The renunciant should wander from door to door, neither seeking out the wealthy nor avoiding the poor (*Ta* 579) and should not seek to fill the stomach: ''While eating moist or dry food, he should not be satisfied. A bhikkhu should wander with unfilled belly, eating in moderation, mindful'' (*Ta* 982). This austere begging practice is most conducive to meditation, for, we are told, ''the mind of one who is greedy for flavours does not delight in meditation *[jhāna]*'' (*Ta* 579–80). The renunciant is also to accept food, as it comes, without judgment. For example, Mahākassapa reports that he came down from his lodging and entered the city to seek alms, coming before a leper who was eating. ''He offered a portion to me with his rotting hand; as he was throwing the piece (into my bowl) his finger broke off there. But near the foot of a wall I ate that portion; no disgust arose in me, either while it was being eaten or when it had been eaten'' (*Ta* 1054–56).

THE IMPORTANCE OF SOLITUDE. One of the most frequently repeated themes in the *Theragāthā* and *Therīgāthā* is that of the necessity, the virtue, and the joy of a life lived away from others, in seclusion. One is to avoid all companions, "not living . . . with householders nor houseless ones alike" (*Ta* 581; see also 54, 577–80, 896). Thus the saints live alone *(ekāsana)* (*Ta* 848), dwell secluded *(pavivitta)* (*Ta* 859–60), find no satisfaction *(asaṃsaṭṭha)* in company (*Ta* 860), and enjoy the "sweetness of solitude" (*Ta* 85). Dwelling "alone in the forest like a tree rejected in a wood" (*Ta* 62), the renunciant is not to grieve, for "if no-one else is found in front or behind, it is very pleasant for one dwelling alone in the wood, . . . alone, companionless, in the pleasant great wood" (*Ta* 537, 541). The solitary retreat of renunciants makes them inaccessible to others, the virtue of which is often stressed (for example, *Ta* 109). It is not only that renunciants are to live in retreat alone; in addition, they wander alone (*Ta* 1122).[17] As in the cases of the other elements of the forest renunciants' lives, their solitude exists in order to facilitate meditation, for *bhikkhu*s and *bhikkhunī*s withdraw into solitude for the purpose of meditation and therefore "should resort to a lodging which is secluded" (*Ta* 577). Significantly, like the other elements of the forest life, such solitude supports meditation not only physically and socially but psychologically and spiritually. The *Theragāthā* and *Therīgāthā* present the belief that, by retiring to solitary retreat, the forest renunciant may purify defilements in a depth and manner not possible "in company."

It should be observed that women ascetics face the particular threat of harrassment and even attack by men, a theme highlighted in the *Therīgāthā*. One woman saint in her forest abode remarks on her fear of this danger but says that such fear is a wile of Māra to which she will not succumb. For her, as for the other renunciants both women and men, courage and tenacious resolve prevail: even if 100,000 rogues were to menace her, she will not move a hair's breadth (*Ti* 230–31). Although complete solitude is the general rule, forest renunciants sometimes live together with one or a few like-minded others (*Ta* 177–78), or in small communities (*Ta* 148 and perhaps 266), or when a disciple lives with or near his or her teacher (*Ta* 66). Such situations are exceptions,[18] however, and in the two texts the general rule applies that where people gather in numbers, be they laity or renunciants, the virtue of the true renunciant life is compromised (*Ta* 245, 898).

"SPEAKING LITTLE." The renunciant is peaceful and taciturn, speaking little. Sāriputta (Skt., Śāriputra), we are told twice, is "calm *[upasanta]*, quiet *[uparata]*, speaking in moderation *[mantabhāṇin]*" (*Ta* 1006, 1007). Gaṇgātīriya tells us, "In two rainy seasons I uttered only one word" (*Ta* 127). Elsewhere in the texts reference is made to the noble *(ariya)* silence *(tuṇhībhāva)* of the renunciants, indicating an implicit characteristic if not an explicit vow (*Ta* 650, 999). The theme of silence is connected not only with the renunciants "on the path," so to speak, but also with enlightened saints. Thus we read in Revata's song, "Having attained to non-reasoning *[avitakka;* Skt., *avitarka]*,[19] the disciple of the fully enlightened one is straightway possessed of noble silence" (*Ta* 650).

THE ELEMENTS OF FOREST LIFE IN CONCERT. These elements of the lifestyle of the forest renunciant are often described in concert, as in Upasena Vangantaputta's *gāthā*, in which he refers to a habitation that is secluded; a coarse robe fashioned from cloth taken from a rubbish-heap, cremation ground, and streets; wandering "for alms from family to family without exception; and not living in company with householders nor houseless ones alike'' (*Ta* 577–81). Sometimes the collection of conventions followed by the renunciant represents one of the classical lists of ascetic requisites, such as the ''four requisites'' (*Ta* 1057) or other lists of *dhutaguṇa*-type practices (*Ta* 842ff.). Another, less standardized description is found in the song of Gaṅgātīriya, who says, ''My hut was made of three palm leaves on the bank of the Ganges. My bowl was only a funeral pot, my robe a rag from a dust-heap'' (*Ta* 127; compare also *Ta* 842–65).

THE RIGORS OF THE FOREST LIFE. The life of forest renunciation is difficult and demanding, something expressed in a verse repeated several times: ''Tormented by gnats and mosquitos in the forest, in the great wood, like an elephant in the van of the battle, one should endure there mindful'' (*Ta* 31, 684). Another song mentions other hardships: ''Brought low by colic, dwelling in the grove, in the wood, where there is restricted food supply, where it is harsh'' (*Ta* 350; compare 435). The forest life is not only onerous, it can pose danger to life and limb, and several songs make reference to the continual threat of wild beasts (for example, *Ta* 524, 577, 1135). Other verses make reference to the difficulty of finding sufficient food and to the loneliness of forest life, the inclement weather one faces in the forest, the threat of attacks by others, and so on, as well as the social disapprobation that seems to go along with and to parallel whatever praise may come one's way (for example, *Ta* 1118). These difficulties are summarized in the following frank appraisal: ''Truly it is hard to go forth . . . sustenance of life is difficult for us with whatever comes our way'' (*Ta* 111). While presenting a realistic picture of the rigors of forest life, the saints are able, at the same time, to affirm its unique value in comparison to the alternatives. As Godatta observes simply, ''There is happiness arising from sensual pleasures and pain springing from seclusion; [but] the pain springing from seclusion is better than happiness arising from sensual pleasures'' (*Ta* 669).

5. *The seeking and finding of a teacher or guru.* In the *Theragāthā* and *Therīgāthā,* the teacher *(satthā)* (for example, *Ta* 214, 912) plays a crucial role in the prospective saint's journey. In many of the songs, it is assumed that a personal teacher is necessary to the forest renunciant in the meditative quest. This is because the teacher has attained enlightenment (*Ta* 747ff.) and can therefore guide the renunciant on the way to realization (*Ta* 66). One renunciant, for example, has been meditating for a long time but has not found the way to release. Anguished by his failure, he says that he seeks one ''who will cause me to experience bond-releasing enlightenment in the world'' (*Ta* 750), one who is ''the doctor who might remove that dart of mine'' (*Ta* 756). Anūpama has found such a teacher and comments to himself on his good fortune: ''You have found the teacher who is hard to find'' (*Ta* 214).

How is a genuine teacher to be recognized? Frequently, it is *seeing* the teacher that is decisive, giving birth to faith and renunciation. Anuruddha recounts many of his former lives and then remarks, ''Then I saw the fully-enlightened one, the teacher with no fear from any quarter'' (*Ta* 912). This seeing gives birth to trust, and Anuruddha goes forth into the houseless state (*Ta* 912). Others similarly recognize the authenticity of the teacher by seeing him or her (for example, *Ti* 22,

160, 154, 148). Authentic teachers may also be known by their trustworthiness (*Ti* 43), the quality of their teaching, or their kindness (*Ti* 148). The woman renunciant Candā emphasizes this latter element in her description of her teacher: "In pity [she] sent me forth; then having exhorted me, she urged me towards the highest goal. . . . The noble lady's exhortation was not in vain. . . . [I am] without āsavas" (*Ti* 124–26).

The disciple responds to the authentic teacher with devotion and veneration. Senaka, speaking of his teacher in a typical way, comments on his joy when he "saw the enlightened one teaching the supreme doctrine" and puts forth a praise of the magnificence of the Buddha (*Ta* 287–90). Others similarly worship the teacher (*Ta* 480), for "would anyone transgress who bowed down his head with hands and feet, worshipping such a teacher when he came?" The devotion of the disciple to the teacher is also expressed in service, and the disciple may stay with the master for periods of time, waiting upon and serving him or her (*Ta* 604, 918). The disciple's devotion ultimately expresses itself in following the teacher's instructions. Sumana has carried out his practice under the direct guidance of such a teacher and has thereby attained realization (*Ta* 330).

It appears that the disciple's devotion to the teacher is not extraneous but is rather inseparable from the meditative path he or she has chosen. This is suggested by the putting of devotion and realization together in a two-part phrase that occurs several times in these songs: "The teacher has been waited on *[pariciṇṇa]* by me, the Buddha's teaching has been done" (for example, *Ta* 1050). In the songs of the *Theragāthā* and *Therīgāthā,* certain of the *thera*s and *therī*s seem called upon to epitomize one or another trait desirable in saints or prospective saints. The quality of devotion to the teacher is such a trait and is nowhere more clearly etched than in Ānanda's song, in which he remarks that for twenty-five years he served the blessed one with loving deeds, loving words, and loving thoughts, "like a shadow not going away from him. . . . I paced up and down behind the Buddha while he paced up and down" (*Ta* 1041–42).

6. *The formulation of aspirations and taking of vows in connection with the quest.* Like the Buddha before them, the renunciants of the two texts make general aspirations and take specific vows as part of their spiritual quests. These include both general aspirations to enlightenment (for example, *Ta* 167) and specific vows, and a revealing epithet of the renunciant is *sīlabbata,* possessed of "virtuous conduct and vows" (*Ta* 12; see also *Ta* 19). In this case, the specific conduct and vows being referred to would appear to be quite different from the classical *prātimokṣa*[20] of settled monasticism but would seem to involve, among other things, obligation to the *dhutaguṇa*s or *dhutaguṇa*-like codes and practices bound up with life in the forest. It may also be that behind some of the other practices attributed to the forest renunciants of these texts, such as living without companions, not speaking, and acting as if insane, lie one or another ascetic convention or vow. The renunciants of these texts are also depicted as taking specific vows in connection with their meditation in strict retreat, much as the Buddha did at the time of his enlightenment. Thus, one renunciant declares: "I shall enter the grove, nor shall I come forth from there until I have gained the annihilation of the

āsavas'' (*Ta* 543), and another: ''I shall not eat, I shall not drink, nor shall I go forth from my cell. I shall not even lie down on my side, while the dart of craving is not removed'' (*Ta* 223; also 312–13). And Mudita similarly declares, ''Let this body be broken willingly; let the lumps of flesh be dissolved; let both my legs fall down on the knee-joints. I shall not eat, I shall not drink, nor shall I go forth from my cell. I shall not even lie down on my side, while the dart of craving is not removed'' (*Ta* 312–13).

7. *The intensive practice of meditation, which makes up the substance of the spiritual quest.* Meditation (*jhāna* [Skt., *dhyāna*], *sati* [Skt., *smṛti*]), not surprisingly, stands at the center of the *Theragāthā* and *Therīgāthā:* one abandons the world, follows the arduous conventions of forest life, and dwells in solitude all for the purpose of meditation. And one meditates because it is the sole road to enlightenment (*Ta* 112). It is uniquely through meditation that one trains one's mind (*Ta* 134), develops good qualities (*Ta* 352–53), cultivates genuine compassion for others (*Ta* 352–53), gains the highest happiness (*Ta* 884), and achieves liberation (*Ta* 112). Thus, in one's solitary retreat, ''one should meditate undistracted'' (*Ta* 37) ''continually putting forth energy'' (*Ta* 266).[21] The sounds of the forest are welcome because they ''awaken the sleeper to meditation'' (*Ta* 22). One should sit down, cross one's legs, and hold one's body erect (*Ta* 29). Then one carries out the practice of meditation to transform the mind's unruliness (*Ta* 355ff.) and gradually bring it into a state of calm (*Ta* 689). Mindfulness *(sati)* is the standard practice of the two texts.[22] Sometimes other standard practices are mentioned, such as the practice of concentration *(jhāna)* (*Ta* 12), ''recollecting the enlightened one'' (*Ta* 354, 382), and practicing the four unlimiteds (*appamaññā;* Skt., *apramāṇa*) (*Ta* 386). There are also references to the classical cremation ground (cemetery) contemplations (for example, *Ta* 567ff., 18).

Meditation is depicted as an arduous practice, requiring commitment and exertion, because the mind is wild and chaotic. Dominated by conflicting and defiling emotions, it is a horse that needs to be tamed and a wild elephant that needs to be put in a pen (*Ta* 355–59). Given this situation, one must exert oneself in order to attain success.[23] Part of the rigor of meditation is the lifelong commitment it entails, seen in Anuruddha's reference to fifty-five years of meditation practice (*Ta* 904). The rigor of meditation is also a day-to-day commitment, as implied by one of the classical *dhutaguṇa* practices wherein the renunciant does not lie down at any time but remains upright, meditating night and day (*nesajjika;* Skt., *naiṣadika*).[24] In addition to expressing the rigors of the solitary meditative path, the songs also speak of the joy and contentment that it brings. Bhūta remarks, ''When in the sky the thunder-cloud rumbles, full of torrents of rain all around on the path of the birds, and the bhikkhu who has gone into the cave meditates, he does not find greater contentment than this'' (*Ta* 522).[25] Meditation is not something abandoned at the time of realization but plays a role for the enlightened ones in two ways. First, although enlightened, one continues to meditate, like Bhaddiya, who, ''having plucked out craving root and all, meditates, happy indeed'' (*Ta* 466). Second, meditation, it would seem, becomes internalized and defines the state of being of the saint.[26]

8. *Personal realization of enlightenment.* As a result of spiritual praxis, the renunciant attains direct and personal experience of enlightenment. In the *Theragāthā* and *Therīgāthā,* in the matters of inspiration, renunciation, lifestyle, and practice under a teacher, there is an assumed parity between the women and the men; the same is true in the matter of realization. In contrast to texts and traditions that reflect the two-tiered model of Buddhism, in the *Theragāthā* and *Therīgāthā* not only are women clearly held to attain enlightenment, but their realization is defined in virtually the same terms as that of the men.[27] Sometimes enlightenment is provoked by some incident or state, as when the *therī* Dhammā remarks, "Having wandered for alms, leaning on a stick, weak, with trembling limbs, I fell to the ground in that very spot, having seen peril in the body. Then my mind was completely released" (*Ti* 17). One of the more interesting of these realization-provoking situations is the *bhikkhunī* Sīhā's desperation, which leads her to the brink of suicide, whereupon she attains realization.[28] In addition, several songs describe a situation of realization that closely approximates that of the Buddha. Sunīta remarks that in the first watch of the night he recollected his previous births, in the second he attained the *deva* eye, and in the last he "tore asunder the mass of darkness," after which the gods came to pay him homage (*Ta* 627–31).[29] Although in most cases realization is obtained only after many years of intense meditation, this is not always the case; sometimes it is obtained much more quickly. In one instance, a *bhikkhunī* attains realization in seven days (*Ti* 43–44). Another woman saint experiences extreme grief at the death of her husband and two sons, and this precipitates an immediate realization (*Ti* 218–22).

Enlightenment in the songs is typically expressed in a series of stock words and phrases. We read, "My defilements have been burned up; all existences have been rooted out; journeying-on from rebirth to rebirth is completely annihilated; there is now no renewed existence" (*Ta* 67) and "looking at the arising and passing away of the elements of existence as they really are, I stood up with my mind completely released" (*Ti* 96).

The specific terms used to describe enlightenment reveal a variety of expression. Sometimes enlightenment is described as the fruition of meditation.[30] Sometimes enlightenment is spoken of apophatically, as the eradication of the three root evils (*Ta* 79), the elimination of karma (*Ta* 80), the removal of "imaginings" (*Ta* 675), and the attainment of "nonreasoning" (*Ta* 650). This style of expression is nicely summed up by a well-known analogy: "He whose āsavas are completely annihilated, and who is not interested in food, whose field of action is empty and signless release, his track is hard to find, like that of birds in the air" (*Ta* 92). Sometimes enlightenment is described in more kataphatic ways as positive knowledge, the purification of the mind, the attainment of the undying, or the winning of good qualities.[31] In a similar vein, enlightenment is sometimes expressed as the attainment of a pure and radiant mind: "Truly my mind is purified, unlimited, well-developed; having penetrated and having been applied, it illuminates all the quarters" (*Ta* 549).[32] In this view, enlightenment may be described as the freeing of the mind. Realization is also expressed as a victory over death (*Ta* 7), the "exchange [of] the ageing for agelessness" (*Ta* 32), and the attainment of the unageing, undying state devoid of grieving (*Ti* 512–13).

Enlightenment is further characterized in terms of the attainment of virtues, of "attributes," and "many qualities" (*Ta* 1251); of the gaining of sets of qualities such as "faith, energy, concentration, mindfulness and wisdom" (*Ta* 745); and of the winning of the meditations *(jhāna),* faculties *(indriya),* powers *(bala),* constituents of enlightenment *(bojjhaṅga;* Skt., *bodyaṅga),* concentration *(samādhi-bhāvanā),* and the three knowledges (*Ta* 1114).

In the songs, the experience of realization is often described in the vivid imagery of light and fire.[33] "See this wisdom *[paññā]* of the Tathāgatas, who, giving light and vision like a fire blazing in the night, dispel the doubt of those who come" (*Ta* 3). Martial images also abound in the two texts in descriptions of enlightenment as a victory over Māra (*Ta* 298) and the breaking of his bonds (*Ta* 336, 680, 888). Like the men, the women are also depicted as defeating Māra (*Ti* 7). For the women, enlightenment is additionally expressed as a state of realization in which the oft-proclaimed "inferiority of a woman's birth" has been transcended once and for all.[34] The diversity of forms of the expression of enlightenment in these texts is significant and stands in marked contrast to such expression in more self-conscious Buddhist philosophical schools within which certain ways of speaking of enlightenment vis-à-vis ultimate reality become characteristic, preferred, and dominant. Of interest also is the important role played by symbolism and concrete imagery, which again contrasts with the often abstract style of the scholastic tradition.

It must be mentioned that, with the attainment of enlightenment, the renunciant's teacher does not cease to be important. After attainment, the renunciant may be identified as the enlightened one of such and such a teacher, as in the case of Sumana, who says of himself that he is "made a thoroughbred by a thoroughbred, made good by one who is good, disciplined, and trained by Anuruddha whose task is done" (*Ta* 433). In addition, the disciple continues to bear the utmost love for the teacher, something well expressed by Cūḷapanthaka in his *gāthā,* in which, having attained realization, he speaks of his teacher with tenderness, reverence, and gratitude (*Ta* 557–66). In a very real sense, the enlightened disciple experiences himself or herself as inseparable from the teacher, through whom and in accord with whose legacy enlightenment has been won.[35]

Postrealization

9. *Recognition of the saint's enlightenment.* The gods acknowledge the saint's realization, as in Sunīta's report that when he achieved enlightenment, "Inda [Skt., Indra] and Brahmā came and revered me with cupped hands [saying] 'Homage to you, thoroughbred of men; homage to you, best of men; to you whose āsavas are annihilated; you are worthy of a gift, sir' " (*Ta* 628–29). In addition, people recognize the saint's realized status wherein the saint's appearance, words, or actions provide incontrovertible proof of realization.[36]

10. *Self-declaration of enlightenment.* As we have seen, the saints themselves proclaim their enlightenment; the *Theragāthā* and *Therīgāthā* taken as a whole

are, in fact, as mentioned, a collection of such declarations by the saints. Typical is Adhimutta's statement that he has lived the holy life, gone to the far shore, annihilated future rebirth, passed beyond suffering, and seen the world as it is (*Ta* 707ff.). Closely related is the lion's roar, made by men and women saints alike.[37]

11. *Compassion identified as a central component in the saint's enlightened personality.* The Buddha is compassionate *(kāruṇika)* (*Ta* 870), one who is kind *(anukampin)* (*Ta* 109), and the realized saints similarly are marked by compassion for all sentient beings. Thus, as a woman cares for her only son, so does the saint for all living creatures (*Ta* 33), protecting all creatures moving and unmoving (*Ta* 876). The saint is compared to an elephant whose "two front feet are gentleness *[soracca]* and mercy *[avihiṃsā]*" (*Ta* 693; see also *Ta* 238).

12. *Miraculous phenomena spontaneously surround the saint's person.* There is no explicit representation of this element in the songs. The reason may be that, because these songs are seen as products of the saints themselves, it was considered inappropriate to refer to this aspect of sainthood, a pattern that is seen elsewhere.[38]

13. *Possession of supernatural powers.* As a result of enlightenment, the saints are in possession of magical powers (*Ta* 375). Uruveḷakassapa knows his former births *(pubbenivāsa),* has purified his *deva* eye *(dibbacakkhu),* has magical abilities *(iddhi),* knows the minds of others *(paracittaññu),* and possesses divine hearing *(dibbasota)* (*Ta* 379).[39] Anuruddha similarly knows his former births and has purified his *deva* eye, enabling him to see the disappearance and reappearance *(cutūpapāta)* (dying and rebirth) of creatures (*Ta* 913–17).[40] Among these powers, recollection of former lives is most often mentioned, as in the case of Sobhita, who says, "In one night, I recollected 500 eons" (*Ta* 165; see also *Ta* 258–60 and 332). The *iddhi*s, the collection of superhuman physical abilities (flying, walking on water, and so on) are also commonly possessed by the saints (for example, *Ta* 379).[41] And just as the attainment of enlightenment of the women is the same as that of the men, so both women and men possess the same supernatural powers. Thus an anonymous *bhikkhunī* has gained the powers: she knows previous births, has had her *deva* eye purified, can see the minds of others, has had her ear element purified, is in possession of the *iddhi*s, and has attained the destruction of the defilements (*Ti* 67–71; see also *Ti* 179–81, 227–28, and 330–31). Although the saints have gained supernatural powers, they have not meditated for the purpose of gaining these, nor are they attached to them. Sāriputta, for example, affirms that although realized and in possession of power, he never had any intent to gain them.[42]

14. *The receiving of darśan.* The saint is depicted as possessing great spiritual presence, most directly experienced by "seeing," or darśan. It is often through receiving the darśan of the Buddha and other saints that prospective saints of the *Theragāthā* and *Therīgāthā* are inspired to renounce the world. The Buddha's charismatic appearance is described in images with which we are now familiar: he is compared to a fire, to gold, to the sun, to a lion, and to a mighty elephant (*Ta* 343, 818–21). The appearance of the other Buddhist saints is described in similar

terms, and they are commonly compared to the full moon: they are like the moon released from a cloud (*Ta* 871) and freed from the grasp of Rāhu (*Ti* 2) and are said to be "filled with things sublime, as the moon on the 15th day [is full]" (*Ti* 3). Darśan is a decisive experience because having seen such a saint, "who would not have faith?" (*Ta* 833). In addition, darśan is precious because "it is hard to obtain the sight of the enlightened ones repeatedly" (*Ta* 829).

15. *A cult with characteristic features that develops around the saint.* The saints, on account of their attainment, are highly to be revered by both humans and gods (*Ta* 186, 690). Humans adore the saints with praises and with offerings; they are privileged to make offerings because of the great merit gained by such donations to an enlightened one (*Ta* 629; *Ti* 111). The *deva*s are enamored of the realized saints because, owing to their attainment, they are above the gods (*Ta* 489) and envied by them (*Ta* 206). Thus, the *deva*s come respectfully before the saints, singly, in twos, and in groups (*Ti* 365), singing their praises and declaring their worthiness of offerings (*Ta* 629). In the case of Sāriputta, ten thousand *deva*s in all "stand with cupped hands," attending upon him who meditates, although they cannot fathom his wisdom (*Ta* 1082–84), and a similar image is given of Mahāmoggallāna (Skt., Mahāmaudgalyāyana) (*Ta* 1178–80). It is, of course, their realization—expressed in their wisdom, compassion, and power—that makes the saints the objects of a cult. Indeed, it is realization that "increases fame and reputation" (*Ta* 551) and renders one "worthy of gifts" (*Ta* 296). So the saints offer themselves as objects of cultic activity for the good of beings and can declare, "Do not hinder the many, belonging to various different countries, who have come to see; let the hearers, the congregation, see me" (*Ta* 1037–38). Various forms of the traditional cult are mentioned in the texts, such as worshiping the feet of the teacher (*Ta* 565), bowing down before and worshiping the saint (*Ta* 510), making offerings of various kinds (*Ta* 565), and sitting down to one side (*Ta* 565). Praise, supplication, and asking counsel are also important forms of the cult of the saints (*Ta* 835–41). It is significant that in the two texts these cultic forms are not engaged in just by the laity but by forest renunciants as well. This veneration is, moreover, performed not only to accrue future merit (as in *Ta* 910–12) but as part of the immediate path to enlightenment itself (*Ta* 1264). It is also significant that renunciants participate in this cult not just in the phase prior to realization but also after they have attained enlightenment (*Ti* 117–21). In spite of the cult that is proffered to them, renunciants are counseled to avoid recognition and riches. "Knowing this fearful peril in honours, a bhikkhu should go forth receiving little gain" (*Ta* 154). Furthermore, one should not seek reverence by crowds, for this only distracts from practice (*Ta* 1051). In fact, the saint must stand beyond praise and blame (*Ta* 159–60).

16. *The teaching of others, including not only humans but supernatural beings as well.* The saints teach others, including both human beings and the gods. The model of the ideal teacher is, of course, provided by the Buddha: he is "the teacher of the world including the devas *[satthā lokassa sadevakassa]*" (*Ta* 870), and his teaching pierces to the heart (*Ta* 26). The saints of the *Theragāthā* and *Therīgāthā* are similarly the teachers of others. First, of course, are the songs

themselves, examples of the teaching of the men and women of the two texts. In addition, many of the songs mention the teaching that master gives to disciple, as in the case of Uttamā, who remarks, "I went up to a bhikkhunī who was fit-to-be-trusted by me. She taught me that doctrine, the elements of existence, the sense-bases, and the elements" (*Ti* 43; see also *Ta* 214, 330, 432–33 and *Ti* 69, 102, 170).

17. *The acceptance of close personal disciples and lay followers.* The saints teach, instruct, and guide close personal disciples. Sumana was, in the previously quoted example, "Anuruddha's novice . . . made a thoroughbred by a thoroughbred, made good by one who is good, disciplined, and trained by Anuruddha whose task is done" (*Ta* 433). In this, as in other examples we have seen, the disciples frequently refer to their training under their teachers. It is significant that while the saints, after realization, accept and teach their own disciples, their connections to their teachers remain important (*Ta* 433, 557–66). The saints also attract lay devotees and teach them. Isidinna refers to lay followers who know the Buddhist teachings well (although their inner understanding is wanting) (*Ta* 187), and in another *gāthā* we are told that the saint "preaches to householders that which [he has] . . . collected over many years" (*Ta* 65).

18. *The absence among the saints of scholarly considerations and particularly of textual study.* The study of texts plays no major role in the lives of the saints of the two texts. This is true both of the period of their training, when their central preoccupation is meditation, and also after realization, when they are not shown as learned in textual matters or as recommending the study of texts to others.[43] Nevertheless, they are not without texts, as the existence of the *Theragāthā* and *Therīgāthā* themselves imply.

19. *The communication of teachings in an oral form.* Although concern for the vocation of texts and scholarship is absent from the *Theragāthā* and *Therīgāthā,* teaching and learning are constantly going on in the oral interchanges between master and followers, both renunciant and lay. In the two texts, doctrine appears less as an abstract and free-standing phenomenon with its own internal logic and more as a clarification of immediate life situations and experience. For example, doctrines appearing in these texts are stated simply and directly, are often connected with the events of a listener's life, and not infrequently emerge as the natural conclusion of a particular event. For example, as we have seen, many saints come to understand the first noble truth through their personal and direct experience of suffering.

20. *The making of conversions.* The saints are effective in converting others. Others are drawn to them by seeing them, hearing their teachings, experiencing their compassion, or witnessing some display of their power. Not infrequently, conversions are accomplished as a kind of by-product of a person simply becoming aware of who the saint is. Adhimutta, for example, is held captive by thieves who prepare to kill him. When he shows no fear, his captors are deeply impressed, take teachings from him, and renounce the world (*Ta* 705–25).

21. *The defeat of evil beings.* The enlightened saint has gained dominion over malevolent demons, chief among whom is, of course, Māra. Not only is enlightenment often described as a victory over Māra, but after realization the saints are shown as vanquishing Māra on every front. Thus in the song of Mahāmoggallāna, we see the *bhikkhu* censuring Māra in the Bhesakaḷā grove, after which "the yakkha, dejected, vanished on the spot" (*Ta* 1208). The saints are also able to overcome other powerful beings. Sumana, for example, states that by his supernatural powers he has overcome the king of the snakes, who himself had magical powers (*Ta* 429).

22. *Association with the lowborn and disadvantaged.* As we shall see, sometimes Buddhist saints, out of compassion, explicitly seek out the most humble of potential donors in order to grant them special blessing. Such is not the case in the *Theragāthā* and *Therīgāthā,* although in these texts the saints are advised against the dangers of close association with the highborn. Thus Piṇḍolabhāradvāja remarks that "respect and homage in high-born families is truly a 'bog.' A fine dart, hard to extract, honour is hard for a worthless man to give up" (*Ta* 124). The reason given is that seeking alms from high-caste families is connected with greed and desire for tasty food and can lead to impediments to spiritual development. Mahākassapa similarly says, "A sage should not visit [highborn] families; he becomes distracted, concentration is hard to obtain. He who is greedy and desirous of flavours misses the goal which brings happiness" (*Ta* 1052; compare 495).

23. *The unconventionality of the saints and their critique of social and religious conventions.* We have already seen that in certain respects the way of the Buddhist saints in the *Theragāthā* and *Therīgāthā* runs counter to convention. Their social unconventionality is seen in their rejection of the conventional values of the world, retreat to the forest, avoidance of highborn families, and view of honor and veneration as potential obstacles to the path. The saints are also, to some extent, religiously unconventional, for they are uninvolved with the values and preoccupations of conventional monastic Buddhism even when, as we shall presently see, these are prominent in their environment. It would appear that the unconventionality of the forest renunciant is sometimes consciously exaggerated. On the path, although a person is intelligent and competent, he or she is sometimes counseled to appear the opposite: Upasena Vaṅgantaputta says that one should make oneself appear as stupid *(jaḷa)* or mute *(mūga).*[44] That forest saints stand apart from worldly values is seen in the fact that although the saints may be enlightened, the world considers them worthless (*Ta* 129–30). Ajina observes, for example, that "even if one has the triple knowledge, has left death behind, and is without āsavas, ignorant fools *[bāla]* despise him as being unknown. But whatever individual obtains food and drink in this world, he is honoured by them even if he is of evil nature" (*Ta* 129–30). The forest saints' critique of conventional values becomes particularly sharp when, as we shall presently see, they point out the self-serving and hypocritical behaviors of certain monastics.

24. *Saints criticized and even persecuted for their sanctity, unconventionality, or explicit critiques.* In spite of their genuine and humble behavior, the saints may suffer disrespect, criticism, insult, and even persecution, hints of which are given in the texts. Godatta remarks that the saints are often ignored by others, while unrealized ones gain honor and praise: "There is the fame of those of little wisdom, and the lack of fame of the wise" (*Ta* 667). Ajina remarks that people despise the realized one (*Ta* 129). Tāḷapuṭa refers to others speaking to the saint with abuse (*Ta* 1100). Those among whom the realized one wanders may revile him or her (*Ta* 1118). Mahāmoggallāna's song refers to attacks on *bhikkhus* (*Ta* 1173). We also learn of non-Buddhists who, instead of offering veneration to realized arhants, attack them (*Ta* 1173). Persecution of the saints may even come from within the *saṃgha* (*Ta* 209, 920–80).

25. *The danger of the numinous power of the saint.* Nevertheless, one does not harm saints with impunity. Nandiya says simply, "Attacking such a bhikkhu, whose mind is like splendour. . . . [Y]ou will come to grief, Kaṇha" (*Ta* 25). Mahāmoggallāna says to that brahmin who would attack *bhikkhus*, "Do not destroy yourself. For, such a one may expect his head to split open" (*Ta* 1173). Those who do injury to saints may face dire consequences in the future.[45]

26. *The saint as principal reference point of the dharma for his or her followers, functioning in place of the Buddha.* In the *Theragāthā,* Mahākassapa is called "heir of the Buddha" (*Ta* 1058), and in this, although he enjoys a special status, he also exemplifies a general trend among the saints: the saints tend to become the principal reference points of the dharma for their disciples and stand in place of the Buddha, enacting his function; they may even be called "buddha." Other saints may similarly be referred to as "heir of the best of the Buddhas" (*Ta* 1168, 1248). In the songs, enlightened disciples are thus assimilated to their own teachers and to the great teachers of their lineages. Ramaṇīyavihārin says, "You should consider me as one possessed of insight, a disciple of the fully-enlightened one, the Buddha's own thoroughbred son" (*Ta* 45). Similarly, *therī* Sundarī remarks, "I am your daughter, brahman, your true child, born from your mouth" (*Ti* 336). And Bhaddā Kapilānī declares her essential identity with Kassapa (*Ti* 63–66). As the disciple is assimilated to the teacher, the teacher is assimilated to the Buddha (for example, *Ta* 1232–33), and the Buddha is assimilated to the previous six buddhas (*Ta* 490). The essential identity of these enlightened ones derives ultimately from the fact that they inherit the very being of their teachers, defined by the enlightenment they experience (*Ta* 490).

27. *Possession of a body that is supermundane in some way.* The body of the saint is seen to be wonderful. Various examples of the marvelous appearance of the saint's physical form have already been cited. In addition, as we have seen, the saints' bodies may be credited with other extraordinary features, such as the many miraculous abilities contained in the *iddhis.* Such abilities may refer to yogic experience of the subtle body as may also Khitaka's remark, "Truly my body is light, touched by much joy and happiness. My body floats as it were, like cotton blown by the wind" (*Ta* 104).

28. *Possession of the power of longevity and the capacity to live even to the end of the* kalpa. This theme, though important in the hagiography of the Buddha, makes no explicit appearance in the *Theragāthā* or *Therīgāthā*. One of the ways in which enlightenment is described is as the attainment of "agelessness" and of "the undying." It is not possible to ascertain to what extent this usage in these texts reflects the experience of realization and to what extent it may also have also been understood as a literal and physical condition attained by the saint.[46]

29. *Association of the saint with millennial expectations.* In the two texts, we find at most only possible allusions to this motif, for example, in the songs of Pārāpariya (*Ta* 920–48) and Phussa (*Ta* 949–80), which are considered in the conclusion to this chapter. The first song laments the present degeneration of the dharma and expresses the belief that the final dark time *(pacchimakāla;* Skt., *paścimakāla)* of the dharma is already at hand (*Ta* 947). The second speaks of the same degeneration that will occur in the future *(anāgatakāla),* when the latter days *(kālapacchima)* of the dharma will have arrived (*Ta* 950, 977).[47] Elsewhere, as we shall see, these same themes may be linked with the coming of Maitreya, but we find no such explicit linkage here.

30. *Anticipation of death.* In the songs, one finds no mention of the saints' foreknowledge of their own deaths, but there is some discussion of the attitude with which they confront the prospect of death, an attitude that is, in itself, extraordinary. In their solitary haunts, the saints regard their own deaths with equanimity: Adhimutta says, "I have no fear at death, just as I would have none at the complete annihilation of disease" (*Ta* 709). Other saints similarly declare their complete equanimity in the face of death (for example, *Ta* 20, 654–55, 606–7, 685–86, 1002–3).

31. *Extraordinary death.* There is no explicit representation of this theme in the songs, presumably because these songs are generally sung to or by the saints under whose names they appear, so that this phase of their lives could not be included. The songs of living saints would not provide information about the next two points either.

32. *Ritual disposition of the body of the saint, usually by cremation.* See theme 31.

33. *The saint's remains enshrined, usually in a stūpa.* See theme 31.

34. *The association of the saint with one or more sacred places.* The saints sometimes refer to holy places associated with other saints, or to places with which they feel a special connection (*Ta* 287, 308). There is, however, no mention of the sacred places of these saints, perhaps because such places tend to take on special significance particularly after the saint's passing.

35. *Development of characteristic kinds of texts, in particular, sacred biography and "sayings" or "songs" of the saint.* The texts of the *Theragāthā* and *Therīgāthā* are, of course, themselves songs containing hagiography and the sayings of the saints. They suggest the connection of the forest saints behind these

texts with traditions in which biography and the collection of sayings are important textual idioms. The antiquity of these texts also suggests a point that was discussed in Chapter 1 and that will be treated again, namely, that hagiography and sayings of the teacher represent textual material that may be placed among the earliest forms of Buddhist literature.

Conclusion

The *Theragāthā* and *Therīgāthā* present images of Buddhist saints of the forest whose traditions existed over a period of some centuries beginning in the early days of Indian Buddhism. Moreover, these saints tend to reflect a distinct and consistent type, which conforms closely to the basic paradigm of the Buddhist saint. As we have seen, the saints of the two texts do not reflect settled monastic values and orientations and, in fact, stand in considerable contrast to the classical type of the monk. Generally speaking, the world of the settled monastic and monastery do not appear in the two texts, in which the primary actors in the Buddhist world are the forest renunciants and their lay devotees.

However, in some important exceptions to this general trend, the existence of nonforest-dwelling renunciants is mentioned. For example, *Theragāthā* 245 may give evidence of town-and-village renunciant (or settled monastic) life, evaluated here as lower than the solitary ideal: "One (bhikkhu) alone is like Brahmā, two (together) are like two devas; three together are like a village; more than this are like a tumult." *Theragāthā* 153 implies the same: the life of poverty of forest renunciation is superior because if one lives in a certain establishment ("with shaven head, wearing his outer robe, obtaining food, drink, clothes and bed"), "he gets many enemies."[48] In Mahācunda's song, we find the remark that "one should make use of solitary beds and seats," although "if one does not gain contentment there, one should dwell in the Order *[saṃgha]*" (*Ta* 142). This appears to suggest, at least at the time of the songs in question, the existence of two contemporaneous and parallel but more or less distinct traditions—that of the forest renunciant and that of the town-and-village renunciant (or settled monastic).[49] Similarly, Phussa remarks on certain renunciants who, "finding their woodland wilderness wearisome . . . will dwell in villages" (*Ta* 962). This passage points to two possible options for the renunciant life: what is considered the superior but more difficult solitary life of the forest; and the nonsolitary life of town and village. These passages may additionally reflect a trend toward movement from the rigorous renunciant ideal, seen here as more ancient and more authentic, to the less demanding, more comfortable renunciation of town and village.[50]

The entire song of Pārāpariya (*Ta* 920–48) explicitly documents such a movement, which the saint regards as bound up with a corruption of the Buddha's authentic dharma. In this song, we find the ascetic engaged in solitary meditation "in the great wood, when it was in flower." Pārāpariya reflects that "the behaviour of the bhikkhus now seems different from when the protector of the world, the best of men, was alive" (*Ta* 921). He then draws a comparison between what he understands as the original and authentic tradition of the Buddha and what he sees as the corruption that is overtaking it. In the Buddha's day, *bhikkhus* dressed simply and modestly (*Ta* 922). They ate moderately and gladly accepted whatever was received as alms (*Ta* 922, 923). Toward the bare necessities of life, they had no greed (*Ta* 924). Their sole passion was for liberation, for "the annihilation of the āsavas" (*Ta* 924). To this end, they dwelt alone "in the forest, at the foot of trees, in caves and grottoes" (*Ta* 925). In these solitary locations, they devoted themselves to meditation as the vehicle of liberation (*Ta* 928). The moral qualities of these renunciants reflected their simple and dedicated way of life. They were "devoted to lowly things, of frugal ways, gentle, with unstubborn minds, uncontaminated, not garrulous, intent upon thinking about their goal" (*Ta* 926). Most important, through their way of life, these renunciant meditators attained their goal, they had "all āsavas completely annihilated" (*Ta* 928). However, Pārāpariya tells us, "Now those elders with all āsavas completely annihilated, great meditators, great benefactors, are quenched.[51] Now there are few such men" (*Ta* 928). In fact, the manner of the behavior of certain *bhikkhus* is now such that the true dharma of the Buddha "is destroyed" (*Ta* 929).

Pārāpariya then goes on to describe the current behavior of *bhikkhus*. Their lifestyle is opposite to that of the forest tradition, for they live not in the forest but rather in places where there are many people and things to keep them occupied. There they fill their bellies with food and are lazy with napping: "Having eaten their fill, they lie down, lying on their backs," after which they awaken (*Ta* 935). Moreover, they are concerned with their adornment (*Ta* 939). In short, "they enjoy the things of the flesh" (*Ta* 940). In addition, these *bhikkhus* have nothing of the moral probity and inner stillness of the forest renunciants: they are "not . . . calm inside" (*Ta* 936). Instead, they are turbulent within, and their states of mind are characterized by the defilements (*Ta* 931), greed (*Ta* 935), anger (*Ta* 933), and ambition (*Ta* 944). Moreover, these *bhikkhus* possess nothing of the silence and reticence of the forest renunciants. "Having abandoned the true doctrine, they quarrel with one another; following after false views they think, 'This is better.' " Moreover, when they are not sleeping, "they tell stories, which were condemned by the teacher" (*Ta* 935).

Behaving in contrast to the forest renunciant sitting motionless in meditation in solitary retreat, these *bhikkhus* cannot keep still but run everywhere, endlessly busy with projects. They "run here and there in the divisions of defilement, as if their own private battle (with Māra) has been proclaimed." They are constantly "running after pretexts, arrangements, [and] strategems" (*Ta* 941). Their impure minds, speech, and actions are reflected in everything they do. They are deceitful in their interactions with others and seek to find ways to acquire wealth such that "those who are outside the Order quarrel about the Order's gain" (*Ta* 943). Worst of all, these *bhikkhus* betray the dharma and use it as a vehicle of their personal ambition. "Having cast aside wealth and sons and wife they go forth: [then] they cultivate practices which are not to be done" (*Ta* 934). "They preach the doctrine to others for gain, and not for the goal" (*Ta* 942). In their renunciant life, they seek principally personal prestige: "some with shaven heads and wearing the outer robe desire only reverence, being bemused by gain and honour" (*Ta* 944). "They cause the assembly to meet for business purposes, not because of the doctrine"

(*Ta* 942). These *bhikkhus* apply themselves to everything but meditation (*Ta* 944). Avoiding meditation, filled with impurity, using the dharma to further their personal ambition, these *bhikkhus* attain no goal. They have succeeded in turning the dharma into another samsaric project, devoid of genuine spirituality. Thus it is, at least among them, that "the conqueror's teaching, endowed with all excellent qualities, is destroyed" (*Ta* 929). Pārāpariya finds himself living in a dark age, a "time of evil characteristics and defilements" (*Ta* 930).

However, says Pārāpariya, even in contemporary times the true dharma is not entirely destroyed, for "those who are ready for seclusion possess the remainder of the true doctrine *[saddhamma;* Skt., *saddharma]"* (*Ta* 930). In other words, there are those who still follow the true dharma of the tradition of the Buddha, namely, those who stand in the lineage of forest renunciation. By emulating this renunciant life of those saints who have gone before, even in these troubled times, one may attain realization: "Remembering the former sages, recollecting their behaviour, even though it is the last hour *[pacchimakāla],* one may attain the undying state *[amatapada]"* (*Ta* 947). Pārāpariya then concludes his song, "Thus speaking in the sāl wood, the ascetic with developed faculties, the brahmin, the seer, was quenched, with renewed existence annihilated" (*Ta* 948).

Some of the themes of Pārāpariya's song are again taken up in the following song of Phussa (*Ta* 949–80). Again we learn about the latter days of the dharma, but for Phussa they are seen to lie in a future degenerate era. Phussa's *gāthā* presents a prophecy concerning what things will be like in a more or less distant time. In that time, we are told, certain renunciants, "desirous of gain, inactive, devoid of energy . . . finding their woodland wilderness wearisome . . . will dwell in villages" (*Ta* 962).

> In the future many will be angry and full of hatred, hypocritical, obstinate, treacherous, envious, and with different doctrines. / Thinking that they have knowledge about the profound doctrine, while only remaining on the brink, fickle and irreverent towards the doctrine, without respect for one another. / Many perils will arise in the world in the future. The foolish will defile this well-taught doctrine. / Although devoid of virtuous qualities, running affairs in the Order the incompetent, the garrulous, and those without learning will be strong. / Although possessing virtuous qualities *[guṇa],* running affairs in the Order in the proper manner, the modest and unconcerned will be weak. (*Ta* 952–56)

When these events occur, the latter days *(kālapacchima)* of the dharma will have arrived (*Ta* 977). Phussa thus observes trends similar to those documented by Pārāpariya, but he prefers to emphasize their function in a future age,[52] in bringing destruction to the true dharma.[53]

Some important conclusions can be drawn from the songs of Pārāpariya and Phussa. First, these songs suggest a time not only when the nonforest renunciant life exists, but when it has in fact become dominant. Pārāpariya's gloom about the true dharma having been destroyed suggests that his tradition is in the minority and has been eclipsed by more dominant nonforest forms of the criticized *bhikkhus*. Second, the authors of the songs clearly see the forest renunciant tradition as retaining the true dharma of the Buddha and regard the kind of Buddhism followed by the *bhikkhus* that they criticize as inferior and even illegitimate. Finally, we see here little evidence of interactions or relationships between the forest renunciants and the nonforest *bhikkhus*. The little interaction that is mentioned notes either the settled monks' ignoring of the forest traditions or open hostility against them.[54] As Pārāpariya and Phussa see it, then, a dramatic change has occurred within Buddhism: there seems to be an increasing tendency for Buddhist renunciants to move from forest into village, abandoning the solitary vocation of meditation in favor of the collective, monastic life defined primarily by other preoccupations, including cultivating correct external behavior and engaging in study and debate. We may refer to this type of movement from forest retreat to village monastery as a process of monasticization. In the history of Indian Buddhism, as we shall see, monasticization occurs in a number of different contexts. In the present instance, the center of gravity of Buddhism seems to be shifting from forest to a nonforest type of renunciation. It is not possible to determine whether the monasticization described in these songs reflects only the growing popularity of town-and-village renunciation within Buddhist circles or whether it reflects a time when the development of what came to be classical monasticism was in full spate. In other cases of monasticization the issue is more clear, for they involve the movement of traditions, specific phenomena, and individuals—originally associated with forest Buddhism—into the context of settled monastic life. In the process of monasticization, these are absorbed and integrated into monastic Buddhism in a way that inevitably involves some transformation of both assimilated and assimilator. Understanding this process of monasticization is essential to an accurate appreciation both of the forest renunciants themselves and of their dynamic relationship with the more conventional forms of Buddhism.

Notes

1. Norman's translations of the *Theragāthā* (1969) and *Therīgāthā* (1971) supersede those of C. A. F. Rhys Davids (1909 and 1913). Rhys Davids's volumes remain useful, however, because the author introduces each song with a translation of the initial, biographical part of Dhammapāla's commentary on that song. On *Ta* and *Ti,* see Norman 1983, 72–77 and Horner 1930, 162–210.

2. These texts contain, respectively, 164 songs in 1,279 verses and 73 songs in 522 verses. These appear to have corresponding texts in Sanskrit in the *Stharivagāthā* and *Sthavirīgāthā,* which do not survive, but which are mentioned in the canonical literature (Lamotte 1958, 177–78). (The Mūlasarvāstivādin *vinaya,* "Bhaiṣajyavastu" section, contains a collection of songs called by N. Dutt "Sthaviragāthā" [*Gms* 3:1.21] and Hofinger "Sthavirāvadāna" [1954], surviving in an incomplete Sanskrit version [*Gms* 3:1.162ff.] and in Tibetan and Chinese [see Hofinger 1954, 9–15 for a discussion of the various editions]. The stories contained in this text are different from those contained in the *Ta* and *Ti,* although there is a small amount of shared material due, Dutt believes, to borrowing [*Gms* 3:1.20ff.]). The *Ta* and *Ti* contain from one to twenty-eight *(Ti)* or one to seventy *(Ta)* verses arranged in each text in sections *(nipāta)* with other verses of the same length. These sections are in turn ordered in each text according to length, beginning with those containing the fewest number of verses up to those containing the most.

3. See references to the forest life throughout the *Suttanipāta* (e.g., 35–75, 165–66, 207–21, 257, 331–34, 338, 388, 405–24, 474, and passim).

4. In *Dp,* for example, see the text's discussion and commendation of the forest life (99, 127, 205, 271, 305, 330; verses in the English translation by Radhakrishnan [1950] correspond to those in the Pāli text) and its view of meditation as the essence of the path (24, 27, 33–43, 144, 157, 205, 209, 276, 282, 293, 301, 350, 386–87, and passim). See also *Dp*'s forest interpretations of certain key terms. Thus, in reference to the term *paṇḍita* (learned person), we read that one is not a *paṇḍita* because he can speak much but rather because he has attained peace *(khema)* (258). Again, one is not a *dhammadhara* (usually, one who has committed the texts to memory; *PTSD* 338.2) because he speaks much but rather because, though with little learning, he has personally experienced reality *(dhamma)* (*Dp* 259). See also *Dp*'s similar interpretations of *thera* (260–61), *samaṇa* (264–65), *bhikkhu* (266–67, 360–82, especially 362, 364, 365, 370, 371, 378), *muni* (268–69), and *ariya* (Skt., *ārya*) (270–71). In a similar vein is *Dp*'s definition of the term *brahmin:* "Him I call a brahmin who wears cast-off garments *[paṃsukūla;* Skt., *pāṃśukūla],* lean, spread over with veins, solitary, and who practices meditation in the forest" (395) and "keeps away from both householders . . . and the houseless [mendicants], who does not frequent houses, and has few wants" (404).

5. The *Ta* presentation of its women saints as forest renunciants is paralleled by other texts in the Pāli canon. The "Suttas of Sisters" section of the *Saṃyuttanikāya,* for example, recounts the stories of ten women saints of the forest, dwelling in certain forests, sitting under particular trees, and meditating (*Syn* 1:128ff. [RW., 1:160ff.]). The images of women saints of the forest in the Pāli canon stand in considerable contrast, then, with the *vinaya* for women, which states rules making the forest life difficult or impossible for nuns (for example, women are never to be alone, they are not to enter the forest, and so on) (Horner 1930, 156ff. and 259).

6. Although the songs of *Ta* and *Ti* are each attributed to a specific saint, it cannot necessarily be assumed that they were composed by or sung to the historical individuals whose names are linked with them. Much more doubtful still is the historicity of the commentaries *(Paramatthadīpanī)* written on *Ta* and *Ti* in the fifth century C.E. by Dhammapāla, a contemporary of Buddhaghosa, which attach to the songs and their authors a variety of legendary material. In discussing these commentaries, Lamotte expresses the view that "their historical value is practically nil" (1958, 766).

7. Composition according to stereotypical plan is, of course, the rule in Buddhist hagiography, on which see Hofinger 1954, 21. For some discussion of the content of these texts see also Gokhale 1976.

8. In this chapter, Pāli terminology will be used.

9. References are to the verses of the Pāli edition of *Ta* and *Ti.* The reader is referred to Norman's translation of *Ta* and *Ti.* As the verses in his translation are given with the Pāli verse numbering, no additional reference to the translation need be given.

10. Thus in *Ta* and *Ti,* the terms *bhikkhu* and *bhikkhunī* generally indicate simply a renunciant rather than one who, among renunciants, has taken a second, higher ordination. *Dp,* for example, exhibits a similar usage, according to which *bhikkhu, pabbajita,* and *samaṇa* are used more or less interchangably (see, e.g., 72, 184, 243, 254–55, 264–67, 283, 302, 313, 361–82, 388). The *Suttanipāta* is similar (see, e.g., 915–34). The same kind of meaning of the term *bhikkhu* or *bhikṣu* is also found in later texts. In the *Jātakamālā,* for example, a certain pratyekabuddha who comes alms-seeking among humans and gladdens them with extravagant displays of his magical powers is referred to as a *bhikṣu* (*Jm* 22 [S., 30]).

11. The term *pāṭimokkha* also occurs at least once in the texts, for a discussion of

which see note 20. This is not to deny that later in Buddhist history there were forest renunciants who followed the classical monastic *prātimokṣa,* for we find them in modern Theravāda Buddhism (see, e.g., Tambiah 1984); rather, at this time and in these texts, there is no evidence that such was the case.

12. See Chapter 9 for a discussion of these practices. *PTSD* does not register the term *dhutaguṇa* (see *PTSD* 324, s.v. *dhutaṅga*), but, as seen here, *dhutaguṇa* occurs in the Pāli canon. The fact that *dhutaguṇa* occurs in *Ta* in preference to the much more common (in Pāli) *dhutaṅga* is additional evidence that *Ta* follows an older and somewhat different tradition from the traditions behind other Pāli discussions of these practices, as discussed in Chapter 9.

13. Norman translates this phrase as "qualities of shaking off" (1969, 99).

14. See Norman's remark on the term as used in this verse (1971, 149, n. 401).

15. Later in Buddhist history *leṇa* comes, of course, to indicate a monastery (Dutt 1962, 92–97).

16. In at least one instance (*Ta* 111), a renunciant has been given a robe by a layperson. This is an example of the lack of uniformity in the life rule expressed in these songs. In most cases where the acquiring of a robe is mentioned, the saints have made their own robes from rags gathered at a dustheap, in conformity with the four *nissaya*s and the *dhutaguṇa*s.

17. See also *Ta* 27, 76, 233, 266.

18. Another kind of exception is found in references in the two places in the songs to large groups of saints surrounding the Buddha. See the mention of five hundred *bhikkhu*s (*Ta* 1234) and one thousand *bhikkhu*s (*Ta* 1238). These, however, would appear to have primarily a cultic meaning, for which, see Chapter 6.

19. Or "nonthought."

20. As mentioned, the term *pāṭimokkha* occurs in these texts but refers to something other than the classical practices as defined in settled monasticism. Thus, in *Ta* 583, the term occurs in a song about solitary meditation in a secluded place, haunted by beasts of prey, where the renunciant is "not living in company" (*Ta* 577ff.). Dhammapāla's commentary uses the term more frequently, however, apparently with the classical meaning in mind, as when Sirimaṇḍa (*Ta* 447–52) is waiting for the recital of the *pāṭimokkha* (*Ta*-c 2:188 [C.R. 1913, 224–25]), Sirimitta (*Ta* 502–6) is preparing to recite the *pāṭimokkha* (*Ta*-c 2:211 [C.R. 1913, 241]), and Upāli (*Ta* 249–51) is depicted carrying out the recital of the *pāṭimokkha* (*Ta*-c 2:101 [C.R. 1913, 169]). Similar examples of the use of the term *pāṭimokkha* in the Pāli canon in a context of forest renunciation may be found in other texts of the *Khuddakanikāya,* e.g., *Dhammapada* 185 and 375 (Radhakrishnan 1950, 212 and 175) and *Suttanipāta* 340.

21. Sumaṅgala urges himself, "Meditate Sumaṅgala, meditate Sumaṅgala, remain vigilant Sumaṅgala" (*Ta* 43). We also read, "In a thicket of trees [one] meditates, happy indeed" (*Ta* 466). Though lightning flashes about the mountain, within, "the son of the incomparable venerable one meditates" (*Ta* 41).

22. For example, *Ta* 30, 31, 39, 40, 42, 66, 351–54, 518, 794, 817. One is advised to make one's mind well concentrated (*Ta* 50, 51, 56) and to guard the sense doors (*Ta* 503). The applications of mindfulness *(satipaṭṭhāna;* Skt., *smṛtyupasthāna)* are mentioned (*Ta* 352), as are practices classically considered under this rubric, such as mindfulness of the body *(kāyagatāsati)* (*Ta* 468; see also *Ta* 636) and of breathing *(ānāpānasati)* (*Ta* 548).

23. This virtue is stressed over and over in the songs (e.g., *Ta* 842–65) and provides the keynote of various injunctions that the renunciants give themselves, e.g., "I will fasten you, mind, like an elephant at a small gate. . . . I shall . . . make you turn. . . . I shall

tame you. . . . I shall bind you with mindfulness'' (*Ta* 355–59). The texts also refer to the process of meditation in martial images: Kātiyāna enjoins himself to ''meditate and conquer'' (*Ta* 415).

24. For example, *Ta* 856, 904, 1120. We are told, ''Night with its garland of lunar mansions is not just for sleeping; this night is for staying awake for one who knows'' (*Ta* 193; see also 84, 200, 203, 627–31, *Ti* 172–73, 179–80). Thus, the meditator may practice over a long period of time, day and night, without any break (*Ti* 44). This practice, of course, recalls the Buddha's meditating through the night under the pipal tree.

25. Mahāgavaccha tells us that he is ''delighting in meditation'' (*jhānarata)* (Ta 12).

26. Thus we read of the awakened one Mahāgavaccha, who is praised as ''concentrated'' and ''possessed of mindfulness'' (*Ta* 12).

27. The equivalence of attainment is the explicit theme of the song of Bhaddā Kapilānī, in which the woman saint's enlightenment not only is said to be the same as that of the men but is equated with that of no less a figure than Kassapa (*Ti* 63–66).

28. ''Thin, pale, and wan, I wandered for seven years: (being) very pained, I did not find happiness day or night. Then taking a rope, I went inside a wood, (thinking) 'Hanging here is better for me than that I should lead a low life again.' Having made a strong noose, having tied it to the branch of a tree, I cast the noose around my neck. Then my mind was completely released'' (*Ti* 79–81; see also *Ta* 405–10). Galloway (1981 and 1985) identifies this type of story with a tradition of ''sudden enlightenment'' in Indian Buddhism.

29. Nearly identical accounts are given in the songs of Uttarā (*Ti* 178–79) and Vijayā (*Ti* 172–73). Taken together, these accounts at least raise the possibility that they may give expression to a kind of meditation practice regularly engaged in by some of the forest renunciants of this tradition.

30. ''I am a great meditator, skilled in the calming of the mind. I have obtained the true goal; the Buddha's teaching has been done'' (*Ta* 112).

31. Thus we read of enlightenment as seeing reality just as it is (*Ta* 87), the attainment of ''the three knowledges'' (*Ta* 117), and knowing the ''five elements of existence'' (*Ta* 120).

32. Elsewhere we read, ''Continually considering my pure mind which has been released from defilements and is undisturbed, I shall dwell without āsavas'' (*Ta* 438).

33. This theme in early Buddhist literature has been explored by Gokhale 1989, 1–10.

34. ''What (harm) could the woman's state do to us, when the mind is well-concentrated, when knowledge exists for someone rightly having insight into the doctrine?'' (*Ti* 61).

35. This spiritual identity is expressed in the woman renunciant Sundarī's song: ''You are the Buddha, you are the teacher, I am your daughter Brahmin, your true child, born from your mouth, my task done, without āsavas'' (*Ti* 337).

36. In the discussion of the Buddha's life, a third kind of recognition of the saint's realization was mentioned, namely, the response of the natural world in miraculous phenomena of various sorts. The absence of this element in the present instance is examined in the discussion of theme 12.

37. For example, *Ti* 332. Upon realization, Bharata remarks to his friend Nandaka, ''Let us go into the presence of the preceptor [to] roar the lion's roar *[sīhanāda]* face to face with the best of the Buddhas. We have now attained that goal for which, in compassion, the sage made us go forth'' (*Ta* 175–76). Rhys Davids and Stede call this ''a song of ecstasy, a shout of exaltation'' *(PTSD* 714, s.v. *sīhanāda).*

38. We shall see a similar pattern when we examine some Mahāyāna *sūtra*s that, like the songs of *Ta* and *Ti,* reflect the forest saints themselves (Chapter 9).

39. In addition to these five mundane powers, Uruveḷakassapa has also attained a sixth,

transcendent accomplishment: destruction of all the fetters, *sabbasaṃyojanakkaya,* equivalent to nirvāṇa. The five or six abilities *(abhijñā)* are frequently found in both the Pāli and Sanskrit texts, although order and precise terminology may vary. In a typical formulation, the five mundane abilities are: (1) *divyacakṣus* (P., *dibbacakkhu*), divine sight; (2) *divyaśrotra* (P., *dibbasota*), divine hearing; (3) *paracittajñāna* (P., *paracittaññāṇa*), knowledge of the minds of others; (4) *pūrvanivāsānusmṛti* (P., *pubbenivās' ānussati*), recollection of former abodes; and (5) *ṛddhi* (P., *iddhi*), supernatural abilities (levitation, etc.). The five Sanskrit terms are listed in *Dhs* (20). The *Mvy* (201ff.) mentions these five, with some variant forms, and the sixth, *āśravakṣayajñāna* (P., *āsavakkhayaññāṇa*), the wisdom of the destruction of the taints.

40. *Cutūpapāta* (Skt., *cyutopapāda*) is typically considered the product of *divyacakṣus* although in Anuruddha's *gāthā* these two are mentioned in two different verses.

41. Cūḷapanthaka comes to his teacher by flying through the air (*Ta* 564). Tāḷapuṭa refers to the saint's ability to "cross over Ganges, Yamunā, Sarasvatī, the Pātāla country, and the fearful Baḷavāmukha sea, by supernormal power" (*Ta* 1104). And Mahākassapa declares, "In a moment I can fashion the bodily form of 100,000 crores (of people); I am skilled in (supernormal) transformations; I am a master of supernormal power *[iddhi]*" (*Ta* 1183). The saints also perform other magical feats, such as making the *deva*s tremble (*Ta* 1194) and discerning the future (*Ta* 547). The realized one Gavāmpati (Skt., Gavāṃpati), "by his supernatural power made the River Sarabhu stand fast" (*Ta* 38). In other texts of the Pāli canon, magical powers are regularly ascribed to the enlightened disciples of the Buddha (Wagle 1985, 64–65).

42. Mentioned here are knowledge of former habitations, the *deva* eye, knowledge of others' thoughts, and the other powers associated with enlightenment (*Ta* 996–97).

43. At the same time, however, one occasionally finds some of the saints credited with being very learned, as one who has "heard much" *(bahussuta)* (*Ta* 235, 373, 988; *Ti* 401, 449). In these cases, *bahussuta* is an isolated epithet and cannot be taken in and of itself to refer to textual learning, at least as that came to be understood in monastic tradition as involving sometimes massive memorization. However, in *Ta* and *Ti,* there is one clear exception to the absence of reference to the vocation of texts and learning among the saints: the case of Ānanda (*Ta* 1018–50), which will be discussed presently.

44. See, however, Norman's preference for "foolish" as a translation for *mūga* (1969, 202, n. 501, and 213, n. 582). On these two terms, see *PTSD* 280, s.v. *jaḷa* and 539, s.v. *mūga*. We also are told that, although one's senses are intact and sharp, one should act as if they are not: "One hears all with the ear, one sees all with the eye. . . . One with eyes should be as though blind; one with ears as though deaf; one with wisdom as though stupid; one with strength as though weak" (*Ta* 499).

45. "There were 100 iron spikes, all causing separate pain; of this kind was the hell where Dussī was boiled, having assailed the disciple Vidhura and the Brahman Kakusandha. Whatever bhikkhu, disciple of the Buddha, knows this, having assailed such a bhikkhu you will come to grief, Kaṇha" (*Ta* 1188–89).

46. Ray 1990 discusses the widespread attribution of longevity to saints in Indian Buddhism.

47. The *Theragāthā* commentary links Phussa's song with one of the traditions of the disappearance of the dharma (3:89). See also Rhys Davids 1913, 339, n. 2.

48. In addition, some songs, e.g. 632ff., speak of certain *bhikkhu*s who do not meditate but instead have their hopes fixed on external things. These *bhikkhu*s are contrasted with the renunciant who is continually engaged in meditation in the forest.

49. The fact that the term *saṃgha* is the specific term used to identify some form of community of town-and-village renunciants and that the term is not used to refer to the

forest life is interesting. At the least, it suggests the possibility that at the time of this song, within Buddhism the term *saṃgha* was used restrictively to designate a type of town-and-village renunciant community.

50. This also appears to be reflected in a passage in the *Milindapañha,* in a *gāthā* that S. Dutt believes to be relatively ancient (1984, 94): "Seek lodgings distant from the haunts of men, / Live there in freedom from the bonds of sin; / But he who finds no peace in solitude, / May with the Order *[saṃgha]* dwell, guarded in heart, / Mindful and self possessed" (*Mp* 402 [T.R. 1890–94, 2:343]). In relation to this passage, Dutt remarks, "The shelter of the *saṃgha,* as is said here, is to be sought only by those who find no peace in solitude, but the unsocial life [i.e., the life in the forest] is preferred to cenobitical society" (1984, 94).

51. *Nibbuta.*

52. Why is this critique projected into the future? One possible reason is that Phussa wishes to criticize the same trends as Pārāpariya but does not wish to do so directly. By talking about the destruction of the dharma in a future age, however, he is perhaps able to make the same points as Pārāpariya, but in a way less directly and explicitly offensive to what is now, perhaps, the Buddhist establishment. Phussa's reference to the future also enables him to make the important point that the final outcome of the current trends that he criticizes will be disastrous. It is interesting that Pārāpariya, while talking about the present, also uses the term for the latter days, *pacchimakāla;* this suggests that in the minds of both him and Phussa, the defects linked with the rise of town-and-village renunciation—perhaps already in its Buddhist form of settled monasticism—are bound up with *pacchimakāla,* Pārāpariya preferring to talk about current trends, Phussa preferring to talk about their final result. For further discussion of the linkage of *pacchimakāla* with the rise of settled monasticism, see Chapter 12.

53. Two *sutta*s contained in the *Aṭṭhakavagga* section of the *Suttanipāta,* the *Pasūra Sutta* and *Māgandiya Sutta* (*Sn* 824–47), voice critiques echoing many of the themes found in the songs of Pārāpariya and Phussa. These two *sutta*s wish mainly to point to the evils implicit in disputation *(vivāda):* the renunciant attracted by "learning" *(suta)* (836) is preoccupied by doctrine (824); in the midst of assemblies (825), he causes disputes (825), seeking praise (825–26) and profit (828). Desirous of conquering others, he claims purity for himself alone (824) and he belittles others (824–26), seeing them as fools (825). If victorious, he becomes elated (828), proud, and conceited (830); if defeated he becomes depressed and angry (826). His elation is, we are told, a cause for downfall *(vighāta)* (830). Thus, one should entirely avoid this way of life (828, 833–34, 844), "leaving his home, wandering homeless, not making acquaintances in a village" (844 [Nr., 141]). Interestingly enough, however, neither of these two *sutta*s mentions *bhikkhu*s as the offending parties but rather, more vaguely, *samaṇa*s (824–34 and 835–47). See also the *Kalahavivāda Sutta* (862–77), the *Cūḷaviyūha Sutta* (878–94), the *Mahāviyūha Sutta* (895–914), and the *Tuvaṭaka Sutta* (915–34), which contain similar themes.

54. Along these same lines, *Ta* 209 remarks that "one should not suspend others (from the order), nor object (to them). One should not revile nor raise one's voice against one who has gone to the far shore."

4

Some Orthodox Saints in Buddhism

This chapter contains discussion of three "orthodox saints" of Indian Buddhism: Mahākāśyapa, Upagupta, and Śāriputra. These saints may be termed orthodox because they are paradigmatic, creative figures at the center of the history of the major Indian Nikāya schools, including those connected with the Mahāsāṃghika, the Sthavira/Theravāda, and the Sarvāstivāda. Also, in the texts of the established monastic traditions, they are cast in a consistently positive light as embodiments of the schools' highest ideals. The first saint to be treated, Mahākāśyapa, is an important saint throughout the Northwestern and Southern sources, with a character that is variously described. The second, Upagupta, is celebrated chiefly, though not exclusively, in the Northwestern sources. The third, Śāriputra, has particular importance for Southern Buddhism of the Sthavira/Theravāda.

A Preeminent Saint among the Buddha's Disciples: Mahākāśyapa

In the *Aṅguttaranikāya,* in a well-known list of the Buddha's foremost disciples that includes the characteristic by which each is renowned, Mahākāśyapa is called "foremost among those who follow the *dhutas [dhūtavāda],*"[1] the code setting forth a lifestyle of forest renunciation and meditation (1:23 [WH., 1:16]).[2] In the *Mahāvastu,* Mahākāśyapa is similarly called *dhutarāja,* "king of the *dhutaguṇas*" (*Mv* 1:77.2 [Jns., 3:55]).[3] In the *Divyāvadāna,* Mahākāśyapa is again known as foremost in the practice of the *dhutaguṇas* (61 and 395). The special character of Mahākaśyapa as forest renunciant, follower of the *dhutaguṇa*s, and meditator of great accomplishment is celebrated in a variety of other texts, including the *Divyāvadāna,* the *vinaya* of the Mūlasarvāstivādins,[4] the Pāli *vinaya, sutta*s, and commentaries, and the Pāli *jātaka*s. Although these texts reflect different times, places, and traditions, they contain certain consistent hagiographical themes, the more important of which are examined in this section.[5]

According to the *Mahāvastu,*[6] Mahākāśyapa, born to a very wealthy family,[7] finds his wealth "cramped and full of defilements" (3:66–67 [Jns., 3:49]). He longs for "the open air" of the renunciant life and, abandoning his wealth, takes up a patched cotton cloak *(paṭapilotika)*[8] and sets out in quest of "whatever arhans there might be in the world'' (3:67 [3:50]). After wandering for a year, Mahākāśyapa encounters the Buddha. Merely seeing the Blessed One, Mahākāśyapa knows that he is in the presence of a fully enlightened saint.[9] As he recounts this experience he remarks, ''I approached the Exalted One, bowed my head at his feet and stood to one side. And as I thus stood to one side, I said to the Exalted One, 'Lord, thou art my Master; I am thy disciple, O Sugata.' When I had thus spoken, O venerable Ānanda, the Exalted One said to me, 'Even so, O Kāśyapa, I am your Master; you are my disciple' '' (3:68 [3:50]).[10]

The Buddha then declares his own enlightened identity to Mahākāśyapa, commenting that he is perfectly enlightened *(samyaksaṃbuddha),* all knowing *(sarvajña),* and all seeing *(sarvadarśāvin)* and that he has absolute knowledge and insight *(apariśeṣajñānadarśana)* (*Mv* 3:68.6–8 [Jns., 3:50]).[11] Following this, the Buddha trains Kāśyapa in correct behavior and meditation. Mahākāśyapa's schooling in behavior, we learn elsewhere in the *Mahāvastu,* revolves chiefly around the *dhutaguṇa*s (3:68–71 [3:51–53]).[12] The Buddha then gives his pupil an extensive instruction in meditation, including the practice of mindfulness[13] and awareness.[14] ''Thus, O Kāśyapa,'' the Buddha exhorts him, for the sake of realization, ''you must train yourself.'' Kāśyapa is then a probationer student for eight days and, on the ninth, attains enlightenment becoming an arhant (3:71 [3:53]).

After this, the Buddha goes to a certain place to sit down, and Kāśyapa spreads his patched robe for him to sit on. When the Buddha expresses his appreciation of the robe, Mahākāśyapa presents it to him. In affirmation of his unique regard for Mahākāśyapa, the Buddha then gives to him his own hempen robe *(śāṇānāṃ pāṃśukūlānāṃ saṃghāṭīm)* (*Mv* 3:72.10 [Jns., 3:54]).[15]

As a realized one, Mahākāśyapa declares his identity as one who has transcended the ordinary human condition. ''I am a genuine son of the Exalted One, born of the dharma, created by the dharma, an heir as to the dharma, not an heir as to the flesh'' (*Mv* 3:72–73 [Jns., 3:55]). After he has attained realization, the general character of Mahākāśyapa as a forest renunciant—and his specific connection with the *dhutaguṇa*s—stand forth prominently in his personality.[16] As a realized saint, Mahākāśyapa is in possession of a variety of magical powers *(ṛddhi)* including the power of flight (1:75.2 [1:54]) and also supernormal sight *(divyanayana)* by which he can see the *tathāgata*'s passing away from afar (1:74.15 [1:53]). About the full measure of his powers, Mahākāśyapa hints to Ānanda:

> He who could imagine that my three knowledges, my six superknowledges and my mastery of the powers could be hidden away, could just as well imagine that a sixty years old elephant could be hidden by a palm leaf . . . could just as well imagine that the flow of the Ganges river could be checked by a handful of dust . . . could just as well imagine that the wind could be imprisoned in a net'' (3:73 [3:55]).[17]

In the *Mahāvastu,* Mahākāśyapa is the proponent of strict observance and a sharp critic of those who are lax. Thus, one day he sees Ānanda wandering abroad, seeking alms with a large group of disciples ''who have no guard on the doors of their senses, who know no moderation in food, who are ever unused to the exercise of vigilance and are irresponsible,'' although, Mahākāśyapa says, it is clear that the Buddha prohibited more than three renunciants to eat together. "It seems to me," he remarks to Ānanda, "that you are like one destroying the harvest" (3:63–64 [Jns., 3:47–48]). Mahākāśyapa is also a danger to those who do not properly acknowledge his sanctity. The nun Sthūlanandā, who has previously blamed Mahākāśyapa for his upbraiding of Ānanda (3:65–66 [3:48]), refuses to be reconciled to him and hardens her heart against him. Finally, she commits open insult against him by uncovering herself in front of him; as a result, she immediately dies and is reborn in one of the great hells (3:74 [3:56]).[18]

Even as an enlightened one, Mahākāśyapa has great devotion to the Buddha, and his relation to him is expressed in a variety of cultic behaviors. For example, when the Buddha dies, Mahākāśyapa, wishing to see his master once more, journeys from afar on foot (out of devotion, for it is acknowledged that he could have flown [*Mv* 1:75.2 (Jns., 1:54–55)]) and pays deep and tender homage to his teacher's remains. It is interesting that, prior to Mahākāśyapa's coming, the Buddha's funeral pyre could not be lit, because until "he who has preeminence comes along," the *devas* will not permit it (1:76.11–14 [1:54]).[19] These events make evident Mahākāśyapa's devotion to the Buddha, his participation in the cult of the Buddha, and various of his magical powers and the miracles that surround him.

These events also reaffirm another important aspect of Mahākāśyapa's person, namely, his preeminence. This is attested to in the Buddha's exchange of his robe with him, an honor given to no other disciple. His preeminence is explicitly affirmed here in the passage just quoted ("one who has preeminence . . ."). It is affirmed again when the pyre cannot be lit until he has arrived. And it is further affirmed when, just after the Buddha's passing, he assumes spiritual leadership of the *saṃgha* and proposes the first council. The funeral pyre has just ignited and the body of the Blessed One is in flames. At this point, the five hundred great arhants in attendance approach and chant a lament to the passing of the Buddha, concluding with their own intentions to pass from the world.[20] Mahākāśyapa tells them that they may not do so but must instead convene for the recitation of the Buddha's teachings, a liturgical event that will provide for the continuation of the Blessed One's dharma in the world (1:80–82 [1:56–57]).[21]

Connected with Mahākāśyapa's preeminence is his assimilation to the Buddha himself, wherein he is implicitly compared to the Buddha and virtually assumes the role of the departed master. After the Buddha's passing, Mahākāśyapa remarks to Ānanda,

> "Whosoever of these five hundred monks harbours doubt or mistrust of me, let him ask a question, and I, in answering the question, shall roar a veritable lion's roar." Then those five hundred monks said to the venerable Mahā-Kāśyapa, "Whosoever, O venerable Maha-Kāśyapa, harbours doubt or mistrust, let him ask a question. And we shall honour you, and henceforth our obedience will be greater and better than before." The venerable Mahā-Kāśyapa then instructed, roused, gladdened and thrilled the monks with a discourse on dharma. (*Mv* 3:73–74 [Jns., 3:56])

The depiction of Mahākāśyapa in the *vinaya* of the Mūlasarvāstivādins[22] parallels the account of the *Mahāvastu* in general outline and also in many details. In the

Mūlasarvāstivādin *vinaya,* Mahākāśyapa is the devoted pupil of his master and the enlightened saint of forest renunciation and asceticism, able in miracles, revered by both renunciants and laity.[23] He is the leader of the *saṃgha* after the Buddha's demise and is assimilated to the Buddha, acting in his stead.[24] The Mūlasarvāstivādin *vinaya* also tells many of the same stories about Mahākāśyapa as does the *Mahāvastu.*[25] For all the similarities, however, in its treatment of Mahākāśyapa, the Mūlasarvāstivādin *vinaya* contrasts with the *Mahāvastu* in at least two important respects. For one thing, it does not linger over Mahākāśyapa's early life. This may be because the main purpose of this section of the text is to depict the events surrounding the death of the Buddha, his cremation, and the first council.[26] Second, the Mūlasarvāstivādin *vinaya* places even more emphasis than does the *Mahāvastu* on Mahākāśyapa's preeminence in the *saṃgha* and his leadership of it, and the reason seems to be, again, the interest shown in the text in his political role. Thus we are explicitly told that of the four greatest elders (*sthaviras*) in the world, Mahākāśyapa is the greatest owing to his wisdom and virtue (*V*-t, D., *'dul.ba,* vol. da, 296a–b [R., 144–45]).[27] This, presumably, partially justifies or at least reflects his leadership of the *saṃgha.* Perhaps more to the point, in the Mūlasarvāstivādin *vinaya,* the Buddha explicitly confirms Mahākāśyapa as his legitimate successor.[28] Similarly, when the convocation of the five hundred arhants occurs, we are given a picture of Mahākāśyapa presiding by acclamation.[29] Mahākāśyapa's preeminent position is further defined in the Northwestern texts; he is listed several times as the Buddha's successor, who in turn is to choose his own successor and even the successor of his successor.[30]

A version of the story of King Aśoka preserved in Chinese, the *Aśokarājāvadāna,*[31] describes the final nirvāṇa of Mahākāśyapa.[32] After the close of the first council, Mahākāśyapa reflects that his work is now complete, that he is very old, and that the time to enter final nirvāṇa has arrived. He transmits his lineage to Ānanda, remarking that just as the Buddha transmitted the dharma to him, so now he does so to Ānanda: "Oh *āyuṣmat* Ānanda! . . . I transmit the dharma to you. Protect it well" (*Ara* 114b [Prz., 328]).[33] He then predicts Śāṇakavāsin as the disciple of Ānanda, giving details of his youth and how Ānanda will know him. Mahākāśyapa then makes a final pilgrimage to those sites made sacred by the Buddha's relics.[34] Returning to Rājagṛha, visiting Ajātaśatru to say farewell but finding this latter asleep, Mahākāśyapa departs to Mount Kukkuṭapāda, where he will pass away. In the middle of three peaks, he sits down in meditation posture on—like the Buddha when he achieved enlightenment—a seat of grass. He reflects that his body is now clothed in the *pāṃśukūla* that the Buddha gave him and that he will wear it until the coming of Maitreya. He further remarks, "If King Ajātaśatru does not visit my body, boiling blood will gush from his mouth and he will die" (*Ara* 114c [Prz., 332]). Then the saint passes into that state from which there is no return,[35] the mountain closes over his body,[36] and a spirit laments, "Today . . . without exception, men and gods lament and weep with grief" (*Ara* 114c–115a [Prz., 332]). Thus, like his life, Mahākāśyapa's death is assimilated to that of the Buddha.

King Ajātaśatru, who has meanwhile learned of his master's passing, hastens with Ānanda to Mount Kukkuṭapāda, desiring to make offerings to the saint. Upon arrival, the mountain opens and, as the two pilgrims draw near Mahākāśyapa's body, celestial flowers, heavenly perfumes, and the best sandalwood miraculously rain down upon it. After prostrating himself before the remains, the king expresses the desire to perform a cremation, but he is dissuaded by Ānanda, who tells him that Mahākāśyapa, plunged in meditation, must not be burned but must remain intact so that he can fulfill his mission when Maitreya comes. When the future Buddha arrives, Ānanda continues, he will come with 9,600,000 disciples, whose faith is wanting. Before these, Mahākāśyapa will leap into space and manifest the eighteen miraculous transformations, making his body immense in size. Maitreya will then receive the Buddha's robe from the saint. At this, the disciples will be ashamed, and, their pride broken, they will all become arhants. Ānanda finishes his account, he and the king leave the place, and the mountain closes again over Mahākāśyapa's body.[37] As they leave, Ajātaśatru cries to Ānanda, "I did not have the joy to witness the *nirvāṇa* of the *tathāgata*. I also was not able to see the entry of Mahākāśyapa into *nirvāṇa*. O Venerable one! When you enter into *nirvāṇa*, let me be there to see it." Ānanda gives his consent.[38]

The fact of Mahākāśyapa's ongoing, tangible presence at Mount Kukkuṭapāda is emphasized in the *Divyāvadāna*, where the saint Upagupta and King Aśoka go to Mount Kukkuṭapāda to visit the stūpa of Mahākāśyapa. Aśoka makes a great offering of gold to Mahākāśyapa, addressing him as one who is alive and present even now: "I honor the elder Kāśyapa / who dwells hidden inside the mountain; / serene, his face turned away from strife, devoted to tranquility, / he has fully developed the virtue of contentedness" (*Da* 395 [St., 254]). The Sarvāstivādin texts affirm the importance and continuity of the lineage founded by Mahākāśyapa, which he transmits to Ānanda, who later transmits it to the promised Śāṇakavāsin, who subsequently teaches Upagupta, the quintessential forest renunciant. Adding one further motif to the portrait of Mahākāśyapa, the Sanskrit *Mahākarmavibhaṅga* provides the information that Mahākāśyapa carried out important missionary work: he converted the populations of the West, beginning with Avanti (Lamotte 1958, 326).

The Northern tradition presents a variety of images of Mahākāśyapa, and these are not always consistent with one another. An example is provided by the *vinaya* of the Mūlasarvāstivādins at the point where the text elaborates the saint's character as a forest renunciant (*Gms* 3.1, 81–84; see also *Da* 81ff.). The Buddha, we are told, has arrived in Śrāvasti to see Anāthapiṇḍika and is inside the wealthy donor's compound enjoying a meal with his monks. Mahākāśyapa arrives, having come to join the Buddha at the feast, but the gatekeeper bars his way, thinking that he is a non-Buddhist renunciant *(tīrthya)*. The reason for this error is that Mahākāśyapa is just coming from his dwelling place *(śayanāsana)* in the forest *(āraṇya)* and has the appearance of a forest renunciant: he has long hair *(dīrghakeśa)* and a beard *(śmaśru)* and wears a coarse robe *(lūhacīvara)*. The gatekeeper informs Mahākāśyapa that the master of the household, Anāthapiṇḍika, has commanded that no non-Buddhist renunciants be allowed to enter until such time as the Buddha and his company of monks *(buddhabhikṣusaṃgha)* have finished their meal. The saint observes that he is being treated in this way because the gatekeeper does not realize that he is a son of the Buddha *(śākyaputrīya)*.

Thus repelled, Mahākāśyapa shows no resentment, anger, or disappointment. Instead, he will show compassion to some poor, miserable person *(kṛpaṇajana)* by accepting gifts from such a one. The saint sees a poor, wretched washerwoman who is painfully afflicted with leprosy and whose limbs show rotting sores. As Mahākāśyapa approaches, she sees him, whose body is handsome, whose charisma attracts her, and whose demeanor is peaceful, and she is moved to make an offering. This unfortunate person has only some water in which rice has been boiled, but this she resolves to give to the saint as a donation. As she is about to offer the water, however, a fly falls into it, and, when she removes it, one of her leprous fingers drops into the bowl. Undismayed, Mahākāśyapa consumes the water anyway and, we are told, takes no other food that day.[39] The washerwoman is so overjoyed at this that she immediately dies and is reborn as a deity in the Tuṣita heaven. This story from the *vinaya* of the Mūlasarvāstivādins is interesting because it presents a picture of Mahākāśyapa that stands in some contrast with the images of the saint from the same text just examined. Here Mahākāśyapa is not the one who stands at the very origin and heart of the Buddhist establishment but is the great outsider, the forest monk who is not admitted into the presence of the Buddha and his monks, and who is even believed to be a *tīrthika*. Nevertheless, he is the figure of realization and compassion, who is unmoved by rejection and simply uses it as an opportunity to help others.

The theme of Mahākāśyapa's preference for the low-caste, diseased, and disadvantaged is further spelled out as the story continues. Wishing to make offerings to Mahākāśyapa, the god Indra and his wife Sacī take on the forms of a poor, low-caste weaver and his wife, clothed in rags, knowing that the saint is most likely to accept offerings from them in this form. Mahākāśyapa, however, recognizes who they are and turns his bowl upside down, so that the offering of the deities falls on the ground. This shows that Mahākāśyapa is loyal to the downtrodden, not because he cannot get other offerings, but because he prefers to receive offerings from those who are most in need of his blessings and the merit gained from offering to him.[40]

The antiestablishment character of this image of Mahākāśyapa is unmistakable, particularly in the contrast of donors. Inside the compound from which Mahākāśyapa is debarred, the Buddha and his tonsured and well-robed monks are enjoying the abundant hospitality of Anāthapiṇḍika, the wealthy, powerful, respected banker. Outside, barred from admittance to the feast, taken for a *tīrthika,* the great saint Mahākāśyapa receives the rice water of a poor, low-caste, diseased washerwoman, which he prefers even to the offerings of the gods. This antiestablishment image of the saint was evidently too off-putting for a monastic contributor to this legend, who blames Mahākāśyapa for rejecting the divine offerings of the gods, having the Buddha ordain that henceforth renunciants must not refuse the donor's offerings.[41]

In the preceding discussion, Mahākāśyapa appears as a fully developed, impressive Buddhist saint with an enlightened, multifaceted personality. However, he does not appear with such a stature in all the "pre-Mahāyāna" Buddhist texts. In the *vinaya* of Pāli tradition, for example, Mahākāśyapa appears but generally tends to play a relatively smaller role. Among a few stories told of Mahākāśyapa in the Pāli *vinaya,* the best-known is the account of the first council.[42] Although the general outlines of the story are the same as in the Mūlasarvāstivādin *vinaya,* the tone is different. Most notably, in the Pāli account, Mahākāśyapa shows little of his saintly personality. His adherence to the *dhutaguṇa*s is not stressed.[43] He is depicted not as one who dwells in the forest, but rather as the conventional monk, who is hardly more than a peer of the other disciples. He also does not reveal his enlightened status in dramatic ways and, most notably, does not tend to show magical powers. For example, in the Mūlasarvāstivādin *vinaya,* Mahākāśyapa learns of the Buddha's passing by seeing wondrous signs in nature and perceiving their cause; in the Pāli account, a wandering ascetic has to tell him that the Buddha has died. In the *Mahāvastu,* Mahākāśyapa presides over the first council by virtue of his personal charisma and there ordains events, whereas in the Pāli account he must ask permission of the assembled *saṃgha* each time he wants to propose something. The few other stories told about Mahākāśyapa in the Pāli *vinaya* are in the same vein, when compared with the stories told about him in the *Mahāvastu* and the Mūlasarvāstivādin *vinaya.* What is significant is not what the Pāli texts say, but what they do not say. In these stories, Mahākāśyapa appears as a bland, mostly urban disciple, who merely provides pretexts—hardly different from those provided by the other disciples—for the Buddha to lay down rules.[44] In the Pāli *Suttapiṭaka,* and particularly in the first four *nikāya*s, Mahākāśyapa is similarly made little of. As in the Pāli *vinaya,* he is generally seen as one among many of the Buddha's main disciples; although his forest character is mentioned a few times,[45] it is obviously not an object of particular concern.

However, some striking exceptions to this general trend appear in the *Udāna* and *Theragāthā* of the *Khuddakanikāya*[46] and chapter 16 of the *Saṃyuttanikāya.* The song of Mahākāśyapa in the *Theragāthā,* for example, paints a detailed picture of Mahākāśyapa and his forest way of life (*Ta* 1051–90). Prominent in this song are various affirmations of the normativity of forest renunciation: the four *niśraya*s are praised, as are dwelling in seclusion and solitude, the practice of meditation, contentment with little, the joys and beauty of life in the forest, avoidance of the highborn, and so on. Mahākāśyapa concludes by declaring his preeminence as a practitioner of the *dhutaguṇa*s.[47] A similar depiction is given in the *Udāna,* in a story that recalls the incident from the *vinaya* of the Mūlasarvāstivādins just recounted. Mahākāśyapa is staying in a certain cave and, during a seven-day period remains in cross-legged posture, ardently meditating. When he finally rises to seek alms, five hundred *deva*s present themselves as potential donors, but the saint rejects them and sets off to seek alms in Rājagṛha. The god Śakra and his consort, assuming the guise of weavers, provide donations to the saint. But Mahākāśyapa sees through the guise and upbraids the god, telling him not to repeat this deceptive action. Then the saint, by his divine ear, hears the god declare, "the monk who quests for alms . . . at peace and ever mindful, such the *devas* envy" (*Ud* 29–30 [Wd., 34–36]). In this story Mahākāśyapa is once again a forest saint; he lives in a cave; he ardently practices meditation; he is a person of great attainment; he is in possession of magical powers; he is revered by gods and humans alike; veneration of him confers merit on donors; he prefers to shun the abundant offerings of the gods to make his begging rounds among the ordinary folk of Rājagṛha; and he is most likely to accept offerings from a humble weaver and his wife, revealed in Śakra's choice of disguise.[48] A close relation may be noted between elements in the portrayal of Mahākāśyapa in the *Udāna* and the *Theragāthā* and those in the *Mahāvastu* and the *vinaya* of the Mūlasarvāstivādins. It is significant that both the *Udāna* and the *Theragāthā* see Mahākāśyapa as strictly a forest saint and neither contains any reference to his settled monastic character.

Particularly interesting in the present context is an extended portrait of Mahākāśyapa in the Pāli canon, this time in the "Kindred Sayings on Kassapa," chapter 16 of the *Saṃyuttanikāya* (2:193–224 [RW., 2:131–52]). The chapter opens with what will be its central theme, namely, the Buddha's praise of Mahākāśyapa's forest way of life and saintly character. In a reference to Kāśyapa's adherence to the four *niśraya*s, the Buddha remarks that Kāśyapa is contented with no matter what robe, no matter what alms, no matter what dwelling place, and no matter what medicine. Moreover, Kāśyapa commends this way of life to others. The Buddha concludes by exhorting his disciples to train in the manner of Kāśyapa (2:193 [2:131]). As chapter 16 continues, we find Mahākāśyapa depicted as a prototypical forest renunciant: he lives aloof, dwells in solitude, wants little, is content, practices meditation, and does not fraternize with the laity. In addition, his renunciant way involves few words, and he criticizes those renunciants for whom Buddhism is primarily a matter of words, arguing, and verbal competition.[49] The Buddha praises the forest features of Kāśyapa and affirms his approval of them.

The Buddha's praise of Mahākāśyapa's forest way of life occurs again in a passage in which the Buddha asks why Kāśyapa follows an ascetic way of life, including the wearing of castoff, coarse rag-robes that are past wearing. Kāśyapa responds,

> I, lord, for many a day have been forest dweller and have commended the forest life; have been almsman and have commended alms-living; have been a rag-robe wearer and have commended rag-robe wearing; have been a three-garment man and have commended the triple-raiment; have wanted little and have commended few wants; have been contented and have commended contentment; have dwelt in seclusion and have commended seclusion; have held aloof from society and have commended such aloofness; have lived in strenuous energy and have commended strenuous energy. (2:202 [2:136–37])

The Buddha then asks what advantages Kāśyapa finds in this way of life, and the saint replies that there are two: his own happiness and his compassion for those who will come after. "For surely these may fall into error. But let them say: They who were disciples of the Buddha and of the followers of the Buddha were for many a day forest dwellers and commended forest life. . . . This for many a day will be for their good and for their happiness" (2:202 [2:136–37]). As we shall presently see, the error into which future generations may fall is the abandonment of the life of forest renunciation, an error to be remedied only by a reaffirmation of the priority of forest values and practices. The passage concludes with the

Buddha confirming that Kāśyapa has indeed practiced "for the happiness of many folk, out of compassion for the world, for the salvation, the good, the happiness of devas and men." "Wherefore, Kassapa," the Buddha says, "wear thou thy coarse rag-robes that are past wearing, go thy rounds for alms and dwell in the forest" (202 [136–37]). From the viewpoint of this passage, then, normative Buddhism is to be found in the life of forest renunciation.

The Buddha is shown praising not only Mahākāşyapa's forest way of life but also his great attainment. Kāśyapa, the Buddha says, is a realized saint and, moreover, one who in his person virtually duplicates his own realization. The Buddha proclaims his own proficiency and attainment in meditation, point by point and step by step, and then affirms that Kāśyapa has the very same proficiency and attainment.[50] The Buddha concludes, "Kassapa too, brethren, by the withering of the intoxicants, has entered into and abides in that sane and immune emancipation of will, emancipation of insight which he has come thoroughly to know and to realize for himself even in this present life" (2:214 [2:145]).

Finally, as if to summarize its portrait of Mahākāśyapa, chapter 16 contrasts Kāśyapa and his forest life with the way of settled monasticism and affirms the temporal priority and the qualitative superiority of forest renunciation. At one time, the Buddha says, the senior brethren were forest renunciants and commenders of the forest life, contented with going for alms and advocating the same; contented with wearing rag-robes and so on and advocating the same; of few wants, contented, secluded, aloof from society, and strenuous in energy. Moreover,

> the brother who lived this kind of life the senior brethren would invite to a seat, saying:—"Come brother! Who may this brother be? Welcome indeed is this brother! Anxious to learn truly is this brother! Come brother, take this seat." They practised that they might so attain; that made for many a day for their good, for their happiness.

But now, the Buddha says, the senior brethren are not forest renunciants nor do they commend the forest life; they do not go for alms, wear rag-robes, and so on; nor are they of few wants, contented, secluded, aloof from society, or strenuous in energy.

> So it is that the brother who is known, is of repute, one who gets presents of raiment, alms, lodging and medical requisites—him it is that the senior brethren invite to a seat, saying:—"Come brother! Who may this brother be? Welcome indeed is this brother! Anxious truly is this brother for companions in religion! Come brother, take this seat." . . . They practise that they may so attain. That makes for many a day for their hurt and for their sorrow. (2:108–10 [2:140–41])

Thus, the Buddha affirms, "they who lead the religious life are harassed by its own dangers." Here the forest way of life embodied by Mahākāśyapa is said to be on the wane, and its prestige has declined to the point at which its exemplars are no longer respected: instead, those who exemplify the ideals and ways of settled monasticism are honored and rewarded. This change, in the view expressed in this passage, is one to be mourned; whereas forest renunciants were "anxious to learn truly,'' their settled monastic counterparts are only ''anxious truly . . . for companions in religion.'' Whereas the way of forest renunciation ''made for many a day for their good, for their happiness,'' the nonforest way ''makes for many a day for their hurt and for their sorrow.'' This passage thus reflects many of the themes of the songs of Pārāpariya and Phussa, but here the virtues of the forest life are exemplified in no less a figure than Mahākāśyapa and the nonforest alternative is criticized by no less a person than the Buddha.

Chapter 16 of the *Saṃyuttanikāya* is not a unified text but is a heterogeneous collection of some thirteen different selections, some complete, others clearly incomplete. These are held together by two themes: first, they all concern Mahākāśyapa; second, they all present him as a forest saint and as the ideal embodiment and proponent of forest Buddhism. Like the *Udāna* and *Theragāthā,* the selections from chapter 16 see Mahākāśyapa strictly as a forest saint and contain no reference to his settled monastic character. It is interesting that a number of these selections share ground with the *Mahāvastu* and *vinaya* of the Mūlasarvāstivādins.[51] The difference is that in the non-Pāli sources, these stories occur as dramatically complete and compelling elements in key texts, whereas here they are often fragmentary and appear randomly assembled. It is as if once the dominant depiction of Mahākāśyapa had begun to take shape in the Pāli canonical texts—emphasizing his role as a central figure in the history of settled monasticism and giving scant attention to his more forest and charismatic attributes—some place had to be found for these traditional aspects of his character. Within the first four *nikāyas*, chapter 16 of the *Saṃyuttanikāya* would seem to fulfill such a role. The close connection, in hagiographical themes and specific legends, of the affirmations of Mahākāśyapa's forest and saintly character in the *Udāna, Theragāthā,* and chapter 16 of the *Saṃyuttanikāya* with similar stories and themes in the Mūlasarvāstivādin *vinaya* and the *Mahāvastu* is interesting and suggests again the tremendous richness of the Pāli canon as a historical document and resource for viewing successive stages in the unfolding of Buddhism in the Theravāda and, more generally, in the larger Indian context.[52]

As suggested by the preceding discussion, the traditions surrounding Mahākāśyapa had not merely literary or hagiographical dimensions but important cultic aspects as well. Further hints of these are found in the *Sūtra on Maitreya's Birth,* an Indian Buddhist text translated into Chinese in the early fourth century by Dharmarakṣa, in which the Buddha specifically enjoins Mahākāśyapa to delay his *parinirvaṇa* until Maitreya's coming, abiding inside his ''cavern of meditation.'' When Maitreya arrives, he will find the cave and will show Mahākāśyapa to the people, who will thereupon become arhants. Then Maitreya will receive the Buddha's robe from Mahākāśyapa, and ''Mahākāśyapa's body shall forthwith be scattered like stars'' (De Visser 1922–23, 68). The gathering of the people where the saint's remains are housed, the showing of Mahākāśyapa, the seeing of the saint by the people, and the attainment thereby of liberation by them doubtless reflect not only future hope but contemporary practice and likely reveal cultic patterns surrounding Mahākāśyapa at the time of the text's composition. Confirmation of this is provided by Fa-hsien, the Chinese pilgrim who visited India in the early fifth century. In his account of a visit to Mount Kukkuṭapāda we read:

> The great Kāśyapa is at present within this mountain. (On a certain occasion) he divided the mountain at its base, so as to open a passage (for himself). This entrance is now closed up. At a considerable distance from this spot, there is a deep chasm; it is in this (fastness as in a) receptacle that the entire body of Kāśyapa is now preserved. Outside this chasm is the place where Kāśyapa, when alive, washed his hands. The people of that region, who are afflicted with headaches, use the earth brought from the place for annointing themselves with, and this immediately cures them. In the midst of this mountain, as soon as the sun begins to decline, all the Rahats [arhant] come and take their abode. Buddhist pilgrims of that and other countries come year by year (to this mountain) to pay religious worship to Kāśyapa; if any should happen to be distressed with doubts, directly the sun goes down, the Rahats arrive, and begin to discourse with (the pilgrims) and explain their doubts and difficulties; and, having done so, forthwith they disappear. The thickets about this hill are dense and tangled. There are, moreover, many lions, tigers, and wolves prowling about, so that it is not possible to travel without great care. (B., 132–33)

Mahākāśyapa's personality and hagiography, then, reflect many features of the paradigm of Buddhist sainthood. For one thing, there is a general continuity of saintly type: like the Buddha—and reflecting the paradigm abstracted from his life—and like the saints of the *Theragāthā* and *Therīgāthā,* Mahākāśyapa is a saint of the forest, who wanders about, follows ascetic practices, engages in meditation, and attains realization. In its details, Mahākāśyapa's life reflects the general structure of the paradigm and many of its specific themes. Thus Mahākāśyapa undergoes a personal crisis in his life (theme 1). In spite of great wealth and a "good marriage," he finds ordinary life unbearable. Longing to follow a spiritual path (theme 2), he renounces the world (theme 3), taking up a life defined by the *dhutaguṇa*s (theme 4), seeking a realized teacher. He wanders abroad; he dwells at the foot of trees or in mountain retreats; he wears a coarse robe; and he begs his food. In his wanderings, Mahākāśyapa finally comes to a place where the Buddha is and, receiving darśan from him, is moved with veneration and devotion, offering himself as a disciple (theme 5), thus fulfilling his initial aspiration (theme 6) to find an enlightened one. The mutual recognition between master and disciple is immediate and intimate. Under the Buddha, Mahākāśyapa is instructed in meditation, practices it (theme 7), and attains realization (theme 8), becoming an arhant. Like the Buddha, as a realized one, Mahākāśyapa continues to be marked by the life of forest renunciation, the *dhutaguṇa*s, and meditation. His attainment is recognized by others (theme 9), and he is not hesitant to proclaim his realization (theme 10). Mahākāśyapa's enlightenment is reflected in his great compassion, expressed in his various postrealization activities (theme 11). Because he is a realized saint, miracles such as earthquakes attend Mahākāśyapa's person (theme 12), and he possesses various powers, including magical flight and miraculous transformations (theme 13). Homage is paid to Mahākāśyapa by all the beings in the cosmos, who come to receive darśan from him, both during his life and at the moment of his final nirvāṇa (theme 14). He is surrounded by a cult (theme 15). He teaches not only humans but supernatural beings as well (theme 16). Mahākāśyapa has two sorts of devoted followers: his chosen successor and his close disciples; and the laity who revere him (theme 17). To his principal disciple (Ānanda), he passes on the authority that he received from the Buddha, such that a line of lineage holders is created.[53] Mahākāśyapa is also devoutly revered by laypeople, best exemplified in the person of King Ajātaśatru. All his devotees participate in his cult, including both his own primary disciple (Ānanda) and his principal lay devotee (Ajātaśatru)—and even the future Buddha Maitreya who will make a pilgrimage to Mount Kukkuṭapāda. He is particularly adored by the gods, who, like Śakra, will go to any lengths to engage in his cult, coming to see him, making offerings, and earning merit thereby. The gods' particular partiality to Mahākāśyapa is shown at the time of the cremation of the Buddha, when they do not allow the pyre to be lit until the saint has arrived.

Mahākāśyapa is a teacher, but (apart from his presidency of the first council, which will be discussed) he is not associated with the study of texts (theme 18) and is depicted as teaching his suppliants in an informal and oral form (theme 19). Mahākāśyapa is known for his conversions (theme 20) in the northwest and for his defeat of evil beings (theme 21), such as the evil nun who would undo him. Mahākāśyapa's compassion is directed especially to those in need. He does not frequent those who are highborn, powerful, and wealthy. By choice and circumstance, he remains distant from the privileged, preferring to show his compassion to the poor and downtrodden (theme 22). Mahākāśyapa can be an unconventional figure and also a critic of religious convention (theme 23), appearing not a little strange, on the outskirts of established Buddhism, with long hair, beard, and coarse hempen robe, mistaken for a non-Buddhist ascetic and debarred from joining a gathering of Buddhist renunciants. He also stands in the posture of critic of those even among his closest disciples who are in need of critique, upbraiding Ānanda, his own lineage holder, for his failure to retain the teachings of the Buddha in their integrity, as measured by Mahākāśyapa's forest criteria. Because of his unconventionality, Mahākāśyapa may be criticized and even persecuted, as in the case of the evil nun (theme 24). The danger implicit in the saint's numinous power becomes evident in the dire consequences experienced by the nun and also in Mahākāśyapa's prediction of Ajātaśātru's horrible end, should he fail to venerate his master's body properly (theme 25).

After the Buddha's passing, Mahākāśyapa becomes the principal reference point of the dharma for his followers, renunciant as well as lay (theme 26). He is, in effect, a substitute for the Buddha, being assimilated to him: he acts like him and is treated like him by his followers, performing an authoritative function within the early *saṃgha.* Of central importance in this respect is his status as lineage holder of the Buddha, indicated by his possession of the Buddha's *pāṃśukūla,* his role in the cremation, and his presidency of the first council. As a realized saint, Mahākāśyapa has a body that is in some respects supernormal (theme 27): his form is particularly pleasing to see; he may travel long distances by flight; and, according to some sources, his body, steeped in meditation in Mount Kukkuṭapāda, will remain intact more or less indefinitely. This also reflects Mahākāśyapa's great powers of longevity (theme 28), as well as his connection with Maitreya (theme 29). Mahākāśyapa anticipates his own passing (theme 30) and departs from this world in an extraordinary way (theme 31). At death, he will not be cremated[54] (theme 32), but his body rests in its stūpa-like enclosure on Mount Kukkuṭapāda (theme 33). This site thus becomes a holy place of pilgrimage for devotees (theme 34), and his ongoing existence there is such that Aśoka can address him as living and present. A cult develops around Mahākāśyapa's remains at this place, and suppliants come there seeking his blessings and the fruits of his compassion. Participants in this cult include both renunciants and the laity, and Ānanda journeys to Mount Kukkuṭapāda just as Mahākāśyapa had visited the places enshrining the Buddha's relics. The development of his hagiography seems clearly an element of his cult (theme 35).

Like the Buddha, then, and in conformity with the paradigm of Buddhist sainthood, Mahākāśyapa is both a credible man in the description of his preenlightenment phase—brief though it be—and a superhuman being, superior to humans and gods, after realization. Mahākāśyapa's life, type, and structure as a saint thus correspond in a quite complete and detailed way with the paradigm of Buddhist sainthood outlined above. This correspondence is not accidental but is rather due, as mentioned, to the fact that the paradigm reflects certain basic Indian assumptions about Buddhist saints. The textual accounts of Mahākāśyapa again reveal that when Indian Buddhists want to talk about their saints, they tend to understand them in ways that approximate the paradigmatic model.

As we have seen, a variety of voices is present in the texts, sometimes even within the same text (for example, the Mūlasarvāstivādin *vinaya*). This suggests that the saint Mahākāśyapa transcends any particular Buddhist group or set of interests. To some, Mahākāśyapa embodies in his person a model that one should personally emulate, by renouncing the world and following the path to realization. To some, he is a saint who is above all to be venerated, one who lives on and will dispense his blessings to those who supplicate him. To others, he is a kind of lawgiver, the chosen successor of the Buddha; he acts in his stead, presiding over the *saṃgha* after the Buddha's death, codifying his teachings, establishing the early church, and, in general, setting the seal of legitimacy on mainstream Buddhist tradition. To others again, Mahākāśyapa presents an aspect that calls the establishment into question, for he is the one who favors the wretched, who rejects the favor of the rich and powerful (as in the story of Indra and Sacī), and who is himself rejected by the established order. And finally, he is the guarantor of future justice, the one who will confer the Buddha's robe on Maitreya, who in a future age will make all things right. Particularly interesting among these different facets of Mahākāśyapa are two seemingly opposed images. On the one hand, more than any other of Buddha's main disciples, Mahākāśyapa is identified as a forest renunciant who practices the *dhutaguṇa*s, a solitary meditator, and an outsider. On the other hand, particularly in the *Mahāparinirvāṇa Sūtra* and the *vinaya*s, he is seen as the representative and upholder of the monastic establishment. One may well wonder how two such seemingly opposed facets could have come to coexist within his person.

An answer to this question is suggested by Przyluski, who in his *Concile de Rājagṛha* (1926–28, 279–305) has examined the position of Mahākāśyapa as chief of the renunciant *saṃgha* and president of the first council. Przyluski observes that in a number of early lists of the Buddha's chief disciples, Mahākāśyapa is not accorded such pride of place but that this honor is reserved instead for Ājñāta Kauṇḍinya. This is, Przyluski tells us, a logical enough choice, as Kauṇḍinya was the one first ordained by the Buddha in Banaras, after his enlightenment, thus making him the senior among renunciant disciples. Thus we find, for example, that in the *vinaya* of the Mahīśāsaka, Kauṇḍinya is the first among Buddha's disciples, whereas Mahākāśyapa is the sixth (300). In one passage in the *vinaya* of the Sarvāstivādins, we find Kauṇḍinya again listed first, with Mahākāśyapa fourth (302). Through examining these and other texts, Przyluski concludes that the tradition placing Ājñāta Kauṇḍinya at the head of the *saṃgha* is the earlier one, and the one placing Mahākāśyapa at the head is later (302–3).[55]

Who then, was Mahākāśyapa originally, and how did he come to gain preeminent honor in the time of the *Mahāparinirvāṇa Sūtra* and the *vinaya*s? Przyluski bids us recall Mahākāśyapa's character as a great ascetic and practitioner of the *dhutaguṇa*s. This part of Mahākāśyapa's character, he suggests, is the earlier one, with the conventional monastic side of the saint developing later. So much may be granted, but the question then arises of how Mahākāśyapa came to stand in the Nikāya *Mahāparinirvāṇa Sūtra* and the *vinaya*s as the prime consolidator of monastic orthodoxy.

According to Przyluski, it was precisely Mahākāśyapa's reputation as a great forest saint and practitioner of the *dhutaguṇa*s that enabled him later to replace Kauṇḍinya as the senior disciple of the Buddha and to play the central roles at the Buddha's cremation and the first council. In this replacement of Kauṇḍinya by Mahākāśyapa, Przyluski remarks, "merit [i.e., sanctity] [Kāśyapa] ends up taking precedence over temporal seniority [Kauṇḍinya]" (Przyluski 1926–28, 303). So Mahākāśyapa can, at a later date, come so decisively to the fore in the *Mahāparinirvāṇa Sūtra* and the *vinaya*s, precisely because he is the great forest saint, whose realization is unquestioned and whose charisma unmatched.[56]

In the replacement of Kauṇḍinya by Mahākāśyapa we have an ironic process: the forest saint, the solitary meditator, the one at home among wild animals and demons but not among ordinary humans, the great outsider, comes to be not only acknowledged but also appropriated by settled monaticism into its own traditions and even celebrated as its chief. This, then, is another example of the process of monasticization by which phenomena connected with the forest saints and their traditions are appropriated by, and integrated into, the traditions of the established Buddhism of the settled monastery.[57] It is this process, perhaps among others, that ends up lending to Mahākāśyapa a personality with complex and sometimes contradictory features.

A Latter-day Orthodox Buddhist Saint: Upagupta

Upagupta is an important saint in Sanskrit Buddhist tradition who lived in the region of Mathurā sometime between the third century B.C.E. and the first century C.E. In Sarvāstivādin tradition, he is the fifth patriarch in the succession beginning with Mahākāśyapa and including Ānanda; Madhyāntika; Upagupta's guru, Śāṇakavāsin; and Upagupta (Lamotte 1958, 150). In his hagiographies, Upagupta is said to have lived during the time of King Aśoka and to have been a special object of his devotions. In the Aśoka cycle, Upagupta receives more attention than any other saint (Przyluski 1923, 8). Although Upagupta is not mentioned in the Pāli canon, via the influence of Sanskrit Buddhism in Southeast Asia, he emerges in about the twelfth century as a prominent saint in legend and cult in Theravādin countries, particularly Burma, northern and northeastern Thailand, and Laos.[58]

Primary sources for Upagupta's hagiography are several texts, mostly of the *avadāna* or legendary type, existing in the original Sanskrit as well as in Chinese and Tibetan translation.[59] Most important among these are the *Divyāvadāna* (chapters 21 and 27 contain the fullest extant version of Upagupta's life);[60] the *Avadānaśataka* (260–63 [F., 430–35]) (containing the earliest known reference to Upagupta); and three versions of the story of King Aśoka preserved in Chinese, the *Aśokarājāvadāna (A yü wang chuan)* (T. 2042, 50:99a–131a [Prz., 225–427]), *Aśokarāja Sūtra (A yü wang ching)* (T. 2043, 50:131b–70a),[61] and several chapters from the *Samyuktāgama Sūtra (Tsa a han ching)*.[62] Finally, the Mūlasarvāstivādin *vinaya,* existing in Sanskrit as well as in Chinese and Tibetan, contains a number of stories about Upagupta.[63] Important for an understanding of Upagupta in Southeast Asia is the Pāli *Lokapaññatti* (162–74 [Denis 1977, 2:144–52]), which draws on the legend as it is found in earlier Sanskrit tradition but also includes material not found there.

The Upagupta legend as set out in the Sanskrit sources contains two distinct cycles of stories that have been more or less combined in the mature legend.[64] First and foremost is a "Mathuran cycle," containing Upagupta's own hagiography, made up of stories located in and around Mathurā. This cycle tells Upagupta's story from the time of the Buddha's prediction of him and his past life; through his birth, youth, training under his guru, realization, and teaching career; to his final days and death. The second is an "Aśokan cycle," in which Upagupta figures as an important actor in King Aśoka's own story, as Aśoka's guru and object of his devotion (Strong 1992, 10–11). The following summarizes the main themes of the mature Upagupta legend as given in the Sanskrit sources.

In many of the texts, Upagupta's legend begins with a prediction made by the Buddha while on a journey to Mathurā with his attendant Ānanda. Pointing to Mt. Urumuṇḍa, a place famous for its meditating hermits, the Buddha remarks that a hundred years after his own *parinirvāṇa* a certain Upagupta will be born who will live on the mountain and make many converts. In the *Divyāvadāna* version, the Blessed One remarks that one hundred years after his *parinirvāṇa,* Upagupta will be born as the son of a perfume merchant of Mathurā. At that time, there will be a certain renunciant named Śāṇakavāsin who will build a hermitage on Mt. Urumuṇḍa. Upagupta will renounce the world under Śāṇakavāsin, will attain realization, and will become a "buddha without marks," carrying on the work of a buddha and guiding many to arhantship.[65] The *Aśokarājāvadāna* adds that the Buddha predicted that Upagupta would be the foremost of all those who teach meditation, suggesting Upagupta's credentials as a forest saint (*Ara* 120b [Prz., 363]).

The sources next recount the story of Upagupta's previous life. In the Mūlasarvāstivādin *vinaya,* where this story is told in its fullest form, the Buddha describes how Upagupta, in his previous life, lived on Mt. Urumuṇḍa as a monkey, leader of a monkey troupe. In the Buddha's narration, the monkey, supplanted and driven away by a young male, goes wandering and comes across a community of five hundred pratyekabuddhas. The monkey offers them food and other things and, when they sit down to meditate, imitates them. The pratyekabuddhas soon decide that the time for their *parinirvāṇa* has come and, rising into the air, they burst into flame and are consumed. The monkey, saddened by their disappearance, goes wandering again, seeking human company. In time, he comes across five hundred Brahmanical ascetics practicing various kinds of self-mortification. After making offerings to them, he shows them the pratyekabuddhas' meditation posture. The ascetics, prompted by their own teacher, abandon the practices they were engaged in and adopt the posture demonstrated by the monkey. In time, they gain the thirty-seven wings of enlightenment and win *pratyekabodhi,* the enlightenment of a pratyekabuddha. The ascetics venerate the monkey with offerings and, after he dies, cremate him with fragrant wood. The Buddha closes his account with the comment that as in that previous life Upagupta worked for the benefit of many, so he is predicted as one who will show compassion for the multitude (*Gms* 3, pt. 1:4–7 [Strong 1992, 44–45]). Strong remarks that one function of accounts of previous lives of great saints is to establish the primary context and characteristics of their present lives as saints (46). In the Buddha's narration, we find the major phases of Upagupta's career: the period of his life as a layperson, his renouncing of the world, living in the forest, veneration of forest saints, study with the meditation masters, practice (more correctly, imitation) of meditation, teaching of others, respect and homage paid by his own students, and concluding with his death and cremation (52–53).

The *Divyāvadāna* provides details concerning the beginning of Upagupta's present life. According to the text, prior to his birth, the elder Śāṇakavāsin is aware of the Buddha's prediction and also of the important part that he himself will play in preparing Upagupta for his destined role. Knowing that the Mathuran perfume merchant Gupta is to be Upagupta's father, Śāṇakavāsin pays a visit and elicits Gupta's promise that when he has a son he will give him to the teacher as an attendant. Gupta has first one son, then another, but in each case he demurs, insisting that he needs each for his business. Śāṇakavāsin knows by his supernatural powers that neither son is Upagupta, so he waits. Eventually a third son is born, and this son, who is Upagupta, the father definitively promises to Śāṇakavāsin—but only when "there will be neither profit nor loss."[66]

Śāṇakavāsin is fourth in the line of Buddhist patriarchs, looking for someone to whom he may transmit the dharma, who may act as his successor. The lineage that Śāṇakavāsin represents is, as Strong points out, one of forest renunciation (1992, 71). The forest character of the first patriarch, Mahākāśyapa, has been noted, and Śāṇakavāsin is no less as a forest renunciant. As we shall presently see, like Mahākāśyapa and other forest renunciants, Śāṇakavāsin can appear dirty and disheveled, with long hair and a beard. He also exhibits a devotion to meditation in the forest. In the *Aśokarājāvadāna,* for example, Śāṇakavāsin is in meditation retreat and enters into *dhyāna,* meditation. Joyful and at peace, he utters this *gāthā:*

> Clothed in robes of *śaṇa* [hempen cloth], I have attained the five branches of *dhyāna*. Seated in *dhyāna* among the mountain peaks and lonely valleys, I meditate. Who could not (thus) abide the wind and the cold? The arhant Śāṇa[kavāsin], his surpassing mind having won liberation, has gained the supreme wisdom. (*Ara* 120b [Prz. 363–64])

In addition, Śāṇakavāsin's institutional role is inseparable from forest Buddhism: central to Ānanda's charge to him is that he go to the region of Mathurā and there build a forest hermitage on Mt. Urumuṇḍa, awaiting the birth of Upagupta. This hermitage, Naṭabhaṭika, is well known in Sanskrit Buddhism as an ideal place for meditation (Strong 1992, 62, 71).

As Upagupta grows up, he remains for some time a layperson helping his father in the family perfume business. This lay phase of Upagupta's life is crucial to his spiritual development. In the course of his life as a layperson, he meets his guru, Śāṇakavāsin; begins his meditative training; develops as a dharmic businessman; preaches the dharma for the first time; makes his first convert; and attains the first of the four paths of liberation. As recounted in the *Divyāvadāna,* Śāṇakavāsin one day comes to the perfume shop, engages Upagupta in conversation, and gives him his first meditation instruction, a mindfulness practice wherein for each defiled mental event a black marker is put aside and for every pure mental event a white one is put aside. At the beginning the black markers outnumber the white but soon there are more white markers than black, and finally white alone (352–53 [St., 178–79; see also Strong 1992, 75–76]). Implicit in this development is the Buddhist idea that defiled states of mind can only exist in an agitated and distracted mind; when the mind becomes settled and calm, positive states are the natural result. Upagupta's mindfulness also has an immediate ethical impact: as we are told in the *Aśokarājāvadāna,* "all of his decisions were then in accord with the Buddha's Teaching and none of them opposed to it" (*Ara* 118a [Prz., 348]).

While Upagupta is still "in the world," he has an important encounter with a famous courtesan of Mathurā named Vāsavadattā. In the *Divyāvadāna* version (353–56 [St., 179–84]), this woman hears of Upagupta and conceives a desire for union with him. Upagupta resists meeting her—until she commits a deed for which she is punished by having her hands, feet, nose, and ears cut off and being left in the cremation ground to die. Upagupta goes to the cremation ground and stays with her, instructing her in the dharma. Hearing his teaching, she is converted and attains the first of the four Āryan paths to liberation, that of a stream enterer *(srotāpanna).* Upagupta, seeing and preaching to Vāsavadattā, has his own eyes opened and attains the third Āryan state, that of a nonreturner *(anāgāmin).*

Upagupta's father now gives permission for him to leave the world. As told in the *Aśokarājāvadāna* (118c [Prz., 352ff.]), Upagupta is ordained by Śāṇakavāsin at the forest hermitage of Naṭabhaṭika and in due course achieves the state of an arhant. Śāṇakavāsin then bids him carry out the work of a buddha, and Upagupta commits himself to do so.[67] Upagupta now demonstrates the depth of his power and realization by converting Māra, who—though repulsed by Śākyamuni on the night of his enlightenment—has yet to be finally conquered. As recounted in the *Divyāvadāna,*[68] while Upagupta is teaching dharma to the laity, Māra interferes by creating various displays that divert the laity's attention. Through his higher perception, Upagupta sees that the evil one is responsible for his listeners' distraction. Using his magical powers, Upagupta appears to honor Māra with a garland of flowers. But, once these are draped on Māra, they turn into the carcasses of a snake, a dog, and a human being, which he cannot remove. This convinces Māra of the power of the Buddha's dharma, breaks his resistance, and leads him to devotion for the Blessed One. Māra prostrates to Upagupta and takes refuge in the three jewels, becoming a follower of the Buddha. Having brought about Māra's conversion, Upagupta requests a favor in return—that Māra, through his own magical powers of transformation and his personal memory of the Buddha, manifest the physical form of the Blessed One. Māra agrees but warns Upagupta not to forget that his manifestation will only be a likeness of the Buddha and not the Blessed One himself; Upagupta must therefore not bow down before this apparition. But when Māra produces a vision of the physical form *(rūpakāya)* of the Buddha, Upagupta, forgetting himself in fervent devotion, venerates it. Called to task, Upagupta responds that his action is admissible because it is no different from paying homage to a statue of the Buddha.

As a result of his taming of Māra, Upagupta is worshipped by humans and by supernatural beings, including (in a standard formula) "the Lord of the Realm of Desire, gods, humans, serpents, *asuras, garuḍas, yakṣas, gandharvas,* and *vidyādharas.*" All these fall at Upagupta's feet and are able to share in the saint's charisma (*Da* 364 [St., 197–98]). Upagupta's success leads his master, Śāṇakavāsin, to feel he can leave Mathurā and this he does, retiring to Kashmir to practice meditation in seclusion. Sometime later, Śāṇakavāsin, returned from Kashmir, transmits the dharma to Upagupta, telling him to confer it in turn upon one named Dhītika.[69] Then he rises into space, manifests the eighteen transformations, and enters into nirvāṇa. Upagupta erects a stūpa over his remains.[70]

A few features of Upagupta's personality as an enlightened saint deserve special mention. After his enlightenment, he continues to dwell in the forest, specifically in the forest *(araṇya)* of Naṭabhaṭa on the remote mountain of Urumuṇḍa (*Ara* 102c [Prz., 247]), "the foremost of all the Buddha's forest-haunts *[araṇyāyatana],* where the lodgings [seats-beds] are conducive to meditation *[śamatha]*" (Strong 1992, 71). This is a lonely place, where wild animals roam, and here Upagupta encounters, subdues, and teaches two tiger cubs (*Ara* 120b–c [Prz., 364]). Like his guru, Upagupta is particularly known for his meditational attainments; in the *Aśokarājāvadāna* it is remarked that he is skilled in "the dharma of meditation" and is foremost of all who teach meditation (102b–c [Prz., 246]). Upagupta is known as a great teacher and maker of conversions, with multitudes being tamed and thousands renouncing the world under him and attaining arhantship (Lamotte 1958, 229). The saint teaches not only humans but supernatural beings, and the *Aśokarājāvadāna* tells us that gods, *nāga*s, and *yakṣa*s all find the way to deliverance through him (102b [Prz., 247]).

Upagupta is also powerful and insightful, and unpredictable and unconventional in manner, as illustrated by the following story. While he is in residence in his forest hermitage, a visitor, a conventional Buddhist monk from south India arrives to see him (*Ara* 120c–121a [Prz., 366ff.]; cf. Lamotte 1958, 227ff.). Unbeknownst to all but the far-seeing Upagupta, this monk has committed fornication and has murdered his mother. He has entered the monastic order because he desired a certain woman's hand in marriage and was repulsed. Though of corrupt character, this monk is an accomplished textual scholar: he has mastered the *Tripiṭaka* and has gathered to himself a multitude of disciples. When he appears in Upagupta's story, he has come as one proud of his own scholarly achievement, perhaps wanting to debate, perhaps seeking the saint's confirmation of his status. Upagupta, seeing clearly the monk's evil deeds and obscurations, refuses even to see him. This behavior upsets Upagupta's disciples, for they believe an impropriety has been committed (Lamotte 1958, 227ff., 303). Upagupta settles their doubts by summoning his own guru, Śāṇakavāsin, while he absents himself. Śāṇakavāsin suddenly arrives—with long hair and beard, a tattered robe, and a disheveled appearance—and seats himself upon Upagupta's own seat.[71] Upagupta's disciples express disbelief that their master, while refusing to speak with a master of the *Tripiṭaka,* would associate with this disreputable character! Śāṇakavāsin, however, reveals to the disciples that he is no ordinary being. The disciples want to drive him away, but he remains as immovable as Mt. Meru. They try to abuse him verbally, but their tongues will not move. When he exhibits other wonders, the disciples gain faith in Śāṇakavāsin, listen to his teaching, and attain arhantship. Thus both Upagupta and his guru Śāṇakavāsin show no hesitation in contravening conventional ideas of what is meritorious and in confounding the understanding of the unaware in order to generate insight.

Particularly important to Upagupta's stature is his renown as a teacher, illustrated in detail in a collection of some twenty-five stories in the *Aśokarājāvadāna* describing Upagupta's training of disciples (121b–126b [Prz., 370–98]). This group of accounts, from which a few representative examples will be examined, is especially interesting because it provides an unusually close and detailed look at the forest saint's guru in pre-Mahāyāna Buddhism. In his hagiography, Upagupta stands as an exemplar of the values, perspectives, and methods of forest Buddhism. It is not surprising, then, that when prospective disciples come to him, they are attracted by his reputation as a great meditation master and seek above all instruction in meditation. A typical story is told of a certain monk who one day encounters a *bhikṣuṇī* of attainment. When she questions the fidelity of his adherence to the dharma, he thinks that she means his tonsure, so he shaves his face and head and washes himself. When she again questions him, he thinks she means his robe, and so he fixes his robe. When she questions him a third time, he asks what remains wrong. She remarks that correctness in the dharma refers not to proper external trappings but rather to the attainment of the stages of holiness. She advises him to go to the forest of Naṭabhaṭa to study meditation with Upagupta. He does so, learns from the meditating monks there, and finally becomes an arhant (121b–122b [371–74]). This example suggests the general character of Upagupta's kind of Buddhism: monks who have previously identified with conventional monastic concerns—in this case, external appearance—may find themselves at Upagupta's door in search of something deeper and more productive of realization.

Sometimes Upagupta is shown training disciples who are already forest renunciants but have encountered obstacles on their meditative paths. For example, a certain renunciant has attained mastery of the fourth *dhyāna,* is in possession of the five mundane *abhijñā,* and is particularly accomplished in being able to cause rain in times of drought. All of this has given birth to overweening pride, and he believes that he has become an arhant. Upagupta determines to bring him to liberation and so, through his magical power, causes a twelve-year drought. When the laity come to Upagupta requesting his intervention, he sends them instead to the rainmaking renunciant. This renunciant causes a great rain, and his pride swells to such an extent that he finally becomes aware of it himself, remarking "an arhant is not proud of himself. I know therefore that I am not yet an arhant." Humbled by this insight, he goes for training to Upagupta, who deals with him in a blunt and uncompromising fashion, and the renunciant eventually becomes an arhant (*Ara* 126a [Prz., 396–97]). This story is perhaps an account by meditators and for meditators, calling attention to the danger of pride, especially among those who have reached a high level of meditative accomplishment. It also illustrates Upagupta's trust in his disciples' own intelligence and the subtlety with which he encourages this intelligence. In this story, he does not directly criticize the disciple but rather brings about a situation in which the disciple himself comes to see clearly the flaws in his own state of mind. Particularly interesting here is the portrayal of Upagupta's power vis-à-vis the phenomenal world: the drought that sets off the entire train of instructive events is directly attributed to Upagupta's action.

A similar story is told of an especially ascetic renunciant who "desires little and is content," eats the simplest fare, and bathes in cold water. As a result, he is emaciated and weak. Looking at this man and realizing that he would be able to attain arhantship but for his feeble condition, Upagupta prescribes warm baths, good food, and other similar "luxuries," and the disciple soon becomes an arhant (*Ara* 123a–b [Prz., 380–81]). This story beautifully illustrates Upagupta's flexibility and freedom from conventional ideas of asceticism in his work with his disciples. In India and in forest Buddhism, desiring little and being content, eating simple fare, and living an ascetic existence are, as we have seen, typically regarded as important indicators of a person's legitimacy as a forest renunciant. Upagupta, undiverted by his disciple's adherence to the ideal norm, sees that something softer and more generous will be of help, something that in the traditional context would have offended some and raised doubts about Upagupta's own legitimacy as a meditation teacher.

Upagupta's skill as a meditation teacher is further revealed in a story about another disciple obsessed with food and drink, to the point at which it obstructs his spiritual progress. Upagupta invites him to a meal where he must sit before his food until it is cold, then eat the food, and then vomit it up. Next he instructs the disciple to eat his vomited food, and when the latter refuses, Upagupta points out that this is in any case the condition of food in the stomach. The disciple is then told to contemplate the body's impurities, and he forthwith becomes an arhant (*Ara* 123a [Prz., 380]).

A particularly interesting account is given of a renunciant disciple who continually tends to fall asleep, especially when the dharma is being preached. Upagupta directs him to go into the forest and sit down beneath a tree to meditate. The saint then magically produces a crevasse a thousand feet deep around the spot where the disciple is sitting. This instantly rouses the disciple, who, filled with terror, calls to mind his teacher, Upagupta. Immediately, he discovers a small passage (a bridge?) across the crevasse, again magically produced by Upagupta, and so passes out of danger. The disciple comes before his master and is instructed to return again to the tree under which he was meditating. Sitting beneath the tree, he experiences great joy and says, "My master has saved me from the danger of this deep crevasse." Upagupta then suddenly appears before him, saying that this crevasse is not nearly as deep or dangerous as that of the three lower realms, of birth, old age, sickness, and death. He further instructs the disciple to realize the four noble truths of suffering, the cause of suffering, the end of suffering, and the path. The disciple does so and, losing all desire to sleep, gains energy *(vīrya)* and attentiveness *(manaskāra)* and becomes an arhant.[72] This story reveals additional aspects of Upagupta's person as a powerful saint. When the disciple experiences a horrifying vision while meditating in the forest, this is attributed to Upagupta. When the disciple calls his teacher to mind, a way out of the horror is provided, and this too is attributed to Upagupta. We have seen that Upagupta is understood to have power over natural phenomena. In this story, we see that he also has the ability to create powerful visions for his disciples. This account also provides insight into the fervent devotion felt by disciple toward teacher. In his extremity, it is the teacher toward whom he turns. The teacher saves him, and this only causes his joy and trust in the teacher to increase.

Upagupta is some generations removed from the first patriarch, Mahākāśyapa, and lives in a time when Buddhism is fully established. As a forest saint in this time, Upagupta can also, as the occasion warrants, be a proponent of the values and preoccupations of settled monasticism, but always from a forest point of view. This is illustrated by several stories depicting prospective disciples who come to the saint to learn meditation but find themselves directed by the teacher for one reason or another, at the least for a time, into other avenues. An accomplished scholar and teacher has grown weary of his usual activity, desiring instead to meditate. He seeks out Upagupta, who, he has heard, is foremost among those who teach meditation. Upagupta, however, looks into this man's character and sees that realization will not best be achieved by meditation. The saint tells the scholar that he will accept him as a disciple only on the condition that he precisely follow the instructions that he, Upagupta, will provide. When consent is given, the master tells his disciple not to desist in his scholarship and teaching, and this advice directly followed leads to realization (*Ara* 121b [Prz., 370–71]). It is significant that only when the scholar agrees to submit himself to Upagupta's instructions, whatever they may be, is he accepted as a disciple. It is also significant that he accepts the conditions without comment or complaint and simply does as Upagupta instructs, even though he is asked to do exactly the thing that he does not want to do. This incident reveals the view that unconditional commitment is required of a prospective disciple desiring to be accepted by a forest meditation master and illustrates the expectation, found rather widely in texts reflecting forest

Buddhism, that such a commitment on the part of the disciple is necessary in order for the relationship to work (see Guenther 1963, x–xii). The prospective disciple's submission is particularly interesting because the individual in question here is not some young and naive renunciant, but rather one who is clearly mature in years with considerable scholarly and teaching accomplishment behind him.

A similar story tells of a skilled monastic administrator who is fatigued by his work and longs to devote himself to the practice of meditation. Hearing of Upagupta's renown, he journeys to Upagupta in his forest hermitage, Naṭabhaṭika, and requests to be accepted as a disciple. Upagupta sees that this man will not be able to attain realization without further accumulation of merit. In responding to the man's request, the master again stipulates that he will accept him as a disciple only if he will do exactly as instructed. The administrator enthusiastically agrees to the conditions, begging for Upagupta's teachings. Upagupta then counsels him not to meditate but rather to do the very kind of work he has been doing. He eventually accumulates enough merit and becomes an arhant (*Ara* 122b–c [Prz., 377–78]). In another story, a monk is accomplished—indeed renowned in the construction of monasteries and stūpas—but becomes fatigued by this work. He travels to Upagupta's forest hermitage and presents himself with the request to be trained in meditation. Upagupta considers by what method this man will be able to attain realization and sees that it will be precisely by continuing in his building of stūpas and monasteries. Again Upagupta's precondition to teaching is the prospective disciple's commitment to do as the master commands. The monk agrees and Upagupta tells him to continue his building work; this leads to his arhantship (122c–123a [378–80]). In these two examples, as in the previous story, we find the same unconditional commitment required as a precondition to acceptance as a disciple by the forest saint. Once again the applicants are not callow youths but people with experience and accomplishment behind them.

In these examples, Upagupta is depicted as encouraging his disciples in a broad range of activities, including—as might not necessarily be expected of a forest saint—textual learning, monastic administration, and the construction of monasteries and stūpas. Nevertheless, these appear in a hierarchically arranged order. In the *Aśokarājāvadāna,* the ultimate goal is always realization, to which meditation is depicted as the most direct path. Textual learning, preaching, monastic administration, and meritorious construction—though clearly less direct means to realization—are not presented in a negative light but are also seen as having important functions within Buddhist soteriology. In directing some of his disciples to engage in these more active preoccupations, Upagupta not only assists them toward their own realization but also implicitly affirms the value of these activities. These images suggest that the Buddhism behind the text is characterized by a harmony of values: on the one hand is the path of forest renunciation and meditation and on the other the more active path of town-and-village monastic life, including scholarship, administration, and institution building; these two paths complement one another as harmonious components of a common faith, here epitomized by Upagupta.

In addition to his close personal disciples, Upagupta also has lay devotees. Primary among these is the great King Aśoka. The meeting and subsequent relationship of king and saint, described in the *Divyāvadāna,* the *Aśokarājāvadāna,* and other texts,[73] provide insight into the lay cult surrounding Upagupta. While the saint is living in his forest hermitage on Mt. Urumuṇḍa with 18,000 arhants, Aśoka hears about him and wants to see him (*Da* 385 [St., 239–40]). A debate is raised between the king, who would go to Upagupta in his hermitage, and his counselors who feel this would be unseemly and who prefer that Upagupta be summoned to the capital. In the context of this discussion, Aśoka observes that Upagupta is enlightened and therefore has an indestructible, adamantine body of *vajra.* If Upagupta were to refuse to come to the capital, the king argues, there would be little that could be done to him. Upagupta solves the problem by coming by boat to Pāṭaliputra; as he approaches, the king goes down to the river to meet him and welcomes him with musical instruments, garlands of flowers, and perfume. When Upagupta arrives, the king himself lifts the saint to the shore and then prostrates to him, kissing his feet. Aśoka remarks upon the great joy of seeing the saint Upagupta, greater even than when he united the world under his aegis: in seeing the master, he is seeing the Blessed One himself. Upagupta then blesses the king, touching him with his right hand (385–87 [240–42]).

Aśoka's joy is so great because Upagupta represents the Buddha in this world, now that the Blessed One is in *parinirvāṇa,* a notion affirmed in the epithet "*alakṣaṇakabuddha,*" "buddha without marks." This notion is also evident in Upagupta's repeatedly being assimilated to the Buddha, as in the *Aśokarājāvadāna,* in which his appearance, teaching, and conversions are all compared with those of the Buddha (*Ara* 102b [Prz., 246–47]). In the *Aśokarājāvadāna* Aśoka says, "Although the Buddha has entered nirvāṇa, you fulfill his office" (102c [248]). Upagupta's stature as Buddha is further affirmed when Aśoka has his crier announce the saint's arrival in the following terms: "If you never saw the foremost of men the greatly compassionate self-existent Master, go and see the elder Upagupta who is like the Master, a bright light in this Triple World" (*Da* 387 [St., 241]). What is to be gained by taking darśan of Upagupta? The proclamation that Aśoka has spread forth, announcing the arrival of the saint, spells several levels of benefit: first, he can help one leave poverty behind; second, seeing him can lead to rebirth in heaven; finally, he can bring release from saṃsāra (387 [241]). Through darśan of Upagupta, Aśoka affirms, all may gain the full benefits of the Buddha's dharma, something known to the king, not because he has himself meditated for years in a cave, but because he has mysteriously participated in the saint's enlightened charisma.

At their meeting, Upagupta gives Aśoka instruction. He teaches the impermanence of all worldly gain, the ineluctibility of karma, and nirvāṇa as the only authentic ultimate value. And he tells the king to venerate the three jewels without ceasing (*Ara* 103a [Prz., 249]). The king replies with a litany of his activities of munificence to the dharma (103a [250]). Aśoka, who has already constructed 84,000 stūpas, wishes to build new ones in the regions sacred to the Buddha, and Upagupta offers to act as guide. Thus the saint and the king set out together as pilgrims to visit the major places made holy by the Buddha's presence and activity (*Da* 389 [St., 244]).[74]

Upagupta must now complete the major task of transmitting his lineage to a successor—a certain Dhītika. He trains his heir culminating with Dhītika's ordination at the age of twenty. Then Dhītika successively attains the first, second, and third stages of holiness and becomes an arhant (*Ara* 126a–b [Prz., 397]).

Following this event, Upagupta reflects to himself that he has now converted beings, paid proper homage to the Buddha, nurtured his renunciant disciples, helped his lay disciples to prosper, and, in this way, seen to the exact transmission of the dharma and its survival without interruption. "Now," he says, "the time has come to enter into nirvāṇā." After confirming Dhītika in the transmission he has received, he predicts that he will enter nirvāṇa in seven days. Then 100,000 arhants assemble along with innumerable laity. At the appointed time, Upagupta rises into the air, exhibits the eighteen miraculous transformations—giving to the assembled renunciants and laity great joy—and enters into nirvāṇa. When Upagupta's body is cremated, 10,000 arhants, seeing this nirvāṇa, themselves enter into extinction. The gods arrive, bringing offerings, and a stūpa is raised over the saint's remains (*Ara* 126b [Prz., 398]). Finally, hagiography develops around the figure of Upagupta.[75]

These images and legends are connected with Upagupta in North Indian Buddhism, where the master is most richly documented, but Upagupta is also an important saint in the Southeast Asian tradition. Here Upagupta is known as one of the great arhants of old, who is guardian of the dharma and patron saint of those who follow the way of meditation. By virtue of his magical power *(ṛddhi),* he is still alive, dwelling in a brazen palace hidden in the depths of the southern ocean. Further, he will remain alive as long as the doctrine of the Buddha is known upon earth (Maung Kin 1903). The story of Upagupta as told in the Pāli *Lokapaññatti* draws on both the Mathuran and Aśokan cycles but adds material not present there,[76] especially discussing Upagupta's longevity.

Upagupta thus represents an exemplar of our paradigm of Buddhist sainthood, whose life reflects the themes seen in the lives of the Buddha, the saints of the *Theragāthā* and *Therīgāthā,* and Mahākāśyapa in some ways, and in others offers some interesting variations. Upagupta's life, as seen in our texts, does not clearly reflect an initial personal crisis (theme 1) or strong early sense of personal vocation (theme 2). Perhaps the stature of the patriarch, reflected in the Buddha's prediction, does not provide room for this most human dimension of the Buddhist saints. Upagupta remains for some time a layperson who nevertheless makes considerable spiritual progress developing dharmic behavior—meeting and beginning to study with his guru, training in meditation, beginning to teach and make converts, and attaining some measure of realization. Upagupta's activity as a layperson is significant, for it brings Upagupta the realized saint closer to the laity and demonstrates what can be accomplished by laypeople (Strong 1992, 75). Upagupta eventually renounces the world (theme 3) and takes up a life of forest renunciation on Mt. Urumuṇḍa (theme 4). The guru (theme 5) plays the same central role in Upagupta's spiritual career as he does in that of Mahākāśyapa, except that Śāṇakavāsin finds Upagupta rather than Upagupta seeking out his master. This variation may reflect the strength of Upagupta's stature and fated destiny, and it also makes dramatic sense: if the saint-to-be has no personal crisis and explicit sense of vocation, then motivation for an ardent search for a guru, as found among other Buddhist saints, would be less expected. The "path" dimension of Upagupta's life similarly tends to be played down, and we do not see him making vows or forming aspirations to enlightenment (theme 6). For Upagupta, meditation practice stands at the center of the dharma, and he meditates both as a layman in the marketplace and as a forest renunciant in the mountain hermitage of Urumuṇḍa (theme 7), but again little insight is provided into the details of his own struggle. In summary, in the prerealization phase of his life, apart from his dramatic encounter with Vāsavadattā, Upagupta appears as a somewhat flat figure, and most of the dramatic focus is upon those contending over him, both the father who is reluctant to let him leave the world and the guru who would help him fulfill his destiny.

Upagupta attains realization (theme 8) in stages: he purifies his mind through separating black and white objects; he realizes the stage of nonreturning in the cremation ground; and he becomes an arhant on Mt. Urumuṇḍa. After realization, others recognize his attainment, and he is widely known as having crossed to the other shore and as a "pure being who enjoys omniscience" (*Da* 385 [St., 239]) (theme 9). If Upagupta does not explicitly declare his own enlightenment in so many words (theme 10), perhaps it is because he does not need to do so: the Buddha has already prophesied his arhantship and Upagupta's charismatic actions (his victory over Māra and so on) leave little doubt about his enlightened status. Now compassion becomes Upagupta's primary motivation (theme 11). Particularly in his encounter with Māra and in teaching his disciples, but at other times as well, miracles surround his person (theme 12), and he possesses extraordinary magical powers (theme 13), all in conformity with the type. Human and supernatural beings of all sorts, including even Māra, pay homage to Upagupta, taking darśan from him (theme 14). They also participate in his cult (theme 15) and receive his teachings (theme 16). As depicted in the Sanskrit texts, the cult of Buddhist saints—in contrast to what the two-tiered model would suggest—is clearly not just for the unenlightened; Upagupta himself participates fervently in the cultic adoration of the image of the Buddha manifested by Māra. If the cult is for renunciants as well as laity, the goal of liberation is evidently not only for renunciants but for laity as well. Upagupta attains a high stage of realization while still a layperson. Moreover, through taking darśan from Upagupta, both renunciants and laity may advance toward mundane and supermundane goals—including even liberation—again contradicting the notion found in the two-tiered model that the laity can hope only for a better rebirth.

Among humans, Upagupta accepts two kinds of followers (theme 17), close personal disciples and lay followers, with Aśoka at their head—all of whom participate in his cult. The portrait of Upagupta as guru for his disciples as presented in the *Aśokarājāvadāna* is particularly rich with its themes of the priority of inner realization over external forms of the dharma, the requirement of unconditional commitment of disciple to master, the master's flexibility and unconventionality in training methods, his skill in guiding disciples advanced in meditation, his power over the phenomenal world and the visions and meditation experiences of the disciples, the intense devotion of disciple for master, and so on.

As a realized forest saint, Upagupta has little directly to do with textual scholarship, something perhaps best left to those living in town-and-village monasteries (theme 18). At the same time, he is quite willing to recommend textual learning when and where appropriate but, it should be stressed, not for its own sake so much as for its ability to advance disciples directly to liberation. As seen in his instruction of Vāsavadattā, Māra, and his meditation students, Upagupta's teaching of the dharma is oral, informal, and situational, rather than based on preexisting texts (theme 19). He converts many beings (theme 20) and defeats those who are evil (theme 21), of whom Māra is the primary example. Upagupta is not shown particularly associating with the lowborn and disadvantaged (theme 22), and this may reflect, as in the case of the Buddha, his role as guarantor of the establishment. At the same time, Upagupta can be unconventional and a critic of the status quo (theme 23), as seen in his criticism of the famous but depraved scholar monk and his often unorthodox methods of training his own disciples. In the uneasiness of Aśoka's counselors in the face of Upagupta's spiritual power, one may perhaps see reflected the image of a saint who is guided by his own inner realization more than by conventional values. Upagupta's establishment role may also explain why he is not depicted as being subjected to persecution (theme 24), although Aśoka's counselors clearly do not trust him and even his own disciples can have doubts about him. The danger of Upagupta's numinous power is hinted at when Aśoka remarks that he cannot be forced to come to the capital (theme 25). Upagupta is clearly assimilated to the Buddha, as a "buddha without marks," and acts in his role; in Strong's words, "Upagupta himself will function as the Buddha in the Buddha's absence" (1992, 38) (theme 26). He possesses a body of *vajra,* implying that he is resistant to harm (theme 27). Longevity is not ascribed to Upagupta in the Sarvāstivādin materials we have examined (although it is a central feature of the saint's character in Theravāda Buddhism) (theme 28). Millennial expections are also not associated with him in the Sanskrit evidence (theme 29), although the saint's presence until the end of the Buddha's teachings, affirmed in the Theravādin evidence, implies such themes. Like the Buddhist saints before him, Upagupta anticipates his own passing (theme 30), dies in a miraculous manner (theme 31), and is cremated (theme 32); and a stūpa is built over his remains (theme 33). Sacred places are clearly an important part of Upagupta's Buddhism, for he can lead Aśoka on pilgrimages to sites holy to the Buddha (theme 34). In addition, sacred places are important to Upagupta's cult in India (and continue to be so in Southeast Asia).[77] Finally, Upagupta is particularly associated with the genre of hagiography (theme 35).

Like Mahākāśyapa, Upagupta is an orthodox saint, seen primarily as a patriarch of Northern Buddhism and representative of the establishment. And like Mahākāśyapa, Upagupta is a forest saint. Although in the *vinaya*s Mahākāśyapa is president of the first council and thus a guarantor of settled monasticism, he lives at the time of origins, while Buddhism is still taking shape. Upagupta, by contrast, lives in a time when monastic Buddhism is fully mature and his identity becomes clear partly in relation to it. Many of his pupils are monks preoccupied with typically monastic concerns, and Upagupta is quite ready to employ conventional monastic means in the service of his soteriological goals. Even more indicative is the way in which, in the texts, Upagupta is contrasted with Yaśas, the prototypical monk and abbot of Kukkuṭārāma, founded by King Aśoka, which is not far from the palace and is the chief royal monastery.[78] Whereas a saint such as Upagupta appeals to Aśoka because of his personal charisma and embodiment of the Buddha's enlightened essence, a conventional monk like Yaśas is important to the king for other reasons.[79] Yaśas is the ever-ready counselor to the king, the royal family, and the court, and this monastic official consults the king before arriving at decisions on important matters. Strong remarks that "Yaśas is presented as a wise, insightful, kindly abbot, but there is little extraordinary about him. Although he is said to be endowed with the six supernatural faculties, he is never pictured [as are Upagupta and the other saints] as flying through the air, or making flames leap out from half his body while water pours down from the other" (St., 87). As a representative of conventional values, Yaśas "is much more thickly involved in the business of royalty, and is the prototype perhaps, of the *saṅgharāja* (supreme patriarch) who in some Theravāda countries was appointed by the king to head the Buddhist community. With Yaśas, Aśoka can pursue an ongoing, routine, symbiotic relationship" (St., 88).

The existence in the *Divyāvadāna* and the *Aśokarājāvadāna* of the images of previously monastic disciples and of the conventional monastic abbot Yaśas alongside that of Upagupta is important because it suggests that for the Buddhist tradition behind the Sanskrit texts, the monastic and the forest renunciant ideals were historically coexistent and more or less harmonious components of a larger Buddhist whole. Moreover, each type of renunciant is depicted as performing certain characteristic functions within the overall economy of Buddhism. But the relationship is not entirely harmonious, as seen in the account of the morally depraved monk who pays a visit to Upagupta. This story is important because of the contrast it draws between the realized forest saint in his hermitage and the scholarly, learned, and popular—but morally corrupt—conventional monk. Ideally speaking (as illustrated by Yaśas and by some of Upagupta's disciples), the institutions of forest renunciation and the town-and-village monastery may exist in harmony, and the forest saint and the conventional monk may complement one another. At the same time, as the story seems to indicate, in practice it does not always work that way.

A Paradigmatic Saint of Settled Monasticism: Śāriputra

Śāriputra,whose hagiography has been studied in detail by Migot (1954),[80] is best known as one of the two chief disciples of the Buddha, the other being Mahāmaudgalyāyana (or Maudgalyāyana). In the Pāli canon, in fact, Śāriputra is preeminent, "the greatest saint of this canon," ranked virtually as a second Buddha (533). What is particularly interesting about Śāriputra is that he appears to represent a basic divergence from virtually all the Buddhist saints we have so far examined and, indeed, from the paradigm of the Buddhist saint itself. As we have seen, central to the personalities of Śākyamuni Buddha, the saints of the *Theragāthā* and *Therīgāthā,* and Mahākāśyapa and Upagupta are the values and orientations of the forest. These Buddhist saints begin as forest renunciants and through forest renunciation attain enlightenment. Having taken on a forest identity, and basing themselves on it, they typically submit to the process of monasticization and may even come eventually to function as revered members of the monastic establishment. In Śāriputra, however, we seem to have a contrary example. For Śāriputra appears to have little to do with forest Buddhism; rather, he is depicted as a settled monastic who attains the pinnacle of sainthood through following the methods of classical monasticism.

The original kernel of Śāriputra's legend, Migot tells us, may be found in the story of his conversion and that of Mahāmaudgalyāyana, documented in its simplest and most primitive version in the Pāli *Mahāvagga* (*V*-p 1:23–24 [H., 4:52–56]); existing in very similar form in the *vinaya*s of the Dharmaguptaka and Mahīśāsaka; and found in more developed form in other *vinaya*s and other texts (Migot 1954, 426–43, 455).[81] The main elements of the story, in the primitive *Mahāvagga* version, are:[82]

1. The ascetic Sañjayin (P., Sañjaya) is in Rājagṛha with 250 disciples, among whom are Śāriputra and Maudgalyāyana.
2. Śāriputra and Maudgalyāyana make an oath that whichever among them first finds the deathless will tell the other.
3. A certain disciple of the Buddha enters Rājagṛha on his alms rounds and is seen by Śāriputra, who is deeply impressed by his charisma.
4. Śāriputra asks the disciple about his master and teaching, and the disciple pronounces the famous stanzas beginning, "*ye dharmā*," upon hearing these Śāriputra attains the dharma eye (dharma-*cakṣus*) and is converted.
5. Śāriputra meets Maudgalyāyana again and recounts his experience.
6. Maudgalyāyana likewise attains the dharma eye and is converted.
7. Śāriputra and Maudgalyāyana decide to find the Buddha and become his disciples.
8. They return to tell the other disciples of Sañjayin of their decision, and these all elect to follow them.
9. Sañjayin tries unsuccessfully to dissuade them, and they all leave.
10. Sañjayin dies of hemorrhage.
11. The Buddha sees Śāriputra and Maudgalyāyana approaching and declares that they will be his principal disciples.
12. Śāriputra and Maudgalyāyana receive ordination from the Buddha.
13. People complain against the Buddha, and he responds with teaching.

It should be noted that throughout this account, when Śāriputra and Maudgalyāyana are mentioned together, Śāriputra is mentioned first, reflecting his preeminence.

In the more elaborate, later accounts of this story in the various *vinaya*s and other texts, other elements are added. Most significant, the more developed versions already emphasize what eventually comes to be Śāriputra's main characteristic in his fully developed legend: in his background and personality, he is the paradigmatic textual scholar and master of doctrine. In the Chinese version of the Mūlasarvāstivādin *vinaya,* for example, it is said that Śāriputra comes from a lineage of learned brahmins, who exhibited great skill in doctrinal debate (Migot 1954, 430). In the *Mahāvastu* we are told that Śāriputra was born a brahmin and was preeminent in Vedic learning, along with his friend Maudgalyāyana (3:57ff. [Jns., 3:57ff.; Migot 1954, 429ff.]). After Śāriputra has renounced the world, the *Mahāvastu* account continues, his training under his first teacher consists in memorizing texts. In this he demonstrates great ability, quickly memorizing "all the *parivrājaka śāstras*" and thereby accomplishing everything his master has to teach (Migot 1954, 447). In the *Mahāvastu,* after meeting and receiving ordination from the Buddha, Śāriputra, in a manner reminiscent of Buddhist scholastic analysis, questions the Buddha concerning the manifestation, endurance, decay, and reconstitution of phenomena, to which, in reply, the Buddha teaches about the four great elements. Śāriputra then asks about causality, and the Buddha replies with a discourse on the origin, duration, breaking up, and reconstitution of phenomena according to causes, including teaching on the *āyatanas*, nonself, and karma (3:65–67 [Jns., 3:67–70]).

In the *Mahāvagga* account, Śāriputra and Maudgalyāyana are simply mentioned as the two main disciples of the Buddha. It is in the more developed versions of the legends that we find Śāriputra and Maudgalyāyana depicted according to their special virtues. Thus Śāriputra is declared to be foremost in wisdom *(prajñā),* Maudgalyāyana foremost in miraculous power *(abhijñā)* (for example, *Mv* 3:63 [Jns., 3:65]) and, in some sources, meditation (Migot 1954, 447, 503ff., 509). This is consonant with the emphasis on Śāriputra's scholastic character in the more developed versions of the conversion story. In the developed legend, Śāriputra is explicitly said to be preeminent over Maudgalyāyana, and his preeminence is typically characterized as scholarly in nature.[83]

Śāriputra's legend is further developed in other Nikāya texts, canonical and extracanonical, that supplement the core conversion story with other legends. What is noteworthy about these additions is their emphasis on Śāriputra as a saint who embodies the scholarly ideals of settled monasticism. He is particularly associated with scholastic matters: he is concerned with "correct doctrine," clarifies obscure points, examines the doctrinal rectitude of the disciples, excels in preaching the dharma, and refutes heresies. Perhaps most indicative, in the Nikāya traditions, he is closely connected with the *abhidharma,* the epitome of pre-Mahāyāna scholastic Buddhism (Migot 1954, 519), and is in fact the paradigmatic saint of the *abhidharma*. In the Pāli tradition, he is related with the origins of the *abhidharma:* when the Buddha is preaching the *abhidharma* in heaven and leaves off, it is Śāriputra who picks up and continues the exposition, and he is also shown preaching the *abhidharma* to Revata (407–8, 446–47). Śāriputra's scholastic primacy is clearly seen in a representative passage from the *Dhammapada* commentary in which the Buddha tests the doctrinal expertise of his disciples. As the questions become more and more difficult, one by one all are eliminated until finally only Śāriputra and Maudgalyāyana are left; then Maudgalyāyana goes down to defeat, leaving Śāriputra as foremost of all (504).

The tendency of Śāriputra to embody the scholarly ideals of settled monasticism reaches a culmination in the Pāli canon, where the texts celebrating Śāriputra's scholastic preeminence "are innumerable" (Migot 1954, 463). Moreover, "it is essentially his qualities as a *dhammasenāpati* (chief of doctrine) that are emphasized in the Pāli canon" (466). Part of Śāriputra's role as preeminent master of doctrine includes frequent questions put to him on matters of dogma by the other disciples. In one typical passage in the *Majjhimanikāya,* Mahākoṭṭhita closely questions Śāriputra on doctrine and, in reply, receives a detailed summary that encompasses the essentials of the dharma (466). Śāriputra's role as progenitor of the *abhidharma* emerges in the final two *sūtra*s of the *Dīghanikaya,* the *Saṅgīti Suttanta* and the *Dasuttara Suttanta,* in which, in response to the Buddha's request that he teach, Śāriputra delivers long lists of doctrine, reminiscent in style of the Pāli *abhidharma* (408; *Dn* 3:207–71 [T.R. and C.R. 1921, 3:201–65]). Beyond this, he is frequently mentioned in Pāli *abhidharma* texts, for example, the *Dhammasaṅgaṇi, Kathāvatthu,* and the *Puggalapaññatti.*[84] In the Pāli canon, Śāriputra not surprisingly upholds the values of orthodoxy—for example, condemning all magical practices (Migot 1954, 466) and defeating heretics. He typically takes an active role in doing battle with heretics, refuting their doctrines and, if possible, converting them to the dharma. This role is, in fact, "one of the great prerogatives of Śāriputra in the Pāli canon" (469). In all these ways, then, Śāriputra functions as the primary saint for Pāli monasticism and paradigmatic embodiment of its ideals.

It is quite interesting, however, that in his legend, already beginning with the story of his and Mahāmaudgalyāyana's conversion, Śāriputra exhibits a number of features that remind us of the paradigm of the forest saint. For example, Śāriputra shows a strong sense of personal vocation: struck by the reality of death, he renounces the world and seeks a realized teacher; after studying with another master, he sees a disciple of the Buddha and, deeply impressed by his charisma, asks for teachings, commenting that he needs only the essential "spirit" (P., *attha;* Skt., *artha,* lit. "meaning"), not the "letter" *(vyañjana)* (*V*-p 1:39–40 [H., 4:52–56]). Receiving this, he attains realization and is later accepted by the Buddha as a disciple. As a realized master, he possesses abundant supernatural powers, is a charismatic reference point for the other disciples, and functions in many ways like a second Buddha. These forest features stand in some tension with the more conventional, monastic dimensions of Śāriputra's personality.

The preceding discussion suggests one possible explanation for this tension in Śāriputra's personality, a tension that is noted but not adequately explained by Migot (1954, 503–18). Śāriputra, precisely because he is the champion of settled monasticism, has been dignified with qualities that, within the Indian Buddhist context, were understood to be characteristic of great saints. It is not surprising that settled monasticism—beyond putting Śāriputra forward as a great master of texts and doctrine—should also see in him not only the same power, charisma, and realization as found in the other great saints but, in some cases, affirm the superiority over all other saints of these same qualities in Śāriputra.[85] No doubt some such dynamic of the attraction of forest qualities to Śāriputra is operative throughout his biography (as, indeed, in the biographies of other "monastic saints").

However, there may be another, more satisfactory explanation of Śāriputra's forest features. Let us note the interesting and significant fact that, in what Migot identifies as the most primitive account of Śāriputra's conversion story, there is no evidence of Śāriputra's scholastic character. In fact this element of Śāriputra's personality begins to emerge only in the more developed strata of the conversion account, gaining momentum in the later, even more developed segments of his legend and reaching a culmination in the Pāli canon. This raises the interesting possibility that Śāriputra was originally not the champion of the values and preoccupations of settled monasticism at all but was a saint along different lines—that he was, in effect, originally a saint of the forest and was only later monasticized. This view could explain at least some of the forest features active in Śāriputra's personality, especially those that seem to run directly counter to his monastic character. Based on the evidence brought forward so far, however, such an explanation, although possible, would seem to have little to recommend it.

Very interesting, then, are some Pāli accounts of Śāriputra that stand in sharp contrast to the main trends of the rest of the Pāli canon; Migot, whose study is otherwise the model of thoroughness and care, has uncharacteristically chosen to mention them hardly at all, perhaps because of their seemingly extraneous nature. These accounts emerge in several early texts contained in the *Khuddakanikāya,* including the *Theragāthā,* the *Udāna,* and the *Aṭṭhakavagga* of the *Suttanipāta.* In the *Udāna,* for example, Śāriputra is a paradigmatic saint of the forest. He is presented as essentially a forest contemplative who is described in the traditional manner: he needed little, was contented, was a recluse, shunned society, had ardent energy, was given over to meditation (43 [Wd., 51]). Similarly in the *Udāna,* Śāriputra is shown on one occasion "seated . . . in cross-legged posture, holding his body upright, keeping mindfulness before him" (27–28 [32–33]; see also 43 [51]) and on another meditating on a moonlit night, having won access to a certain stage of meditation (39 [47]). Moreover, Śāriputra is a realized saint who is praised by the Buddha for his accomplishment (3–4 [4–5] and 27–28 [32–33]). Like other realized saints, he is possessed of numinous power such that, when a *yakṣa* (P., *yakkha*) attempts to harm him, "instantly that *yakkha,* screaming 'I burn! I burn!' fell into the great hell" (39–40 [47–48]).

The *Theragāthā* presents a similar image of Śāriputra as paradigmatic forest saint. In Śāriputra's *gāthā,* we read, "Near the foot of a tree, with shaven head, clad in an outer robe, the elder Upatissa [Śāriputra], supreme in wisdom, truly meditates. Having attained to non-reasoning [*avitakka,* absence of conceptual thought], the disciple of the fully enlightened one is straightway possessed of noble silence" (*Ta* 998–99). This *gāthā* extolls other virtues of forest renunciation, such as solitude (981), wandering "with an unfilled belly" (982), meditation (981ff.), calm (1006, 1007), quiet (1006, 1007), and "peace of mind" (988). In this song, we are further told that "forests are delightful" (992), but also that "whether in the village or the forest, on low ground or high, wherever the arahats live, that is delightful country" (991).

The *Sāriputta Sutta,* in the *Aṭṭhakavagga* of the *Suttanipāta* (*Sn* 955–75), likewise identifies Śāriputra with forest Buddhism: he receives from the Buddha a dharma of forest renunciation and preaches the same himself. Thus, Śāriputra tells us, a *bhikṣu* is to resort to a lonely seat, such as a cave in the mountains, the foot of a tree, or a cremation ground (958). Although in his silent and solitary retreat there may be many things to fear, nevertheless there he may overcome the perils of the world (959–60). For in his retreat, through practicing meditation (962), he may go to the "place" beyond death (960). In responding to Śāriputra's words, the Buddha in this *sutta* echoes the same themes: one should "wander homeless," not becoming preoccupied with questions of where he will sleep the night or what food he will obtain (970–71); the renunciant should resort to a lonely seat (963); there various sorts of obstacles will arise, such as insects, animals, heat and cold, hunger, even attacks from humans (964–66); in spite of these, the renunciant should not be deterred, but should persevere, making great effort (964–69); in his retreat, the renunciant should avoid wrong behavior (967–69); there he should meditate (962, 964); he should be mindful (973, 975); "intent on meditation, he should be very wakeful . . . with self concentrated" (972); and when wandering in a village, he should remain restrained, not uttering a harsh word even to those who may offend him (971). In this way, he may achieve realization (975).

The consistency of the image of Śāriputra as a forest saint in the *Udāna, Theragāthā,* and *Suttanipāta,* and moreover the contrast of this image with that of Śāriputra as the scholarly ideal and champion of settled monastic tradition in the majority of other texts in the Pāli canon arrests our attention. At the least, it indicates that the Pāli texts reflect at least two distinct hagiographical traditions connected with Śāriputra, one dominant in the Pāli canon—reflecting Śāriputra as paradigmatic monastic scholar—and a second, more recessive one—reflecting Śāriputra as a paradigmatic forest saint.

If, as seems not unreasonable, the *Udāna, Theragāthā,* and *Aṭṭhakavagga* accounts of Śāriputra reflect a stratum of Śāriputra's personality predating his monastic, scholarly character, then the earliest evidence shows him as a forest saint. As mentioned, Migot believes that the conversion story represents "the primordial element in [Śāriputra's] legend" (1954, 455). However, the preceding discussion, seen in light of Chapters 1 to 3, suggests a somewhat different way of framing the matter. Śāriputra's forest traits in the conversion story—and even more strikingly in the *Udāna, Theragāthā,* and *Aṭṭhakavagga*—suggest a background and presupposition to the story, namely, Śāriputra's personality as a forest saint. It is not impossible that it was because of, and dependent upon, his forest personality that the conversion story was able to develop in the first place. It is Śāriputra's forest personality, then, that likely provides the real "primordial element" of his legend, although, as we have seen, this element becomes gradually obscured as it is taken into the primitive form of the conversion story, as that story undergoes development, and as Śāriputra's legend as a whole becomes more and more fully monasticized. However, Śāriputra's more or less complete monasticization does not represent the end of his journey. At a relatively advanced time in his history, Śāriputra appears at center stage in certain early Mahāyāna *sūtras* in which his early forest personality comes once again to the fore. For in the *Aṣṭasāhasrikā-prajñāpāramitā Sūtra* we find Śāriputra willing to open himself to the contemplative values of the *prajñāpāramitā.*[86]

Conclusion

As we have seen, there are some clear differences in the ways in which the Sanskrit and Pāli traditions treat Mahākāśyapa. Both traditions know of two facets of

Mahākāśyapa's personality, forest saint and settled monastic. In the Northwestern texts affiliated with the Sarvāstivāda his forest quality is acknowledged while his role as progenitor of established monastic tradition is affirmed, within the same texts and without any particular sense of incompatibility. Mahākāśyapa is essentially a forest saint who, without losing his forest character and even partially because of it, has come to play a central role in the history of settled monasticism. The same kind of pattern is evident in the *Mahāvastu,* also of Northwestern provenance. If we may take Mahākāśyapa's hagiography as a reflection of larger historical trends and attitudes, it appears that within the Sanskrit Buddhism, established tradition viewed forest Buddhism and settled monasticism as compatible elements within a larger whole, standing in generally harmonious relation to one another.

The Pāli sources, by contrast, reflect more tensions and oppositions. Although both aspects of Mahākāśyapa's personality are evident in the Pāli texts, unlike the case of the Sanskrit tradition, these aspects do not appear side by side in the same texts. It is as if the texts are forced to make a choice: the *Theragāthā, Udāna,* and chapter 16 of the *Saṃyuttanikāya* depict Mahākāśyapa as a forest saint with no reference to settled monasticism, whereas the Pāli *vinaya,* setting the tone for the *Dīghanikāya, Majjhimanikāya, Aṅguttaranikāya,* and rest of the *Saṃyuttanikāya,* has him scaled down nearly to the level of the rest of the disciples, with his forest and charismatic saintly character barely hinted at. Again taking Mahākāśyapa as a cipher for larger trends, we find a tension between forest and settled monastic points of view. As reflected in the Pāli *vinaya* treatment of Mahākāśyapa, it would appear that the monastic church finds in itself the norm for renunciant Buddhism and does not willingly admit the legitimacy of the forest wing. The silence in the *Theragāthā, Udāna,* and chapter 16 of the *Saṃyuttanikāya* regarding the monastic Mahākāśyapa raises an interesting question. Does this silence result from the fact that the material in these texts antedates the *vinaya* appropriation of Mahākāśyapa? Or is it to be explained by the fact that it represents a separate tradition unaware of—or perhaps aware of but uninterested in—the settled monastic interpretation? Be this as it may, in the experience of Pāli tradition as reflected in the Pāli canon, settled monasticism and forest Buddhism appear at considerable remove from one another.

The contrast between these two different ways—Northwestern and Southern—of viewing the relation of settled monastic and forest Buddhism evident in Mahākāśyapa's personality is even more striking when one compares the two other saints discussed in this chapter, Upagupta and Śāriputra. In the Northwestern traditions surrounding Upagupta, we have seen that Upagupta is, like Mahākāśyapa, both a forest saint and a lineage holder of the established church. As in the case of Mahākāśyapa, Upagupta's character as a forest saint appears to be part of what legitimates his role as lineage holder. In Upagupta's hagiography, when he trains his disciples, the saint affirms the legitimacy of both forest and settled monastic values. In addition, although settled monasticism is depicted as a distinct kind of Buddhism from that with which Upagupta is most closely associated, it is nonetheless seen (vide Yaśas) as not only legitimate, but also necessary (along with forest and lay Buddhism) to a larger Buddhist whole. However, in Upagupta's hagiography, forest Buddhism clearly takes precedence. The patriarch Upagupta is himself a forest saint. The forest value of the realization of enlightenment in the present life is the ultimate value according to which the utility of various renunciant preoccupations is to be judged. And the practice of meditation in the forest is regarded as the most direct path toward this aim—the activities of settled monasticism are employed less commonly and only when called for in individual cases. Taking Upagupta's hagiography as reflective of larger attitudes and historical trends, we find in Northwestern Buddhism the notion, again, that forest and monastic (and lay) Buddhism are indispensable aspects within the Buddhist whole, each performing a dual role. On the one hand, each element speaks with a particular voice and contrasts with each of the other elements; on the other, each performs its own characteristic functions in more or less harmonious relation to the others and complements them.

If Upagupta may be seen as a prototypical Northwestern Buddhist saint embodying the ideals of that tradition, Śāriputra plays the same role for Southern Buddhism. This is true in the historical sense. From an ancient time, Śāriputra was a—if not *the*—primary saint of Southern Buddhism, which arose in the region of Kauśāmbī among the Sthavira branch of schools and particularly the Vātsīputrīya.[87] Migot believes that Śāriputra was an ancient saint in the Kauśāmbī region; that his charisma expanded with time; that at a certain point he was adopted by the old Sthaviras and set within the early conversion legend; that the Sthaviras developed and augmented Śāriputra's scholarly side—which reflected their own monastic and scholarly orientation—and that this tendency reached its apex in the Pāli canon (1954, 408). Such an explanation is, of course, compatible with the preceding analysis and with the idea that Śāriputra was originally a forest saint who, over the course of time, became more and more fully monasticized.[88]

The Pāli sources are unique in the emphasis they place upon Śāriputra as the preeminent and paradigmatic disciple of the Buddha, seeing him virtually as "a second Buddha" (Migot 1954, 408).[89] And it is in the Pāli sources that Śāriputra most quickly, surely, and completely moves away from being a saint of the forest to becoming the ideal saint of settled monasticism. In this character of Śāriputra, one finds—in Migot's words—a "quasi-unanimity of the Pāli canon on Śāriputra"; and the reason is "because the canon represents the monastic Buddhism of the Sthavira sect" (408). This quasi-unanimity (leaving aside, of course, the *Khuddakanikāya*) is consonant with the role of Pāli tradition as the most conservative of the monastic sects and the one in which the monastic establishment has most clearly and definitively stated the precedence of settled monastic values over those of the forest life.

In the Pāli treatment of Śāriputra, we find the same kind of pattern as in its treatment of Mahākāśyapa. Although in the Pāli literature taken as a whole Śāriputra is depicted with both forest and settled monastic features, these are typically not found side by side within the same texts. In the *Mahāvagga,* Śāriputra's scholarly side is not yet evident, but his forest side is hinted at. In the *Khuddakanikaya,* his forest side is prominent, but there is no mention of his monastic, scholarly side. In the majority of canonical texts in Pāli, Śāriputra's monastic side does not admit the forest as a critical dimension of his personality. One may not be wrong to read in these divergent portraits a more pervasive belief—at least in the monastically oriented texts of the *vinaya*—that forest Buddhism does not have a central role to play within normative Buddhism.

Such a belief is more explicit in certain negative attitudes toward meditation and forest Buddhism evident in the Pāli versions of the conversion story. A particularly revealing example is provided by the treatment of Sañjayin, the heretic teacher to whom Śāriputra and Maudgalyāyana first go when they leave the world. As Migot shows, this teacher is most likely a forest renunciant who teaches meditation or yoga (1954, 447). In the Pāli sources, Sañjayin is presented in an extremely negative light. Śāriputra and Maudgalyāyana attain everything that Sañjayin has to teach and, having ascertained that he has nothing further to offer, abandon him, seeking another, better teacher. In the Pāli sources, Sañjayin, who is presented as frankly hostile to the dharma of the Buddha, does everything in his power to prevent Śāriputra, Mahāmaudgalyāyana, and the rest of his five hundred disciples from studying with the Buddha. When they finally go to the Buddha, they repudiate Sañjayin and break with his tradition. After they leave, Sañjayin—owing to his inveterately evil nature, which has now been revealed—dies vomiting blood (447–48).

The Northwestern treatment of Sañjayin stands in sharp contrast to that of the Pāli.[90] While Śāriputra and Maudgalyāyana are still his disciples, the teacher falls ill. As they are caring for him, Sañjayin predicts the arrival of the Buddha and affirms the Blessed One's sanctity, enjoining his two disciples to study with him. When Sañjayin's dies, Śāriputra and Maudgalyāyana feel great appreciation for their former teacher and realize that his dharma was truly marvelous. In the Northwestern texts, then, Sañjayin is not, as in Pāli tradition, a confirmed heretic hostile to the Buddha but rather a precursor—in Migot's words, a kind of John the Baptist—who paves the way for the one to follow, announcing his coming and bidding his disciples to follow him. Migot is surely right that in the Pāli and the Northwestern treatments of Sañjayin, "one has certainly here a reflection of two opposed tendencies," the one more scholarly, the other more meditative or yogic. Migot continues,

> For, we have seen that the doctrine of Sañjayin is probably that of yoga; are the sects which are favorable to him not the same that are favorable to this tendency? The first group, unfavorable to Sañjayin, contain above all Theravāda texts, and it is known that the monastic Buddhism of the Sthavira was not kindly disposed toward magic and yoga. In contrast, the Chinese and above all Tibetan canon of the Mūlasarvāstivāda is much more strongly impregnated with yoga. . . . (1954, 448)

Migot's observation may be generalized. The positive treatment in the Northwestern texts of Sañjayin reflects the generally positive evaluation on the part of Northwestern monasticism of forest Buddhism, its central meditative preoccupation, and its rightful and necessary place within the whole. It is ultimately this that explains the affirmation, noted by Migot, of magic and yoga in the Northwestern texts, of which we shall presently see other examples. By contrast, the negative attitude toward Sañjayin within the Pāli sources reflects a correspondingly negative evaluation of forest Buddhism, interpreted as separate from, and in some sense inimical to, the normative Buddhism of settled monasticism.

The preceding summary makes possible some further insight into the two-tiered model of Buddhism. As mentioned, the two-tiered model in contemporary scholarship was developed primarily out of a study of Pāli materials and, among these, those that reflect settled monasticism. The two-tiered model is, in effect, a reflection of the attitudes and beliefs of the monastic establishment in Pāli Buddhism. The fact that the forest saints are ignored in the two-tiered model and that the forest dimensions of Mahākāśyapa and Śāriputra are ignored by Pāli monastic tradition are thus reflections of the same thing: Pāli Buddhism's particular attitudes toward forest Buddhism.[91] This discussion also makes clear the limitations of the two-tiered model: not only does it not necessarily apply to other Buddhist traditions, for example, that of the northwest—it has little applicability to the forest dimensions of Pāli Buddhism itself.

It is important to reformulate our understanding of early Buddhism and that of the Nikāya schools to include in an integral way the forest traditions not only in service of a more balanced and accurate view of the "pre-Mahāyāna" traditions themselves, but also for the considerable impact that this recasting can have on our conceptualization of the relation of earlier to later Buddhism in India. The portrait of Upagupta as guru for his disciples as presented in the *Aśokarājāvadāna* is a case in point. That depiction is, as noted, particularly rich in its themes of the priority of inner realization over external forms of the dharma; the sometimes implicit, sometimes explicit critique of the conventional values of settled monasticism; the requirement of unconditional commitment of disciple to master; the master's flexibility and unconventionality in training methods and skill in guiding disciples advanced in meditation; the beliefs that the guru has power over the phenomenal world and is ultimately behind the visions and meditation experiences of the disciples; the intense devotion of disciple for master; and so on. All of these illustrate common assumptions and expectations of what a teacher is in forest Buddhism and how such a person works.

Modern buddhology, of course, is not unfamiliar with such images of the guru, but it generally has seen them as characteristic of Tantric Buddhism in India and Tibet and not of the earlier, more "conservative" traditions.[92] The particular conformation of the Tantric guru is, in turn, often explained as the result of non-Buddhist influences.[93] It must come as a surprise, then, that here, in the heart of the lineage of the patriarchs of Northwestern Buddhism is to be found an image of the Buddhist teacher that in many of its essential characteristics mirrors that found in the Vajrayāna. This discrepancy is to be explained, of course, by the fact that buddhology has derived its understanding of the teacher in earlier Buddhism from monastic models, whereas the teacher in the Vajrayāna is essentially a forest figure. When forest images of the teacher in earlier Buddhism are compared with the forest images in the Vajrayāna, then, as we have seen, there is a much closer correspondence.

Notes

1. For a detailed discussion of these, see Chapter 9. On Mahākāśyapa, see Lamotte 1944–80, 87–103, 190–96, 287, 615, 654, 1046–47, 1399, 1761, and 2332–34; 1958, 19, 24, 71, 101, 137, 226–27, 191–92, and passim; and 1962, 149–50. For additional references, see below in this chapter.

2. The Theravāda commentary on the *Aṅguttaranikāya,* the *Manorathapūraṇī,* follows suit (*Mrp* 1:161). The passage in the Chinese *Ekottarāgama* parallel to the *Aṅguttara* portrays Mahākāśyapa as typically preeminent among those who follow the *dhutaguṇa*s (Lamotte 1958, 765–66, citing the *Ekottarāgama.*

3. In *Mv,* he is several other times explicitly connected with these practices (*Mv* 1:64.14 [Jns., 1:53]; *Mv* 1:66.16 [Jns., 1:55]; *Mv* 1:71.12 [Jns., 1:57]).

4. Lamotte provides a useful summary of this material (1958, 191–92, 226–27).

5. No reference is made here to texts dealing with Mahākāśyapa composed outside of India. Of particular interest in this regard are the "Five Records of the Lamp," five texts dating from the Sung dynasty (960–1279) in China that trace the lineage of transmission from Śākyamuni. These texts, which contain biographic images of Mahākāśyapa, have been helpfully summarized by Dumoulin (1988, 7–10). The materials presented in these texts appear sometimes to duplicate material found in the Indian texts summarized above and sometimes to provide stories and images not found in those texts. See also McRae 1986, 79–82.

6. The *Mahāvastu* provides an account of the saint, beginning with a former life, in which his reputation as a meditating ascetic living in solitude in the Himalayas is already reflected (*Mv* 2:160 [Jns., 2:110]).

7. We are told that he himself owned eighty cartloads of gold, five hundred bondsmen, five hundred bondswomen, five hundred head of cattle, five hundred fields and villages, and so on (*Mv* 3:67 [Jns., 3:49]).

8. *Mv* 3:67.5 (Jns., 3:49); cf. *BHSD* 346, s.v. *pilotika.* See also *Mv* 3:53.14, 16 (Jns., 3:54). See also *BHSD* 354, s.v. *pailottika,* and 395, s.v. *plotikā.*

9. He remarks, "And when I saw him, there came to me the unambiguous awareness that I was looking on the perfect Buddha, on the Exalted One, who was all-knowing, all-seeing, and possessed of absolute perfect knowledge" (*Mv* 3:67 [Jns., 3:50]).

10. See Hofinger 1954, 195. Hofinger remarks on the relative antiquity of these verses (193, n. 3).

11. The Buddha says, "If a man should accept a disciple in complete possession of his mind, and then, though he was not perfectly enlightened should claim to be so; though not all-seeing, should claim to be so; though he was limited in knowledge and insight, should claim to have absolute knowledge and insight, his head would split in seven. As for me, O Kāśyapa, I claim to be perfectly enlightened, because I am so; I claim to be all-knowing, because I am so; I claim to be all-seeing because I am so; I claim to have absolute knowledge and insight, because I have them" (*Mv* 3:68 [Jns., 3:50]). This appeal to a magico-religious phenomenon (the heads of those who lie about such matters split in seven) is reminiscent of the story of the Buddha's enlightenment, where he appeals, not to human authority, but to the earth divinity.

12. Elsewhere in *Mv* we are told that Kāśyapa was purified through the *dhutaguṇa*s *(dhutadharmaviśuddha)* (*Mv* 1:80.3 [Jns., 1:56]), and as his personality in the text is closely bound up with them, one cannot think of his training under the Buddha apart from the forest life in general and these practices in particular. As the organ of restraint the text specifically mentions here the *prātimokṣa.* The prominence of forest renunciation in general and in particular the *dhutaguṇa* in relation to Mahākāśyapa's personality, as defined else-

where in the text (see references to the *dhutaguṇa* just below), raises the question of how the term *prātimokṣa* is to be understood in this passage.

13. He is to practice mindfulness of the body and to guard the doors of his six senses. When he sees an object with his eye, he is not to make it an object of thought and is to avoid desire for it, thus practicing restraint of sight. He shall practice the same with sounds, scents, tastes, sensations of touch, and objects of thought (*Mv* 3:69–70 [Jns., 3:51–52]).

14. Kāśyapa is further to train in the awareness of the rise and fall, in turn, of each of the five *upādānaskandhas* (personality aggregates associated with grasping). He shall observe that such and such is material form *(rūpa),* the uprising of material form, the cessation of material form, and observe the same for feeling *(vedanā),* perception *(saṃjñā),* the karmic formations *(saṃskāra),* and consciousness *(vijñāna).*

15. Pāli tradition similarly says that Mahākāśyapa accepted from the Buddha hempen, rag robes *(sāṇāni paṃsukūlāni)* (see H., 2:143, n. 3).

16. Thus *Mv* calls him *dhutadhura,* "foremost in the *dhuta(guṇas)*" (or perhaps, "he whose burden [= discipline] is the *dhutaguṇas*") (*Mv* 1:82.7 [Jns., 1:57]), *dhutadharmasamañgī,* "provided with the *dhutadharmas (= dhutaguṇas)*" (*Mv* 1:82.11 [Jns., 1:57]), *dhutaraja,* "king of the *dhuta (guṇas)*" (*Mv* 1:77.2 [Jns., 1:55] and 1:82.6 [Jns., 1:57]), *dhutadharmaviśuddha,* "purified through the *dhutadharmas*" (*Mv* 1:80.3 [Jns., 1:56]), and, very frequently, *dhutadharmadhara,* "maintainer of the *dhutadharmas*" (*Mv* 1:99.8, 14; 100.1, 4, 7, 10, 13; 101.4, 8, 11, 14; 102.3, 6, 9, 12; 103.1; and 123.7 [Jns., 1:66–70 and 83] and passim). (Jones renders these terms very vaguely and thus the specific character of the *dhutaguṇas* is not evident in his translation. Thus *dhuta* in *dhutadhura, dhutadharmasamañgī,* and *dhutadharmadhara* is translated as "pious," in *dhutadharmaviśuddha* as "piety," and in *dhutara[ā]ja* as "saintly.")

17. These two declarations, of his transcendent identity and of his magical powers, call to mind the similar "self-declarations" made by the Buddha mentioned in Chapter 2. What is important here is that Mahākāśyapa is referring to no human authority but is speaking on his own authority, as a realized saint. Particularly interesting here is Mahākāśyapa's bold claim of stupendous powers that cannot possibly be concealed. Could this perhaps be an oblique reference to the *vinaya* rules discouraging the claim of powers in general (cf. Chapter 1)?

18. The image of Ānanda articulated in these sections of *Mv* is quite interesting and contains several traits: first, he wanders around with a large group of disciples, and Mahākāśyapa finds this blameworthy: the Buddha said that no more than three renunciants can eat together. Second, his disciples are immature and unattained in meditation: they do not guard the doors of their senses and are greedy. Third, Ānanda has a special connection with the *vinaya,* and particularly the nuns' *vinaya:* he received it. Moreover, Ānanda has defenders among the organized monastic *saṃgha:* his loyal follower is a nun, who attacks Mahākāśyapa in the most shameless and aggressive manner, precisely for his critique of Ānanda. The pattern has some coherence: the monk, who, associated with the *vinaya* and the organized *saṃgha,* is connected with large groups of undisciplined monks and is indirectly associated with vicious and unfair attacks on the forest renunciant, embodied in the figure of Mahākāśyapa. Does this story in the *Mahāvastu* reflect a certain tension between the Buddhism of the settled monastery and the Buddhism of the forest renunciant? The evidence of this account is too fragmentary to be sure, but such a possibility is suggested by the frequency with which the same configuration of themes arises in other texts, such as the songs of Pārāpariya and Phussa in the *Theragāthā* (discussed in Chapter 3), as well as in other texts to be considered, in which, it is clear, just such a tension is in question.

19. When Mahākāśyapa arrives, suddenly the encasements of the corpse break open at the feet and Mahākāśyapa pays his last obeisance, taking the Buddha's feet in his hands

and touching them to his head. "Kāśyapa, his mind full of the greatest reverence for the Master, fell on his face, and again and again caressed with his hands the Sage's feet which were marked with perfect circles" (*Mv* 1:77.13–16 [Jns., 1:55–56]). At this, miraculously, the pyre spontaneously bursts into flame.

20. This funeral lament is one example of a more general pattern of specific verses chanted in the context of a cremation rite. For other examples of similar verses, see Chapter 11.

21. The liturgical nature and magical dimensions of the event cannot be doubted. The chanting, which is to be done "without a break and in perfect unison," will unite the Buddha's teaching, will allow it to have renown among gods and humans, and will allow saints to appear in the future (*Mv* 1:80.15–18 [Jns., 1:56]). When the teaching is recited, the *devas* assemble to hear the recital, the earth quakes, and celestial drums sound and garlands of flowers rain down (1:81–82 [1:57]). Then the *devas* chant joyful verses.

22. The material cited here is to be found in the *Kṣudrakavastu (phran.tshegs.kyi.gshi)* section of the Tibetan *vinaya ('dul.ba),* in the Derge edition, cited here, volume da, 290a, ff. In his *Life of the Buddha* (1884), Rockhill has presented some of this material, working from the "East India Office copy of the Bkah.hgyur" (vi) (edition unspecified). In this work, Rockhill sometimes translates word for word, sometimes summarizes several pages of Tibetan in a few sentences, and often omits large sections altogether. Nevertheless, his work is useful in indicating some of the major themes of this section of the Tibetan version.

23. For the account of Mahākāśyapa's previous lives, cf. *Gms* 3:1, 172–74 (Hofinger 1954, 193–97).

24. Thus, for example, when Ajātaśatru first sees Mahākāśyapa, he is reminded of the Buddha so strongly that he falls senseless to the ground (*V*-t, D., *'dul.ba,* da, 305a [R., 151]).

25. For example, as in *Mv,* when the Buddha dies, there is an earthquake and Mahākāśyapa, using his magical powers, divines its cause (*V*-t, D., *'dul.ba,* da, 290a [R., 141]). Like *Mv, V*-t tells the story of the funeral pyre that will not light and repeats Aniruddha's explanation that this was because Mahākāśyapa had not yet arrived (da, 295b [R., 144]). As in *Mv,* Mahākāśyapa uncovers the body of the Buddha and worships it, after which the flame spontaneously leaps up (da, 296b [R., 144–45]). As in the case of *Mv,* so here Mahākāśyapa is concerned that the Buddha's teachings will be lost and therefore convenes a council to ensure their preservation. Again as in *Mv,* in *Vms,* throughout the description of the events of the first council, Mahākāśyapa is clearly presented as the leader of the *saṃgha.* He gives directives to Ānanda, Pūrṇa, and the other great arhants, and he decides where and how this great event shall occur (da, 301b [R., 149–50]). See also *Gms* 3:1.172–74 (parts missing) (Hofinger 1954, 193–97).

26. As we shall see, it falls to other texts of the Northwestern tradition to deal with the other phases of Mahākāśyapa's life.

27. See Rockhill's comment, p. 148.

28. Mahākāśyapa has just rebuked Ānanda for his many errors and omissions while he was the Buddha's attendant. Then, "great was Ānanda's grief, but he called to mind what the Blessed One had said to him shortly before his death. 'Ānanda,' he had said, 'sorrow not, neither be distressed nor afflicted. Thou must turn to the *bhikṣu* Mahākāśyapa (as to the head of the order). Be patient and do as he shall tell thee' " (*V*-t, D., *'dul.ba,* da, 309a [R., 155]).

29. The five hundred arhants request him to preside over the assembly, and he therefore takes his seat on the lion throne.

30. Thus Ānanda says that the Buddha transmitted the lineage to Mahākāśyapa, who, in turn, transmitted it to himself, Ānanda (*V*-t, D., *'dul.ba,* da, 321a [R., 166]). And the

one to whom Ānanda transmitted the lineage, Śāṇakavāsin, remarks to his chosen disciple, Upagupta, on this same lineage: the Buddha—Mahākāśyapa—Ānanda—Śāṇakavāsin (da, 323a–b [R., 170]).

31. In Chinese, the *A yü wang chuan* (T. 2042) translated into Chinese by Fa-ch'in the early third century C.E., translated by Przyluski (1923).

32. The following summarizes the "Avadāna du Nirvāṇa de Mahākāśyapa," *Ara* 114a–116b (Prz., 327–40). Lamotte provides a list of sources treating Mahākāśyapa's final nirvāṇa (1944–80, 191, n.1).

33. It is interesting that Ānanda seems quite the devoted disciple of Mahākāśyapa, just as elsewhere in the tradition he is the devoted disciple of the Buddha. We see an image of Ānanda's devotion when, after receiving transmission from Mahākāśyapa, "Ānanda followed [Mahākāśyapa] constantly and did not leave him. He was afraid that [Mahākāśyapa] would enter *nirvāṇa,* or else that he would not see him again, and that is why he followed him" (*Ara* 114c [Prz., 330]).

34. Relics that, the texts says, are "authentic and marvellous, which are charged with merits that are good, pure and innumerable" (*Ara* 114b [Prz., 329]). Mahākāśyapa then travels by magical flight to various places, including the four holy places and the eight great stūpas, prostrating himself and making offerings. He also flies to the palace of Sāgara in the ocean and venerates a tooth of the Buddha. Next he journeys to the heaven of the thirty-three *deva*s and worships another Buddha's tooth there, whereupon the multitude of *deva*s with their chief Śakra (Indra) prostrate before the saint and make offerings to him. Realizing that Mahākāśyapa is near the end of his days, they hang their heads with grief.

35. As the time for the final nirvāṇa of Mahākāśyapa draws near, the earth quakes in six ways. The saint predicts that when Ānanda and King Ajātaśatru come to the mountain, it will open to enable them to enter, and when they leave, it will close again. At this point, Śakra and his innumerable *deva* followers arrive, showering offerings of celestial flowers and perfumed powders on the body of Mahākāśyapa. When they have prostrated and made their offerings, the saint passes away.

36. Thereupon, Śakra cries, "The pain caused by the entrance of the Tathāgata into *nirvāṇa* has just begun to subside. Today the venerable Kāśyapa, in entering *nirvāṇa,* has redoubled our grief" (*Ara* 114c–115a [Prz., 332]). Upon the saint's passing, the spirit of Pippala Cave declares, "Today this cave is deserted and bare. In the kingdom of Magadha, all is empty and silent. In the streets of the villages, the unfortunate are weakened and afflicted. He always took pity on the poor and helped them. Now, this multitude of destitute have lost their protector. Henceforth, the wretched and the downtrodden are deprived of the good dharma" (*Ara* 115a [Prz., 332]).

37. An interesting parallel to this event of the opening of the mountain and revelation of the saint is provided by the *Saddharmapuṇḍarīka Sūtra.* In the *stūpasaṃdarśana* chapter (*Sps* 149–65 [Kn., 227–54, trans. from Skt.; Hurwitz 1976, 183–94, trans. from Ch.]), the central stūpa of the text opens, revealing the ancient Buddha Prabhūtaratna sitting inside. Like Mahākāśyapa, this Buddha has in one way passed beyond but in another he is alive and ever present.

38. Lamotte, drawing upon the *Divyāvadāna, vinaya* of the Mūlasarvāstivādins, the *Kṣudrakavastu,* the *Saṃyuktāgama* and the *Fen pieh Kung tê lun* (T. 1507), gives an account of Mahākāśyapa's passing that repeats the essential elements of this account (1958, 226–27; 768). Lamotte adds the detail that Mahākāśyapa, in his mountain, has entered into nirvaṇa or *nirodhasaṃāpatti,* the attainment of cessation (768).

The close connection between Mahākāśyapa and Maitreya receives elucidation in another text from the Sanskrit tradition, the *Maitreyavyākaraṇa* (Lamotte 1958, 777–78), which, Lamotte tells us, is found in a number of versions showing little variation. In this text, we are told that in the distant future, when human life has attained a span of eighty thousand years, a son will be born to a certain man and woman of brahmin caste. Like his father, this child will teach eighty thousand students. However, moved by the fragility of life, he will retire into the forest and, radiating compassion, will attain enlightenment as the *samyaksaṃbuddha* Maitreya. After converting many, accompanied by a crowd of followers, he will ascend Mount Kukkuṭapāda. The mountain will open, revealing the skeleton of Mahākāśyapa, who—in this variant of the story—appears quite dead. Maitreya will hold this tiny skeleton in his hand, saying that it is of Mahākāśyapa, disciple of Śākyamuni, who lived in an epoch when people lived for no more than a hundred years. This Mahākāśyapa, he will explain, was first among those following the *dhutaguṇa*s and codified the dharma after the passing of Śākyamuni. This revelation will provoke the amazement of those present, and all will attain the state of an arhant.

39. Is this a sign of his honoring of her offering? Is this perhaps also an indication of his observance of "one eating," a member of the *dhutaguṇa* list (see Chapter 9)?

40. This story is also recounted in *Da* 80–84. This facet of Mahākāśyapa's personality is mentioned in Buddhaghosa's *Visuddhimagga* (*Vsm* 403–4 [Nyāṇamoli 1976, 441]) quoted below. *Dp*-c tells a similar story (1:423–30 [Bg., 2:86–89]).

41. When the Buddha is made aware of Mahākāśyapa's rejection of the gods' offering, so the author of this text informs us, he directs that his disciples must take the food that is given them.

42. *V*-p 2:284ff. (H., 5:393ff.). Cf. Lamotte 1958, 136–38.

43. However, it is alluded to in a story concerning his rag robe, cited below.

44. One story has him finding the laity unfriendly to the *saṃgha,* which the Buddha on investigation discovers has occurred because the *bhikṣus* are behaving improperly. The discovery leads to a rule (*V*-p 3:144–46 [H., 1:246–48]). In another story, a man comes to Mahākāśyapa for ordination, and when Ānanda declares he cannot proclaim the person's name because he is his teacher, the Buddha allows proclamation by clan name (*V*-p 1:92–93 [H., 4:118–19]). In another story in the same location, two people want to be ordained by Mahākāśyapa and cannot agree on who should go first. The Buddha allows them to be ordained together. In yet another story, Mahākāśyapa gets his robe wet, and another rule emerges from this event (*V*-p 1:109–10 [H., 4:142–45]). In another, Mahākāśyapa's robe becomes heavy, and various rules are laid down concerning robes (*V*-p 1:297 [H., 4:423]).

45. E.g., *Mn* 1:214 (Hn., 1:266); *An* 1:23 (WH., 1:16); and *Syn* 2:156 (RW., 2:109).

46. Materials on Mahākāśyapa in the later books of the *Khuddakanikāya* are not considered here, as they fall outside the scope of the present discussion.

47. In more detail, the account in the *Ta* includes the following themes:

a. The highest life is one of forest renunciation, defined by the four *niśraya*s: "For whom leftover scraps suffice as food, smelly urine as medicine, the root of a tree as lodging, a rag from a dustheap as robe, he truly is a man of the four quarters" (*Ta* 1057).

b. One goes clad in a robe from a dustheap (*Ta* 1080, 1081).

c. The saint resides in a mountain retreat, dangerous and difficult to reach (*Ta* 1058).

d. His is a life of perpetual wandering (*Ta* 1090).

e. The practice of meditation is the heart of the Buddha's teaching, and it is this upon which one is engaged in retreat (*Ta* 1058, 1059–61, 1066, etc.).

f. Solitude is necessary for the successful practice of meditation by the forest retreatant (*Ta* 1069, 1072).

g. One should be wary of associating with a crowd, where one is distracted and concentration is hard to attain (*Ta* 1051).

h. One should be on guard against being greedy for good food, as this undermines the spiritual life (*Ta* 1052).

i. The saint follows the practice of complete nondiscrimination regarding food. Here the story is told of the eating of a leper's finger, reminiscent of the story told of the leper washerwoman, although the setting, the donor, and the actual story are different (*Ta* 1054–56). The same story is told in the *Milindapañha* (395 [T.R. 1890–94, 2:330]).

j. One should avoid visiting homes of the highborn, as this interferes with concentration (*Ta* 1052).

k. One should avoid visiting the homes of the highborn, as this involves one with considerations of honor, which are hard to give up (*Ta* 1053).

l. The saint extols the forest life, with its solitude and its beauty (*Ta* 1062ff.).

m. The goal of realization is won by the forest life (*Ta* 1077).

n. The saint declares his preeminence as a practitioner of the *dhutaguṇas*: "Except for the great sage himself, I am outstanding in the qualities of [the *dhutaguṇas*]. There is none like me" (*Ta* 1087).

48. See *Dp*-c retelling (1:423–30 [Bg., 2:86–89]).

49. Mahākāśyapa's reticence is revealed in a passage, repeated several times in chapter 16, about two monks who talk a great deal, try to outtalk one another, and argue over "which will speak the more? which will speak the better? which will speak the longer?" The Buddha strongly rebukes these monks, indicating that talking about what one has learned is not the dharma that he teaches and that such practice is "futile" (2:105 [2:138]). The two brethren are overcome with remorse, prostrate themselves at the Buddha's feet, confess their transgression—"so foolish, so stupid, so wrong were we"—and vow that they will not act in such a manner in the future (2:203–6 [2:137–39]). Here the reticent way of the forest saint Mahākāśyapa is defined as the true dharma, whereas the more loquacious and contentious approach is rejected. That this latter is intended to refer to practice current within nonforest renunciation is suggested by the fact that one version of this passage is followed by the Buddha's remark, "Yes, Kāśyapa, there was a time when the senior brethren were forest dwellers and commenders of the forest life," and his comment that this is no longer the case (2:108 [2:140–41]).

50. The Buddha says, "I, brethren, according as I desire [can], aloof from sense and evil, attain to and abide in First Jhāna, wherein thought is applied and sustained, which is born of solitude and filled with zest and pleasant emotion. Kassapa too brethren, can so attain and abide." The same is said in turn of each of the three next *jhāna*s, the four formless meditative states, *nirodhasamāpatti,* the attainment of cessation, the five mundane *abhijñā*s or superknowledges, concluding with the Buddha's confirmation that Mahākāśyapa has also, like himself, won the sixth, transcendent attainment (2:214 [2:145]).

51. E.g., 2:218–22 contains a biography of Mahākāśyapa that in its themes duplicates many found in the *Mahāvastu* account. The story of the exchange of robes is found at *Syn* 2:219–22 (2:149–50). Mahākāśyapa's declaration of his magical powers in the *Mv* is paralleled by *Syn* 2:216 and 222 (2:146 and 150). The criticisms in the Mūlasarvāstivādin *vinaya* of Ānanda for having young, ill-trained, and ill-behaved disciples are found at *Syn* 2:217 (2:147). The conflict between the partisans of Ānanda and the partisans of Kāśyapa is reflected at *Syn* 2:215 (2:145).

52. The Pāli commentaries also contain legendary material with connections to the non-Pāli sources. Cf. *Mrp* 1:133–34, 161–83, and passim; *Ta*-c 121–43 (C.R. 1937 359–68); *Vsm* 15 (N., 1:16), 68 (N., 1:68–69), 403–4 (N., 1:441), and 430 (N., 1:472); *Dp*-c 1:258–60 (Bg., 1:311–12) and 1:423–30 (Bg., 2:86–89). For example, Buddhaghosa tells a story illustrating Mahākāśyapa's special regard for the poor. "The Elder Mahā-Kassapa, it seems, after spending seven days in attainment, stood at the house door of a man in poor circumstances called Kākavaḷiya in order to show favour to the poor. His wife saw the Elder, and she poured into his bowl the unsalted sour gruel that she had cooked for her husband. The Elder took it and placed it in the Blessed One's hand. The Blessed One resolved to make it enough for the Greater Community of *bhikkhus*. What was brought in

a single bowl became enough for all. And on the seventh day Kākavaḷiya became a rich man'' (*Vsm* 1:403–4 [N., 1:441]. See a similar story in *Dp*-c 1:423–30 [Bg., 2:86–89]).

53. It may be thought that to place Ānanda in this role involves a contradiction, because Ānanda is quite clearly the Buddha's disciple, not that of Mahākāśyapa. It could be argued that in question here is succession rather than discipleship: Ānanda succeeds Mahākāśyapa in the hierarchy of masters, but this does not imply a relation of discipleship. This point of view has merit, but the issue is debatable. These texts do not deal with historical persons with consistent personalities or roles but with images of saints that may conflict with or even contradict one another. It may make logical sense that Ānanda is the Buddha's, not Mahākāśyapa's, principal disciple, but in the *Aśokarājāvadāna* Ānanda is clearly placed in the role of the subordinate disciple, when he is criticized by Mahākāśyapa, when he exhibits devotion and deference to the master, and when he receives the transmission from him.

54. Although, as we have seen, upon Maitreya's coming he may leap into the air and effect an autocremation.

55. This tendency is seen in the *Sthirāvadāna,* where the stories of the previous lives of thirty-six great arhants are told. In this text, where the arhants are arranged in order of importance, Mahākāśyapa is listed first, whereas Kauṇḍinya is found toward the end of the series, as number thirty-three (Hofinger 1954, 9, 17–20).

56. In his discussion of the first council, Bareau seems to favor such an interpretation, remarking that ''[Mahākāśyapa's] vast wisdom and his good qualities attract to him the veneration and the offerings of all the faithful, monks and laity, and set him in fact, if not by right, at the head of the community'' (Bareau 1970–71, 2:232).

57. Migot believes that it is this monastic personality of Mahākāśyapa that accounts for his unrelenting critique of Ānanda. Thus, Migot sees in these critiques the movement to the fore of the established monastic church, with the concomitant displacement of another kind of Buddhism, embodied in Ānanda, characterized by devotion and a close personal relationship with the guru (Migot 1954, 407).

58. The following discussion of Upagupta is indebted to the fine recent study of this saint by John Strong 1992 (see my review [Ray 1993]). This section also draws on Waddell 1897; Maung Kin 1903; Lamotte 1944–80, 572–73 and 1958, 226–32 and passim; Witanachchi 1976; and Strong 1983 and 1985.

59. See Strong's summary of texts containing information on Upagupta (1992, 9–10). See also Lamotte 1958, 232 and Maung Kin 1903, 219–42.

60. *Da* 348–418. These two chapters are also contained in the *Aśokāvadāna,* ed. Sujitkumar Mukhopadhyaya, 1–28 and 75–93 (Strong 1983, 173–97, 238–56). Mukhopadhyaya's edition contains four chapters from the *Da,* the two in question here along with two others, collectively presenting the legend of King Aśoka.

61. Partial trans., Ernst Waldschmidt in Lüders 1926, 77–83.

62. T. 99, 2:161b–70c (partial trans. Przyluski 1914, 518–22).

63. *Gms* 3, pt. 1:3–7; T. 1448, 24:41c–42b (partial trans., Przyluski 1914, 558–59; abridged trans. of part of the Tibetan, Rockhill 1884, 164–70). For a listing of additional texts containing information on the Indian legend and cult of Upagupta, see Strong 1992, 9–10.

64. Przyluski argues that these stories were all part of a common Mathuran tradition (1923, 8). Strong sees these two cycles as quite possibly having originally existed separately, with the mature Upagupta legend being the result of their combination at some point (1992, 11).

65. *Da* 348–49 (Strong 1983, 174; translation quoted and commented on, Strong 1992, 24ff.).

66. *Da* 351–52 (Strong 1983, 176–78; translation quoted and commented on, Strong 1992, 58–60).

67. *Da* 356 (Strong 1983, 184–86); see also *Ara* 118c–119a (Prz., 353).

68. *Da* 356–64 (Strong 1983, 185–97). See also *Ara* 118c–120b (Prz., 353–62). For a list of other soures treating this famous encounter, cf. Strong 1992, 315, n. 2.

69. Frauwallner (1956, 28ff.) believes that Upagupta's legend at this point shows an obvious insertion.

70. Lamotte 1958, 230. Lamotte in the same place tells us that this legendary material concerning the five masters of the dharma, from Mahākāśyapa to Upagupta, has no counterpart in the Sinhalese tradition. Lamotte concludes, "Of the silence of the Pāli sources one must conclude that the legend of the five masters forms no part of the primitive tradition, but has been elaborated subsequent to the evangelization of Ceylon." However, Lamotte says, it is nevertheless true that the legend "on the other hand is solidly implanted on the Indian subcontinent in the testimony of both texts and of monuments." He mentions Mt. Kukkuṭapāda, the modern Kurkihar some twenty miles north of Bodh-Gayā, as well as other physical remains (1958, 230). In contrast to the wide acceptance of these five masters, those depicted as succeeding them differ in the sources. For example, in the Mūlasarvāstivāda tradition, Upagupta is succeeded by Dhītika, Kṛṣṇa, and Sudarśana (Lamotte 1958, 770–71).

71. He is called by the derogatory name *mahallaka,* "an old person" (*BHSD* 421); cf. Durt 1980 and Strong 1992, 68–70.

72. *Ara* 122b (Prz., 376–77). See Strong's slightly different rendition of this event (1992, 122–23).

73. Cf. Strong 1992, 145ff.

74. These include Lumbinīvana, where he was born; Kapilavastu, where he made the "great departure" from home; Bodh-Gayā, where he attained enlightenment; Sārnāth, where he preached his first sermon; Śrāvastī, where he carried out "the great miracle;" Sāṃkāśya, where he descended from the sky in the company of the gods; and Kuśinagarī, where he entered into final nirvāṇa. Lumbinī, Bodh-Gayā, Sārnāth, and Kuśinagarī are the "four great places of pilgrimage" marking the locations of the four major events of the Buddha's life (birth, enlightenment, first sermon, passing away). Kapilavastu, Śrāvastī, and Sāṃkāśya represent three additional pilgrimage places of somewhat less renown. Mitra (1971, 8–9) mentions the four great places and then another set of four lesser pilgrimage places associated with the life of the Buddha: two from the list given in *Da,* Śrāvastī and Sāṃkāśya, and two additional sites not mentioned there, Rājagṛha, where he tamed the elephant Nālāgiri, and Vaiśālī, where he was offered a bowl of honey by a monkey.

75. On Upagupta's special ties with hagiography as a genre, see Strong 1985.

76. See Strong's discussion, 1992, 186–208. See also Maung Kin 1903, 232–41; Duroiselle 1904; and Denis 1977.

77. Cf., e.g., Strong 1992, references to Hsüan-tsang and 253ff.

78. Cf. Strong 1983, 86–87.

79. Cf. Strong's discussion, 1983, 86–89.

80. On Śāriputra, also see Lamotte 1944–80, 87–103, 118–121, 190–96, 287, 621–49, 701, 1630–32, 1760, and 2331–32; 1958, 19, 201, 372 and passim; and 1962, 141–42; and Nyanaponika 1966. In the interests of stylistic consistency, the Sanskrit rendering, Śāriputra, is used in this discussion.

81. Migot points out that the *Mahāvagga* does not represent the "original text" of this legend, but rather itself shows some development. Instead, the hypothesized original text provides the common source for the earliest versions, including that of the *Mahāvagga* (1954, 455).

82. Following Migot's useful summary, 1954, 427.

83. The developed versions of the conversion story then suggest a split between scholarly and meditative, not evident in the primitive conversion story. Such a split may explain the significance of the pair of chief disciples, Śāriputra and Maudgalyāyana, the former credited with unequaled *prajñā,* the latter with unparalleled *abhijñā.* As we shall see, the early texts acknowledge two ways within Buddhism—that of meditation and that of textual learning. The identification of two chief disciples would appear to represent another acknowledgment, this time in a hagiographic frame of reference, of these same two trends. Moreover, Śāriputra's preeminence is what one would expect in the Pāli and other texts reflecting primarily the views of settled monasticism.

84. For many other examples of this scholastic character of Śāriputra in the Pāli canon, see Migot 1954, 466–69.

85. Such would seem to explain the apparent contradiction, noted by Migot (1954, 503ff.), that although Maudgalyāyana is said to be foremost in miraculous powers—which, as we have seen, are traditionally believed to accompany meditational attainment—such powers are also abundantly attributed to Śāriputra and, in some texts, are even said to surpass those of Maudgalyāyana himself (504).

86. See, e.g., *Asp* 1ff. (Cz., 83ff.).

87. Przyluski believes that the region of Kauśāmbī is the place of origin for the western schools, separated from the eastern group of the Mahāsāṃghikas after the first schism (see also Frauwallner 1956, 54). Kauśāmbī was therefore the seat of the pre-Theravāda, the old Sthaviras, including both of the two great sectarian groups that split apart, the Sthavira who went southwest to Ujjayinī and the Sarvāstivādins who went to the northwest (Migot 1954, 455).

88. Very interesting in the present context are images of Śāriputra in Jain tradition depicting him as originally a forest renunciant but one who is in the process of moving into—and justifying—a nonforest way of life. In the Jain *Isibhāsiyāiṃ,* in a very early poem, Śāriputra is seen as the ideal forest renunciant, one who lives in a cozy hermitage (P., *assama*) (see Nakamura 1987c, 58). However, elsewhere in this text, one finds passages in which Śāriputra exhibits a change of venue to a more settled environment. What is particularly interesting about these passages is that in them Śāriputra does not question the primary value of forest renunciation and meditation but rather is concerned to affirm that these can be carried out without actually living in the geographical forest itself. "What use of forests and huts *(assama)* for the hero who has conquered his senses? Wherever one feels happy, there one finds a forest. That place is also his hermitage. . . . For the one who has disciplined himself well, forests . . . are vain. The whole (world) is for his meditation" (Nakamura 1987c, 58–59). These early passages lend credence to the idea that Śāriputra was originally a forest saint, but one who later becomes monasticized. What is particularly interesting about the *Isibhāsiyāiṃ* is that it reveals Śāriputra in the very midst of this transformation, with one foot in each world, something not seen clearly in the Pāli sources.

We have already seen an example, in the person of Asita, discussed in Chapter 2, of the notion that one may retain forest values while living in a nonforest environment. Such has also been seen in the *Milindapañha.* Other examples of this same notion will be seen below in both Nikāya and Mahāyāna texts (cf., e.g., Chapter 8). The *Isibhāsiyāiṃ* expression of this idea raises the interesting question of whether this relatively common affirmation may not have originated at the time of and among those attempting to affirm the normativity of town-and-village renunciation (or settled monasticism) over and against forest renunciation. Both of these images—the one of the specific saint Śāriputra and the other of the justification presented by Buddhist renunciants for leaving the forest—suggest the potential value of the Jain sources for shedding light on early Buddhist history and particularly the history of early forest Buddhism.

89. Śāriputra is an important saint for Northwestern Buddhism, but he never came to have the same paradigmatic role there as in the Pāli tradition.

90. See Lamotte's discussion of these differences, 1958, 729–30.

91. This trend is all the more striking because, as is now strongly suspected, many of the geographical regions where Theravāda Buddhism has been prominent have contained more or less continuous Buddhist traditions of forest renunciation that may well date back to ancient times. Tambiah's *Buddhist Saints of the Forest and the Cult of Amulets* (1984) is an interesting and suggestive study of forest Buddhism in modern Thailand and of its relations with the more established Buddhism of the village/town/city monastery. Michael Carrithers (1983) examines the same phenomenon in Sri Lanka. Juliane Schober has recently completed a study that includes discussion of forest Buddhism in Burma (1989).

92. Cf., e.g., Conze 1951, 180.

93. Cf., e.g., Conze 1962b, 270.

5

Saints Criticized and Condemned

Mahākāśyapa, Upagupta, and Śāriputra are preeminent saints, presented in a positive light within their respective traditions. Quite in contrast to them are other important saintly figures toward whom Indian Buddhism has a much more ambivalent attitude. This chapter contains discussion of two such masters, Piṇḍolabhāradvāja and Devadatta.

A Critical Saint: Piṇḍolabhāradvāja

Piṇḍolabhāradvāja as a Saint

Throughout his hagiography, Piṇḍolabhāradvāja[1] is depicted as a realized master, conforming to the paradigm of the Buddhist saint. Piṇḍola is not only a saint but one of the great enlightened disciples of the Buddha, characterized in the *Aṅguttaranikāya* list of disciples and their specialties as "foremost among the lion-roarers" (*An* 1:23 [WH., 1:17]).[2] His conversion story is recounted in the *Damamūkanidāna Sūtra* (T., 202).[3] At one time, when the Buddha was staying in the park of Anāthapiṇḍada at Śrāvastī, there was a brahmin named Piṇḍoladvāja who had an ugly and abusive wife who regularly reviled him. In addition, Piṇḍola was forced to support his seven daughters and their husbands. One day, he borrowed an ox to work his rice field, but the ox became lost in the marshes. This unfortunate event threw him into great anxiety, and in this state he wandered about in a forest. There Piṇḍola chanced upon the Buddha sitting under a tree and, seeing him, was inspired to renounce the world and become his disciple. Here we find reference to a number of features of the paradigm, including personal crisis (theme 1), renunciation of the world (theme 3), the idea of the forest (theme 4), the experience of darśan (theme 14), and the finding of a teacher (theme 5).

Like the Buddha, Mahākāśyapa, and Upagupta, and other exemplars of the paradigm, Piṇḍola becomes a forest renunciant who follows the *dhutaguṇas* (theme 4) and practices meditation in solitude. The *Udāna,* for example, describes him as "[sitting] in cross-legged posture, holding his body upright, being a forest-dweller, an alms-quester, a rag-robe wearer, using three robes, needing little, contented, a recluse shunning society, one of ardent energy, upholding the scrupulous life *(dhutavāda),* given to the higher thought *(adhicitta)*" (42 [Wd., 50–51]). Piṇḍolabhāradvāja as an exemplary forest renunciant is mentioned in other texts, such as the *Theragāthā* (123–24), the *Theragāthā* commentary (2:4–6 [C.R. 1913, 110–11]), and the *Milindapañha*. In this last text, the saint remarks on the delights of solitary meditation:

> Alone, with no one near, the man of insight,
> Searching into and finding out the nature,
> Of this body, can lay him down to rest,
> On the sweet bed of contemplations deep.
> (398 [T.R. 1890–94, 2:335])

Piṇḍolabhāradvāja's forest-renunciant character is indicated in another legend, told in the *Suttanipāta* commentary and in the *Jātaka,*[4] in which he is shown sitting under a tree meditating. Here he is found by some women from the harem of King Udayana (P., Udena), returns from his *samādhi* to ordinary consciousness, and preaches the dharma to them. Others of the harem report this meeting to the king, describing Piṇḍola as a *śramaṇa* and as a wandering renunciant. Like other forest saints, Piṇḍola is sometimes depicted living in places that are far away and hard to get to. In the *Divyāvadāna* (402 [St., 264]), for example, his main place of residence is specified as Gandhamādana, the mountain in the north, in the Himalayas, a place famous for those other forest contemplatives, the pratyekabuddhas (see Chapter 7). In the tradition of the sixteen arhants, it is said that he lives in the mythical land of Aparagodānīya in the West, along with 1,000 enlightened followers (theme 17) (LC., 10–11), a place that is equally far off and inaccessible.

Like the other Buddhist saints, Piṇḍolabhāradvāja's spiritual path is essentially defined by meditation (theme 7). This is not only implied by his life of forest renunciation, his dwelling on Mount Gandhamādana, and his following of the *dhutaguṇa*s but is also an explicit part of his image, as in *Udāna* 42: when the Buddha points Piṇḍola out to his monks, Piṇḍola is sitting in meditation posture. When Piṇḍola is seen by King Udayana's harem, he is also sitting under a tree meditating. In a Pāli *sutta* in the *Samyuttanikāya* entitled "Bhāradvāja," when Piṇḍola preaches the dharma to King Udayana, his teaching consists in meditation instruction, including the cemetery contemplations and the practice of mindfulness (*Syn* 4:110–12 [RW., 4:68–70]).

As a result of his meditation Piṇḍolabhāradvāja attains realization as an arhant; as in the case of the other Buddhist saints, his enlightened status is central to his identity (theme 8). In the *Milindapañha,* for example, Piṇḍola expresses his realization: "How great and how deep is Nirvāṇa's bliss!" (404 [T.R., 1890–94, 2:346]). Upon attaining realization, Piṇḍola utters his famous lion's roar. Piṇḍola "roamed about roaring his lion's roar: 'Whoever has any doubts about the path or the fruit, let them ask me!' And when he stood in front of the Buddha, he roared again: 'In this *sāsana,* O Bhadanta, I have done what is to be done, I have reached the summit!' Therefore he got the name 'foremost of the lion roarers.' "[5] In declaring his own enlightenment, and in presenting himself as the authority for questions concerning "the path or the fruit" of the dharma, Piṇḍola is fulfilling two other features of the paradigm, namely, self-declaration of enlightenment (theme 10) and assimilation to the Buddha and acting in his role as principal reference point for the dharma (theme 26). As a result of his enlightenment, like the other saints, Piṇḍola is credited with extraordinary supernatural powers (theme 13). The *Theragāthā* commentary (2:4 [C.R. 1913, 111]), for example, says he possesses the six *abhijñā*s, which include enlightenment itself, and the five mundane powers, the *ṛddhi*s, remembrance of former lives, etc. In particular, he can fly, an ability he uses to exhibit the supremacy of the Buddha's teaching or just to travel from place to place.

Several *vinaya*s recount the most famous story associated with Piṇḍolabhāradvāja's flying.[6] In the Pāli version (*V*-p 2:110–12 [H., 5:149–52]),[7] for example, we are told that a rich man of Rājagṛha has a begging bowl made from a block of sandalwood. Wishing to give the bowl to a highly attained saint, he suspends it from the top of a bamboo pole and declares that whichever ascetic can obtain the bowl by magical powers may keep it. "If there is a *śramaṇa* or brahmin who is an Arhat and who has supernatural powers, let him take the bowl; I give it to him." At this, the non-Buddhist master Pūraṇa Kāśyapa (P., Pūraṇa Kassapa) comes forward and claims arhant status. However, when invited by the rich householder to take the bowl,[8] he cannot. In turn, the five other non-Buddhist teachers—who with Pūraṇa Kāśyapa form the stereotyped list of the six heretic masters—similarly come forward[9] but are unable to produce the powers necessary to take the bowl.[10] Then Piṇḍola and Maudgalyāyana (P., Moggallāna) chance by on their alms-seeking rounds, and Piṇḍola remarks, "The Venerable Moggallāna is an *arhat;* he has supernatural powers; go Venerable Moggallāna, take this begging bowl; it is yours" (*V*-p 2:111.12–15 [H., 5:150; LC., 94–95]). But the saint defers, replying instead, "The venerable Piṇḍola Bhāradvāja is an Arhat; he has supernatural powers; go, Venerable Bhāradvāja, take the bowl; it is yours" (*V*-p 2:111 [H., 5:150; LC., 95]). To this, Piṇḍola acceeds: he ascends into the air, takes the begging bowl, and flies around the city of Rājagṛha three times. At this time, the rich householder is in his house with his family. He joins his hands, prostrates, and supplicates, "O venerable one, noble Bhāradvāja, do stop at my house." Then Piṇḍola comes to the house of his suppliant, and the rich householder, taking the bowl of Piṇḍola, fills it with costly food and gives it back to the saint, who then departs. The word has spread that Piṇḍola has taken the sandalwood bowl by miraculous means, and people collect about him, following him, hanging on him, cheering him, and making a great noise (*V*-p 2:111 [H., 5:151; LC., 95]). This episode illustrates a number of further elements of our paradigm, including Piṇḍola's acceptance of lay devotees (theme 17), the existence of a cult around him (theme 15), and the defeat of enemies of the dharma (theme 21).

The Dharmaguptaka version presents a slightly different account of this story (LC., 96ff.). After the heretical masters reveal themselves incapable of taking the bowl, and Piṇḍolabhāradvāja and Maudgalyāyana, seated on a large rock, exchange invitations to one another,

> Then Pin-t'eou-lóu [Piṇḍola] having heard these words of Mou-lien [Mahāmaudgalyāyana], with the rock, leaped into the air and flew around the city of the

> Royal-residence [Rājagṛha] seven times. The people of the region fled in all directions crying out that the rock was going to fall. At this time, the master of the house was on the roof of his dwelling. He saw from afar Piṇḍola in the air; forthwith he joined his hands, paid him homage and uttered these words: "Take the bowl, Piṇḍola." Thereupon, Piṇḍola took the bowl. The master of the house said to him: "Descend here, for a bit, Piṇḍola." Piṇḍola then came down for a bit (near him). Then the master of the house took the bowl from his hands, filled it with excellent food, and gave it to him. Having taken the bowl, Piṇḍola again ascended into the air by his supernatural powers, and departed. (LC., 97–98)

This story illustrates again the saint's great power and, in addition, his potentially dangerous character (theme 25). The Sarvāstivādin *vinaya* generally follows the Pāli and Dharmaguptaka accounts, but adds two interesting details. First, it tells us that even before Piṇḍola obtains the bowl by magical power, the master of the house, Jyotiṣka, is deeply impressed by Piṇḍola's appearance, which he finds to be handsome and majestic, whether the saint is walking or motionless, seated or standing (LC., 105), thus emphasizing the saint's charisma and the good fortune of seeing him (theme 14). Second, it provides further insight into the cult surrounding such a person as Piṇḍola. The nobleman gets up from his seat, bares his own right shoulder, joins his two hands together, turns in the direction of the saint, and supplicates him thus: "Welcome! It has been a long time since you came here." Then he invites him to take a seat and honors the saint's feet (LC., 105). Following this, the saint gets the bowl, but this time by miraculously stretching out his hand and elongating it to reach the bowl (LC., 244). In these various versions Piṇḍola, responding to Maudgalyāyana's wish, reveals himself to the lay devotee, enables the layperson to participate in his cult, attracts the faith of many, exhibits the supremacy of the Buddha's teaching, and defeats the heretics.[11]

Piṇḍolabhāradvāja is particularly skillful in making conversions (theme 20). In the Mahīśāsaka *vinaya,* immediately following the account of the taking of the begging bowl is found another story concerning the four great disciples *(śrāvaka)*— Kāśyapa, Aniruddha, Piṇḍolabhāradvāja, and Maudgalyāyana (LC., 99ff.). According to this story, the four great disciples remark that in Rājagṛha there is a nobleman and his elder sister who are unsympathetic to the Buddha and his teaching. The first three disciples say that they will convert the nobleman, and Piṇḍola says he will convert the elder sister. When the first three fulfill their commitment[12] and it is Piṇḍola's turn, he puts on his robe and goes into the town to seek his alms, coming in turn to the door of the nobleman. The rich man's elder sister comes to the door but, seeing Piṇḍola the Buddhist, declines to make an offering. When Piṇḍola uses his supernormal abilities to issue smoke from his body, she remains unmoved. Then in succession, he emits flames from his body, levitates, and turns upside down in the air, remaining there. After each exhibition, she reaffirms her refusal to honor the master with alms. Piṇḍola then takes a huge boulder and, flying up into the sky with it, suspends it over her house. Finally the housewife gives in, her heart made pliable by fear, if not by devotion, and she makes a donation to the master. At this juncture, however, she attempts in various ways to skimp on her offering, but Piṇḍola's magic is again too much for her, with small cakes becoming larger, and so on. Finally, she submits entirely and tells Piṇḍola she will give him whatever he wants. To this, he replies, "I have no need of cakes. . . . We four had together decided to save you and your younger brother at the same time. The three have already converted your brother. I must convert you and that is why I have acted in this way" (LC., 102–3). This story illustrates a number of features of the paradigm, including, again, the saint's magical abilities (theme 13) and his dangerous aspect (theme 25). We also see the saint's compassion: here as elsewhere, the enlightened master goes seeking alms not out of his own desire for food but rather out of his concern to be of benefit to others (theme 11). He wanders for alms in order to provide beings with opportunities to make donations to him and thus to earn great merit (De Visser 1922–23, 4)[13] and, as in this case, to make conversions (theme 20). In the *Theragāthā* (123–24), in a passage already quoted above, we are also told that in seeking donors, Piṇḍola prefers to avoid high-caste people (theme 22).[14]

Piṇḍolabhāradvāja is sometimes the object of persecution (theme 24). When King Udayana hears that some of his harem are with the wandering saint, he becomes enraged and determines to kill him by setting loose red ants to eat him. However, when the king attempts to bring this about, he himself ends up being attacked by the ants, with Piṇḍola flying off. Finally, the king realizes the error of his ways and pays reverence to the master (Strong 1979, 60, n. 44).

In the various accounts, Piṇḍolabhāradvāja, at the end of his story, is not depicted as dying but rather as going to the mythical land of Aparagodānīya and there greatly prolonging his life (theme 28). As recounted in the Sarvāstivādin *vinaya,* the saint makes this journey by sitting in meditation posture, entering into meditation, and departing from Jambudvīpa. Once in Aparagodānīya, he continues his works of compassion: he teaches and converts multitudes of laymen and laywomen, trains a great many disciples, and builds dwellings for renunciants. In particular, he trains disciples and teaches the full extent of the dharma (theme 16) (LC., 105–7).

A relatively late account, but one with many similar themes, is found in the *Nandimitrāvadāna* (Chin., *Ta a lo han nan t'i mi to lo so shuo fa chu chi,* T. 2030; [LC., 6–24]), attributed to Nandimitra. According to this text, the Buddha, shortly before entering *parinirvāṇa,* entrusts the good dharma to Piṇḍolabhāradvāja and the fifteen other great arhants of whom Piṇḍola is the leader, asking them to remain in the world, living to a vast age (theme 28), maintaining the dharma and protecting it from decay until such time as, in a future age, the dharma will be extinguished forever, leading to the time when Maitreya shall appear (theme 29).

The cultic dimensions of Piṇḍola's identity receive particularly strong delineation in the *Divyāvadāna, Nandimitrāvadāna,* and Chinese tradition. In the *Divyāvadāna,* for example, we learn that Piṇḍola may miraculously appear, in response to the invitations and needs of sentient beings.[15] King Aśoka is giving a great Pañcavarṣika feast for the *saṃgha,* but although a great assembly of renunciants has gathered, the place of honor remains vacant. The elder Yaśas is asked the reason for this and he replies, "This seat of honor belongs to Bhāradvāja . . . foremost of lion-roarers" (*Da* 399 [St., 260]). The subject of Piṇḍolabhāradvāja's longevity comes up at once. Aśoka says, "Is there a monk still alive who has seen the Buddha?" Yaśas replies in the affirmative, and Aśoka expresses his overwhelming desire to see the saint. Yaśas confirms that Piṇḍola will soon arrive. What Aśoka fervently desires is precisely to *see* the saint: "Great would be my gain, and unprecedented my great bliss unsurpassed on earth, were I to see with my own eyes that exalted being of the Bhāradvāja clan" (*Da* 400 [St., 260]).

Aśoka gazes into the heavens, and soon the saint Piṇḍolabhāradvāja miraculously appears, in the midst of several thousand arhants, his body like that of a pratyekabuddha (theme 27), his hair white and his eyebrows so long they hang down over his eyes. Aśoka, as he did upon meeting the saint Upagupta, prostrates himself to Piṇḍola and kisses his feet. Then the king kneels before the elder, declaring his great joy and remarking, "by looking at you, I can, even today, see the *tathāgata*. You show yourself out of compassion" (theme 11). Aśoka then asks Piṇḍola a crucial question: has he, in fact, actually seen the Buddha with his own eyes? Piṇḍola replies that he has: "Indeed, I saw him many times—that great incomparable Sage." Thus, through the medium of seeing, there is a link of unbroken continuity of transmission between the Buddha himself and Aśoka: Piṇḍola has seen the Buddha, Aśoka has seen Piṇḍola, and thus Aśoka has seen the Buddha (*Da* 401–2 [St., 261]),[16] again affirming Piṇḍola's assimilation to the Buddha (theme 26).

According to the *Nandimitrāvadāna,* Piṇḍola may appear at any time, in a hidden and anonymous form. He may turn up, for example, as an ordinary renunciant, and if a layperson makes offerings to such a one he may receive the great merit deriving from offerings to the saint (De Visser 1922–23, 63). This notion of the anonymous appearance that Piṇḍola may take is amplified in the Chinese sources. The story is told of a layperson who wishes to make donations to Piṇḍola and so extends an invitation to the renunciant, providing several feasts to this end. Piṇḍola appears not to arrive, but later the layperson learns that a certain old monk, in a tattered robe, who had been beaten and turned away from each feast by the layperson's own servant, was none other than the revered master himself. The servant had thought that Piṇḍola was "a good-for-nothing *śramaṇa* who had been expelled from the community" (De Visser 1922–23, 79). Thus, as was true of Mahākāśyapa, Piṇḍola may look quite different from what is conventionally expected for Buddhist renunciants (theme 23), and he may consequently suffer abuse, even from upstanding Buddhists (theme 24). Piṇḍola may also appear from his mythical residence, even though uninvited, in order to help meditators. Paramārtha tells us that while the Yogācārin master Asaṅga was still a Sarvāstivādin monk, he came to despair over his meditation practice and his inability to attain wisdom. When he was about to commit suicide, Piṇḍola came to him from Pūrvavideha and taught him.[17]

Chinese tradition, quite possibly reflecting Indian usage,[18] knows a variety of legends and cultic activities surrounding the figure of Piṇḍolabhāradvāja. In the *sūtra* on the *Method of Inviting Piṇḍola,* for example, the main outlines of Piṇḍola's legend are given as the ideological basis for the cultic activities surrounding him. If one intends to invite Piṇḍola, one burns incense and makes prostrations in a pure environment. Facing in the direction of a certain Indian mountain, one invokes his name with all one's heart, saying, "Man of great virtue,

Piṇḍolabhāradvāja, you have received from the Buddha the order to be a field producing happiness for men in these final days of the dharma. We wish that you will accept our invitation and that you will eat in this place." This and other texts allude to various other cultic contexts in which Piṇḍola's presence is to be invoked, including when building a new house, when inviting the *saṃgha* to bathe, and when the *saṃgha* itself partakes of a meal (De Visser 1922–23, 77). Lévi and Chavannes cite another text in which it is remarked that cultic activity surrounding Piṇḍola includes the construction of his image and the carrying out of various cultic activities of worship to it, in the belief that Piṇḍola himself will become present (LC., 75).

Piṇḍolabhāradvāja as an Object of Criticism

In this array of sources, representing different regions, time periods, and Buddhist traditions, we find Piṇḍola depicted as a Buddhist saint, in many respects conforming to the paradigm. In type, then, Piṇḍola bears a close resemblance to the Buddha, Mahākāśyapa, Upagupta, the forest Śāriputra, and the saints of the *Theragāthā* and *Therīgāthā*.[19] However, unlike these saints, Piṇḍola is the subject of a distinctly ambivalent attitude on the part of surviving tradition; this is seen most clearly in certain criticisms that are leveled at him (see Lamotte 1958, 354–55).[20] These criticisms are never final, for after he is castigated, mildly or severely as the case may be, through certain events he redeems himself and becomes a member in good standing of the *saṃgha*. However, the criticisms are curious, because in the sources they are widespread, they touch different defects in Piṇḍola's character, and they seem at direct variance with much of his saintly personality. Most curious, it is often precisely the very elements of Piṇḍola's sainthood that provoke criticism.

Although Piṇḍolabhāradvāja's saintly character is reflected in virtually all the sources in which he appears, the criticisms are not as similarly widespread. They are absent in particular from earlier, briefer mentions of the saint—for example, in the *Udāna, Theragāthā, Samyuttanikāya,* and *Aṅguttaranikāya* passages cited. And they are absent from texts that attest to Piṇḍolabhāradvāja's cult, for example—the *Nandimitrāvadāna* and the *Divyāvadāna*.[21] However, the criticisms are present in some of the earlier and most of the later discussions of Piṇḍola, being particularly pronounced in the various *vinaya*s and in the Pāli commentaries.

Early expression of this attitude of reservation toward Piṇḍola is found in the conclusion of various *vinaya* stories concerning his miraculous taking of the sandalwood begging bowl, studied by Lévi and Chavannes (1916, 94ff.). In the Pāli account (*V*-p 2:110–12 [H., 5:149–52]), the Buddha hears the great noise of the crowd voicing its adulation of Piṇḍola. When he asks Ānanda what the source of this great noise may be, Ānanda explains that Piṇḍola has taken the bowl of the merchant by magical means and that a crowd is following him.[22] Then the Buddha gathers the community of renunciants together and asks Piṇḍola, "Is it true, as is said, Bhāradvāja, that the bowl of the (great) merchant of Rājagaha was fetched down by you?" "It is true, Lord." Then the Buddha castigates him, saying, "It is not suiting, Bhāradvāja, it is not becoming, it is not fitting, it is not worthy of a recluse, it is not allowable, it is not to be done." The Buddha then censures Piṇḍola for exhibiting his magical power merely to gain a bowl, an act he compares to a prostitute who exhibits herself merely for money. Then the Buddha lays down the *vinaya* rule that the monastic is forbidden from exhibiting miraculous powers before the laity. If one does so, it is a *duṣkṛta* (P., *dukkaṭa*) sin. Thus Piṇḍola's miraculous taking of the begging bowl becomes the occasion for a laying down of a formal and binding *vinaya* rule (see Strong 1979, 72).[23] The other *vinaya*s tell essentially the same story, adding various details. The Pāli commentaries give their own versions of the story of the taking of the begging bowl, adding further information, and also provide other legends that elaborate on the theme of Piṇḍola's blameworthiness.[24]

This criticism is curious because, in some important respects, it sets up contradictions in the texts. For example, the criticisms in the *vinaya* run counter to central elements of the story (see Strong 1979, 72–73). In the Pāli account, Piṇḍola initially wants Maudgalyāyana to perform the feat, and it is only at the latter's insistence that Piṇḍola reveals his magical powers at all. Moreover, his action is at once a demonstration of the validity of the Buddhists' claim to genuine attainment and a defeat of the heretics who have been trying to prove their own superiority.[25] Interestingly, the claim to genuine attainment, the manifestation of supernormal powers, and the defeat of heretics are all, as we have seen, constitutive of Buddhist sainthood as such. Thus it appears that the *vinaya* criticizes Piṇḍola precisely because he is, and shows himself to be, a saint in the classical mold.[26]

Why, then, do the *vinaya*s and the Pāli commentaries, in particular, blame Piṇḍolabhāradvāja? Strong offers a psychosocial explanation, suggesting that the tension between the saintly and retrograde elements of Piṇḍola's character represents a healthy admission of tensions within the Buddhist *saṃgha* and within the minds of the laity. Some monks, it is admitted, fall short of the ideal of renunciation and cause doubts among the laity. Nevertheless, once in the *saṃgha,* they are purified and, the laity may be assured, become worthy fields of merit (Strong 1979, 67–68, 77–78, 87–88). This explanation is undoubtedly valid as far as it goes.

In addition, certain historical patterns in Piṇḍola's legend can be discerned. For example, the *vinaya* story clearly presupposes that Piṇḍola is a Buddhist saint in the classical conception, thus suggesting that his identity as a saint is historically antecedent to the uses made of him in the *vinaya,* which would blame him. Moreover, in Piṇḍola and in those who would criticize him, are reflected the two historical strands of early Buddhism, namely, forest Buddhism and the more collective ideal of monasticism as represented by the *vinaya*s. On the one side is Piṇḍola, the forest renunciant, for whom asceticism, intensive meditation, attainment, and magical powers are the norm. On the other is the monastic renunciant here defined by a communal lifestyle and behavioral purity. In the preceding chapters, we have seen several examples of just such an emerging dichotomy between the traditions, values, and ideals of settled monasticism and those of forest Buddhism. Mahākāśyapa's legend reveals, for example, a tension between Mahākāśyapa the solitary forest saint—whose discipline is perfect, who is proficient in meditation, and who is fully realized—and Ānanda—himself unrealized, with his crowds of undisciplined disciples, who are immature and unattained in meditation. A similar dichotomy exists between Upagupta the forest saint—living in his remote hermitage, impeccable in discipline, attained in meditation, and fully realized—and Upagupta's learned visitor, the monastic scholar—who is adept in textual matters and surrounded by disciples, but who is morally corrupt within. Most explicit of all is the relatively detailed description of this tension between forest Buddhism and that of the settled monastery given by Pārāpariya and Phussa in the *Theragāthā.* All these examples reveal tensions between the ideal of forest renunciation and that of the more settled forms from the viewpoint of the forest tradition, in which the values of the settled forms are held as blameworthy. In the *vinaya* accounts of Piṇḍola, there is the same phenomenon but viewed from the opposite side, from the vantage point of settled monasticism, from which it is the forest ideal that appears flawed.

The *vinaya* story reflects, in fact, a process of monasticization, wherein Piṇḍola, the revered forest saint of the *Theragāthā, Udāna, Samyuttanikāya,* and *Anguttaranikāya,* is appropriated by the *vinaya* and brought into its sphere. A similar process of monasticization was evident in the case of Mahākāśyapa who came to function as chief disciple in the *Mahāparinirvāṇa Sūtra* and president of the first council in the *vinaya.* In the different *vinaya*s, the process of monasticization was more or less intense: in the Northern sources, Mahākāśyapa as leader of the *saṃgha* retains much of his forest-saintly character, whereas in the Pāli *vinaya* his monasticization is more thorough and he becomes little more than a primus inter pares with little of the dominating charisma visible elsewhere in the early texts. The same kind of process was visible in the case of Śāriputra, whose monasticization, particularly as it gains momentum in the Pāli sources, leads to the almost entire elimination of the forest elements of his personality.

The process of monasticization in Piṇḍolabhāradvāja's case is brought about by a somewhat different mechanism. In the *vinaya*s and Pāli commentaries, Piṇḍola is monasticized, not by the elimination of references to his forest character or his sainthood, but rather by subjecting the elements of his sainthood to criticism. Thus the *vinaya* nowhere tries to deny the reality of Piṇḍola's attainments. It accepts them as given but tries to present them so that they will be taken not at face value but as making some point other than Piṇḍola's sanctity. In the case of the exhibition of magical powers, Piṇḍola does something that is blameworthy and must not be done. Even his dwelling in Aparagodānīya, as stated by the Sarvāstivādin *vinaya* (Strong 1979, 76), is seen to be a result of his blameworthy behavior and of his having fallen short of the collective, monastic ideal propounded by the Buddha. In the *vinaya*s, then, the manifestations of Piṇḍola's saintliness are reinterpreted as signs of spiritual lapse.

The evidence suggests some of the forces that may have led to this reinterpretation. In the *Milindapañha,* as we have seen, the existence of the forest type of Buddhist renunciation naturally raised important questions for settled monasticism. Which was the truly normative Buddhist tradition—that of the settled monastery or that of the forest hermit? The monks had their claims of moral and scholarly attainment, but how could their ascendency be maintained in the face of certain charismatic forest masters with acknowledged attainment, compassion, and power?

It seems that in the *vinaya* treatments of Piṇḍolabhāradvāja, we have before us a characteristic response. As the central institutionalized carrier of Buddhist tradition, monastic Buddhism does not choose to put forward claims for itself that rival those made by the forest-renunciant traditions. Rather, it seeks to maintain its own forms and to see everything in light of the Buddha himself, defined here strictly as the one who founded and guaranteed the normativity of the monastic form of Buddhism. Thus Piṇḍola's realization and its attendant magical powers cannot be taken on their own terms and say nothing for themselves. They can only be properly understood when seen in light of the *vinaya* and its rules, the stories being ingeniously placed so as to confirm the authority of the *vinaya* rules prohibiting such saintly manifestations!

It is interesting that the tradition of criticism of Piṇḍola becomes so pervasive that it can appear even in texts representative of his cult, which otherwise reflect a positive attitude toward him. Thus, in one translation into Chinese of the *Method of Inviting Piṇḍola,* we read that the reason that Piṇḍola has delayed his nirvāṇa, remains in Aparagodānīya, and acts compassionately is precisely because the Buddha told him to do so, as punishment for his having revealed supernatural powers to the laity. The *Divyāvadāna* refers to a similar view, as do other texts of Indian origin (Strong 1979, 76). In this reading of Piṇḍolabhāradvāja's legend, it is ultimately and only because of the Buddha himself—because he chose to punish Piṇḍolabhāradvāja in a certain way—that Piṇḍola is now available and helpful to human beings. These various attempts to limit the saint's charisma and to reduce it back to (by making it depend upon) that of the Buddha *in his specific role as founder of the monastic saṃgha* is a theme to which we shall return.[27]

The pattern of Piṇḍolabhāradvāja's representation in the various sources is particularly revealing. In the non-*vinaya* Pāli canonical sources *(Ta, Ud, An,* and *Syn),* he is an accomplished saint of the forest, pure and simple. In the Pāli and other *vinaya*s, Piṇḍola undergoes a process of monasticization, being scaled down and subordinated to *vinaya* perspectives and values. In the Pāli commentaries, which extend and intensify trends present in the *vinaya*s, the criticism of Piṇḍola reaches a kind of climax. In the case of Piṇḍola, as in those of both Mahākāśyapa and Śāriputra, the Pāli tradition reflects the most consistent and intense reservations concerning forest Buddhism and its saints. In the treatment of Piṇḍola, Mahākāśyapa, and Śāriputra, there is a direct line from the *vinaya*—not just the Pāli but the other early *vinaya*s as well—to later Pāli tradition. It appears that the polarization between forest and monastic Buddhism, along with the antipathy toward forest Buddhism and its saints evident in later Pāli tradition, has its roots in the same trend in the early *vinaya*s. This polarization reflects the extreme development of the same conservative, communal, settled monastic tendency already clearly evident in the *vinaya*s of the early schools—a tendency that, though sometimes mitigated, is still visible in one form or another in the other early Nikāya schools.

In conclusion, it may be mentioned that the general pattern of Piṇḍolabhāradvāja's legend—of a great saint who is rebuked and criticized through the application of monastic norms, precisely for characteristics of his sainthood—is not unique to this saint alone. The *Lokapaññatti,* another Pāli text, recounts a legend of Upagupta that repeats a number of themes of Piṇḍola's story, including Upagupta's character as a forest renunciant, his residence in an inaccessible location, his meditative attainment, his magical powers, his surpassing charisma, and his vow to postpone his nirvāṇa indefinitely in order to help others (Maung Kin 1903, 219ff.). One story told in the text is of particular interest—namely, the account of the festival planned by King Aśoka for the dedication of the 84,000 stūpas he has had constructed. It is feared that Māra will try to disrupt the festivities, and Upagupta's name is mentioned as one who could provide the requisite protection. When Upagupta is thought of, "the monks [are] glad and joyous beyond all bounds . . . exclaiming *'sādhu, sādhu.'* " Two arhants then journey to Upagupta's far-off hermitage to invite him to come to render the needed protection against Māra. Upagupta agrees, promising to come to the monastery. He does so and, arriving by magical means, is immediately rebuked by the monks for his nonmonastic behavior and priorities: "Shin Upagupta, you have not attended the Assembly of Bhikkhus for the purpose of performing the rites of Uposatha and Pavāraṇā; you do not take interest in the affairs of the Saṃgha; you care but for your own happiness and are mindful only of your salvation" (Maung Kin 1903, 237). The monks then announce their determination that Upagupta be punished for his "forest"[28] ways. His punishment is that he must protect against Māra's depredations during the forthcoming festival.

We see here some of the same dynamics as in Piṇḍolabhāradvāja's story. As in Piṇḍola's case, this story clearly presupposes the existence of the powerful, realized, and respected forest saint. When, like Piṇḍola, Upagupta exhibits his magical powers to protect the dharma, he is criticized by the monastic *saṃgha.* In both cases, it is offense against the *vinaya* that provides the logic of the critique. As Piṇḍola is blamed and becomes the occasion for a *vinaya* rule against this type of behavior, so Upagupta is blamed because he does not participate in the *prātimokṣa* recitation of the *uposatha,* or the *pavāraṇā.* The fact that his sin has been to act against the conventions of settled monasticism is further revealed in the critique of his nonmonastic lifestyle and values: he does not engage in or show interest in the affairs of the *saṃgha.* Like Piṇḍola, Upagupta is punished by having to vow to protect the dharma—in Upagupta's case by combating Māra. Furthermore, as in Piṇḍola's legends, this story finishes by exhibiting some dramatic inconsistencies. Upagupta is a great saint and people are attracted to him; at the same time, he is criticized when he reveals his sainthood. In this story of Upagupta, there is also the strange spectacle of Upagupta originally coming of his own free will to combat Māra and ending up subjected to a punishment that consists in nothing other than fulfilling his original intention! Why is there criticism in this story and why is Upagupta's protection of the festival regarded as a punishment, as a sign of his blameworthiness, rather than more simply (and logically, from a dramatic standpoint) as an expression of his power as a realized saint?

Here, as in the case of Piṇḍola, we detect the imprint of the values of settled monasticism. In fact, settled monasticism appears to be incorporating the charismatic forest saint into its own story but revealing considerable ambivalence in the process. Forest saints may be assimilated, we seem to be told, provided that their lifestyles and values are clearly subordinated to those of classical monasticism. That the stories of both Piṇḍola and Upagupta reveal the same dynamic suggests that the pattern of accepting but criticizing and punishing the forest saint is not an isolated phenomenon but a more general hermeneutical strategy employed by settled monasticism. We may refer to this particular process of monasticization as incorporation but subordination, wherein the forest saints' traditions are incorporated into the monastic way but clearly subordinated to the values and orientations of settled monasticism.[29]

A Condemned Saint: Devadatta

Devadatta[30] appears prominently in the Nikāya texts as the Buddha's cousin and archrival, who consistently competes with the Blessed One and tries to overthrow him. As depicted in his legends, Devadatta is, in fact, an inveterate evildoer who is driven by ambitious and hateful intentions and performs a variety of pernicious deeds. Thus he tries, at various times, to supplant the Buddha, to bring the *saṃgha* to ruin, and even to kill the master through one or another diabolical scheme. Referring to Devadatta, Rockhill rightly remarks that "his name became in later times synonymous with everything that is bad, the object of the hatred of all believers" (1884, 83).

But the portrait of Devadatta as an evildoer is, within the Indian Buddhist corpus, not entirely consistent. In fact, there are indications, however slight, of another, quite different Devadatta, an impeccable saint whose sanctity is acknowledged by other Buddhist saints, including Śāriputra and even the Buddha himself. In the *vinaya* of the Sarvāstivāda, for example, we learn that for twelve years following his admission into the order, Devadatta conducts himself with faultless deeds and thoughts. He reads and recites the *sūtras,* lives according to proper discipline, and strives in his practice of dharma; in the *Aṅguttaranikāya* Devadatta reveals himself as one who has the right view and can preach the correct doctrine (Mukherjee 1966, 120; Bareau 1988–89, 541). Little wonder, then, that Śāriputra praises Devadatta for his saintliness: "Godhi's son is of great psychic power, Godhi's son is of great majesty" (*V*-p 2:189 [H., 5:265]), a praise that the Buddha affirms is spoken with truth.[31]

The theme of Devadatta's saintliness is affirmed in the *Udāna,* where it is the Buddha who praises him. Devadatta is mentioned as a Buddhist saint among other great Buddhist saints. In this account, eleven saints approach the Buddha, Devadatta and ten others—including the greatest disciples of the Buddha, listed, in the Pāli, as (1) Sāriputta, (2) Mahāmoggallāna, (3) Mahākassapa, (4) Mahākaccāyana, (5) Mahākoṭṭhita, (6) Mahākappina, (7) Mahācunda, (8) Anuruddha, (9) Revata, and (11) Ānanda; Devadatta is tenth in this list, between Revata and Ānanda.[32] The Buddha refers to these eleven as brahmins, declaring, "Monks, these are brahmins coming, these are brahmins coming." When asked to define what he means by *brahmin,* he replies that they are awakened saints: "Barring out evil things, who are ever mindful fare, Awakened, bond-free,—such in the world are surely brahmins" (4–5 [Wd., 4–5]).

Devadatta also appears with many of the characteristics of a saint even in passages that are openly hostile toward him. For example, he is depicted as one who meditates in solitude (*V*-p 2:184 [H., 5:259]). Moreover, as we shall presently see, he espouses the *dhutaguṇa*s, including living in the forest, dwelling under a tree, begging food, and wearing patched clothes. Devadatta is also a realized master and, through his awakening, is in possession of magical power. The laity are enamored of him and show their devotion through elaborate donations. He is a master who has disciples. He is an eloquent preacher, who "gladdened, rejoiced, roused, delighted the monks far into the night with talk on *dhamma*" (*V*-p 2:200 [H., 5:280]). Taken together, these features define not an evildoer but a realized master who in many respects conforms to the paradigm of the Buddhist saint of the forest. This raises the question of why Devadatta is on the one hand vilified as the very embodiment of evil and on the other depicted as a realized saint. In order to address this question, let us consider the main themes of Devadatta's legend as found in the extant literature.

Legends

According to Mukherjee, who provides a detailed analysis of the texts surrounding Devadatta, the components of Devadatta's biography fall naturally into three parts: the main traditions, the secondary traditions, and the individual reports (Mukherjee 1966, 6–7).

Main Traditions. These include fifteen episodes found in the Pāli *vinaya,* in the *Vibhaṅga* (*Saṃghādisesa* 10) and the *Skandhaka (Cullavagga)* and, in more or less complete form, also in the *Vibhaṅga* and *Saṃghabhedavastu* of the *vinaya*s of the Dharmaguptaka, Mahīśāsaka, Sarvāstivāda, and Mūlasarvāstivāda. The content of these main traditions, shortly to be summarized, includes the Devadatta legend from the time of his admission into the order, through his efforts to split the community and his attempts on the Buddha's life, until his death.

Secondary Traditions. These include four episodes found primarily in the Mūlasarvāstivādin *vinaya* and the *Mahāvastu,* which include a résumé of Devadatta's family tree, his attempt to kill an elephant, his participation in an archery competition, and also his attempt to poison the Buddha and his fall into hell.

Individual Reports. These include an additional fifteen episodes each of which is found only in one text: nine are found in the Mūlasarvāstivādin *vinaya,* and the other six are scattered in the *Aṅguttaranikāya,* Dharmaguptaka *vinaya,* Mahīśāsaka *vinaya,* Sarvāstivādin *vinaya,* and *Ekottarāgama.* These depict episodes from various periods of Devadatta's life from his childhood onward.

According to Mukherjee, the fifteen episodes of the main traditions, contained in the *vinaya*s of the five schools, represent the oldest stratum and the essential foundation of the Devadatta biography. Both the secondary traditions and the individual reports clearly represent later additions to this material, a judgment in which Bareau (1988–89), who has examined the Devadatta legends in detail, concurs.[33] The two contradictory facets of Devadatta's personality, saintly and diabolical, are unmistakably articulated already in the main traditions. Thus the question of the reasons for the contradictions in Devadatta's depiction may best be addressed in terms of the early stratum of the legend, as found in the fifteen episodes of the main traditions. The following summarizes the Pāli account, with differences from the other *vinayas* noted where appropriate.

In the *Vibhaṅga, Saṃghādisesa* 10, we read that one day in the Bamboo Grove in Rājagṛha, Devadatta, who is himself a renunciant in the Buddha's order, approaches four other of the Buddha's renunciants (in the Pāli rendering), Kokālika, Kaṭamorakatissaka, the son of lady Khaṇḍā, and Samuddadatta. He proposes to them the splitting of the order. When Kokālika asks how they might carry out this intention, Devadatta suggests that he and his four compatriots approach the Buddha and ask him to institute five *dhuta*[34] practices that shall be mandatory on all his renunciants, saying,

> Lord, the lord in many ways speaks in praise of desiring little, of being contented, of expunging (evil), of being punctilious, of what is gracious, of decrease (of the obsctructions), of putting forth energy. Lord, these five items are conducive in many ways to desiring little, to contentment. . . .
>
> [1] It were good, lord, if the monks for as long as life lasted, should be forest dwellers; whoever should betake himself to the neighborhood of a village, sin *[vajja]* would besmirch him.
>
> [2] For as long as life lasts let them be beggars for alms; whoever should accept an invitation, sin would besmirch him.
>
> [3] For as long as life lasts let them be wearers of robes taken from the dust-heap; whoever should accept a robe given by a householder, sin would besmirch him.
>
> [4] For as long as life lasts let them live at the foot of a tree; whoever should go under cover, sin would besmirch him.
>
> [5] For as long as life lasts let them not eat fish and flesh; whoever should eat fish and flesh, sin would besmirch him. (*V*-p 3:171 [H., 1:296–97])

Devadatta then explains the rationale of his proposal: "The recluse Gotama will not allow these things. Then we will win over the people by means of these five items. It is possible, your reverence, with these five items, to make a schism in the Order of the recluse Gotama, a breaking of the concord. For, your reverence, people esteem austerity" (*V*-p 3:171 [H., 1:297]).

Following this, Devadatta with his four coconspirators approach the Buddha, and Devadatta puts forward his proposal. As anticipated, the Buddha is not receptive:

> Enough Devadatta. . . . Whoever wishes, let him be a forest-dweller; whoever wishes, let him dwell in the neighbourhood of a village; whoever wishes, let him be a beggar for alms; whoever wishes, let him accept an invitation; whoever wishes, let him wear rags taken from the dust-heap; whoever wishes, let him accept a householder's robes. For eight months, Devadatta, lodging at the foot of a tree is permitted by me [i.e., during the rains]. Fish and flesh are pure in respect of three points: if they are not seen, heard or suspected (to have been killed for him). (*V*-p 3:171–72 [H., 1:298])

The Buddha, in effect, will allow Devadatta's austerities as optional practices for *bhikṣus* but will not make them compulsory on all and certainly not "for as long as life lasts."

Receiving the Buddha's rejection, Devadatta is "joyful and exultant" (*V*-p 3:172 [H., 1:298]). Then, having paid reverence to the lord, he departs, journeying with his four friends to Rājagṛha. There, he proclaims to the laity that whereas he and his followers adhere to the rigorous practices, the Buddha and his followers do not. Some of the laity respond by praising Devadatta and his company. "These recluses, sons of the Sakyans, are punctilious *[dhuta]* and practice the expunging of evil; but the recluse Gotama is luxurious and strives after abundance" (*V*-p 3:172 [H., 1:299]). However there are other laity who, loyal to the Buddha, are distressed that a schism is in the making. When other renunciants of the Buddha hear of this incident, they make a report to the Blessed One, accusing Devadatta of fomenting a schism. The Buddha asks Devadatta if this report is true, and when Devadatta admits that it is, the Buddha castigates him and lays down the rule that if a *bhikṣu* should seek to foment a schism, he should be spoken to three times. If he does not pay heed, there is an offense entailing a formal meeting of the order, *saṃghāvaśeṣa* (P., *saṃghādisesa*) (*V*-p 3:172–73 [H., 1:299–300]).

In the *Vibhaṅga, Saṃghādisesa* 11, we read of a further incident leading to a rule pertaining to those who support the fomenter of a schism. Kokālika, Kaṭamorakatissaka, the son of lady Khaṇḍā, and Samuddadatta overhear certain renunciants criticizing Devadatta for fomenting a schism: "Devadatta is not one who speaks *dhamma,* Devadatta is not one who speaks *vinaya.* How can this Devadatta proceed with a schism in the Order, with a breaking of the concord?" The four then respond, "Do not speak thus, venerable ones; Devadatta is one who speaks *dhamma,* Devadatta is one who speaks *vinaya,* and Devadatta having adopted our desire and objective, gives expression to them; he knows that what he says for us seems also good to us." This is reported to the Buddha, who institutes the rule that if certain *bhikṣus* support one who foments a schism, they should be admonished three times, after which, if they do not desist, there is an offense entailing a formal meeting of the order (*V*-p 3:174–75 [H., 1:304–5]).

In *Cullavagga* 7, the story told in the *Vibhaṅga, Saṃghādisesa* 10, appears again but as part of a much fuller account of Devadatta's life and designs, summarized here according to Mukherjee's fifteen episodes of the main tradition. In chapter 7, we see Devadatta renouncing the world, along with six other Śākya youths (*V*-p 2:182–83 [H., 5:257]) (Mukherjee, episode 1), after a year following which Devadatta obtains supernatural power (*V*-p 2:183 [H., 5:257]) (episode 2). Subsequently, Devadatta schemes to win lay converts and satisfy his desire for honor and material gain and decides to manifest his magical powers to the crown prince Ajātaśatru. Devadatta manifests himself to the prince as a young boy clad in a girdle of snakes, and Ajātaśatru, "greatly pleased with this wonder of psychic power on Devadatta's part," becomes his loyal patron, lavishing offerings upon him morning and evening (*V*-p 2:184 [H., 5:259–60]) (episode 3). Devadatta, inflated with his success, conceives a desire to become leader of the order in the Buddha's place, at which point his psychic powers diminish. This evil wish, known by a certain *deva,* is reported to the Buddha (*V*-p 2:185–87 [H., 5:260–62]) (episode 4), as are Devadatta's successes with Prince Ajātaśatru (*V*-p 2:187–88 [H., 5:262–63]) (episode 5). The Buddha is not troubled by these reports, for he remarks that Devadatta's mental states will decline and not grow.

Devadatta then approaches the Buddha and, pointing out that the master is now old, suggests that he, Devadatta, assume leadership of the order. The Buddha utterly rejects this request, remarking that "I, Devadatta, would not hand over the Order of monks even to Sāriputta and Moggallāna. How then could I to you, a wretched one to be vomited like spittle?" (*V*-p 2:188 [H., 5:264]).[35] After Devadatta has departed, angry and displeased, the Buddha tells the *bhikṣus* to carry out a formal act of information against Devadatta in Rājagṛha: "whereas Devadatta's nature was formerly of one kind, now it is of another kind; and that whatever Devadatta should do by gesture and by voice, in that neither the Awakened One nor *dhamma* nor the Order should be seen, but in that only Devadatta should be seen" (*V*-p 2:189 [H., 5:264–65]) (episode 7). The act being carried out, the Buddha asks Śāriputra to inform against Devadatta in Rājagṛha. When Śāriputra expresses hesitation because he had formerly spoken in praise of Devadatta, the Buddha allows that just as Śāriputra's former praise had been true, now his condemnation will be equally true (*V*-p 2:189 [H., 5:265]). When Śāriputra enters Rājagṛha and proclaims the act of information against Devadatta, Devadatta's lay devotees express the view that "these recluses, sons of the Sakyans are jealous, they are jealous of Devadatta's gains and honours," while others express willingness to trust the Buddha's judgment (*V*-p 2:190 [H., 5:266]) (episode 8).

Following this, in the *Cullavagga* account, Devadatta attempts to instigate Ajātaśatru to kill his father Bimbisāra in order to become king, while he, Devadatta, plots to kill the Buddha in order to usurp his position as leader of the *saṃgha* (*V*-p 2:190 [H., 5:266]) (episode 9). Ajātaśatru is discovered but, instead of being punished, is given the kingship by his father. Devadatta then convinces Ajātaśatru to send assassins against the Buddha, but they are dissuaded from their intended act by the Lord's charisma, insight, and kindness (*V*-p 2:191–93 [H., 5:268–71]) (episode 10). Devadatta next attempts to roll a boulder from a mountain height down on the Buddha. Although the boulder is miraculously destroyed, fragments draw blood from the Buddha's foot, which prompts the Buddha to remark, "You have produced great demerit, foolish man, in that you, with your mind, malignant, your mind on murder, drew the Truth-finder's blood" (*V*-p 2:193 [H., 5:271]) (episode 11).[36] Following this incident, the Buddha's *bhikṣus* are anxious lest Devadatta succeed in murdering their master. In order to prevent against this, they pace up and down on every side of the Buddha's dwelling, reciting their texts, "doing their studies together with a loud noise, with a great noise for the protection, defence and warding of the Lord." The Buddha hears this cacophony and asks Ānanda what is going on. Upon being told, he replies that the *bhikṣus* are not to worry, as a Buddha cannot be killed before his time by such a one as Devadatta (*V*-p 2:194 [H., 5:271–72]). Next, Devadatta arranges to have a mad, man-killing elephant let loose against the Buddha, but this design also fails, as the Buddha tames the elephant with his loving-kindness and the elephant responds with acts of reverence (*V*-p 2:194–95 [H., 5:272–74]) (episode 12). The *Cullavagga* account next reports of Devadatta's "eating in groups." He wanders among the households, making requests, and is criticized by the people for eating with his friends and "having asked and asked among the households." The *bhikṣus* report this to the Buddha, who institutes a rule against the practice (*V*-p 2:196 [H., 5:274–75]) (episode 6).

Then follows the incident reported in the *Vibhañga:* Devadatta approaches his four companions and proposes the splitting of the order through advancing the five ascetic rules as obligatory (episode 13). The story is told in the same words except that it concludes not with the *saṃghāvaśeṣa* rule but rather with the Buddha simply enjoining Devadatta not to bring about a schism, warning, "whoever [does so] . . . is boiled in hell for an aeon" (*V*-p 2:196–98 [H., 5:275–79]). Devadatta, however, pays no heed and shortly thereafter announces to Ānanda in Rājagṛha that he plans to split the order by carrying out the *poṣadha* ceremony, "both in contradistinction to the Lord and in contradistinction to the Order of monks and will (so) carry out the (formal) acts of the Order" (*V*-p 2:198 [H., 5:278]). Devadatta next gives out the *śalākā* (P., *salāka*), voting sticks or tickets, remarking in reference to the obligatory observance of the five rules, "The recluse Gotama does not allow these, but we live undertaking these five items." He continues, "If these five items are pleasing to the venerable ones, let each one take a voting ticket." Five hundred *bhikṣus*, thinking, "this is the rule, this is the discipline, this is the Teacher's instruction," take the tickets. Thus is the order split (*V*-p 2:199 [H., 5:279]) (episode 14). These *bhikṣus* are not irreparably lost, however, for the Buddha, knowing what has transpired, sends Śāriputra and Maudgalyāyana to Devadatta's camp. After arriving, these two seem to approve of Devadatta's dharma. However, when the usurper goes to sleep, they convince the five hundred *bhikṣus* to return to the Buddha (*V*-p 2:199–200 [H., 5:279–81]) (episode 15). Kokālika then wakens Devadatta and tells him what has happened, whereupon hot blood issues from Devadatta's mouth and he dies (*V*-p 2:200 [H., 5:281]).[37] The Buddha subsequently remarks that Devadatta "is doomed to the Downfall, to Niraya hell, staying there for an aeon, incurable" (*V*-p 2:202 [H., 5:283]) (episode 15).[38]

The four other *vinaya* accounts parallel the Pāli version quite closely. Apart from incidents that are idiosyncratic and can be left aside as likely later additions and not part of the early tradition, these accounts differ mainly in the details of the incidents and in their order. For example, whereas the four other accounts agree that Devadatta promoted five ascetic practices (with the exception of the Chinese version, which mentions four), there is disagreement on the precise members of the list. Thus the Dharmaguptaka *vinaya* agrees with the Pāli in mentioning begging food, wearing robes made of rags, and eating no fish or flesh but does not mention living in the forest or under trees, including instead living in the open and taking neither butter nor salt. The other traditions similarly show some agreement and some disagreement with the Pāli and Dharmaguptaka lists.[39] Nevertheless, here, throughout the variations, the dramatic intent and meaning of the story are the same: Devadatta uses the proposal of the ascetic practices to bring about a split in the order.[40]

One also finds differences among the five *vinaya* traditions in the arrangement of the incidents. Mukherjee points to two subgroupings within the five traditions: on the one hand are the Theravāda, Dharmaguptaka, and Mahīśāsaka; on the other, the Sarvāstivāda and Mūlasarvāstivāda. It will be recalled that the Pāli account in the *Cullavagga* describes Devadatta's attempted murder of the Buddha and follows this with his efforts to cause a schism in the order by proposing compulsory adherence to the five ascetic rules. This same sequence is followed by the Dharmaguptaka and Mahīśāsaka. Mukherjee points out that this does not make sense, because after Devadatta had attempted to kill the Buddha, he certainly would have been expelled from the community, thus making it impossible for him to have approached the Buddha as a *bhikṣu* in good standing who could propose a matter of discipline. The Sarvāstivāda and Mūlasarvāstivāda accounts, on the other hand, have these incidents reversed in the dramatically more logical order.

Interpretations

As mentioned, within the overall corpus of Devadatta legends, the fifteen episodes just summarized in their Pāli version, are, with some alterations, also found in the Dharmaguptaka, Mahīśāsaka, Sarvāstivādin, and Mūlasarvāstivādin *vinayas*.[41] This raises the question of what the earliest form of the Devadatta legend may have been. In addressing this question, Mukherjee examines the fifteen episodes as they appear in the five *vinayas*. He notes that whereas in the Pāli version, for example, all fifteen episodes appear in the *Cullavagga,* only episodes 13 (the attempt to have the ascetic practices made obligatory) and 14 (splitting of the order) appear in the *Vibhañga*. Moreover, the configuration of the legend in the *Cullavagga* suggests that episodes 13 and 14 were originally identified as a *saṃghāvaśeṣa* offense. From this Mukherjee concludes that these two episodes represent the earliest core of the Devadatta legend.[42] In addition, it may be observed that episodes 13 and 14 represent the necessary dramatic core—the basic theme of proposed and effected schism—around which the other episodes could crystalize as a further elaboration and explanation of the core.

The identification of episodes 13 and 14 as the earliest core of Devadatta's legend raises the further question of the time period in which these episodes may have originated. Mukherjee notes the important fact that the Mahāsāṃghika *vinaya* contains mention of Devadatta but does so in a form entirely different from the *vinayas* of the Theravāda, Dharmaguptaka, Mahīśāsaka, Sarvāstivāda, and Mūlasarvāstivāda (1966, 144). In fact, there is no overlap between the Mahāsāṃghika treatment and that of the five schools. It will be recalled that the so-called first schism within Buddhism occurred between the Sthaviras—from which the Theravāda, Dharmaguptaka, Mahīśāsaka, Sarvāstivāda, and Mūlasarvāstivāda all derive—and the Mahāsāṃghika. The fact that the Devadatta legend, including its core (episodes 13 and 14) and its elaboration (episodes 1 to 12 and 15), is common to the *vinayas* of the five schools deriving from the Sthavira but is not found in the Mahāsāṃghika *vinaya* suggests that the legend arose among the Sthaviras, after they split from the Mahāsāṃghika in the fourth century B.C.E.[43] Thus, the Devadatta legend is, in Mukherjee's view, in its earliest form a production of the Sthaviras.

In what circumstances might this earliest core have arisen among the Sthaviras? In a recent article, Bareau (1988–89) has examined the early part of the Devadatta legend as found in the *vinayas* of the Theravāda, Dharmaguptaka, Mahīśāsaka, Sarvāstivāda, and Mahāsāṃghika (he has left aside that of the Mūlasarvāstivāda because it contains a considerable amount of later material). Bareau tells us that schism *(saṃghabheda),* is treated in the *vinaya*s of the various schools in two sections, that of the *Skandhaka* (in which the *Cullavagga* account is found) and the *Vibhaṅga.* Bareau begins with an examination of the *Skandhaka* treatment of Devadatta, noting that the core of the account is a very brief conversation held at Śrāvastī in which the Buddha, at the request of Upāli, defines *saṃghabheda.* In the Mahāsāṃghika *vinaya,* this brief passage forms the totality of the chapter, whereas in the *vinaya*s of the other schools it forms the conclusion of the extended legend of Devadatta. Bareau concludes that the tradition concerning the *saṃghabheda* in the *Vinayapiṭaka* may be reduced to the single, simple conversation between Buddha and Upāli. The complete silence of the Mahāsāṃghika *vinaya* concerning Devadatta in this discussion of *saṃghabheda* suggests that the linkage of Devadatta with this offense in the *vinaya*s of the schools deriving from the Sthaviras is a later addition (539–40). Bareau's observation tends to confirm Mukherjee's conclusion that the core of the Devadatta legend arose among the Sthaviras after the first schism.

Bareau identifies the same earliest core of the Devadatta legend as Mukherjee (episodes 13 and 14) but adds Mukherjee's episode 15, the conclusion of the story wherein the wayward *bhikṣu*s return to the fold. He makes this addition because he does not assume—as does Mukherjee—that the *Vibhaṅga* version is the earlier. Unlike Mukherjee, Bareau begins his analysis with the legend of the schism as it appears in the *Skandhaka,* as the more authentic earlier version. Bareau's argument makes good sense, among other reasons because the *Vibhaṅga* version clearly leaves the story of the schism incomplete and dangling—in order to interject the rule that this story is supposed to have provoked—whereas the *Skandhaka* account gives the story in a dramatically complete form. Based on his analysis, Bareau tells us that three core elements of Devadatta's legend are present in all four *vinaya*s. Found in a simpler form in the Mahīśāsaka and the Dharmaguptaka *vinaya*s, they are: (1) Devadatta's proposal of the five rules as obligatory, which the Buddha rejects; (2) the departure of the five hundred *bhikṣu*s, effecting the schism; and (3) the winning back of the five hundred by Śāriputra and Maudgalyāyana (1988–89, 540ff.). These three elements are also found in the Theravādin *vinaya,* with elaborations that tend mainly to further blacken Devadatta's reputation with additional crimes, and in the *vinaya* of the Sarvāstivāda, also in more elaborate form, in a slightly different order.

This analysis enables Bareau to identify three stages in the development of the Devadatta legend in the *Skandhaka* section of the *vinaya*s of the schools:

1. In the earliest, preschism account of *saṃghabheda* in the *Skandhaka,* Devadatta does not appear at all (Mahāsāṃghika).
2. Devadatta enters the postschism *Skandhaka* of the schools deriving from the Sthaviras. Here he provokes the division of the community because he wishes to insist on a certain standard of rigor for all *bhikṣu*s. Bareau comments, "the only fault of this person is having caused a temporary rupture in the *saṃgha* and revealing himself more strict than the Buddha. Nothing leads to doubt about his sincerity or permits the attribution to him of bad motives."
3. Finally, in the latest stratum, Devadatta is accused of being filled with

greed, pride, and ambition and of attempting various crimes, to set himself in the Buddha's stead, to induce Ajātaśatru to kill his father, to himself murder the Buddha, and so on—all in spite of his (in some accounts) previously saintly character. Bareau remarks, "the desire to condemn Devadatta and to make him completely odious is too clear for one to have confidence in this new portrait, which is nothing but pure calumny" (1988–89, 542).

Bareau next deals with the passages that discuss *saṃghāvaśeṣa* in the *Vibhaṅga*. All the versions accord major responsibility for the division in the community to Devadatta but differ in their explanations. In the Mahāsāṃghika version, Devadatta tries to break the community by any and all means, wanting to throw out all the rules of monastic discipline and the doctrinal teachings. Refusing to listen to advice and warnings of the virtuous *bhikṣus* and even of the Buddha, he recruits a body of unvirtuous disciples. Here is a portrait of Devadatta as the paradigmatic schismatic type, with no details given as to why he acted thus or what methods he used (1988–89, 542). The Mahīśāsaka and Dharmaguptaka give much the same extended account as presented in the Theravādin *Skandhaka* version. The Theravādin version is much briefer, containing only Devadatta's proposal to the Buddha, the bulk of the other episodes being found in the Pāli *Skandhaka*. The Sarvāstivādin *Vibhaṅga* account is also short. In neither the Theravādin nor the Sarvāstivādin version do we find the least allusion to Devadatta's intrigues with Ajātaśatru or his attempts to kill the Buddha. Thus, the personality of Devadatta in the *Vibhaṅga* of these schools presents the same configuration as in the *Skandhaka* of the Mahīśāsaka and Dharmaguptaka: he is simply a saint who wishes that all *bhikṣus* follow a rigorous lifestyle. Bareau completes his discussion of the texts by observing that it is only upon this single depiction of Devadatta as a virtuous, "rigorist" *bhikṣu* that all the early *vinaya* texts agree (1988–89, 544).[44] The original Devadatta, Bareau concludes, was simply a saint whom Buddhist tradition, over the course of time, came more and more to hate.

This conclusion raises an important question: what is it about Devadatta that sets his Buddhist attackers on such a literary rampage? It is significant that Devadatta, in the earliest stage of his legend, is a forest saint[45] in the classical mold. He has renounced the world under the Buddha. He has practiced a forest style of Buddhism, including some form of the *dhutaguṇas*, retreat into solitude, and meditation, and he has reached some attainment. His attainment is given Buddhist legitimacy in being recognized by no less than Śāriputra (Pāli) or Ānanda (Sarvāstivāda),[46] and even by the Buddha himself. In his biographies, his realization is also indicated by his effortless and sometimes elaborate magical displays. In addition, a cult surrounds his person such that he may count among his devoted patrons even the crown prince and later king Ajātaśatru. Devadatta's cultic popularity is also clearly evidenced in the hostile witness of the Buddhist account, which acknowledges at several points the faith and enthusiasm of his lay supporters.

Devadatta is not only a forest saint but one who strongly advocates forest Buddhism as the only authentic type of Buddhist renunciation, seen in his proposing the *dhutaguṇa*-type practices as obligatory for all renunciants. His unwavering advocacy of forest Buddhism is also seen in the issue of leadership. Unlike his Buddhist critics, Devadatta—in his request to the Buddha to become leader after the Buddha is gone—assumes that the transmission of authority in Buddhism must pass from teacher to disciple; the more collective, textual, and institutional forms that came to characterize settled monasticism are not part of his thinking. Devadatta's identification with forest Buddhism is seen finally in the fact that—as explicitly seen in his rules—he is deeply distressed to see some *bhikṣus* taking up residence in villages, living in dwellings, receiving robes as gifts from the laity, accepting invitations from the laity to come to meals, and so on. As Bareau remarks, he is concerned that certain *bhikṣus* are enjoying the donations of rich laity too much and are becoming too attached to the things of this world, phenomena he "considers as a form of laxity, a danger for the future of the community and of Buddhism altogether" (1988–89, 546). In this, his reaction is not dissimilar to the distress felt by Pārāpariya and Phussa in the *Theragāthā* over a similar movement to the village in their day. Like these two, Devadatta feels that the true dharma is to be found solely and strictly in the forest, and he appeals to the Buddha to back him up. Devadatta, then, is a classic forest saint who, like the other Buddhist renunciants we are examining in this book, identifies normative Buddhism with forest Buddhism. This strict identification of Devadatta with forest Buddhism undoubtedly provides one important reason for his vilification by later Buddhist authors. It is not just that he practices forest Buddhism, is a forest saint, and advocates forest renunciation. Even more, and worse from the viewpoint of his detractors, he completely repudiates the settled monastic form, saying in effect that he does not judge it to be authentic at all. Moreover, his loyalty to forest Buddhism cannot be shaken: even when he meets with intense resistance, he will not be moved.

This explanation is confirmed when we notice that his attackers are, among the Buddhists, precisely those most identified with settled monasticism. His most enthusiastic vilifiers are, first of all, those monastic schools deriving from the conservative, monastic Sthaviras. In addition, it is in precisely their *vinaya*s—those texts in which the form of settled monasticism is consolidated and articulated—that this critique is carried out. In other words, Devadatta becomes significant as an enemy within the specifically monastic context and set of concerns. Further, it is clear that settled monastic values drive the Devadatta story even in its earliest form: the issue in question has to do with central authority and institutional unity, something that more or less presupposes just the kind of centripetal force provided by settled monasticism. Finally, the predominant values evinced by Devadatta's attackers are those of settled monasticism: although toleration of forest life is given lip service, the preferred—indeed, assumed—renunciant form is clearly the settled monastic one. It is no accident, then, that when the monks are worried about the Buddha's safety, they wander back and forth in front of his cave, reciting their *sūtra*s, studying. The Buddha may be alone in his cave (may we guess that he is meditating?), but his disciples exist in a large group noisily going over their homework. It is also typical that the dramatis personae of the conflict square off as the solitary individual—Devadatta (his four friends and his gain and loss of the five hundred only highlight his aloneness)—versus the crowd of the Buddha's disciples. It seems clear that the core of the Devadatta legend, and particularly the vitriolic nature of the condemnation of this saint, is best understood as the expression of a controversy between a proponent (and his tradition) of forest Buddhism and proponents of settled monasticism, a controversy that in the sources is seen from the viewpoint of the monastic side.[47]

There can be no doubt that Devadatta's schism is not an event imagined by Buddhist authors but is a historical fact, as shown by the evidence provided by the two Chinese pilgrims, Fa-hsien and Hsüan-tsang.[48] Fa-hsien, for example, reports that near Śrāvastī there was a community of disciples following Devadatta who rendered homage to the three previous buddhas but not to Śākyamuni (B., 82). As Bareau notes, this information gives indirect confirmation to the historicity of the ancient controversy that resulted in the disciples of Devadatta separating themselves from the mainstream, monastic Buddhist tradition. Hsüan-tsang, some two hundred years later, in the seventh century C.E., confirms the existence of disciples of Devadatta living in three monasteries in Bengal "in which, in accordance with the teaching of Devadatta, milk products were not taken as food" (Wts., 191). This passage suggests adherence to a code more strict than those typical of Buddhist monks (although in Hsüan-tsang's time Devadatta's disciples live in monasteries!) and reveals a rule similar to one attributed to Devadatta in the Mahīśāsaka and Mūlasarvāstivādin *vinaya*s (Mukherjee 1966, 76–77). It also suggests that the reason for Devadatta's schism was indeed his adherence to certain austerities of the *dhutaguṇa* type, which the mainstream community from which he and his group seceded were not willing to follow. These references also reveal the great success of Devadatta and his tradition: it was still in existence long (at least a millennium) after its separation from mainstream Buddhism (Bareau 1988–89, 544).[49]

The recognition of the historicity of Devadatta's schism leads naturally to the question of its rough date. The *Skandhaka*s of the various Sthavira-derived schools, of course, depict this schism as having occurred during the lifetime of the Buddha. They wish us to believe that the essential conflict occurred between Devadatta and the Buddha himself. However, as mentioned, in the earliest core of the *Skandhaka* discussion of *saṃghabheda,* as reflected in the Mahāsāṃghika version, Devadatta does not appear. This raises at least the possibility that Devadatta's schism arose not only after the death of the Buddha but also after the split between Mahāsāṃghikas and Sthaviras.[50] The fact that this story suggests the existence of settled monasticism in a dominant form, which took some time to occur, also perhaps points to a similar conclusion.[51]

As far as the Nikāya *vinaya*s are concerned, Devadatta is more or less totally condemned as "incurable" and relegated to outer darkness.[52] It is interesting, then, that Devadatta is not always condemned in Indian Buddhism. In the *Saddharmapuṇḍarīka Sūtra,* for example, Devadatta is presented in a former life as a forest renunciant who assisted Buddha Śākyamuni to buddhahood.[53] In chapter 11 of the text the Buddha is preaching the Mahāyāna to an assembled gathering, among whom is the *bhikṣu* Devadatta, whom the Buddha now praises.[54] In a former life, the Buddha says, there was a forest renunciant, a *ṛṣi,* whose spiritual life was oriented around the *Saddharmapuṇḍarīka Sūtra* itself. At that time, this *ṛṣi* taught the *Saddharmapuṇḍarīka Sūtra* to the bodhisattva in return for which the bodhisattva acted as his devoted servant for a thousand years. This seer was none other than Devadatta, whom the Buddha terms his *kalyāṇamitra* (*Sps* 158.25–26 [Kn., 246]), or "spiritual friend"—in effect, his teacher. It was through training under Devadatta as his teacher, the Buddha tells us, that he was able to perfect the qualities[55] by which he eventually became a buddha (*Sps* 158.26ff. [Kn., 246]). In future times, the Buddha continues, Devadatta will be greatly revered and honored and shall become no less than the greatly revered *tathāgata* Devarāja, who shall lead innumerable beings to enlightenment. After he has passed away, the dharma of this Buddha shall remain for twenty intermediate *kalpa*s. Moreover, his relics will not be divided but will be kept together in a single, gigantic stūpa, worshiped by gods and humans. So holy will be this stūpa that those who circumambulate it may hope for realization as an arhant, a pratyekabuddha, or a buddha. Finally, in the future, a great blessing shall come to those who hear about Devadatta: for those hearing this chapter of the *Saddharmapuṇḍarīka Sūtra* and gaining from it shall be liberated from rebirth in the three lower realms.[56] For at least one Buddhist tradition, then, Devadatta is clearly neither a *vinaya*-breaker nor the archenemy of the Buddha but is a simple *bhikṣu* in good standing, present in an assembly in which the Buddha is preaching the Mahāyāna of the *Saddharmapuṇḍarīka Sūtra*. Moreover, he is identified as having been in a previous lifetime a forest saint devoted to the principal Mahāyāna text of this tradition, one who made possible the present Buddha and his central Mahāyāna teaching. Does this textual image of Devadatta, though written down much later, retain a tradition relating to this saint that antedates or is contemporaneous with his vilification in the various *vinaya*s? This question, particularly in light of the Mahāyāna associations of Devadatta in the *Saddharmapuṇḍarīka Sūtra,* is intriguing.

Notes

1. For information on Piṇḍolabhāradvāja, see Watters 1898; Kumagusu 1899; Kern 1901–3, 1:152; Lévi and Chavannes 1916; De Visser 1922–23; Przyluski 1923, 75–88, 191–92, 208–11, 264–66, and passim; Shan Shih Buddhist Institute 1961; Strong 1979 and 1983, 83–87, 260–61, and passim; for bibliographical information on the sixteen and eighteen arhants, see Strong 1979, 52, n. 6, and the notes to this chapter, below.

2. The *Manorathapūraṇī* typifies him in this same way (*Mrp* 1:196). See also *Da* 399 (St., 260). Piṇḍolabhāradvāja's previous lives are discussed in *Vms* 3.1, 183–84 (Hofinger 1954, 212–15).

3. Translated into Chinese in 445 C.E. Following De Visser's summary (1923, 74).

4. *Suttanipāta* commentary (*Sn*-c 2:570) and *Jātaka* (*J* 4:263), summarized by Strong 1979, 60, n. 44.

5. In the *Aṅguttaranikāya* commentary (Strong 1979, 69). The motif of lion-roaring has two different faces in the tradition. On the one hand, as here, it is uttered by the saint who has broken through to realization. On the other, it is a mark of those who defeat heretics (LC., 112).

6. Translated by Lévi and Chavannes (1916, 94ff.).

7. Following the translation of Lévi and Chavannes (94–96).

8. In the Pāli version, the householder says, "If you are an *arhat* and if you have supernatural powers, then take the begging bowl" (*V*-p 2:110.34–35 [H., 5:149; LC., 94]). In the Dharmaguptaka version of the story, there is assumed an indissoluble linkage of one's status as an arhant and one's magical powers: the rich householder says, "If you are an *arhant,* then you are in possession of magical power and will be able to take the bowl" (LC., 97).

9. Maskarin Gośālīputra (P., Makkali Gosāla), Ajita Keśakambala (P., Ajita Keśakambala), Kakuda Kātyāyana (P., Pakudha Kaccāyana), Sañjayin Vairaṭīputra (P., Sañjaya Belaṭṭhiputta), Nirgrantha Jñātiputra (P., Nigaṇṭha Nātaputta). For a brief discussion of this stereotyped list of six heretical teachers, see Lamotte 1958, 21.

10. The Dharmaguptaka *vinaya* adds that the rich householder is the disciple of all six masters, suggesting more explicitly that the taking of the bowl is bound up with the struggle of Buddhism against rival traditions for converts and the material support of wealthy patrons (LC., 96).

11. De Visser 1922–23, 72–73. A commentary on the *Ekottarāgama* says that as a result of his having defeated heretics, Piṇḍola was known as "first in suppressing heresy," and the *sūtra* collection itself quotes the Buddha as calling Piṇḍola "(first in) suppressing the heretical doctrine and walking in accordance with the *saddharma*" (De Visser 1922–23, 73).

12. The story unfolds in this way. The nobleman has established seven successive doors and he has three troupes of musicians. When he takes his meals, the seven doors are all shut. At each meal, a different troupe of musicians plays. While he is eating a meal, Aniruddha presents himself before him for alms. The nobleman asks, "How did you get in?" Aniruddha replies, "I entered by the door." The nobleman then asks the guard, "How is it that you permitted this mendicant to enter?" The guard replies, "The doors were locked as usual and I saw no one enter." Thereupon, the nobleman gives alms to Aniruddha and he departs. At the second meal, the same events and words transpire with Kāśyapa and at the third meal with Maudgalyāyana. Finally, the man is converted (LC., 100–103).

13. An interpretation presented in the *Theragāthā* commentary and in the *vinaya* of the Mahīśāsaka (see Strong 1979, 64–65).

14. "They know that this respect and homage in highborn families is truly a bog. A fine dart, hard to extract, honor is hard for a worthless man to give up" (*Ta* 124).

15. Chinese tradition comments on this aspect of Piṇḍola's character. In the seventh century, Tao-shih remarks that a number of disciples wish to see the venerable Piṇḍolabhāradvāja again. Therefore, the Buddha authorizes Piṇḍola to return "occasionally and to take his seat when invited" (Strong 1979, 78).

16. The authenticity of the lineage of seeing is a matter of further concern in the text. Aśoka would know more about the nature of Piṇḍola's seeing. He asks the saint, "Where did you see the Blessed One, and how?" Piṇḍola replies, indicating that he has seen the Buddha at those climactic moments when the Blessed One's full majesty was revealed. "I saw him first after he had conquered Māra's host and was spending the rains retreat in Rājagṛha together with five hundred arhats. I was there at the time and could see him perfectly. . . . I was then right there in front of the enlightened Sage, and I saw him face to face just as you see me now with your own eyes." Similarly, Piṇḍola saw the Blessed One when he performed the great miracle at Śrāvastī, magically creating a vision of buddha images in space and thereby defeating the heretics. He also saw the Buddha when he descended the miraculous stairway, in brilliantly transfigured form, from the Trāyastriṃśa heaven, where he had been preaching the dharma to his mother. And Piṇḍola saw the

Buddha when he accepted an invitation from Anāthapiṇḍada's daughter and miraculously flew to Puṇḍavardhana with five hundred arhants. Piṇḍola, having taken hold of a mountain boulder, flew along with the Buddha and his retinue (*Da* 401–2 [St., 261–63]).

17. Strong 1983, 71, citing Takakusu 1904, 273. It is significant that it is Piṇḍola, the forest renunciant and practitioner of meditation, who appears to Asaṅga, the great renunciant and meditator. Wayman similarly reports, "Asaṅga, after entering the Sarvāstivādin school, sought in vain to understand voidness *(śūnyatā)* and fell into profound despair. Then came the *arhat* Piṇḍola from eastern *(pūrva)* Videha, and with his instruction Asaṅga penetrated the 'small vehicle' *(hīnayāna)*" (1961, 31).

18. Lévi and Chavannes, having studied the Indian texts relating to this saint, conclude that the legends and rites attaching to Piṇḍolabhāradvāja in China originally came from India, brought by Indian missionaries (De Visser 1923, 79).

19. Like Mahākāśyapa and Upagupta, Piṇḍola possesses some significant features that I have not included in the paradigm of Buddhist sainthood because, although these are closely connected with the phenomenon of the realized saint, they represent more limited traditions pertinent to some but not all types of saints. For example, Piṇḍola is known as chief among the lion-roarers, a motif that turns up particularly among forest saints, such as those of the *Theragāthā* and *Therīgāthā,* following *dhutaguṇa*-like codes and meditating in seclusion for the purpose of realization.

20. King 1980, 28–29. The *Theragāthā* commentary depicts him as having become a renunciant in the first place because he is gluttonous by nature and sees that the *bhikṣu-saṃgha* receives a lot of food (*Ta*-c 110–11). Strong mentions that in at least two Pāli texts the word *piṇḍola* is used as a term of abuse by laypeople against renunciants (1979, 61).

21. Although in these two texts there is passing reference to the negative evaluations of Piṇḍola.

22. The Dharmaguptaka *vinaya* describes quite differently the manner in which the Buddha finds out about Piṇḍola's actions. Some *bhikṣus* who have learned of these events reproach Piṇḍola and then go to the Buddha, telling him what has happened. It is revealing that in this account, those monks who reprove Piṇḍola and report him to the Buddha are described as adhering to the *dhutaguṇas*: "having few desires, knowing themselves content with little, practicing the *dhutas*" (LC., 98). The Sarvāstivādin *vinaya* puts the matter in similar terms (LC., 106). Why is it *bhikṣus* following the *dhutaguṇas* who are made to criticize Piṇḍola, first to his face and then to the Buddha? Surely the fact that it is precisely these renunciants who censure him makes the strongest argument against Piṇḍola's credentials as a great *dhutaguṇin* and saint.

23. It is interesting that the various *vinayas* arrive at the same conclusion by sometimes different routes. In the Mahīśāsaka *vinaya,* the story of the taking of the bowl by magic is mentioned briefly but is not connected with the *vinaya* rule. Then follows the much longer account, summarized above, of Piṇḍola's conversion of the elder sister of the nobleman, in which he exhibits a variety of miraculous powers. It is at this point that the Buddha gathers the *saṃgha* together, questions and rebukes Piṇḍola, and lays down the *vinaya* rule about not exhibiting magical powers in front of the laity (LC., 103–4). For another kind of magical feat performed by Piṇḍola, for which he is also criticized by the Buddha, see Strong 1979, 74.

24. The *Ta*-c, for example, depicts Piṇḍola as a learned brahmin plagued by gluttony, prior to his conversion to Buddhism. Seeing how well the *bhikṣu saṃgha* was supported, he renounced the world under the Buddha, who finally tamed him. The *An*-c recounts essentially the same story (Strong 1979, 62).

25. One text says that, after the heretics were unable to obtain the bowl, the donor

became convinced that there were no more enlightened ones (arhants) in the world. Piṇḍola's demonstration puts this doubt to rest.

26. Strong 1979, 76. The logical inconsistencies between the positive image of Piṇḍola as a saint and his condemnation multiply. Piṇḍola's "misdeed" and punishment as described in the *vinaya* do not really make sense, as Piṇḍola's story is itself the occasion for the formulation of the *vinaya* rule in the first place; thus we are to believe that he is blamed for an infraction against a rule that was not even in existence at the time of his act. Again, Lamotte notes that the Pāli *vinaya* has the Buddha denying the specific effect that magical power in Buddhist tradition is often held to accomplish: the Buddha says, "This kind of conduct has the result neither of leading unbelievers into the faith nor confirming the faithful in their belief" (Lamotte 1958, 56).

27. In any case, it would appear that in the legends surrounding Piṇḍola, we are dealing with texts reflecting different viewpoints. The Northern sources tend to present Piṇḍola as a saint pure and simple, whereas the Southern want to reduce or dismiss his sainthood in various ways. Again, it is the *vinaya* or more monastically oriented texts that tend to take the more negative approach, whereas it is the more hagiographically oriented texts, such as the *Divyāvadāna,* that promote the more positive images. Nevertheless, the matter is complicated, because both Northern and Southern texts—including *vinaya, avadāna,* and *jātaka* texts—contain both positive and negative elements. This suggests (1) an original hagiographical complex surrounding Piṇḍola; (2) negative critiques of him that were more or less known in different forms by most of the traditions; and (3) a bringing of positive and negative elements into various configurations, some more positive, some more negative, by the texts as we have them.

28. This term is my interpolation and is not used in the text.

29. A further example is provided by the treatment of Maudgalyāyana in the legends surrounding Śāriputra. It will be recalled that Maudgalyāyana, exhibiting not scholarly but rather forest values, is contrasted with and put in a secondary position to Śāriputra. Particularly interesting in the present context, Maudgalyāyana, like Piṇḍola and Upagupta, is implicitly criticized because of his saintly traits. Migot, for example, recounts a legend according to which Maudgalyāyana's connection with longevity is seen as blameworthy: he is said to be inferior to Śāriputra *because* "he desires to live until the end of the *kalpa*" (Migot 1954, 509).

30. On Devadatta, see particularly Mukherjee's analysis of the corpus of legends surrounding this saint (1966) and Bareau's discussion of the early material (1988–89). See also Frauwallner 1956, 117–19, Lamotte 1958, 19–20, 69–70, 374, 572 and 728–29, Bareau 1959, 357–58, Waldschmidt 1964, and Lamotte 1980, 868–78.

31. It is not always Śāriputra who has this role. In a Sanskrit fragment of the *vinaya* of the Sarvāstivāda found in Chinese Turkistan, it is Ānanda who makes this praise (Waldschmidt 1964, 552ff.).

32. This list, containing the same saints given in the same order, appears in the *Majjhimanikāya* (3:78–79 [Horner 1954–59, 3:121])—except for the fact that Devadatta is absent from his position as number ten. The two most reasonable explanations for this discrepancy are (1) that the *Mn* list represents the original list and that Devadatta was later added to the *Ud* list and (2) that the *Ud* list represents the earlier confirguration, with Devadatta being removed in the *Mn* version. This latter option seems more likely for three reasons: (1) the antiquity of *Ud* in relation to the *Mn* (Lamotte 1958, 172); (2) given Devadatta's odious character in developed Buddhism, he is much more likely to be removed from a list like this than added to it; and (3) Devadatta does have a positive side, as we have seen, but as time goes on, it is increasingly hidden under a covering of vitriolic condemnation.

33. See especially Bareau 1988–89, 540.

34. In the Pāli account, these five conventions are explicitly called *dhuta* (*V*-p 3:171 [H., 1:296–97]). In other accounts, they are similarly identified as *dhuta* or *dhutañga* (Bareau 1988–89, 540).

35. *V*-p 2:188 (H., 5:264). For a discussion of this insult, see Lamotte 1970.

36. One of the most heinous deeds in Buddhism.

37. The Sarvāstivādin tradition has Devadatta not dying, the significance of which will become evident below (Bareau 1988–89, 541).

38. See Buddhaghosa's rendition of these events, *Dp*-c 133–50 (Bg., 1:230–42). Hsüan-tsang visited a place to the east of Jetavana monastery where there was a deep pit through which Devadatta was said to have dropped into hell (Watters 1904–5, 1:390). See also *V*-t, D., *'dul.ba,* nga, 292a–93a (R., 106–9).

39. For discussion of the different lists, see Chapter 9, pp. 312–14.

40. A version of Devadatta's proposed ascetic practices occurs in the Mūlasarvāstivādin *vinaya* preserved in Tibetan (Mukherjee's "Sanskrit tradition"):

> 1) The *śramaṇa* Gautama makes use of curds and milk; henceforth we will not make use of them, because by so doing one harms calves. 2) The *śramaṇa* Gautama makes use of meat; but we will not use it, because, if one does, living creatures are killed. 3) The *śramaṇa* Gautama makes use of salt; but we will not use it, because it is produced from a mass of sweat. 4) The *śramaṇa* Gautama wears gowns with cut fringes; but we will wear gowns with long fringes, because by his practice the skilful work of the weavers is destroyed. 5) The *śramaṇa* Gautama lives in the wilds; but we will live in villages, because by his practice men cannot perform works of charity. (*V*-t, D. *'dul.ba,* nga, 289a–b [R., 87–88])

This list has two items not found in the others (numbers 4 and 5). The fifth point in particular is interesting, for it directly contradicts the rules to live in the forest (in the "forest," "under trees," or "in the open"), at least one instance of which is found in each of the other traditions. That this list is more than simply a spurious attribution to Devadatta of a list of ascetic practices is suggested by Hsüan-tsang's report that there existed in his own time a sect that traced itself back to Devadatta in which milk products were not taken (Watters 1904–5, 2:191) (see later discussion in this chapter).

41. For a discussion of these *vinaya*s and that of the Mahāsāṃghika, see Lamotte 1958, 181–88.

42. To this he tentatively adds episode 6, Devadatta's practice of group begging and eating, which is present in most of the other *vinaya*s and is briefly mentioned in the Mahāsāṃghika (Mukherjee 1966, 146).

43. Many features of the Devadatta legend are found in the *Ekottarāgama*. Frauwallner believes that these features were originally contained in the Mahāsāṃghika *vinaya* and later separated from it. Mukherjee rejects this proposal, pointing out that the treatment of Devadatta in the *Ekottarāgama* in fact differs markedly from that accorded him in the *vinaya*s of the five schools, making Frauwallner's hypothesis unlikely (1966, 144).

44. Bareau points out that neither the Mahāsāṃghikas nor the Sarvāstivāda in either their *Skandhaka* or *Vibhañga* versions, nor the Mahīśāsaka nor Dharmaguptaka in their short versions *(Skandhaka),* link Devadatta with the Śākya family, and his family linkage with the Buddha is not mentioned in either *Skandhaka* or *Vibhañga* of any of the four schools. Bareau therefore finds it doubtful that this renunciant was a Śākya or a relation of the Buddha, as later held (1988–89, 544–45).

45. The same identification is also suggested by the existence near old Rājagṛha of a sacred place, a cave known as the Devadatta *samādhi* cave mentioned by both Hsüan-tsang (Watters 1904–5, 2:155) and Fa-hsien (Beal 1869, 118).

46. See note 31.

47. There should be no surprise that the later monastic authors who set down Devadatta's legend in the form that we have it failed so thoroughly to understand this saint's person and motives. In this regard, Bareau observes,

> The authors of the texts of the *Vinaya-piṭaka* lived a long time after the *parinirvāṇa,* as proved by the numerous differences which separate their accounts, in an epoch in which the mode of monastic life had greatly changed. Like their confreres, or at least the majority of these, they lived in monasteries where they enjoyed a material comfort far superior to that which had been known by the first disciples of the Blessed One. They judged the conditions of their existence as completely normal and in conformity with the rules set forth by the Buddha, because the *saṃgha* had become little by little habituated to these over the course of time. [The monastic authors] could not therefore comprehend the meaning of the reform which Devadatta had wished to impose on all the monks one or two centuries earlier, and this return to primitive austerity seemed to them insupportable. For them, the intentions of this person could not therefore be anything but malevolent, dictated not by an excess of virtue, but by envy, pride, and hatred of the Buddha. Incapable of giving up their lifestyle, so much less demanding than that of the first disciples, they slanderously accused him who had wished to impose such a renunciation on their precedessors of having acted from pure malice. Later on, their own successors slanderously accused Devadatta of further crimes, the most grave they could imagine, in order to further justify their resentment in relation to him and their condemnation of his action. (1988–89, 546)

48. See Bareau's discussion of this evidence (1988–89, 544).

49. Other scholars tend to agree with this interpretation (cf., e.g., Lamotte 1958, 374 and 572; Warder 1970, 62; and Shastri 1965, 44–45).

50. The presence of Devadatta in the Mahāsāṃghika discussion of *saṃghāvaśeṣa,* then, would be the result of a later borrowing. This is suggested by the complete difference in the way in which the events surrounding this episode are portrayed in the Mahāsāṃghika version.

51. Consistent with his belief in the early and normative character of settled monasticism, Bareau puts the Devadatta schism during the lifetime of the Buddha (1988–89, 544).

52. One exception, however, is provided by the Mūlasarvāstivāda *vinaya,* which says that one day Devadatta will be a pratyekabuddha.

53. The importance of the *Sps* mention of Devadatta to a full discussion of Devadatta's identity has been noticed by Sugimoto 1982.

54. *Sps* 157.15–161.33 (Kern 1884, 243–48). In the Chinese version of Kumārajīva, this section takes the form of its own chapter (cf. Hurwitz 1976, 195–201).

55. The six *pāramitā*s, great compassion *(mahākaruṇā),* the thirty major and eighty minor marks, the ten powers, the four confidences, the eighteen special dharmas, and so on.

56. A text preserved in Mongolian attempts to reconcile the good and evil personalities of Devadatta thus: "Stupid men believe wrongly and assert that Devadatta has been an opponent or enemy of the Buddha. That the sublime *bodhisattva* Devadatta during five hundred births, in which Buddha was going through the career of a *bodhisattva,* inflicted on him all possible evil and suffering was simply in order to to establish the excellence and high qualities of the *bodhisattva*" (Thomas 1949, 135, citing I. J. Schmidt, *Geschichte der Ost-Mongolen,* Saint Petersburg, 1829, 311).

6

Cults of Arhants

The phenomenon of the Buddhist saint is typically defined by the intersection of a particular paradigm of sainthood, characteristic traditions of forest renunciation, and an active cult. The preceding chapters have focused primarily upon the paradigm of Buddhist sainthood and have offered no more than glimpses of the saints' traditions of forest renunciation and their cults. The present chapter contains a discussion of the cult of the Buddhist saints through an examination of the cults of the arhants, as expressed in two quite different but converging bodies of evidence: textual evidence of the cult of the sixteen arhants and the reports of the Chinese pilgrims on the general cult of arhants.[1] As we shall see, the arhants depicted in this evidence possess many of the major features of the paradigm of the Buddhist saint outlined in previous chapters. However, in the evidence of the cult, almost the entire focus of attention is upon the arhants as fully realized saints. Although the postrealization careers of the arhants are depicted in the cultic evidence in bold and vivid colors, there is little discussion or even acknowledgment of their prerealization lives.

The Sixteen Arhants

A tradition of sixteen great arhants is documented in a number of Indian texts translated into Chinese,[2] particularly important among which is the *Nandimitrāvadāna*. This text, referred to in Chapter 5, is attributed to the great arhant Nandimitra who is depicted as living in Sri Lanka; it was in existence sometime prior to the seventh century,[3] when it was translated into Chinese by Hsüan-tsang.[4] According to the *Nandimitrāvadāna,* when the Buddha was about to enter *parinirvāṇa,* he entrusted his dharma to sixteen arhants and their followers, asking them to protect and maintain it from extinction (LC., 8). At the head of the arhants[5] stands Piṇḍolabhāradvāja, and their number also includes Kanakavatsa, Kanakaparidhvaja, Subinda, Nakula, Bhadra, Kālika, Vajraputra, Śvapāka, Panthaka, Rāhula, Nāgasena, Iṅgada, Vanavāsi, Ajita, and Cūḍapanthaka (9). These sixteen arhants are Buddhist saints in the classical mold, reflecting in their persons the major features of the paradigm, particularly its postrealization elements. Thus, these arhants all possess the characteristics of enlightened people, including wisdom, compassion, and power (9). The Buddha, we are told, asked these sixteen enlightened beings to present themselves to the laity as worthy objects of donation, so that those who make offerings to them may gain great reward. In order to fulfill the Buddha's injunction, the sixteen arhants, by means of magical power, have extended their lives indefinitely, remaining in various places and responding to the supplications of beings (8–10).[6]

The *Nandimitrāvadāna* tells us that the sixteen arhants now dwell in various abodes, along with groups of arhant disciples. Thus Piṇḍola lives with one thousand enlightened disciples, the other fifteen with five hundred, six hundred, seven hundred, eight hundred, nine hundred, one thousand, eleven hundred, nine hundred, thirteen hundred, eleven hundred, twelve hundred, thirteen hundred, fourteen hundred, sixteen hundred, and sixteen hundred disciples, respectively (LC., 10–11). This presents considerable contrast, of course, with some of the traditions examined in previous chapters, in which the saints dwell alone. This difference is consistent with the fact that the sixteen arhants represent saints in their realized phase. Whereas solitude is emphasized in the case of the saint-to-be, the fully realized, enlightened saint is at least sometimes depicted as surrounded by many disciples, who, in cultic contexts such as this, are stereotypically counted in the many hundreds.[7]

The sixteen arhants are each said to live in a particular locale, which tends to be nonordinary, either a sacred site or a remote or even mythical place.[8] On the continent of Jambudvīpa, they often live on holy mountains, including Gandhamādana, the Himalayan refuge of pratyekabuddhas; Gṛdhrakūṭa in Magadha, the Vulture Peak Mountain famed for its caves of meditating ascetics; Potalaka in the south; or the mountains of Vipulapārśva, Vatsa, or Nemiṃdhara.[9] On Jambudvīpa, they also live in Kashmir in the north (LC., 10–11). They also inhabit the mythical lands of Tāmradvīpa, Saṃghaṭa or Siṃhaladvīpa, Paraṇa, and Priyañgu (Shan Shih 1961, 10). The sixteen arhants are also explicitly said to inhabit each of the four continents of the world, Pūrvavideha in the east, Aparagodānīya in the west, Uttarakuru in the north, and Jambudvīpa in the south (this is perhaps mentioned for symmetry, for several arhants are said to live in specific places on Jambudvīpa). One arhant lives in the realm of the gods, Trāyastriṃśa (LC., 10–11).[10]

These habitations of the sixteen arhants identify them as quintessential forest saints—they are not of the known and civilized world but live in places that are remote and even completely inaccessible to ordinary folk. All their abodes, whether mountain top, island, far-off land, another continent, or the realm of the gods, are other. If ordinary forest renunciants live in jungles, caves, or mountains that have only a vague geographical relation to centers of "civilization," the sixteen arhants, owing to their unsurpassed sanctity, tend to live in places that are even further removed. The would-be devotee of the ordinary forest saints knows that they are hard to search out in their domains, but the sixteen arhants cannot be visited at all, at least not by ordinary people.[11] The character of the sixteen arhants as forest saints is also reflected in their association with *dhutaguṇa*-like practices and with meditation.[12] In another textual discussion of the arhants, in the *Ekottarāgama,* we find Vakula (Nakula) sitting alone in his mountain retreat, patching an old garment. The same text tells us that "he who tortures his body and sits in the dew, and who does not flee wind and rain, is the *bhikṣu* Vatsa" (De Visser 1922–23, 81, 89). Such retreat places and the meditation that one does there, in Indian conception, provide access to other realms, and thus it is that we find the sixteen arhants able to come and go between this world and others.

According to the *Nandimitrāvadāna,* the sixteen arhants may be remote and nearly impossible to search out, but they are not entirely otiose, for when properly invited they will of their own accord come to provide blessings, protection, and help of all kinds, reflecting the compassion that is central to their personalities. In fact, it is precisely out of their compassion for sentient beings that the arhants have in the first place prolonged their lives.[13] The same altruistic motivation also explains their offering of themselves as worthy objects of donation and their protection of the dharma. The *Nandimitrāvadāna* says further that one invites the presence of the arhants by offering great feasts, and the categories of people who are to make such offerings is broad: "kings, ministers, elders and lay Buddhists, whether male or female," who have a devout and pure mind (LC., 11). One is to offer a great feast to renunciants of the four quarters. In addition, one may hold a quinquennial assembly; arrange a meeting in celebration of a monastery, an image of the Buddha, or a scriptural pennant; invite monks to one's house or go to a monastery where, at the place of walking, one spreads beddings of the finest quality and food and drink as offerings to the monks (11–12). One may also offer "temples, images, and *sūtra* flags . . . chairs and beds, clothes and medicine" (11–12). When one does this, one may expect miraculous results. At such a time, the sixteen great arhants along with their entourages will appear in different forms, secretly receive offerings as ordinary renunciants, and thus allow whoever makes donations to them to receive great merit (12; see also Shan Shih 1961, 11).[14]

The sixteen arhants are typically not shown with any particular connection to the memorization and study of texts, nor to the activity that is typically connected with this, the public expounding or preaching of the dharma.[15] In fact, the arhants are sometimes explicitly depicted as far removed from such preoccupations. An example of this tendency is Vakula, depicted in the *Ekottarāgama* as sitting alone in the mountains, engaged in patching an old garment. Śakra, king of the gods, comes to him and asks, "Why [did] Vakula, an arhant, who had dissolved all bonds, whose length of life was immeasurable, who constantly suppressed his thoughts himself, who was not attached to worldly matters, . . . not explain the Law to others and preferred a solitary self-practice?" Vakula explains that this is not his kind of dharma, and the preaching he can leave to Śāriputra, Ānanda, and the other like-minded disciples. When, in another text, he is challenged as to why he does not preach, he responds that it is not through lack of intelligence or knowledge but because he prefers to progress directly to liberation (De Visser 1922–23, 81–82).[16] This distance from the world of texts, learning, and exposition is also a feature in Cūḍapanthaka's story. He is challenged by a learned brahmin to a debate, and although he is unable to answer the brahmin with words, "decided to do so by deeds. By means of his divine power he flew up into the air and there sat down cross-legged" (84–85).[17] Cūḍapanthaka is described as someone who left the world at an old age and is very stupid. Although caused by the

Buddha to be instructed by the five hundred arhants daily for three years, he has been unable to learn even a single verse. Nevertheless, he attains arhantship. At a nunnery where he goes to preach the dharma, the women renunciants all laugh, but on hearing him preach, they are "very much rejoiced and edified" (86).[18]

The arhants are able to shower their suppliants with blessings owing to their superhuman status. They are enlightened sages who, as we have seen, possess great longevity. Of particular importance, they are understood to possess various kinds of wisdom, compassion, and supernatural power, including the three knowledges *(vidyā),* the six *abhijñā*s, the eight meditative stages *(vimokṣa),* and immeasurable merits and virtues. The *Ekottarāgama* says of the tenth and sixteenth arhants in Nandimitra's list, "He who by means of his divine magic power can hide himself is the *bhikṣu* Panthaka, and he who can transform his body and perform very many miracles (metamorphoses) is the *bhikṣu* Cūḍapanthaka" (De Visser 1922–23, 83). In another text we are told that Cūḍapanthaka can cause five hundred apparitions of himself to appear, such that all of them seem to be real (85). In another version of his story, though able to explain only one *gāthā,* Cūḍapanthaka's magical powers are revealed to be prodigious: "He divided his body into innumerable bodies and then rejoined these into one shape. He jumped over stone walls, walked upon water as if it were earth, entered the earth like water, showed a half body or a golden body or caused smoke and fire and water to come out of his body. He sat and lay down in the air and flew like a bird. With his hands he reached to his seat and explained the *gāthā* like before" (86).

The roles of the sixteen great arhants will change with the changing world ages. Now, they dwell in remote regions, coming among people only on special occasions. Later, when the life of human beings will have decreased to ten years and war and strife prevail, the Buddha's dharma will temporarily disappear from the world. Subsequently, the life of human beings will increase to one hundred years, and humans, becoming tired of the chaos of their lives, will again begin to practice virtue. Then, the sixteen great arhants will return among humankind, again preach the unsurpassable dharma, cause people to leave their homes and enter the renunciant life, and act for the benefit of all living beings. Their work will continue until the length of human life is sixty thousand years and the dharma will be widely propagated in this world without cessation. This will go on until the span of human life has reached seventy thousand years, at which point the dharma will be extinguished forever (LC., 12).

At this point in their legend, the sixteen great arhants are explicitly connected with the coming of Maitreya and with millennial themes (LC., 13–14). At this time, the arhants and their disciples will make a great stūpa of the seven precious substances and place within it all the relics of the *tathāgata.* Having circumambulated the stūpa and made offerings and sung praises, they will ascend into the air and declare, "Homage to the Bhagavat, Śākya, the Tathāgata, the Arhat, the Samyaksaṃbuddha! We have been ordered by you to protect and maintain the good law [dharma] and to accomplish all kinds of beneficial actions for gods and humans. Now the baskets *(piṭaka)* have come to an end; the cycle of causes [of our presence] has come to its end; and we beg leave to enter nirvāṇa" (13). Having said this, the arhants will enter nirvāṇa without remainder in the following fashion: based on a former vow, flames will spontaneously arise and cremate their bodies, leaving no trace of their remains.[19] Then the stūpa will sink underground, until it reaches the stratum of the Golden Wheel. The dharma of Buddha Śākyamuni will then disappear forever from the three thousand great chilicosms (LC., 13).[20] At this point, seventy thousand *koṭis*[21] of pratyekabuddhas will emerge in this buddha field. When human life has reached eighty thousand years, the pratyekabuddhas will also enter nirvāṇa. Then Maitreya, the future Buddha, will come into this world. At his arrival, this world will be transformed, becoming broad and pure, without thorns or thistles, without valleys or hills, covered with golden sand, ponds of pure waters, verdant forests with grasses and beautiful flowers, and heaps of jewels radiant with light. The people of this world will be kind, ever performing the ten virtuous actions and, as a result, will enjoy happiness, abundance, and long life. In this world, Maitreya will preach the dharma to innumerable disciples (13–14).

The *Nandimitrāvadāna* closes with the dramatic *parinirvāṇa* predicted for the sixteen arhants, prefigured now by Nandimitra. By the power of his *abhijñā,* Nandimitra rises into the air and displays various miracles to the assembly. Then he sits, legs crossed in meditation posture, and enters *parinirvāṇa.* By the power of his vow, fixed beforehand, the flame of *samādhi* comes out from his body and he is spontaneously cremated. A rain of relics falls upon the earth, and the crowd of people assembled there erect a stūpa for the relics and make offerings to them (LC., 23–24).

What was the Buddhist context of the sixteen arhants, at least in so far as can be determined from the Indian texts? As we have seen, the arhants themselves possess many of the typical features of the paradigm of the forest saint and are not depicted as associated with Buddhist monasticism or its ideals. Thus, it seems that they were understood as renunciants who, through their forest life of meditation, have attained perfection and have become worthy of the cult that surrounds them. This does not, however, answer the question of the context of the cult of these arhants. Nandimitra's text is centrally concerned with the making of offerings to the sixteen arhants, through making offerings to renunciants of the four quarters, and with the benefits to be obtained thereby. In a discrete section of the *Nandimitrāvadāna,* which follows a discussion of Maitreya's coming, three other kinds of religious activities are mentioned from which great benefits are to be derived. We are told that when Maitreya arrives, he will teach the dharma in three assemblies. Moreover, one will earn merit to be in the first, second, or third assembly depending on the kind of cult in which one has previously participated.

In first place is the cult of the Buddha. In this type of activity connected with the first of the three jewels (Buddha, dharma, *saṃgha*), one should perform or cause others to perform the making of images of the Buddha and stūpas, in various media, including the seven precious substances, or in other less valuable substances, or by weaving or painting. Through this meritorious activity, suppliants will be born as human beings in Maitreya's time and, attending the first assembly offered by Maitreya, will renounce the world and realize nirvāṇa. "This is what is called, in the first place, the recompense of the reward obtained by those who have planted an excellent root in practicing the cult of the Buddha'' (LC., 15–16).

In second place is the cult of the dharma, meaning in this case the study, recitation, and veneration of texts. In this second type of activity, connected with the second of the three jewels, one should oneself perform or cause others to perform the study of the Mahāyāna *sūtras* of the Mahāyāna *Sūtrapiṭaka* that are in harmony with emptiness. The *Nandimitrāvadāna* goes on to mention by name some fifty Mahāyāna *sūtras*, including the *''Prajñāpāramitā Sūtra,''* the *Avataṃsaka Sūtra,* the *Saddharmapuṇḍarīka Sūtra,* and the *Suvarṇaprabhāsa Sūtra (Suvarṇaprabhāsottama Sūtra).* It also mentions the Mahāyāna *Vinayapiṭaka* and *Abhidharmapiṭaka* contained in the *Bodhisattvapiṭaka;* the Śrāvakayāna *Tripiṭaka* including the *Sūtrapiṭaka* containing the five *āgamas;*[22] the *Vinayapiṭaka* with its various subdivisions; the *Abhidharmapiṭaka* with the six sections and the *Jñānaprasthāna;* the *Jātakamālā;* the *Pratyekabuddhamālā;* and other works. These texts should not only be studied but recited, read, practiced, or explained. In addition, one should respect and make offerings to preachers or pay homage and make offerings to the scriptures—fragrant flowers, music, lamps, and so on. Those who do so will be born as human beings in the time of Maitreya and, present in the second assembly offered by Maitreya, will renounce the world and attain nirvāṇa. ''This is what is called, in the second place, the recompense of the reward obtained by those who have planted an excellent root in practicing the cult of the *dharma*'' (LC., 16–21).

In third place is the cult of the *saṃgha.* In this third type of religious activity connected with the third of the three jewels, one is to perform, or cause others to perform, the making of offerings to the *bhikṣus* and *bhikṣuṇīs* on the first, eighth, or fifteenth day of the month. Food should be offered to them or should be taken to the monastery to one or all the monks. One is also to act as attendant or make offerings to those who practice meditation or who preach the dharma. One should additionally support those who wish to study the dharma and make offerings to monasteries. Those who do so will be reborn as human beings in the time of Maitreya, will renounce the world, attend the third assembly of Maitreya, and will attain nirvāṇa. ''This is what is called, in the third place, the recompense of the reward obtained by those who have planted an excellent root in practicing the cult of the *saṃgha*'' (LC., 21–23).[23]

Among these three types of religious activities, the first, the cult of the Buddha, stands in close relation to the cult of the arhants. As has been suggested, and as shall be seen in more detail, the building and veneration of stūpas and the fashioning of images occupy a central place in the larger Buddhist cult of saints, whether buddhas, arhants, or other types of saints. However, the second and third types of activity enjoined by the *Nandimitrāvadāna* are less closely related to the cult of arhants, for the dharma is explicitly associated with the study of texts, and the term *saṃgha* clearly includes the world of settled monasticism. The mere fact that the *Nandimitrāvadāna* can mention such a vast array of texts from various traditions suggests the developed scholarly traditions of settled monasticism, as does the fact that one may also gain merit by making offerings to monastics and monasteries. These two taken together suggest that by the time of Nandimitra's text, at least in the recension in which we have it, the cult of arhants was understood to be part of a greater whole within which the world of monastic Buddhism was prominent.

In fact, structurally the *Nandimitrāvadāna* seems somewhat at odds with itself. The earlier and major portion of the text presents the sixteen arhants, the context of their worship, and the benefits to be derived therefrom. None of these benefits mentions human birth in Maitreya's time. This is followed by the section on the three types of gifts that describes these divergent activities and their goals. Oddly enough, nowhere does it say in the text that worship of the sixteen arhants leads to the goal of rebirth in Maitreya's time. One has the impression, in fact, of dealing with two different texts that have been put together, one focusing on the sixteen arhants and their cult, the other discussing various religious activities, each with its reward. These facts suggest that the cult of the sixteen arhants, as expressed in the *Nandimitrāvadāna,* developed in stages. In its earlier phases, it perhaps represented a cult of Buddhist saints not particularly aligned with monasticism or institutionalized Buddhism. In its later, monasticized phases it is clearly tied in with the values and orientations of settled monasticism.

Texts such as the *Nandimitrāvadāna* and *Ekottarāgama* make it clear that the cult of the sixteen arhants played a role in Indian Buddhism, but we have very little direct evidence of that cult in India.[24] By contrast, we have considerable information on the practice of the cult in East Asian Buddhism, and there need be little doubt, as Lévi and Chavannes suggest (for example, 1916, 79), that many elements of this extra-Indian cult of the sixteen arhants reflect Indian practice. Further study of the non-Indian evidence may well provide insights into the Indian cult. A few brief examples will suggest the kind of insights this material can provide. In China, for example, tradition reports that the Ch'an renunciant Kuan-hsiu (832–912) was a devoted and leading practitioner of the cult of the sixteen arhants. Among other things, he is said to have established a *lohan* (arhant) hall and painted an early set of the sixteen arhants that became quite famous in subsequent times. In order to paint the arhants, Kuan-hsiu would pray for a dream, and when the desired dream occurred, he would see the arhants vividly. Elsewhere we are told that he would enter *samādhi* and see the arhants, after which he could paint them (De Visser 1922–23, 105–8). We are also told that there was a special ritual connected with the leader of the sixteen arhants, Piṇḍolabhāradvāja, traced by Lévi and Chavannes to Indian origins (1916, 79), wherein an image was made of Piṇḍola and he was offered food. He might also be invited to partake in a bath provided for the renunciant *saṃgha* (78–79). Piṇḍola might accept these invitations and come into the presence of his suppliants, conferring on them blessings.[25] This and other similar evidence raises the question of whether the cult of the sixteen arhants may not have had special connections with Ch'an tradition and its meditators from an early time, which raises the interesting possibility that the cult was similarly aligned with forest meditative traditions in India.

The motif of the longevity of the sixteen arhants is a particularly striking one and invites reflection about its possible relation with another Buddhist tradition concerned with the saints' longevity—if of a slightly different kind—namely, the classical Mahāyāna and its bodhisattva ideal. It is often held that the bodhisattva ideal is modeled on the paradigm of the Buddha, in his former and final lives. Certainly, at least to some extent, this seems a reasonable hypothesis. The bodhisattva, like the Buddha, vows to attain full enlightenment for the good of beings and progresses through a long series of births as a bodhisattva in fulfillment of that vow. At the same time, there is a major discrepancy that suggests a more complex origin for the bodhisattva ideal. Unlike the Buddha, in the tradition of the *Daśabhūmika Sūtra,* for example, the bodhisattva, upon winning the sixth *bhūmi,* attains the level of realization of an arhant. However, the bodhisattva does not exit the world but continues on to attain the full enlightenment of a buddha.[26] Thus, unlike the Buddha, this saint takes rebirth as a virtually enlightened being whose primary purpose for remaining in saṃsāra is to help others. In the Buddha's lives, by contrast, the Buddha cannot attain enlightenment until he in fact does so, in his final life, and there is no notion of an earlier, arhant-type realization available to him with a concomitant delay of his final realization.

This raises the question of the origin of the notion of the bodhisattva's delay, out of compassion, of an enlightenment that is already available. In seeking an answer, let us note a series of intriguing congruities between the ideals of the arhant (of the type of the sixteen arhants) and the bodhisattva, with respect to their ongoing presence among human beings. Like the sixteen arhants, the bodhisattva explicitly postpones *parinirvāṇa,* which otherwise could be taken at the present time. Both arhants and bodhisattvas do so on account of a vow made in the presence of *the* Buddha (arhants) or *a* buddha (bodhisattvas). Like the sixteen arhants, the bodhisattva's motivation is compassion and a desire to help sentient beings. Both the arhants and the bodhisattva will come among human beings again and again; but whereas the arhants arrive from remote and inaccessible places in this life, the bodhisattva comes from beyond death, through the vehicle of repeated and intentional rebirth in accord with the bodhisattva vow.[27] Like the arhants, bodhisattvas may appear to humans in guises in which they are not necessarily recognized; as Asaṅga tells us in his *Bodhisattvabhūmi,* they adopt the manners and speech of ordinary people, making themselves indistinguishable from them (40ff.).[28] Both arhants and bodhisattvas thus maintain an active presence among human beings and respond to people's supplications (Ray 1990).

It may be argued that these similarities are a result of the modeling of the arhant of the cult on the classical bodhisattva ideal of the Mahāyāna. However, this is unlikely, because the tradition of, for example, the longevity of the arhants and other saints is early—appearing in the *Mahāparinirvāṇa Sūtra*—and widespread (for example, Mahākāśyapa, Piṇḍolabhāradvāja, Upagupta). All of this suggests two interesting options. First, the ideal of the bodhisattva developed partly out of that of an early saintly arhant type similar to the later type of the sixteen arhants. Second, the ideals of the bodhisattva and the sixteen arhants, as we have them, both reflect and are developments of features of an earlier, common understanding of what makes a saint within Buddhism. According to this option, the saint's longevity and the features of belief and practice closely implied by it were not considered possessions of one or another type of holy person but were understood as potential characteristics of the Buddhist saint as such.

The Chinese Pilgrims on the Cult of Arhants

During the fifth to the seventh centuries C.E., four Chinese pilgrims visited India and left accounts of their experiences. Two of these in particular, Fa-hsien (fl. 399–418 C.E.; journey to India, 399–412) (Beal 1869) and Hsüan-tsang (596?–664 C.E.; journey to India, 627–645) (Watters 1904–5) provide a considerable amount of information on the Indian Buddhist cult of arhants at the times of their visits in various places.[29] The reports of these two are important because to a large extent they are based on what they saw and heard, rather than on written texts.[30] As foreign travelers seeking the roots of Buddhism, they are mainly interested in the Buddha, and they report in detail on his sacred places and cult. They take some (but less) notice of the former buddhas (B., 67, 72, 82–83, 84; cf. 88), the pratyekabuddhas (47, 69–70, 97–99, 134–35), and the great arhant disciples of the Buddha and even less notice of later well-known or more strictly local arhants. As foreign travelers, Fa-hsien and Hsüan-tsang also tend to seek out established and renowned centers of the saints' cults, visiting well-known monasteries and stūpas, and reporting on legends connected with them. Understandably, they have little to say about contemporary living saints, who would have tended to be less visible and available to them. In spite of such limitations, however, these two pilgrims provide important glimpses of the cult of arhants as it existed in India in the fifth and the seventh centuries C.E.

Fa-hsien

Fa-hsien[31] explicitly discusses three types of Buddhist saint: buddhas, pratyekabuddhas, and arhants.[32] Like the other two categories of saints, the arhants are, in type, to be distinguished from settled monastics. The arhants tend to be forest saints, who meditate in solitude, whereas the monks are associated with settled monasteries. Fa-hsien appreciates these two in different ways. As we shall see, he praises the arhants for their realization, compassion, and power. The monks, Nikāya and Mahāyāna alike, he particularly compliments for recitation of texts (see, for example, B., 6, 56, 105)[33] and purity of behavior (for example, 9, 105, 126).[34]

The arhants mentioned by Fa-hsien are understood as realized beings, different in degree from the buddhas and pratyekabuddhas. As noted, Fa-hsien treats the arhants as realized, superhuman beings and focuses on the postrealization phase of their careers, taking little notice of their humanity or their prerealization lives. The arhants have attained realization, and Fa-hsien usually discusses aspects of their persons that presuppose that realization. However, in a few instances he discusses the moment of realization itself and includes a glimpse of the transition from human to superhuman status. For example, Fa-hsien tells the story of a certain *bhikṣu* who enters the gate of Aśoka's hell, a prison of torture built by

Aśoka before his conversion, from which it is said no one ever comes out alive. Once inside, this *bhikṣu* is seized by the jailer and, while awaiting his own torture and witnessing the torture of another poor soul, attains nirvāṇa (B., 129). We shall see another description of the moment of realization, in which a renunciant attains nirvāṇa through self-immolation.

In Fa-hsien's account, after realization the arhants are typically associated with meditation and the Buddhism of the forest, living in remote and secluded places, such as deep forests, caves, and mountains (B., 103, 114–15). Thus, on Vulture Peak Mountain, where the Buddha meditated, there is a stone cave facing south where Ānanda practiced meditation (114).[35] Moreover, "each of the arhants likewise has a cave (in this neighborhood) celebrated as the place where he practiced meditation. . . . Altogether there are several hundred of these" (115). In another place, the pilgrim finds "very many other stone cells used by all the Rahats [arhants] for the purpose of meditation" (118). Similarly, King Aśoka's brother, who became an arhant, finds "his chief delight in silent meditation" (103). As at the Vulture Peak Mountain, so at other hills and mountains, arhants live in caves meditating (139–41).

By virtue of their attainment, the arhants come into the possession of miraculous powers. In the story just cited, for example, the arhant in Aśoka's prison is put into a caldron of boiling water. He is full of joy and his countenance is radiant. The fire is miraculously extinguished, the water becomes cold, and a lotus springs up in the middle on top of which the arhant takes his seat (B., 129–30). When Aśoka comes to see this miracle, the arhant preaches the dharma to him, and Aśoka is converted and orders the place of torture destroyed (130).[36] The arhants also have the powers typically associated with enlightened saints in Buddhism. For example, they can fly, and Fa-hsien reports of a certain hill where many arhants dwell, where the local villagers often see persons flying in the area (140). The arhants also have supernatural sight, as when the arhant Anuruddha sees from far off the Buddha, who is just descending from the Tuṣita heaven where he was preaching to his mother, and the arhant bids Mahāmaudgalyāyana pay reverence to him (62–63).

By virtue of their *ṛddhi,* the arhants can fly and can visit the heavenly realms, and they can also take other people there. A certain arhant is, by his magical power, able to take a sculptor to the Tuṣita heaven to see the bodhisattva Maitreya in person and to observe his size, color, and general appearance. The purpose of this adventure is to enable the sculptor, upon his return, to carve an accurate wooden image of the buddha-to-be (De Visser 1922–23, 103–4, 106, 108). The sculptor requires three visits to complete the massive statue, but the result is miraculous, for on festival days, it emits effulgent light and the princes of the countries all around vie with one another in making offerings to it (B., 19–20). The arhants, by virtue of their enlightenment, are also charged with a special holy power, which may manifest itself in a physical way. Fa-hsien reports that at the time of the dedication of a certain *vihāra,* an arhant spilled some of the water with which he was washing his hands. The place where the water fell was still visible in Fa-hsien's time, and no amount of sweeping and cleansing could remove it (68–69).

As Fa-hsien sees it, one establishes one's connection with the arhants through worship. All the faithful participate in the arhant's cult, including both laypeople and renunciants—even renunciants after they have attained realization. Thus, Mahāmaudgalyāyana prostrates himself in adoration of the footprints of the Buddha (B., 63). Kings are frequently shown interacting with arhants by making offerings (104). The arhants anticipate their deaths and die in extraordinary ways (101–2). Repeating the well-known story, Fa-hsien reports that Ānanda, for example, in the process of crossing a river, entered into "the *samādhi* called the 'brilliancy of flame,' " which consumed his body, and entered into nirvāṇa "in the very midst of the river" (101–2). Suicide figures in some legends of the passing of arhants, as in the case of a forest renunciant who, near a certain mountain cave, spends his time "walking forward and backward . . . meditating" on the suffering of his life. He determines to commit suicide as a way to root out the three poisons, and, setting about the work of cutting his own throat, he progressively attains the stages of a once-returner, a nonreturner, and an arhant and enters nirvāṇa (119). When arhants die, they are typically cremated; Fa-hsien describes the cremation of a particular arhant in Sri Lanka:

> After his death, the King immediately examined the Sacred Books, with a view to perform the funeral obsequies according to the rules for such as are Rahats [arhants]. Accordingly, about 4 or 5 li to the east of the Vihāra, they erected a very great pyre of wood, about 34 feet square, and of the same height. Near the top they placed tiers of sandalwood, aloe, and all kinds of scented wood. On the four sides they constructed steps by which to ascend it. Then, taking some clean and very white camlet cloth, they bound it around and above the pyre. Then they constructed a funeral carriage, just like the hearses used in this country, except that there are no dragon-ear handles to it. Then, at the time of the cremation, the King, accompanied by every class of his people, assembled in great numbers, came to the spot provided with flowers and incense for religious offerings. The multitude followed the hearse till it arrived at the place of the funeral ceremony. The King then in his own person offered religious worship with flowers and incense. This being over, the hearse was placed on the pyre, and oil of cinnamon poured over it in all directions. Then they set light to the whole. At the time of kindling the fire, the whole assembly occupied their minds with solemn thoughts. Then removing their upper garments, and taking their wing-like fans, which they use as sun shades, and approaching as near as they can to the pyre, they fling them into the midst of the fire, in order to assist the cremation. When all was over, they diligently searched for the bones and collected them together, in order to raise a tower [stūpa] over them. (159–60)

From this passage, it appears that the cremation of arhants was to be carried out according to certain specifications, that these might be found in written texts, that the king had a special role, and that the assembled devotees participated in the cremation mentally (their "solemn thoughts") and physically (by throwing certain garments and possessions into the flames).

For Fa-hsien, stūpas are primary manifestations of the dharma and are encountered everywhere. Although by far the great majority are stūpas to Buddha Śākyamuni, other buddhas, and pratyekabuddhas, the pilgrim also tells us that he visited a number of stūpas built to arhants. Most of the time, these are constructed to particular arhants, as in a certain locale where he found stūpas built to Śāriputra, Maudgalyāyana, and Ānanda (B., 56–57). Stūpas might also be constructed to the arhants in the collective, like a stūpa in Nagrāk built to all the arhants and pratyekabuddhas, of whom as many as a thousand were said to have dwelt at that place (47). The more important of these stūpas each has its own history and peculiarities. At Vaiśālī, for example, are two stūpas, one on each side of the river, each containing one half of the body of Ānanda; this double interment reflects the story just recounted, of Ānanda's autocremation in the middle of the river, leaving half of his relics on one side and half on the other (96, 100–101). The stūpas of the arhants are worshiped in the same general fashion as those of the Buddha. For example, after the chanting of texts, certain monks present religious offerings to the stūpa of Śāriputra, offering "every kind of incense and flowers" and burning lamps "throughout the whole night" (58). One worships the stūpa of this or that arhant depending upon one's interests and orientation. *Bhikṣuṇīs* worship the stūpa of Ānanda, because it was through his good offices that women were allowed to enter the order. *Śrāmaṇeras* worship the stūpa of Rāhula (58–59).

For Fa-hsien, the arhants are not figures of merely past importance but are understood to be present even now. In reference to Mount Kukkuṭapāda, a place of dense and tangled thickets and dangerous wild animals, Fa-hsien says that Mahākāśyapa "is at present within this mountain," in a chasm where his entire body is preserved (B., 132). Suppliants journey from far countries to worship him there, and they may also meet other arhants who dwell there. For example, Fa-hsien tells us that "as soon as the sun begins to decline, all the Rahats come and take their abode" (133). If pilgrims have doubts or difficulties, the arhants help them and then disappear (133).

Fa-hsien's arhants thus closely approximate many features of the general paradigm of Buddhist sainthood outlined in Chapter 2. His discussion of buddhas and pratyekabuddhas and their cults, as we shall see, also shows these saints conforming to the general paradigm. Thus, the three categories of Buddhist saints discussed in detail by Fa-hsien—buddhas, pratyekabuddhas, and arhants—are all of a piece, offering variations upon the theme of the Buddhist saint.

Fa-hsien generally sees arhants and orthodox monks as separate categories of renunciants typically operating in separate contexts, with the arhants depicted as typically living in remote and solitary settings. One interesting exception occurs in his account of the cremation of the arhant in Sri Lanka. In the Mahāvihāra (great monastery) reside some three thousand monks, among whom is an eminent *śramaṇa* so pure in his observation of the disciplinary rules that he is presumed to be an arhant. At the time of this man's death, the king inquires of the monks whether he was indeed an arhant and, having obtained a positive response, prepares the cremation (Legge 1886, 107–8). This reveals that in Fa-hsien's time a person could be considered an arhant who was a monk living in a monastery, who followed the conventional monastic way of life, and whose sanctity was based on the belief in the perfection with which he fulfilled the *vinaya* ideal.

Hsüan-tsang

Hsüan-tsang,[37] like Fa-hsien, also generally discusses the arhants only in the post-realization phase of their careers. However, he tells a few stories that depict the attainment of arhantship—for example, the realization of the mendicant in Aśoka's hell and the story of Aśoka's brother Mahendra, who is locked up by Aśoka, attains arhantship, exhibits miraculous powers, and goes into solitary retreat in a mountain gorge (Wts., 2:94). Having attained realization, the arhants, according to Hsüan-tsang, continue to be forest renunciants, living "on the hills and in the vales" (1:267), in caves, and in other remote places. It is significant that Aśoka, in the hope of luring his arhant brother back from his forest abode to the palace, promises to build him "a cave dwelling there" (2:94).

The realization of the arhants is expressed in compassion (Wts., 1:222), and it is out of compassion that, even after realization, they remain in the world and continue to provide help to sentient beings. Attesting to the realization of the arhants, various miraculous phenomena spontaneously surround their persons. For example, the twelve hundred arhants who form the Buddha's retinue cast away their tooth sticks in a certain place. These all take root and, by the time of Hsüan-tsang's visit, have become a dense forest (1:129). Hsüan-tsang tells us that Śāṇakavāsin, Ānanda's successor, is born already wearing the hempen robe of a renunciant, which grows with him as he matures. At his novice ordination, the robe miraculously becomes the appropriate clerical robe, and when he receives full ordination it becomes a nine-striped robe *(saṃghāṭī)*. When he is about to pass away, Śāṇakavāsin leaves his robe, which will last as long as the dharma lasts in this world and will be destroyed when the dharma disappears (1:120). As realized ones, the arhants have various sorts of magical powers. Most typically, they can fly (1:388), and they know the previous births of others (1:222). They may also make their appearance to teach, and miraculously disappear when they have finished (1:222; 2:44). Further, arhants have the power to visit the heavenly realms (1:239 and 323) and to take others there, as in the case of the arhant Madhyāntika who takes an artist to the Tuṣita heaven—apparently a popular motif in Indian Buddhism—to see Maitreya so that he can better fashion his likeness (1:239). The arhant Devasena similarly takes a famous scholar to visit Maitreya to resolve his difficulties (1:323).[38] Aśoka wants the relics he has collected from the eight great stūpas to be deposited simultaneously in the eighty-four thousand stūpas. The relics are given to the gods, and Upagupta signals the right instant by putting his hand over the sun, darkening the land (2:91). Although arhants possess and freely use their miraculous powers, in one story told by Hsüan-tsang the limited value of such abilities is stressed in relation to the attainment of ultimate wisdom (1:388).

Hsüan-tsang tells us that the arhants have both personal disciples, who wait upon them and attend them (Wts., 1:127), and lay devotees. The arhants instruct others and are active in making converts, as when a certain Kashmirian arhant converts a disciple of Pāṇini (1:222) and another converts a king of Jālandhara who has patronized non-Buddhist systems (1:296). These conversions often occur as the result of a display of magical power (1:222). We learn that in the future, it is only when a group of obdurate unbelievers witnesses the levitation and spontaneous cremation of Mahākāśyapa that they will be converted (2:144). The arhants use their powers to convert evil beings and propagate the dharma, as in the case of the arhant Madhyāntika who, fifty years after the death of the Buddha, comes and sits in a certain wood, by a large lake, alongside a great mountain. Here he performs miraculous exhibitions and, when asked by the local *nāga* what he wants, replies, "I want to have as much dry land in the lake as will enable me to sit cross-legged." The creature agrees, but the saint's legs grow bigger and bigger, until the creature is forced to turn the entire lake into solid earth (1:265). At this, the creature is converted and begs the saint to remain there and accept his offerings. This place will remain dry land, it is said, as long as the dharma exists on earth, after which it will again become a lake.

Hsüan-tsang connects the vocation of books and learning with settled monasticism (for example, Wts., 1:162, 2:109), and typical is his description of Nālandā, quoted in Chapter 1, as a place of eminent scholars who spend their time in textual pursuits and whose knowledge of the sacred scriptures is detailed and vast, a place where those without textual learning are ridiculed and cast out (2:164–65). Significantly, although Hsüan-tsang is himself an avid and accomplished textual scholar, in his report, textual learning sometimes appears with an ambiguous character: it can be used for good or ill and is no guarantee of sanctity. These points emerge clearly in the pilgrim's description of Mahādeva, an ordinary monk living among ordinary *bhikṣu*s (thus not an arhant), "a man of great learning and wisdom, a subtle investigator of name and reality" who composes treatises. This man has in fact taught heresy, deceived his fellow monks, and led Aśoka to attempted murder of the *saṃgha* in which Mahādeva dwelt (1:267). In addition, according to Hsüan-tsang's account, the vocation of texts and scholarship can also present serious obstacles to the spiritual life, as in the story of one Guṇaprabha, a brilliant young *bhikṣu* with great intellectual abilities and wide learning, who becomes a "*śāstra*-master" and composes over one hundred treatises. On one occasion, he wants to visit Maitreya in Tuṣita heaven to put some questions to him. He approaches a certain arhant named Devasena, who is in the habit of traveling to the Tuṣita heaven, and asks to be conducted into the presence of Maitreya. The arhant obliges, but the scholar is so full of pride and arrogance that he will not give the bodhisattva due reverence, and no teaching from Maitreya is forthcoming. Repeated visits to Maitreya's residence produce similar results. When the scholar refuses to heed the arhant's counsel, the arhant declines to conduct him to Maitreya anymore. The scholar then, filled with disgust, retires to the forest to dwell in solitude. However, he does not renounce his pride and arrogance and is unable to attain arhantship (1:323).

The arhants may not be recognized or respected as such and may even suffer criticism and persecution (Wts., 1:281). In Magadha, for example, in the story about Mahādeva just cited, King Aśoka has five hundred arhants and five hundred ordinary monks in his capital but—unable to tell the difference between monks and arhants—does not pay the arhants special honor. One day, deceived by Mahādeva's heretical teachings, he decides to drown them all and so summons them to the River Ganges. Seeing their lives in danger, the arhants leave Magadha and fly to Kashmir where they remain, in spite of Aśoka's later repentance (1:267).

The arhants have the power of longevity. When, in Kashmir, the arhant Madhyāntika is about to pass away, he is asked by a suppliant to remain but replies he cannot do so as the time for his *parinirvāṇa* has arrived. However, he promises to leave his five hundred arhant disciples behind him in Kashmir, to remain there as long as Buddhism continues to exist in that land (Wts., 1:265), motifs reminding us of the sixteen arhants. In their prolonged existences, the arhants continue to frequent various places. At a certain mountain in Kashmir, for example, there are hoofprints left on the top of the mountain by the arhants and their disciples when "out on parties of pleasure." Moreover, "such traces left by them as they rode to and fro were too numerous to mention" (1:280).[39] As another example, the five hundred arhants live on Mount Buddhavana and "those who moved them to an interview might see them going as *śramaṇas* into a village to beg food" (2:146), again reminding us of the sixteen arhants.

This same theme of long-lived arhants appearing among humans occurs in another story told by Hsüan-tsang. A certain wealthy brahmin has exhibited generosity to the Buddhist *saṃgha*s in his region, but these have been destroyed by the depredations of a hostile ruler. One day, sometime before Hsüan-tsang's visit, a strange old Buddhist renunciant with bushy eyebrows and white hair appears at the brahmin's door. Upon drinking the brahmin's offering of milk, he sighs and remarks that the milk is "more insipid than the water in Rājagṛha in which he, when attending the Buddha, had cleansed his bowl and washed." The saint then reveals himself to his host as Rāhula, the son of the Buddha, "who for the maintenance of the true religion [has] abstained from passing into final extinction." After making this statement, he suddenly disappears (Wts., 2:44).

The same theme of the longevity of the arhants appears with equal vividness in Hsüan-tsang's telling of another legend connected with a stūpa built on the summit of a certain mountain.[40] This legend is particularly interesting because of its close resemblance to that of Mahākāśyapa. Centuries ago, Hsüan-tsang was told, the mountain suddenly opened, revealing an arhant with eyes closed, sitting in meditation. "His body was of gigantic stature and his form was dried up; his hair descended low on his shoulders and enshrouded his face" (Beal 1884, 2:305). Upon being told of this marvel, the local king and townspeople come and venerate the saint. In response to their queries, a certain *bhikṣu* informs them that this arhant is one of those who have entered "the *samādhi* which produces extinction of mind." Such saints will awaken only at a certain signal, such as a bell ringing, and until this occurs, "they rest unmoved and quiet, whilst the power of their ecstasy keeps their bodies from destruction" (2:305). Upon hearing this, the king causes a bell to be rung and the arhant returns to ordinary consciousness, asking, "And now where dwells my master Kāśyapa *tathāgata?*" Upon being informed that this Buddha has long since passed into nirvaṇa and that, moreover, even Śākyamuni Buddha has come and gone, the saint rises into the air, exhibits various miraculous transformations, and is spontaneously consumed by fire. His relics then fall to the ground and are collected and enshrined in a stūpa (2:305–6).

The arhants are well aware of the approach of the time of their own passing—for example, Madhyāntika knows that the time of his *parinirvāṇa* has arrived (Wts., 1:265). The arhants may pass away as did the Buddha, in *samādhi,* as in the case of Śāṇakavāsin who, when about to die, goes "into the 'Border-limit *samādhi*' " (1:120). Sometimes their deaths can be dramatic indeed, as in the example of autocremation just cited. A similar example appears in a story told by Hsüan-tsang of a certain arhant who, during his life, has manifested a huge appetite, for which he has been ridiculed by the laity. When his time to die comes, he gives an account of his life to the laity, including his last life as an elephant who performed service to Buddhism—hence his present appetite—his spiritual struggles, and his attainment of enlightenment. Then, in the presence of "the scoffing and unbelieving spectators," he rises into the air, bursts into flame, and goes to his final extinction (1:281). The declaration of his realization, report of his memory of former births, levitation, and spontaneous cremation are apparently enough for the skeptical laity, for after his passing they erect a stūpa over his remains (1:281).

The building of stūpas to departed arhants is, of course, typical. It is interesting that the Mahāyānist Hsüan-tsang finds it important to report that outside Mahāyāna monasteries there are stūpas to great arhants (Wts., 1:280). The stūpas of the arhants are objects of cult; even monkeys and other animals come to venerate them and make offerings (1:280). In addition, after their passing, the arhants are associated with certain holy places, sometimes marked by stūpas; Hsüan-tsang mentions a number of these, such as the place where Ājñāta Kauṇḍinya and his four companions sat down to meditate (2:50), a forest hermitage of Upagupta containing a cave in which many renunciants are reported to have meditated and attained realization (1:306), and a certain forest locale where Śāriputra and the others of the Buddha's twelve hundred fifty great disciples practiced meditation (1:311; see also 1:373). The stūpas to the arhants generally mark places associated with one or another important moment in their lives (for example, Wts., 1:311, 2:50, 2:65, 2:80).

In Hsüan-tsang's seventh-century account, generally speaking, the forest arhant is acknowledged as an unimpeachable Buddhist ideal. However, the pilgrim's work also shows the forest ideal being challenged by the less contemplative ideal of the textually proficient monk. This is seen in Hsüan-tsang's description of the encounter between the great monastic scholar (Ārya) Deva Bodhisattva and a reknowned saint, the arhant Uttara, who lives in bare simplicity in an out-of-the-way place.[41] The arhant possesses the six supernatural powers and the eight meditational attainments *(vimokṣa)*. Deva Bodhisattva comes from a distance to see this saint. Deva arrives and is greeted by the arhant, who then enters into *samādhi,* and comes out of it only after midnight. Then Deva puts various questions to the arhant, who takes up each difficulty and explains it (Beal 1884, 2:227–28). So far, this story conforms to the paradigm explored in this and previous chapters, of the forest arhant as a paradigmatic Buddhist saint. However, there comes a point in this exchange—which has the marks of a debate—when the forest arhant finally cannot further reply to the challenges of the monastic scholar and holds his silence.[42] "Deva, closely examining each word, pressed his difficulties in the way of cross-examination, till after the seventh round of discussion the Arhat closed his mouth and declined *(was unable)* to reply" (2:228; the insertion and emphasis are Beal's). At this point, Hsüan-tsang tells us, the arhant, using his supernormal powers, journeys to the Tuṣita heaven to consult with Maitreya. The celestial bodhisattva provides the arhant with the answers to Deva's questions. Then he adds that this Deva "for a succession of *kalpas* has practised religion, and in the middle of the Bhadra-*kalpa* ought to attain the condition of Buddha. . . . You should greatly honour him and pay him reverence" (2:228). The arhant returns to his seat and gives forth with a clear and precise reply to Deva. Deva, however, is unwilling to accept the reply as proceeding from the arhant, remarking, "this is the explanation of the holy wisdom of Maitreya Bodhisattva. It is not possible for you, revered sir, to have discovered such profound answers." The arhant admits this to his questioner and then, rising from his mat, he offers "him worship and profound reverence and praise" (2:228). Deva's attitude could not be more clear: he acknowledges the legitimacy of the arhant's response, yet he does not see this as reflecting upon the arhant himself. In addition, Deva clearly holds other, noncontemplative values as more important, foremost among them the ability to speak from one's own knowledge and to vanquish others in debate. Of particular significance, it is the contemplative arhant who finally pays homage to the scholar, Deva, not vice versa. As so often in Buddhist legends, this story appears to recapitulate, within the frame of a dramatic episode, broadscale historical developments: here is reflected, it seems likely, a twofold process within Buddhism. First, the more purely contemplative ideal is no longer seen as being supreme and now "defers" to the monastic ideal. Second, we undoubtedly also see here the dominance of the bodhisattva, depicted as a monastic ideal, over the arhant, defined as a forest ideal.[43]

In Chapter 4, it was observed that, particularly in the Pāli canon, Śāriputra is understood as an arhant who represents the scholastic ideal of settled monasticism. This suggests that the term *arhant,* from a relatively early time, could be understood to have associations with monastic scholasticism. Similarly, in this chapter's discussion of Fa-hsien, we saw an instance of *arhant* referring to a renunciant living in a monastery, whose sainthood was defined in terms of purity of behavior. In these two examples, we see *arhant* used for individuals who excel in the settled monastic ideals of textual learning and behavioral purity and who are understood as settled monastics. This use of the term not only for forest saints but also for settled monastics appears more frequently in Hsüan-tsang's account. For example, King Aśoka cannot tell the difference between arhants and ordinary monks living in his city, and not only fails to give the saints due honor but actually tries to kill them. This story depicts arhants as living along with ordinary *bhikṣus* and as not being particularly distinguishable from them.[44] In some circles, then, the term *arhant* could be applied to those living as conventional monks and following their way of life, rather than being restricted to forest contemplatives alone.

The same phenomenon is indicated in Hsüan-tsang's description of an old temple where a great many arhants had lived in which "one could not tell which was common monk and which was arhat" (Wts., 1:109).[45] In Hsüan-tsang's time, arhants could include those who particularly excelled in the study of texts. Thus, Hsüan-tsang tells us that when Kaniṣka wanted to convene his council, he gathered together all who had attained the four paths; from among these he selected arhants; from among those he chose the arhants who had attained to the "threefold intelligence" and the "sixfold penetration"; and, from among those, he dismissed "all of them who were not thoroughly versed in the Tripiṭaka and well learned in the 'Five Sciences' " (1:270)—that is, in both the scriptural corpus of Buddhism as well as "secular" studies.[46] Here *arhant* is clearly being employed as a term that, in at least some of its usages, designates scholastically trained renunciants, monks whose breadth and depth of learning clearly imply a lifetime devoted to the vocation of texts and scholarship. To be sure, we are told that there are other fully attained arhants who do not have this scholarly knowledge, *but they are not wanted and are dismissed* (1:270; see also 2:73–74). The king here seeks to establish normative Buddhism, and his method of establishing it—his council—draws on those who excel in textual matters. We see the pattern again: the scholastically trained renunciant has more or less replaced the forest renunciant as primary authority and definer of normative Buddhism. These examples in Hsüan-tsang's work represent the replacement of the contemplative ideal of the arhant by the ideal of settled monasticism. In examples of this phenomenon cited earlier in this chapter, the way of life of the monastic (albeit bodhisattva) scholar appears to be more valued than that of the forest arhant. In the examples just referred to, *arhant* is defined so that it may be applied to the monastic scholar who not only follows, but excels, in the textual learning.

Some settled monastics who were called arhant must have been saints of the highest attainment. Others apparently were not. Hsüan-tsang, for example, remarks that at a certain monastery, it became necessary to make a distinction between those arhants who were most holy and those who were less so. This distinction could be made, we are told, when the time came for arhants to die. If, at that time, they made a public exhibition of miraculous powers, then they were deemed most worthy among arhants, and a stūpa would be built to them. However, if no such exhibition was made—as was true of some one thousand monks to whom the term *arhant* had been applied—then no stūpa would be built (Wts., 1:109).[47] This shows again that, in Hsüan-tsang's time, the term was applied not only to forest saints but also to settled monastics, and not only to those who were most highly attained but to those who were not.[48] Whereas in Fa-hsien's account, written in the early fifth century, the arhant ideal is relatively consistently defined, in Hsüan-tsang's account, we find a more complex situation, wherein the term *arhant* can mean either one of two distinct types and can refer to people at various levels of attainment. Hsüan-tsang's report makes it clear that this diverse and uneven application of the term caused some uncertainty and confusion among would-be devotees of the arhants.

Not unrelated to this difference between the reports of Fa-hsien and Hsüan-tsang is another. In Fa-hsien's account, there are only three kinds of Buddhist saint: buddhas, pratyekabuddhas, and arhants—the first two being essentially ancient ideals and the third being an ideal with both past and contemporary application. The Mahāyāna is occurring in Fa-hsien's day, and he mentions the existence of Mahāyāna monasteries as well as the worship of bodhisattvas. However, as far as human ideals are concerned in this account, Fa-hsien finds nothing wanting among these arhants and needs no further ideal.[49] In Hsüan-tsang's text, however, a fourth human ideal, the bodhisattva, becomes prominent, particularly in the persons of Aśvaghoṣa, Deva Bodhisattva, and Nāgārjuna. It is interesting that the first two of these are in type monastic scholars in the classical mold. Nāgārjuna, however, possesses additional features that bring him great stature and realization: he is recognized as a saint, has a "majestic face" that renders those who see it silent, possesses magical powers, has personal disciples, communicates in a secret way with his chief disciple, has lay devotees, is particularly venerated by the king, possesses powers of longevity, and so on (Wts., 2:200–201). In other words, this saint—unlike the other two bodhisattvas—approximates in several ways the forest ideal of the arhant.

Conclusion

The materials found in the *Nandimitrāvadāna* and reports of the Chinese pilgrims are primarily cultic, with attitudes and actions of devotion and veneration occupying center stage. Most striking is the particular emphasis placed by the cultic evidence on the supernatural dimensions of the Buddhist saints. As we have seen, these beings have power over the cosmos, time and space, and life and death. They can travel anywhere at will, seem to live on and on, and so forth, giving them a stature that equals and surpasses that of the gods. In contrast, the *Theragāthā* and *Therīgāthā,* for example, present a much more restrained view of the saint—there one finds claims of enlightenment (theme 8) and supernatural powers (theme 13) but not of dazzling miracles (theme 12) or longevity (theme 28). The *thera*s and *therī*s are depicted as human beings, realized and possessing power, but their ultimate achievement is the ability to see things as they are and to face death with courage and equanimity. It would be a mistake to assume that such differences necessarily represent conflicting conceptions about the Buddhist saints or that they evidence a clean split between lay and renunciant Buddhists. We have already seen that both laypeople and renunciants participate in the Buddhist cult of saints, with renunciants not infrequently exhibiting the greater enthusiasm.

There is another, more sensible explanation for the differences between the more strictly cultic materials and the more restrained evidence of the Buddhist saints: this has to do with the function of different kinds of religious activity within the cult of saints as a whole. For example, the adoration of the saints—as articulated in the *Nandimitrāvadāna,* the reports of Fa-hsien and Hsüan-tsang, and other evidence considered in previous chapters—involves various perspectives and ritual actions that articulate the relationship of lay and renunciant devotees to the realized saint. In this context, the saint is seen to be identified with and virtually to embody ultimate reality. This is the reason for the emphasis on the superhuman dimension of the saints' personalities. By contrast, the autobiographical songs of the *Theragāthā* and *Therīgāthā* are intended to express the saint's own journey toward emulation of the saintly ideal and therefore tend to emphasize their human side.

These are different, but not necessarily opposed, perspectives. Both laypersons and renunciant disciples are deeply attracted to the saints and respond in a similar way to them, desiring to see them and to participate in their cults. Through participation, they hope to experience interchange with the saints and to imbibe something of their enlightened charisma. For laypersons, this kind of interchange must generally be enough, at least for the time being. For renunciants, the experience of the saint's charisma can lead to increased longing and aspiration, to further renunciation, and to pursuing the path of meditation so that they may themselves come into permanent possession of the charisma experienced momentarily in the saint. There is, then, an unmistakable continuity between the evidence considered in this chapter and that examined in previous chapters. It would appear that whether we are dealing with the classical *vinaya* of monastic Buddhism or the less monastically oriented *jātaka* and *avadāna* literature; whether we are considering monastic histories, hagiographies, or cultic evidence; whether we are examining buddhas or other saints, there is a sameness of religious understanding, a consensus about who saints are, how they come to be saints, and what one should do in their presence.

In the preceding, we saw that in the evidence provided by Hsüan-tsang, the term *arhant* could be applied ambiguously to two quite different kinds of ideals—the one of the forest, the other of settled monasticism. To what extent was this ambiguous usage of the term simply current in Indian society of the seventh century and to what extent was it a significant trend in earlier Indian Buddhism? Moreover, if an ambiguous usage can be found in the earlier tradition, to what cause may it be traced?[50]

In the Pāli *Kīṭāgirisutta* of the *Majjhimanikāya* the Buddha categorizes his disciples into seven types (*Mn* 1:477 [Hn., 2:150–52]). At the top of this list and given in order of precedence are two classes of arhants: those who attain nirvāṇa through practice of both the eight liberations (P., *vimokkha;* Skt., *vimokṣa*)[51] and *paññā* (knowledge) and are thus "liberated in two ways" (P., *ubhatobhāgavimutta;* Skt., *ubhayatobhāgavimukta*);[52] and those who do not practice the liberations and are freed by knowledge alone (P., *paññāvimutta;* Skt., *prajñāvimukta*).[53] The eight *vimokkha*s are a set of meditative attainments, the highest of which is *nirodhasamāpatti*—in Pāli canonical tradition, the attainment of nirvāṇa itself.[54] According to the *Kīṭāgirisutta,* the *ubhatobhāgavimutta* is described as follows:

> Some person is abiding, having apprehended with [his] person [*kāyena,* lit., by means of his body] those peaceful Deliverances *[vimokkha]* which are incorporeal having transcended material shapes; and having seen by means of wisdom his cankers are utterly destroyed. (*Mn* 1:477 [Hn., 2:152–53])

Other texts in the Pāli canon characterize the *ubhatobhāgavimutta* in a similar fashion. A passage in the *Mahānidāna Sutta* of the *Dīghanikāya,* for example, also associates the *ubhatobhāgavimutta* with the practices of the *vimokkha*s (*Dn* 2:70–71 [T.R. and C.R. 1899–1921, 2:68–70]). The *Mahānidāna Sutta* passage concludes,

> Now when once a brother, Ānanda, has mastered these eight stages of Deliverance in order, and has also mastered them in reverse order, and again, in both

> orders consecutively, so that he is able to lose himself in, as well as to emerge from, any one of them, whenever he chooses, wherever he chooses, and for as long as he chooses—when too, by rooting out the Taints, he enters into and abides in that emancipation of heart, that emancipation of the intellect which he by himself, here in this present world, has come to know and realize—then such a brother, Ānanda, is called "Free-in-both-ways."

Similar laudatory characterizations of the *ubhatobhāgavimutta* are given at *Dīghanikāya* 3:105 (T.R. and C.R. 1899–1921, 3:101), *Saṃyuttanikāya* 1:190 (RW., 1:190), and *Aṅguttaranikāya* 2:73, 4:10, and 4:77 (WH., 2:69, 4:7, and 4:44).[55] The principal distinguishing feature separating the two types of arhant is that the *ubhatobhāgavimutta* practices the *vimokkha*s and attains *nirodhasamāpatti,* whereas the *paññāvimutta* does neither. In the *Kīṭāgirisutta,* for example, the *paññāvimutta* is defined as one who has *not* apprehended with the body "those peaceful Deliverances *[vimokkha]* which are incorporeal having transcended material shapes" (*Mn* 1:477–78 [Hn., 2:152]). In the Pāli *sutta*s, then, the *ubhatobhāgavimutta* is typically depicted as superior to the *paññāvimutta* (see N. Dutt 1960, 267). The hierarchically arranged set of seven types listing the *ubhatobhāgavimutta* first, ahead of the *paññāvimutta,* appears a number of times in the *Suttapiṭaka.*[56]

The meaning of this precedence is illustrated in the *Saṃyuttanikāya,* in the story of Musīla and Nārada (*Syn* 2:114–17 [RW., 2:81–83]). The venerable Musīla, the venerable Saviṭṭha, and the venerable Ānanda are staying at Kosambī in Ghosita Park. One day, Saviṭṭha asks Musīla whether, apart from hearsay and opinion, he has "as his very own the knowledge that decay-and-death is conditioned by birth." Saviṭṭha's question refers, of course, to the twelve *nidāna*s, or links in the chain of conditioned coproduction *(pratītyasamutpāda).* Musīla responds in the affirmative, naming not only the two *nidāna*s mentioned by Saviṭṭha but the other ten as well and concluding, "I know each of these, I see each of these." Saviṭṭha then asks whether Musīla does not also similarly know the ceasing of becoming that is nirvāṇa, and Musīla again responds in the affirmative. Saviṭṭha then declares, "Well then, the venerable Musīla is an Arahant, for whom the intoxicants are perished." This being said, Musīla, in assent, remains silent.

There is now a shift in the narrative for which we have not been prepared. Without warning, a new figure suddenly appears, the venerable Nārada, who requests that Saviṭṭha ask him the same questions that were just asked of Musīla. Saviṭṭha puts forward the questions, and Nārada responds in exactly the same terms as Musīla. This leads Saviṭṭha to remark, as he did in the case of Musīla, "Well then, the venerable Nārada is an Arahant, for whom the intoxicants are perished." Nārada unexpectedly demurs, replying that, in spite of what he has seen and knows, he is *not* an arhant, and he gives the following analogy in explanation:

> It is just as if, friend, there were in the jungle-path a well, and neither rope nor drawer of water. And a man should come by foredone with heat, far gone with heat, weary, trembling, athirst. He should look down into the well. Verily in him would be the knowledge:—Water!—yet would he not be in a position to touch

> it. Even so, friend, I have well seen by right insight (paññā) as it really is that the ceasing of becoming is Nibbāna, and yet I am not Arahant for whom the intoxicants are perished. (*Syn* 2:116–17 [RW., 2:83])

Nārada, in a humble and tactful but unmistakable way, here affirms that, as far as he is concerned, the kind of knowledge that Musīla has and for which he is praised as an arhant is not sufficient for the attainment of liberation. To know is not the same as to taste and experience for oneself, and this, Nārada insists, is required in order for one truly to be an arhant.

This story reveals among Buddhist renunciants two different understandings of what makes an arhant. We also learn what these are. One trend, evident in Musīla, holds that seeing and knowing *(paññā)* of the Buddhist doctrines is sufficient for arhantship. This trend is explicitly associated with the Buddhist doctrine of *pratītyasamutpāda* and the *nidānas*—this is what Musīla sees and knows. Musīla, then, is a representative of the viewpoint of the *paññāvimutta* trend. The other trend, embodied in Nārada, holds that this kind of knowledge—which Nārada is depicted as also possessing—does not, in and of itself, make one an arhant becuase it remains too abstract: one needs not just to see water *(nibbāna)* but to touch and taste it for oneself. In the Pāli canon, this kind of direct experience is typically associated with Buddhist meditation; as La Vallée Poussin has noted, Nārada clearly embodies the viewpoint of the *ubhatobhāgavimutta,* for whom both *paññā* and meditative attainment are necessary for full realization (1936–37, 189ff.).

The dramatic positions of these two figures in the story are also significant. The introduction makes it clear that the story is about Musīla, with Saviṭṭha and Ānanda as supporting characters. Moreover, Musīla as central character is respectfully asked various questions. Nārada, by contrast, is a recessive figure—he is not one of the dramatis personae mentioned in the introduction; he suddenly appears unannounced midway through the story; and he has humbly to request Saviṭṭha to pose the questions to him also. This raises the question of why Nārada is introduced into the story at all. The conclusion suggests an answer. Ānanda asks Saviṭṭha, "Holding the view you do . . . what say you to the venerable Nārada?" Several facts indicate that the interpretation of arhantship of the community behind this story is the one expressed in the person of Musīla: the story is about Musīla, and Nārada is put in the position of the dissenter; in speaking to Saviṭṭha, Ānanda refers to "holding the view you do," and Saviṭṭha's reverence for Musīla indicates that his view is partial to Musīla; and Ānanda wants to know what Saviṭṭha will say by way of response to Nārada. Saviṭṭha's response to Ānanda's question is intriguing: "Holding the view I do, friend, Ānanda, I say nothing that is not lovely and good of the venerable Nārada." We seem to be told, in effect, "Musīla is our kind of saint and represents our view, but we also want to acknowledge the sanctity of the meditator, Nārada."

La Vallée Poussin, in two important articles (1929 and 1936–37), has described in more detail the two Buddhist trends embodied in Nārada and Musīla and the two interpretations of the arhant they represent. In order to focus his argument, in both articles Poussin draws our attention to *Aṅguttaranikāya* 3:355–

56 (WH., 3:252–53), which makes a distinction between two quite different groups of Buddhist renunciants. On the one hand are the practitioners of meditation, or *jhāyin;*[57] on the other, the practitioners of *dhamma (dhammayoga bhikkhu),* the "dhamma zealots" in Woodward and Hare's translation. The meditators have, through their practice, "touched the immortal *(amata)* with their bodies." The practitioners of *dhamma,* by contrast, are not characterized as meditating but rather as having penetrated and seen the truth. These two groups of renunciants are not on good terms with one another, and the *Aṅguttaranikāya* passage acknowledges animosity between them. The *dhamma bhikkhus* ridicule the meditators for their meditation, claiming that it gets them nowhere. The meditators criticize the *dhamma bhikkhus* for lacking the meditative virtues and way of life: they are not mindful, their thoughts wander, they lack self-awareness and composure, they have no control over their senses, they talk too much, they are excitable, and they are puffed up and proud.

According to La Vallée Poussin, Nārada is to be understood as exemplifying the ideal of the *jhāyins*, whereas Musīla exemplifies the ideal of the *dhamma bhikkus*. Moreover, these two groups embody two different and opposed tendencies: they are two distinct types of renunciant, follow differing soteriological methods, and conceive of enlightenment in two quite different ways (1929, 135–36). The *jhāyins* are renunciants of the forest, follow a severe diet and ascetic way of life, engage in meditation, and have attained the liberation of *nirodha-samāpatti,* which "puts them in contact with the transcendent reality of nirvāṇa" (1936–37, 191). The *dhammayogins*—the rationalists, intellectuals, or philosophers (1936–37, 190)—are settled monastics living according to the collective, communal rule *(vinaya),* engaging in textual study, reciting texts, and preaching the dharma. These latter monks follow a method that is intellectual, engage in discursive knowledge, develop a metaphysic, study the nature of things, and attach themselves to the Buddhist truths of suffering and *pratītyasamutpāda* (1929, 135–36). They believe that desire is suppressed by studying the impermanent and unsatisfactory nature of those things that provoke thirst (1929, 135). "They think that it suffices to render nirvāṇa present through the intelligence" (1936–37, 191–92). These two, La Vallée Poussin proposes, correspond to the *ubhatobhāgavimutta* and *paññāvimutta* arhants (1929, 136).

N. Dutt, in discussing the *ubhatobhāgavimutta* and the *paññāvimutta* arhants, agrees with and summarizes the essentials of this argument:

> There are two types of Arhants, called Ubhatobhāgavimutta and Paññāvimutta. These are the two ultimate ends of two classes of adepts, one adopting the path of meditation *(vipassanā-dhura)* and the other that of study and knowledge *(gantha-dhura* and *paññā).* The former called Saddhānusārī depends more on faith in the Triratna and in their spiritual teacher and seeks emancipation mainly through meditational practices. The latter called Dhammānusārī studies the *Sutta* and *Abhidhamma Piṭakas* and tries to comprehend the philosophical tenets embedded in them. . . . The distinction between the two classes is due to the emphasis laid by one group on meditation for purification of mind *(cetovimutti)* and elimination of attachment, hatred and delusion, and by the other on study and knowledge and elimination of ignorance *(paññāvimutta).* (1960, 270–71)

It is telling that the criticisms made of these "*dhamma* zealots" by the meditators in *Aṅguttaranikāya* 3:355–56 are virtually the same as those directed toward town-and-village renunciants (or settled monastics) in the forest traditions of both Nikāya Buddhism (for example, in the songs of Phussa and Pārāpariya in the *Theragāthā*) and the Mahāyāna (see Chapter 8): these *dhamma* zealots do not meditate and, in fact, lack the inner moral and spiritual development to which meditation leads. These various facts, taken together, indicate that the *ubhatobhāgavimutta* and *paññāvimutta* represent the arhant ideals of the two contrasting types of Buddhist renunciant—that of the *jhāyin* and that of the *dhammayoga bhikkhu*. Further, in the context of the typology being developed in this study, the *jhāyin* is the representative of forest Buddhism, whereas the *dhamma bhikkhu* is the representative of settled monasticism. This distinction suggests answers to the questions posed at the beginning of this section: the ambiguous use of the term *arhant* by Hsüan-tsang reflects a phenomenon with a considerable antiquity within Indian Buddhism. Moreover, the primary cause of the ambiguity in the earlier sources reviewed in the present discussion is the same as that lying behind the usage documented by Hsüan-tsang—namely, the application of the term to two different ideals, the one of the forest, the other of settled monasticism.

The recognition that the *ubhatobhāgavimutta* trend and the *paññāvimutta* trend represent, at least in early Buddhism, ideals respectively of forest and town-and-village renunciation helps explain their curious relationship in developed Buddhism, noted by Griffiths (1981, 605). Although various commentators attempt to fit the two into one consistent scheme, such efforts have not been successful, and unresolved tensions and ambiguities remain. When viewed as elements of a classical system, this lack of resolution is puzzling. When seen in the light of Buddhist history, however, these tensions and ambiguities make more sense.

In the *sutta* presentation of the two ideals in the story of Musīla and Nārada, we noted a conciliatory tone. This is also present in *Aṅguttaranikāya* 3:355–56. After acknowledging the conflicts between the *jhāyin*s and the *dhamma bhikkhu*s, the central figure, Mahā Cunda, counsels his listeners that if they are *dhamma bhikkhus* they should praise the meditators and if they are meditators they should praise the *dhamma bhikkhu*s, because "wondrous persons are hardly found in the world—they who with insight penetrate and see the truth" (*Aṅguttaranikāya* 3:355–56 [WH., 3:252–53]).[58] These texts, though reflecting a settled monastic orientation, exhibit a concerted effort to retain the positive evaluations of the *ubhatobhāgavimutta*s and to affirm the legitimacy of the meditative traditions that they follow.

Commentarial texts in both the Theravāda and Sarvāstivāda are, however, not so generous and tend to reinterpret earlier tradition such that the *ubhatobhāgavimutta*s and the trends they represent are, at best, subordinated to the *paññāvimutta*-type or dismissed as irrelevant or, at worst, condemned as illegitimate. La Vallée Poussin tells us that, among the Sarvāstivādins, two paths to nirvāṇa are acknowledged: that of *prajñā* (the *dhamma bhikkhu*-type, involving the review of the four truths) and that of meditation. Now meditation is divided into "worldly meditation," the practice of the four *dhyāna*s and four formless attainments, and "supermundane meditation" presented as meditation legitimized by the path of *prajñā*. However, one may now accomplish "supermundane meditation" without practicing the eight stages at all, simply by reviewing the four truths and abandoning the defilements associated with each of the eight. La Vallée Poussin remarks that this scheme reflects the incorporation and devaluation of the path of meditation by those advocating the superiority of the path of *prajñā*. This formulation is, La Vallée Poussin notes, clearly artificial and contradicts more positive evaluations of the path of meditation found in other Sarvāstivādin literature (1936–37, 192–98). Among the Theravādins, the *ubhatobhāgavimutta* is sometimes identified as entirely devoid of wisdom and as pursuing the same path of the eight stages (excluding *nirodhasamāpatti*) as non-Buddhist heretics. Although initially "liberated in both ways" indicated the gaining of both the eight attainments and knowledge, now it can be claimed that the *ubhatobhāgavimutta* does not possess any wisdom at all but only the stages. In this interpretation, "both ways" indicates the four *jhāna*s and the four *āruppa jhāna*s (see T.R. and C.R. 1899–1921, 2:70, n. 1). These reinterpretations and demotions of the *ubhatobhāgavimutta* are, then, an example of the process of monasticization wherein an element of forest Buddhism is incorporated into the conceptual framework of settled monasticism and, in the process, reinterpreted. The particularly negative recasting of the ideals of the forest arhant by the Theravāda is, of course, consistent with the other negative evaluations that we have examined of forest Buddhism and its ideals in the developed Theravāda.

We saw some striking parallels between members of the sixteen arhant group and the bodhisattva as a type. That observation may now be further generalized to include the forest arhant type altogether. In a number of fundamental respects, the forest arhant and the bodhisattva, particularly in his forest manifestation (to be examined in Chapter 8), are congruent ideals: both are forest renunciants; follow the *dhutaguṇa*s; meditate in seclusion; are understood as realized; exhibit wisdom, compassion, and power; and so on. This congruency raises the question of what explanation may be given for the similarities between these two ideals. One possible hypothesis is that such similarities reflect a syncretism between Nikāya Buddhism and the Mahāyāna.[59] This explanation is unsatisfying, however, because it does not take into account the antiquity of the specific arhant type reflected in the evidence.

Another possible explanation begins with the observation that the Mahāyāna possesses two minds on the matter of the arhants. On the one hand, it lauds them in the cult, something reflected in the tradition of the sixteen arhants and in the cult of arhants as presented with approbation by both Fa-hsien and Hsüan-tsang.[60] At the same time, it can also be sharply critical of arhants, seeing them as interested only in their own salvation, uncompassionate toward others, overly concerned with concepts, deficient in realization, and ready for extinction (that is, to exit saṃsāra for good).[61] These two attitudes may perhaps be explained simply as Mahāyāna responses to the two understandings of the arhant, forest and monastic, active in its environment. As will be suggested in more detail in later chapters, it may be strongly suspected that it is the ideal of the arhant as exemplifying the values and orientations of settled monasticism that comes in for particularly sharp attack by the early Mahāyāna.[62] Toward the ideal of the arhant as the prototypical forest saint, the Mahāyāna—again as we shall see in more detail—seems to be much more appreciative: the arhant may not only be an object of the Mahāyāna cult, as seen in the present chapter, but may even be said to fulfill some of the highest values of Mahāyāna Buddhism. This is suggested in a passage from the *Ratnaguṇasaṃcayagāthā,* which mentions four kinds of persons who are not alarmed by the teaching of *śūnyatā*. One of these four types includes "arhants free from defilements and taints, and rid of their doubts" (*Rgs* 2.6).[63] The same is suggested in the *Laṅkāvatāra Sūtra* in which we read that the term *arhant* has traditionally been applied to three different types of persons: (1) "one who makes straightway for the path of cessation"; (2) "one who neglects all his accumulated stock of merit *[kuśalamūla]* for the sake of his vow to enlighten others *[bodhipraṇidhāna]";* and (3) "one who is a form of the Transformation (Buddha) *[nirmitanairmāṇika]*." The first of these is identified as a *śrāvaka* and is not preferred; the second two are seen as conforming to Mahāyāna ideals (*Las* 49.24–27 [Sz., 104]).

The ambiguity in the usage of the term *arhant* clearly created some difficulties for Mahāyānists, which the *Laṅkāvatāra Sūtra* seeks to resolve. In the text, when Mahāmati expresses some confusion over this ambiguity in the term, the Buddha replies that, in fact, *arhant* should really be applied *only* to the first type, to those *śrāvaka*s who strive directly for cessation. The two others are really bodhisattvas (*Las* 49.26–27 [Sz., 104]). "Mahāmati, as for the [two] others, they are those who have finished practising the deeds of a Bodhisattva; they are forms of the Transformation Buddha. With skilful means born of their fundamental and original vows, they manifest themselves among the multitudes in order to adorn the assemblages of the Buddhas" (49.27–29 [104]). The latter two types of arhant have the correct view of the Mahāyāna (49.29–30 [104]).[64] The solution to the ambiguity in the use of the term represents, in fact, what became the dominant hermeneutical trend in the Mahāyāna, in which the arhant tended to be virtually identified with a narrow, self-serving, often scholastic ideal of conservative monastic "Hīnayāna."

The preceding discussion raises a final question: can one discern any sequence in the development of the term *arhant* within Buddhism? The forest evidence suggests the following possible major stages in the development of the ideal: (1) In pre-Buddhist days, *arhant* was a general designation of those "worthy" or "deserving of merit," including both humans and gods (Swearer 1987, 403). (2) In early Buddhism, the term was used in a more limited sense to indicate specifically liberated saints, including the Buddha, pratyekabuddhas, and the disciples of the Buddha.[65] (3) With the passing of Buddha Śākyamuni and the pratyekabuddhas not present by definition, *arhant* came to indicate those past and presently living, fully realized ones following Buddha Śākyamuni's tradition. In this early Buddhist phase, did the term indicate only forest saints, or could it have applied to town-and-village Buddhist renunciants as well? In the absence of any definitive evidence, the early Buddhist (and Jain) restriction of the term to enlightened saints suggests that the arhant was, in Buddhism, probably initially a forest ideal. (4) At some point, possibly still quite early, the term *arhant* took on the twofold meaning that is present in the Pāli and Sarvāstivādin sources and in Hsüan-tsang's report, referring to two different types—those who have gained realization through the meditative way and those who have followed a nonmeditative path. *Arhant* can now refer not only to a forest meditator but also to a town-and-village renunciant or settled monastic understood to have reached a certain level of attainment. (5) The monasticization of the term may well have contributed to the diminishing of the charisma of the arhant, at least in the eyes of some, beginning at an early time.[66] In any case, *arhant* came to have multiple meanings and different evaluations by different traditions, and debates arose concerning the definition and status of the arhant (Bareau 1957). As noted, it was not only the Nikāya schools that became involved in struggling with the issue of the arhant but also the Mahāyāna traditions. The case of the *Laṅkāvatāra Sūtra* is particularly revealing. As we have seen and shall see in more detail, the text prefers to define the arhant as the conservative, scholastic, monastic ideal of the *śrāvaka*s. At the same time, it admits but disfavors the use of the term for more bodhisattva-like figures. In doing so, it reveals the considerable continuity between the forest arhant and the bodhisattva of the forest. This in turn suggests that the bodhisattva, at least as interpreted as a forest ideal, represents a less dramatic innovation than might otherwise be thought. Rather, the forest bodhisattva may be seen as the Mahāyānist way of continuing to breathe life into the ancient ideal of the Buddhist saint of the forest, the integrity and charisma of which were being diminished, so it is suggested here, by the monasticization of the arhant.

Notes

1. On the arhant ideal, see Horner 1936; Ling 1972, 24–25; Nyanatiloka 1980, 20–22; Katz 1980; and Bond 1984 and 1988; these provide useful summaries of the dominant canonical definitions of the arhant in the Pāli canon. Some intriguing studies draw attention to other understandings of the arhant in Indian Buddhism: Lévi and Chavannes 1916; De Visser 1922–23; Strong 1979 and 1991; Keyes 1982; Carrithers 1983; and Tambiah 1984. Malalasekera (1961– , 2:41–54) and Swearer (1987) have provided overviews of the arhant that attempt to do justice to both dominant and recessive understandings.

2. In his introduction to the English translation of *Na* (Shan Shih 1961), Chao Pu-chu mentions some of the Indian texts, translated into Chinese, that give evidence of the sixteen arhants in the late fourth or early fifth centuries C.E. (Shan Shih 1961, 1). Lamotte (1958, 769–70) believes that idea of arhants who remain in the world as protectors of the dharma, which is embodied in the sixteen arhants, developed in stages: first there were four arhants, later increased to eight, then sixteen, and then eighteen.

a. A set of four arhants is found in the *Ekottarāgama* (T. 125, K. 44, 789a), the *Mi lê hsia shêng ching* (T. 453, 422b) and the *Śāriputraparipṛcchā* (T. 1465, 902a): Mahākāśyapa, Piṇḍolabhāradvāja, Kuṇḍopadhānīya, and Rāhula.

b. Two sets of eight arhants are given in the *Mañjuśrīmūlakalpa* (ed. T. Ganapati Sastri, 1:64 and 111). The first list contains Śāriputra, Maudgalyāyana, Mahākāśyapa, Subhūti, Rāhula, Nanda, Bhadrika, and Kaphiṇa. The second list contains Śāriputra, Maudgalyāyana, Gavāṃpati, Piṇḍolabhāradvāja, Pilindavatsa, Rāhula, Mahākāśyapa, and Ānanda.

c. The set of sixteen arhants (the grouping examined here) found in texts such as the *Mahāyānāvatāra* (T. 1634, chap. 1, 39b) and the *Nandimitrāvadāna,* extant in both Chinese (T. 2030, 13a) and Tibetan (*Pk., mdo. 'grel ('dul.ba)* [U] 300b): Piṇḍolabhāradvāja, Kanakavatsa, Kanakaparidhvaja, Subinda, Nakula, Bhadra, Kālika, Vajraputra, Śvapāka, Panthaka, Rāhula, Nāgasena, Iṅgada, Vanavāsi, Ajita, and Cūḍapanthaka.

d. A set of eighteen arhants, in the Chinese sources studied by Lévi and Chavannes (1916).

The Mahāyana often replaces the sixteen arhants listed here with sixteen bodhisattvas of Indian origin who were "promoted to the same function and designated by the name of Ṣoḍaśasatpuruṣa, 'the sixteen worthy persons' " (adapted from Lamotte 1988, 694).

3. Lévi and Chavannes 1916, 27–28. Lévi and Chavannes point out that it is difficult to avoid uncertainty regarding the dates and identity of the author (1916, 24–27). Nandimitra, "the great *śrāvaka,*" is also a key figure in the *Ajitasenavyākaraṇanirdeśa Sūtra* (Williams 1989, 26–28).

4. Hsüan-tsang's translation has been rendered into French by Lévi and Chavannes, with extensive notes and commentary (1916), and has been summarized by De Visser (1922–23). It has more recently been translated into English, without apparatus, by Shan Shih (1961). On the sixteen arhants, see also Watters 1898; Doré 1914–38, 7:332–87; Lamotte 1958, 768–70; Malalasekera 1961– , 2:48–51; and Tate 1989. De Visser (1922–23) has shed light on the Indian side of the traditions of the sixteen arhants, drawing on the *Ekottarāgama* and other Indian texts surviving in Chinese. He has also studied the literary, cultic, and artistic evidence of the traditions of these saints in China and Japan. The *Nandimitrāvadāna* and the other closely related texts enable us to construct a credible picture of the main features of the sixteen arhants.

5. The following spelling of the names of the sixteen arhants follows Lévi and Chavannes (1916, 9). There is some variation in the way scholars have rendered the names in Sanskrit (see, e.g., Shan Shih 1961, 9).

6. The *Ekottarāgama,* providing information on the sixteen arhants, similarly refers to the longevity of these saints (De Visser 1922–23, 81).

7. Aśvaghoṣa, as we saw, occasionally depicts the Buddha in such a fashion; see Chapter 2, p. 54.

8. The following names have been reconstructed from the Chinese text by Lévi and Chavannes, with some uncertainty as noted.

9. Also Nimiṃdhara, one of the eight great mountains surrounding Sumeru in the center of the world (*BHSD,* 298). Listed as first of twenty famous mountains in *Mvy* (4140–59).

10. Other Buddhist saints may also live there, e.g., Gavāṃpati (Przyluski 1926–28, 242; Shorto 1970, 16).

11. This theme also appears, of course, in the hagiography of Buddha Śākyamuni, found in both Pāli and Sanskrit Buddhism. Thus the Buddha spends time at Lake Anavatapta (P., Anotatta, "without warmth"), in the extreme north, in the Himalayas, a place frequented by gods and saints but where ordinary people cannot go (Hofinger 1954, 7). The image of Buddha Śākyamuni as inaccessible to all but divine beings and saints obviously presents some contrast with the image of his accessibility in much of Nikāya Buddhist literature.

12. The forest character of the sixteen arhants is emphasized in the iconographic traditions surrounding these figures in China and Tibet. Tate, for example, remarks that in Tibet the sixteen arhants

> are generally shown seated at ease in a mountain landscape of crags and waterfalls, their faces serene, or animated with ecstatic insight. Far from "civilization" and from monastic

institutions, they live a wandering spiritual life like that of the early Buddhist monks, accompanied by an enlightened attendant, and with wild beasts as their pets. (1989, 196)

13. In one text cited by De Visser, the Buddha refers to the connection between longevity and compassion when he tells Ānanda that Vakula will have a longer then normal life on account of his merciful heart in a former existence (1922–23, 81).

14. The theme of a saint miraculously appearing before a devotee in response to a supplication is an ancient one in Indian Buddhism. In the *Mahāvagga* section of the *Suttanipāta,* for example, we read, "those who are arahats, fully enlightened ones, reveal themselves when their own praise is being spoken" (*Sn* pr., 108 [Nr., 97]).

15. In the ancient Buddhist context preaching is often particularly associated with texts and textual expertise. As S. Dutt remarks, in the early period a Buddhist group would "memorize and also specialize in its own section [of texts], not as mere reciters *(bhāṇakas),* but as professors, expositors, commentators,—in short as custodians of both the texts and their true meaning" (1957, 92). Thus the *kathika* ("speaker" or "expounder" of the dharma) is typically characterized as one who is learned in textual matters, *bahuśrutya* (e.g., *Rps* 28.7; see *BHSD* 166, s.v. *kathika*). In contrast to town-and-village renunciants, forest renunciants are not typically depicted as specializing either in the memorization of texts or in expounding texts to the laity. In the early tradition, the *dharmakathika* and those specializing in specific types of texts *(sūtra, vinaya, mātṛkā)* are characteristically contrasted with meditators *(dhyāyin),* as distinct types (Lamotte 1958, 164). We will see some examples of this in Chapters 7 and 8. For examples in modern times, see, e.g., Tambiah 1984, 16.

16. De Visser remarks that the other of the sixteen arhants show more active compassion than does Vakula and that, in his lack of activity, Vakula is somewhat anomalous (1922–23, 82).

17. Cūḍapanthaka's lack of adeptness with the textual tradition is reinforced by the way in which the story continues. At this point, in De Visser's words, "Śāriputra, who by means of his celestial ear had heard the discussion, and who was afraid that the *bhikṣu* would give in and the Brahmin would not be converted, by means of his divine power assumed Cūḍapanthaka's shape and caused the latter to disappear himself. Then he took up the discussion with the Brahmin and convinced him" (1922–23, 87). It is no accident that it is Śāriputra who comes to Panthaka's rescue; as we have seen, he is so well known for his expertise in doctrinal matters.

18. A kind of teaching suited to his capabilities? The same kind of scholastic ineptitude and inability to learn texts is ascribed to Cūḍapanthaka in *Vms* 3:1, 206–7 (Hofinger 1954, 249–50) and *Ta* (557–66). If the *Theragāthā* and *Therīgāthā* are any reflection of the actual situation, they would suggest that forest renunciants typically entered their way of life after attaining majority, when they could have a genuine sense of spiritual vocation; they also often came to such a way of life without any previous textual training. The late age at which they entered the renunciant life and their ignorance of textual learning appear to take shape in the derogatory term *mahalla* (or *mahallaka*) that, as mentioned, is sometimes applied to these saints (see Durt 1980 and Strong 1992, 68–70).

19. The themes of autocremation and religious suicide in general are present elsewhere in the Buddhism of India and beyond; see Gernet 1960, Filliozat 1963, and Lamotte 1965.

20. *Trisāhasramahāsāhasralokadhātu* (P., *tisahassī mahāsahassī lokadhātu*). The classical definition of the scope of a buddha field *(buddhakṣetra,* P., *buddhakhetta),* or the vast collection of worlds under the aegis of a buddha, in this case Buddha Śākyamuni. For a detailed definition and discussion of *trisāhasra* . . . see Kloetzli 1987, 115–16.

21. A *Koṭi* is ten million.

22. *Dīrghāgama, Madhyamāgama, Ekottarāgama, Samyuktāgama,* and *Kṣudrakāgama* are mentioned; see Lamotte (1958, 170) for comments on this particular arrangement.

23. For a reference in Fa-hsien's account to a similar legend about Maitreya, see Beal 1869, 163–64. The person who recounted this legend to the Chinese pilgrim remarked, "This is no sacred book, but only what I have learnt by memory, and repeated orally" (163–64).

24. There are some exceptions, e.g., the cults of Mahākāśyapa, Rāhula, Devadatta, and other arhants, as described by the Chinese pilgrims; for discussion of these, see this chapter and index.

25. Particularly interesting is the theme of the incarnation of the arhants in living human beings. Thus the story is told of the painter Kuan-hsiu, who saw in a dream only fifteen arhants and who was subsequently informed that his own face was that of the sixteenth. Thereupon he used a water-mirror and painted his own reflection as the sixteenth arhant. De Visser remarks, "This evidently means that Kwan-hiu [Kuan-hsiu] himself was a reincarnation of the sixteenth Arhant" (1922–23, 110–11).

26. Williams has recently suggested that the notion of the bodhisattva's "delay" of his own *parinirvāṇa* in order to help sentient beings (sometimes until all sentient beings are saved), attributed to "the Mahāyāna" by many modern authors, needs to be seriously reexamined both because in many ways it does not make sense (did the Buddha then break his bodhisattva vow when he entered *parinirvāṇa?*) and also because there is little textual justification for this concept (1989, 52–53). Williams's observation is well taken and will lead, it may be hoped, to more careful and accurate descriptions of the Mahāyāna bodhisattva ideal. At the same time, the present discussion does make clear that the bodhisattva's postponement of what otherwise would be possible is as important an idea within the classical Indian Mahāyāna as within traditions connected with the arhants. However, the term "delay," although appropriate in the case of the arhants, is misleading in the case of the bodhisattva, for the bodhisattva, as a future buddha, would seem to have no choice. Because of his vow, he cannot attain the awakening of the arhant style but must continue on to full enlightenment.

27. This difference is not as great as at first might appear. One of the arhants lives in the heavenly realm, one of the destinies for beings after they die and the place where bodhisattvas may await rebirth.

28. This is a theme that already appears in relation to Śākyamuni in *Mps*-p 3.21–23.

29. The cult of arhants is, in fact, a central theme in the accounts of both Fa-hsien and Hsüan-tsang (see Snellgrove 1989, 13). Sung Yün (518 C.E.) and I-ching (671–95 C.E.) provide very little information, the former because of the brevity of his account and his seeming lack of interest in the arhants (and the saints in general), the latter because of his understanding of *vinaya* as defining normative Buddhism and his focus on *vinaya* in his composition.

30. At the same time, it is clear that what the pilgrims say about arhants is sometimes either taken from or informed by textual tradition. However, it is not always easy to distinguish where the pilgrim is reporting what he has seen or heard from where he is relying on his own knowledge of the texts. In the present context, it is not necessary to make this distinction, as we are interested in finding out what the Chinese pilgrims, given all these sources, feel it is important to say about the arhants.

31. For a discussion of Fa-hsien with bibliographic references, see Yün-hua 1987.

32. Fa-hsien does not treat the bodhisattva as a prominent human ideal, one explicitly followed by individuals. However, he does make at least one reference to a Mahāyāna saint without using the term *bodhisattva,* a certain saintly Mahāyānist living in seclusion, whom

the king of the country revered and served as his teacher (Legge 1886, 78). This raises the question of whether this person may not have been understood as a bodhisattva. At the same time, however, Fa-hsien does refer to images of bodhisattvas as superhuman beings (e.g., Legge 1886, 19, 27). He also makes several references to Mahāyāna *bhikṣus* and monasteries (16, 21, 41, 79).

33. Of the monasteries in Madhyadeśa, Fa-hsien notes three preoccupations, remarking that "the regular business of the monks is to perform acts of meritorious virtue, and to recite their Sūtras and sit wrapt in meditation" (Legge 1886, 44).

34. It is interesting how far the monk Fa-hsien tends to identify his Buddhism with correct performance of the precepts (see Beal 1884, 142–46).

35. In previous chapters, we have seen examples of Ānanda's "settled monastic" personality; e.g., in the accounts of the first council, he is the textual specialist par excellence; in the *vinayas* he is responsible for the origination of the order of nuns; in *Vms* he is the leader of a crowd of undisciplined, unrealized *bhikṣus* and is criticized by Mahākāśyapa. Here, however, Ānanda clearly has a forest personality and stature. In this he is like many other of the Buddha's disciples who possess both forest and monastic dimensions in their hagiographies (e.g., Mahākāśyapa, Upagupta, and Śāriputra). See also B., 101–2, where some of his saintly traits are emphasized.

36. See Hsüan-tsang's telling of this legend (Watters 1904–5, 2:88–90).

37. For a discussion of Hsüan-tsang with bibliographic references, see Sponberg 1987.

38. These accounts of visits to Maitreya's abode recall another visit—namely, that of Asaṅga, who similarly ascends to see Maitreya, receiving (according to Tibetan tradition) the "five *dharmas* of Maitreya," three of which provide important textual foundations for the Yogācāra (Chattopadhyaya 1970, 158–59).

39. Sung Yün repeats a similar theme in one of his infrequent mentions of arhants, remarking on a certain temple, where arhants and *yakṣas*—equally supernatural in aspect—"continually come to offer religious services, to water and sweep the temple, and to gather wood for it" (B., 196).

40. This legend is not given by Watters (1904–5, 2:289–90).

41. This summary is based on Beal's version (Beal 1884, 2:227–28). Watters's treatment (Wts., 2:224–25) is abbreviated.

42. This theme of the forest saint who, when confronted by those who would discuss and debate with him, rests in silence and does not reply is, of course, found in Buddhist textual tradition as well. See, e.g., the beginning of the *Milindapañha,* in which King Milinda journeys to a hermitage and aggressively presses a forest renunciant named Āyupāla to discuss and debate various topics with him. Āyupāla, however, responds to the king with complete and unmoving silence. Just as in the story told by Hsüan-tsang, so in the *Mp* account this silence is the undoing of the forest renunciant, for the king ridicules and rejects Āyupāla and sets off to find one who *can* debate and discuss. Such a one he finds in the highly accomplished textual scholar Nāgasena (*Mp* 1–24 [T.R. 1890–94, 1:1–39]); *Mp* is the account of their conversations.

43. This legend deals not with an isolated instance but with a general pattern of thought within Indian Buddhism. This is suggested in another story, very similar to this one in dramatic structure and dynamics, that occurs in the *Rathavinītasutta* in the *Majjhimanikāya.*

When the Buddha is staying near Rājagaha, he asks his *bhikṣus* who, in their native district, is most esteemed for desiring little and for advocating to the *bhikṣus* the desiring of little; for being himself content and for advocating being content; for being himself aloof and advocating the same; for being unsociable *(asaṃsaṭṭha)* and for advocating the same; for being endowed with energy, moral habit, concentration, wisdom *(paññā),* freedom, and the knowledge and vision of freedom and for advocating the same. These virtues of poverty, contentment, seclusion, meditation, and realization, of course, identify a saint and, moreover, a forest saint. The assembled *bhikṣus* name Puṇṇa, Mantāṇī's son, as the one most esteemed for these things. Śāriputra, who in the Pāli canon represents, as we have seen, the ideal embodiment of the virtues of settled monasticism, is in the assembly and is impressed that the *bhikṣus* thus praise Puṇṇa and that the Lord approves of him. Śāriputra therefore decides that he would like to meet this Puṇṇa and speak with him. Subsequently, he expresses his devotion to Puṇṇa, the saint, by continually extolling him.

One day, Śāriputra hears that the saint, Puṇṇa, is nearby, having left the Jeta grove and retired to Blind Men's Grove (the commentary remarks that "the Jeta grove was crowded . . . and it was impossible to find solitude. But the Blind Men's Grove was secluded" [Hn., 1:189, n. 1]). Śāriputra "hurriedly tak[es] his piece of cloth to sit upon, follow[s] close after the venerable Puṇṇa, Mantāṇī's son, keeping him in sight" (*Mn* 1:147 [Hn., 1:189]). In this forest locale, Puṇṇa sits down under a tree and enters into meditation for the rest of the day; Śāriputra does the same. Toward evening, Puṇṇa emerges from meditation; Śāriputra follows suit. Then Śāriputra puts a series of questions to Puṇṇa about why Puṇṇa has entered the religious life under the Buddha. As possible motives Śāriputra suggests religious life lived for the sake of the purity of moral behavior, purity of mind, purity of view *(diṭṭhi),* crossing over doubt, knowledge of what is the way and what is not the way, and knowledge of the course (*paṭipadā,* "practice," "method"). Puṇṇa rejects all of these and replies instead with the one thing that Śāriputra has not thought of: it is for "utter *nibbāna* without attachment" that the religious life under the Buddha is lived.

Up to this point in the story Puṇṇa represents the forest saint associated with seclusion and meditation and devoted to the goal of liberation. Moreover, he is depicted as the ultimate human ideal and religious authority. Śāriputra, by contrast, represents other values as possibly the appropriate reason for living the religious life, including purity of behavior, correct view, and knowledge of various aspects of the path—all concerns that are consistent with Śāriputra's role elsewhere in the Pāli canon as the ideal embodiment of the settled monastic way. The implication of this story, so far, is clear: Śāriputra is in the position of the unenlightened disciple, who represents lesser values and whose understanding is deficient, who is attracted by the charisma of the forest saint and who seeks his counsel.

At this point there is a sharp—indeed illogical—shift in the story. Puṇṇa asks Śāriputra who he is. When Śāriputra tells him, Puṇṇa replies, "I have been counselling the worthy disciple whom they liken to the Teacher without knowledge that it was the venerable Sāriputta. If I had known it was the venerable Sāriputta, I would not have spoken at such length." Then Puṇṇa puts Śāriputra in the position of a realized saint, using exactly the same words of praise to characterize Śāriputra that Śāriputra has previously used to characterize Puṇṇa, concluding, "It is profitable for us and it is well gotten for us that we have a chance to see, that we have a chance to visit the venerable Sāriputta" (*Mn* 1:145–51 [Hn., 1:187–94]).

Migot notices this dramatic inconsistency in the *Rathavinītasutta* and is puzzled about why Śāriputra, the "second Buddha" in Pāli tradition, plays, for most of this story, the role of the deferential, even obsequious, disciple ("C'est . . . une chose curieuse . . . [qu'] il semble donc bien être présenté comme inférieur à Puṇṇa, et recevant son enseignement . . . [il] est assez étrange" [1954, 468]). It should be clear, however, that within the present context a fairly simple explanation for this suggests itself. In the first part of the story, we find the prototypical forest saint and his kind of Buddhism being established as the highest norm for renunciants. At the same time, Puṇṇa's devotion to "utter *nibbāna* without attachment" is contrasted with other, less ultimate, less contemplative ends, namely, those put forward by Śāriputra. The conclusion of the story, in which Śāriputra and Puṇṇa switch roles, appears to represent a revision of the original story, in which the forest saint is placed in clear subordination to Śāriputra. The replacement at the end of the story of Puṇṇa, the typical forest saint, by Śāriputra—in the Pāli canon so predominently the prototypical embodiment of the ideals of settled monasticism—appears to reflect a process, if implicit, of the diminution of forest Buddhism at the expense of the values and orientations of settled monasticism.

44. In contrast to Fa-hsien's monastic arhant, this story presents a large group of renunciants in which arhants and nonarhants are mixed.

45. This may also include reference to the anonymity of arhants, similar to that in the cult of the sixteen arhants.

46. On the five *vidyās*, see Dutt 1962, 323–24 and Sankalia 1934, 65ff. Holding a council with the aim of establishing normative texts is obviously an activity characteristic of those within the Buddhist world who represent textual concerns. In this context, we may recall Frauwallner's belief that another council, the first one (in legend or in historical occurrence), represented part of the attempt of settled monasticism to establish an aura of legitimacy for its texts.

47. Of course this is one of the main distinguishing characteristics between those who do meditate (they have supernatural powers) and those who do not (they do not have them). Here, we seem to be told, those who have the supernatural powers are the *real* arhants, whereas the others are not!

48. The periodic lack of clarity of the term *arhant* reported by Hsüan-tsang seems connected with another kind of confusion in his account, namely, the blurring of the type of the forest saint. In most of the literature examined in this study, Buddhist saints are typically identified as forest saints, and the type of these is etched, as we have seen, in a relatively clear and consistent—indeed, almost stereotyped—fashion. The foreigner Hsüan-tsang at least once presents a confused image of the saint. For example, he remarks on certain Mahāyānists in Udyāna "who occupied themselves with silent meditation" and were expert in magical powers. However, to this typical characterization of the forest renunciant, he adds, "They were clever at reciting their books without penetrating their deep meaning; they lived strictly according to their rules" (Wts., 1:226).

49. This, in spite of the fact of his Mahāyāna allegiance and his mentioning the worship of bodhisattvas.

50. A number of studies are pertinent to the following discussion, including La Vallée Poussin 1929 and 1936–37; Dutt, 1960, 267–69; King 1980; Barnes 1981; Griffiths, 1981 and 1986; Katz 1982, 78–83; and Cousins 1984. The more recent of these studies have generally not tried to separate viewpoints of canonical tradition from those of later commentators, although as we shall see, such a separation sheds considerable light on this issue.

51. See below, p. 393n. 86.

52. T.R. and C.R. 1899–1921, 2:70, n. 1.

53. Dutt 1971, 267–71. See also Katz 1982, 78ff.

54. See below, pp. 369–72.

55. Again, the *ubhatobhāgavimutta* is listed ahead of the *paññāvimutta*.

56. See, for example, *Dīghanikāya* 3:105 (T.R. and C.R. 1899–1921, 3:101), *Majjhimanikāya* 1:439 (Hn., 2:110) and 1:477 (Hn., 2:150–52). In *Saṃyuttanikāya* 1:190 (RW., 1:190), the two classes of arhant are listed together, with the *ubhatobhāgavimutta* again being given precedence; also *Aṅguttaranikāya* 4:10 and 4:77 (WH., 4:7 and 4:44); see also *Dīghanikāya* 2:70–71 (T.R. and C.R. 1899–1921, 2:68–70).

57. In this context, the term *jhāyin* refers to meditation in general. It can also indicate one who is practicing the *jhāna*s (see *PTSD* 287, s.v. *jhāyin*).

58. Mahā Cunda picks out what is common to both types, seeing the goal through *paññā,* and does not deal with the distinctiveness of the *jhāyin,* suggesting the affiliation of the text with a group representing the *dhamma bhikkhus.*

59. Suggested by Lévi and Chavannes in their study of the sixteen arhants (1916, 50).

60. Presuming, as seems likely, that their basic attitudes toward arhants are congruent with those of the Indian Mahāyāna.

61. As is well known, in dominant Mahāyāna usage, the term *arhant* serves to indicate a follower of the "Hīnayāna," who has striven for and attained the individual liberation of the lesser vehicle, a liberation that is vastly inferior to the great enlightenment to which the bodhisattva aspires. An extreme form of this standard Mahāyāna usage is perhaps found in the *Bodhicaryāvatāra,* as interpreted by the Tibetan commentary of *rTog med bzang po* (twelfth century C.E.), which remarks that arhants as such do not even attain a real liberation but have won merely a false freedom and will in fact eventually be reborn in saṃsāra (*Bca* 9.49–50 [Batchelor 1979, 142]).

62. Werner (1983) argues along similar lines. The chief Mahāyāna complaint is, of course, that these arhants are not realized. In this context, one is reminded of a much earlier similar criticism of arhants, made by Mahādeva, who, we are told in reports of the "second, second Buddhist council," put forward five points that maintain, among other things, that arhants can be seduced and are subject to ignorance and doubt—in other words, that their realization and sainthood are somehow deficient (Prebish and Nattier 1977, 250–65). For a summary of controversies surrounding the arhant ideal, see Bareau 1957.

63. "Four kinds of persons are not alarmed by this teaching: / Sons of the *jina* skilled in the truths; saints unable to turn back; / Arhants free from defilements and stains, and rid of their doubts; / Those whom good teachers mature are reckoned the fourth kind" (*Rgs* 2.6).

64. Lama Tāranātha (writing in 1500 C.E.) similarly remarks on more than one definition of the term *arhant* in tradition, saying that according to tradition, Nāgārjuna said that there were arhants who understood the doctrine of voidness (*Kbdd* 368).

65. See, for example, Conze 1959, 93 and 1962b, 166–67; *PTSD,* s.v. *arhant;* and Swearer 1987.

66. This is suggested by Mahādeva's critique of the arhant ideal (Prebish and Nattier 1977; Williams 1989, 17–18).

7

The Solitary Saint, the Pratyekabuddha

The pratyekabuddha[1] (P., *paccekabuddha;* "solitary Buddha" or one "enlightened on his own"[2]) is frequently mentioned in Indian Buddhist texts.[3] Pāli tradition, for example, attributes several characteristics to him. First and foremost, he[4] is like a buddha, an enlightened being by virtue of having comprehended the four noble truths on his own, without the help of any teacher (*Mp* 105 [T.R. 1890–94, 1:158]). However, he does not have the capacity to proclaim the dharma to others and is not a teacher, and this separates him from a buddha. In addition, the pratyekabuddha cannot coexist in the same time period with a buddha and thus does not arise in the era when the teaching of a perfect buddha is known (Nyanatiloka 1980, 140).[5] In terms of his personal style, the pratyekabuddha enjoys solitude and speaks little (La Vallée Poussin 1908–27c, 152). Among the well-known and frequently appearing triad of arhant, pratyekabuddha, and buddha,[6] he is superior to an arhant but inferior to a buddha (*Mn* 3:254 [Hn., 3:302]).[7] Sometimes, he is closely linked with the buddhas, whereas the arhant seems to stand off to the side as a markedly lower ideal.[8] The Sarvāstivādin definitions follow closely upon the Pāli.[9]

The Mahāyāna accepts the major features of the Nikāya definitions, setting them within a characteristically Mahāyāna framework.[10] Candrakīrti, for example, remarks,

> *Pratyekabuddhas* . . . , owing to their merit and knowledge, are greater than the *śrāvakas*. But, as they lack the equipment of merit and knowledge (of the perfect Buddhas), the great compassion, the universal knowledge, they are inferior to the perfect Buddhas. They are intermediary. And as knowledge (i.e., knowledge that brings *nirvāṇa*) is born in them without a teacher, as they are Buddhas by themselves, isolated and acting for their own sake, they are *pratyekabuddhas*.[11]

In the Mahāyāna, although the pratyekabuddha retains precedence over the arhant, he and the arhant tend to be put together as two self-centered ideals of the "Hīnayāna," strictly inferior to the Buddha and also to the bodhisattva, who is on the way to buddhahood.[12] Thus, the Mahāyāna sometimes sees the pratyekabuddha and *śrāvaka* as members of the same vehicle (La Vallée Poussin 1908–27c, 153).[13] Both Nikāya and Mahāyāna definitions of the pratyekabuddha tend to be abstract, stereotyped, and repetitive. Such differences as exist among them appear to be subtle variations of the generally accepted definitions of the pratyekabuddha. The definitions, clearly reflecting a Buddhism relatively removed from the cult of the pratyekabuddhas, are useful in providing information about what learned tradition thought about them. They do not, however, depict the pratyekabuddhas as actual, living saints, and they leave room for the possibility that, as some researchers believe, these saints never really existed at all but are rather a dogmatic category invented to perform a particular doctrinal function (King 1980, 30).

However, there is another range of texts, quite different from the doctrinal or scholastic works where the definitions primarily occur, in which we find the pratyekabuddha presented in a quite different, much more embodied way—as a saint around whom a rich legendary tradition has formed.[14] This largely hagiographical literature includes texts such as (1) the Pāli *Jātakas*, the *Apadāna,* and Pāli commentaries, particularly the *Suttanipāta* commentary; (2) the Sanskrit *Avadānaśataka, Divyāvadāna,* and *Mahāvastu;* (3) some texts surviving in Chinese, for example, those collected by Chavannes (1910–35); and (4) some Pāli *suttas*, including the *Khaggavisāṇa Sutta,*[15] the *Isigili Sutta,* and some other Pāli *suttas*.[16] This chapter contains an examination of the legendary material in these texts for the understanding it may yield of the pratyekabuddha as a Buddhist saint. In the first section I examine the mass of legends as an undifferentiated whole and attempt to identify the more important hagiographic themes associated with the pratyekabuddha within the larger frame of Indian Buddhism. Owing to the character of the evidence, except in some specific cases, the following discussion will not attempt to discriminate the treatment of one source, tradition, or time period from that of another.[17] At the conclusion of this section and in the following section, some differences will be identified in the ways the various traditions depict and interpret the pratyekabuddha. Finally, in the concluding section of this chapter, three questions will be raised that are crucial to an understanding of what kind of figure the pratyekabuddha was within the context of Indian Buddhism: his type as a saint, his actual or theoretical nature, and the precise nature of his ''Buddhist'' identity.

Images of Pratyekabuddhas

The Path to Realization

Tradition holds that pratyekabuddhas are born in a time when no buddha exists in the world (*Sn*-c 51 [K., 19 and 37]).[18] In general, then, if one attains enlightenment during a buddha period, one becomes an arhant; if one attains enlightenment during a period with no buddha, one becomes a pratyekabuddha (K., 37).[19] However, the legends reveal that in his prior lives a pratyekabuddha may live when a buddha is on earth and, as a realized pratyekabuddha, he may have dealings with those destined to be buddhas in the future. The would-be pratyekabuddha—sometimes called *pratyekabodhisattva* (P., *paccekabodhisatta*)—may begin his career at a lowly station. The *Suttanipāta* commentary remarks that whereas buddhas and *śrāvakas* are born in the families of the two highest castes, the *pratyekabodhi-*

sattva may also be born in lower castes (*Sn*-c 51 [K., 18]). This view is confirmed, for example, in the *Avadānaśataka*'s portrayal of ten pratyekabuddhas (two past and eight future) among whom the lower castes predominate: servant in a household, vendor, merchant, gardener, ferryman. There appears to be one well-to-do person among them, but no brahmins or kings are mentioned (*As* 119–67 [F., 93–111]; see Feer's analysis, 1891, 112). It is not only in his caste that the pratyekabuddha is unassuming. He typically begins his spiritual career enmeshed in saṃsāra, afflicted with impure states of mind—such as ignorance, lust, and anger—and performing evil actions—such as lying, stealing, and drinking alcohol to inebriation (*J* 4:113–19 [C., 4:71–75]).

The pratyekabuddha typically leaves the world through a *pravrajyā* ceremony. However, this is unlike the *pravrajyā* of Buddhist monasticism, for in the case of the *pratyekabodhisattva,* his is a complete ordination, not merely a preliminary to be followed later by another, further initiation. Sometimes the *pravrajyā* ceremony involves leaving the world for solitary wandering, whereas at other times it constitutes entry into a community of pratyekabuddhas; in this case, the initiate must be approved by them before gaining entry (K., 45). Having renounced the world, the *pratyekabodhisattva* lives in the forest (*J* 3:156–57 [C., 3:156]; cf. Ch., 3:17) and is consequently designated by terms such as *śramaṇa* and *ṛṣi* (seer) (Fujita 1975, 100–101). He thus lives in secluded and out-of-the-way places such as forests and mountains (Ch., 3:17, 51), following ascetic practices (Ch., 3:51). By virtue of his forest life, the pratyekabuddha is also a wanderer and is allowed to go where he will: from the time of *pravrajyā* onward, "ascetics are indeed allowed for the sake of effecting their own salvation to go to any place they wish and desire."[20]

When the pratyekabuddha leaves the world, he assumes an appearance characteristic of an ascetic. His hair and beard are typically shaved off (*J* 5:251 [C., 5:130]). He may also appear with hair and beard of a characteristic length, usually specified as two *aṅgula*s. He wears the robes of an ascetic, either yellow or red, perhaps made from discarded rags (*J* 4:114 [C., 4:72]), and he also carries a begging bowl (K., 24), sometimes of brown earthen color (*J* 4:114 [C., 4:72]). "Their hair and beards are shaved, they are dressed in yellow robes, they are not attached to family or tribe, they are like clouds torn by wind or the moon's orb freed from Rāhu" (*J* 3:377 [C., 3:229]). The pratyekabuddha is allowed the "eight requisites": three robes (1 to 3), a begging bowl (4), razor (5), needle (6), girdle (7), and water-strainer (8) (*J* 3:377 [C., 3:229]; *J* 4:342 [C., 4:215]; [K., 26]). As a forest renunciant, he may be exceedingly unappealing in appearance (Ch., 3:20), but he is also sometimes depicted as very handsome (Ch., 3:220). As the pratyekabuddha moves about, it is said that his demeanor is one of gentleness and that he has an air of stillness about him (*J* 6:520 [C., 6:270]).

In leaving the world, the pratyekabuddha thus follows a code in essence like that of other Buddhist saints: he lives in the forest, begs his food, and has the appearance of a mendicant, with shaved head and simple robe. In addition, "silence" is attributed to him: he is described as *tūṣṇīkaśobhana*—one "having the glory of a silent ascetic" (*Mv* 1:301.3 [Jns., 1:249–50])—with *tūṣṇīka* indicating, in Edgerton's rendering, "one engaging in a vow of silence" (*BHSD* 256, s.v.

tūṣṇīka). A vow of silence appears, moreover, to have been a particular and characteristic feature of the pratyekabuddha's traditions, for it forms part of stock descriptions of him.[21] Pratyekabuddhas might observe silence not only while in retreat but also when going among the laity for alms (*Mv* 1:301.14 [Jns., 1:250]). In addition to such ascetic conventions, the pratyekabuddha is also depicted as following specific codes of conduct (K., 42), which include conventions of how to dress, obtain one's food, comport oneself in sitting, standing, walking, and lying down, and so forth.[22] The further place of the formal behavioral conventions of the pratyekabuddha in relation to his entire spiritual path is suggested in outlines of the path to enlightenment associated with him. One such outline, a list of "eight ways of behavior" given in the *Suttanipāta* commentary, begins with rules relating to external behavior (deportment) (1), then moves on to the guarding of the sense doors (2), mindfulness (3), concentration (4), realization (wisdom) (5), the four ways of the noble ones *(ārya)* (6), supreme attainment (7), and compassion for the world (8) (*Sn*-c 64–65 [K., 65]). Interestingly enough, this list articulates a triad of concerns that parallels the threefold Buddhist path *(triśikṣā)* of *śīla, samādhi,* and *prajñā* referred to in Chapter 1. However, whereas in the *triśikṣā, śīla* constitutes a center of gravity, in the pratyekabuddha path more emphasis is placed on meditation and realization, with a relatively lesser place given to concerns of *śīla.*

In the hagiographical evidence, the *pratyekabodhisattva* is not a strictly solitary figure: he often takes a pratyekabuddha as guru, under whom he leaves the world, enters into solitary or community life, and is given the vows that he will follow as a renunciant. His teacher also gives him various kinds of instructions, presently to be examined. This guru instructs him in a generally informal and personal way, suiting his teaching to the psychology and situation of the disciple (*Sn*-c 105 [K., 105]). Although individuals are often depicted as attaining *pratyekabodhi* without the help of a teacher or guru, sometimes such a one is instrumental in the pratyekabuddha's awakening. *Pratyekabodhisattva*s may seek a teacher but be unable to find one. In such cases, a pratyekabuddha will sometimes miraculously arrive from Gandhamādana to provide the needed instruction (*Sn*-c 105 [K., 105]).

The pratyekabuddhas live in remote and out-of-the-way places. Their principal residence is in the north, in the Himalayas, on Mount Gandhamādana[23] (*J* 3:470 [C., 3:280]). There they live in caves such as the Gold Cave, the Jewel Cave, the Silver Cave, and the Nandamūlaka Cave (*J* 4:114 [C., 4:71–72]), where they engage in continual meditation (K., 61). They are also depicted in other activities, such as attending to their caves by plastering the walls with clay (*J* 5:440 [C., 5:237]), or outside their caves, sitting, walking about, dyeing and mending their robes, participating in ceremonies, and so on (*Sn*-c 105 [K., 105]). Mount Gandhamādana is described as an ideal locale: it is crowned with a plateau covered with medicinal plants, shines from afar, and is filled with the sweet odors of perfume. At the opening of the Jewel Cave is a gigantic tree called Mañjūṣaka, which is one *yojana* high and one *yojana* wide. When a pratyekabuddha arrives there, all the flowers of the area burst into bloom at once. The sand and mud in that place consist of jewels. A sweeping wind keeps the area clean of debris; other winds bring water from Lake Anotatta (Skt., Anavatapta), sweet perfumes from fragrant trees in the mountains, and flower blossoms, which are strewn all around (*Sn*-c 61–67 [K., 60–61]). The pratyekabuddha generally remains in his isolated retreat—whether in ordinary forests, mountains, or caves, or on Mount Gandhamādana—only appearing among people when he wanders in search of alms (*Jm* 19–22 [S., 26–30]).

In his mountain hermitage, the pratyekabuddha follows a reclusive meditative way of life and is thus called *muni* (silent one) or *pratyekamuni* (solitary, silent one) (*Mn* 3:68–69 [Hn., 3:110–11]; see K., 22 and W., 56–116). When one chances upon a pratyekabuddha in the forest, it is typical to find him sitting motionless, deep in meditation (Ch., 2:127). Like other forest renunciants, he is often found meditating at the foot of a tree (*J* 5:251 [C., 5:130]). The pratyekabuddha takes joy in his practice and typically meditates for long periods of time; in one story, he is depicted as rising from "a seven days' trance" (*J* 1:232 [C., 1:103]). In fact, the pratyekabuddhas are known as ones who spend nearly all of their time meditating. In this, they are depicted as following the standard practices outlined in the classical Buddhist meditation manuals: the preparations for the *kasiṇa* (P.) meditations (*Sn*-c 71–72), the use of *kasiṇa* devices (*Sn*-c 67), the practice of the four foundations of mindfulness (K., 48), the four *brahmavihāra*s (*Sn*-c 87), and the development of the *dhyāna*s (K., 38). One is enjoined to use whichever method will prove most effective, given one's makeup and needs (K., 48).

The *pratyekabodhisattva*'s contemplative practice is often based on an "object of meditation," some key theme or subject upon which he may meditate, such as some element of the world, the path, or the goal. Frequently, this object is some ordinary situation or fact of life. Sometimes this meditation subject may be given to the *pratyekabodhisattva* by his teacher; sometimes it arises spontaneously within his field of experience, such as some fault of his, the difficulty of living in saṃsāra, some tragic occurrence, and so on. One may take this meditation subject wherever one goes, contemplating it in seeking insight. For example, a certain king observes a jungle fire relentlessly burning everything in its path. This impresses him deeply, and, taking this as his subject of meditation, he sees saṃsāra as an insatiable fire causing suffering for all beings and nirvāṇa as the fire of wisdom that burns all defilements. Again the king sees a fish caught in a fisherman's net bite through the net and escape. He takes this as a mental image and sees that he may bite through the net of thirst and false views, thus escaping the entrapment of saṃsāra. Thereupon, he abandons his kingship, enters upon the religious life, attains insight and realizes *pratyekabodhi* (*Sn*-c 114–15 [K., 113–14]).

The ascetic and meditative way of life of the *pratyekabodhisattva* is characterized as very rigorous: "Hard is the entrance upon religious life, like walking up and down upon the edge of a razor" (*Sn*-c 98). To follow the path, one must endure cold, wind, vexatious insects, uncomfortable sleeping places, hunger, thirst, and so on (*Sn*-c 97). The psychological challenges of the *pratyekabodhisattva*'s life are no less steep. For example, a certain prince and his attendant friend leave the world together. The prince soon learns that in this renunciant life, his own pride of caste and the deference formerly paid to him by his friend have no place.

This causes him no little regret and resentment, and these he must overcome (*Sn*-c 92–94 [K., 97–98]). In short, the *pratyekabodhisattva* must free his mind from dependence on external conditions and circumstances.

The hardships of the *pratyekabodhisattva* sometimes make it difficult to maintain the renunciant life. Thus the son of a wealthy merchant desires to enter the religious life and will not be dissuaded by his parents. Having entered it, he finds his shelter mean and his bed of straw uncomfortable. In the morning, he goes seeking alms but finds that only the senior renunciants get the desirable seats and the best food, while his are poor. After a few days, he cannot abide these sufferings and abandons the religious life. However, after a short time he tries the renunciant life once more but again cannot endure it. Finally, he enters upon the renunciant life a third time and is able to remain upon the way (*Sn*-c 98–99 [K., 101–2]).

In his renunciant life, the *pratyekabodhisattva* must avoid entangling attachments to patrons, whether ordinary layfolk or royalty. Thus a certain son of the king of Banaras enters the religious life and, at his parents' insistence, remains in the royal park, receiving offerings from his parents. However, the security of the regularized donorship creates problems for his spiritual practice, for he is never alone, day or night, and cannot carry out a life of meditation. A pratyekabuddha sees his predicament and comes to the royal park, revealing the limitations of the prince's situation. After this saint departs, the young prince manages to escape, going into the forest where he will be able to meditate properly (*Sn*-c 103–5 [K., 104–6]).

Through his contemplative practice, the pratyekabuddha gains various levels and types of attainment well known in the literature of Buddhist meditation. He passes through the four classical stages of stream enterer, once returner, nonreturner, and, here, pratyekabuddha (*Sn*-c 64). He also gains meditative expertise through practicing the thirty-seven wings of enlightenment (*As* 119–22 [F., 93–95]; *As* 134 [F., 99–102]) and is experienced in the various levels of *dhyāna,* the four lower *dhyāna*s corresponding to the four stages of the world of form and the four higher *dhyāna*s corresponding to the world of nonform. Thus he also experiences the eight *dhyāna*s and the nine *samāpatti*s (attainments), including the final goal of the attainment of cessation *(nirodhasamāpatti)* (*Sn*-c 128–29 [K., 123–24]; see K., 47–53).

Some beings are antagonistic to the *pratyekabodhisattva*'s way of life and foremost among these is the demon Māra, who dogs his heels, in the same way he dogs the heels of Śākyamuni, trying to cause him harm and to dissuade him from his aim (K., 24). When the *pratyekabodhisattva* attains enlightenment, his realization is often depicted as a victory over Māra (K., 58). Even after his enlightenment, Māra remains to be dealt with, for he attempts to deceive the unenlightened disciples of the pratyekabuddha; in one story, he tries to force a potential donor to turn his back on the saint (*Jm* 19–22 [S., 25–30]).

The Pratyekabuddha as a Realized Saint

The *pratyekabodhisattva* attains enlightenment, *pratyekabodhi*[24] (*J* 3:239–40 and 307 [C., 157 and 191]), "all his faults destroyed, (their) roots cut, (like) palm trees uprooted, conditionings that will not again exist in the future, in this way completely free from faults'' (*Sn*-c 64 [K., 54]). The *Isigili Sutta* (*Mn* 3:68–71 [Hn., 3:110–13]), in what Wiltshire calls ''one of the earliest doctrinal pronouncements on the *paccekabuddha*,'' extols this realization: ''These and other *paccekabuddhas* are of great power; they have stopped the flow of phenomenal existence. Praise all these immeasurable, great seers who are freed from all fetters, completely cooled'' (*Mn* 3:71 [W., 7]).[25] In enlightenment the pratyekabuddha, according to the *Jātaka,* is ''free of all attachments, possessed of all virtues'' (*J* 6:45 [C., 6:29]), has escaped rebirth (*J* 5:248 [C., 5:128]), and is liberated in heart, independent, and master of himself (*Mv* 1:467 [C., 1:303]), which brings joy, happiness, and peace (*Sn*-c 69 and 74). The pratyekabuddha's nirvāṇa, representing wisdom gained by direct insight rather than textual learning, is thus ''not sown, not strewn, not explained, not taught, not made known, not established, not unveiled, not explained in detail and not made manifest nor shown'' (K., 55).

Although the pratyekabuddha's enlightenment is typically the fruit of meritorious actions and meditation in this or a previous life, it may be provoked by some ordinary situation or incident (K., 42–44). Thus, Darīmukha, while standing in a garden, sees a withered leaf fall to the ground and comes to see the principles of decay and death, grasps the three marks of things, and making the earth reecho with joy, enters on *pratyekabodhi* (*J* 3:239 [C., 3:157]). Similarly, a king is blessed with a son, whom he loves greatly. One day, when the king has gone to his pleasure garden, the son takes ill and dies. When the king learns of his son's death, he reflects on the nature of causality and attains enlightenment (*Sn*-c 85–86 [K., 92]). Candana, seeing how the lotus flower is beautiful upon first opening yet dies under the rays of the burning sun, reflects that so also is the fate of human beings. Thus he achieves enlightenment (*As* 119–23 [F., 94]). Again, a man is entranced by seeing the beautiful wife of another man. He reflects on his mental entrapment and sees its inevitable karmic consequences if allowed to proceed; this insight provokes *pratyekabodhi* (*J* 4:114 [C., 4:72]).[26] These few examples are typical and reflect the sources' abundance of stories of enlightenment in the midst of ordinary life (*Sn*-c 84–85 [K., 91–92]).[27]

Sometimes a *pratyekabodhisattva* will meditate and attain realization unbeknownst to others. Thus, a certain king of Banaras, while sitting on his throne, secretly follows the path of the pratyekabuddha (*Sn*-c 52–63 [K., 79–81]). He experiences various difficulties, including the distractions of his family and affairs of state, yet nevertheless he persists in his contemplative way, sometimes going to the roof of his palace to meditate. Eventually, he attains realization and, when pressed by his ministers, declares, ''Look here, I am not a king, I am one who is called a paccekabuddha.'' When they object that he does not look like a pratyekabuddha, he touches his head with his right hand and at once miraculously assumes the appearance of a pratyekabuddha, his hair and beard two *aṅgula*s long, and possessing the eight requisites (robes, bowl, etc.). Then he rises in the air and appears seated on a lotus flower.

The renunciant status is important to the pratyekabuddha, particularly after enlightenment. When as a layman he attains realization, as in the previous example, he is typically magically transformed into a fully equipped renunciant (*J* 4:114 [C., 4:71–72]). Thus when Darīmukha achieves enlightenment, ''the character[istics] of a householder vanished from him, a miraculous bowl and frock fell from the sky and clave to his body, at once he had the eight requisites and the perfect deportment of a centenarian monk'' (*J* 3:239–40 [C., 3:157]).

The state of a realized pratyekabuddha is described in classical Buddhist terms. Thus, it is said that the pratyekabuddha, through this or that teaching or circumstance, attains insight into one or another of the three marks *(anitya, anātman, duḥkha)* and into conditioned coproduction *(pratītyasamutpāda),* a feature that becomes, as we saw, particularly important in the doctrinal definitions of the pratyekabuddha. Again, the pratyekabuddha understands what is meant by saṃsāra and what is meant by nirvāṇa (K., 49).

When the pratyekabuddha attains *pratyekabodhi,* his realized status does not depend on the validation of others but is based instead on his own declaration that he has in fact attained the status of a pratyekabuddha. In another story, the bride of a certain king is traveling to meet him and dies along the way. The king's grief leads him to reflect on the nature of existence, and this leads to enlightenment. When his ministers try to console him, he replies, ''I am not distressed. I am a *paccekabuddha,* who is without distress'' (*Sn*-c 67–72 [K., 82]). In another story from the *Suttanipāta* commentary, a prince seeks a certain pratyekabuddha and, not finding him in his hut, enters, sits down, and attains realization. When the prince's attendants find him and remark that they can try to find the saint again another day, the prince replies, ''I do not worry, I became a person without worry [*acintaka,* lit., 'without conceptual thought']'' The attendants inquire, ''What does this mean, Lord?'' His reply: ''I became a *paccekabudda*'' (*Sn*-c 80–82 [K., 89–91]).

Upon the attainment of enlightenment, the pratyekabuddha may be miraculously transported to Mount Gandhamādana (*J* 3:239–40 [C., 3:157]). In one example of this, when the newly attained pratyekabuddha has arrived, other pratyekabuddhas come and sit with him, and the elder of the group asks him: ''How is (this enlightenment of yours) attained?'' He then responds by speaking his own verse with explanation (*Sn*-c 66–67 [K., 60–61]). Upon achieving enlightenment, the pratyekabuddhas also remark upon their identity. When asked who he is, he may answer, ''I am a pratyekabuddha,'' but he may also reply in other ways. Thus two pratyekabuddhas say, ''We are called 'Unattached' '' (*Sn*-c 75 [K., 86]). In another example, four pratyekabuddhas reply to a king's inquiry, ''We are, O great king, called 'those of the four regions.' '' When the king asks what they mean by this, they say, ''Nowhere in the four regions is there any fear or anxiety for us, O great king'' (*Sn*-c 87 [K., 93]). The king is, of course, also one ''of the four directions'' but from a different viewpoint: he has a kingdom to protect and enemies to fear.

Like buddhas and arhants, the pratyekabuddha is typically credited with various supernormal powers, concomitants of his realization, and this feature is one of the dominant themes in depictions in both earlier and later Buddhist literature (W., xiv). Chief among these powers is that of flying, and it is by this *ṛddhi* that the pratyekabuddha travels through the sky, coming and going from his mountain retreat on Mount Gandhamādana (*J* 3:472 [C., 3:281]). He may also, when teaching, rise in the air, sit cross-legged, and deliver his discourses (*J* 3:304–5 [C.,

3:190]). Upon occasion, he may rise into the air and perform the "18 magical transformations" (Ch., 3:51). The pratyekabuddha also possesses other *abhijñā*s: he can foresee events that are to take place (*J* 4:332 [C., 4:209]).

The pratyekabuddha uses his magical powers in a variety of situations and for a variety of purposes. He may employ his powers as a convenience, as when he travels by flying. After he has been given donations, he may respond by displaying his powers to gladden the laity (*Jm* 22 [S., 30]; *J* 1:233 [C., 1:105]). He may also take the initiative, using his powers to demonstrate his attainment, either to instruct his disciples or to engender faith in others (K., 52–53, 73).[28] In relation to this latter purpose, the *Divyāvadāna* and *Pratyekabuddhabhūmi* both comment that "magic converts the ordinary person quickly" (see the references in W., 304). In addition to the powers under his own control, the pratyekabuddha is also surrounded by various kinds of spontaneous occurrences that attest to his sanctity, as when he achieves enlightenment and his appearance is miraculously transformed and bowl and robe fall from the sky; or when he arrives at Mount Gandhamādana, and all the flowers spontaneously burst into bloom.

The pratyekabuddha's solitude is one of the central features of his personality, both while he is a renunciant and after his enlightenment. Thus, he is typically compared to the single horn of the rhinoceros, which has no companion, or to the rhinoceros itself, which travels alone and avoids company. The pratyekabuddha is also called solitary or alone *(eka)*.[29] A phrase found in the *Divyāvadāna, Avadānaśataka,* and *Pratyekabuddhabhūmi* has him "inhabiting remote places" *(prāntaśayanabhakta)* (see the references in W., 303). The pratyekabuddha also sometimes lives in community,[30] and the *Khaggavisāṇasutta* can praise the solitary renunciant's good fortune in having worthy companions and can extol the virtues of finding such to dwell with (*Sn* 8). Elsewhere, the pratyekabuddhas are mentioned as living and traveling about in large groups (*Jm* 40 [S., 55]), as at Mount Gandhamādana, where they dwell in caves in groups of up to five hundred (*J* 4:116 [C., 4:73ff.]). Pratyekabuddhas also wander about together in their alms-seeking and may spend the rains retreat dwelling with their fellows (Ch., 3:135). The pratyekabuddhas' community life is also seen in the *poṣadha,* which they celebrate with their companions in their retreat settings (*Sn*-c 51–52). In fact, on Mount Gandhamādana, seats are always prepared for the arrival of the pratyekabuddhas for the *poṣadha* ceremony on *poṣadha* day (*Sn*-c 67).[31]

Pratyekabuddhas also frequent other places. For example, sometimes they are seen at Ṛṣipatana, the Deer Park near Banaras, where they come together on special days (*Sn*-c 80). Again, they are found at other holy mountains, such as Mount Urumuṇḍa, where the saint Upagupta in a former life made offerings to five hundred pratyekabuddhas (*Da* 349 [St., 175]). Pratyekabuddhas may also be found in cremation grounds, and one story depicts a number of them officiating at a cremation, chanting texts throughout the night (*J* 5:54 [C., 5:30]).

The pratyekabuddhas, as buddhas, become the focus of an intense cult. It is this cultic importance of the pratyekabuddhas that explains why they are also found wandering abroad in the world, appearing among the laity. Thus, they go on their alms rounds seeking offerings individually or traveling in groups, usually of five hundred (Ch., 3:135). A pratyekabuddha may suddenly appear unannounced at one's door, sometimes—like the sixteen arhants and Upagupta—in the anonymous form of an ordinary *śramaṇa* (Ch., 2:33). Pratyekabuddhas may also be invited from their far-off retreat on Mount Gandhamādana, and invitations may be made purely mentally or by casting flowers as offerings in the direction of the Himalayas (*J* 3:470–71 [C., 3:280–81]). One can also attract pratyekabuddhas by generosity, moral virtue, and truthfulness (*J* 3:470–71 [C., 3:280]). When pratyekabuddhas appear at one's door, it is appropriate to offer them water, food, robes, and medicines (*J* 4:117 [C., 4:74]).

During the rainy season, the pratyekabuddhas will sometimes consent to settle in one place, in a hut built for them by laypeople where they will stay receiving offerings, meditating, and interacting with the lay donors (*Mrp* 1:338–39 [K., 64]). In one account, a layman basket weaver and his son build a hut on their property and invite pratyekabuddhas to stay in the hut during the rainy season, feeding them and giving them three fresh robes at the end of that time (*J* 4:317–18 [C., 4:200]). Sometimes, it appears, they may stay as a donor's guest for a prolonged period, like the pratyekabuddha who resides in the pleasure ground of a king, then living in his palace and receiving offerings for a long time (*J* 3:439 [C., 3:263–64]). In another similar example, a village headman offers to provide a certain pratyekabuddha with donations for the rest of the saint's life and instructs his daughter to bring him food every day (*Mv* 1:387 [Jns., 1:251]). Sometimes the pratyekabuddhas will perform specific liturgical services for the layperson, as in the story in which several pratyekabuddhas conduct a cremation (*J* 5:54 [C., 5:30]).

The pratyekabuddha is willing to submit himself to the cultic attentions of the laity because of his compassion, a prominent and important characteristic of his enlightened personality.[32] Compassion is the main reason that the pratyekabuddha comes out of his attainment of cessation on Mount Gandhamādana. He wishes to afford others the opportunity of making offerings to him and participating in his cult (*Mrp* 185 [K., 28]). "The wish to bring happiness . . . and the wish to remove suffering" (*Sn*-c 73–74 [K., 76])—this intention frequently forms the central theme in stories of the pratyekabuddha's activity (e.g., *J* 4:16 [C., 4:10]). In the *Mahāvastu,* for example, we are told that the pratyekabuddha develops "equanimity and pity, cultivating sympathy with others, with love in [his] heart [and is] friendly and compassionate" (*Mv* 1:466–67 [Jns., 1:303]). So it is that, when the pratyekabuddha arrives at one's door, he comes not out of a desire for donations but because he wants to provide the donor with an opportunity to earn great merit (*Jm* 19 [S., 26]). In making himself available to the laity through alms-seeking and staying with them for the rains retreat, the pratyekabuddha aims not to please himself but rather to show compassion to others (*Jm* 19 [S., 26]; *J* 4:16 [C., 4:10]; K., 70). The laity, in fact, fervently desire that the pratyekabuddha accept alms from them and are distressed lest he should pass on without receiving their gifts (*Jm* 19–20 [S., 27]). When he takes their offerings, they feel gladness and joy (*Jm* 21–22 [S., 30]). Like Mahākāśyapa, he is indifferent to the food he obtains, whether it is good or vile (Ch., 2:51).

Interesting also, as in the case of Mahākāśyapa, the compassion of pratyekabuddhas is often shown especially to those who have entered a bad form of existence—the poor, low-caste, and distressed.[33] In an epithet frequently found in the Sanskrit sources, he is said to be "compassionate to the unfortunate" *(hīnadīnānukampaka)* (see the references in W., 303). Similarly, the Pāli sources characterize him as "compassionate to the wretched" *(duggatānukampaka)* (W., 106). When a pratyekabuddha starts on his alms rounds, he considers who would most benefit from the merit accrued by making offerings to him, and it is to such persons that he goes for alms (*Mrp* 2:5 and *Da* 538), consistent with his favoring of the lowborn and disadvantaged. Such considerations are congruent with the previous low-caste status of many pratyekabuddhas (K., 28) and suggest the question as to whether the pratyekabuddhas were not sometimes the special objects of devotion of the low-caste.[34]

In showing his compassion by appearing among the laity, the pratyekabuddha brings them many boons, including the chance to see him, to receive teachings from him, to have their wishes granted, and to be protected from danger both in the present and the future (*J* 4:116 [C., 4:73] and K., 40). The benefits of revering and making offerings to a pratyekabuddha are thus said to be great indeed, both in the present life (Ch., 3:220–21) and in future births (Ch., 3:112). Thus the pratyekabuddha is called "a field for merit" and "worthy of the best gifts" (*J* 4:16 [C., 4:10]; *J* 3:470–71 [C., 3:280]). In a standard epithet in the Sanskrit sources, he is known as one "whose worthiness of offerings is unique in the world" (see references in W., 303).

Through the cultic setting, the pratyekabuddha first and foremost offers himself as an enlightened saint to be seen by the laity. The theme of the participatory "seeing" of the pratyekabuddha is, in fact, central to the laity's relation to him. Thus, his overall appearance is wonderful; in the phraseology of the *Divyāvadāna* and *Avadānaśataka,* he is "graceful in body, serene in mind, tranquil in movement" (see references in W., 303). The pratyekabuddha's body is also described in terms of light symbolism: he is radiant *(śobhana),* so powerfully that objects that have been in contact with him themselves shine (W., 68). In addition, his faculties are said to be very bright and his complexion immaculate (W., 68).[35] The opportunity for darśan of the pratyekabuddha enables his suppliants to participate in his enlightened charisma. In this context, as Wiltshire observes, "alms giving is not simply a perfunctory deed of charity but a ritual act with a deep religious significance" (W., 62). As in the case of other Buddhist saints, so for the pratyekabuddha the offering becomes a vehicle of exchange:

> There is a quid pro quo basis to it: the donor surrenders a physical object or material possession and in return the *paccekabuddha* imparts an element of his spirituality or interior transcendence, that is, he effects a change of consciousness in the donor. Within the procedure of alms-giving, a form of "transmission" may be said to take place between the donor and the recipient. (W., 62)

Thus, typically, when the pratyekabuddha appears at the door of a layperson, the layperson, simply by seeing the saint and making offerings to him, experiences a joyful and tranquil mind (*J* 3:471–72 [C., 3:281]).[36] The salvific implications of the layperson's encounters with the pratyekabuddha should not be missed for "they can significantly influence a person's spiritual destiny. They are situations with 'transforming' possibilities" (W., 82).

The display of magical powers is an important part of the pratyekabuddha's compassionate revelation of himself to the fortunate. We read in the *Divyāvadāna* of the pratyekabuddha's showing of magical feats to his donor: "Out of compassion for him, rising into the air like a regal swan with its wings outspread, he commenced to perform magical feats, creating fire, heat, rain and lightening" (*Da* 583 [W., 304]). To the fortunate donor, the pratyekabuddha may even show the "eighteen miraculous transformations" (Ch., 3:51).

In placing these magical displays within their cultic context, we notice a difference in the way that they are treated in the sources. "Whereas the Pāli tradition is only prepared to admit the value of [the use of magical powers] subsequent upon the offering of the gift, the Avadāna [that is, Sanskrit] tradition sometimes ascribes a value to the use of magic prior to the act of giving" (W., 65). In the Pāli accounts, it is generally only *after* the layperson has responded positively with faith and has made a donation that the pratyekabuddha deigns to reveal his magical powers. Thus in Pāli tradition, the display of powers is a kind of response to, and vindication of, the layperson's devotion and generosity. The subsequent effect of the display on the layperson is to increase or expand his or her devotion. The Sanskrit sources contain stories of magical displays that exhibit the same features as the Pāli. In addition, they also contain stories in which the pratyekabuddhas intentionally use their magic powers—uninvited and without prior conditions—to generate initial faith in the hearts of prospective donors. In some stories, a person either fails to recognize the pratyekabuddha's realization or is ill-intentioned toward him. In this case, the pratyekabuddha takes the initiative and uses magical power to transform the person's attitude (W., 79–80).[37] For example, we read in the *Mahāvastu* that when a certain husband reprimands his wife for making donations to a pratyekabuddha, the pratyekabuddha demonstrates his sanctity by flying through the air, and the husband gains faith (*Mv* 3:35 [Jns., 3:25]). The possible significance of this difference between Pāli and Sanskrit understandings of magical power will be considered shortly.

Through the activity of presenting himself for darśan by the laity, the pratyekabuddha is in fact teaching the dharma. It is this kind of direct, visual teaching, rather than verbal instruction, that primarily characterizes what the pratyekabuddha has to transmit to the laity. We read in the *Divyāvadāna* and the *Avadānaśataka* that "these majestic ones teach *dhamma* [Skt., *dharmadeśanā*] by means of the body not by means of words."[38] Nevertheless, in the cultic setting, words are sometimes exchanged between the pratyekabuddha and his suppliants. For example, after receiving the donation proffered to him, the pratyekabuddha will often invite the donor to make a wish, and—if the giving has been pure—it will often be granted (K., 67). The wish may be for wealth, a better rebirth, or even the attainment of the state of an arhant, a pratyekabuddha, or a buddha. In the *Dhammapada* commentary, a pratyekabuddha responds thus to such a wish: "May you attain quickly what has been wished and requested, may all intentions be fulfilled like the moon (full) on the fifteenth day" (*Dp*-c 1:198; 3:92 [K.,

89]).[39] In addition, the pratyekabuddha gives utterances that will protect suppliants from harm or otherwise guard them against danger (*J* 4:15–22 [C., 4:9–13]; W., xxii).

The pratyekabuddha is sometimes also shown giving explicit verbal instruction to those with whom he interacts, including his renunciant disciples or compatriots, and also the laity, both those whom he wishes to inspire to renounce the world and those to whom he more simply provides guidance. He may enjoin his lay hearer to a life of virtue and lead him or her to insight (*J* 3:471–72 [C., 3:281]). His most characteristic verbal teachings are, however, certain verses *(gāthā)* that he utters, either in the presence of other pratyekabuddhas or to the laity, who may be simple suppliants or prospective pratyekabuddhas.[40] To other pratyekabuddhas, as when he has just arrived at Mount Gandhamādana, he expresses the essence of his enlightenment. To laypersons who are prospective pratyekabuddhas, he may utter similar verses designed to provoke renunciation (W., xxii).

In teaching those close to him, his teaching is direct and personal. In one story, a pratyekabuddha perceives an ascetic full of caste pride and helps him overcome this pride and arrive at attainment (*J* 4:328 [C., 4:207]). The pratyekabuddha as spiritual teacher often works in ways that are not perceived by his student. A certain prince comes looking for a pratyekabuddha to receive instruction; the saint arranges his footprints so that it appears that he has gone into his hut, has not emerged, and is thus inside. The prince enters, finds the place empty, sits down on the pratyekabuddha's meditation place, and attains enlightenment (*Sn*-c 81–82 [K., 90]). Abstract definitions to the contrary notwithstanding, the pratyekabuddha's teaching activities in fact occupy a prominent place in the hagiographies. In these, the pratyekabuddha knows nothing of memorized or written texts, and his instruction is spontaneous and situational, suited to the time, place, and needs of the listener.[41]

The pratyekabuddha's teaching may take the form of uttering the spontaneous verses that express his realization. For example, as we saw, when the pratyekabuddhas attain realization, they go to Mount Gandhamādana and are expected to express their realization to the company of elder pratyekabuddhas. When the time comes for their final nirvāṇa, they declare their realization in verse form. The pratyekabuddha's teaching is also sometimes described as privileged, in that it is only one who has passed through the pratyekabuddha *pravrajyā* who is authorized to receive instruction.[42]

The pratyekabuddha teaches his suppliant, using the situation at hand to instruct in the path to enlightenment and the practice of meditation, or to provoke realization. The style in which such teachings are given is often subtle and suggestive. In relation to the character of the teaching given by the pratyekabuddhas, Kloppenborg pertinently remarks that it involves "subtle influences, instigations, pushes into the right direction, rather than thorough instruction" (K., 40). Doctrine, in and of itself, is not the major interest of the pratyekabuddha.[43] In addition, the pratyekabuddha's instruction often relies on examples, and sometimes these are not verbal. This is perhaps part of the implication of the statement that he teaches by means of his body—*kāyika* (see *PTSD* 209)—not by words (*Da* 133 [K., 41 and 78]). The pratyekabuddha, like the saint Upagupta, may give his teaching in another nonverbal form—namely, visions. A pratyekabuddha wants his young disciple to understand the renunciant way of life; so, although they are far from the place, he reveals to him a vision of Mount Gandhamādana (*Sn*-c 105 [K., 47]).

The emphasis on the bodily teaching of the pratyekabuddhas indicates how far their dharma is from textual interests and preoccupations. The same is reflected in the story, told in the *Suttanipāta* commentary, of a king of Banaras who engages his ministers in a conversation about the nature of saṃsāra and nirvāṇa. The ministers come forward with all sorts of theories about the nature of the world. The king realizes that these men are not speaking from experience and that what needs to be known is something much more practical. Thereupon, he abandons his kingship, enters upon the religious life, and attains *pratyekabodhi* (*Sn*-c 106 [K., 106]). The precedence of direct experience over doctrine has an impact on the way in which doctrine is presented by the pratyekabuddhas. This is illustrated in the story of a king who is very learned but who is dissatisfied with this mode of knowledge. He invites several pratyekabuddhas to give him a talk on dharma. The first does so, but in a disarmingly simple way, saying, "Let one be happy, O great king, let there be destruction of passion." The king finds this "not very learned" and hopes on the morrow for a more "differentiated" discourse. Yet the next day and on the following days, each of the pratyekabuddhas teaches in the same way, with a few equally simple and apparently unlearned words: "Let there be destruction of hatred, destruction of delusion, destruction of coming into existence, destruction of saṃsāra," and so on. In the course of this, the king begins to reflect upon what they are saying. Eventually, he concludes, "These ascetics are very learned without explaining (the teaching); as by a man, while pointing with (his) finger at the great earth or at the sky, not only a spot of the measure of a finger is pointed out, but more the earth (or) the sky as such are pointed out, in the same way by these, while explaining one thing each, an immeasurable (number of) things has been explained." The king wishes to be learned like this and so abandons his throne, enters upon the religious life, and attains *pratyekabodhi* (*Sn*-c 109–10 [K., 110]). Here we see an implicit critique by a meditative tradition of a preoccupation with doctrine: it is simplicity and penetration to the core meaning that are important, not sophistication of words and complex arguments.

The pratyekabuddha possesses a superhuman body. Like the body of a buddha, it may be miraculously marked with the signs of the *mahāpuruṣa*.[44] It is also typically colored like gold and gives off divine scents.[45] The pratyekabuddha who abides in *nirodhasamāpatti* possesses a miraculous body in another way: it is considered invulnerable (*Sn*-c 128–29 [K., 123–24]). The *Dhammapada* commentary tells the story of a pratyekabuddha whom antagonists try to burn but cannot: "Even after having brought a thousand cartloads of wood and having kindled (that), they could not even make a show of heat; therefore he, having risen (from his meditation) on the seventh day, went as he wished" (*Dp*-c 1:2.224–26 [K., 51]).

Like the other Buddhist saints, the pratyekabuddha is sometimes unconventional in appearance, values, and actions. His appearance may be quite unsettling, as one potential donor observes: "This man is frightful, his body seems covered with fish scales and his hair is like a horsetail'' (Ch., 3:21). As a realized saint, he is not bound by the dictates of saṃsāra, he respects neither caste nor wealth (Ch., 3:51), and his actions often represent an affront to conventional values (K., 69). Because of his unconventionality, the pratyekabuddha may be mistrusted (Ch., 3:25), insulted (Ch., 3:20–21), refused offerings (Ch., 3:270–71 and 4:181), falsely accused of crimes (Ch., 3:17), and otherwise injured (*J* 2:194–95 [C., 2:137] and W., 84).

By virtue of his power and sanctity, however, the pratyekabuddha is powerful and dangerous, and one must act in a way appropriate to his person. Those who are foolish enough to try to harm him by word or deed will suffer the consequences, including even rebirth in hell for countless eons (Ch., 2:22 and 3:25; K., 67–68). A woman who expresses anger at a pratyekabuddha becomes terribly ugly as a result of her deed (*J* 5:440 [C., 5:237]). Another who falsely accuses a pratyekabuddha of a crime falls into the three lower realms and suffers innumerable torments (Ch., 3:17). And a king who, jealous of a pratyekabuddha, calls him a leper in rags and spits at him is reborn in hell.[46]

The pratyekabuddha is possessed of extraordinary spiritual charisma, indicated by a number of similes applied to him. He is like a fire consuming grass and wood that cannot be put out (*Sn*-c 114–15 [K., 35]). The pratyekabuddha is also like an elephant, because he remains ''in the forest,'' he walks alone, and he is fully mature (K., 34–35). The pratyekabuddha is like a lion because he is not afraid, he is powerful, he is master of all living beings in the realm of the humans by means of his wisdom, and he has slain passion, aggression, and ignorance (K., 34). The pratyekabuddha's very name elicits reactions of awe. He is compared to the splendor of the sun (*J* 6:41 [C., 6:27]). One is fortunate, for example, to be able to kiss his feet (*J* 4:327–28 [C., 4:207]). A man fortunate enough to have met pratyekabuddhas says that ''he remembered them always till his death'' (*J* 3:408 [C., 3:246–47]). These examples indicate the pratyekabuddha's great stature as an enlightened one; he is thus sometimes called simply ''buddha'' (Ch., 2:58). In one text he is called ''a stainless buddha who was like a flowering royal Sal tree'' (K., 75) and in others, *pratyekajina, saṃbuddha,* and *tathāgata* (*J* 1:304 [C., 1:253]).[47] His postrealization features taken together, the pratyekabuddha has far transcended the human condition. Like the Buddha, he is in his majestic appearance, his sanctity, and his great power, closely assimilated to the *deva*s. However, unlike the *deva*s, he has escaped from the web of saṃsāra.[48]

Eventually, the time comes for the pratyekabuddha to enter final nirvāṇa and to relinquish his human form. One such attainment of *parinirvāṇa* is described in the texts: ''Having played the game of the *jhānas* for three night-watches, taking hold of the plank of the meditation-support at the rise of dawn, based on this the *paccekabuddha* Mahāpaduma entered the sphere of the *nibbāna* without residue of substratum. In this way all other *(paccekabuddhas)* also entered *nibbāna*'' (*Mrp* 1:174 [K., 55]). Pratyekabuddhas may also choose their own time of death and even be the agents of it. Mount Mahāpapāta in the Himalayas is known as a place where pratyekabuddhas may enter final nirvāṇa by throwing themselves down from a precipice (*Sn*-c 128–29). When the pratyekabuddha has passed into final nirvāṇa, his body is to be honored with flowers, perfumes, and so on. When a king of Banaras is shown the body of a pratyekabuddha who has just entered *parinirvāṇa,* he performs *pūjā* to it.[49] Then the body of the pratyekabuddha is cremated (*J* 3:434 [C., 3:260]; see W., 72). Sometimes the pratyekabuddha may be the agent of his own cremation (Ch., 4:98–99). As an example of this, five hundred pratyekabuddhas enter final nirvāṇa at the time of the birth of the Buddha. These beings declare their verse summations of their attainment of realization, as recounted in the *Suttanipāta* commentary, then fly up into the air and burst into flame. After entering into final nirvāṇa and spontaneous cremation, their relics fall to the earth at Ṛṣipatana (P., Isipatana), thus explaining the name of the place (*Mv* 1:357 [K., 63–64]).

After the pratyekabuddha's passing and cremation, his relics are collected and made the object of cultic veneration. Typically, the relics of the pratyekabuddha are enshrined in a stūpa, as when five hundred brothers who are pratyekabuddhas pass away, and their mother erects five hundred stūpas to them (Ch., 4:99). In the story of Candana, the process of the building of a stūpa is recounted: he "attained Nirvāṇa; his disciples made a Caitya in his name; and so one calls it the Caitya of Candana" (see F., 95). The stūpa of a pratyekabuddha is to be placed in a prominent location, such as the place where four roads cross (*J* 3:434 [C., 3:260]). Subsequently, the regular worship of his stūpa should be performed (K., 23). Great benefits are said to accrue to those who perform such worship. In the *Mahāvastu,* when a pratyekabuddha has passed away, his devotees build a stūpa for him, make offerings, "and honor . . . the great seer with dance and music and song" (*Mv* 1:391 [Jns., 1:254]).

There is also an interesting connection made in the *Avadānaśataka* between the hagiography of the pratyekabuddhas and their stūpas. In the case of the two former pratyekabuddhas Candana and Daśaśiras, the life of each is narrated by the Buddha when his disciples come upon the pratyekabuddha's stūpa and ask about who is enshrined within. When the Buddha and his disciples are wandering about the region of Magadha, not far from the Ganges River, they come upon an old stūpa in ruins. The disciples ask, "Blessed One, whose stūpa is this?" The Buddha replies, "There was a pratyekabuddha by the name of Candana, and it is his." This leads to further questioning: "Concerning this pratyekabuddha Candana, what was his origin, from where came his name, what did he do?" The Buddha then tells the story of the pratyekabuddha Candana (*As* 93–95 [F., 95]). Accounts of the lives of saints being told at their stūpas are confirmed by the Chinese pilgrims, who appear to have heard legends of various saints when they visited their stūpas. This intimate connection of hagiography and stūpa no doubt reflects the actual situation in which it was largely at, and by virtue of, stūpas that Buddhist hagiography developed and was preserved (see Chapter 10). In this context, it should be mentioned that the pratyekabuddhas are sometimes understood to be enclosed within a mountain. In the *Majjhimanikāya,* it is said that five hundred pratyekabuddhas dwelt in a cave on the mountain called Isigili. Sometimes people would see them entering the cave after their round of seeking alms, and such folk would remark, "The mountain swallows the seers." In the commentary, we read further that when the seers returned from their round of almsbegging the mountain would open like a huge pair of doors and allow them to enter (*Mn* 3:68–69 [Hn., 3:110–11]). The images of the saint within the stūpa-like mountain and of the ediface opening and closing recall similar images in the hagiography of Mahākāśyapa and in the *Saddharmapuṇḍarīka Sūtra*.[50]

In the preceding analysis of texts concerned with the Buddhist saints, a contrast and sometimes a tension between the values and preoccupations of settled monasticism and those of forest renunciants was occasionally noted. In the hagiographies of the pratyekabuddhas, we find similar phenomena. As we have seen, the pratyekabuddha is a forest renunciant; monks, monasteries, and their ways do not play a role in his life. When he enters the religious life of the forest, he typically does so directly from having been a layperson. However, this is not always the case; he is also depicted as entering from a way of life approximating that of town-and-village renunciation or settled monasticism. According to the *Suttanipāta* commentary, a king enters the religious life accompanied by many ministers and attendants, and donors present him with excellent offerings.

> The king ordered the many excellent requisites to be distributed according to age. Those who on that occasion obtained a beautiful thing, were satisfied; others grumbled: "We, who do all the work, sweeping the cells, etc., obtain (only) lumpy food and worn-out clothes." When he got to know this, he (thought): "Well, although it has been presented according to age, they grumble. Oh! This community is hard to help," and having taken bowl and robes and having entered the forest alone, he, having attained insight, realized *paccekabodhi*. (*Sn*-c 89–90 [K., 94–95])

This legend, as contained in the *Suttanipāta* commentary, tells us a number of interesting things. First, it depicts, in the pratyekabuddha's context, two forms of renunciant life: town-and-village renunciation or settled monasticism, and forest renunciation. Second, the pratyekabuddha's path is presented as the forest alternative to the settled and collective ideal. Third, there are certain limitations to the settled life, at least as seen from the viewpoint of the prospective pratyekabuddha: one might be attracted by the material comforts; seeking comforts could become a preoccupation in itself and a source of satisfaction; it might also produce resentment in those who did not receive as much as others; and this could distract from the religious life. The *Suttanipāta* commentary is, of course, late, and there is no telling the precise historical origin of the legends it recounts. Still, it is interesting that in the mind of later tradition, the pratyekabuddha could be seen as taking an alternative path to a more settled renunciant life, and that the more settled life could be seen as a steppingstone in the road to the radical renunciation of the pratyekabuddha.[51]

In this examination of the hagiographies of the pratyekabuddhas, we have seen some of the aspects of the cult surrounding these figures. On the one hand, as living saints, they were revered by the laity and by their own disciples as realized beings of great dimension. On the other hand, after they departed, their stūpas stood at the center of a lively cult with, as we shall see, the same features that were typical of the cult of stūpas of buddhas and other saints. There is other evidence of the historical importance of the pratyekabuddhas' cult. The Chinese pilgrims report visiting the stūpas of pratyekabuddhas.[52] These were particularly understood to possess special powers of protection, and Kloppenborg mentions evidence that images of pratyekabuddhas were used to ward off negative influences and afford protection and also indicates the connection of the pratyekabuddha with a Sinhalese (P.) *paritta* ceremony (K., 49).[53]

In conclusion, the pratyekabuddha, like the saints already discussed, is a figure at once human and divine. As in the case of the other saints, his humanity tends to be emphasized in the prerealization phase of his career, whereas his divinity takes prominence in the postrealization phase. Nevertheless, even as a realized being, he retains the character of a human ascetic, as reflected in this account of his going for alms:

> The *paccekabuddha,* having clothed himself in the morning, having taken bowl and robe, enters a village or hamlet for alms: his body controlled, his speech controlled, his mind controlled, his mindfulness fixed, his senses restrained, his eyes down-cast, perfect with regard to the way of deportment, approaching high and low families, he walks (to collect) alms. (*Cd* 267 [K., 66])

Nevertheless, such a humble appearance is not human in the ordinary sense, for it masks the superhuman identity of the saint, as seen in another description of a pratyekabuddha going for alms:

> The *paccekabuddha* Tagarasikhin . . . spending (his) time on Mount Gandhamādana in the happiness resulting from the attainment of the fruit, rose in the morning and, having washed his mouth in lake Anotatta, having clothed himself in Manosilātala, having put on his waistband, having taken bowl and upper robe and having entered the fourth *jhāna,* which forms the basis of supernatural knowledge, flew through the air by means of higher power and came down at the city-gate. Having covered (himself) with (his) robe, he gradually reached the door of the house of a wealthy merchant with his bowl. (*Sp* 1:160 [K., 67])

The hagiographical images of the pratyekabuddha reviewed in the preceding discussion are drawn from the sources of three traditions, those of the Pāli, the Sarvāstivāda, and the Mahāsāṃghika. There is a considerable degree of continuity among the sources of these different traditions in their manner of depicting the pratyekabuddha. However, there are a few exceptions to this general trend. One example, noted by Wiltshire, concerns the particular role of gifts to *samyaksaṃbuddhas* in the pratyekabuddhas' careers. Thus, in the third decade of the *Avadānaśataka,* the ten stories of which all concern present or future pratyekabuddhas, we find that in every story gifts to a former buddha (two stories) or the present Buddha (eight stories) produce merit that leads eventually to the donor's attaining *pratyekabodhi*. This theme is not present in the earlier Pāli sources but is only found at a much later time (W., xxvii–xxix, 79, 88–89). Wiltshire believes that this shows that the cult of the pratyekabuddha was made an explicit part of the cult of the Buddha in the Sanskrit tradition, whereas the same did not occur in the Pāli (W., 78–79ff.). This suggests a more positive overall evaluation of the pratyekabuddha in the developed Sanskrit tradition and a greater willingness to affirm his central cultic importance.[54] This greater Pāli ambivalence toward the pratyekabuddha and resistance to including him in the cult of the Buddha is reminiscent of a trend already noted—of the generally greater ambivalence of Pāli tradition, when compared with that of the Sanskrit, to forest saints.

One also finds an interesting difference between Sarvāstivādin and Pāli texts regarding the issue of the merit that can be obtained through donations to pratyekabuddhas. In the *Avadānaśataka* and the *Divyāvadāna,* for example, one can attain arhant status through a pious act toward a pratyekabuddha (W., 89). In other words, through seeing and making offerings to a pratyekabuddha, one can attain a supramundane result. In contrast to this, Pāli tradition generally denies that supramundane benefits can be won by pious acts to pratyekabuddhas.[55] This tends to conform to the general Pāli viewpoints of cult and merit, at least in texts that reflect the two-tiered model of Buddhism. Normative Pāli texts tend to affirm that veneration of saints is of particular interest to the laity and that the attainment of supramundane status is the specific provenance of the monks. Therefore it would not be surprising that a supramundane result of the veneration of the pratyekabuddha, although not logically ruled out, would not be emphasized by the Pāli sources (W., 89).[56] We have already seen examples of this difference between Pāli and Sarvāstivādin sources. In contast to what we have found in Pāli tradition, in the Sarvāstivādin texts we have noted the supramundane benefits won by Aśoka and promised by him to others through his veneration of Upagupta and Piṇḍolabhāradvāja, which includes the attainment of liberation.

Finally, there are distinctions among traditions treating the pratyekabuddha in the matter of magical power. The preceding discussion referred to a difference in the way in which Pāli and Sanskrit sources treat the role of the pratyekabuddha's magical power within the cult: for Pāli tradition magical display generally comes only after a gift has been made; in the Sanskrit tradition it may precede the act, as a way of initially arousing the faith of a prospective donor. Wiltshire believes that this difference reflects a larger distinction in the way in which the Pāli and Sanskrit traditions assign salvific value to displays of magical power. For the Pāli sources, magical power tends not to operate salvifically. It is the sight of the realized pratyekabuddha alone that generates devotion. By contrast, in the Sanskrit tradition, magic can, in and of itself, have transformative power: even when the sight of the pratyekabuddha does not convince, magical power can be applied to effect the needed transformation within the donor. This reflects an attitude on the part of the Sanskrit sources that is more liberal and also "more tolerant of the exhibition of 'magic powers' by Buddhist ascetics" (W., xxvii, 81–82). The general validity of the distinction drawn by Wiltshire certainly seems to be confirmed by other examples of the Pāli denigration of magical displays by Buddhist ascetics. It was noted that, in contrast to the Sanskrit sources, the Pāli condemnation of Piṇḍolabhāradvāja for his exhibition of magical feats is uniquely harsh and uncompromising. In a similar vein, whereas the Sanskrit sources freely extol the magical powers of Mahākāśyapa, the Pāli texts, and particularly the *vinaya,* downplay them.

It is significant that this particular Pāli denigration of magical power is seen not only in the tradition's treatment of hagiography but also more generally in doctrinally oriented texts.[57] In the *Kevaddha Sutta,* for example, the Buddha expresses himself to be troubled *(aṭṭiyati)* and vexed *(harāyati)* in regard to *iddhi-*

pāṭihāriya ("the miracle of magical physical transformation") and avoids it because he sees peril *(ādīnava)* in it (W., 42). A more extended discussion of magic occurs in the *Aṅguttaranikāya,* "Book of Threes," in a discussion of the powers of physical transformation *(iddhipāṭihāriya)* and mindreading *(ādesanāpāṭihāriya)* *(An* 1:168ff. [WH., 1:153ff.]). In Wiltshire's words,

> Here, *iddhipāṭihāriya* together with *ādesanāpāṭihāriya* (the phenomenon of mindreading) are placed a poor second to *anusāsanapāṭihāriya* (the miracle of teaching or instruction) as devices for converting people. We are told that *iddhipāṭihāriya* and *ādesanāpāṭihāriya* seem like an illusion. . . . They belong to the phenomenal world which is characterized by change and impermanence. By contrast, *anusāsanapāṭihāriya* provides others with the possibility to achieve a state of permanence outside the phenomenal world. (W., 41)

Wiltshire is correct to see in this denigration of magic in favor of verbal teaching "a trend away from emphasis on the acquisition of magic power [that] accompanied the growth of the *sāvaka* [settled monastic] tradition" (1990, 43); "an increasing trend in the direction of monachism but, at the same time, a corresponding decline in yogic powers" (15–16); and a "growing effeteness of the powers of *samādhi* and *abhiññā [abhijñā]* within the *sāvaka* tradition" (280). This concomitant to the growth of Buddhist monasticism is all the more interesting precisely because it is found so strongly in the Theravāda, yet is not present, at least to anywhere nearly the same extent, in the sources of the Sarvāstivāda or Mahāsāṃghika. Significantly, all three of these examples of differences between the Pāli and other traditions reflect the same general trend: toward resistance to the charisma of forest saints and a downplaying of them and of those religious characteristics most typically associated with them.

Some Questions of Interpretation

This summary of some of the major themes that appear in the lives of the pratyekabuddhas makes it clear that, as a number of scholars have observed, the pratyekabuddha is an enigmatic figure within Buddhism.[58] Who he is, what kind of traditions he represents, where he may have originated and flourished, and what his relation to Buddhism may have been are all difficult questions. However, the preceding summary provides a starting point for the formation of some tentative hypotheses concerning the pratyekabuddha's identity.

The Pratyekabuddha as a Forest Saint

As La Vallée Poussin pointed out long ago, "there is little doubt that this theory of the pratyekabuddha . . . embodies the old ideal of a solitary and silent life" (1908–27c, 153). This view has been echoed by others, including Conze (1962, 168–69), Kloppenborg (1974, 3–6), King (1980, 30, 72), and Wiltshire (1990, 30–31, and passim). The preceding analysis of the pratyekabuddha's hagiographical image certainly confirms this point. Not only is the pratyekabuddha a saint of the forest, but—as we have seen—his specific type conforms closely to the types of the Buddha and the forest arhant. The career of a pratyekabuddha often begins with some personal crisis that leads to a desire to enter the religious life. He leaves the world through a *pravrajyā* ceremony and becomes a renunciant, living in places conducive to meditation and wandering abroad. The specific path of the pratyekabuddha again reflects features of the saintly paradigm, including a sometimes important role played by the personal teacher, the following of behavioral conventions, retreat into the forest, the practice of meditation, the motif of silence, an absence of scholarly pursuits, and realization. A close conformity with the Buddha and arhant types, and with the general paradigm, continues after realization. The pratyekabuddha's attainment is recognized by others, he teaches would-be renunciants (if usually in small numbers), he accepts the devotions of the laity, he is understood as a buddha, he possesses magical powers, miracles surround his person, he possesses a supernatural body, he converts others and conquers evil spirits, and so on. His hagiographies present a contrast and sometimes a tension with a religious life defined largely by textual and doctrinal expertise. The pratyekabuddha is also powerful and dangerous to those who fail to respect his charisma. He anticipates his own death and may die in an extraordinary way. His body is ritually cremated, as in the case of Buddha and arhant, and his remains, enshrined in stūpas, become objects of cultic activity. Finally, a rich hagiography develops around him during life and, if the example of the *Avadānaśataka* is characteristic, around his stūpa after his passing.

The Historicity of the Pratyekabuddha

The identification of the pratyekabuddha as a forest saint in the classical Buddhist mold (leaving aside for the time being the issue of his "Buddhist" or "non-Buddhist" identity) leads to another question, namely, that of his historical status. In brief, is the pratyekabuddha connected with a living tradition, or is he merely a fictional creation? Some scholars believe that the pratyekabuddha never existed but was—in King's words—"purely an intellectualized category to explain how one may attain enlightenment even in Buddhaless world epochs" (1980, 30). Several pieces of evidence, however, suggest that the pratyekabuddha was, at some point, an actual saint connected with a living tradition.[59]

First, the pratyekabuddha seems to have been a viable ideal for Buddhist renunciants during at least some periods of Buddhist history. In the *Mahāparinirvāṇa Sūtra,* of course, the Buddha speaks about pratyekabuddhas as one of three types of actual saints who should, upon death, be treated in a particular way. We also find the Buddha predicting pratyekabuddhahood for different individuals—for example, when he sends Śāriputra and Mahāmaudgalyāyana to hell to visit Devadatta and console him by announcing that he will one day be a pratyekabuddha. Statements such as these at least suggest the existence at one time of a renunciant way thought to lead to pratyekabuddhahood. More explicit are references in the early Buddhist schools indicating that the path of the pratyekabuddha may be followed by orthodox Buddhists. Although saying that there can be no pratyekabuddhas during the time of a Buddha—in other words, there can be no living, human pratyekabuddhas once the Buddha has appeared—these traditions do not exclude the possibility of taking the vow to become a pratyekabuddha in a future life and of following the corresponding path. The Sarvāstivāda show, as we have seen, that the future attainment of pratyekabuddhahood is an important karmic result of current pious acts to the Buddha. In addition, they mention the pratyekabuddha as one of three legitimate enlightened ideals after which people may strive (in addition to the arhant and the Buddha). Corresponding to the three ideals are three vehicles: one may follow the Buddhayāna, Pratyekabuddhayāna, or Śrāvakayāna (N. Dutt 1930, 26, n.36). The early Mahāyāna takes a similar view: both the *Aṣṭasāhasrikāprajñāpāramitā Sūtra* and the *Saddharmapuṇḍarīka Sūtra* take it for granted that there are people taking the vow of the pratyekabuddha and following the vehicle of the pratyekabuddha; in response, each text offers its characteristic critiques.[60] More recently, in Theravādin tradition, one finds evidence of people vowing to become pratyekabuddhas in a future life, right down to modern times.[61]

The second major piece of evidence suggesting that the pratyekabuddha is connected with a living tradition is the cult of the stūpa that surrounded him in India. In the canonical texts, there are a great many references to the cult of the pratyekabuddha's stūpa, in monastic histories such as the *Mahāparinirvāṇa Sūtra* and in hagiographies, in which the Buddha is shown recommending veneration of pratyekabuddha stūpas and even engaging in the cult himself. A similar cult of pratyekabuddhas is also indicated in the *Mahāvastu,* where it is said that the bodhisattva, although following a different path from that of the pratyekabuddha, nevertheless should, as part of his own path, render devotions to pratyekabuddhas (*Mv* 1:54 [Jns., 1:40]). The widespread character of the cult of the pratyekabuddha in later times is clearly seen in the reports of the Chinese pilgrims. For example, when Fa-hsien visited India in the early fifth century, he found many stūpas and other places sacred to pratyekabuddhas.[62] Hsüan-tsang, as noted, visiting India during the seventh century, similarly reports on his visits to many pratyekabuddha stūpas.[63] These reports confirm the existence of a cult of pratyekabuddha stūpas important enough to mainstream Buddhism to be on the itinerary of foreign devotees. Further evidence of the cult of the pratyekabuddha is an array of archaeological evidence, including the discovery of pratyekabuddha images and of references to them in rock inscriptions.[64] Thus, the pratyekabuddha is connected with a living tradition in at least these two senses: people could aspire to become pratyekabuddhas and follow a path thought to lead to that goal; and the cult of the pratyekabuddha was popular and widespread.

However, this leads to a further question: in Buddhist times, did saints exist who were believed to be pratyekabuddhas? The doctrinal definitions, of course, say that pratyekabuddhas do not exist in the time period of buddhas, claiming that actual pratyekabuddhas were not known to exist once Buddhism had come on the scene. If this is the case, the pratyekabuddha would in this be similar to the Buddha, for in his case also, although there were renunciant traditions aspiring to buddhahood—for example, the early Mahāyāna—yet after Śākyamuni, in our world there are no more human buddhas; for a human buddha, one must await a far-distant future time when Maitreya will come. On the other hand, tradition holds that although pratyekabuddhas are rare, they are not as rare as buddhas. Yet this does not really explain the fact that there is no evidence to suggest that a person believed to be a pratyekabuddha did in fact exist after the inception of Buddhism. In order to explain this fact, we must consider the question of the "Buddhist" sectarian affiliation of the pratyekabuddha.

The Question of the "Buddhist" Identity of the Pratyekabuddha

A number of scholars, including La Vallée Poussin (1908–27c, 152–53) and Kloppenborg (1974, 4–5), believe that the pratyekabuddha represents a "non-Buddhist phenomenon." Kloppenborg, for example, holds that the pratyekabuddhas are "non-Buddhist" ascetics, who have been retrospectively incorporated into Buddhism.[65] La Vallée Poussin articulates a central assumption behind such a belief: "Śākyamuni did not favor [the ideal represented by the pratyekabuddha] . . . he, indeed, condemned the vow of silence, and did his best to encourage spiritual exercises in common—reading, teaching, and social activities of many kinds" (1908–27c, 153). Kloppenborg, with others who deal with the pratyekabuddha, follows La Vallée Poussin in taking the commentarial viewpoint at face value: "Although the Buddha attained enlightenment by means of an ascetic way of life, and made renunciation and entrance upon religious life a condition for the attainment of insight, he rejected the ideas of austere asceticism and practice of ritual in the way in which these were followed by the *śramaṇas* of his time" (K., 5). By "austere asceticism," Kloppenborg, typifying prevailing interpretations, seems to mean not only the extreme practices of self-mortification observed by Gautama prior to his enlightenment but more simply and generally the life of forest renunciation as such, by which he attained realization; for, she continues, the Buddha "was in favour of a less rigid separation from society and encouraged the monks to engage in occupations other than the practice of asceticism and meditation, e.g. preaching, teaching, study, and discussion with others, and social activities of various kinds" (K., 5). As the preceding discussion should have made clear, however, the forest nature of the pratyekabuddha ideal is not, in and of itself, sufficient evidence to resolve the question of the pratyekabuddha's Buddhist identity. Because there is, as we have seen, a forest saint type that is legitimately Buddhist and there are many Buddhist saints of the forest, the question must be answered on other grounds.

Some of the evidence suggests that the pratyekabuddha is, in fact, a Buddhist saint of the highest order. For one thing he does not reflect the values and orientations of settled monasticism, but rather conforms closely to the type of the Buddhist forest saint. Second, in Nikāya Buddhism and, to a lesser extent, in the Mahāyāna, the pratyekabuddha is explicitly acknowledged as a great saint—standing with the Buddha and the arhants and above the arhants in stature. This is significant, for early Buddhism is generally clear about the sectarian affiliation of the saints who turn up in its texts; when "*tīrthikas*" appear on the scene—whether with Jaina, Ājīvika, or other *śramaṇa* affiliation, on the one hand, or brahmin, on the other—they are clearly identified as such and either converted or dealt with in a usually uncompromising fashion. Can we assume that in the pratyekabuddha early Buddhism has made an exception to this procedure, admitting a whole variety of non-Buddhist saints and then covering its tracks so thoroughly? Third—and this is a particularly telling fact—the pratyekabuddha is closely assimilated to the Buddha. Both made a vow long ago to attain enlightenment, both are bodhisattvas, each acts as disciple and teacher of the other, each must conquer Māra, each attains *bodhi (anuttarasamyaksaṃbodhi* or *pratyekabodhi),* each sits under a tree to attain enlightenment, each is enlightened by himself, and so on (K., 24, 25, 39). If the pratyekabuddha were really essentially non-Buddhist, then how is it that he approximates the Buddha so closely and why is he given nearly the honors of the Buddha himself?

Although the pratyekabuddha may not be clearly non-Buddhist, the obverse—namely, that he is strictly Buddhist—is not so easily decided. In this respect, it is particularly interesting that the pratyekabuddha's tradition, as evidenced in the texts of both Nikāya and Mahāyāna Buddhism, has no direct linkage to any of the historical Buddhist traditions, seeming instead to stand apart from them. This makes him different from the other renunciants of the forest we have considered, all of whom, in one way or another, trace themselves, without doubt or hesitation, back to Śākyamuni Buddha and see themselves as fulfilling, in an authentic manner, the ideals of his lineage.

If in fact the pratyekabuddha represented an early Buddhist tradition, begun by the Buddha, one would expect different things from the evidence. For example, his *not* appearing in the proximity of a buddha would not be such a central feature of his definition. There should be some evidence, if not in the definitions, at least in the hagiographies, connecting the pratyekabuddha with a lineage of the Buddha. The evidence consistently indicates that the pratyekabuddha has no connection with the Buddha in his final life. Thus the pratyekabuddha represents a forest renunciant tradition, with at least a quasi-Buddhist identity, but one that in its separation and independence from the Buddha and his lineages is unlike any other tradition known in Buddhism. But this appears to leave us in a perplexing position. How can the pratyekabuddha represent a tradition that is strictly neither non-Buddhist nor Buddhist?

In order to address this issue, it is necessary to raise the larger question of the precise processes by which the pratyekabuddha may have come to play the role that he does in developed Buddhism. Let us begin by noting that the designations of all three categories of early Buddhist saints—buddhas, pratyekabuddhas, and arhants—appear to have been known outside of Buddhism in the religious environment of the *śramaṇa* movement. As we have already seen, the term *arhant* was in general use among the *śramaṇa* schools and was applied to realized people in Jainism and Buddhism. The term *buddha* was similarly a class name used in Jainism and Buddhism to refer to enlightened saints, foremost among whom were the enlightened founders in contemporary and former times.[66] Even in later Buddhism, the term continued to be used in a less restrictive sense (see Reynolds and Hallisey 1987, 319) to indicate various individual and sets of former buddhas who preceded Śākyamuni as well as the future buddha, Maitreya. The pratyekabuddha also appears to have been part of the heritage that Buddhism shared with other *śramaṇa* schools.[67] Several researchers have pointed to the important fact that the pratyekabuddha, in a configuration very similar to the one found in Buddhism, was also known in Jainism as the *patteyabuddha* (Pkt.).

It is significant that in Jainism as in Buddhism, the pratyekabuddha is not only known but is often paired with the enlightened founder (Buddhist, *samyaksaṃbuddha*-pratyekabuddha; Jain, *svayambuddha-patteyabuddha*) (W., 117–25, esp. 123–24; see also Norman 1983). Moreover, a threefold hierarchical typology of founder buddha-pratyekabuddha-disciple also exists in both traditions. Finally, legendary material connected with the pratyeka*(patteya)*buddha is very similar in both traditions (W., 117–225; Norman 1983). The evidence makes it unlikely that either Jainism or Buddhism borrowed this legendary material from the other (W., 123–24)[68] and suggests rather that it goes back to a common source.[69]

The Buddhist and Jain notions of the founder buddha and pratyeka*(patteya)*-buddha obviously have in common the notion of buddha as a fully enlightened person. This implies, as Norman has suggested, that what was originally a single concept of buddha likely predated and then bifurcated into two types of buddha (1983, 94; W., 16, 47). If this is so, then at some point, out of a unitary buddha type, there developed two subtypes: on the one hand, the buddha who is known for teaching others and founding a tradition; and on the other, the buddha who simply achieves enlightenment without being particularly known for these activities.

The differences in the way these two concepts of buddha come to be defined—differences upon which the later commentators capitalize—raises the important questions of what the original concept of buddha may have been and which of the two subsequent types more closely approximates the original ideal. In the Buddhist sources, the pratyekabuddha is depicted as a very ancient tradition. Moreover, he always lives in the age preceding the birth of a buddha and then disappears. The concept of an enlightened one without world-redeeming features is also structurally the simpler of the two types of buddha, for whereas the notions of the pratyekabuddha and *samyaksambuddha* both imply enlightenment, only the latter additionally teaches and founds a *saṃgha*. These facts suggest that the simple notion of buddha as an individual saint represents the original notion out of which the other developed. But why would this simpler buddha ideal have given rise to another, more complex one? And why would it then have receded into the background?

Let us recall that individual wandering ascetics were a feature of Indian religious life since Vedic times. The fact that the term used for Vedic sages, *muni* (silent one), was used in early Buddhism (for example, the *Suttanipāta, Muni Sutta* [*Sn* 207–21]; W., 226ff.) to refer to certain wandering *śramaṇa*s suggests a possible continuity of some kind between the more ancient and the later figures. Be that as it may, the sixth century B.C.E. was a time of profound religious change in northeastern India, spurred on by unprecedented social and economic events including the development of cities, increased trade, a growing middle class, and newly available wealth. These events were paralleled by the development of sizable groups of renunciants, the town-and-village *śramaṇa*s described in Chapter 2, who were supported by wealthy laity. Perhaps when society gained the ability to offer material support not just to one or two or three renunciants but to increasingly sizable bands that began to congregate in and around towns and villages, a transition occurred in the unitary notion of the buddha figure. Perhaps the buddha figure with more solitary and reclusive connotations (the pratyekabuddha in concept, if not in name), which was more appropriate for renunciant traditions that were more strictly forest oriented, became, in this increasingly collectivized *śramaṇa* religious environment, insufficient at least for some. Perhaps with the rise of *śramaṇa* groups living in towns and villages the need arose for another, more collectively oriented buddha ideal, one that corresponds to the Buddhist notion of *samyaksaṃbuddha*.

Reading backward from the Buddhist case, we may hypothesize that, unlike the original, more purely forest buddha ideal, the more collective buddha ideal would have included under its aegis town-and-village *śramaṇa*s. The more collectively oriented ideal would likely not have represented a strict alternative to the original ideal but merely a development and expansion of it. Thus, the buddha as a more collective ideal would have been understood as master of both town-and-village groups of *śramaṇa*s and forest renunciants. Status as leader of forest renunciants would have remained a necessary element in the conception of the collectively oriented buddha ideal because of the linkage of the forest with meditation and realization. Any buddha figure would have had to retain his forest credentials simply as part of his stature as a buddha. Thus, the forest credentials of Śākyamuni Buddha, as he is portrayed in the Nikāya texts, remain intact and important, however much he may come to be seen as an essentially urban religious figure: *first* he is a forest renunciant, *then* he can become an urban master teaching a form of religion stressing urban values (settled communities, socially laudible behavior, regularized relations with the laity, textual scholarship, close relationships with individuals and institutions of wealth and power, and so on). According to this line of thinking, then, the new, more collectively oriented buddha ideal represents the old forest ideal of leadership of forest renunciants to which has been added leadership of town-and-village *śramaṇa* groups and, through them, of large numbers of laity, particularly those of influence. Seen in this way, the *samyaksaṃbuddha* is truly a teacher of the many *(bahujana)* and protector of the world *(lokanātha)*.

As the new social, political, economic, and religious developments of the sixth century B.C.E. gained momentum, the more collectively oriented buddha ideal—of which Śākyamuni is the paradigmatic example—would have gained popularity. As part of the development and increasing popularity of the *samyaksaṃbuddha* ideal, the pratyekabuddha would have been given a sharper and more specific definition. For the idea of the pratyekabuddha as a buddha who specifically does *not* found a *saṃgha* or teach a world-redeeming dharma makes sense only in relation to the other kind of buddha who *does* teach such a dharma and *does* found a *saṃgha*. The particular emphasis on the pratyekabuddha's isolated and asocial character must thus have developed only after the *samyaksaṃbuddha* notion had increasingly come to be understood as identified with urban, monastic values and, in that increasingly urban guise, had begun to move to center stage in settled monastic tradition. In addition, as a natural corollary to these developments, the more forest-oriented buddha ideal would likely have suffered a decline, losing its charismatic prestige and cultic popularity to the new kind of buddha, perhaps at first in the town-and-village context, later more generally. Is this not what the Buddhist evidence itself communicates to us regarding the cult of the pratyekabuddha, that he was in the Buddha's time already seen as a figure pertinent mainly to a time since passed, a figure that had ceased to be relevant now that Śākyamuni had made his appearance?

The possibility must additionally be admitted that Śākyamuni was historically not the first to exemplify the *samyaksaṃbuddha* type. The bifurcation of an original buddha type into pratyekabuddha and *samyaksaṃbuddha* may have occurred prior to the arrival of Śākyamuni. Buddhist tradition itself holds that Buddha Śākyamuni was preceded not only by pratyekabuddhas, who depart from his type in the ways mentioned, but also by former buddhas who are *samyaksaṃbuddha*s and duplicate his type exactly.[70] Buddhist texts depict the cults of both former buddhas and pratyekabuddhas as ancient already in the time of Śākyamuni. In addition, the existence of former saints of the universal saviour type is found in both Jainism and Buddhism, allowing for its existence prior to both. The *Mahāparinirvāṇa Sūtra,* in the Pāli (5.12) and two Chinese versions (Bareau 1970–71, 1:2.50–53), states that there are three types of holy persons to whom stūpas should be built: buddhas, pratyekabuddhas, and arhants. Buddha and pratyekabuddha are distinguished and each is considered as a type rather than an individual. Specific discussion of former buddhas also exists in relatively early examples of Buddhist literature, for example, the introduction to the *Suttavibhaṅga* (*V*-p 3:7–9 [H., 1:14–17]) and the *Mahāpadāna Sutta* of the *Dīghanikāya* (2:1–54 [T.R. and C.R. 1899–1921, 2:1–41]). These various strands of evidence, then, raise the possibility that the bifurcation of an originally more reclusive buddha ideal and the development of a more expansive ideal of the *samyaksaṃbuddha* were elements in the inheritance received by Buddha Śākaymuni and his followers.

Be this as it may, developed Buddhism held that the pre-Sākyamuni buddhas are understood to fall into two groupings: the *samyaksaṃbuddha*s (including the former buddhas understood as those who teach and found *saṃgha*s) and the pratyekabuddhas (understood as those who do not). Following this reasoning, it is not quite correct to say, then, that the pratyekabuddha represents a Buddhist way of including "non-Buddhist saints" within the Buddhist fold. Rather, the pratyekabuddha and former buddhas together represent the two categories of saint with which Buddhism sees a direct and lineal connection. These two are both examples of the particular type of saint, buddha, of which Śākyamuni—both as type and as an individual—is the decisive example for this particular period of history. The former buddhas and the pratyekabuddhas, then, are neither "Buddhist" nor "non-Buddhist" saints but, rather, *proto-Buddhist saints* in the specific sense indicated here.[71]

Thus it is that the legitimacy of these two types of buddhas within the developing Buddhist context was not questioned and that the texts accept, as legitimately Buddhist, not only Buddha Śākyamuni and his cult but the sets of "former buddhas" with their cults and the pratyekabuddhas with theirs. Much later, the Chinese pilgrims reflect the same view and visit the sacred places, not only of Buddha Śākyamuni and his enlightened disciples (the arhants), but also of the past buddhas and pratyekabuddhas. For the texts, for the Chinese pilgrims, and—no doubt—for the collection of Indian Buddhists themselves, the tradition of Buddha Śākyamuni was to be legitimately defined not by Śākyamuni in isolation but by this heritage of buddha saints, of which, to be sure, Śākyamuni—as a self-enlightened and world-redeeming buddha in this world age—is foremost.

Authenticity here is clearly not defined by historical derivation, that is, by those saints who can be shown to derive historically from the individual Buddha Śākyamuni. When one takes the historical individual Śākyamuni as the reference point, in the strict sense, for normative Buddhism, of course the pratyekabuddhas (and the former buddhas) must be seen as non-Buddhist. But from the Buddhist viewpoint in which the historical individual Śākyamuni is, from the beginning, an example of a type, the former buddhas and pratyekabuddhas are as legitimately Buddhist (or, more accurately, as dharmic) as Buddha Śākyamuni himself.[72] In other words, it is the collection of saints that make up authentic Buddhism, not the individual Śākyamuni Buddha, and the pratyekabuddha figures high in the hierarchy of these saints.[73]

Let us return to the abstract definitions of the pratyekabuddha summarized at the beginning of this chapter. A comparison of them with the hagiographic images epitomized in the body of the chapter reveals some interesting discrepancies. For example, the definitions say that the pratyekabuddha has no teacher, yet we have found him sometimes studying with a master; the definitions generally see him as solitary, yet in his lives he may live in community; he is said to be deficient in compassion, yet the hagiographies can depict compassion as crucial to his enlightened motivation; he is said to be silent and not to teach dharma to others, yet the legends present him as instructing both laity and renunciants. Differences such as these make it clear that in the evidence of the pratyekabuddha, there are two major levels of tradition, that of story and legend (which would appear to stand relatively closer to the cult of the pratyekabuddha) and that of learned commentaries (which is more removed from the cult and for which the saint performs much more limited and specific doctrinal functions).[74] The commentators clearly developed a stereotype of the pratyekabuddha that did not always fit the facts as expressed in the more legendary evidence. At the same time, they stayed close enough to the facts of the pratyekabuddha as a solitary forest saint to remain credible.

Thus the abstract stereotype of the commentators reflects the hagiographic image of the pratyekabuddha in some important ways. For example, there is some accuracy in the remark that the pratyekabuddha is alone, for he does spend much of his time meditating in isolation. The contention that he has no teacher may well reflect the fact that his is a dharma of personal discovery, not one defined by living in community and being preoccupied with received tradition. The notion that he does not speak and does not teach may reflect the fact that he does not do so in the manner that is customary in classical monasticism—that is, based on and relying upon the *prātimokṣa* and textual tradition.[75]

The evidence in the commentaries reflects a process of monasticization in which the monastic and particularly the monastic commentarial traditions have assimilated the pratyekabuddha, retaining something of his charisma but reducing him so that the figure he presents is harmonious rather than at odds with Buddhism as then understood. As we have seen, the pratyekabuddha himself reflects an ideal of forest renunciation that is perhaps close indeed to the ideals of the Buddha and earliest Buddhism. In his assimilated state, however, the pratyekabuddha has been quite thoroughly woven into the logic of established Buddhism.

Notes

1. Two full-length modern studies on the pratyekabuddha in Buddhism have appeared: Kloppenborg 1974, which focuses almost exclusively on Pāli texts, and Wiltshire 1990, which, although emphasizing the Pāli sources, includes discussion of Sanskrit texts. The primary value of Kloppenborg's work in the present context consists in her attempt to identify some of the principal themes associated with the pratyekabuddha in the Pāli texts. Wiltshire's study is particularly valuable both for pointing to principal hagiographic themes and for attempting to discern particular patterns and structures in the pratyekabuddhas' lives. For some other scholarly discussions of the pratyekabuddha, see Charpentier 1908; La Vallée Poussin 1908–27c; Dutt 1930, 80ff.; Fujita 1975; de Jong 1976; Gombrich 1979; and Norman 1983.

2. Tib., *rang.sangs.rgyas* (enlightened by oneself).

3. For a summary of these definitions, see La Vallée Poussin 1908–27c and Conze 1962, 167.

4. Pratyekabuddhas are always depicted as men.

5. For some textual references, see *PTSD* 385, s.v. *paccekabuddha.* See Wiltshire's summary of these three points (W., xi–xii).

6. *Vsm* 376 (N., 412); La Vallée Poussin 1971, 1:2.

7. See also *Vsm* 116 (N., 120); *Vsm* 234 (N., 251–52); La Vallée Poussin 1971, 4:176, 267, 273; 5:8–9, 124.

8. *Vsm* 443 (N., 488).

9. La Vallée Poussin 1971, 2:193–96 and 5:73; La Vallée Poussin 1908–27c, 152–54; Fujita 1975. Vasubandhu explicity identifies a second category of pratyekabuddhas alongside that of solitary renunciant, namely, those who live together in a group *(vargacārin)* (La Vallée Poussin 1908–27c, 153; and La Vallée Poussin 1971, 2:194 and 4:177).

10. See, e.g., *Asp* 3ff. (Cz., 84ff.) and *Sps* 30ff. (Kn., 30ff.). See also La Vallée Poussin 1908–27c, 152–54 and Dutt 1930, 80–81.

11. La Vallée Poussin's translation and additions (1908–27c, 153).

12. Dutt 1930, 81; *Asp* 115–18 (Cz., 162–65); Candrakīrti, cited by La Vallée Poussin 1908–27c, 153; Lamotte 1980, 2234–35.

13. La Vallée Poussin remarks that many additional "technical details" concerning the pratyekabuddha are found in the works of both Nikāya and Mahāyāna Buddhism (1908–27c, 153–54). There is some disagreement among Mahāyāna schools concerning the enlightenment of the pratyekabuddha. The *Saddharmapuṇḍarīka Sūtra,* for example, holds that ultimately there is not a separate vehicle for pratyekabuddhas and *śrāvaka*s, but that both will eventually become bodhisattvas and enter the Mahāyāna, the only true vehicle. The *Prajñāpāramitā,* by contrast, maintains that pratyekabuddhas and *śrāvaka*s each have their own vehicles through which they may attain nirvāṇa.

14. Wiltshire is thus quite right, in his analysis of the pratyekabuddha, to classify the Buddhist sources as falling into two quite distinct genre types: "narratives (stories and

legends) and expositions of doctrine'' (W., xx), a distinction Kloppenborg fails to make. At the same time, Wiltshire also correctly notes that ''it is often the case that doctrinal expositions are integrated into the narrative.''

15. This text exists in nearly the same form in *Sn* (35–75) and the *Paccekabuddhāpadāna* section of *Ap* (7–14) and in a somewhat different version in *Mv* 1:468–70 (Jns., 1:303–4). In the *Mv* version, the verses are attributed to pratyekabuddhas, whereas in the Pāli version they are not, although they are so attributed in *Sn*-c. This raises the question of whether in its older form the text may not have been explicitly connected with pratyekabuddhas. Fujita believes that the Pāli *Sn* represents the more ancient version and that it was only with the rise of the Buddhist schools that the verses of the text were identified as having been spoken by pratyekabuddhas (1975, 101–3). Wiltshire takes a similar view (W., xxii). Be this as it may, in both *Mv* and the Pāli *Sn*-c, *Ks* is understood as providing important definition to the figure of the pratyekabuddha. See Wiltshire's discussion of these three versions (W., xxii–xxiv).

16. For a summary of this literature, particularly that preserved in Pāli, see W., xx–xxix. Wiltshire also includes a useful discussion of Jain literature on the pratyekabuddha (W., xxix–xxxii). The fact that no Mahāyāna texts are mentioned in this listing reflects the fact that the Mahāyāna generally takes little interest in the lives of the pratyekabuddhas and treats them mainly in a doctrinal perspective (W., xxvi).

17. The texts reflect widely differing times, places, traditions, and contexts. This suggests that it might be possible to separate out the various depictions of the pratyekabuddha according to the different time periods and textual traditions. This is perhaps particularly so because it has proved not only possible but also quite revealing in the cases of some of the individual arhants discussed in previous chapters. However, this kind of tradition-specific, historical analysis is rendered difficult in the case of the pratyekabuddha. For one thing, historical distinctions in the texts that treat the pratyekabuddha are hard to make because of the difficulties in dating the legendary material contained in them. It is often the later tradition that contains the most legendary material on the pratyekabuddha, yet it cannot be assumed that this legendary material itself derives from or reflects a later time. In addition, tradition-specific analyses are difficult because there is a relatively high degree of consistency in the major themes of the pratyekabuddhas' hagiographies from one tradition to another. The reason for this seems to be that the Buddhist authors are generally interested in the pratyekabuddha as a type rather than as an individual. Thus, the marked individualizing tendency that shows up in, for example, the treatment of particular arhants within specific contexts is not commonly seen among the pratyekabuddhas. In addition, the pratyekabuddhas are, by definition, figures of the ancient past and have no direct role in the immediate history of Buddha Śākyamuni or of the *saṃgha*. This means that, in contrast to the case of the arhants, there appears to have been relatively little temptation to work the pratyekabuddhas into the history of any school or to make them reflect any sectarian viewpoint (although some exceptions will be noted). Thus, one finds Buddhist authors, editors, and scholastics taking relatively less interest in the pratyekabuddhas, and one suspects that the legends were left more intact as received than was the case for the other Buddhist saints.

These limitations of the evidence of the praytekabuddha can also be an asset. Migot sheds some light on this issue when he remarks that in presentations of the Buddha, ''each time that a school assembled its canon, it was obliged to put the entire system in accord with the new orthodoxy, attributing to the Buddha its own interpretations.'' (One need only think of the very different images of the Buddha and his teachings in the Nikāya schools, the Mahāyāna, and Vajrayāna Buddhism.) Migot then observes that the legends of the great disciples have been subjected much less to the kind of sectarian, revisionist tendencies that one finds in the depictions of the Buddha: "The difficulties that we have pointed to for the Buddha do not exist for the saints; they were not judged sufficiently important to drastically modify . . . and [from their hagiographies] we can often gain a fairly accurate picture of the epoch in which they were in favor" (1954, 407). Migot's optimistic assessment regarding the absence of major modifications in the legends of the great disciples is, as we have seen in a number of instances, overdrawn. However, such an absence of revision would seem to apply to the hagiographies of the pratyekabuddhas. Thus, in the legendary material, we may gain an accurate glimpse of the kind of saints that these figures represented in a fairly ancient time.

Factors such as these suggest that, given the present state of our knowledge as presented in this study, we shall do best to examine the legendary tradition as an entity, taking some note where possible of differences among traditions. At the same time, it is possible to imagine a more precise method that may produce more specific results.

18. Kloppenborg has provided a useful summary of textual images of the pratyekabuddha (1974). However, as mentioned, she examines only Pāli materials, although in an appendix she includes a translation of Asanga's *Pratyekabuddhabhūmi.* For reviews of Kloppenborg's book, see Strong 1975, de Jong 1976, and Gombrich 1979.

19. See *Mv* 1:385 (Jns., 1:249).

20. *Sn*-c 105 (K., 105); see also W., 19, 128, 159, 183, 227, and 237.

21. See, for example, *Mv* 1:385 (Jns., 1:249–50): pratyekabuddhas are "splendid in their silence *[tūṣṇīka],* of great power *[mahānubhāva],* live in loneliness like a rhinoceros" and the nearly identical description at *Mv* 3:553 (Jns., 3:415). See also W., 277. Wiltshire remarks that the pratyekabuddha's "silence" may be seen as due to (1) the difficulty of communicating in words transcendental experience (also reflected in the Buddha's hesitation about teaching and the characteristic silence of other forest saints); and (2) the restraint of speech that "is regarded as a necessary condition of self-discipline and a natural corollary of meditation" (W., 277). To these may be added a possible additional factor of the commentarial tradition's assumption that all authentic doctrinal teaching resides with the Buddha and his disciples and thus its reluctance to allow the capacity for this to pratyekabuddhas (W., 277).

22. Kloppenborg refers us to *Sn* 45, 46, and 72: "i.e., what is called the 'minor precepts,' as they are expounded in the *Khandhaka* section of the *vinaya. Vsm* 11 equates this practice with the third, fourth, and fifth stages of the noble eightfold Way, right speech, right behaviour, and right living" (K., 19). In *Mrp,* a certain initiate is instructed thus in the *abhisamācārika:* " 'Thus you should dress, in this way you should cover yourself' and similar ways of conduct" (*Mrp* 2:192 [K., 76]). The *Sn*-c also associates the pratyekabuddha with the *abhisamācārika* (*Sn*-c 92–94 [K., 97] and *Sn*-c 126–27 [K., 121–22]).

23. The *Sn*-c places Mount Gandhamādana north of seven mountains: the Cullakāḷa, the Mahākāḷa, the Nāgapaliveṭhana, the Candagabbha, the Suriyagabbha, the Suvaṇṇapassa, and the Himavanta (*Sn*-c 66–67 [K., 60–61]).

24. Wiltshire observes that in the earlier stratum of literature on the pratyekabuddha, enlightenment is referred to not by *pratyekabodhi* but by other terms such as *subodhi.* It is only in the later strata of literature that *pratyekabodhi* is used (W., 11).

25. Pāli terms in Wiltshire's translation not included.

26. Gombrich (1983, 98–100) articulates the commonly held view that the pratyekabuddha's early identity may be connected with enlightenment through causes *(pratyaya).*

27. Chance occurrences thus play a typically important role in the path and realization of the pratyekabuddha.

28. Wiltshire remarks on the use of powers as initiated by the pratyekabuddha or as strictly responses to the laity's devotion: "The difference is important because in one case

it is the *[pratyeka]buddha* and in the other the devotee who instigates the 'religious' or 'revelatory' experience; a difference functionally corresponding to the distinction between prevenient and cooperating grace in Christian theology'' (W., xxvii).

29. *Eka,* however, has not only a literal but also a figurative meaning: ''*Eka* means alone in what is called the entrance upon a religious life *(pabbajjā),* alone in having no second (i.e., no companion), alone in the annihilation of thirst, alone in being completely free of faults, alone in being fully enlightened to perfect *paccekabodhi.* Even if [a *pacceka-buddha* should] live amidst a thousand ascetics, he is alone. . . . He stands alone, he goes alone, he sits down alone, he lies down alone, he walks alone'' (*Sn*-c 64 [K., 32]). For a discussion of the pratyekabuddha's solitary nature, see K., 58ff.

30. Something noticed by the Sautrāntikas, who were led to make a distinction between two types of pratyekabuddhas, those who live alone *(khaḍgaviṣāṇakalpa)* and those who live in groups *(gaṇa) (vargacārin)* (La Vallée Poussin 1971, 4:176, n. 3). No such explicit distinction appears in the hagiographies, and pratyekabuddhas are depicted in both ways as if these were simply two modes of the same way of life.

31. This *poṣadha* is, of course, different from that of the Buddhist monks who recite the *prātimokṣa* on *poṣadha* days. Kloppenborg remarks that ''one should keep in mind that the ceremony as described in the *vinaya* is of course not meant for *paccekabuddhas''* (K., 20, n. 38).

32. For a list of references to the Sanskrit sources, see W., 303.

33. See Wiltshire's remarks on this topic (W., xxvii–xxviii).

34. Wiltshire believes that ''the *paccekabuddha* was assigned a special function with regard to votaries from the less privileged or lower social orders'' (W., 103). The pratyeka-buddha may also appear for alms at doors of the highborn, such as the palaces of kings (*J* 1:395 [C., 1:233]), and we are told that making offerings to him is one of the most important things a king can do (*J* 6:44 [C., 6:28]).

35. Wiltshire explains, ''The mind-states which are cultivated in meditation manifest themselves in bodily dispositions and faculties: grace and gentleness of bodily movement, and a calm and radiant countenance. When the *paccekabuddha* is mentioned in the context of alms-giving invariably his imposing beauty is mentioned'' (W., 66).

36. Wiltshire suggests the following as the mechanics of this transmission: ''The source of his spirituality, his pure mind *(mano suddhaṃ),* expresses itself in a physical dimension as 'radiance' or an 'aura of light.' . . . When a prospective almsgiver or donor espies, that is, experiences a *paccekabuddha* visually, the light or aura which the *paccekabuddha* emits is transmitted to him . . . [this] spiritual energy . . . 'illuminates,' that is . . . makes serene the mind *(citta)* of the prospective donor'' (W., 70).

37. In remarking that examples of this sort ''are not found'' in the Pāli texts (W., 81), Wiltshire overstates his case. To give one example, there is the story from *Sn*-c (52–63 [K., 79–81]) of the king who attains *pratyekabodhi* and who demonstrates his attainment to those around him by magical means.

38. Wiltshire picks up this theme, remarking that the transmission from pratyekabud-dha to layperson is generally nonverbal, as the *paccekabuddha* rarely attempts to teach or instruct the donor (W., 303).

39. *Mrp* states that giving can result in arhantship, *pratyekabodhi,* or even the realm of a buddha (1.56 [K., 71]).

40. See Wiltshire's discussion of this element (W., xxi–xxiv).

41. The *Khaggavisāṇasutta* commentary relates the story of three *pratyekabodhisattvas*, all kings, who are friends. In a subsequent life, two of them leave the world and attain *pratyekabodhi.* One day, the two pratyekabuddhas decide to help their friend to liberation and so station themselves at the gate of his pleasure garden by a bamboo grove.

When he comes along, they compare the king's mental defilements to the bamboo thicket, hard to pull out and destroy. Upon hearing this, the king attains insight and becomes a pratyekabuddha (*Sn*-c 74–76 [K., 86–87]).

42. The story is told of a brahmin youth who wanted to receive teaching from the pratyekabuddhas and so went to Ṛṣipatana to make his request. He asked the pratyekabuddhas whether they knew the beginning and origin of all things. They replied to him that they did. He then asked them to teach that to him, whereupon they replied, "For this purpose, Sir, you should enter upon religious life, (because) it is not possible for some one who did not enter upon religious life to learn" (*Mrp* 2:192 [K., 76]). Kloppenborg remarks, "*Pabbajā,* entrance upon religious life, is mentioned in many cases as a necessary condition for instruction, but in other places this is omitted" (K., 77–78).

43. In Kloppenborg's words, it is "very limited, and provides the person striving for enlightenment only with vague indications regarding the stages he will have to pass and the difficulties attached to these" (K., 42).

44. Kloppenborg (27, n. 78) citing *Mmk* 1:63. When a certain pratyekabuddha goes flying off to Mount Gandhamādana, he departs "with a visible body," perhaps pointing to the fact that he makes his journey in a miraculous physical body (*Sn*-c 105 [K., 105]).

45. Candana, as described in *As,* has a body that is handsome and colored like gold, possessing the thirty-two marks of a great man, as well as the eighty distinctive signs. His breath is that of the perfume of a lotus, and his body gives off the scent of sandalwood. When he walks upon the ground, ravishingly beautiful lotuses spring up. He is called a pure being (*As* 120 [F., 94]).

46. *Sp* 1:349 (K., 68). The karmic consequences of maligning a pratyekabuddha may be more immediate. A certain king has a son of whom it is predicted that he will die of lack of drinking water. The king consequently has lakes and tanks everywhere his son might go. However, one day when the prince has grown up, he passes by a pratyekabuddha and becomes jealous of the veneration shown to him. He takes the saint's begging bowl, just filled with food for his daily meal, and smashes it on the ground, stamping on it and taunting the pratyekabuddha. Immediately after, a burning fire arises in the prince's body, and he dies, being reborn in hell (summary of story told by the *Jātaka* "scholiast" provided by C., 2:137, n. 1).

47. Rahula 1978, 78. In one story, a villager wants to make offerings to a pratyekabuddha, and, the text says, he "treated the Buddha with repeated acts of kindness [saying], 'I shall invite the *tathāgata* to live with me in ease and comfort' " (*Mv* 1:390 [Jns., 1:253]).

48. This superhuman character is perhaps reflected in the *Isigili Sutta,* in which the pratyekabuddha, as a *ṛṣi* (P., *isi*), is contrasted with "human beings" *(manussa).* Wiltshire, in what appears a reasonable supposition, remarks, "The alignment here of *manussa* and *isi* possibly has the implication that the *paccekabuddhas* qua *isi* are a different (higher) category of being" (W., 9).

49. In a possible reference to the rite of *śarīrapūjā,* for a description of which see Chapter 10.

50. One additional, less typical yet important hagiographic theme is related to the birth of the pratyekabuddha and again connected with his bivalence as both human and divine, namely, a miraculous birth. *Sn*-c relates the story of Mahāpaduma, who in a previous life had made offerings to a pratyekabuddha and, as a result, is born in heaven in a lotus flower as the god Mahāpaduma. Meanwhile, the virtuous queen of Banaras greatly desires a son and fervently supplicates the god Śakra to that end. He goes to Mahāpaduma and tells him that although merit earned on earth results in rebirth in the land of the gods, it is only on earth that the perfections can be brought to fruition and that therefore Mahāpaduma must

return to the realm of humans. As Mahāpaduma cannot endure the travails of the womb, he is reborn in the heart of a lotus in the pond named Silapatta in the pleasure garden of the king of Banaras. There he is found by the queen and raised as a prince, the son of herself and the king (*Sn*-c 76–84 [K., 87–91]). A similar story is told in the *Avadānaśataka* of the pratyekabuddha Candana (*As* 119–23 [F., 93–95]). A certain king of Banaras named Brahmadatta has no son and, desiring one, makes supplications. Soon a lotus appears in the pond of his pleasure garden and it daily grows larger and larger. One morning it opens, and in the pericarp of the lotus is a young boy, sitting with his legs crossed in meditation posture. He has a wonderful appearance, handsome and of the color of gold, with the thirty-two marks of a *mahāpuruṣa*. This child will one day be the pratyekabuddha Candana. In another story in *As* that repeats many of the details of Candana's story, it is the pratyekabuddha Daśaśiras who is the miraculous lotus-born child (*As* 134–38 [F., 99–102]). *As* also tells the story of a small child who accompanies his mother to market. The Buddha comes along the same way on his begging rounds. The small child sees the Blessed One and makes expressions of joy. He reaches out his hands, takes a lotus blossom from the stall of a lotus vendor, and tosses it upon the head of the Buddha. This lotus assumes the size of a chariot wheel and floats in the air, following the Blessed One when he moves, stopping when he stops. This small child, the Buddha predicts, will one day be the pratyekabuddha named Padmuttara (*As* 134–38 [F., 96–97]).

51. The question of whether the contrast presented here may reflect an old tradition or a later interpolation would depend upon an assessment of the historical status of the legendary material contained in this part of *Sn*-c.

52. For example, Watters 1904–5, 2:51, 71, 198. The connection of the pratyekabuddha with the cult of the stūpa appears throughout his hagiography. When he dies it is appropriate to build a stūpa over his remains. In addition, he is a wandering *yogin,* and he evidently comes to stūpas in the course of his peregrinations. Thus, he is found at holy places, of which the centers are usually marked by stūpas. In *As,* a renunciant under Kāśyapa who later becomes a pratyekabuddha is shown performing devotions at a stūpa (119–23 [F., 93–95]).

53. On *paritta,* see La Vallée Poussin 1908–27b.

54. At the same time, it is difficult to tell for certain the extent to which this phenomenon may be explained by a difference in textual genre and to what extent it reflects an actual difference in the conception of the pratyekabuddha between Pāli and Sanskrit Buddhism.

55. As Wiltshire notes, Pāli tradition does contain examples of this feature, but they are found in *Dp*-c and the *Nettipakaraṇa,* both late compositions (W., 89). See note 39.

56. Wiltshire remarks that "to recognize [as the Northern sources do] that the householder could perform devotional acts which conduced in the long term toward transcendental consequences, was to admit that the lay-monachist distinction is not so absolutely crucial. In other words, the laity is given access in the long term to what the *bhikkhusaṃgha* has access to in the shorter term. In the growth and expansion of Buddhism there were increasingly pressures to narrow the gap between lay and monachist salvific goals" (W., 89).

57. Some good examples are pointed out by Wiltshire (W., 39–42).

58. Conze remarks that "the traditions about the *Pratyekabuddha* are not always very clear" (1962b, 167), and King observes that "what this figure represents . . . is difficult to determine" (1980, 30). Fujita remarks that "the *pratyekabuddha* can be characterized only as a being concerning whose historical personality no direct conclusions may be drawn" (1975, 88). Also see Eliot 1921, 1:344–45 and W., ix.

59. Both Kloppenborg (K., 5) and Wiltshire (W., ix, and passim) take this view.

60. *Asp* accepts the discrete nature of the three vehicles, while advising its adherents to avoid the vehicles of the *śrāvaka* and pratyekabuddha and to follow that of the bodhisattva (1–3 [Cz., 84–85] and 115–16 [Cz., 163]). The *Lotus Sūtra,* by contrast, holds that the appearance of three separate vehicles is finally not real and that all people apparently following the three vehicles are actually part of the one great vehicle, the Buddhayāna, leading to the one great enlightenment of *anuttarasamyaksaṃbodhi* (see, e.g., *Sps* 21–43 [Kn., 30–59]).

61. The ideal of the pratyekabuddha has been a viable one in more modern times, sometimes being followed by forest monks in contemporary Theravāda Buddhism. Tambiah cites the example of a certain Theravadin forest monk who took a vow to follow the pratyekabuddha tradition and attain *pratyekabodhi* (1984, 86).

62. Thus he reports seeing near Sāṃkāśya the place where a pratyekabuddha used to take his food. "The *nirvāṇa* ground (where he was burned after death) is as large as a carriage wheel; and while grass grows all around, on this spot there is none. The ground also where he dried his clothes produces no grass, but the impression of them, where they lay on it, continues to the present day" (B., 69). In another place, he saw two stūpas of two royal fathers who had become pratyekabuddhas and there heard a legend connecting these two with a former life of Buddha Śākyamuni (B., 98–99).

63. See note 52.

64. Wiltshire cites the example of a rock inscription dating from the first century C.E. in Sri Lanka that mentions the existence in the place of "the stūpa of the tenth *pacceka-buddha*" (W., 50).

65. "The adaptation of the concept of the *paccekabuddha* in Buddhism . . . presented the opportunity to include pre-buddhist recluses and seers in Buddhism. . . . [It arose] to give an answer to the question which arose regarding the validity of the achievement of the ascetics and sages of pre-buddhist times" (K., 6). Wiltshire similarly contends that the term is a designation for *śramaṇa*s who lived before the time of the Buddha, which Buddhism wanted to acknowledge within its system.

66. Reynolds and Hallisey 1987, 319. Gombrich points out that the notion of former buddhas existed in early Jainism and early Buddhism (1980, 64). This suggests that the notion of buddha represents part of the common heritage of Jainism and Buddhism.

67. First indicated by Charpentier (1908, 35ff.), who shows legends of pratyekabuddhas being held in common by Buddhist and Jain traditions (cf. Norman 1983, 93–94).

68. Jainism, according to Fujita, "preaches the *pratyekabuddha* in a form analagous to his Buddhist form," and, Fujita adds, as it seems clear that neither borrowed the term from the other, this points to a common heritage (1975, 102). See also Norman 1983, 93.

69. Wiltshire believes that the concept of the pratyekabuddha, but not the actual term, existed in Jainism and Buddhism. He believes that the term did not exist because it is found neither in *Sn* nor in other Pāli texts deemed to derive from earliest times. This is not a decisive argument, however. In this context, it may be pointed out that other reasons for the absence of the term from such texts can be adduced (e.g., a lack of interest in the issues implied by discussion of the pratyekabuddha, for a discussion of which see note 73). By contrast, Fujita believes that "the word *pratyekabuddha* was already in general use by the time Buddhism and Jainism made their appearance" (1975, 103), with which Norman agrees (1983, 92).

70. For a discussion of the past buddhas, cf. Vogel 1954 and Gombrich 1980. In the canonical literature of both Pāli and Sanskrit tradition, for example, seven former buddhas are mentioned: Vipaśyin (P., Vipassin), Śikhin (P., Sikhi), Viśvabhū (P., Vessabhū), Krakucchanda (P., Kakusandha), Kanakamuni (P., Koṇāgamana), and Kāśyapa (P., Kassapa), who is then followed by Śākyamuni. For references in the Sanskrit tradition, see

BHSD, s.v. the names; for references in Pāli, see *PTSD,* idem. For an indication of the importance of the cult of these saints in later times, see Hsüan-tsang's many references to sites and stories connected with the past buddhas throughout the account of his journey, for example, Watters 1904–5, 1:203, 214, 302, 311, 331, 332, 334, 351, 359, and 369; 2:5–6, 23, 51, 52, 60, 80, 105, 141, 154, 171, 190, 198, and 226. Jainism presents a similar structure: Vardhamāna Mahāvīra is preceded by twenty-two saints of his type, the *tīrthaṅkaras*, of which he is number twenty-three. See Tatia's comparison of early Jainism and Buddhism (1980).

71. Wiltshire has put forward a different hypothesis concerning the origins of the pratyekabuddha concept. It is unfortunately not possible in the present context to provide a summary or discussion of Wiltshire's detailed argument. However, it will be worthwhile to mention some of its salient points. Wiltshire proposes that the concept of the pratyekabuddha (though not necessarily the term) should be understood as a designation for *all* pre-Buddhist *śramaṇas* ("*paccekabuddhas* . . . are to be identified with the ascetico-religious tradition out of which Buddhism and Jainism both evolved. . . . [They] are synonymous with the earliest *śramaṇas,* themselves the originators of the Śramaṇic Movement" [W., 117–18]; they are "the ascetic forerunners of Buddhism" [132]). Through the concept of the pratyekabuddha, Wiltshire contends, Buddhism was able to acknowledge the pre-Buddhist *śramaṇa* tradition out of which it arose, while at the same time putting distance between itself and that preexisting tradition. One difficulty with the hypothesis as stated is that the *śramaṇa* tradition contained—so the various sources make clear—a great variety of different sorts of figures, some solitary, some in groups, some realized, some beginners, some meditators, some philosophers. By contrast, the pratyekabuddha concept is a strictly limited one: it indicates a solitary, fully enlightened person. It is difficult to see how a concept so limited in definition would have been used to designate such a multifaceted phenomenon. Moreover, this hypothesis does not adequately explain the existence of the stūpas of the pratyekabuddhas. For Wiltshire's hypothesis to work, all these would have to have been renamed, well after the term entered Buddhism. Indian religious life would seem far too conservative for his hypothesis to be plausible; moreover, in India, religious life does not usually follow the dictates of learned commentaries. The hypothesis of Wiltshire (and of La Vallée Poussin, Kloppenborg, etc.), then, needs to be limited in order to be acceptable: the pratyekabuddha represents the acknowledgment of one facet of the pre-Buddhist *śramaṇa* tradition; among renunciants, he is an enlightened one, a buddha; among buddhas, he is that buddha who is solitary.

Another difficulty with Wiltshire's hypothesis is that it represents a logical conclusion built on the questionable foundation of the two-tiered model of Buddhism. Wiltshire believes that early Buddhism is a tradition exhaustively defined by settled monasticism. In his conception pre-Buddhism is, by contrast, a disorganized movement of individual *śramaṇas*, of which the pratyekabuddha is a representative (W., 131). Thus, forest traditions, as such, by definition belong to pre-Buddhist times and represent non-Buddhist phenomena. As we have seen, examples of forest phenomena cannot automatically be assumed to be pre-Buddhist and non-Buddhist. Moreover, it cannot be assumed the *śramaṇa* movement was entirely nonsectarian in character. Wiltshire's model also prevents him from seeing the actual significance of the pratyekabuddha within Buddhism—i.e., this figure represents a trend within Buddhism with which settled monasticism is struggling.

72. Indian Buddhist origins, then, would appear to present quite a different configuration from those of Christianity, at least as popularly understood. In the case of Christianity, a founder arrives who, while fulfilling the past, also to a large extent presents a dramatic and qualitative innovation over what came before. By contrast, in Indian Buddhism, we would appear to have a preexisting tradition that is accepted as legitimate and is simply

given less or more distinctive shape by Śākyamuni Buddha in his time. It is incorrect to say that Jesus Christ is a prophet like other prophets or a saviour like other saviours, whereas it is quite appropriate to say that Buddha Śākyamuni is like, indeed is identical to, other buddhas. Buddha Śākyamuni has an old message for a new age (as Eliade notes, "The Buddha himself proclaimed that he had 'seen the ancient way and followed it' " [1969, 162]), whereas Jesus Christ has a message that is radically new. See Gombrich's remarks (1980, 62–63). One might suggest that this represents a diminishing of the figure of Buddha Śākyamuni in terms of his uniqueness and individual creativity, a devaluation of the historical Buddha, in favor of other enlightened ones. This is, of course, reminiscent of the "devaluation" that is often said to have occurred in the historical Mahāyāna, and it is surprising that it is found relatively early, if implicitly, in Buddhist history. However, the use of the term *devaluation* in this context is not accurate, for it is possible to argue that the conservative, monastic (particularly Pāli) emphasis on the "historical Buddha" represents one trend within early Buddhism but not necessarily early Buddhism as such. It is possible, then, that those who set up the "historical Buddha" as the single, relatively exclusive criterion of Buddhist authenticity do so, as already suggested, to some extent by turning away from the dominant perspectives of earliest Buddhism and heading off into new, institutionally driven directions.

73. The pratyekabuddha—as noted in the preceding analysis of his legends—gives birth to other pratyekabuddhas who repeat his type. By contrast, a *samyaksaṃbuddha,* at least as seen in the Nikāya traditions, gives birth to *śrāvaka*s, receivers of his teaching. These do not duplicate his type (the Buddha's type and accomplishment are incomparable in this historical period) and, unlike their teacher, represent a collective ideal. The nonconformity of the *śrāvaka* to the buddha type and the collectivity of the ideal perhaps provide further indication of the important role of town-and-village renunciation in the formation of the *samyaksaṃbuddha* concept.

The important role of town-and-village renunciation in the birth of the *samyaksaṃbuddha* type is also indicated by the fact that it is in the lineal descendant of town-and-village renunciation—settled monasticism—that the greatest interest is taken in comparing the pratyekabuddha and *samyaksaṃbuddha* and in making distinctions between them. Wiltshire has pointed out, for example, that different historical strata of the Pāli sources treat the pratyekabuddha in different ways. In the earliest documents, the *Suttanipāta* and other texts and sections of texts deemed to represent the same general historical vintage (as noted, showing Buddhism as essentially a forest tradition), there is no explicit mention of the pratyekabuddha at all (W., xi–xii). Later are texts from the "main *nikāya* period," including the first four *nikāya*s, which speak of the pratyekabuddha but do not discuss the doctrinal definitions by which he is later chiefly known (his nonteaching, his noncoexistence with a *samyaksaṃbuddha,* and so on). Still later are the texts of the fifth *nikāya* together with the post-*nikāya* commentarial literature, in which the doctrinal definitions contrasting buddha and pratyekabuddha, including systematic denigrations of the latter, are fully developed (W., xii, 48–49, 130). These include the affirmations that (1) both buddha and pratyekabuddha are enlightened without a teacher; (2) unlike the *samyaksaṃbuddha,* the pratyekabuddha does not teach a dharma and does not found a *saṃgha;* and (3) the pratyekabuddha cannot live at the same time as a *samyaksaṃbuddha* and therefore belongs to a bygone era (W., xi–xii). This suggests that Buddhist tradition takes an interest in the pratyekabuddha, as a figure comparable but inferior to a buddha, *in proportion to its own degree of monasticization.* The preceding discussion helps us to understand the anomaly that, although the pratyekabuddha probably existed (again, in structure if not in name) in pre-Buddhist times, he does not appear in the earliest Buddhist texts. For these earliest, forest-oriented texts, the bifurcation of pratyekabuddha–founder (urban) buddha would have not been interesting or important. However, with time, as Buddhism became more and more fully monasticized and the Buddha became increasingly seen as the founder of a large and expanding settled monastic tradition, with its emphasis on textual scholarship and regularized relations with society, the situation would have changed. Now the elevation of the urban buddha and the diminution of the forest-oriented buddha would have become matters of considerable doctrinal importance. Thinking on previous saints would have been one arena where this was worked out: former *samyaksaṃbuddhas* thus came to be given highest honors, whereas the solitary buddhas increasingly became the butts of criticism, a process that is, according to Wiltshire, particularly evident in the later Pāli commentarial tradition. The absorption of the pratyekabuddha into Buddhist dogma and the increasingly sharp contrast of him with the *samyaksaṃbuddha* reflect, then, the same kinds of processes of which we have seen several examples. In this, settled monasticism is asserting the normativity of its particular orientation, and part of this affirmation includes showing forest Buddhism as an old, outmoded style of spirituality.

It is also pertinent to observe that the teaching structure associated in the Nikāya texts with the *samyaksaṃbuddha*—of buddha producing *śrāvaka*—is not universal within developed Buddhism. There is another important tradition in which the teaching structure associated with the pratyekabuddha—of buddha producing buddha—remains the norm, namely, that of the Mahāyāna. It is significant that in several early Mahāyāna texts another feature of the teaching structure of the pratyekabuddha is retained (which will be examined in the next chapter): buddha produces buddha in a context of forest renunciation and solitary meditation. In the next and final chapters of this study, we shall need to consider the possible reasons for the curious proximity of the teaching structure of the Mahāyāna to that of the pratyekabuddha.

74. This distinction in viewpoint and presentation between hagiography and learned commentary has generally *not* been made in most discussions of the pratyekabuddha. See, e.g., Kloppenborg, who remarks in the introduction to her work on the pratyekabuddha that "the explanations of the commentary have simply been followed" (K., 12), an approach that de Jong is quite right to criticize (1976, 322). For other similar examples of an overvaluation of commentarial tradition, see Eliot 1921, 1:344–45 and Conze 1962b, 167–68.

75. Wiltshire argues along similar lines, although he arrives at different conclusions (W., xvii).

8

Bodhisattva Saints of the Forest in Mahāyāna *Sūtras*

In the preceding chapters, the three major types of Buddhist saint prominent in pre-Mahāyāna Indian Buddhism have been examined: the buddha, the pratyekabuddha, and the arhant. This chapter contains discussion of a fourth type of Buddhist holy person, who comes into prominence only in the Mahāyāna *sūtras*, the bodhisattva.[1] The bodhisattva is not unique to the Mahāyāna; in the Nikāya traditions, as we have seen, this type is understood as defining the ideal of a buddha from the time of his vow to complete enlightenment until the moment when he attains buddhahood. The Nikāya evidence, in fact, preserves an extensive tradition of stories *(jātaka)* told about Śākyamuni as a bodhisattva prior to his final life and similarly attributes to all other world-redeeming buddhas previous existences as bodhisattvas. In addition, as is well known, the Nikāya texts also contain descriptions and discussions of the bodhisattva and his career.[2] For the pre-Mahāyāna, the bodhisattva is an important type of saint but is relatively rare, because the arhant functions as the primary enlightened ideal of Nikāya Buddhism, whereas buddhas were few and those who aspired to become buddhas were not commonly known. The distinctive Mahāyāna doctrine of the bodhisattva represents, then, not so much the invention of a new type of saint as the bringing into prominence and fleshing out of a type that was already understood to exist, but that had been—at least in the evidence—recessive.

Three types of bodhisattvas—those of forest, city, and monastery—are documented in the Mahāyāna. In earlier texts, the bodhisattva of the forest, to be examined in this chapter, frequently has a unique normativity. It may at first glance seem contradictory that the highest form of this compassionate, self-giving, and other-oriented ideal should be a solitary figure, withdrawn from the world, meditating in a remote forest hermitage. The *Mahāprajñāpāramitā Śāstra,* however, shows how the contradiction is only apparent:

> Question: For the Bodhisattva, the rule is to save all sentient beings. Why does he seclude himself in the forests and fens, solitude and mountains, preoccupied with only himself, thus abandoning beings?
> Answer: Although the Bodhisattva is physically secluded from others, his mind never abandons them. In his solitary retreat *(śāntavihāra),* he practices meditation

> *(samādhi)* and gains true wisdom in order to save others. It is like when taking medicine for the body, one temporarily interrupts his household duties. Then, when one's health is restored, one again takes up one's duties as before. The meditative retreat of the bodhisattva is like that. Through the power of his meditative states *(dhyāna),* he avails himself of wisdom; when he has obtained the power of the superknowledges *(abhijñā),* he returns among beings and becomes, among them, father, mother, husband or son, master, servant, school master, god, man, or even animal; and he guides them by all manner of teachings and salvific methods *(upāya).* (Lamotte 1981, 984)[3]

Śāntideva on the Bodhisattva as Forest Renunciant

An overview of the major themes associated with the Mahāyāna discussion of forest bodhisattvas may be gained by considering some fragments of Mahāyāna *sūtras*[4] treating forest bodhisattvas, contained in the eleventh, or "Praise of the Forest" *(araṇyasaṃvarṇana),* chapter of the *Śikṣāsamuccaya,* attributed to the Buddhist monk Śāntideva. Although such an attribution places the text in the eighth century, much of the material it contains is taken from a considerably earlier time.[5] The *Ugraparipṛcchā Sūtra,* for example, tells us that the life of forest renunciation represents the normative Buddhist way of life for bodhisattvas: "The bodhisattva who has left the world must reflect that dwelling in the forest *[araṇyavāsa]* was ordained by the Buddha *[buddhānujñāta],* and therefore he must live in the forest; for thus there is fulfillment of the pure Law [dharma]" (*Ss* 110.17–19 [BR., 193]). The *Candrapradīpa Sūtra (Samādhirāja Sūtra)* adds that none of the buddhas of past, present, or future have been able to attain their goal without leaving the world and following the solitary life of forest renunciation (107.7–8 [188]). According to the *Ugraparipṛcchā Sūtra,* one should abandon household life and take up a life of forest renunciation (107.1–2 [188]). The *Candrapradīpa Sūtra* adds that the bodhisattva cannot attain supreme wisdom while he is enmeshed in attachments and "follows the household life which he ought to loathe" (107.3–4 [188]). Terrified of the dangers of household life, one should flee to the forest. Like Śākyamuni and the buddhas of the past, one should dwell in the forest, having love for solitude *(vivekakāma)* (107.7–10 [188]). This is the best way to honor the buddhas (107.11–12 [188]).

The *Candrapradīpa Sūtra* tells us that in the forest, one dwells in caves (*Ss* 107.28–29 [BR., 189]). The *Ratnakūṭa Sūtra* adds that one's forest retreat should be located where there are caves and mountain slopes, near enough to human settlements so that one may seek alms, but not too near, so that it is still quiet and undisturbed. It should have a source of pure water nearby, be shaded by trees, and be without danger from rabid dogs (109.3–7 [190]). The *Candrapradīpa Sūtra* continues that in the forest, one is alone and should always seek solitude (108.7–10 [189]) and "walk the world lonely as a rhinoceros *[khaḍgasama]*" (108.2 [189]). Again we read, "Be always like the solitary rhinoceros; soon ye will obtain the boon of tranquility" (108.18–19 [190]). The *Rāṣṭrapālaparipṛcchā Sūtra,* as quoted by Śāntideva, says further that the forest bodhisattva associates with neither women nor men but is solitary, living like a rhinoceros (108.21–26 [190]). According to the *Ratnarāśi Sūtra,* he thinks, "I have come into the forest alone, without a fellow. . . . I have no companion to do well or ill by me" (111.19–21 [195]). In the forest, the bodhisattva practices meditation, purifying his mind *(Up)* (108.29–30 [190]), eliminating his defilements *(Rps)* (108.21–22 [190]), and developing tranquility *(Cp)* (108.12–13 [189]). Ardent meditation, indeed, fulfills the true aim of the forest life *(Up)* (110.32–33 [194]). It is through meditation that he will attain the Buddha's salvation *(Rr)* (111.11–12 [194–95]). The *Ratnakūṭa Sūtra* also refers to the forest bodhisattva's recitation of textual material "thrice in the night and thrice in the day" (109.7–9 [190]), implying a limited body of textual material that he repeats as part of his practice.

Life in the forest is difficult and often dangerous. For example, noisesome beasts may appear, but the bodhisattva should not fear, remembering that he has already renounced his life *(Rr)* (*Ss* 111.1ff. [BR., 194]). The *Candrapradīpa Sūtra* notes that the forest bodhisattva owns nothing and has no belongings (108.1–2 [189]). Nevertheless, the *Rāṣṭrapālaparipṛcchā Sūtra* adds, one takes no pleasure with what one gets, nor is one depressed with what one does not get. Of modest desires, he is content with whatever comes his way (108.25–26 [190]). The *Ugraparipṛcchā Sūtra* additionally remarks that although one has entered the forest, this is no guarantee of virtue or realization. Many there are who live in the forest who are "untamed, uncontrolled, not devoted, not diligent" (109.21–22 [191]). Therefore, one must be vigilant and examine oneself constantly (109.24–26 [191]). Only when the self has been utterly abandoned will the goal of forest renunciation be fulfilled (110.7–8 [192]).

But in spite of its rigors, the forest life clearly has great advantages, which are spelled out in the *Candrapradīpa Sūtra.* The bodhisattva has abandoned the world and is no longer enmeshed in its defilements. Never quarreling or entering into disputes, he is delighted with peace (*Ss* 107.17ff. [BR., 188–89]). He is restrained in body, speech, and mind. And deliverance comes easily to him. The *Candrapradīpa Sūtra* adds that the forest life is conducive to freedom, and the bodhisattva dwelling by himself and meditating goes "like the wind in the sky" (107.28–29 [189]). For the renunciant who lives in the forest, there is great praise (108.10–11 [189]). The realized bodhisattva is gentle *(sūrata)* (*Rps*-s) (108.22 [190]) and he shows his compassion to gods, humans, beasts, and demons. To deities, he preaches the dharma, to help them understand it *(Rr)* (111.8–10 [194]). To human beings, he shows a gracious and respectful face *(Up)* (110.20–22 [193]). To beasts, he is willing to offer even his body as food *(Rr)* (111.1–7 [194]). He refrains from both attacking and conciliating spirits *(amanuṣya)* who come into his presence *(Rr)* (111.7–8 [194]).

According to the texts cited in Śāntideva's compendium, the life of the forest bodhisattva is not without its counterpoint elsewhere in renunciant Buddhism. The *Ugraparipṛcchā Sūtra,* for example, mentions Buddhist renunciants (*bhikṣu*s, *ācārya*s, *upādhyāya*s) who are found in groups in towns and villages and who engage in textual recitation *(svādhyāya)* and exposition *(uddeśa)* (*Ss* 110.20–22 [BR., 193]). The *Ratnakūṭa Sūtra* refers less explicitly to certain *śramaṇa*s and brahmins who are not forest renunciants but have learned and studied many scriptures and yet remain filled with defilements (108–9.30–34 [190]). Like those who, although carried along by a great flood, perish of thirst, so these, though carried along "by the great flood of the dharma," are defeated by the *kleśa*s and will fall into the lower realms *(durgati)*. Less explicitly still, the *Candrapradīpa Sūtra* refers to fools *(bāla)* who are filled with impurities and who become angry and distrustful if admonished by others (107.17–26 [188–89]).

Interestingly, we learn that the bodhisattva of the forest has something to do with the settled renunciants. The *Ugraparipṛcchā Sūtra* says that once he has achieved some realization, the forest bodhisattva may descend "into the village and town and market-town, kingdom and capital." But if the bodhisattva thus goes "amongst the multitude," he is to be courteous to *ācārya*s and *upādhyāya*s and respectful to *bhikṣus*[6] (*Ss* 110.20–22 [BR., 193]). Purposes mentioned include listening to the preaching of the dharma by these town-and-village *bhikṣu*s and attending the sick (110.29–31 [194]). During this time, however, "he must keep a cave-and-forest mind, as when he dwells in his hermitage" (110.29–33 [194]). In any case, in the evening he is to return to his forest abode. Thus, Śāntideva's extracts show a fairly strict division of labor between forest and village renunciants: the village renunciants are textual specialists, who know the texts and engage in preaching them, whereas the forest renunciants primarily meditate.

Although in Śāntideva's *sūtra* extracts, it is generally not possible to ascertain the extent to which the original texts behind the extracts reflect a homogeneous view of their saintly subjects, some divergences at least are evident. For example, the *Ugraparipṛcchā Sūtra* uses the term *forest (āraṇyaka) bodhisattva* and not *bhikṣu* to designate the forest renunciant (*Ss* 110.3–4, 18, 29 [BR., 193–94]). By way of contrast, the saints discussed in both the *Ratnakūṭa Sūtra* and the *Ratnarāśi Sūtra* are termed *forest bhikṣu (Rk: āraṇyakasya bhikṣu)* (109.9–10 [191]) *(Rr: āraṇyaka-bhikṣu)* (111.9, 11 [194–95]). Neither text, however, refers to this forest *bhikṣu* as a bodhisattva. The *Candrapradīpa Sūtra,* although espousing ideals associated with the Mahāyāna (for example, aspiration to the enlightenment of a buddha), refers to its own human ideal of forest renunciation by the term *śramaṇa* and uses neither *forest bodhisattva* nor *forest bhikṣu* (107.29 [189]). However, the types of both the forest *śramaṇa* of the *Candrapradīpa Sūtra* and forest *bhikṣu* of the *Ratnakūṭa Sūtra* and *Ratnarāśi Sūtra* are clearly homologous in type with the forest bodhisattva of the *Ugraparipṛcchā Sūtra,* which enables Śāntideva to consider all three types equally to be representatives of the classical type of the forest bodhisattva. At the same time, the forest *bhikṣu* of the *Ratnakūṭa Sūtra* and *Ratnarāśi Sūtra* is sharply different in type from the monastic *bhikṣu*s described in the *Ugraparipṛcchā Sūtra* that the bodhisattva meets in the villages among the multitudes. This diversity of terminology raises the distinct possibility, to be discussed further, that we are here dealing with relatively independent traditions of forest renunciation that, in later times, equally came to be understood as expressions of the Mahāyāna.

The Bodhisattva in the *Ratnaguṇasaṃcayagāthā*

The *Ratnaguṇasaṃcayagāthā,*[7] a compilation of verses on the *prajñāpāramitā,* closely related to the *Aṣṭasāhasrikāprajñāpāramitā,*[8] represents early evidence of Mahāyāna Buddhism.[9] For this reason, information about the bodhisattva in the *Ratnaguṇa* will be of interest for the light it may shed on early Mahāyāna conceptions of this figure. To begin with, the ideal in this text is most often termed *bodhisattva* (*Rgs* 1.5, 7, 11, 16, and passim). The bodhisattva may be either a renunciant or a layperson, and the text takes into account both ideals, making it clear that either is valid.[10] However, the renunciant is a forest practitioner, not a monk. That the renunciant bodhisattva represents the forest type is indicated by the facts that he is described as living alone in the forest and meditating and that he is nowhere shown in monastic settings or following the *prātimokṣa* or as reflecting monastic values. The forest identity of the renunciant bodhisattva is also suggested by the fact that the term *yogin* is used interchangeably with *bodhisattva* in contexts of forest renunciation, meditation, and realization (e.g., 10.9–10, 20.10–13, 21.3, 29.5). Chapter 21 specifically identifies the primary environment of the renunciant bodhisattva: he may "practise quite detached from villages or cities in a mountain cave, in a remote forest, or in isolated woods" (21.4), dangerous environments where wild beasts roam (21.6). Although, as mentioned, the text accepts both lay and renunciant ideals, it is clear that, of the two, the life of forest renunciation is considered the higher, and it is primarily the forest renunciant that the text addresses. This is seen in the primary emphasis on the forest habitat of the *yogin,* in the stress that is placed upon meditation, and in explicit statements of the preferability of forest renunciation.[11] For example, we are told that *even* if one is a devoted *yogin* who practices in the forest, if one develops pride and does not course in *prajñāpāramitā,* one's practice is of little account. By the same token, *even* if one dwells in towns all the time, if one's understanding and aspiration are pure, then one practices rightly (21.4–6).[12]

How is the ideal of the *yogin*-bodhisattva who dwells in the forest characterized? Of the Buddha, it is said approvingly, "freely he wandered without a home" (*Rgs* 2.3) and this is what the *yogin* should do (20.12). The *yogin*-bodhisattva is a devoted *yogin* who observes the ascetic practices *(dhuta)* (21.3). He may live in mountain caves infested with wild animals for many years (21.6). In addition, like other forest renunciants examined in previous chapters, the bodhisattva lives out his renunciant life under the direction of a master (guru) who acts as his spiritual friend *(kalyāṇamitra)* (15.1–2). The guru trains the bodhisattva, schooling him in the perfection of wisdom and helping him develop good qualities. Therefore, the bodhisattva should respect and revere his master (15.1–2). Under the guidance of his guru, the bodhisattva takes various vows in connection with his spiritual journey, foremost among them his vow to attain enlightenment for the sake of all beings (e.g., 20.6, 23). In doing this, he rejects the ideal of personal salvation embodied in the ideals of arhant and pratyekabuddha (2.2; 5.4; 30.9). These two other ideals the text generally sees as inferior to the ideal of complete buddhahood (e.g., 6.1).[13]

The bodhisattva's life is additionally defined by various prescriptions of morality *(śīla)*. On a specific level, the text mentions the *daśakuśalakarmas*, or ten wholesome actions (*Rgs* 17.2; 31.5), a set of behavioral norms that concern actions of body, speech, and mind.[14] On a more general level, the text devotes considerable attention to the six *pāramitās* (perfections) as types of action that should be cultivated by bodhisattvas (28–31). Both the specific *daśakuśalakarmas* and the six *pāramitās* would appear to apply to both renunciant and lay bodhisattvas. Beyond these, more specific conventions are suggested for each of the two ideals. The renunciant bodhisattva should follow the *dhutas* (21.3), and the *dhutaguṇas* are presented as the major defining behavioral code of the renunciant bodhisattva as such (21.3).[15] In the *Ratnaguṇa,* special conventions are suggested for householders, including nonattachment to their possessions, the avoidance of inappropriate livelihoods, the development of benevolence to others, and complete devotion to the dharma (17.5–6). Noteworthy in the present context, monastic *śīla* appears to play no role in the bodhisattva's path. Of particular importance is the nonliteral dimension of *śīla* in the text: if a bodhisattva develops a longing for the attainment of the arhant or pratyekabuddha, even if he is practicing the ten virtuous actions, "he becomes one whose morality is broken, and faulty in his morality" (31.5).

The bodhisattva, particularly in his primary incarnation as a bodhisattva of the forest, represents an essentially meditative ideal, for it is through meditation that he develops the perfection of wisdom (*Rgs* 29.1). Thus, he develops mindfulness, such that he is collected (17.3), quiet, and calm (20.7). He also cultivates the four meditative states, or *dhyānas* (17.4), including the four formless *dhyānas* (29.1–2). The four *dhyānas* are particularly important, for they "will in their turn become the basis for the attainment of the supreme and unsurpassed enlightenment" (29.1). "One who is established in the trances *[dhyānas]* becomes one who obtains foremost wisdom" (29.2). Meditation is, then, the way in which the bodhisattva gives birth to supreme wisdom. Thus, he meditates on the foremost wisdom (18.5) and "courses in this most excellent quietude of the concentration *[samādhi]* on emptiness" (20.7). According to the *Ratnaguṇa,* the motivation of the bodhisattva to meditate is different from that of the arhant or pratyekabuddha. These latter two meditate to gain peace alone and to effect only their own liberation, whereas the bodhisattva meditates in order to develop wisdom and compassion for the benefit of all beings (29.6).[16] It is through the *dhyānas* that he develops his excellent qualities *(guṇas)* (29.3) by which he can help others. Although meditation is the basis and vehicle of his attainment of the perfection of wisdom and of enlightenment, he does not settle down in meditation nor make it into a home (29.1). Thus, in his meditation he should not enter into either signs or signlessness (20.7). For the bodhisattva, meditation is not an end in itself, but a means to another end; "having let go the acquisition of the joy and ease of trance and concentration, [he enters] again into the sensuous world, compassionate for all that lives" (29.8).

Through his practice, the *yogin*-bodhisattva realizes the perfection of wisdom. "The *yogin* who has set out for the best enlightenment . . . moves forward, and swiftly he comes to the [state of] Bliss" (*Rgs* 22.13). Nevertheless, while still on the path to buddhahood, the bodhisattva's realization remains ambiguous. On the one hand, though still a bodhisattva, in the *Ratnaguṇa* he is depicted as a realized being, one with wisdom, compassion, and powers, very like the other Buddhist saints. On the other hand, his journey remains incomplete, for he continues to move forward, aspiring to the goal of complete and perfect enlightenment of a world saviour *(lokanātha)* (2.5; 10.6). Nevertheless, though not yet a buddha, the saintly bodhisattva is assimilated to the Buddha in various ways. For example, it is the Buddha's wisdom that he has sought (1.1). Moreover, all genuine teaching he may do is ultimately that of the Buddha (1.3), and everything the bodhisattva does comes from the might of the Buddha (1.4).

The realized but not yet perfectly realized bodhisattva is characterized in ways now familiar to us. Most important, his postrealization being is marked by compassion (*Rgs* 29.8). United with wisdom, he gives birth to great compassion (1.24) and *maitri* (20.19) and exhibits pity and concern for others (3.6). He does not retire into rest (1.7), but works to free gods and humans and shows beings the way to liberation (23.4), in fulfillment of his vow to release the world (26.6). Most important, though free of saṃsāra's shackles, abiding in neither the conditioned world nor the realm of rest (20.8), he takes rebirth again and again, according to his wish, to aid beings (29.3), all the while remaining unstained (29.5). Thus he will wander in birth and death for a long time in order to work for the purification of beings (30.1).

The bodhisattva manifests his compassion in many ways. He is a teacher of the world, giving instruction in dharma (*Rgs* 27.3). The bodhisattva also possesses magical powers of various sorts, including powers *(bala)* and the supernatural abilities *(ṛddhi)* (21.7 and 20.12).[17] By the power of the "declaration of truth" *(satyādhiṣṭhāna),* he can instruct beings (20.24) and even overcome fire (20.23). He has attained victory over the Māras, and they cannot harm him (27.2–3).[18] All such abilities and powers the bodhisattva uses to help sentient beings, and this help is discussed from two angles. On the one hand, he helps beings individually. On the other, his compassion is ultimately directed toward the purification of the (buddha)field *(kṣetra),* in which he has taken rebirth (30.1). The purity of beings and the purity of the buddhafield are thus the two dimensions of his compassionate activity (32.5).

In contrast to the type of the conventional monk, the bodhisattva of the *Ratnaguṇa* is not associated with textual study and scholarship as a primary preoccupation. However, the text and, moreover, the written text *(pusta)* have an important role to play in his Buddhism. We are told in chapter 3 that one who copies out the text,[19] bears it in mind, and venerates it with flowers and ointments will receive incomparably greater merit than the one who venerates stūpas (*Rgs* 3.4). The reason for this great merit clearly rests upon the fact that this text not only articulates and celebrates but also magically embodies the *prajñāpāramitā*. Thus, the text represents the *prajñāpāramitā,* the mother of the *sugata*s from which the buddhas come forth, in a written form (3.4). In the same chapter, we read that one who takes up the *prajñāpāramitā* and masters it is virtually assured the status of a saint: he cannot be harmed by fire, poison, sword, and water and will be safe from the attacks of Māra and his host (3.1). Clearly it is the text's magical embodiment of the *prajñāpāramitā* that justifies the various cultic activities and the incomparable benefits accruing therefrom. Thus the bodhisattva's relation to the text is defined by his goal of identification with the enlightenment of the buddhas, and the copying, understanding, and veneration of the text are primary agents, along with meditation, that bring this about.

Because of his wisdom, compassion, and power, the bodhisattva "becomes worthy of the offerings of the whole world" (*Rgs* 22.10) and is "dear to gods and men" (23.4). Thus, he is praised by human beings and gods and by the buddhas themselves (27.1). In spite of his sanctity and repute, some may hate the bodhisattva and speak harshly and offensively to him, but he is to think nothing of it (30.8). In addition, although a saint to humans, he remains unfathomable and mysterious, beyond conventionality and the grasp of the conceptual mind: "He becomes one who, like a cloud, stands in the sky without anywhere to stand on, / As a sorcerer who, like a bird, rides on the wind which offers him no support, / Or as one who, by the force of his spells, miraculously produces a tree full-blown flowers out of season" (27.5).

What of the cult of the bodhisattva after his death? The text mentions the worship of stūpas (*Rgs* 3.2–4) and the cult of relics (4.1–2), but although it remarks on the salvific validity of this cult, it avers—as just seen—that it is more to the point and far more meritorious to attend to the *prajñāpāramitā* and to copy and revere the *Ratnaguṇa* (4.2). Nevertheless, there is no doubt that the legitimacy of the cult of relics is accepted (4.2), and it is those who participate in this cult and do nothing else who are particularly criticized (3.3). However, it is stūpas of buddhas that seem to be indicated here, and there is no direct evidence in this text that human bodhisattvas had stūpas built to them.[20] As in Śāntideva's *sūtra* extracts, the bodhisattva in the *Ratnaguṇa* repeats many aspects of the paradigm of sainthood, with its themes of forest renunciation, practice of various nonmonastic codes, including the *dhutaguṇa*s, absence of prototypical monastic preoccupations, focus on meditation, realization, compassion, magical powers, and so on.

It is interesting that in the *Ratnaguṇa,* as in the Nikāya evidence and in Śāntideva's extracts, we find criticism of other Buddhist renunciants who follow a different and inferior path. It will be recalled that the text mentions three enlightened ideals: arhant, pratyekabuddha, and buddha. Significantly, the *Ratnaguṇa* is of two minds about the relationship of these ideals to one another. In some places, it acknowledges all three as legitimate—that each implies liberation; in others the text takes a more purely negative attitude toward the pratyekabuddha and arhant. On the positive side, for example, we read of arhants "free from defilements and stains, and rid of . . . doubts" who are not alarmed by the teaching of *śūnyatā* (*Rgs* 2.6; see also 5.4; 12.3). The text also mentions offspring of the *śrāvaka*s (contrasted with those of the Buddha), who are *aśaikṣa* (beyond learning) (6.4)—that is, realized ones ("adepts" in Conze's translation, 1962, 137). In a particularly interesting passage, we are confronted with the example of a *bhikṣu* who is clearly a realized saint: he can manifest the *ṛddhi*s, standing in the sky and performing miracles *(prātihārya),* going, coming, lying down, and sitting, with no fatigue, and he is compared with the wise bodhisattva, clearly a figure distinct from this *bhikṣu,* who stands in emptiness (20.11).

However, this positive evaluation tends to be the exception, and the ideals of both arhant and pratyekabuddha are much more frequently criticized in the *Ratnaguṇa* as being different from and vastly inferior to the ideal of a buddha (*Rgs* 23.2), both in their goals (5.4; 14.1) and their paths (11.4–5), or vehicles *(yāna)*.[21] Whereas the "profound vehicle" *(gambhīrayāna)* (18.2) of the *Ratnaguṇa* leads to buddhahood, the path of the *śrāvaka*s that leads to arhantship (2.2–5 and 5.4) is criticized as being inferior and is associated with betrayal of the true dharma and a cultivation of the antidharma *(adharma)* (9.6). This negative evaluation is developed in chapter 11, when Subhūti asks the Buddha whether there will be any obstacles to the precious qualities *(ratnaguṇa)* being enumerated in the text (11.1). The Buddha responds that there will indeed be many obstacles and proceeds to mention some of them. In the future, the Buddha says, certain bodhisattvas will have difficulty understanding the *Ratnaguṇa* and will conceive doubts about its teaching. They will desire the enlightenment of the level *(bhūmi)* of an arhant, will abandon the *prajñāpāramitā* in favor of the *sūtra*s (of the *śrāvaka*s) (11.4), and will enter a wrong path, that of the *śrāvaka*s. Such a bodhisattva will be deluded,[22] preferring the branches of a tree when he has the root, an elephant's foot when he has the elephant, and inferior food when he has the best fare (11.4–5). Moreover, in entering the lower path, those deluded bodhisattvas will desire honor *(satkāra)* and gain *(lābha)* and will seek close relations with (high-caste) families (11.5–6). In so doing, they will abandon the right path and follow a wrong one (11.6). At this time, "many *bhikṣus* will be troubled . . . and will not bear in mind the *prajñāpāramitā*" (11.8). Elsewhere, we read of those who, deficient in wisdom and skill in means, fall down to the *śrāvaka* level (16.5).[23]

As we have seen, the *Ratnaguṇa* propounds an ideal of forest renunciation and does not itself reflect the values or preoccupations of settled monasticism. This raises the important question of whether we find any references to settled monastics in it. Although the text does not describe the *śrāvaka* tradition explicitly in terms of monks and settled monasticism, several factors suggest that the *śrāvaka*s it criticizes are settled monastics. Thus, as just mentioned, unworthy *bhikṣu*s are connected with the *śrāvaka*s. The desire for honor and gain, as well as familiarity with high-caste families (appearing in the Nikāya texts, examined in Chapter 3 of this book in connection with critiques of a nonforest renunciant life), are mentioned. The noncontemplative nature of the *śrāvaka* ideal, again suggestive of settled monasticism, is also implied in the chapter on meditation (*Rgs* 29), in which we are told that it is owing to meditation that the bodhisattva will escape the vehicles of the arhants and pratyekabuddhas. As long as the bodhisattva rests in meditation, he gives rise to no interest in the vehicles of the arhants and pratyekabuddhas; but if he becomes unconcentrated, then he becomes vulnerable (29.9). Just as the text does not propound the values of settled monasticism and clearly reflects another (predominantly forest and, to a lesser extent, lay) context, so in the text the *śrāvaka*s are generally not credited with forest values or contexts. The *Ratnaguṇa* thus repeats, in an abbreviated and largely implicit way, some of the same kinds of criticisms, even using some of the same terminology, that we have already seen. Admittedly, the *Ratnaguṇa* presents no more than bits and pieces of evidence, but it provides enough to suggest that the *śrāvaka*s it criticizes are probably primarily settled monastics.[24]

If this is correct, the *Ratnaguṇa* in contrast to the Nikāya evidence, reflects some major differences in the way this criticism is articulated. Most important, the "wrong path" is now linked with the arhant ideal, with the *śrāvaka*s, with corresponding *sūtra*s, and, finally, with a rejection of the teachings of the bodhisattva ideal, the enlightenment of the Buddha, the *prajñāpāramitā,* and so on. In other words, the Mahāyāna of the *Ratnaguṇa* appears to be making the same kind of critique of settled monasticism as a deviation from the true dharma that we have seen in the Nikāya evidence, except that—at least in this text—the Mahāyāna appears to be equating settled monasticism with the *śrāvaka* traditions and identifying the arhant as the *śrāvaka* ideal. The text can do this because it is itself nonmonastic, and the only monasticism that it makes allusion to is that connected with the *śrāvaka*s. At the same time, the ambiguity in its presentation—for example, mentioning arhants and *bhikṣu*s of a clearly saintly character—suggests that it is aware of non-Mahāyāna traditions that cannot be reduced to the settled monastic path of the *śrāvaka*s of which it is particularly critical.

The Bodhisattva of the Forest in the *Rāṣṭrapālaparipṛcchā Sūtra*

A similar description of the bodhisattva as a forest saint is presented in another early Mahāyāna text, the *Rāṣṭrapālaparipṛcchā Sūtra,* contained in the *Ratnakūṭa* collection,[25] surviving in Buddhist Hybrid Sanskrit, edited by Louis Finot (1901),[26] and also in Tibetan, an edition of which has been prepared by Ensink (E., 60–125),[27] and Chinese translations.[28] It has been translated into English by Ensink (1952), who terms it "the longer *Rāṣṭrapāla Sūtra*" to distinguish it from another text of the same name (see the Appendix to this chapter). The *Rāṣṭrapāla Sūtra* opens with the Buddha on Vulture Peak Mountain near Rājāgṛha accompanied by a *bhikṣusaṃgha* (order of monks) composed of 1,250 *bhikṣu*s and by 5,000 bodhisattvas.[29] Nothing further is said here about the *bhikṣu*s, but the bodhisattvas are credited with excellent qualities: they have destroyed Māra; they are near the *buddhadharma*s; they will have only one more rebirth (that is, they will achieve buddhahood in the next life); they have gained mastery of the *dhāraṇī* (mantra formulas), *samādhi,* and the *ṛddhi;* and so on (*Rps* 1.6–10 [E., 1–2])—all marking them as saints of great attainment.

The Buddha sits in the midst of this gathering, in a state of the utmost beatification. At this time, a certain monk named Rāṣṭrapāla arrives from Śrāvastī and, approaching the Buddha, honors him with salutation to his feet, circumambulation, and respectful and eloquent praise (*Rps* 5.4ff. [E., 6ff.]). Then, with the Buddha's permission, Rāṣṭrapāla poses a series of questions concerning the bodhisattva ideal. He says that his own aspiration for enlightenment lies behind these questions and asks the Blessed One to explain the supreme way *(uttamacari).*

The text from this point onward is divided into two sections: the first, which shall concern us here, describes the career of the bodhisattva; the second presents stories of former lives. The first section is divided into two parts. The first details the excellent qualities of the good bodhisattva, who is a forest-dwelling renunciant and whose qualities are to be emuluated. The second describes, by contrast, various bad traits and practices most, if not all, of which define certain "*bhikṣu*s" who live in monasteries; the bodhisattva is to avoid these traits and practices at all costs. These *bhikṣus*, we are told, will in a future age bring the dharma to ruin. The prophetic nature of this statement notwithstanding, as in the case of the song of Phussa in the *Theragāthā*, it is clear that the text is criticizing certain practices that are occurring in its own environment.

The Qualities of the Bodhisattva as Saint

The bodhisattva is marked by aspiration to the full enlightenment of a Buddha (*Rps* 10.6–9 [E., 12]; 15.15 [16]), and he will follow this path to enlightenment *(bodhimārga)* (10.10–11; 11.1–2 [12]) as have all the buddhas (11.11 [13]). He wants to gain the Buddha's wisdom *(buddhajñāna)* (13.11 [14]), and his goal is to attain the unsurpassed enlightenment *(anuttarabodhi)* (15.15 [16]). He aims to reach the omniscience *(sarvajñatā)* of the Buddha (13.15 [14]) and strives for wisdom of the buddhas (14.8 [15]). When he hears of the qualities of the Buddha, he thinks, "In no long time at all, they shall be mine" (15.7 [16]). He aspires to this goal for the sake of all beings (12.7 [13]). He says, " 'I will bring all sentient beings to liberation.' Thus I vow to attain supreme enlightenment" (14.12 [15]). His resolve is like a diamond *(vajropama)* (13.13 [14]).

The bodhisattva has left ordinary life behind and has gone forth from the world *(pravrajita)* (*Rps* 12.16–17 [E., 15]; 16.2 [16]). He has abandoned the life of the householder (12.17 [14]) and no longer cares about living in a house (12.17 [14]). Having renounced the world, he lives in the forest *(araṇya)* and follows the way of the forest renunciant. He dwells in the desolate forest (14.5 [15]), in which he finds joy (13.5 [14]). He does not abandon dwelling in the forest (13.17 [14]), but, solitary, he lives undefiled like a rhinoceros (13.7 [14]; 16.7 [17]). He remains alone, shunning the company of both men and women (13.6 [14]). As a mark of his living in the forest, he is free of hypocrisy, babbling, and trickery (15.10–11 [16]). Sometimes the bodhisattva's dwelling in the forest is described more specifically. We are told that he remains always in forests *(vana)* and in caves *(kandara)*[30] (15.1 [15]). He also dwells in the mountains *(giri)* (16.2 [16]). He lives in various forests in remote border regions *(araṇyavividhaprānta)* (16.3 [17]). He is happy having his seat and bed in border areas (14.14–15 [15]).[31] Living in the forest, the bodhisattva follows the *dhutaguṇa*s (30.15 [30]).[32] In fact, so important are the *dhutaguṇa*s to the *Rāṣṭrapāla Sūtra* that in one place it defines its Buddhism as "the vehicle of the *dhuta*s" *(dhutayāna)*, which has been taught by the buddhas (27.17 [28]). Thus the bodhisattva holds the *dhutaguṇa*s as dear to him (33.1 [31]) and is devoted to them (20.6 [20]).[33]

Living in the forest, the bodhisattva also follows, and teaches others to follow, other behavioral and moral norms. In this respect, the text mentions the supreme *śīla* of the buddhas (*Rps* 11.17 [E., 13]; see also 14.4 [15]). The "ten virtuous actions" *(daśakuśala)* (15.6 [16]) are said to be particularly important to him. The six *pāramitā*s are also mentioned as central to this path (21.7 [21]). Various other specific moral principles are given in connection with the bodhisattva. For example, he acts according to his words (10.8 [12]), and he is faithful to what he says (11.1 [12]). In spite of his high moral attainment, the bodhisattva does not take pride in his accomplishments. He does not think, "I am well restrained in my *śīla*" (14.3–4 [15]). Living in the forest, the bodhisattva has completely renounced the world, including everything that belonged to him (12.2 [13]). He has given up his attachment to any relatives (16.3 [17]; see E., 17, n. 84), his village, kingdom, land, sons, wife, even his life (12.14–15 and 13.8–11 [14]). He does not care about his body or his life (13.1–2 [14]). He becomes joyful when he sees a beggar come near (12.12–13 [14]). Even having given everything away, he does not desire recompense (15.10–11 [16]).

Thus, the life of the bodhisattva in the forest is austere. He is satisfied with whatever he finds (*Rps* 16.5 [E., 17]). He does not try to create stores for himself (16.5 [17]). In his way of life, he bears hundreds of sufferings (16.16 [17]). Living in the forest, the bodhisattva truly has no abode. He has no place of his own in all the world; he has sacrificed all for the sake of enlightenment (16.6 [17]). Like a frightened deer, he finds no rest (16.8 [17]).

The bodhisattva is deeply devoted to the Buddha. There are four things that cause joy to the bodhisattva while he is in saṃsāra, and the first of these is to see a buddha *(buddhadarśana)* (*Rps* 12.1 [E., 13]). The bodhisattva thus sees him who is supreme among human beings, who is fully enlightened, who is radiant with light and illumines the world (12.4–5 [13]), and he does *pūjā* to him (12.4–6 [13]). The bodhisattva does extensive *pūjā* in the context of striving after the wisdom of the victorious ones (12.4 [13]). When he hears of the qualities of the Buddha *(buddhaguṇa),* he is happy (15.7 [16]). In addition, central to the bodhisattva's path is the human representative of the Buddha, his own guru. The bodhisattva obtains a spiritual friend *(kalyāṇamitra)* (11.4 [12–13]; 11.10 [13]), a guru (14.14 [15]) who teaches him the most excellent path (11.10–11 [13]), the very same path followed by the buddhas (11.11 [13]). He must be obedient to his guru and serve him without concern for worldly things (14.14 [15]).[34]

The bodhisattva follows his path, witnessed by all the buddhas. By his actions, he pleases countless multitudes of *sugatas* (*Rps* 15.4 [E., 16]). The first element in the bodhisattva's path is his conduct. In this regard, we are told that he is completely pure in his morality (11.4 [12–13]). He guards the stainless *śīla* (14.3 [15]). His *śīla* is uninterrupted (11.16 [13]). He is always free from sin (11.1–2 [12]). He does not break his *śīla* (13.16–17 [14]). The central practice of the bodhisattva's path is meditation. He takes delight in *śamatha (śamada)* (16.14 [17]). It is through meditation *(dhyāna)* and the quality of exertion *(vīrya)* that he achieves realization (13.11 [14]). The bodhisattva is well accomplished in meditation. He is tranquil and tamed (11.2 [12]).[35] His mind is mighty (16.14 [17]). The path of the bodhisattva is also marked by the practice of the *dhāraṇī* (11.3–4 [12–13]). He strives to attain the *dhāraṇī* (16.16 [17]), by which he is able firmly to establish the excellent dharma taught by the Blessed One (11.6–7 [13]).

The bodhisattva's path is marked by a variety of practices that he is to carry out. He is to apply himself to the six *pāramitās*, the qualities of the bodhisattva stages *(bhūmiguṇa),* the powers *(bala),* the faculties *(indriya),* and wisdom *(jñāna)* (*Rps* 21.7 [E., 21]). The bodhisattva's path is further characterized by doctrinal instruction. The regular hearing of the dharma is a thing that causes the bodhisattva joy (12.1 [13]). He possesses learning *(śruti)* (14.8 [15])[36] and has learned much *(bāhuśrutya)* (13.18 [14]).[37] He understands the noble truth of suffering (14.9–10 [15]). He is deeply schooled in the subject of *śūnyatā* (11.14 [13]). In spite of these characterizations, the bodhisattva does not follow a vocation of books and scholarship, as revealed by a passage that says that he is not to criticize those who memorize and recite texts (*dharmabhāṇaka*s) (15.11–12 [16]), a comment that would probably not be made unless the *dharmabhāṇaka*s represented a type and tradition different from those of the forest-renunciant bodhisattvas of the *Rāṣṭrapāla Sūtra*.[38] The same is indicated by the text's critique, shortly to be reviewed, of those who follow the vocation of texts, *bhikṣu*s who are attached to the external letter of the dharma but do not penetrate to its inner core.

The bodhisattva, having meditated, moves toward the goal of full buddhahood (*Rps* 21.6 [E., 21]). Upon realization, he will have understood that in ultimate reality there is no self and there are no beings (10.16 [12]).[39] He will have realized *śūnyatā* (10.7 [12]) and be liberated (21.8 [21]). This is the realization of the profound dharma *(gambhīradharma)* (11.14 [13]), which will mark the attainment of the Buddha's wisdom *(buddhajñāna)* (13.11 [14]) and the possession of all the good qualities *(sarvaguṇa)* of a buddha (21.8 [21]). Nevertheless, the "not-yet" is also an "already" in two respects. First, as the bodhisattva traverses his path, he is continually defined in terms of the goal toward which he strives, that of completely realized buddhahood. Thus, even on the path, he is assimilated to the ideal of the Buddha, as in passages such as those already cited. More explicitly, "When they have heard of the virtues of a buddha, they are contented: 'They will be mine in a short time' " (15.7–8 [16]). Second, many statements make it clear that the high-level bodhisattva, though still on the path, is also a realized saint in the classical Buddhist mold. It is said of the renunciant bodhisattva residing in the forest that he is like an immaculate rhinoceros, pure and without stain, and that he has gone to perfection *(pāramigata)* (13.7, 11 [14]). He unresistingly accepts the profound dharma *(gambhīradharma)* (11.4 [12]), the dharma that is inconceivable (12.2 [13]).

The state of mind of the bodhisattva as a realized saint is also depicted at various places in the text. The bodhisattva, for example, "has no harshness, nor impurity, nor angry thought; neither does he look for a fault with anyone. He is not wicked, nor hypocritical, his mind [dwells in] the nonconceptual *[niṣprapañca],* while he wishes to obtain the unsurpassed enlightenment *[anuttarabodhi]"* (*Rps* 15.14–15 [E., 16]). He has left behind both what is dear and what is not dear to him, as well as gain *(lābha),* fame (*yaśa*s), quarrels, pride, and jealousy (19.14 [20]).

Various other laudatory statements are also made about the realized bodhisattva. He is the supreme individual (*Rps* 10.15 [E., 12]). Among gods and humans, he is the chief (15.5 [16]). He behaves like a lion (16.4 [17]) and like a lion has no fear (16.7 [17]). The bodhisattva's compassion for the world is boundless. He sees the suffering of all beings, and looks upon them as he would upon his only son. He makes the resolve to free all beings (10.12–15 [12]). He acts for the welfare of beings (13.10 [14] and 19.13 [20]) and teaches them the dharma. He is said to turn the ultimate, excellent wheel (of the dharma) (19.12 [20]). The bodhisattva is also widely renowned among gods and humans. As bearer of the dharma *(dharmadhara)*,[40] he is revered among all beings on earth (20.1 [20]). As a mark of the bodhisattva's attainment, however, in spite of receiving all manner of reverence from gods and humans, he remains indifferent to honor *(satkāra)* and material gain *(lābha)* (12.17–13.1 [14]; 14.14–15 [15]). He is not joyful when he receives offerings, nor disheartened when he does not (13.8 [14]). He is content with whatever he receives (13.9 [14]). In particular, he does not care about close association with high-caste families *(kulasaṃstava)* (13.1 [14]). In an image familiar from the characterization of saints in the Nikāya evidence, the bodhisattva is compared with the wind: "like the wind, he does not remain" (16.10 [17]).

The Faults of Unworthy Renunciants

The bodhisattva, according to the *Rāṣṭrapāla Sūtra,* is not without counterpart. In fact, he lives in a world where his own Buddhism of forest renunciation is under pressure from another kind of renunciant Buddhism, and the conflict of the two versions of the dharma is sharply etched in the text. This other kind of Buddhism, with which the text sees itself in fundamental conflict, is embodied in the *bhikṣu.* The *bhikṣu,* virtually the mirror opposite of the bodhisattva, is defined in several lists of negative qualities that the good bodhisattva must avoid. As in the songs of Phussa and Pārāpariya, it is said in the *Rāṣṭrapāla Sūtra* that the *bhikṣus* who exhibit these kinds of behavior will, in the latter time *(paścimakāla)* (*Rps* 17.14 [E., 18]), utterly destroy the Buddha's dharma.[41]

These *bhikṣus* are associated with settled monasteries *(vihāra)* (*Rps* 18.8 [E., 18]) and connected with the two typical preoccupations of settled monastics, behavioral purity and the vocation of texts and scholarship. Thus, these *bhikṣus* claim for themselves behavioral purity and insist that no one surpasses them in the accomplishment of *śīla* (17.11 [18]). However, such claims involve fraud and wickedness (17.9 [18]) and are made out of self-serving motives (17.11 [18]). In fact, the *bhikṣus*' actions are unrestrained (17.9 [18]), and they are far from the genuine virtues of *śīla* (17.14 [18]). The *bhikṣus* also preoccupy themselves with the study of texts and the exposition of doctrine. Thus, they have knowledge, but it is not ultimate knowledge (19.17–18 [20]). They are, moreover, proud of their relative knowledge *(jñāna*; Tib., *shes.pa)* (19.15–16 [20]).[42] They strive after the enjoyment of impure knowledge *(apariśuddhajñāna)* (19.17–18 [20]) and find delight in impure knowledge (20.3 [20]). They are bound by hundreds of philosophical views *(dṛṣṭi).* These *bhikṣus* are confused (or deluded, *mūḍha*) (17.9 [18]).

These countertypes are hostile to meditation. If they see a patient *bhikṣu* in the monastery *(vihāra)* absorbed in meditation, they will expel him from the monastery, beating him with a stick (*Rps* 18.8 [E., 19]).[43] As they are hostile to meditation, so are they far from its attainments. Their state of mind *(citta)* is deluded (18.7 [18]) and unstable (18.9 [19]). They engage in conceptualizing what they experience (19.6 [19]). Their minds are unrestrained (20.12 [21]), grasping (21.1 [21]), and devoid of wisdom *(jñāna)* (20.13 and 21.2 [21]). Like those criticized in the *Theragāthā* and *Ratnaguṇa,* these countertypes are motivated primarily by a desire for honor *(satkāra)* and gain *(lābha)* (17.4–5, 10 [17–18]). They are intent upon begging bowls *(pātra)* and robes *(cīvara),* and on objects of enjoyment (19.10 [20]). They continually curry the favor of the high-caste *(kula-saṃstava)* (19.10 [20]). Their minds are attached to familiarity with the high-caste (20.14 [21]), and they are bound by ties of familiarity with high-caste families (21.1 [21]).

These antitypes are proud (*Rps* 18.7 [E., 18]) and have no devotion *(adhimukti)* to the Buddha (20.5 [20]). They are always disrespectful *(agaurava;* Tib., *ma.gus.pa)* to the holy gurus *(āryaguru)* (17.8 [18]). They do not revere the gurus or other holy persons *(āryajana)* (20.4 [20]). They hate those marks of the realized person, the good qualities *(guṇa)* (18.11 [19]). Moreover, they become upset when they see others venerated, jealousy arising in them when they see worship *(pūjā)* being paid to another (18.9 [19]). In general, they are without faith *(aśraddha)* (18.1–2 [18]). The *bhikṣus* also have no devotion to the dharma nor to the community of lay and renunciant bodhisattvas *(gaṇa)* (20.5 [20]).[44] They despise the good bodhisattvas (20.2 [20]).[45] In a similar fashion, the *bhikṣus* have no devotion to the morality followed by the bodhisattvas, to the general rules of conduct *(śikṣa)*,[46] or to the ascetic code *(dhuta)* of renunciant bodhisattvas (20.6 [20]).[47]

Moreover, the *bhikṣus* are always angry (*Rps* 18.7 [E., 19]). They are not only hostile to bodhisattvas but are jealous and quarrel with one another (17.15ff. [18]), always looking for faults (17.12 [18]), so that they may criticize a person (18.10 [19]). Even abstention from livelihood is not sacrosanct, for these *bhikṣus* will become involved in plowing and trade (17.13 [18]). Because of their antidharmic behavior, *śramaṇas*[48] stay far away from them (17.13 [18]). These *bhikṣus* have abandoned the teaching of the victorious ones (18.12 [19]) and are far away from the doctrine of the Buddha (18.11 [19]). They condemn the good dharma *(saddharma)* (19.1 [19]). They are far away from the path to enlightenment (17.16 [18]) and from the wealth of the saints *(āryadhana)* (17.16 [18]). They have given up the path to liberation *(mokṣa)* (17.17 [18]). As a result, in the future, they will wander throughout the five samsaric destinies *(pañcagati)* (17.17 [18]), inhabit states of woe *(apāya)* (18.11 [19]), and suffer in the realms of hell and among the hungry ghosts *(preta)* and animals (20.7–8 [20]).

The *Rāṣṭrapāla Sūtra* thus presents the ideal of the bodhisattva as saint in much the same way as the *Śikṣāsamuccaya* and *Ratnaguṇasaṃcayagāthā*. On the one hand, the bodhisattva generally conforms to the type of forest saint as described in the Nikāya literature. On the other, in contrast to the saint of the Nikāya evidence, the Mahāyāna saint is given the name bodhisattva; he is explicitly associated with the ideal of the Buddha; compassion is more self-consciously and more insistently attributed to him; and he is clearly depicted not only as a realized saint of the classical type but also as one awaiting the full perfection of a future buddhahood.

In the evidence of the forest saints we have examined, we have seen a repeated critique of certain practices and values of settled monasticism. In the songs of Phussa and Pārāpariya in the *Theragāthā,* we saw a full-blown critique of some *bhikṣus* living in settled monasteries who are constantly busy with various projects, preoccupied with scholarly learning and disputation, and concerned with wealth and status. These *bhikṣus*, moreover, shun solitude and meditation, are filled with defilements, and have no genuine wisdom. In other Nikāya Buddhist evidence and in the *Śikṣāsamuccaya* and *Ratnaguṇa* we saw a similar critique voiced, if in a more fragmentary way.

The *Rāṣṭrapāla Sūtra* picks up this critique and develops it in two ways: first, by making it a central theme of its message; and, second, by presenting a particularly complete description of the antidharmic renunciant, sometimes explicitly called *bhikṣu,* sometimes referred to by other, less explicit designations, but in any case unified in characterization and consistent in type with the *bhikṣu* criticized in the other evidence. The major themes have already been seen but are presented in a more systematic form: preoccupation with scholarly learning, but neglect of meditation; pretension to ethical purity, but inward moral corruption; thirst for wealth and recognition along with a cultivation of high-caste families, but absence of inspiration for realization; cultivation of, and pride in, "impure knowledge," but absence of wisdom; and so on.

The *Rāṣṭrapāla Sūtra* also makes more of another characteristic of the settled monastic *bhikṣu* that we have seen, namely, his antipathy to forest saints and their traditions. Thus, the *bhikṣu* is presented as actively and aggressively opposed to the bodhisattvas: he is disrespectful to the group *(gaṇa)* of bodhisattva renunciants and saints, he has no respect for their forest codes *(dhuta),* he does not revere the gurus, and he is jealous of the veneration received by genuine saints. In the *Rāṣṭrapāla Sūtra,* the antidharmic *bhikṣu* has hardened into a type, perhaps reflecting not only the ascendency of settled monasticism but also its unwillingness to countenance the bodhisattvas and their forest traditions.

Significantly, the *Śikṣāsamuccaya* assumes a considerably more conciliatory tone than the *Rāṣṭrapāla Sūtra,* in spite of the fact that Śāntideva quotes the latter text. Although Śāntideva likely had before him in the *Raṣṭrapāla Sūtra* material severely critical of monastic life and its values and preoccupations, he chose somewhat less potentially offensive passages to cite. Thus, the general tone of his chapter comes rather close to that of the *Ratnaguṇa.* There should be nothing surprising in this, when it is recalled that Śāntideva was a conventional monastic of the Mahāyāna.

The *Saṃdhinirmocana Sūtra* on the Bodhisattva as Saint

The *Saṃdhinirmocana Sūtra,* according to Lamotte,[49] came into being by the second century C.E. as a collection of a number of short, originally independent *sūtras*.[50] Among these, an earlier stratum, comprising chapters 1 to 4 can be identified,[51] and it is this that is taken for analysis here. This older section advances a meditative ideal, generally called *ārya*[52] (saint) (*Sns* 35.17–18 [L., 170]), *yogin*[53] (45.12 and 24 [177]), or, occasionally, *bhikṣu* who meditates (or "practices *yoga*"; *bhikṣu yogācāra*);[54] (51.9 [181]). In passages of chapters 1 to 4 actually describing the saint and his realization, the term *bodhisattva*[55] is rarely used, raising interesting questions about the origins of these sections of the text.[56] Unlike the *Ratnaguṇa, Rāṣṭrapāla Sūtra,* or *Śikṣāsamuccaya,* chapters 1 to 4 do not mention the specific religious context and lifestyle of the saintly ideal, and there is thus little explicit discussion of the forest, the retreatant way of life, or forest disciplines such as the *dhutaguṇas*.[57] These must rather be inferred from the primarily contemplative values, interests, and preoccupations of the text, and their contrast with those that more clearly reflect settled monasticism.

The *yogin* understands the Buddha to have taught a way to direct and concrete realization of the ultimate, the way of meditation (*Sns* 39.1ff. [L., 172–73]). The *yogin*'s major preoccupation is thus the practice of meditation, notably *śamatha*[58] and *vipaśyanā*[59] (47.14–15 [178]). As a contemplative, he knows the interior joy of solitude *(praviveka)*[60] (41.2 [174]). As a solitary meditator, he knows the inner joy of holy silence *(āryatūṣṇīm)*[61] (41.6 [174]). He realizes the ultimate that can only be known through individual, direct experience *(pratyātmavedanīya)*[62] (40.3–4 [173]). He possesses the holy wisdom *(āryajñāna)*[63] and holy seeing *(āryadarśana)*[64] and is perfectly enlightened *(abhisaṃbuddha)*[65] (35.18–21 [169–70]). In light of this, one may understand a central affirmation of the *Saṃdhinirmocana Sūtra:* the various doctrinal terms and categories taught by the Buddha are misunderstood when taken in a purely intellectual and conceptual way. Rather, they correspond to nothing in reality and have been used by the Blessed One only to lead others toward awakening (34.1ff. [169–71]). In fact, the ultimate transcends all speculation *(sarvatarka)*[66] (39.24ff. [173–74]).

The *yogin* belongs to a minority who make meditation their chief preoccupation, and he is set in opposition to another kind of renunciant who, by contrast, makes up the majority and engages in scholastic pursuits (*Sns* 47.18–53.3 [L., 178–82]). However, the scholastic learning of the majority is unnecessary to the *yogin* because he has realized the ultimate, the insubstantiality of the dharmas *(dharmanairātmya)*[67] or suchness *(tathatā)*[68] (51.10 [181]). Thus, he does not need to acquaint himself separately with the ultimate, the insubstantiality of the dharmas, the *tathatā* of all the *skandhas*, *āyatanas*, and so on (51.8–52.17 [181–82]).

> The ultimate is not multiplicitous *[abhinna]*.[69]
> Everywhere, it has one taste, so has the Buddha said.
> Whoever conceives of it as multiplicitous is confused and afflicted with pride.
> (52.26–53.2 [181–82])

Who are the scholastic renunciants who make up the majority? According to the text, they are settled monastics, *bhikṣus*, and they are characterized in an exchange between the Buddha and Subhūti (*Sns* 47.19–53.3 [L., 178–82]). The Buddha has asked Subhūti about the relative strength of numbers of those who express their knowledge with pride *(abhimāna)*[70] compared to those who express their knowledge without pride. Subhūti says that those who express their knowledge without pride are few, whereas those who express their knowledge with pride are a vast and incalculable number (47.19–48.9 [178]). In order to clarify what he means, Subhūti tells the following story. In a solitary forest retreat *(araṇyamahāvanaprastha)*,[71] he once observed a great crowd of *bhikṣus* who had gathered to teach and discuss their knowledge. All of them were expounding their concepts of things. Different *bhikṣus* were expounding various concepts of the *skandhas*,[72] the *skandhas*' characteristics *(nimitta)*,[73] their origin *(utpāda)*,[74] their decay *(vināśa)*,[75] their cessation *(nirodha)*,[76] and realization of their cessation *(nirodhasākṣātkāra)*.[77] *Bhikṣus* held forth on the concepts of the (twelve) bases of consciousness *(āyatana)*[78] and conditioned coproduction *(pratītyasamutpāda)*.[79] Other *bhikṣus* displayed their knowledge of the concepts of the (four) foods *(āhāra)*.[80] Others expatiated on the concepts of the (four) noble truths *(satya)*,[81] the (eighteen) *dhātus*,[82] the (four) foundations of mindfulness *(smṛtyupasthāna)*,[83] the (four) abandonments (or strenuous exertions [*BHSD* 389, 2]) *(samyakprahāṇa)*,[84] the (four) bases of miraculous power *(ṛddhipāda)*,[85] the (five) faculties *(indriya)*,[86] the (five) powers *(bala)*,[87] the (seven) limbs of enlightenment *(bodhyaṅga)*,[88] and the noble eightfold path *(āryāṣṭāṅgamārga)*[89] (48.9–49.25 [178–80]).

At this sight, Subhūti reports, he thought to himself that the *bhikṣus* were expounding their knowledge of the different aspects of the Buddhist teaching while remaining ignorant of the ultimate *(paramārtha)*,[90] which has everywhere just one taste *(ekarasa)*.[91] In so doing, Subhūti says, these monks were guilty of expounding their knowledge with pride. The passage concludes with the remark that if members of the Buddha's own religion, who are *bhikṣus*, find it so difficult to understand the ultimate that has everywhere just one taste, what can be said about the heretics *(tīrthika)*[92] (*Sns* 50.1–15 [L., 180])? The contrast presented in this story is one with which we are already familiar: on the one hand is the individual forest renunciant, symbolized by Subhūti, alone in the forest, the silent observer, whose understanding of the dharma is deep and confident; on the other are the innumerable *bhikṣus*, unaware even of the solitary renunciant's existence, preoccupied with words and concepts, busily debating and arguing with one another, engaged solely with the external dharma, and lacking inward realization of ultimate reality.

Other characterizations are given of this kind of understanding of the dharma that remains purely conceptual and therefore superficial. One of the most important revolves around the term *bāla*,[93] immature one, child, or fool,[94] defined in this way:

> The profundity *[gambhīra]*[95] (of the ultimate) is not the domain *[gocara]*[96] of the immature. Although the Victorious one has taught the ineffability *[anabhilāpya]*[97] and nonduality *[advaya]*[98] (of the ultimate), the immature *[bāla]* remain ignorant *[moha]*[99] and deluded *[mūḍha]*. Delighting in the complexities of discourse *[vādaprapañca]*,[100] they establish themselves in duality. They are either unrealized *[asaṃbodha]*[101] or have a perverted realization *[vipratipatti]*,[102] and are reborn among cows and sheep. Having abandoned the discourse of wisdom, they will continue for a long time to transmigrate in saṃsāra. (*Sns* 38.22–29 [L., 172])[103]

Who are these *bāla?* Let us note that in chapters 1 to 4, the term *bāla* is not explicitly used in conjunction with the term *bhikṣu*. However, the similarity in the characterizations of these two suggests a close relationship. Both are said to miss the profound *(gambhīra)*[104] dharma; both are far from the ultimate teaching of the Buddha; both are preoccupied with dharma as dualistic, external, conceptual knowledge; both are caught up in verbal presentations; and both lack realization.

From the passage just cited, it would appear that the *bāla* are Buddhists; otherwise their contravening the real intention of the Buddha and the inauthenticity of their realization would not be such central issues. More specifically, these *bāla* would appear to be, or at least to include, the *bhikṣus* that the text has elsewhere been criticizing.

It is clear that *bāla* and *bhikṣu* are not quite synonymous, for the primary intention of the term *bāla* is to identify not a specific group, but rather a way of understanding the dharma that the *Saṃdhinirmocana Sūtra* sees as deficient. In other words, it is not a specific renunciant ideal *(bhikṣu)* that the *Saṃdhinirmocana Sūtra* is set against so much as a kind of superficial, overly conceptual and external understanding, although this is admittedly particularly characteristic of a certain renunciant lifestyle. If this be so, it would not be surprising to find the term also used to refer to a group with a different designation. Such a group turns up in chapter 3 (*Sns* 42.1ff. [L., 175ff.]), where the bodhisattva Suviśuddhamati tells the Buddha that in a certain place he has seen bodhisattvas gathered in a great crowd (like the *bhikṣus*), engaged in hot debate (again like the *bhikṣus*) about whether the *samskāras* and the ultimate *(paramārtha)* are the same. Some maintain that they are the same, others that they are different. Others again are confused and perplexed, asking, "Who is right? Who is wrong? Whose reasoning is accurate? Whose reasoning is inaccurate?" At this sight, Suviśuddhamati thinks to himself (as Subhūti did when he saw the *bhikṣus*), "None of [these] sons of good family understands the profound *[gambhīra]* ultimate truth *[paramārtha]*, the character of which transcends difference with the *samskāras* and also identity. They are immature *[bāla]*, confused, ignorant,[105] and uninformed"[106] (42.1–30 [175]). In other words, the scenario, the activities, and the criticism closely resemble those articulated in connection with the *bhikṣus*.

This suggests that, in the time of chapters 1 to 4, there were bodhisattvas who were understood to have departed from the normative path of the forest bodhisattva (who relies on meditation and who understands the dharma of one taste). Who are these bodhisattvas who are thus being criticized in virtually the same terms as the *bhikṣus*? Are they bodhisattvas who, though not called *bhikṣus*, are living some kind of town-and-village renunciation? Although in characterizing these bodhisattvas in virtually the same terms as the *bhikṣus*, the text certainly seems to suggest this, it may be pointed out that so far there is no clear archaeological evidence of the Mahāyāna as a discrete monastic entity until several centuries after the date proposed for the *Saṃdhinirmocana Sūtra* 1 to 4 (see Chapter 12).

Conclusion

The Mahāyāna *sūtras* examined in this chapter all take as their central ideal the bodhisattva who is a saint of the forest. In addition, the major features of this bodhisattva—including his way of life, his preoccupations, and his realization—are described in markedly similar terms from one text to another. At this point it will be useful to draw some general comparisons between this Mahāyānist forest saint and those seen in the Nikāya evidence examined in previous chapters. In many ways, the bodhisattvas of the forest are not so very different from their Nikāya counterparts. All these saints are motivated by a strong sense of personal vocation; all have renounced the world and, desiring tangible results, have retired to the forest; all aspire after realization, all meditate, and all are understood as, in one way or another, realized. As realized saints, all have compassion as a primary motivation, have powers, make themselves available to their suppliants, and do not prefer people of high caste. All are set apart from monastic life with its preoccupations of pure behavior, as defined by the *vinaya,* and from textual learning.

In spite of such similarities, however, there are some important differences between the bodhisattvas of the forest, as defined by these texts, and their Nikāya counterparts. First, and most obviously, the forest saint is now called bodhisattva, not arhant or pratyekabuddha, and we are told that his goal is nothing less than the enlightenment of a world-redeeming buddha. Thus, although the forest ideals of arhant and pratyekabuddha in many respects implicitly involve emulation of the way of life and ideal of the Buddha, they are explicitly held to be different in type. By contrast, the bodhisattva of the Mahāyāna is explicitly identified with the type of the Buddha.[107]

Second, the Mahāyāna *sūtra*s more explicitly present the compassion of the bodhisattva as integral to his type. In the Nikāya evidence, compassion tends to be assumed, rather than explicitly emphasized, as a central part of the personality of either arhant or pratyekabuddha. In the *Ratnaguṇa* and other *sūtra*s examined in this chapter, however, compassion is more self-consciously brought to the fore as defining the relationship between the saintly bodhisattva and others. This undoubtedly has to do with the emphasis, from early times, on compassion as a central and defining feature of the ideal of buddhas.

Third, and related to these points, there is the ambiguity in the way the realization of the bodhisattva is presented. On the one hand, in his wisdom, compassion, and power, he is clearly depicted as a realized saint whose stature is in no way less than the saints of the Nikāya traditions. On the other hand, his realization is neither final nor complete, for he looks forward to the time when, like his ideal, Śākyamuni Buddha, he will attain the realization of a world-redeeming buddha. What is strange is that, at least as seen in the texts promoting this ideal, this already-but-not-yet character of the bodhisattva's realization does not diminish his charisma in relation to that of the arhants and pratyekabuddhas; it actually seems to have the opposite effect. Although the bodhisattva's realization lies ahead, he already takes on something of the unparalleled charisma of the Buddha himself, and this—not separable, of course, from the decline of the charismatic prestige of the non-Mahāyāna ideals—leads to his being understood as superior to arhants and pratyekabuddhas.

There is a final interesting difference between the bodhisattva as a saint and the non-Mahāyāna ideals. The bodhisattva of the forest is to some extent distinctive because of certain attitudes toward language bound up with him, that become central in the developed Mahāyāna. As we have seen, the forest traditions in general seem to exhibit a characteristic attitude toward language. No doubt because of their emphasis on meditation, language, including the language of Buddhist doctrine and dogma, is for them relative and must be viewed in the context of the silence of realization. In the preceding discussion, we have seen this kind of understanding of language in the Nikāya evidence in the silence of the realized ones; in the vows of silence of the meditators; in the few words of the pratyekabuddhas; in the often epigrammatic songs of the saints of the *Theragāthā* and *Therīgāthā;* in the exclamations of the lion-roarers; in Śāriputra's remark that he needs only the essential meaning *(artha)* and not the letter *(vyañjana)* of the dharma; and, perhaps most explicitly, in the critique, found throughout the texts reflective of forest Buddhism, of those who take the dharma in a scholastic way, putting concepts and categories before the dharma of realization and even identifying the dharma with its verbal expression.

The Mahāyāna of the forest bodhisattva continues this understanding of language, but it is more explicit, systematic, and unrelenting in its approach. As we have seen, it now becomes the leading edge of Mahāyāna doctrine that language is "empty" of substance, that it refers to no thing in ultimate reality, and that genuine realization transcends all concepts and categories. We are also told that those who understand the dharma primarily in terms of words and ideas have missed the main point. As in the other differences from the Nikāya evidence, this is not so much an innovation as an explication of what was already implicit in the non-Mahāyāna forest traditions. Although this attitude toward doctrine is clearly implicit in the lives of the pre-Mahāyāna saints, it generally remains hidden in hagiography and, for various reasons, does not emerge with clarity in developed Nikāya dogmatics. In the Mahāyāna, by contrast, this attitude comes to center stage and becomes a basis—if emptiness can be called a basis—of the entire dogmatic tradition of the Mahāyāna from the Prajñāpāramitā onward.

However, the distinction drawn here between the Mahāyāna and pre-Mahāyāna forest traditions with regard to the relativity of language, although generally true, must be qualified. In fact, as is well known, both the term *śūnyatā* and its meaning, as found in the early Mahāyāna, are already present in some strands of Nikāya Buddhism. This trend is mentioned in the *Ratnaguṇa;* the text attributes to certain realized arhants a genuine understanding of emptiness, remarking that they are not alarmed at the teaching of *śūnyatā.* There is no reason not to believe that the *Ratnaguṇa* understands this as an acceptance of *śūnyatā* in its own sense, not in some primitive, pre-Mahāyāna form. Particularly interesting in the present context is some striking evidence suggesting that the Nikāya teaching of *śūnyatā* is specifically linked with forest Buddhism. For example, Luis Gomez has argued in detail and with cogency that a "proto-Mādhyamika" exists in the Pāli canon, precisely in the *Suttanipāta,* as we have seen, an early text reflective of forest renunciation (1976). In the *Suttanipāta,* particularly in its two oldest sections, the *Aṭṭhakavagga* and the *Pārāyanavagga,* there is clear expression of many themes central to the later Mahāyāna and, more specifically, Mādhyamika teaching of emptiness. Equally interesting are two *sutta*s in the *Majjhimanikāya,* the *Cūḷasuññata Sutta* and the *Mahāsuññata Sutta,* describing enlightenment specifically as a realization of emptiness, for both texts are clear representatives of forest Buddhism and depict the realization of emptiness as an attainment won by forest renunciants, living in solitude in the forest, adhering to behavioral patterns characteristic of forest Buddhism, and following a path defined by intensive meditation.[108] These examples raise the possibility that the teaching of emptiness as found in the early Mahāyāna *sūtras* was hardly, if at all, an innovation, and that it was already embodied in an articulate way in some forest texts of early Nikāya Buddhism. This possibility has important implications for the question of the origins of the Mahāyāna, discussed in Chapter 12.

The centrality of the teaching of *śūnyatā* within the early forest Mahāyāna enables a kind of sustained flexibility and absence of dogmatism that, even among Buddhist forest traditions, is particularly striking. We see this quite clearly in the *Ratnaguṇa* and the *Ugraparipṛcchā Sūtra,* which counsel against the danger of absolutizing the forest lifestyle. The former text, in particular, tends to see the forest life as embodying, most essentially, an attitude of renunciation and independence that may be effectively transferred to nonforest (in its case, lay) life. The *Saṃdhinirmocana Sūtra,* in its critiques of other Buddhists, sets itself against not so much a particular form of renunciation as a way of understanding that is overly conceptual and externalized. Even the *Rāṣṭrapāla Sūtra,* which comes the closest of the Mahāyāna texts examined here to identifying legitimate dharma with the forest lifestyle and which sometimes exhibits a vitriolic condemnation of *bhikṣus*, is ultimately critical not of a particular external form but of a state of mind.

In these cases, a realization that was originally gained in the forest is nevertheless not strictly identified with the external form of forest life.[109] Nor, conversely, is delusion strictly identified with either lay life or settled monasticism. This kind of nondogmatism and flexibility clearly opened up the possibility of translating the essential realization of forest Buddhism, *śūnyatā,* as termed in the texts examined here, into any number of other environments and external forms. This is articulated with particular clarity in the *Ratnaguṇa*'s comment that even if one lives in a village, one may do so with a fully "forest state of mind," whereas living in the forest—with all that implies—is no guarantee of sanctity. This kind of flexibility, evident in the forest Mahāyāna texts, may of course be seen as characteristic of Mahāyāna Buddhism as a whole, nonforest manifestations included.

The tendency toward doctrinal flexibility on the part of forest traditions clearly opened the way, at least theoretically, for the translation of forest values into other contexts as evident in the *Ratnaguṇa.* This could lead to a deemphasis, perhaps even the disappearance in some traditions, of the forest ideal, at least as an external form. But it is another question to what extent this kind of change involved a betrayal of the essence of forest Buddhism. Since the forest traditions emphasize as most essential the actual realization itself, not the attendant forms of forest renunciation, however much these may be praised, the question of whether the essential values of forest Buddhism have been effectively translated into one or another alternative form becomes simply the question of whether realization is still a living value in the translation. In any case, the ability to distinguish between the forest life as an external form and the forest life as an inward state opens the door to some fascinating transformations of forest Buddhism, many interesting examples of which are seen in the later history of the Indian Mahāyāna and Vajrayāna.

In the preceding discussion, we have seen that the Mahāyāna forest texts are engaged in developing the classification of Buddhist human ideals along two different lines. On the one hand, the texts have made a more or less clear division between forest renunciants and settled monastics.[110] On the other hand, as Mahāyāna texts, they have also been at pains to distinguish between the bodhisattva ideal, which they regard as superior, and the non-Mahāyāna ideals. The simultaneous presence of both methods of classification clearly poses special interpretive problems, for we are confronted with the potential need to discriminate six rather than three ideals—namely, arhant, pratyekabuddha, and bodhisattva of the forest and those same ideals understood in a nonforest manner. At any given point in the texts, one needs to know who among these six is being praised and who is being criticized, and why.

This same pattern of classification into two renunciant lifestyles and three ideals, along with their attendant interpretive challenges, is found in later Mahāyāna texts of the forest. An example striking both for the energy devoted to carrying out the two types of classification and also for the clarity of the result is provided by the *Laṅkāvatāra Sūtra,* a Mahāyāna forest text particularly important for East Asian Buddhism.[111] It is worthwhile briefly to examine this text both because it reveals a further stage in the way in which forest Mahāyāna texts handle the need to carry out the twofold classification and because consideration of this pattern sheds considerable light on some important dynamics in the *Laṅkāvatāra Sūtra,* linking it up with earlier trends.

Like the other Mahāyāna *sūtras* we have considered, the central human ideal of the *Laṅkāvatāra Sūtra* is the bodhisattva, who aspires to full buddhahood, and the *sūtra* presents this ideal as superior to the non-Mahāyāna ideals of arhant and pratyekabuddha (*Las* 20.23–21.3 [Sz., 41]; 23.9–17 [46]; 27.18–28.10 [56–57]; and passim). At the same time, the text sees Buddhist renunciants as falling into two categories—forest and settled monastic. The bodhisattva, whom it typically calls *yogin,* is a contemplative ideal of the forest. He is to retire from the world, go into seclusion *(rahogata),* and dwell alone *(ekākin)* in a remote and hidden forest retreat *(vanagahanaguhā),* relying only on himself (20.29–32 [41]; 54.30–31 [115]). He may dwell in an open place, on a heap of straw, under a tree, in a cave, in a cemetery, or in an abandoned dwelling (129.17–18 [253]). As a forest renunciant, he is to keep away from turmoil and social intercourse (22.25–28 [44]), to abandon the life of *bhikṣus* (142.11 [265]), and to avoid monasteries (129.27–28 [253]). In his retreat, he is to keep away from texts (23.5 [45]). He is to maintain a life of poverty (129.3–4 [252]), not preoccupy himself with thoughts of food and drink (131.1–2 [254]), and is "not to approach for food kings, princes, ministers of state, or persons of rank" (129.25–26 [253]). In his retreat, his central preoccupation is meditation, and he is to strive in his practice to develop a "meditation *[samādhi]* body" (23.5 [45]). Further, like forest renunciants before him, he is counseled to forego sleep (22.25–28 [44]).[112] He is skilled in the trances (*dhyānas*), meditative states (*samādhis*), and attainments (*samāpattis*) (20.23ff. [41]). As a forest renunciant, his goal is direct, personal, nonconceptual realization. He traverses the stages of spiritual development (*bhūmis*), progressing on toward great enlightenment (for example, 20.23ff. [41]).

Like the *Ratnaguṇa*, the *Rāṣṭrapāla Sūtra*, and the *Saṃdhinirmocana Sūtra*, the *Laṅkāvatāra Sūtra* also criticizes those who follow a more scholastic kind of Buddhism (for example, *Las* 19.1ff. [Sz., 36–37]).[113] They are preoccupied with study, logic, argumentation, and disputation. They habitually identify the genuine dharma with mere words and concepts. They are far away from the practice of meditation. In this, they miss the highest reality, which is "an exalted state of bliss . . . to be attained by the inner realization of noble wisdom" (37.3–8 [77]; see also 10.23ff. [23ff.]). They are called fools or ignorant ones *(bāla)* (38.1–3 [79]) and termed logicians *(tārkika)* (18.3 [33]).

Who are these scholastic Buddhists? Without actually calling them *bhikṣus*, the text makes it clear that they are settled monastic renunciants following textual pursuits. We have seen that the scholastic Buddhist renunciants are explicitly called *bhikṣu* in the *Rāṣṭrapāla Sūtra* and the *Saṃdhinirmocana Sūtra*, chapters 1 to 4.[114] The *Laṅkāvatāra Sūtra*, however, places the scholastic Buddhists within the context of a slightly different kind of typology. Moreover, this typology is complicated by the fact that the text integrates the twofold division of forest and settled monastic with the threefold division of bodhisattva/buddha, *pratyekabodhisattva*/ pratyekabuddha, and *śrāvaka*/arhant. According to the *Laṅkāvatāra Sūtra*, then, there are two sorts of *śrāvaka*s—those who are meditators and achieve a form of authentic realization and those who are scholars and are preoccupied merely with texts, words, and concepts. The *śrāvaka* meditators are clearly the saints of the forest of non-Mahāyāna traditions who follow the vocation of meditation, whereas the scholastic *śrāvaka*s are settled monastics who do not meditate but occupy themselves with textual study and scholarship.

These two types of *śrāvaka*s are described at various points in the text. One such description credits the meditator *śrāvaka*s with the attainment of the holy, personal, spiritual realization—*pratyātmāryādhigama,* a term frequently used in the text to indicate the realization of the bodhisattvas. In addition, they are contrasted with the scholastic *śrāvaka*s, who are characterized by attachment to substantialistic conceptions (*Las* 25.30–26.12 [Sz., 52–53]). Along the same lines, the text applies the prized term *yogin* not only to bodhisattvas but also to these meditating *śrāvaka*s (and also to pratyekabuddhas) (40.28–41.1 [85]). As this characterization suggests, the text looks favorably upon the realization of the meditator *śrāvaka*s who, along with the pratyekabuddhas, are lauded for having won a genuine attainment. At the same time, the text is careful to point out that these are non-Mahāyānists (for example, 42.1 [87])[115] whose realization is only partial, and that although the bodhisattva will attain these *śrāvaka*s' level of realization in the course of his development, he must transcend it as he progresses onward toward full enlightenment (25.30ff. [52–53]). Thus, these *śrāvaka* meditators are rebuked in a more gentle way than their scholastic counterparts for their incomplete attainment. Such a strategy enables the *Laṅkāvatāra Sūtra* to affirm the values of the forest life and meditation, while reminding us that these exist in a (in its view) lesser form in the Śrāvakayāna and Pratyekabuddhayāna (55.8–12 [115]; see also 55.14 [116]).

The scholastic *śrāvaka*s come in for a more direct and acerbic critique. On the one hand, in contrast to some of the texts we have examined, the *Laṅkāvatāra*

Sūtra is willing, if reluctantly, to grant Buddhist authenticity to those following the scholastic path. Thus the text quotes the Buddha as remarking, "I have two forms of teaching the truth: self-realisation and discoursing. I discourse with the ignorant *[bāla]*and [disclose] self-realisation to the Yogins" (*Las* 70.20–21 [Sz., 149]). On the other hand, as this passage makes clear, the text regards the path of scholarship as the inferior one, fit only for *bāla.*[116] This term is, in fact, frequently used to refer to Buddhist scholastics (for example, 22.119 [44]; 53.9 [112]). It is interesting that the text reflects a blanket criticism of scholarship, criticizing those ignorant ones, heretics, *śrāvaka*s, and pratyekabuddhas[117] who remain attached to words and letters (8.12 [18]). Further, although no Mahāyānist scholastics are explicitly referred to in the text, there are several mentions of doctrines, reminiscent of the scholastic Madhyamaka, against which the *Laṅkāvatāra Sūtra* inveighs (41.2–7 [85]; 39.1ff. [85]; 67.30ff. [144]). Thus, the threefold division of bodhisattva, pratyekabuddha, and *śrāvaka* is found throughout the *Laṅkāvatāra Sūtra* interwoven with the twofold classification.[118]

Appendix: The Minor *Rāṣṭrapālaparipṛcchā Sūtra* on Forest *Bhikṣus*

Another different and revealing perspective on forest renunciation, as seen by the Mahāyāna, is provided by another *Rāṣṭrapālaparipṛcchā Sūtra,* preserved in Tibetan, a text roughly one-tenth the size of the *Rāṣṭrapāla Sūtra* just examined, called by Ensink the "minor *Rāṣṭrapālaparipṛcchā Sūtra*" (E., 133–38). The shorter text is closely related to the longer in several ways: it is called a Mahāyāna *sūtra*, and the term *Mahāyāna*[119] is used in the body of the text (*Rps*-m 132.21 [E., 138]); Rāṣṭrapāla is again the interlocutor; the text espouses full and complete enlightenment as its highest ideal (126.26–27 [133]); it frequently mentions emptiness *(śūnyatā),*[120] (132.19–20 [138]); and it extols the forest life. In spite of such continuities, the minor *Rāṣṭrapāla Sūtra* shows some important differences in terminology and perspective from the *Rāṣṭrapāla Sūtra.*

The text begins with a question to which the rest of the text will provide a response: "Exalted One, of what character are the beings that bring the teaching of the Tathāgata to ruin?" (*Rps*-m 126.12–13 [E., 135]). The text begins the main section of its response to this question by telling us that an individual should reflect, "Am I desirous to destroy the mass of my own suffering or am I desirous to reach the unsurpassed, complete enlightenment *[anuttarasamyaksaṃbodhi]?*"[121] (126.25–28 [133]). These two, we next learn, correspond respectively to, on the one hand, the vehicle of the *śrāvaka* (Śrāvakayāna)[122]—discussion of which occupies most of this text—and, on the other, the "great vehicle" or Mahāyāna, explicitly mentioned but not discussed in any detail. The text then continues, "When he wishes to reach nirvāṇa by the career of the *śrāvakas* he must practise the teaching of the *śrāvakas:* he must accept the restrictions of the *prātimokṣa*"[123] (126.28–127.3 [133]). In other words, if one is interested in following the Śrāvakayāna, he will become a *bhikṣu* and follow the rules of the *prātimokṣa.* For the minor *Rāṣṭrapāla Sūtra,* apparently, the *prātimokṣa* is definitive of the Śrāvakayāna. The text then initiates its discussion of the Śrāvakayāna by telling us that the Buddha has made a distinction between two stations—that of the *bhikṣu*[124] and that of the lax person[125] (126.18–19 [133]). As the text progresses, we learn that both of these parties are actually *bhikṣus*. The first is the good *bhikṣu* who follows the Buddha's teachings, whereas the second is a counterfeit *bhikṣu* (Tib., *dge.slong.ltar.bcos.pa*),[126] and it is he who corrupts the Buddha's teachings and will eventually bring the dharma to ruin.

The good *bhikṣu* is the person of good conduct who abides by the moral precepts *(śīla)*[127] (*Rps*-m 130.11 [E., 137]) and follows the *prātimokṣa* (130.13, 20 [137]). He purifies his conduct of body, speech, and mind. He does not hanker after good robes and bowls, nor does he long for delicious food (130.23–34 [137]). He is temperate in taking the monk's robe, and he is not attached to savory food, seeing food as an impure substance necessary to life but nothing more (127.6ff. [134]). The good *bhikṣu* is also a forest renunciant. He dwells in the forest and takes joy in the forest *(araṇya)*[128] hermitages of the remote border regions *(prānta)*[129] (130.17 [137]). He praises dwelling at the foot of trees (130.29 [137]).[130] He dwells in a solitary *(vivikta, rahogata)*[131] place (128.5 [135]), a locale that is peaceful (130.12 [137]). "He must have pleasure in complete solitude and the jungle; in a place where it is quiet to sit and lie, where there is little noise, where there are few sounds" (127.28ff. [134]). In his forest retreat, the good *bhikṣu* must continually and without ceasing generate the thought of renunciation *(skyo.ba)*.[132] To fulfill his needs, he begs simply, from house to house (131.1–4 [137]). The virtuous *bhikṣu* does not look to the world for comfort (131.19 [137]). In his solitary abode in the forest, the good *bhikṣu* dwells alone (*ekākin*).[133] The good *bhikṣu* "must be lonely. He must have pleasure in solitude" (127.21 [134]). He must remain ever alone, relying neither on his mother and father, much less on other families, avoiding association with householders, with women, and with other renunciants (128.2ff. [134–35]). In particular, the *bhikṣu* is to avoid other *bhikṣus* who are not of good family *(kula)*[134] (127.34–36 [134]). In his solitary retreat, the good *bhikṣu* observes silence and does not talk (128.6–7 [135]). He does not take pleasure in useless talk, nor is he addicted to worldly talk (127.18ff. [134]). He does not talk to others in a peaceful way, much less in an unpeaceful way (128.6–7 [135]). This life in the forest is, we are told, the normative way of life of the virtuous *bhikṣu*. "Living alone in the forest; endowed with virtue, striving with vigor; seeing no support in the world; this is the ultimate truth *(dharmatā)*[135] of the *bhikṣu*" (131.17–20 [137]).

The good *bhikṣu* dwells in this solitary retreat for the purpose of meditation. His forest abode is a place "abandoned by men, suitable for complete absorption" (*Rps*-m 127.29–30 [E., 134]). There, for the purpose of attaining liberation from all suffering, he practices meditation (131.23–24 [137]). What sort of meditation does the good *bhikṣu* follow? He examines the sense organs and sees that each of them cannot be dualistically conceived. The eye is not thus conceived, nor is the visible form nor the eye consciousness (128.14 [135]). Why? Because no dharmas are dualistically conceived. Similarly, the bases of the ear, the nose, the tongue, the body, and the mind are not to be dualistically thought of (128.15–17 [135]). This meditation reveals that all existents (dharmas) are empty *(śūnya)*, and by it, one should exert oneself to realize the emptiness of dharmas. The good *bhikṣu* adheres to and meditates on the emptiness of all existents (127.33–34 [134]). He is not afraid of emptiness (132.4 [137]).[136] Striving in this way, one's morality *(śīla)* will be completely purified, as will one's meditation *(samādhi)*[137] and wisdom *(prajñā)*[138] (128.19–21 [135]). Striving to realize emptiness is, we are told, the proper dharma of the *bhikṣu:* "Dharmas are without life and without vitality; they are empty, void and without essence; [virtuous *bhikṣus*] are devoted to emptiness; this indeed is the final truth *[dharmatā]* of the *bhikṣu*" (131.13–16 [137]).[139] In addition, the text twice specifically tells us that the virtuous *bhikṣu* does not "preach the [discrimination of] dharmas" (131.4, 36 [137]), possibly referring to the scholastic discrimination and analysis of dharmas, as in the *abhidharma.*[140]

Through his practice, the good *bhikṣu* will attain his goal. He will obtain the result of a stream-enterer *(srotāpanna),*[141] once-returner *(sakṛdāgāmin),*[142] nonreturner *(anāgāmin),*[143] and arhant (*Rps*-m 128.22–24 [E., 135]). Having achieved his goal, he will have obtained the destruction of the *āśravas.*[144] Having reached nirvāṇa, the virtuous *bhikṣu* is a worthy recipient of veneration (132.11–12 [138]).[145] Finally, we are told that the good *bhikṣu* follows in the footsteps of the Buddha, does not go against the teachings of the Buddha, and causes the Buddha's dharma to flourish. He feels deep veneration for the Buddha, and day and night shows great devotion *(bhakti)*[146] to the best of human beings (130.22 [137]). He indeed is a *śrāvaka* of the Buddha[147] (130.26, 30 [137]). In fact, this one, who dwells in solitude, "is the best *śrāvaka*"[148] (128.23–24 [135]).

The bad *bhikṣu* is a *bhikṣu* in outward appearances, but he is in effect a counterfeit of the real thing (*Rps*-m 128.25 [E., 135]). He shaves his head, wears robes, and begs his food, but he is driven by desire for material objects. Though beholden to his vows, he breaks his moral principles and contravenes his *prātimokṣa* (128.25ff. [135]). The bad *bhikṣu* also rejects the forest life, and thus he "rejects all the seats and beds suitable for an ascetic which are authorized by the Buddha" (129.3–5 [135–36]). He also criticizes the solitary life (129.10 [136]). Having rejected the forest life, the bad *bhikṣu* also abandons the practice of not speaking *(tūṣṇīm)*[149] (128.29 [135]).[150] In fact, he indulges in useless talk and even goes so far as to praise this practice (129.11–13 [136]).

In addition, the bad *bhikṣu* knows many people of all sorts. He is acquainted with householders (*Rps*-m 129.6 [E., 136]). He also associates with women in an inappropriate way (129.18ff. [136]). The bad *bhikṣu* teaches and instructs these people. Moreover, he teaches those *sūtras* that are not to be publicly taught. Adopting the outward appearance of a *bhikṣu,* he teaches "in a place where there are many people" (129.34 [136]). Through his teaching, the bad *bhikṣu* attracts many people and holds sway over them (129.14–18 [136]). In this way, teaching what should not be taught, he is a robber of the dharma (129.20–21 [136]).

The bad *bhikṣus* are associated with monasteries (*Rps*-m 129.30, 31 [E., 136]). They take food with their own hands. They store food, millet, corn, and the like. They prepare and cook their food themselves. They procure gold and silver. They even trade in property of houses, land, and monasteries. "They apply themselves to this work, on this they are intent, to this they devote their energy, this they think to be true. This is their daily life" (129.27ff. [136]).

These bad *bhikṣus* do not purify their minds, and they are far from the teaching of emptiness. They have little use for emptiness and, in contrast to the wise, do not meditate (*Rps*-m 132.19–20 [E., 138]). In fact, "having conceptualized that sphere of activity of the Buddha[s], the dwelling place of the Tathāgata[s], [which is] emptiness, they abandon it; it is to be expected that they will revile it";[151] thus, these persons reject the profound dharma, reviling it and criticizing it (130.3–4 [136]). They turn their backs on the genuine dharma, and do not praise the Mahāyāna (132.21–22 [138]). So it is that the unvirtuous *bhikṣu* is a counterfeit and a hypocrite. "Shaving their heads they are hypocritical, frauds; donning the yellow robe they are hypocritical. For what reason must one know that they are hypocritical? What is blamed by the Buddhas, the exalted ones, is allowed by those fools" (129.23–26 [136]). Thus, the unvirtuous *bhikṣus* are morally corrupt. "Suffering heavily from the *kleśas*[152] his condition is such that he is doing great or little sins" (128.33–129.1 [135]). They are filled with arrogance and delight in evil deeds *(pāpa)*[153] (132.13–16 [138]).

What will be the fruit of this false *bhikṣu?* He will bring suffering on himself and will take rebirth in the lower realms. And, most grievous of all, he will destroy the teaching of the *tathāgata* and bring it to ruin (*Rps*-m 126.12–13 [E., 133]; 130.7–8 [136]). This, then, is the answer to the question posed at the beginning of the minor *Rāṣṭrapāla Sūtra:* "Of what character are the beings that bring the teaching of the Tathāgata to ruin?"

The preceding discussion raises the important question of the relation of the minor *Rāṣṭrapāla Sūtra* to the longer text. Several options immediately suggest themselves: (1) that the two texts were originally parts of a single, unitary composition, the position preferred by Ensink (1952, xi); (2) that they were not parts of one text but are closely related, with one being an abbreviation (if the longer text is earlier) or expansion (if the shorter text is earlier) of the other; and (3) that they were composed independently of one another. Owing to the marked difference in the understanding of the term *bhikṣu* in the two texts (in the longer text, all *bhikṣus* are bad; in the shorter text, the distinction between good and bad *bhikṣus* is crucial), it seems unlikely, as in option 1, that the two were originally part of one composition. The content, form, and concerns of the two texts are sufficiently different also to suggest that neither is an adaptation of the other (option 2). The peculiar relationship of the content of the two texts makes it unlikely, as in option 3, that the two texts are entirely independent of one another.

There is another possibility, namely, that development of the shorter text, as we now have it, reflects a process more complex than that suggested by any of the preceding options. Let us begin by noting the curious fact that the minor *Rāṣṭrapāla Sūtra,* although in its present form a Mahāyāna text, is principally concerned with discussing good *bhikṣus* and bad, both of whom belong to the Śrāvakayāna. Moreover, although various Mahāyāna topics are mentioned, these provide the frame for the rest of the text and, apart from the discussions of *śūnyatā,* are not present except as window dressing. Let us note further that in its concerns and argument, the text reveals some striking parallels to the songs of Phussa and Pārāpariya in the *Theragāthā,* including the discrimination between good and bad *bhikṣus*, the attribution to bad *bhikṣus* of the decline of the dharma, and even many of the specific criticisms made of the bad *bhikṣus*. Taken together, these facts suggest the possibility that the central portion or core of the text was originally a composition of a Nikāya forest tradition, with a viewpoint similar to that behind the songs of Phussa and Pārāpariya. If this is deemed plausible, then at a later time this core could have been adapted as a Mahāyāna text, with a reworking of the context and logic of the minor *Rāṣṭrapāla Sūtra* into its present form.

Such an explanation raises an important question: what could have been the motivation on the part of some Mahāyānists to accept and rework the minor *Rāṣṭrapāla Sūtra* into a Mahāyāna text? Let us assume, for the sake of argument and as seems reasonable, that the Mahāyāna group behind such an adaptation would have been a Mahāyāna forest community either identical to or similar to the original forest community behind the *Rāṣṭrapāla Sūtra.* Perhaps, at a certain point, the shorter text appeared within this group of forest Mahāyānists. Admittedly, this proto–minor *Rāṣṭrapāla Sūtra* was a text of the Śrāvakayāna that lauds the good *bhikṣu.* At the same time, however, the text could recommend itself very well to such a Mahāyāna community particularly for two reasons. First, it eloquently articulates and praises the life of forest renunciation. Second, like certain forest *śrāvaka*s evidenced in the Pāli canon *(Suttanīpāta, Cūḷasuññata Sutta,* and *Mahāsuññata Sutta)* and certain other forest *śrāvaka*s mentioned in the *Ratnaguṇa* and *Laṅkāvatāra Sūtra,* it holds certain values that come to be seen as Mahāyānist, most particularly its identification of *śūnyatā* as the central realization of the forest renunciant. As to the immediate cause of adaptation, it may be noted that the shorter text as we now have it appears to represent a softening of the longer text's harshly negative attitude toward *bhikṣus*. This raises the interesting possibility that the shorter text was adapted by the community in question and put with the longer text, partly to counteract the blanket condemnation of *bhikṣu*s found in the longer text.

Be this as it may, the minor *Rāṣṭrapāla Sūtra* gives the appearance of being a response—indeed, rebuttal—to the *Rāṣṭrapālaparipṛcchā Sūtra*'s view that the *bhikṣu* as such will bring the dharma to ruin. The shorter text thus retains the same explanation for the destruction of the dharma as the longer—namely, the abandonment of the normative way of forest renunciation. But by showing that some *śrāvaka bhikṣu*s follow the normative path of forest renunciation and are therefore good, the shorter text does not attribute the blame for the destruction of the dharma to the *śrāvaka bhikṣu*s as such, but rather to the abandonment of what it considers the normative Buddhist way of forest renunciation.

This approach enables the shorter text, as we now have it, to take a view of its religious context that is, in comparison to many other Mahāyāna *sūtra*s, relatively uncluttered by Mahāyāna polemics. For the shorter text the usual conceptual barriers and dividing lines between the Mahāyāna and the Śravakayāna do not apply. As we have seen, the text criticizes certain *bhikṣu*s who do conform to the Mahāyānist stereotype of the *śrāvaka bhikṣu.* But, as we have also seen, it describes other *śrāvaka bhikṣu*s who follow the same way of life as the bodhisattva forest renunciant described in the longer text and other Mahāyāna forest texts. Moreover, like this bodhisattva they are virtuous, possess a genuine understanding of emptiness, are endowed with good qualities, are genuinely realized beings, and are worthy of praise and veneration. Finally, like the forest bodhisattva, the forest *bhikṣu* is seen as upholding authentic renunciant Buddhism, which here, as in the other texts we have examined, is identified with the way of forest renunciation. The main differences between the *śrāvaka bhikṣu* of the forest of the shorter text and the bodhisattva renunciant of the forest of the longer text are that the *śrāvaka bhikṣu* follows the *prātimokṣa* and seeks an end to his own suffering rather than aspiring to *anuttarasamyaksaṃbodhi*.[154]

In its final Mahāyāna configuration, then, the minor *Rāṣṭrapāla Sūtra* exhibits the same kind of flexibility with regard to language as is seen in the forest texts of the pre-Mahāyāna and the Mahāyāna that we have examined, in its reluctance to give too much substance to the terms *Śrāvakayāna* and *Mahāyāna* as necessarily opposed phenomena. The text thus stands forth as a sustained critique of the view that all *śrāvaka bhikṣus* conform to the conceptual stereotype of the *śrāvaka bhikṣu* as presented in Mahāyāna texts such as the *Rāṣṭrapāla Sūtra*. It wants to say, in effect, that this talk of "vehicles" has its place, but it is a limited place and must not blind one to similarities and alliances that, at first glance, do not appear to conform to type.

In all of this, the shorter text, like the *Ratnaguṇa* and the *Laṅkāvatāra Sūtra*, provides us with insight into the time and the situation in which what finally became understood as the Mahāyāna was in the process of sorting out its own self-identity in relation to existing traditions. In addition, the shorter text is also like the other two texts, both of which clearly admit the existence of non-Mahāyānist renunciants of the forest who come close to the ideal of the forest-renunciant bodhisattva. What makes the shorter text distinctive is the strength of its affirmation of the authenticity and value of the forest *bhikṣu* of the Śrāvakayāna, while still managing to affirm its own sense of the superiority of the bodhisattva path. The minor *Raṣṭrapāla Sūtra* makes some other important contributions to the present discussion, but these will best be reserved for Chapter 12.

Notes

1. On the bodhisattva ideal in Mahāyāna Buddhism see Suzuki 1930, 202–36; Dayal 1932; Rahula 1971; Snellgrove 1970; Basham 1981; Kajiyama 1982; and Lopez 1988. These studies discuss the doctrinal definitions, classical practices, and stages of development of the bodhisattva. They generally give little treatment to the image of the bodhisattva as a saint, particularly in the *sūtra* literature. The term *bodhisattva*, of course, is sometimes used in a nonrestrictive sense in Buddhism. Thus, the term may, as noted, refer to the person aspiring to become a pratyekabuddha, after his initial vow and prior to realization, as in *pratyekabodhisattva*. This study, unless otherwise noted, follows conventional usage, employing the term *bodhisattva* to refer to that person who aspires to and has taken the vow to attain the complete and perfect enlightenment of a buddha.

2. See, e.g., Dutt 1930, 31, 34, 66–67, and passim; Dayal 1932, 30–49, 273–75; Bareau 1955, 260, 296–305, and passim; Dutt 1970, 81–84, 110–13; Nakamura 1987b.

3. Some Sanskrit terms supplied by Lamotte have been deleted.

4. In the Bendall and Rouse translation, these texts are identified as follows: the *Ugraparipṛcchā* (cf. Schuster's discussion of the full text in Chinese translation; Schuster 1985); *Candrapradīpa Sūtra* (= *Samādhirāja Sūtra* [*Ss* 199]); *Rāṣṭrapālaparipṛcchā Sūtra;*

tra; the *Ratnakūṭa Sūtra;* and the *Ratnarāśi Sūtra.*

5. See also the eighth, *"Dhyāna"* (meditation), chapter of the *Bodhicaryāvatāra,* which extols a lifestyle of forest renunciation, especially *Bca* 25ff. and 85ff. (Batchelor 1979, 103ff. and 113). In keeping with the practice of the texts summarized and quoted in this chapter, the masculine pronoun will be used. Of course, bodhisattvas may be either male or female.

6. Implying, of course, that these represent a different category of renunciant from himself.

7. Sanskrit editions include Obermiller 1937 and Yuyama 1976 (review by Schopen 1978). See also Yuyama 1977. The text is translated by Conze 1962a and incorporated into Conze 1973b. References are to chapter and verse of Yuyama's edition. As the numbering in Conze's translation corresponds, references to the translation may be omitted.

8. Conze believes that *Rgs* is the earliest textual expression of Mahāyāna Buddhism, presenting a reliable picture of the early Mahāyāna (Conze 1973b, ix). He further remarks that although the arrangement of the text is not the original one, nevertheless its content has likely remained relatively unchanged: "The verses themselves, as distinct from their arrangement, cannot have been altered very much because their archaic language and metre would resist fundamental changes" (1973b, ix; cf. 1967a; reprinted from 1960). Conze further identifies *Rgs* chapters 1 and 2 as the earliest sections of the text (1958b). Some scholars have expressed doubts concerning the adequacy of Conze's view of the relation of *Rgs* and *Asp* (see Yuyama 1976 [*Rgs* edition], xiv–xvii, and Schopen 1978, 112). A resolution of this question is not a necessary prerequisite to the present discussion for two reasons: (1) no one has yet disputed that *Rgs* represents *an early* (if not the earliest) expression of the Prajñāpāramitā; and (2) whatever the relation of *Rgs* to *Asp, Rgs* was clearly composed or assembled by an agent for some purpose and can therefore be treated as a discrete document reflecting certain intentions of composition or compilation. It may be noted, for example, that on at least one matter of importance in the present discussion, *Rgs* and *Asp* present differences: on the one hand, as we shall presently see, *Rgs* reflects an essentially forest context. On the other hand, *Asp* contains important evidence of an urban context. One example may be taken from *Rgs* 17.7 in comparison to its corresponding passage at *Asp* 167.18–25 (Cz., 206). *Asp* mentions that the bodhisattva, as a token of his irreversibility, is born in Madhyadeśa, "for in the border countries *[pratyantajanapada]* there are only a few beings with a good knowledge of the arts, of poetry, of *mantras,* of secret lore, of the standard treatises, of portents, and of the meaning of religion, but in the middle region they [irreversible bodhisattvas] are reborn in abundance. But those who are reborn in the border regions are at least reborn in the big towns *[mahānagara]*" (*Asp* 167.18–25 [Cz., 206]). Conveying a different meaning is the corresponding passage in *Rgs,* in the section of the qualities of irreversible bodhisattvas, where we read that the irreversible bodhisattvas "are not associated with the barbarous peoples of the border regions *[pratyantamlecchajanavarjita],* of the hinterland *[antadeśa]*" (*Rgs* 17.7). Unlike *Asp,* the *Rgs* passage does not explicitly mention rebirth (i.e., the issue here is not one's birth), nor does it say that dwelling in the midst of civilization is preferred or that high-caste, "civilized" values and preoccupations of learning and the arts are ideal. The *Asp* passage seems clearly to indicate an urban context, whereas the *Rgs* passage does not contradict a forest venue. (Thanks to Jan Nattier for drawing my attention to this reference.)

9. See Lancaster 1975.

10. The same two ideals are articulated in another early Mahāyāna *sūtra,* the *Ugrapariprcchā Sūtra,* first translated into Chinese in the second century C.E. (Schuster 1985, 31ff.).

11. This is, of course, consistent with other early Mahāyāna *sūtra*s (Harrison 1987, 76–77).

12. The *Ugraparipṛcchā,* although seeming to emphasize the householder bodhisattva's way, likewise sees the forest life as the higher (Schuster 1985, 35).

13. As mentioned, Conze considers chapters 1 and 2 to represent the earliest parts of *Rgs* (1958b). Interestingly enough, in chapter 2 of *Rgs*, where the three ideals are first mentioned, although the bodhisattva ideal is clearly considered the highest of the three (being called "the king of dharma," *dharmarāja* in relation to the other two), still the arhant and pratyekabuddha appear to be presented as legitimate ideals, parallel to the ideal of the bodhisattva and valid each in its own way (2.2–4). The less polemical tone of this discussion, when contrasted with *Rgs*'s later discussions of the three ideals (e.g., 6.1), suggests the possibility that in earliest Mahāyāna times the three ideals were accepted as separate and legitimate, yet still hierarchically arranged. On this point, see Fujita 1975. Later, though still in the times of the later sections of *Rgs,* increased polemical rancor becomes evident, suggesting more explicit and open hostility among proponents of the different ideals, a phenomenon to be explored further in Chapter 12.

14. The corresponding section of *Asp* (161.20–162.1 [Cz., 200–201]) mentions the *daśakuśalakarma,* or ten virtuous actions, followed by a list of eleven members, given here with comparisons to lists of the *daśakuśalakarma* in the *Dharmasaṃgraha* (entry 56) and the *Mahāvyutpatti* (entries 1685–98):

a. Abstention from *prāṇātipāta,* taking life.
Dhs: same
Mvy: prāṇātighāta

b. Abstention from *adattādāna,* taking what is not given.
Dhs: same
Mvy: same

c. Abstention from *kāmamithyācāra,* wrong conduct as regards sensuous pleasures.
Dhs: same
Mvy: same

d. Abstention from *surāmaireyamadyapramādasthāna,* intoxicants as tending to cloud the mind.
Dhs: not included
Mvy: not included

e. Abstention from *anṛtavacana,* lying speech.
Dhs: mṛṣāvāda
Mvy: mṛṣāvāda

f. Abstention from *piśunavacana,* malicious speech.
Dhs: paiṣunyav . . .
Mvy: paiśunyav . . . (the order of this and next item are reversed).

g. Abstention from *paruṣavacana,* harsh speech.
Dhs: pāruṣyav . . .
Mvy: pāruṣyav . . .

h. Abstention from *saṃbhinnapralāpa,* indistinct prattling.
Dhs: same
Mvy: same

i. Abstention from *abhidhyā,* covetousness.
Dhs: same
Mvy: same

j. Abstention from *vyāpāda,* ill will.
Dhs: same
Mvy: same

k. Abstention from *mithyādarśana,* wrong views.
Dhs: mithyādṛṣṭi
Mvy: mithyādṛṣṭi

It will be observed that this list in *Asp* differs somewhat from the classical Mahāyāna list of the *daśakuśalakarma* as found in both *Dhs* and *Mvy*. In particular, neither of these latter include *Asp* item d, abstention from *surāmaireyamadyapramādasthāna,* a convention found, of course, in the list of five precepts, as for example, in Pāli tradition (P., *surāmeraya-majjapamādaṭṭhāna) (PTSD* 712, s.v. *sīla).*

15. Although not enumerated in *Rgs, Asp* (21 [Cz., 231]) mentions various *dhutaguṇas* taken by the forest-renunciant bodhisattvas; see the discussion in Chapter 9.

16. Quite interesting is the assumption in *Rgs* that the arhant and the pratyekabuddha, like the bodhisattva, represent essentially meditational ideals. This would tend to support the idea that originally, in at least one tradition, there were three distinct and valid ideals accepted within (what became) the Mahāyāna, and further that each of these was understood as a forest ideal.

17. Although, in *Rgs* as in other texts that emphasize the bodhisattva as an ascetic ideal, such abilities are not stressed. For the role of these in relation to the bodhisattva ideal, see Gomez 1977.

18. The *Rgs*'s treatment of the magical powers of the saint is indicative. Like the *Theragāthā* and *Therīgāthā, Rgs* describes the life of forest renunciation from the viewpoint of the renunciants themselves. We know from other Buddhist texts, even those where magical powers are given relatively positive evaluation (e.g., *Csp* 74–81 [Rb., 81–85]), that for renunciants although the existence of magical powers is acknowledged, they are regarded with ambivalence. At best, they are useful but secondary manifestations of wisdom and, at worst, side tracks from the primary task at hand, that of attaining realization. For texts reflecting a more cultic viewpoint, of course, the magical powers of the realized saint typically play a larger and more important role.

19. This reference to the existence of a written text shows writing penetrating forest Buddhism, just as it did settled monasticism.

20. The *Ugraparipṛcchā Sūtra* is worth mentioning in this context. This text, dated to the first century C.E. or earlier (Schuster 1985, 28–31), provides an image of the forest-renunciant bodhisattva's path that is in many ways closely similar to the one given in *Rgs.* Thus in *Up,* we are told that there are two legitimate bodhisattva ideals, that of the householder and that of the forest renunciant (30ff. and 36ff.). In one sense, the latter is the higher ideal, as all bodhisattvas must eventually become forest renunciants in order to attain buddhahood. Nevertheless, just to live in the forest is not enough, for one's attitude must be correct (37). In the forest, the renunciant bodhisattva practices an ascetic regimen, defined principally by the "four practices of the noble ones" *(āryavaṃśa)* (see Chapter 9). The forest-renunciant bodhisattva must practice meditation ardently, generate great compassion, practice the six *pāramitās*, penetrate emptiness, practice the three gates to deliverance, etc. One important difference between *Up* and *Rgs* is the relative emphasis placed upon the household life. In *Up*, the interlocutor is the householder Ugra, whom the Buddha praises above forest renunciants because he is willing to stay in the world to assist beings (37–39).

21. The "three vehicles" are mentioned at *Rgs* 15.5. For similar patterns in other early Mahāyāna texts, see Harrison 1987, 83–84.

22. *Rgs* 31.5 tells us that one who longs for arhantship or pratyekabuddhahood will have broken his morality *(śīla).*

23. In this context, see Harrison 1987, 82.

24. *Rgs* 31.5; we learn that the bodhisattva will break his *śīla* if he longs for arhantship or pratyekabuddhahood and that this is more serious even than a *pārājika* offense. We may suspect that the *pārājika* referred to here is the *prātimokṣa* category, as functioning within classical monasticism of the time. In reference to the typically monastic connotations of

the term *śrāvaka,* La Vallée Poussin points to certain features of the *śrāvaka* implying activities of scholarship and preaching of the settled monastic establishment: "*śrāvaka* . . . is commonly translated 'auditor,' 'disciple,' but it also means 'preacher' . . . [and] points out one of [their] features . . . they are preachers. They are the fathers and doctors of the Church" (1908–27c, 152).

25. Warder remarks that although there is no external evidence for its great antiquity, this text, judging from its content, would appear to be among the earliest of extant Mahāyāna *sūtra*s (1970, 359).

26. Reprinted *IIR* 1957. In an appendix, the *IIR* reprint lists emendations to the Sanskrit text suggested by Finot, La Vallée Poussin, Ensink, Bailey, and de Jong (the appendix is reproduced in de Jong 1979, 421–27). Further emendations are suggested by de Jong 1968, 4–7.

27. E.g., in the *dkon.brtsegs* section of the Peking edition of the Tibetan *Tripiṭaka (shi),* 192a–226b. Ensink's edition of the Tibetan translation was made on the basis of the Derge, Narthang, Peking, and Lhasa editions of the Kanjur.

28. The text was translated into Chinese three times, by Dharmarakṣa in 270 C.E.; by Jñānagupta at the end of the sixth century (Taisho 310); and by Dānapāla in 994 (Taisho 321) (Ensink 1952, ix; de Jong 1968, 1). For a discussion of the texts of the *Rps,* see de Jong 1953, 1957, and 1968.

29. References are to the Sanskrit edition of Finot. In his edition of the Tibetan, Ensink provides cross reference to Finot's Sanskrit edition so that the references here may be used readily to locate passages in either Sanskrit or Tibetan. This analysis generally follows the Sanskrit version. In a few instances where the Sanskrit leaves room for differing interpretations, the Tibetan is consulted. Except as noted, I quote Ensink's generally sound translation.

30. Not translated by Ensink.

31. The stereotypical notion that forest saints live in border regions is also found in Nikāya Buddhism, e.g., in the *vinaya* of the Mūlasarvāstivādins, where no less a figure than Gavāṃpati is said to be "foremost among those who dwell in the border regions" (Przyluski 1926–28, 243). On this saint and his cult, see Przyluski 1926–28, 239–47; Lévy 1957, 82–90; and Shorto 1970.

32. The term *dhuta* is often used in Mahāyāna texts to refer to the *dhutaguṇa*s (*BHSD* 286.1). In the four passages cited here, and throughout this text, Ensink translates this term vaguely as "morality." This, however, misses the specific sense intended here, namely, the set of ascetic practices that specifically define the life of the forest renunciant, specifying the obtaining of food, clothing, and habitation.

33. This, by implication, where the text critiques those who are not devoted to the *dhutaguṇa*s.

34. The Sanskrit reads *nirāmiṣasevanatayā* (*Rps* 73.19–20). See *BHSD* 299, s.v. *nirāmiṣa*.

35. Again, his mind is tranquil and tamed (*Rps* 11.16 [E., 13]).

36. Following the Tibetan, which takes the compound *śrutiguṇa* as a *dvandva* (*Rps* 73.7) rather than Ensink who prefers a *tatpuruṣa* (E., 15).

37. Mentioned only once in the text and clearly not a central element in the bodhisattva ideal being articulated here.

38. *Dharmabhāṇaka* is used in both Nikāya Buddhism and the Mahāyāna to refer to those who recite texts (*BHSD* 280). Although in *Rps,* the term appears to indicate people different from the ideal promoted by the text, in other Mahāyāna texts that espouse a less strictly forest ideal, the term *dharmabhāṇaka* can be used to indicate something done by

the ideal bodhisattva, for which see *Asp* 55.14, 16 (Conze 1973b, 118); *Sps* 12.18 (Kn., 20), 142ff. (213ff.), and 143.10 (214); and *Daśabhūmika Sūtra* 29.19 (Honda 1968, 180). This suggests that although it may be suspected that in the context of *Rps* the *dharmabhāṇakas* are monastics following Nikāya traditions, one cannot be certain, for the text may rather intend to include more broadly Mahāyāna preachers as well. On the use of the term in early Buddhism, see Lamotte 1958, 164.

39. Again, he will see that there is no self in either beings or dharmas (*Rps* 12.11 [E., 13]).

40. In early Buddhism, this term indicates those who memorize, recite, and maintain the continuity of the passing on of the *sūtras*, in contrast, for example, to the *vinayadhara,* who memorize, recite, and pass on the *vinaya* (cf. Lamotte 1958, 164). Ensink appears correct in translating the term here as indicating the bodhisattva's custodianship of the dharma in the sense of the general Mahāyāna teaching of the Buddha, rather than as referring to a specific text or corpus of texts.

41. This section of the text identifies this antibodhisattva type in several ways: at the beginning of the section and following, he is explicitly called "*bhikṣu*" (e.g., *Rps* 17.14 [E., 18]); sometimes he is called "ignorant" *(alpabuddhi)* (e.g., 17.2 [17]); sometimes he is mentioned as "one whom the bodhisattva must avoid" (e.g., 18.17 [19]); sometimes we simply find the text mentioning qualities that the bodhisattva must shun, qualities that would lead to his downfall (e.g., 19.16 [20]). Several facts make it clear that these passages are referring to a renunciant of a non–forest-dwelling type: (1) the section opens with an explicit critique of the *bhikṣus* (17.3–15 [15–17]); (2) the *bhikṣus* return as the explicit object of critique elsewhere in this section; (3) the opening section makes it clear that the "downfalls *[prapāta]* of the bodhisattvas" are principally found in the way of life of the *bhikṣus* and their faults (17.3–15 [15–17]); (4) even where the explicit term *bhikṣu* is not used, the specific values, qualities, and preoccupations criticized are those that elsewhere in *Rps* are attributed to settled monastic life; and (5) this section embodies a consistent presentation of the antitype of the bodhisattva, and the type described throughout emerges as a unified and coherent type of the settled monastic. In a review of Ensink's translation, de Jong remarks in passing that "la prophétie de la future décadence de l'église" does not occur in the Chinese version of the text in its earlier translation (de Jong 1953, 546).

42. In this text, *jñāna* generally refers to the wisdom of the buddhas and is typically translated by the Tibetan as *ye.shes*. Here, however, *jñāna* clearly means relative knowledge, reflected in the Tibetan rendering of *jñāna* simply as *shes.pa*.

43. Buddhaghosa similarly cites examples of *bhikkhus* trying to meditate in a settled monastic context who become objects of others' jealousy and who are criticized and even driven out (*Vsm* 119–20 [N., 23–24]). Here *Rps* clearly acknowledges the existence of monks within settled monasteries who attempt to practice meditation, although unsuccessfully.

44. Ensink translates *gaṇa* (group) as *saṃgha,* by which he appears to mean monastic *saṃgha*. This usage must, however, be questioned. The term *gaṇa* is frequently used in Mahāyāna *sūtras* to refer to the community of bodhisattvas and is often set in opposition to the term *saṃgha,* meaning the order of *bhikṣus*. The term *gaṇa,* as used in these texts, appears to refer to both lay and renunciant bodhisattvas. Thus in the *Laṅkāvatāra Sūtra,* in the opening sections of the text, we are told that the Buddha is surrounded by the *saṃgha* of *bhikṣus* and by the *gaṇa* of bodhisattvas *(bhikṣusaṃghena . . . bodhisattvagaṇena)* (*Las* 1.5 [Sz., 3]). The *Sukhāvatīvyūha Sūtra* similarly refers to Amitābha surrounded by *śrāvakasaṃgha* and *bodhisattvagaṇa* (Hirakawa 1963, 70). In the same fashion, the *Saddhar-*

mapuṇḍarīka Sūtra speaks of the *śrāvakasaṃgha* and the *bodhisattvagaṇa* (Hirakawa 1963, 81). The term *gaṇa* is also used in specific reference to the group of bodhisattvas in the *Daśabhūmika Sūtra* (Hirakawa 1963, 80). In *Rps,* the use of the term *saṃgha* for the monastic order of *bhikṣu*s or *śrāvaka*s is seen, for example, in the way in which in its opening section *Rps* uses the term *saṃgha* to refer to the *bhikṣu*s but not to the bodhisattvas (*Rps* 1.1ff [E., 1ff.]). Similar are the *Vimalakīrtinirdeśa Sūtra* (Lamotte 1962, 97ff., 83) and the *Aṣṭasāhasrikāprajñāpāramitā Sūtra* (*Asp* 1.5 [Cz., 83]). Although, as Hirakawa has pointed out, the Mahāyāna texts show some variation in the way they present their dramatis personae, it is significant that the two groups, the *bhikṣu*s (or *śrāvaka*s) and the bodhisattvas, are often presented as distinct and separate bodies (Hirakawa 1963, 79ff.; see also Nakamura 1987a and 1987b). This understanding of the frequently mutually exclusive meanings of the terms *saṃgha* and *gaṇa* provides the necessary tools for a proper understanding of this passage in *Rps*. What is being said here is, in effect, not that these *bhikṣu*s disrespect community as such, much less the monastic *saṃgha,* but rather that they show no devotion for the community of lay and renunciant bodhisattvas. At the same time, it should be pointed out that there are exceptions to these trends, for the term *gaṇa* is sometimes used to refer to gatherings of monks in the Mahāyāna (e.g., *Ss* 160.20 [BR., 193]; *Rgs* 6.1). Likewise, the term *saṃgha* may occasionally be used to refer both to the group of *śrāvakas*/*bhikṣu*s and to the group of bodhisattvas, such as in the *Saṃdhinirmocana Sūtra* (31.14 and 33.1 [L., 167–68]).

45. The epithet *dharmadhara* is used here making it clear that the bodhisattva is intended.

46. =*śikṣā*. The behavioral meaning of this term seems clear (see, e.g., *BHSD* 527.1). It is not clear whether or not a specific code is being referred to here, such as the *daśakuśalāni* mentioned at 15.6.

47. Ensink again renders *dhuta* as "morality" and *śīkṣā* as "teachings." *Dhuta* should, as mentioned in note 32, be taken to refer to the *dhutaguṇa*s, whereas in this context it seems likely that *śīkṣā* refers to the conduct of the bodhisattvas. By contrast, the term *prātimokṣa,* which refers to the moral code of the *bhikṣu*s, is not used in *Rps* to refer to the bodhisattvas. The specific terminology in *Rps* thus reflects a clear separation between the tradition of the bodhisattvas and that of the *śrāvaka*s, but Ensink's translation at key points renders this separation invisible. In this, Ensink's work reflects the two-tiered model and stands as a good example of how this model can have a major impact on an otherwise fine translation, such that the phenomenon of the saints is obscured.

48. The text reads *śravaṇa*. Finot remarks that "d'après les 2 versions chinoises, *śravaṇā* = *śramaṇā*" (1901, 17, n. 2). The Tibetan reads *dge.sbyong,* confirming this reading (E., 76.12). From context, it appears that this term is intended to refer to, or at least to include, renunciant bodhisattvas. If so, this suggests that although the term *bhikṣu* is not applicable to the renunciant bodhisattva of this text, the term *śramaṇa* is.

49. The *Saṃdhinirmocana Sūtra,* including the introduction and ten chapters of the text, represent according to Lamotte "a complete summary of the Buddhist Great Vehicle" (1935, 24). The text has long been recognized as an important Mahāyāna *sūtra,* because of its antiquity and also because it is the principal *sūtra* upon which the early Yogācārin masters, including Asaṅga, Vasubandhu, and Sthiramati, base their thinking (L., 14–15). Lamotte provides a useful summary of the central ideas of Asaṅga's thought and its grounding in *Sns* (L., 16–17).

50. For remarks on *Sns* in the context of early Yogācāra, see Weinstein 1958 and Schmithausen 1987, 1–33.

51. Although acknowledging the difficulty of definitively dating the text and its various components, Lamotte believes that the short *sūtra*s of which *Sns* is composed were in

existence at least by the second century C.E. and were collected into a single text by the end of the second century (L., 24–25). He sees the text itself as divided into three large blocks, identifiable as units through both their form and their content. These blocks developed, Lamotte believes, in three successive stages: chapters 1 to 4, followed by chapters 5 to 8, and finally chapters 8 to 10 (L., 18).

52. Tib., *'phags.pa*. Although *Sns* does not survive in Sanskrit, in notes to his Tibetan edition of the text, Lamotte has provided a nearly exhaustive list of common Sanskrit equivalents to Tibetan technical terms. The present analysis includes, where pertinent, references to these hypothesized equivalents.

53. Tib., *rnal. 'byor.pa*.

54. Tib., *dge. slong. rnal. 'byor. spyod.pa*. Lamotte, "moines mystiques" (1935, 181). These are clearly the Mahāyānist ideal of the text, for they are defined as having realized the *tathatā* and understood the selflessness of the dharmas (*Sns* 51.9ff. [L., 181]).

55. *byang. chub. sems. dpa'*.

56. Perhaps these sections reflect a forest origin, but one not originally understood as connected with the ideal of the bodhisattva or as "Mahāyānist." As in the case of *Ss*, the *Sns* may have originated as a forest tradition similar to those reflected in the Nikāya evidence, which only subsequently came to be included within, and to be understood as an expression of, Mahāyāna Buddhism. For another possible example of the same phenomenon, see the appendix at the end of this chapter.

57. Except in a story recounted by Subhūti, shortly to be summarized.

58. Tib., *zhi.gnas*.

59. Tib., *lhag.mthong*.

60. Tib., *rab.tu.dben.pa*.

61. Tib., *mi.smra.ba.'phags.pa*.

62. Tib., *so.so.rang.gis.rig.pa*.

63. Tib., *'phags.pa'i.shes..pa*.

64. Tib., *'phags.pa'i.mthong.pa*.

65. Tib., *mngon.par.rdzogs.par.sangs.rgyas.pa*.

66. Tib., *rtog.ge.thams.cad*.

67. Tib., *chos.bdag.med.pa*.

68. Tib., *de.bzhin.nyid*.

69. Tib., *tha.dad.ma.yin*.

70. Tib., *mngon.pa'i.nga.rgyal*.

71. Tib., *dgon.pa.nags.khrod.chen.po*.

72. Tib., *phung.po*.

73. Tib., *mtshan.ma*.

74. Tib., *skye.ba*.

75. Tib., *'jig.pa*.

76. Tib., *'gog.pa*.

77. Tib., *'gog.pa.mngon.du.bgyid.pa*.

78. Tib., *skye.mched*.

79. Tib., *rten.cing.'brel.par.'byung.ba*.

80. Tib., *zas*.

81. Tib., *bden.pa*.

82. Tib., *khams*.

83. Tib., *dran.pa.nye.bar.bzhag.pa*.

84. Tib., *yang.dag.par.spong.ba*.

85. Tib., *rdzu.'phrul.gyi.rkang.pa*.

86. Tib., *dbang.po*.

87. Tib., *stobs.*

88. Tib., *byang.chub.kyi.yan.lag.*

89. Tib., *'phags.pa'i.lam.yan.lag.brgyad.pa.*

90. Tib., *don.dam.*

91. Tib., *ro.gcig.*

92. Tib., *mu.stegs.can.*

93. Tib., *byis.pa.*

94. *Bāla* is, of course, also a preferred term of derision applied by Buddhists to members of other traditions (Bollée 1974, 28).

95. Tib., *zab.mo.*

96. Tib., *spyod.yul.*

97. Tib., *brjod.med.*

98. Tib., *gnyis.min.*

99. Tib., *gti.mug.*

100. Tib., *smra.ba'i.spros.*

101. Tib., *ma.rtogs.pa.*

102. Tib., *log.par.rtogs.pa.*

103. From the Tibetan.

104. The term *gambhīra* is commonly used in Mahāyāna texts to characterize the Great Vehicle in contrast to the other, lesser vehicles of *śrāvaka*s and pratyekabuddhas. We have seen *Rgs* define its Buddhism as *gambhīrayāna* and *Rps* characterize the core Mahāyānist realization of emptiness as the "profound dharma" *(gambhīradharma).* On the term *gambhīra,* see also Conze 1973b, 164, s.v. *gambhīra.* For its use in Pāli texts, see *PTSD* 245, s.v. *gambhīra.*

105. Tib., *mi.gsal.ba.*

106. Tib., *mi.mkhas.pa.*

107. In a sense, then, the Mahāyāna movement represents a resurgence or renaissance of the cult of the Buddha (see Chapter 12).

108. The *Cūḷasuññata Sutta,* for example, portrays a gradual awakening to the full realization of emptiness; the context within which this awakening is described, as well as the analogies it employs in its argument, reflect forest Buddhism. Thus the Buddha explains the experience of emptiness to Ānanda in the following way: "A monk [*bhikkhu*], not attending to the perception of village, not attending to the perception of human beings, attends to solitude grounded on the perception of forest. His mind is satisfied with, pleased with, set on and freed in the perception of forest. He comprehends thus: 'The disturbances there might be resulting from the perception of village do not exist here; the disturbances there might be resulting from the perception of human beings do not exist here. . . . This perceiving is empty of the perception of village . . . of human beings . . . [but it is not empty of] solitude grounded on the perception of forest' " (*Mn* 3:104 [Hn., 3:147–48]). In other words, the renunciant's realization of emptiness must go to deeper levels. Next, the renunciant attends to the solitude of the perception of earth beneath him and imagines it empty of trees, growing things, and everything else upon it, but this is still not subtle enough. Next he attends to solitude of the perception of space, then of infinite consciousness, of no-thing, and of neither-perception-nor-nonperception. Finally, he attends to the solitude grounded on the concentration of a mind that is signless. Then he comprehends that "this concentration of mind that is signless is effected and thought out. But whatever is effected and thought out, that is impermanent, it is liable to stopping." At this moment, he attains liberation. "Thus," the Buddha concludes, "this comes to be for him a true, not mistaken, utterly purified and incomparably highest realization of emptiness" (3:105–9 [3:148–52]). Thus the *Cūḷasuññata Sutta* reveals the presence of *śūnyatā* within Nikāya

Buddhism as a teaching practiced by forest renunciants, within a forest context, using forest analogies, and following a meditative path.

The *Mahāsuññata Sutta* presents similar evidence, commenting that the *bhikṣu* who remains within and delights in the collectivity, the body of *bhikṣus*, either his own or another, does not excel. The one who excels is, rather, the one who acquires the happiness of renunciation, of aloofness, of calm, of self-awakening, and the one who does so "dwells alone, remote from a group" (*Mn* 3:110 [Hn., 3:153–54]), "in a forest, at the root of a tree, on a mountain slope, in a wilderness, a hill-cave, a [cremation ground], a forest-haunt, in the open air or on a heap of straw" (3:115–16 [3:160–61]). This forest renunciant, moreover, practices meditation: "That *bhikkhu* . . . should steady, calm, make one-pointed and concentrate his mind precisely on what is inward . . . , an inward emptiness. . . . This abiding, Ānanda, has been fully awakened to by the Tathāgata, that is to say, by not attending to any signs, the entering on and abiding in an inward emptiness." It is to this realization of emptiness that the renunciant in the forest should aspire (3:109–18 [3:152–62]). The text also mentions certain restrictions of speech characteristic, as we have seen, of other forest texts (3:113 [3:157]). Further, it warns that both forest teacher and forest disciple face a particular danger—namely, that they will be besieged by the laity, by townsfolk and country folk, and will become enamored of the attention, thus losing their way. Finally, the *Mahāsuññata Sutta* specifically rejects textual pursuits as a focus of attention for the forest renunciant: "Ānanda, it is not fit that a disciple should follow after a teacher if it is for the sake of an exposition of the Discourses that are in prose and in prose and verse" (3:115 [3:159]). For a discussion of Nikāya Sanskrit texts treating *śūnyatā,* or emptiness, see Lamotte 1973.

109. This trend is, of course, not entirely absent from Nikāya Buddhist texts extolling the forest life. For an example, see *Dhammapada* 141–42.

110. In the preceding discussion, we have seen some variations in the way in which the bodhisattva is defined as a forest saint, and in the way in which his way of life is contrasted with that of the monastic *bhikṣu.* In *Rgs,* the bodhisattva is primarily a forest saint, and the contrast between him and the settled monastic, his way of life, and his understanding are alluded to but not spelled out. In *Sns,* the forest identity of the bodhisattva is not explicitly stated but is implied; moreover, although his way of life is not explicitly extolled, his major preoccupation (meditation) and his understanding (nonconceptual realization) are, and these are favorably compared with the scholastic preoccupations and conceptual understanding of (monastic) *bhikṣus* and (it was suggested) certain bodhisattvas. In *Rps,* the bodhisattva is also a forest saint, and he is sharply and boldly contrasted with the monastic *bhikṣu.* In *Up, Cp, Rps, Rk,* and *Rr* selections of Śāntideva's *Ss,* the central ideal is similarly a forest saint, but one finds here no blatant criticism or even strong contrast with monastic life, consonant, as mentioned, with Śāntideva's monastic status.

111. According to Suzuki, the *Laṅkāvatāra Sūtra* was compiled sometime before 433 C.E., when it was translated into Chinese. However, the complete text as we now have it dates from a later time, and Suzuki mentions in this respect that translations done in 513 and 700–704 contain the *dhāraṇī* and *sagāthakam* sections of the text not present in the earlier translation (1932, xlii). On the development of *Las,* see Takasaki 1980 and 1982.

112. Reference to the type of practice reflected in the last member of the classical *dhutaguṇa* lists. See Chapter 9.

113. This critique is, of course, part of the larger polemical intention of *Las,* for some major themes of which see Kunst 1980.

114. It may be noted that in the introduction to *Sns,* which Lamotte judges to reflect a later time than chapters 1 to 4, the term *śrāvaka* is used to refer to the scholastic Buddhists of settled Nikāya monasticism. As the text opens, the Buddha is preaching to a great

gathering of *śrāvaka*s and a great gathering of bodhisattvas. Four major themes dominate the description of the *śrāvaka*s (*Sns* 32–33 [L., 168]): (1) *śīla*, or exemplary behavior; (2) textual learning; (3) teaching; and (4) *prajñā*. Thus we are told (1) that the *śīla* of the *śrāvaka*s is completely pure *(suviśuddhaśīla;* Tib., *tshul.khrims.shin.tu.rnam.par.dag.pa*); (2) that they have studied much *(bahuśruta;* Tib., *mang.du.thos.pa),* are specialists in that which they have studied *(śrutadhara;* Tib., *thos.pa.'dzin.pa*), and accumulate that which they have studied *(śrutasaṃnicaya;* Tib., *thos.pa.bsags.pa*); (3) that they conceive good thoughts *(sucintitacintin;* Tib., *legs.par.bsams.pa.sems.pa*), speak in good speech *(subhāṣitabhāṣin;* Tib., *legs.par.smra.ba.brjod.pa.),* and perform good deeds *(sukṛtakarmakārin;* Tib., *legs.par.bya.ba'i.las.byed.pa);* and (4) that their *prajñā* is lively *(āśuprajñā;* Tib., *shes.rab.myur.ba*), swift *(javanap.;* Tib., *shes.rab.mgyogs.pa),* sharp *(tīkṣṇap.;* Tib., *shes.rab.rno.ba),* prudent *(niḥsaraṇap.;* Tib., *nges.par.'byung.ba'i.shes.rab.can),* penetrating *(nairvedhikap.;* Tib., *nges.par.rtogs.pa'i.shes.rab.can),* great *(mahāp.;* Tib., *shes.rab.che.ba),* extensive *(pṛthup.;* Tib., *shes.rab.yangs.pa),* etc. The emphasis here is clearly on noncontemplative values. The nature of the *śrāvaka*s is thrown into particular relief by the entirely different ways in which the bodhisattvas are characterized (*Sns* 34 [L., 168–69]):

> They are marked with meditational accomplishment: they are free from all conceptualizing *[kalpa;* Tib., *rtog.pa],* conceptual thought *[vikalpa*; Tib., *rnam.par.rtog.pa],* and defiling thought *[parikalpa;* Tib., *yongs.su.rtog.pa].*
>
> They are spiritually highly attained: they have transcended the five great fears *[mahābhaya;* Tib., *'jigs.pa.chen.po];* they tend toward those *bhūmi*s where one does not regress.
>
> They are victorious over supernatural and other enemies: they have conquered Māra and all adversaries.
>
> They possess charisma, being firm in the joyful experience and great bliss of the dharma.
>
> They exhibit compassion for sentient beings: they are even-minded *[samacitta;* Tib., *sems.mnyam.pa]* toward all sentient beings; they are directed toward those *bhūmi*s that pacify the sufferings of all beings.
>
> They dwell in other realms, the buddha fields: they come from the various buddha fields where they dwell.
>
> They belong to a separate tradition from that of the *śrāvaka*s: they are established in the Mahāyāna dharma; they remain far removed from the habitual attitudes *[manasikāra;* Tib., *yid.la.byed.pa]* of the *śrāvaka*s and pratyekabuddhas.

115. The fact that *śrāvaka* is not used to refer to these scholarly types is seen in the way in which the text frequently contrasts the *tarkika*s and the *śrāvaka*s (e.g., *Las* 24.25–26 [S., 49]).

116. The term *bāla* is applied to unworthy *bhikṣu*s also in the *Dhammapada;* for an example see *Dp* 73–74.

117. So far has the original meaning of the pratyekabuddha as a silent forest hermit been obscured.

118. To the obvious question as to which division is the more ancient, there is no clear answer. The hierarchical arrangement at least of bodhisattva/buddha (in reference to Śākyamuni, if not to others) and *śrāvaka*/arhant may well reflect the time period of the Buddha himself. At the same time, as noted, it is unclear whether original Buddhism was purely a tradition of forest renunciants with their lay devotees or whether the Buddha himself accepted town-and-village renunciants as legitimate members of his renunciant *saṃgha*. If the latter is true, then the two different classification systems may in fact derive from the same period.

In addition, can one be sure that, just as some advanced the *śrāvaka*/arhant ideal, there were not from earliest times also partisans of the bodhisattva ideal? We may recall that at a later time, the Sarvāstivāda held that there were three legitimate ideals and paths to realization, those of bodhisattva, pratyekabuddha, and arhant. We have also seen that the early Mahāyāna, as reflected in *Rgs,* accepts this view. It is significant that even in Theravāda Buddhism, where the arhant ideal reigns supreme, there is similarly a recognition that all three ideals are legitimate and that devotees may aspire to any of the three. In the previous chapter we saw that the pratyekabuddha was an ideal for some in Thailand even in modern times. Spiro similarly tells us that, in Burma, there was a tradition, restricted in numbers but nevertheless long-standing, of those who aspired to full buddhahood, "who refer to themselves as Embryo Buddhas *(hpaya: laung:),*" that is, bodhisattvas (1982, 61–63). Harrison views the matter similarly (1987, 85).

119. Tib., *theg.pa.chen.po.* The text does not survive in Sanskrit. However, standard Sanskrit equivalents are given here for terms appearing in their Sanskrit forms elsewhere in this study.

120. Tib., *stong.pa.nyid.*

121. Tib., *bla.na.med.pa.yang.dag.par.rdzogs.pa'i.byang.chub.*

122. Tib., *nyan.thos.kyi.theg.pa.*

123. Tib., *so.sor.thar.pa.*

124. Tib., *dge.slong.gi.gnas.*

125. Tib., *lhod.pa'i.gnas.*

126. Tib., *dge.slong.ltar.bcos.pa; ltar.bcos.pa* is the Tibetan rendering of the Sanskrit *prativarṇika* ("counterfeit, [false] imitation [of something, which usually precedes it in comp]," *BHSD* 366). For variants and references, see *BHSD,* s.v. *prativarṇika.*

127. Tib., *tshul.khrims.*

128. Tib., *dgon.pa.*

129. Tib., *bas.mtha'.*

130. *Shing.drung.rnams,* or, perhaps, following Ensink, ascetics who dwell at the foot of trees.

131. Tib., *dben.pa.*

132. Tib. Ensink translates "disturbance," the literal meaning of *skyo.ba* (Skt., *udvega*), but this fails to catch the meaning of this term as commonly used in Buddhist texts to indicate revulsion toward an object of grasping and consequent inward renunciation.

133. Tib., *gcig.pu.*

134. Tib., *rigs.pa.*

135. Tib., *chos.nyid.*

136. Once again, we find a Mahāyāna forest text crediting other forest practitioners who follow non-Mahāyāna traditions (here Śrāvakayāna) with an understanding of *śūnyatā.*

137. Tib., *ting.nge.'dzin.*

138. Tib., *shes.rab.*

139.

> *Chos.rnams.srog.med.gso.ba.med*
> *gsob.dang.gsog.dang.snying.po.med*
> *stong.pa.nyid.la.mos.byed.pa*
> *de.ni.dge.slong.chos.nyid.do.*

140. *Chos.rnams.ston.par.mi.byed.do.* Ensink translates vaguely "do not preach the doctrines" (1952, 137), but the meaning appears more specific, namely, not that the good *bhikṣu* refrains from teaching altogether, but rather that he abstains from a certain *kind* of teaching—that concerned with scholarly (abhidharmic) analysis (of the dharmas, *chos.rnams.*).

141. Tib., *rgyun.du.zhugs.pa.*

142. Tib., *lan.cig.phyir.'ong.ba.*

143. Tib., *phyir.mi.'ong.ba.*

144. Tib., *zag.pa.zad.pa.thob.pa.*

145. Tib., *mchod.pa'i.gnas.su.'os.par.'gyur.*

146. Tib., *bkur.sti.chen.po.*

147. Tib., *sangs.rgyas.nyan.thos.*

148. Tib., *dang.po'i.nyan.thos.*

149. Tib., *mi.smra.ba.*

150. Ensink translates "abandoning taciturnity."

151. Ensink translates this as "the land of the *tathāgata* is *void,*" but the text gives the substantive "voidness" or "emptiness" *(stong.pa.nyid).*

152. Tib., *nyon.mongs.*

153. Tib., *sdig.pa.*

154. There are, of course, a number of other examples of early Mahāyāna *sūtra*s that similarly show a lack of antagonism toward *śrāvaka*s as such. See, e.g., Williams's summary of the *Ajitasenavyākaraṇanirdeśa Sūtra* (1989, 26–28).

9

Ascetic Traditions of Buddhist Saints

The *Dhutaguṇas*

So far this study has dealt primarily with two of the three dimensions of the Buddhist saints, their hagiographic paradigms and their cults. This chapter raises the issue of the third dimension, the specific ascetic traditions typically followed by the saints themselves. The preceding chapters have already indicated what is most important about these ascetic traditions: they are traditions of forest renunciation. The Buddha himself emerges from a tradition of retirement to the forest and homeless wandering. Mahākāśyapa, at least in most sources, also follows a wandering, ascetic way of life in the forest. The later patriarch Upagupta is a forest saint who lives on Mount Urumuṇḍa—famed for meditation—far from Aśoka's capital. Piṇḍolabhāradvāja is a forest saint who wanders about, begging food and meditating. Devadatta is a forest renunciant, who is criticized for wanting to reconfirm the ancient forest way of life in its purity in the face of change. And even Śāriputra, prototypical embodiment of settled monastic values and orientation, has forest features in his history and personality.

We also saw that the saints of the *Theragāthā* and *Therīgāthā* live in the forest, as do many of the arhants mentioned by the Chinese pilgrims. The pratyekabuddha likewise follows a forest way of renunciation and so do the the bodhisattvas examined in the previous chapter. The habitual association of saint with forest is important; it is the forest, we seem to be told, that is the natural habitat of the saint, the environment where saints are produced. The converse is also suggested: living saints are not typically or naturally associated with the settled monastery of town and village.[1] In light of the preceding chapters, this should come as no surprise. As we have seen, it is by meditation that, in Buddhism, realization and realized people become possible, and those who would practice meditation intensively must withdraw to the forest.[2]

An important aspect of the identity of Buddhist forest traditions are specific codes of ascetic practice that relate to, among other things, a forest renunciant's dress, sustenance, and habitation and sometimes speech, meditation, seclusion, and basic attitudes of renunciation. As we shall see, these codes appear in a considerable variety of forms and are found in a wide selection of texts of both Nikāya and Mahāyāna Buddhism. This chapter sets out some of the more prominent types of such codes and attempts to discern some historical relationships among them.

Early Buddhism knows of a number of different sets of ascetic practices that define a life of forest renunciation. In the *Dīghanikāya,* for example, we are told that a renunciant who is true to the "four noble families" (P., *ariyavaṃsa;* Skt., *āryavaṃśa*) (in the Pāli terminology) (1) is content with any robe *(cīvara);* (2) is content with any alms food *(piṇḍapāta);* (3) is content with any place for sitting and lying *(senāsana);* and (4) has pleasure and delight in abandoning and meditation *(pahānārāmo pahānarato bhāvanārāmo bhāvanārato)* (*Dn* 3:224–25 [T.R. and C.R. 1899–1921, 3:217]).[3] Chapters 1 and 5 contained reference to several variations of the set of five practices attributed to Devadatta that similarly give specifications regarding food, apparel, and dwelling. Also mentioned in previous chapters is the set of four *niśraya*s,[4] or "requisites," followed by early forest renunciants; these specify that renunciants are to (1) sleep only at the foot of trees *(vṛkṣamūla);* (2) live only by begging food *(piṇḍapāta);* (3) wear only clothes made from cast-off rags (*pāṃśukūla;* P., *paṃsukūla*); and (4) use as medicine only cow's urine (*pūtimuktabhaiṣajya;* P., *pūtimuttabhesajja*).[5]

The four *niśraya*s, in particular, seem to have played a pivotal role at an early time in Buddhist history. So much is suggested by their frequent mention in the Buddhist texts and by their appearance at a crucial place in the ordination ceremony, as described in the *Mahāvagga* (see Chapter 1). The same is also suggested, according to Frauwallner, by the way in which they appear in the *vinaya*s. Thus, in the *Bhaiṣajyavastu* of the *vinaya* of the Dharmaguptaka and of the Mahīśāsaka, we are told that five monks[6] ask the Buddha what should serve them as food. The Buddha replies that they should eat only food that they have received as alms in their begging bowls. Similarly, in the *Bhaiṣajyavastu* of the *vinaya* of the Dharmaguptaka, five monks ask which medicine they should employ. The Buddha tells them that they should use only cow's urine. Further, in the *Cīvaravastu* of the *vinaya* of the Sarvāstivādins and of the Dharmaguptakas, five monks ask what garb they should use, to which the Buddha responds that they should use only picked-up rags. Finally, in the *Śayanāsanavastu* of the Sarvāstivādins and of the Dharmaguptakas, the five monks ask where it is appropriate for them to live. The Buddha says that they should dwell in forests, caves, the foot of trees, and so on (Frauwallner 1956, 133–34).

Who are these five monks and what is the historical importance of the practices thus enjoined upon them? Frauwallner believes that these five are none other than the original five monks to whom the Buddha first preached the dharma in the Deer Park in Banaras and that the practices are none other than the four *niśraya*s enjoined upon the Buddha's original disciples. Frauwallner sees this interpretation confirmed by the fact that Banaras is mentioned in these accounts, although it is otherwise seldom mentioned in the *Old Skandhaka* (1956, 134–35). Whether or not one accepts the full extent of Frauwallner's interpretation,[7] one can agree with him that the antiquity of these practices is suggested by the particular way in which they are introduced in the *Old Skandhaka.* According to Frauwallner, these questions and answers appear abruptly, with no real introduction and no inherent connection with the flow of the rest of the text, and they disappear with equal suddenness; thus, they appear to be "foreign intrusions." Moreover, the nonmonastic, renunciant life that they imply stands in sharp contrast to the settled, communal context of the *Old Skandhaka,* where the Buddha typically appears, in Frauwallner's words, "in front of the mass of meetings of the most different sorts and of a community organization developed down to the smallest details" (134–35). In Frauwallner's view, these discourses on the requisites attest to a world very different from that of the *Old Skandhaka,* a world essentially of the forest of which there is expression in texts available to the author of the *Old Skandhaka* but in which he himself is not a direct participant.

Another closely related but more detailed code became accepted—with minor variations—as standard in Indian Buddhism. This is the code of the *dhutaguṇas*[8] (ascetic practices; lit., "[good] qualities of shaking off [impurities]"), the twelve (Sanskrit) or thirteen (Pāli) behavioral conventions[9] frequently attributed to the Buddhist renunciants of the forest.[10] These renunciants, then, are typically styled in Sanskrit as *dhutadhara* (holders of the *dhutaguṇas*) or *dhutaguṇin* (those who practice the *dhutaguṇas*) and in Pāli as *dhutavāda* (adhering to the *dhutaguṇas*) or *dhutadhara* (holders of the *dhutaguṇas*). The *dhutaguṇas* are referred to, although not always under this designation, in the early and later Nikāya and Mahāyāna literature, in both *sūtras* and commentaries.[11] In these texts, the *dhutaguṇas* are frequently mentioned by name without an enumeration of the individual practices. We have already seen frequent reference to the *dhutaguṇas* as the primary defining code of the saints of the forest. Thus, Buddha Śākyamuni himself is held to have taught the *dhutaguṇas* to his disciples. Mahākāśyapa is foremost among the *dhutaguṇins*, Piṇḍolabhāradvāja and Upagupta are said to follow the *dhutaguṇas*, the saints of the *Theragāthā* and *Therīgāthā* are associated with the *dhutaguṇas*, and some of the sixteen arhants are shown following practices that imply the *dhutaguṇas*. We further saw that the bodhisattvas of the forest also follow the *dhutaguṇas*: the *Ratnaguṇasaṃcayagāthā* mentions the *dhutaguṇas* in connection with the renunciant bodhisattva and the *Rāṣṭrapāla Sūtra* says that the bodhisattva follows the vehicle of the *dhutaguṇas (dhutayāna)* taught by the Buddha.

The *dhutaguṇas* are also mentioned prominently in other Mahāyāna texts. In the *Pañcaviṃśatisāhasrikāprajñāpāramitā,* for example, the *dhutaguṇas* define the forest life and are inseparably connected with meditation and realization (Conze 1975, 120).[12] In the commentary on this text, the *Mahāprajñāpāramitā Śāstra,* we find the *dhutaguṇas* defining the pure *śīla* of the forest renunciant, providing the basis of meditation that, in turn, leads to wisdom. Thus, the text can say that realization "is the reward of the [*dhutaguṇas*], and the two are related like cause and effect" (Conze 1975, 170, n. 28). The *Mahāprajñāpāramitā Śāstra* also explicitly connects the *dhutaguṇas* with the standardized epithets of the forest renunciant *(araṇyavāsin)*—few desires and contentment with little (Lamotte 1980, 195). The *Samādhirāja Sūtra* similarly connects the *dhutaguṇas* with "pure *śīla*" and says that the renunciant is always to practice them because they provide the basis for meditation (19.23–26). In the *Saddharmapuṇḍarīka Sūtra,* we are told that the *dhutaguṇas* provide the path to realization (wisdom, *prajñā*) and to the acquisition of good qualities *(guṇa).* In this text, a man asks certain sages *(ṛṣi)* how he may acquire these attributes, and they reply, "If you desire that, go and live in the forest *[araṇya]* or dwell in mountain caves *[parvataguhā]* and meditate on the dharma, and you will destroy the *kleśas*. There, relying on the *dhūtaguṇas*, acquire the supernatural powers *[abhijñā]*" (92.12–15).[13] The *Daśabhūmika Sūtra* (66.31–67.1; 98.2) mentions the *dhutaguṇas* as practices possessed by the perfected bodhisattva. The *Pañcaviṃśatisāhasrikāprajñāpāramitā Sūtra* says that one should not abandon the *dhutaguṇas* (Conze 1975, 170) and that irreversible bodhisattvas should take upon themselves the twelve *dhutaguṇas* (Conze 1975, 391). The *dhutaguṇas* are similarly referred to as normative in a variety of other texts, both Nikāya and Mahāyāna, such as the *Mahāvastu* (see Chapter 4); the *Divyāvadāna* (Lamotte 1980, 195, n. 1); the *Kāśyapaparivarta* (36, 91, 126, 139, and 153); the *Śikṣāsamuccaya* (106.16 [BR., 186] and 174.25 [BR., 292]); and the *Pratyutpannabuddhasaṃmukhāvasthitasamādhi Sūtra* (Harrison 1987, 76). The frequent mention of the *dhutaguṇas* in the canonical and extracanonical Buddhist literature suggests the central role that these practices and the forest life they define must have played in the formative periods of Indian Buddhism. Their particular prominence in such a broad selection of Mahāyāna literature does nothing but confirm the impression gained in Chapter 8 of the importance of the forest life in the early days of the great vehicle.

In contrast to this frequent mention of the *dhutaguṇas* in both Mahāyāna *sūtra* and commentarial literature, except for their appearance in texts specifically dealing with forest renunciation, in the classical set of practices or under the term *dhu(ū)taṅga* these practices are hardly mentioned in the Pāli canon (*PTSD* 342). The list appears and is termed *dhūtaṅga* in a rare instance in the relatively late *Parivāra,* shortly to be examined, and in a context that reveals a decidedly ambivalent attitude toward these practices (*V*-p 5:193 [H., 6:310–11]). The Pāli commentarial literature, however, provides a contrast with the canon. Sometime in the early centuries of our era, the *dhutaguṇas* became a popular subject of discussion in texts such as the *Vimuttimagga,* the *Visuddhimagga,* and the *Milindapañha.* Presently, we shall consider some possible reasons for these differences of emphasis in the Pāli canon and commentarial tradition.

The individual ascetic practices conventionally designated by the term *dhutaguṇa* are frequently mentioned, often without the word *dhutaguṇa, dhutaṅga,* or a variant being applied to them, in both the Mahāyāna and Nikāya literature. Sometimes, these practices are referred to individually in the texts. We read in the *vinaya* concerning the rule of three robes (*V*-p 1:295–96 [H., 4:423]); in the *Milindapañha* about *ekāsana* (one-eating) (20 [T.R. 1890–94, 1:32] and 216 [2:9]);[14] in the *Saddharmapuṇḍarīka Sūtra* of the *āraṇyadhuta* (the *dhutaguṇa* of dwelling in the forest) (185.24–27 [Kn., 293]);[15] and in the *Śikṣāsamuccaya* of dwelling in cremation grounds (75:12 [BR., 132]). The *Śikṣāsamuccaya* in fact mentions several individual *dhutaguṇas* (N. Dutt 1930, 319). At other times, the *dhutaguṇas* are listed in groups of one, two, or a few other regulations, as in the *Rāṣṭrapālaparipṛcchā Sūtra* (57.10 [E., 55]), where we are told that three robes, begging food, and not lying down are practices for the worthy renunciant to develop.[16] The *Milindapañha* gives a list of five practices connected with living in the forest, including dwelling at the foot of trees, living in the open air, living near cremation grounds, not lying down, and sleeping on heaps of straw (which is not an item in either Pāli or Mahāyāna lists) (342 [T.R. 1890–94, 2:231]).[17] Similarly, the *Majjhimanikāya* mentions a set of nine practices (3:40–42 [Hn., 3:91–92]). The *Aṅguttaranikāya* enumerates a list of several dozen ascetic conventions, including some later considered legitimately Buddhist and also many others in addition (1:294–96 [WH., 1:272–74]). The many and varied ways in which the members of the *dhutaguṇas* and similar practices are mentioned in the texts suggest that originally the practices composed a fund of ascetic conventions and that, in time, they came to be formed into various groupings with, at last, the classical groupings coming to be regarded as the normative ones.[18]

Two formulations came, as mentioned, to be standard, a twelve-member group in the Mahāyāna and a thirteen-member list in Theravāda tradition. The Mahāyāna list[19] is as follows:

1. *Pāṃś(s)ukūlika,* one who wears the *pāṃśukūla,* or rags taken from a refuse heap (for textual references, see *BHSD* 338)
2. *Traicīvarika,* one who wears the three (monastic) robes (*BHSD* 259)
3. *Nāma(n)tika,* one who wears garments of felt (or wool) (*BHSD* 293)
4. *Paiṇḍapātika* (*piṇḍapātika*), one who lives on alms food (*BHSD* 345)
5. *Aikāsanika (ekāsanika*), one who follows one-eating (eats in one place) (*BHSD* 154)
6. *Khalupaścādbhaktika,* one who does not eat after (the time when one should cease) (*BHSD* 204)
7. *Āraṇyaka (araṇyaka),* one who dwells in the forest (*BHSD* 102)
8. *Vṛkṣamūlika,* one who lives at the foot of a tree (*BHSD* 506)
9. *Ā(a)bhyavakāśika,* one who lives in the open air (*BHSD* 99)
10. *Śmā(a)śānika,* one who lives in cremation grounds (*BHSD* 534–35)
11. *Naiṣadika* (*naiṣadyika*), one who remains in a sitting posture, not lying down (*BHSD* 313)
12. *Yāthāsaṃstarika* (*yathā . . .*), one who accepts any seat that may be offered (*BHSD* 443)

Pāli tradition knows a nearly identical list:[20]

1. *Paṃsukūlika,* one who wears *paṃsukūla,* or rags taken from a refuse heap (for textual references, see *PTSD* 378–79)
2. *Tecīvarika,* one who wears the three (monastic) robes (*PTSD* 306)
3. *Piṇḍapātika,* one who lives on alms food (*PTSD* 458)
4. *Sapadānacārika,* one who carries out uninterrupted alms-seeking (*PTSD* 679)
5. *Ekāsanika,* one who follows one-eating (eats in one place) (*PTSD* 159)[21]
6. *Pattapiṇḍika,* one who eats only measured food (eating from one bowl only) (*PTSD* 406)
7. *Khalupacchābhatika,* one who does not eat after (the time when one should cease) (*PTSD* 235)
8. *Āraññaka* (*araññaka*), one who dwells in the forest (*PTSD* 107)
9. *Rukkhamūlika,* one who lives at the foot of a tree (*PTSD* 571–72)
10. *Abbhokāsika,* one who lives in the open air (*PTSD* 61)
11. *Sosānika,* one who lives in cremation grounds (*PTSD* 726)

12. *Yathāsanthatika,* one who accepts any seat that may be offered (*PTSD* 550)
13. *Nesajjika,* one who remains in a sitting posture, not lying down (*PTSD* 378)

The Pāli list and the Mahāyāna list differ in only very minor respects. The Pāli list omits Mahāyāna item 3—wearing garments of felt or wool—while including two rules not in the Mahāyāna list concerning the taking of food, one requiring "regular alms round" (item 4), the other insisting on "measured food" (item 6). The other items are the same, including even the order in which they are listed, except that the last two are reversed in the two groupings.

Two Pāli Depictions of the *Dhutaguṇas*

Upatissa on the Dhutaguṇa*s*

An early discussion of the *dhutaguṇa*s is found in the third, or *dhuta*, chapter of the *Vimuttimagga,* a Pāli composition by Upatissa, who in Bapat's view lived in south India in the first or second century C.E. (Bapat 1964, xvii).[22] The text was later accepted by the Abhayagiri sect.[23] Upatissa's text exists in Chinese translation,[24] and the *dhuta* chapter survives in a Tibetan version (Skt. title, *Dhutaguṇa-nirdeśa*), which shows some differences when compared with its counterpart in Chinese.[25] The *Vimuttimagga* as a whole generally reflects its monastic context, and the lifestyle that it prescribes for renunciants is defined by the *prātimokṣa* and classical *vinaya* (Eh., 16, 18, 24). Nevertheless, the *dhuta* chapter of the text is important because part of it provides us with a glimpse of life in the forest, as seen within its own frame of reference and not from the viewpoint of the monastic commentators.

The *dhuta* chapter, as we have it, contains two sections that appear to reflect different time periods and contexts. The bulk of the chapter contains a description of thirteen *dhutaguṇa*s, much as they must have been practiced by forest renunciants. The practices described in this section are rigorous, the renunciants following them have little if any demonstrable connection to monastic life, and the virtues of the life in the forest are extolled. A second, relatively small section occurs at the end of the chapter, as a commentary on what precedes it; in this section the settled monastery and the monastic order are mentioned frequently. Here a list of exceptions to each rule is appended, and these exceptions tend drastically to modify the rules to which they refer and generally to cancel out their rigor.[26] Thus, a rule (item 1) says the renunciant must wear "dirt rags" that are not given by the laity and that one fails to observe this rule if one accepts robes given by the laity (Eh., 28–29). The exception given at the end of the chapter, however, says that, if expedient, the renunciant may receive robes from the laity (34). The other exceptions follow suit.[27]

In the earlier and by far larger main section of Upatissa's chapter on the *dhutaguṇa*s, the author tells us that the thirteen *dhutaguṇa*s are practiced as supports for meditation. He further emphasizes the solitary, free, and meditative life made possible by the *dhutaguṇa*s. The *dhutaguṇas* lead specifically to a life of freedom from dependence on others, one that is conducive to meditation and promotes inner development. Upatissa continues that the *dhutaguṇa*s may be divided into four groups: the first two connected with robes; the next five with alms; the next five with dwelling place; and the last one with energy (Eh., 27).

Two practices connected with robes

1. DIRT RAGS *(paṃsukūlika).* "How does one undertake to observe (the austerity of) 'dirt-rags'? One sees the fault of asking householders for robes and the merit of 'dirt-rags' (and undertakes thus): 'I refuse the offerings of householders and observe (the austerity of) "dirt-rags." ' " Thus, the renunciant may wear rags that are either made out of cast-off (ownerless) scraps of cloth found in a cremation ground, dirt heap, or street, or material that has been thrown away by others. The benefits of this practice are that "one does not depend on others" and thus engages in a happy and independent life (Eh., 28–29). The Tibetan version, the *Dhutaguṇanirdeśa,* noting that this practice is identified with the first of the four traditional *niśraya*s, comments that "dirt rags" is consonant with the best *niśraya.* Also, when one practices it, one will elicit faith from others (Bp., 11).

2. THE THREE ROBES *(tecīvarika).* "How does one undertake to observe (the austerity of) 'three robes'? One immediately gives up extra robes. Knowing the fault of keeping (extra robes) and seeing the benefits of the observance of 'three robes,' (one undertakes thus): 'I refuse extra robes from today and observe (the austerity of) "three robes." ' " Thus one is to have only three robes—the shoulder cloak, the upper garment, and the waist cloth—and refuses a fourth robe. The benefits of this practice are that one is free of the hoarding of what is unnecessary and thus free to wander at will, "as a bird on the wing that does not yearn for what it leaves behind." Through this practice, one will also get a following of worthy lay devotees (Eh., 29).

Five practices connected with alms

3. BEGGED FOOD *(piṇḍapātika).* "How does one undertake to observe (the austerity of) 'begged food'? If a *bhikkhu* accepts an invitation, he[28] interrupts his activities and is not at ease. One sees these drawbacks and the merits of the observance of 'begged food' (and undertakes thus): 'I refuse invitations from today and observe (the austerity of) "begged food." ' " Thus, one does not accept invitations for meals from the laity but gains alms only by begging. The benefits of this practice are that one does not have one's own meditation interrupted by having to fulfill obligations to the laity, nor does one have to be any particular place at any time and "is free to go or stay according to one's wishes." Moreover, one can benefit others impartially, without attachment to any quarter. Through this, one will get a following of good lay donors (Eh., 30). The Tibetan version again notes that this practice is identified with the second of the traditional set of four *niśraya*s. It is further remarked that this practice enables one to avoid being dependent on others (Bp., 21).

4. REGULAR ALMS ROUND *(sapadānacārika).* "How does one undertake to observe (the austerity of) 'regular alms-round'? When a *bhikkhu* is able to obtain

tasty food from any house by making a 'regular alms-round,' he does not go again (in that direction). If he goes again, it is an ordinary alms round [as in 3]. If there is a doubtful place he avoids it. One sees these faults (of going again, etc.) and the benefits of the observance of 'regular alms-round' (and undertakes thus): 'I abandon the irregular alms-round from today and observe (the austerity of) "regular alms-round." ' " Thus, the renunciant begs alms going from house to house, not going particularly to one house and not skipping other houses. He simply takes the houses in order as they come, not preferring one over the other: "When a renunciant enters a village for alms, he begs in regular order from the last house backwards. How does one fail? Skipped begging." The benefits of this practice are that one thinks of all beings equally, does not call on householders and does not look for invitations from householders, and destroys the fault of hankering. One is also able to benefit all beings equally, and one gains a following of good lay donors (Eh., 30). The Tibetan version mentions that one who has abandoned clinging to any family avoids the dangers that derive from visits to a family and enjoys freedom from attachment to people. Through this, one has "compassion in one's heart" for beings (Bp., 25).

5. ONE-EATING *(ekāsanika).* "How does one undertake to observe (the austerity of) 'one-eating'? Eating in two places, eating frequently, taking food frequently, washing the bowl frequently—the opposite of these is 'one eating.' . . . One sees the faults (of eating in two places, etc.) and the merits of the observance of 'one-eating' (and undertakes thus): 'I abandon eating at two places from today and observe (the austerity of) "one eating." ' " After the renunciant washes his bowl or intends that his meal is finished, he cannot eat again. The benefits of this practice are that it undermines greed, and one lives free and happy regarding one's livelihood (Eh., 31). The Tibetan version comments that one-eating has the advantage of minimal interference with one's own activities *(rang.gi.las)* (Bp., 29).

6. MEASURED FOOD *(pattapiṇḍika).* "How does one undertake to observe (the austerity of) 'measured food'? If a *bhikkhu* drinks and eats too much, he increases sleepiness, always hankers for much food, and sets no limit to his appetite. One sees these faults and the merits of the observance of 'measured food' (and undertakes thus): 'From today, I will take food without greed, and observe (the austerity of) "measured food." ' " Thus, one takes a measured amount of food in light of the amount that appropriately fulfills one's needs. One does not exceed this limit. The benefits of this practice are that "one does not eat for the belly's sake" and thus avoids fatigue, disease, and rigidity (Eh., 31).

7. NO FOOD AFTER TIME *(khalupacchābhatika).* "How does one undertake to observe (the austerity of) 'no food after time'? One abandons expectation and avoids extra food. One knows these faults (expectation, etc.) and sees the benefits of the observance of 'no food after time' (and undertakes thus): 'I abandon extra food from today and observe (the austerity of) "no food after time." ' " Thus, the renunciant eats only once and does not have another meal. The benefits of this practice are that "one abandons greed, and experiences the joy of self-restraint. One protects the body, and avoids taking food in advance, does not hanker, does not ask others for things, does not follow his inclinations" (Eh., 32). The Tibetan

version comments that through this practice, one can be easily supported and there is "no dependence on others" (Bp., 39).

Five practices connected with residence

8. DWELLING IN THE FOREST *(āraññaka)*. "How does one undertake (the austerity of) 'dwelling in the forest'? When the village is crowded, one's mind is touched by the five objects of sense and saturated with the desire for pleasure. When one dwells in a crowded place, one is disturbed by people going and coming. One sees these faults and the merits of the observance of 'dwelling in the forest' (and undertakes thus): 'I abandon dwelling in the village from today and observe (the austerity of) "dwelling in the forest." ' " Thus, the renunciant dwells in solitude, in the forest. The benefits of this practice are that dwelling in the forest, one will not be disturbed by people coming and going. "One does not wish to become worldly, and wishes to gain tranquility. One dwells in solitude, speaks little and meditates, according to one's bent of mind" (Eh., 32–33). About the advantages of this practice, the Tibetan version remarks on the beauties of nature and says that one will gain the assistance of the gods in the form of admonitions. In addition, one will experience the joy of solitude and find it conducive to meditation owing to its being so quiet.[29]

9. DWELLING UNDER A TREE *(rukkhamūlika)*. "How does one undertake to observe (the austerity of) 'dwelling under a tree'? One avoids roofed places. One does not keep animals. One does not build or long for (roofed places). One does not search (for roofed places). One sees the faults (of dwelling in roofed places) and the merits of the observance of '(dwelling) under a tree' (and undertakes thus): 'I abandon roofed places from today and observe (the austerity of) "dwelling under a tree." ' " Thus, the renunciant dwells under a tree. The benefits of this practice are that one can dwell in a place in accordance with one's wishes, one is not bound to interaction with the world, one is freed from work, "one dwells with the gods, cuts down resentment [of others] due to residence, and is free from attachment" (Eh., 33). The Tibetan version again remarks on the identity of this practice with the third of the traditional set of four "reliances," thus having the advantage of "consonance with the best *niśraya*" (Bp., 47).

10. DWELLING IN THE OPEN AIR *(abbhokāsika)*. "How does one undertake to observe (the austerity of) 'dwelling in the open air'? One does not desire to dwell in roofed places, under trees, and in places where animals and goods are kept. One sees the faults of these, and the benefits of 'dwelling in the open air' (and undertakes thus): 'I avoid unpleasant places from today and observe (the austerity of) "dwelling in the open air." ' " Thus, the renunciant avoids roofed places and the shelter of trees. The benefits of this practice include the fact that "one goes whithersoever one wills, like a forest-deer and is not attached to any particular place" (Eh., 33–34). The Tibetan version comments that one can go in all the four directions and does not have dependence on anything (Bp., 51).

11. DWELLING IN THE CREMATION GROUNDS *(sosānika)*. "How does one undertake to observe (the austerity of) 'dwelling in cremation grounds'?[30] One who dwells in other places becomes careless and does not fear wrongdoing. One

sees the faults of these and the merits of 'dwelling in cremation grounds' (and undertakes thus): 'I avoid other places from today and observe (the austerity of) "dwelling in cremation grounds." ' " Thus, the renunciant dwells in cremation grounds, without hut or bed, with his back to the wind, without sleeping. He is not to eat the flesh of animals or of fish or certain other foods. If where he is meditating there is too much weeping and wailing and smoke and fire, it is recommended that he move to a quieter place. The benefits of this practice are that "one understands the feeling of the time of death. One perceives that all is impure. One acquires the homage of non-humans. One does not cause heedlessness to arise, overcomes passion, and is much detached. One does not fear what common folk dread. One contemplates on the emptiness of the body and is able to reject the thought of permanence" (Eh., 34). The Tibetan version emphasizes that this practice wins the respect of gods and humans alike. The advantages of this practice include "being highly revered by men" and "being highly revered by supernatural beings" (Bp., 55).[31]

12. ANY CHANCED-UPON PLACE *(yathāsanthatika).* "How does one observe (the austerity of) 'any chanced-upon place'? One does not like the place which men want greedily. One is not troubled when others wish him to leave any place. One sees these faults (greed for place, etc.) and the merits of the observance of 'any chanced-upon place' (and undertakes thus): 'I abandon the greed for residence and observe (the austerity of) "any chanced-upon place." ' " Thus, the renunciant renounces the longing that depends on dwelling. The benefits of this practice are that one is satisfied with any place, can leave comforts behind, and "dwells with a heart of compassion" (Eh., 35).

One practice connected with energy

13. ALWAYS SITTING AND NOT LYING DOWN *(nesajjika).* "How does one undertake to observe (the austerity of) 'always sitting and not lying down'? One sees the faults of sleeping and idling in the dwelling place and the benefits of 'always sitting and not lying down' (and undertakes thus): 'I abandon sleeping and lying down from today and observe (the austerity of) "always sitting and not lying down." ' " Thus, the renunciant abandons sleep and does not lie down. The benefits of this practice are that one avoids the place where laziness arises and removes concern for the body. In addition, one diminishes torpor, is always at peace, and becomes fit for the practice of meditation (Eh., 35). The Tibetan version remarks on the advantages of this practice, that one takes only a little sleep and that this practice is conducive to yoga (Bp., 63).[32]

The commentarial section of the text follows, with the list of exceptions. This concludes with various additional remarks, including mention of time specifications for the observance of dwelling under a tree, in the open, and in the cremation grounds: "How many seasons are there for the observance of austerities? Eight months are the period for [these] three austerities. . . . The Buddha has permitted dwelling in roofed places in the rainy season" (Eh., 38; cf. Bp., 81).

The *dhutaguṇas*, as presented in the main section of the *dhuta* chapter of Upatissa's text, represent an essentially meditative and ascetic ideal of forest renunciation. The very raison d'être of the various *dhutaguṇa*s is clearly to make the reclusive, solitary, meditative life possible. Renunciants wear certain garments to minimize their possessions and to eliminate, as much as possible, their contact with and dependence upon the laity.[33] They follow certain patterns of begging food so as to undercut their own psychological dependence on the laity, to eliminate special relationships with particular laity, and to keep obligations to them and thus interruptions to meditation practice to a minimum. Renunciants live in certain places that are isolated and quiet, where they may practice meditation in an undistracted way.[34] Apart from the specific lifestyle enjoined by the text, one finds other themes connected with the Buddhist saints, with which we have become familiar in previous chapters. Thus, these practices are said to help one to develop impartiality toward all and, through this, to enable compassion to arise for beings. In addition, these practices will lead others to take faith in one, such that one will be venerated by gods and humans, and will gain a following of virtuous persons.

Buddhaghosa's Treatment of the Dhutaguṇas *in the* Visuddhimagga

As noted in Chapter 1, already in the *Mahāvagga,* the four *niśraya*s no longer define the normative way of life of the Buddhist renunciant. And so, as we have also seen, the texts take an ambivalent attitude toward them. On the one hand, something of the original normativity of these "reliances" is suggested in the ordination ceremony as described in the *Mahāvagga:* there the ordinand is reminded of the four *niśraya*s lest he look upon his new status as necessarily implying a comfortable and secure lifestyle. On the other hand, in the *Mahāvagga,* the *niśraya*s are not accepted at face value: the Buddha allows various exceptions that end up by rendering them inoperative. As noted, this handling of the *niśraya*s permitted the retention of the theoretical ideal while subordinating it to the norm of settled monastic life.[35]

This same kind of ambivalence toward forest renunciation and its way of life is found expressed in the *vinaya,* in the *Parivāra,* this time in terms of the thirteen *dhutaguṇa*s. The Pāli text begins by mentioning five types of reasons for following the practice of dwelling in the forest:

1. "One is a forest-dweller from stupidity, from confusion."
2. "One of evil desires, filled with covetousness, is a forest-dweller."
3. "One is a forest-dweller from madness, from a deranged mind."
4. "One is a forest-dweller at the thought, 'It is praised by Buddhas and disciples of Buddhas.' "
5. "One is a forest-dweller because he is of few wishes, because of contentment, because of subduedness, because of aloofness, because this is of good avail." (*V*-p 5:131 [H., 6:210–11])

The text then similarly lists these five reasons in relation to the other members of the *dhutaguṇa* grouping; there are "five alms-food-eaters, five refuse-rag-wearers, five tree-root-dwellers, five charnel-ground-dwellers, five open-air-dwellers, five three-robe-wearers, five house-to-house-seekers," and so on (*V*-p 5:131 [H., 6:210–11]).[36] In this passage, on the one hand, the *Parivāra* acknowledges the high stature of the *dhutaguṇas* and those who practice them and that one may be a *dhutaguṇin* out of worthy motives. On the other, it wants to affirm that one may be following the *dhutaguṇas* for invalid reasons, because one is stupid or confused, overcome by evil desire, or insane. It is interesting that the deplorable reasons are listed first, suggesting that they were uppermost in the mind of the author, who seems more than ready to attribute one or another of these motives to some forest renunciants and to condemn them.[37]

This discussion of the *dhutaguṇas* in the *Parivāra* is immediately followed by a second one, which restricts those who may be considered legitimate forest renunciants. "A man who is possessed of five qualities should not live independently: if he does not know the Observance, if he does not know the (formal) acts for Observance, if he does not know the Pātimokkha, if he does not know the recital of the Pātimokkha, if it is less than five years (since his ordination). A monk who is possessed of five qualities may live independently: if he knows the Observance . . . if it is five years or more than five years (since his ordination)" (*V*-p 5:131 [H., 6:210–11]). In other words, the only legitimate forest renunciant is one who is a fully ordained monk of at least five years' standing and who is thoroughly knowledgeable and accomplished in monastic discipline. In these two passages, then, the *Parivāra* demeans and diminishes the life of forest renunciation by calling into question the motives of those who would pursue it and by denying the legitimacy of any following it who are not fully ordained monastics in good standing.

The *Milindapañha* devotes chapter 9 to a discussion of the *dhutaguṇas* (348–62 [T.R. 1890–94, 2:244–74]). This Pāli text exhibits a similar ambivalence to forest renunciation and the *dhutaguṇas*. We are told that the *dhutaguṇas* are difficult but uniquely worthy practices. All the buddhas have longed for them and held them dear (351 [2:251]). Through their practice, one fully renounces the world and is joyful in solitude, one is tamed and purified, one transcends all fear, one attains realization, one generates compassion for others, one gains the magical powers, and one is honored by gods and humans alike (351–52 [2:251–54] and 358–59 [2:264–65]). So crucial are the *dhutaguṇas* that "there is no perception of the truth for those not purified by the practice of the vows *[dhutaguṇa]*" (353 [2:255]), and "there is no realization of arhatship . . . in one single life, without a previous keeping of the vows" (353 [2:254]). At the same time, however, the *Milindapañha* imposes an important restriction on the practice of the *dhutaguṇas* similar to that imposed by the *Parivāra:* they may be practiced only by one who is qualified—that is, only one "whose conduct is consistent with membership in the order . . . who has entered the order from belief (in the doctrine)" (358–59 [2:264–65]). Others, "whose conduct is inconsistent (with membership in the order), unworthy of it, inappropriate to it—whosoever being such shall take upon himself the *[dhutaguṇa],* he shall incur a twofold punishment" (357 [2:263]). On the one hand, "in this world, he shall receive disgrace, and scorn, and blame, and ridicule, and suspension, and excommunication, and expulsion, and he shall be outcast, rejected, dismissed." On the other hand, "in his next life, he shall suffer torment in the great Avīci [hell]" (357–58 [2:261–64]), a remark followed by a list of tortures that the errant forest renunciant will undergo in his future hellish rebirth.[38]

Like the *Parivāra,* then, the *Milindapañha* says that only monastics, and among these only those deemed worthy, are permitted to practice the *dhutaguṇa*s without incurring negative consequences. For the *Milindapañha,* only a select few have the right to practice them, and the text explicitly mentions only virtuous members of the monastic order as qualified. It seems, moreover, that they may retire to the forest only when their obligations to the monastic order are fully in order (that is, they remain in good standing). In addition, membership in good standing in the order is the only criterion mentioned for adjudging one's worthiness. It may be noted how easily this restriction can provide a basis for the repudiation of Buddhist renunciants following the *dhutaguṇa*s who may not be *prātimokṣa*-following *bhikṣu*s at all or who are otherwise deemed unfit according to canons of settled monasticism. Here, the process of monasticization is thorough: not only are the ascetic practices integrated into the normative form of settled monasticism, but their legitimate existence in a nonmonastic form is not even admitted.

This process of the monasticization of the *dhutaguṇa*s reaches a climax in Buddhaghosa's *dhutaguṇa* chapter of the *Visuddhimagga.* At first glance, the treatments of the *dhutaguṇa*s in the *Visuddhimagga* and the *Vimuttimagga* are very similar.[39] Not only are the same thirteen *dhutaguṇa*s mentioned in the same order by each author, but the descriptions given of each, the benefits to be obtained, and the exceptions are sometimes nearly the same. Nevertheless, there are some important differences between the presentations in the two texts. Most important, as we have seen, the body of the treatment of the thirteen *dhutaguṇa*s in the *Vimuttimagga* reflects a context of forest renunciation: the various exceptions, which set the *dhutaguṇa*s within a monastic context, appear added as an afterthought, as a kind of appendix to the main presentation of the *dhutaguṇa*s.

In contrast, in treating these same practices in the *Visuddhimagga,* Buddhaghosa is clearly the proficient monastic scholar writing for scholastically trained monks who live in settled monasteries. In his treatment, the exceptions are worked into the very core of his presentation, and it is clear that every section of his discussion takes entirely for granted from the beginning the monastic context of the *dhutaguṇa*s. For Buddhaghosa, the *dhutaguṇa*s, if put into practice at all, are clearly exceptions to the monastic norm and are to be carried out in the context of monastic life in temporary and usually only partial separation from its normal routines. The image of the monastery appears throughout Buddhaghosa's treatment, and it is always in relation to the monastery and to the exigencies of monastic life that the various *dhutaguṇa*s are explained. The settled monastic ambiance of Buddhaghosa may be brought into focus by considering the ways in which he defines the practices, the exceptions he allows, and his practice of presenting each *dhutaguṇa* in three grades of rigor—strict, medium, and mild. Buddhaghosa's initial definition of each *dhutaguṇa* and its strict grade usually most closely approximate the treatment in Upatissa's main section, and his exceptions and his medium and mild grades represent a substantial softening and monasticizing of the ideal. Buddhaghosa's division into three grades is particularly interesting because of the dual function it performs. On the one hand, the medium and mild grades give monastics great latitude, allowing them to be considered as followers of the *dhutaguṇas*, all the while remaining close to the concerns and ways of settled monastic life and in minimal separation from the monastery. On the other hand, by retaining the category of the strict grade within the definition, even if this grade were rarely followed, some of the charisma attaching to the *dhutaguṇas* as practiced by true forest renunciants could be retained. Let us consider as examples three *dhutaguṇas*, one from each of Upatissa's main categories of robes, food, and dwelling.

In the first *dhutaguṇa* (*Vsm* 62–64 [N., 63–65]), that of wearing only cast-off rags, the strict grade is very similar to Upatissa's rendition of the rule. However, in the medium grade, one may take a robe left by the laity for an unspecified monk; in the mild grade, one may accept a robe from another monk who has had the robe left at his feet by a layperson. Buddhaghosa mentions many of the same benefits as Upatissa (''he is independent of others,'' and so on), but in this context there are so many loopholes that allow one to continue to receive donations from laypeople that it is clear that in its modified forms the rigor of the rule has been canceled out. With such economic dependence, how much real independence of others could the renunciants really have enjoyed? Similarly, in the alms-food eater's practice, Buddhaghosa allows this general exception: ''If instead of saying 'take a meal given to the Order' [which is forbidden under this rule], (meals) are given saying, 'The Order is taking alms in our house; you may take alms too,' it is allowable to consent. Tickets from the Order that are not for actual food, and also a meal cooked in a monastery, are allowable as well'' (66–67 [66–67]). After this, the three grades are once again given. Under the strict practice, one may take alms brought to the refectory in the monastery and given there. Under the medium, one may sit and wait for food to be brought to him there. Under the mild, one ''consents to alms [being brought] on the next day and on the day after.'' In other words, one can remain at the monastery and even receive alms brought day after day and still fulfill this *dhutaguṇa*. As in the cases of the other *dhutaguṇas*, so here Buddhaghosa recites the ''benefits'' of the practice: ''His existence is independent of others,'' but again in this context this benefit is hard to take seriously (66–67 [66–67]).[40]

In the third example, Buddhaghosa says that the tree dweller must avoid certain types of trees, including those in the middle of a monastery! However, ''he can choose a tree standing on the outskirts of a monastery'' (*Vsm* 74 [N., 74]). This practice also has three grades. According to the strict one, a monk is not allowed to have others tidy up the area around the tree that he has chosen. In the medium, he can ask those who come along to fix up his abode. ''The mild one can take up residence there after summoning monastery attendants and novices and getting them to clear it up, level it, strew sand and make a fence round with a gate fixed in it'' (74 [74]).

As one might expect, the essentially monastic setting of these three *dhutaguṇas* is repeated in the other practices. In the house-to-house seeker's practice, there are also three grades. In the strict grade, the monk does not take food brought to the refectory. In the medium one, he may take food brought to the monastery, but he may not wait for it there. In the mild one, he may wait at the monastery for the arrival of food (*Vsm* 68–69 [N., 68–69]). In the forest dweller's practice, in the strict grade, even if one has been to the monastery, by the next sun up he must be back in the forest. In the medium grade, he may spend the rainy season in the village. In the mild one, he may live in the village in the winter months too (73 [73]).

It is not only Buddhaghosa's explicit formulations of the *dhutaguṇa*s that exhibit a clear monastic setting but also his style and idiom of presention and exposition. Ehara, Soma Thera, and Kheminda Thera, in the introduction to their translation of the *Vimuttimagga,* pertinently observe that the *Visuddhimagga* "is more comprehensive than the *Vimuttimagga* and in every sense more scholarly, with a wealth of material drawn from every imaginable source" (Eh., xliv). A comparison of the *dhutaguṇa* chapters of the two texts certainly confirms this judgment. Buddhaghosa clearly comes at the topic of the *dhutaguṇa*s as, above all, a monastic scholar. He is interested in definitions, distinctions, and conceptual clarifications. In his formulation of the first *dhutaguṇa,* for example, Buddhaghosa gives a description similar to—although much longer than—Upatissa's, of where one may legitimately obtain a robe. Then Buddhaghosa takes the key words in this description and subjects each of them to definition, in the style of scholarly commentary on a *sūtra.* This section, which consists of nineteen definitions, is followed by a section of exceptions and then a discussion of the three grades (*Vsm* 62–63 [N., 63–64]). The vocabulary of Buddhaghosa's chapter is also laced with and presupposes a knowledge of scholastic *abhidharma* terminology. For example, Buddhaghosa, quoting tradition, remarks that "he who does the undertaking is a person. That whereby he does the undertaking is states of consciousness and conscious-concomitants. The volition of the act of undertaking is the ascetic practice. What it rejects is the instance. All have the function of eliminating cupidity, and they manifest themselves with the production of non-cupidity. For their proximate cause they have the noble states consisting of fewness of wishes, and so on" (61 [62]). Thus, Buddhaghosa presents a version of the *dhutaguṇa*s that, although agreeing in many particulars with that given in the main body of Upatissa's text, clearly represents a different sort of tradition in many ways. Whereas the main discussion in the *Vimuttimagga* appears as an expression of a wandering and solitary meditative way of life, Buddhaghosa's version is an expression of the life and concerns of the settled monastery.

Some Other Groups of *Dhutaguṇa*s

Upatissa and Buddhaghosa agree on the number, order, and content of the thirteenfold list of *dhutaguṇa*s. However, as we have seen, the Mahāyāna knows a twelvefold list that differs in some respects from the Theravādin list, omitting the practices of moving in succession for food and of measured food and including a practice of wearing woolen or felt cloth. The latter practice is probably connected with the climate of the regions to which certain renunciants following the *dhutaguṇa*s went. Bapat remarks, "The monks living in the cold regions of the Himalayas, Tibet and China, probably thought it necessary to permit the use of a woolen cloth on account of extreme cold in those regions'' (Bp., xxi–xxii; see also Conze 1959, 307). Other texts present other lists of *dhutaguṇas*. The Sanskrit *Dharmasaṃgraha,* for example, contains the same twelve members as the *Mahāvyutpatti,* enumerated earlier in this chapter,[41] but presents these in an entirely different order (*Dhs* 13).[42] The *Pañcaviṃśatisāhasrikāprajñāpāramitā* gives a twelvefold list that is the same as the standard Theravādin list except for its omission of measured food (Conze 1975, 338). As mentioned, the Pāli canon gives a ninefold list of *dhutaguṇas*, including *Vimuttimagga* items 1, 3, and 7 to 13 (*Mn* 3:40–42 [Hn., 3:91–92]). Bapat mentions yet another twelvefold list found in the Chinese version of the *Dvādaśadhuta Sūtra* (T. 783), which follows the Theravādin version but omits ''any chanced-upon place'' (Bp., xxii). In addition to fairly minor variations in the *dhutaguṇas* such as these, other lists show greater variation, and it is to two of these that we now turn.

Dhutaguṇa*s in the* Theragāthā

A group of nineteen ascetic conventions, closely resembling the classical list of the thirteen *dhutaguṇas*, is given in the *Theragāthā* 842–65. However, in the text, the group is not connected with the term *dhuta*. In all nineteen verses, the ascetic practice is followed by the same refrain: ''Persevering, delighting in whatever scraps come into his alms bowl, Bhaddiya, son of Godhā, meditates without grasping.'' In the *Theragāthā,* these practices are listed in an apparently random order, with rules relating to food, robes, and habitation intermingled. However, to facilitate analysis, practices will be organized in groups, according to the categories of the *dhutaguṇas*. Each item in the list is followed by the verse number in the text (843, etc.) and by its place in the order of nineteen (1, etc.).

Introduction

1. ''Now fortunate, persevering, delighting in whatever scraps come into his alms-bowl, Bhaddiya, son of Godhā, meditates without grasping.'' (verse 843, item 1 in list)

Food

2. ''Living on alms-food *[piṇḍapātin]*, persevering, delighting in whatever scraps come into his alms-bowl, Bhaddiya, son of Godhā, meditates without grasping.'' (845, 3)

3. ''Going on a begging round of every house without exception *[sapadānacārin]*, persevering. . . .'' (847, 5)

4. ''Eating one bowlful only *[pattapiṇḍin]*, persevering. . . .'' (849, 7)

5. ''Never eating after time *[khalupacchābhattin]*, persevering. . . .'' (850, 8)

Apparel

6. ''Wearing rags *[paṃsukūlin]*, persevering. . . .'' (844, 2)

7. ''Wearing the triple robe *[tecīvarin]*, persevering. . . .'' (846, 4)

Dwelling

8. "Living in the forest *[āraññika]*, persevering. . . ." (851, 9)
9. "Living at the foot of a tree *[rukkhamūlika]*, persevering. . . ." (852, 10)
10. "Living in the open air *[abbhokāsin]*, persevering. . . ." (853, 11)
11. "Living in a [cremation ground] *[sosānika]*, persevering. . . ." (854, 12)
12. "Accepting whatever seat is offered *[yathāsanthatika]*, persevering. . . ." (855, 13)

Solitude

13. "Sitting alone *[ekāsanin]*, persevering. . . ." (848, 6)[43]
14. "Secluded *[pavivitta]*, persevering. . . ." (859, 17)
15. "Not living in company *[asaṃsaṭṭha]*, persevering. . . ." (960, 18)

Meditation

16. "Remaining in a sitting position *[nesajjika]*, persevering. . . ." (856, 14)
17. "Putting forth energy *[āraddhaviriya]*, persevering. . . ." (861, 19)

Attitude

18. "Desiring little *[appiccha]*, persevering. . . ." (857, 15)
19. "Satisfied *[santuṭṭha]*, persevering. . . ." (858, 16)

In verses 862 to 865, the song concludes with a brief biographical statement.[44] As we see by the rules themselves and by the song's conclusion, the context of this group is clearly the life of forest renunciation. Consonant with this setting, in each verse, the particular item is specifically related to the basic goal of the forest life—meditation—which it serves to support. A comparison of the specific rules with those of Upatissa is instructive:

Theragāthā	Upatissa
1 (introduction)	—
2	3
3	4
4	6
5	7
6	1
7	2
8	8
9	9
10	10
11	11
12	12
13	5 (but different interpretation
14	—

Theragāthā	Upatissa
15	—
16	13
17	—
18	—
19	—

1. Upatissa's rules are all concrete modes of behavior, whereas the *Theragāthā* group represents a mixture of concrete practices and attitudes to be maintained.

2. All Upatissa's rules are represented in the *Theragāthā* group, except that in the *Theragāthā, ekāsanin* seems to refer to solitary dwelling, whereas in Upatissa's list *ekāsanika* is taken to mean "one eating."[45] This and point 1 suggest that, in relation to the *Theragāthā* group, Upatissa's list represents a reduction and a concretizing.

3. Not including the introduction, the *Theragāthā* list contains five items not mentioned in the conventional list of the *dhutaguṇa*s and one interpreted differently. Three of these six differences have to do with solitude (13, 14, 15), two have to do with an attitude of acceptance of poverty (18, 19), and one has to do with exertion (17), probably in relation to meditation.[46] This further suggests that Upatissa's list is a reduction and concretizing in relation to the *Theragāthā* list.

4. The *Theragāthā* passage clearly represents a listing of traditional ascetic practices. This is revealed by the stereotypical nature of the list: each member is followed by the same stock refrain, "persevering, delighting in whatever scraps. . . ." In addition, each of these practices is given with what appears to be a standard technical term. This is suggested by the fact that the terms all appear frequently in designating forest renunciants and also by the fact that a number of them, including the more attitudinal items on the list, are used even though they do not fit the meter and throw off the *pāda*s.[47]

5. The *Theragāthā* group appears not to betray the standardizing influence that we sense behind the classical set of *dhutaguṇa*s for three reasons: first, its components are given in no particular order; second, there is an intermixing of concrete behavioral conventions with more attitudinal ones; and third, there appear to be duplications ("sitting alone," "solitude," and so on).

Dhutaguṇa*s in the* Aṣṭasāhasrikāprajñāpāramitā Sūtra

As we have seen, the *dhutaguṇa*s were evidently important in the Mahāyāna from an early time. In this context, particularly interesting is chapter 21 of the *Aṣṭasāhasrikāprajñāpāramitā Sūtra,* which refers to a total of seventeen ascetic practices, explicitly designated by the term *dhutaguṇa,* engaged in by the bodhisattva, which closely resemble but are not quite the same as the classical list of *dhutaguṇa*s of Upatissa (*Asp* 192 [Cz., 231]). In the text these various ascetic rules are not systematized by category but, as in the case of the *Theragāthā* group, are given in an apparently random fashion.[48] Again for facility of analysis, the following summary presents them by category, indicating their original position in the list by number:[49]

Food

1. Begging food *(piṇḍapātika)* (2)
2. Never eating any food after times *(khalupaścādbhaktika)* (4)
3. Eating one's meal in one sitting *(ekāsanika)* (5)[50]

Apparel

4. Wearing clothes made of rags taken from a dust heap *(paṃsukūlika)* (3)
5. Possessing no more than three robes *(traicīvarika)* (7)
6. Wearing a garment made of felt or wool (*nāmantika* [*BHSD* 293]) (12)

Dwelling

7. Dwelling in the forest *(āraṇyaka)* (1)
8. Sleeping at night wherever one may happen to be *(yāthāsaṃstarika)* (6)
9. Living in and frequenting cemeteries *(śmaśānika)* (8)
10. Dwelling at the foot of a tree *(vṛkṣamūlika)* (9)
11. Living in an open, unsheltered place *(abhyavakāśika)* (11)

Solitude

12. Dwelling alone *(pravivikta)* (15)[51]

Meditation

13. Even in one's sleep, remaining in a sitting posture *(naiṣadyika)* (10)

Speech

14. Being of soft or gentle speech *(mṛdubhāṣin)* (17)

Attitude

15. Having few wishes *(alpeccha;* P., *appiccha)* (13)
16. Easily contented *(saṃtuṣṭa;* P., *santuṭṭha)* (14)
17. Frugal *(apagatapādamrakṣaṇa)* (16)[52]

As in the case of the *Theragāthā* list, the context of this passage is clearly forest renunciation: the purpose of these practices is to facilitate a life of meditation. A comparison of this list with that of Upatissa and that of the *Theragāthā* yields some further insights.

Aṣṭa	*Theragāthā*	*Upatissa*
1	2	3
2	5	7
3	13 (different interpretation)	5
4	6	1
5	7	2
6	—	—
7	8	8

Aṣṭa	*Theragāthā*	*Upatissa*
8	12	12
9	11	11
10	9	9
11	10	10
12	14	—
13	16	13
14	—	—
15	18	—
16	19	—
17	—	—
—	4	6
—	15	—
—	17	—

The *Aṣṭasāhasrikāprajñāpāramitā Sūtra* grouping is like that of the *Theragāthā* in several respects. It represents a listing of ascetic practices but is different from the classical list of thirteen (or twelve) *dhutaguṇa*s. Like the *Theragāthā* group, this listing includes several items not contained in Upatissa's set (items 6, 12, 14, 15, 16, and 17), and it lacks one of Upatissa's items (6, "measured food"). Like the *Theragāthā* and unlike Upatissa, the *Aṣṭasāhasrikāprajñāpāramitā Sūtra* listing also contains at least one rule concerning dwelling alone. And like the *Theragāthā,* it contains not only specific behavioral conventions but also attitudinal ones. Some of these are shared by the two texts. There are also several differences between them. The *Aṣṭasāhasrikāprajñāpāramitā Sūtra* contains one item concerning apparel not found in Upatissa or in the *Theragāthā,* namely, wearing a garment made of felt. It also includes a rule concerning limitation on speech not contained in the *Theragāthā.*

Devadatta's Conventions of Forest Renunciation

The preceding discussion suggests that the *dhutaguṇa*s, as they appear within the Indian Buddhist texts, essentially define a life of forest renunciation. Mention of them in the literature suggests that the basic concept of specific practices that define forest renunciation is found in Indian Buddhism both early and later. Moreover, traditions of *dhutaguṇa*s were considered sufficiently important to be featured even in texts that do not reflect a forest context (for example, the *Milindapañha* and the *Visuddhimagga*). We have also seen that when these practices are set out in list form, there is evidence of considerable diversity. Such variation in the lists in the earlier period is noteworthy, particularly when compared with the high degree of uniformity in the *prātimokṣa* lists of the different schools. This difference would appear to be related to the different contexts in which the *prātimokṣa,* on the one hand, and the *dhutaguṇa*s, on the other, were primarily practiced. In the consistency of the *prātimokṣa* (particularly in all but the *śaikṣadharma* category of rules), we see the standardizing and leveling influence of the monastic institution, where accuracy of transmission of the literal text was so important and where behavioral purity was defined primarily in terms of adherence to the received set of rules. By contrast, the diversity in the different lists of the *dhutaguṇas* no doubt reflects the primary context in which these practices were carried out—forest renunciation. The relative isolation of individual practitioners, the trend toward independence of guru and disciple from institutional constraints, the emphasis on meditation and concomitant preference for efficacy of method over that which is orthodox, the loyalty to practice and realization, and the lack of a single, defined institutional focus for the various practitioners of the conventions all would have served to encourage the kind of diversity we find in the texts that make reference to the *dhutaguṇas*.

At the same time, however, there is a very significant, perhaps surprising, level of consensus among the *dhutaguṇa* lists. In fact, all the lists agree on several things. First, they agree on certain categories of rules, specifically those regulating food, dress, and habitation. Second, they agree on the majority of the rules, with the *Parivāra, Milindapañha, Vimuttimagga, Visuddhimagga, Theragāthā,* and *Aṣṭasāhasrikāprajñāpāramitā Sūtra* all agreeing on ten rules (Upatissa's items 1, 2, 3, 5,[53] 7, 8, 9, 10, 11, 12, 13).[54] As it is very unlikely that this consensus can be explained as institutionally driven, we may conclude that within Indian forest Buddhism there was considerable agreement on what general forms of behavior were considered appropriate for Buddhist forest renunciants.[55]

There is another, more divergent group of ascetic practices in the Buddhist texts also explicitly styled *dhuta*—namely, those conventions of Devadatta, existing in the Pāli and other *vinayas*. Leaving aside the Mūlasarvāstivādin list (because of its discrepant and in some respects later character),[56] taking the Pāli and other *vinayas* together, we find the following rules mentioned:[57]

Dwelling

1. One should dwell in the forest, not in villages (Pāli).
2. One should dwell under trees, not under roofs (Pāli).
3. One should dwell out in the open (Dharmaguptaka, Sarvāstivāda, Mahīśāsaka).[58]

Food

4. One should beg one's food (Pāli, Dharmaguptaka, Sarvāstivāda, Mahīśāsaka),[59] not accept invitations (Pāli only).
5. One should accept neither flesh nor fish (Pāli, Dharmaguptaka, Mahīśāsaka, Sarvāstivāda).
6. One should eat no salt (Mahīśāsaka).
7. One should take neither sweet nor sour milk (Mahīśāsaka).
8. One should eat neither butter nor salt (Dharmaguptaka).
9. One should eat only once a day (Sarvāstivāda).

Clothing

10. One should wear only rag robes and accept no clothes from householders (Pāli, Dharmaguptaka, Sarvāstivāda).[60]

These practices, we are told in the Pāli version, are conducive to desiring little *(appiccha)*, to contentment *(santuṭṭha)*, to expunging evil *(sallekha)*, to being punctilious *(dhuta)*, and to putting forth energy *(viriyārambha)*: (*V*-p 3:171–72 [H., 1:296–97]). These qualities are, of course, the same as ones found connected with the *dhutaguṇa* lists we have already examined.

Devadatta's list suggests some additional perspectives on the *dhutaguṇas*. Six practices (1, 2, 3, 4, 9, 10) duplicate members of the common core of the *dhutaguṇas*. On the other hand, Devadatta's group mentions four practices regarding food that are not found in the common group: the prohibitions against the eating of (1) flesh and fish,[61] (2) salt, (3) butter, and (4) sweet and sour milk. As noted, some of these practices turn up in later history. The prohibition against eating milk products was found among monasteries that followed Devadatta in Hsüan-tsang's time. Of particular note, the injunction against eating meat turns up in the Mahāyāna. Whereas the practices attributed to Devadatta obviously shared common ground with the other lists discussed, they also show significant differences. Without further research, it is not possible to say much about the precise historical process that Devadatta's departure may have involved, but the Mahāyāna connection, taken in conjunction with the positive image of Devadatta in the *Saddharmapuṇḍarīka Sūtra*, is intriguing.

In addition, an examination of the *dhuta* practices of Devadatta again confirms his reputation as a rigorist. For example, in the Pāli rendering, the Buddhist renunciant is to live in the forest and, in addition, to avoid villages. Moreover, Devadatta wishes these rules to be binding on all Buddhist renunciants "for as long as life shall last." That four of his restrictions regarding eating are not found in any of the Buddhist *dhutaguṇa* lists suggests again, from a different angle, that Devadatta was a rigorist, even compared with other Buddhist forest renunciants.

Conclusion

The appearance of the classical *dhutaguṇas*, *dhutaguṇa*-like groups, as well as subgroups of and individual *dhutaguṇa*-type practices in the Nikāya and Mahāyāna texts raises the question of what historical development may lie behind the evidence. Any adequate response to this question will have to await a thorough cataloging of these phenomena as they appear not only in the Pāli canon but also in the Sarvāstivādin texts in Sanskrit and translation, other Nikāya Buddhist evidence, and the Mahāyāna literature in Sanskrit, Tibetan, and particularly Chinese—something far beyond the scope of the present study. In spite of this limitation, however, certain historical patterns are suggested by the evidence we have discussed.

First, let us consider the issue of the early development of the *dhutaguṇas*. Bapat tells us that a Tibetan version of Upatissa's text contains only ten items, omitting *tecīvarika, sapadānacārika,* and *piṇḍapātika* (one member shy of being identical with the ten items the different traditions have in common). Upatissa remarks that the *dhutaguṇas* may also be understood in an eightfold and a threefold form. In the eightfold form, "measured food" and "one-eating" are included within "no food after time"; and "dwelling under a tree," "dwelling in the open," and "dwelling in cremation grounds" are included in "forest dwelling"

(Bapat 1937b, 23 and 1964, 37). When reduced to a threefold form, the *dhutaguṇas* include forest dwelling, wearing of rags, and begging for food. This threefold form is interesting because it amounts, in effect, to three of the four ancient *niśrayas*. Moreover, each of these three *dhutaguṇas* are, as we have seen, explicitly identified by Upatissa with the corresponding member of the *niśrayas*, which are several times explicitly praised in Upatissa's text (Bp., 11, 21, 47). The facts that three of the *niśrayas* appear in the *dhutaguṇa* list, that Upatissa explicitly identifies these three *dhutaguṇas* with three of the four *niśrayas*, and that the *dhutaguṇas* may be reduced to that threefold list are significant. They suggest that the *niśrayas* represent an early stage in the line of development of the Buddhist ascetic ideal that culminates in the *dhutaguṇas*.[62] That three practices attributed to Devadatta are the same as the *niśrayas* suggests that these practices are likely the common ancestors both of the Buddhist lists of *dhutaguṇas* we discussed and also of Devadatta's conventions.

We may also see some later patterns of development. The agreement of Upatissa and Buddhaghosa may be due to the latter's reliance on the former or on a similar tradition. The *dhutaguṇa* list given in the *Mahāvyutpatti* is also closely similar in several ways to the Upatissa-Buddhaghosa lists: like their lists, the *Mahāvyutpatti* list is systematized according to category (all food items are together, and so on), is listed in the same order, contains almost the same number of items (twelve and thirteen), and contains the same items but for two that Upatissa has that the *Mahāvyutpatti* lacks and one the *Mahāvyutpatti* has that Upatissa lacks. These facts suggest a close filiation between the *Mahāvyutpatti* list and the lists of Upatissa and Buddhaghosa.

The enumerations of the *Theragāthā* and the *Aṣṭasāhasrikāprajñāpāramitā Sūtra* both stand at some remove from these standardized lists. It is interesting that the *Theragāthā* group and the *Aṣṭasāhasrikāprajñāpāramitā* list—on the surface deriving from "Hīnayāna" and "Mahāyāna"—are in fact much more similar to one another than the *Aṣṭasāhasrikāprajñāpāramitā* list is to the Mahāyāna list of the *Mahāvyutpatti* or the *Theragāthā* list is to those of Upatissa and Buddhaghosa. On the other hand, the lists of the *Mahāvyutpatti* and of Upatissa and Buddhaghosa—though again ostensibly deriving from "Hīnayāna" and "Mahāyāna"—are much more similar to one another than either the *Mahāvyutpatti* list is to the *Aṣṭasāhasrikāprajñāpāramitā* list or the *Theragāthā* group is to the enumerations of Upatissa and Buddhaghosa. How may one account for these curious facts? It is significant that the *Theragāthā* and the *Aṣṭasāhasrikāprajñāpāramitā Sūtra* both contain material that is considered to be among the oldest textual expressions of Nikāya Buddhism and the Mahāyāna, respectively. The lack of rationalized organization and the terminological variations suggest that these may, in fact, represent older versions of the *dhutaguṇas*. At the same time, the fact that these two lists share the same general categories and many of the same components suggests that they both participate in a common context, the context of forest Buddhism.

The following may be advanced as a possible way to organize the evidence in a developmental sequence:

1. The four *niśrayas* define an early normative form of forest Buddhism. Moreover, they leave their influence on later times, for their threefold concern for

begging of food, apparel, and habitation will provide the underlying structure of the later *dhutaguṇa* lists. These *niśraya*s precede the division into what later come to be understood as Nikāya and Mahāyāna Buddhism. In any case, the *niśraya*s are not universally definitive of forest Buddhism; as we have seen, other simple lists of forest practices within Buddhism are also known.

2. Devadatta's "schism" occurs, with its rigorist interpretation of the *dhutaguṇa*s, stricter than that evidenced by any other known tradition of forest Buddhism.

3. At perhaps roughly the same time, the more conventional codes of forest Buddhism are in development, with each of the *niśraya* categories being expressed in larger but still loose groupings, containing perhaps some of, perhaps all the rules that the different traditions share, perhaps along with some others. This development occurs as common ground of forest traditions later understood as Nikāya and Mahāyānist and precedes the split that this terminology reflects.

4. This leads to some early, unsystematized versions of what later become the classical *dhutaguṇa*s, such as those of the *Theragāthā* and the *Aṣṭasāhasrikāprajñāpāramitā Sūtra,* without evident connection to the life of the settled monastery.[63]

5. Upatissa's basic text, exclusive of the exceptions given at its end, also generally reflects a nonmonastic context. At the same time, in relation to the larger and looser lists of the *Theragāthā* and *Aṣṭasāhasrikāprajñāpāramitā Sūtra,* Upatissa's list represents, as noted, a reduction and concretizing of the list.

6. The set of *dhutaguṇa*s is monasticized, a process reflected in Upatissa's text in its final form and in the *Visuddhimagga* of Buddhaghosa. This development need not have occurred after those enumerated above but could have occurred at a very early time, with town-and-village renunciants or perhaps even settled monasticism proper having had a version of *dhutaguṇa*-type practices, seen as temporary (and relatively permissive) modifications of this kind of renunciation.

7. Later Mahāyāna lists of the *dhutaguṇa*s *(Mahāvyutpatti* and *Dharmasaṃgraha)* appear to reflect a similar process of the monasticization of the *dhutaguṇa*s.

This ordering of the facts is, obviously, no more than hypothetical: other interpretations could no doubt be drawn from the same material and further research will likely suggest other perspectives. But the preceding reveals at least some of the kinds of issues that a study of the *dhutaguṇa*s can raise. By way of example, the kinds of patterns that the *dhutaguṇa*s suggest make it clear, once again, that the attempt to clarify the phenomena of early and later Indian Buddhism by terms such as "Hīnayāna" and "Mahāyāna" is of limited value. Far from always shedding light on the formation of Indian Buddhism, such polemically driven terminology may sometimes actually have the opposite effect, by concealing what is a much more interesting and revealing dichotomy—namely, that between the Buddhism of the forest and the Buddhism of the monastery.

The *dhutaguṇa*s, as an explicit class of practices, are rarely mentioned in the Pāli canon. At the same time, they are a subject of considerable interest to monastic commentators in the early centuries of the common era and after. This has led numerous researchers to judge the *dhutaguṇa*s to be a relatively tardy Buddhist phenomenon. Thus T. W. Rhys Davids remarks that the "doctrine of the thirteen *dhutaṅgas* is at variance with primitive Buddhism" (1890–94, 2:268, n. 1), and Przyluski tells us that "the Buddha appears to have had a completely different ideal from those of the ascetics, strict observers of the *dhutaguṇa*s, preoccupied above all with solitary meditation" (1926–28, 292). Dayal similarly believes that the *dhutaguṇa*s represent the late intrusion of non-Buddhist ideas into the heart of Buddhism (1932, 137–38). Others have more recently voiced similar opinions (for example, Carrithers 1983, 62–63). However, such interpretations are based upon the assumption that settled monasticism, as defined by the final form of the *vinaya,* constitutes normative Buddhism from the earliest times, rather than on an examination of the *dhutaguṇa*s themselves and the texts in which they appear.

In addition, this kind of view fails to answer some important questions. For example, as the texts themselves tell us so clearly that the four *niśraya*s, the *dhutaguṇa*s, and allied practices defined the lifestyle of at least some early Buddhist renunciants, one wonders what justification there is for seeing the *dhutaguṇa*s as strictly later. Furthermore, as we have seen, the *dhutaguṇa*s in all but their latest and most monasticized formulations virtually imply the meditative life in the forest. Are we really to suppose that the Buddha, who had attained realization by following a way of life centered on meditation and *dhutaguṇa*-like practices (he lived in the forest, and so on), taught something else to his earliest disciples? And, finally, if the *dhutaguṇa*s were really a peripheral and essentially non-Buddhist concern, why are they mentioned in the literature of all periods of Indian Buddhist history, and why are so many Buddhist saints, even down to the present day (for example, Carrithers 1983, 75–76; Tambiah 1984, 175–76), closely associated with them? Surely a much more logical explanation of the presence of the *dhutaguṇa*-oriented traditions within Indian Buddhism is that they formed a central focus of Buddhism in its earliest days and were pushed to the side (at least in the evidence) only later, by the development and rise to dominance of settled monasticism.[64]

This view permits a simpler and more logical explanation for the relative absence of the *dhutaguṇa*s in the Pāli canon. The monastically oriented compilers of the Pāli canon, as we have it, simply did not consider the *dhutaguṇa*s sufficiently important to their kind of Buddhism to merit serious discussion. Nevertheless, the many examples of the individual items of the *dhutaguṇa* list in the Pāli canon show that such practices provided an important part of the background of this collection, a background that those immediately responsible for the compiling of texts of the canon could not entirely dismiss. By contrast, for those more forest-oriented renunciants reflected in the *Theragāthā* and the earlier Mahāyāna *sūtra*s, practices like those found in the *dhutaguṇa*s clearly played a much more essential role.

It is curious, then, that Theravādin tradition begins to take considerable notice of the *dhutaguṇa*s as such at the same time that the Mahāyāna is beginning to appear in India. It may well be that the Theravādin commentators begin to acknowledge the *dhutaguṇa*s in a major way as a response to the growing popularity of the Mahāyāna and its forest saints. In the writing of the *Milindapañha,* the *Vimuttimagga* (in its final form), and the *Visuddhimagga,* we may be observing settled monasticism in the process of appropriating something of the charisma of the saints and their forest way of life, while subjecting them to the process of monasticization—and here Buddhaghosa is the past master—to make them more harmonious with the particular institutional exigencies of its kind of Buddhism.

Notes

1. Here, as elsewhere with regard to the Buddhist saints, this is a tendency toward type but not an invariable rule, for there are exceptions. For some examples, see the Conclusion. Although the texts cited in this chapter typically refer to the renunciant as a male, as we have seen, female forest renunciants are also known.

2. The close connection between the forest life and the Buddhist saints was noticed long ago by La Vallée Poussin (1929).

3. For other references in the Pāli texts, see *PTSD* 78, s.v. *ariyavaṃsa.* The four *āryavaṃśa*s are mentioned in the Sanskrit Nikāya sources. In the *Abhidharmakośa,* for example, we find the list *cīvara, piṇḍapāta, śayanāsana,* and *prahāṇabhāvanārāmatā,* which La Vallée Poussin equates with *nirodhamārgārāmatā* (1923–31, 6:146). The *āryavaṃśa*s are mentioned in the Mahāyāna *sūtras* such as *Rps* (13.17–18 and 14.7) and *Kp* (6.17, 123.3, and 126.7). They are also mentioned in the *Ugraparipṛcchā* translated by Schuster as "1) being content with one robe, 2) being content with one meal a day, 3) being content with one couch, and 4) being content with one medicine for illness"; see Schuster's discussion of this list (1985, 36–37). On the *āryavaṃśa*s, see also Ruegg 1969, 457ff. and *BHSD* 105, s.v. *āryavaṃśa.*

4. For a list of references to the four in the Pāli and Sanskrit literature, see *PTSD* 374, s.v. *nissaya* and *BHSD* 306–7, s.v. *niśraya.*

5. Listed in their Sanskrit form in *Mvy* 8670–73. In *Ta,* song of Mahākāśyapa, we read a typical expression of the ideal: "For whom left-over scraps suffice as food, smelly urine as medicine, the foot of a tree as lodging, a rag from a dust heap as robe, he is truly a man of the four quarters" (1057).

6. I follow Frauwallner's usage here; the renunciants referred to are, of course, not settled monastics.

7. See, e.g., Prebish 1973, 676–77.

8. *PTSD* lists the following as meanings of the term *dhuta* (and *dhūta*): "1. shaken, moved . . . 2. lit., 'shaken off,' but always expl. in the commentaries as 'one who shakes off' either evil dispositions *(kilese),* or obstacles to spiritual progress *(vāra, nīvaraṇa)"* (342, s.v. *dhuta).* The term has similar meanings in Sanskrit, listed by Edgerton as "purified, got rid of (evil . . .)" *(BHSD* 285, s.v. *dhuta).*

9. The code itself is designated in Sanskrit and Pāli by a number of closely related terms and variations of them. For a discussion of the major Sanskrit designations, see *BHSD* 285, col. 2, s.v. *dhuta; dhutaguṇa* (*dhūtaguṇa*); *dhutaguṇin; dhutadhara;* and *dhutadharma;* and 286, col. 1, s.v. *dhutaguna.* For Pāli terms, see *PTSD* 342, s.v. *dhutañga;* this entry includes discussions of *dhutadhara, dhutavata,* and *dhutavāda.* Edgerton comments that *PTSD* contains some important gaps in its summary, for a few of which see the *BHSD* 285, col. 2 listings mentioned here.

10. For some discussions of the *dhutaguṇa*s, see Kern 1886, 75–76 and 1901–3, 2:16–

18; Bapat 1937a and 1937b; Khantipalo 1965; Lamotte 1980, 195, n. 1; Tambiah 1984, 28–37; and references below.

11. See later in this chapter for some of the more important of these references.

12. In this chapter, Conze's *Large Sūtra on Perfect Wisdom* is, following Conze, referred to as the *Pañcaviṃśatisāhasrikāprajñāpāramitā Sūtra.* In fact, as Schopen has pointed out, Conze's work also includes the addition of material from other *Prajñāpāramitā* texts (Schopen 1977).

13. Kern 1884, 132 offers a somewhat different translation.

14. See also *Mp* 20 (T.R. 1890–94, 1:32–33).

15. Kern translates this not very specifically as "hermit life."

16. *PTSD* 342 provides references for the Pāli sources where examples of one or another of them are given.

17. In Chapter 8, we saw mention of such practices in *Rgs, Rps, Rps*-m, *Sns,* and *Las.*

18. This is also suggested by the fact that the *dhutaguṇa*s, as a set and under this or an analagous term, are not mentioned in early forest texts such as *Sn, Dp, Iv,* and *Ud.*

19. Mentioned in *Mvy* 7011, with the full list of twelve members given in *Mvy* 1127–39. Listed in *BHSD* 286, col. 1, s.v. *dhūta-guṇa.*

20. This standard Pāli list is found in both canonical and extracanonical texts, the *Parivāra* (*V*-p 5:131, 193 [H., 6:209–11, 310–12]) being an example of the former, and the *Milindapañha* (6.20 [T.R. 1890–94, 267–68]), *Vmm,* and *Vsm* (see below) examples of the latter.

21. The *PTSD* translates this more literally as "one who keeps to himself" (*PTSD* 159). Thus, the same term might be understood in different ways. In the present case, one must wonder whether the original meaning of *ekāsanika* might not have had to do with dwelling in solitude rather than with eating all one's food at one sitting. For a discussion of this term, see note 43.

22. In the interests of sylistic consistency, in discussing the Pāli materials, I use the term *dhutaguṇa.* The preferred term in Pāli for these practices is, of course, *dhutaṅga.* Although not listed in *PTSD,* the term *dhutaguṇa* does appear in the Pāli texts both early (*Ta* 1087) and late (*Dp*-c 4:30.13). In quotations in this section from Ehara, Soma, and Kheminda 1961, I have replaced their translations of some of the *dhutaguṇa* practices with renderings that reflect current usage: *āraññaka* is translated as "dwelling in the forest" (rather than "in a peaceful place"); *abbhokāsika* as "dwelling in the open air" (rather than "in a dewy place"); and *sosānika* as "dwelling in cremation grounds" (rather than "among the graves").

23. The *Vimuttimagga* was connected with the Abhayagiri School in Sri Lanka, which was composed largely of monks who had migrated from India and of those who did not agree with the viewpoints of the Mahāvihāra *saṃgha.* Although a large and well-organized monastic tradition, the Abhayagiri sect appears to have had special linkages with the forest renunciant ideal (cf. Tambiah 1984, 73).

24. T. 1648. Translated into English by Ehara, Soma Thera, and Kheminda Thera 1961.

25. Edited and translated into English by Bapat (1964). For a summary of the publication history of this text, see Bechert 1989a, 11–14.

26. The fact that the exception presupposes: the rule (1), the contradiction between rule and exceptions (2), and the placement of the contradictions in a commentarial section at the end (3)—all suggest that the main section of this chapter reflects a forest tradition, whereas the exceptions reflect a time when this chapter, perhaps in the context of the entire *Vmm,* was used by monastic tradition.

27. Gunawardana in fact mentions the view that *Vmm* as we have it is the monastic (Abhayagiri) recension of an earlier work (1979, 23). Such an interpretation seems plausi-

ble, at least in terms of the basic structure and content of the *dhuta* chapter. For a discussion of *Vmm* and its texts, see Gunawardana 1979, 22–23.

28. Although the texts discussed here typically use the masculine gender, and although the *vinaya* specifically forbids *bhikṣuṇīs* from following the life of forest renunciation, women adhering to *dhutaguṇa*-like practices have been known in Indian Buddhism from the time of the *Therīgāthā* down through the Vajrayāna period (eighth to twelfth centuries C.E.).

29. *Sgra.chung.bas.rnal.'byor.dang.mthun.pa.nyid.dang.*

30. As mentioned, this is also considered a forest practice.

31. In this rule, we find an interesting discrepancy between the Pāli and Tibetan versions of this text. In the Pāli version, in this section, we find the only reference to a monastery in this main section of the text. Thus, the text says that in the morning the renunciant returns to the *saṃghārāma,* avoiding other places, suggesting that one dwelt in the cremation grounds at night and returned to the monastery in the morning (when did one sleep?). In the Tibetan version, however, a different picture is presented. The text specifically says that one should not stay in a hut or house of any kind and that living in the cremation ground involves giving up residence in any other place. Conversely, one breaks the rule if one takes up one's abode in any other place. The Tibetan text appears to say that one stays permanently in the cremation ground (*Dgn* 57).

32. As we see here, Upatissa explicitly connects this practice with yoga, or meditation, as does Buddhaghosa in *Vsm,* where he remarks about one who engages in this practice that "his state is suitable for devotion to any meditation subject" (*Vsm* 79 [N., 79]). In later tradition, in Tibet, for example, this practice was similarly understood to exist for the purpose of facilitating meditation. These examples indicate the status of *naiṣadika* as a meditative discipline.

33. The need for the forest renunciant to reduce contact with the laity to a minimum in order to fulfill the meditative vocation is well known in Indian Buddhism. As mentioned in Chapter 1, for example, Buddhaghosa, in his enumeration of the potential faults of the settled monastery as a place for meditation, puts his finger on the key obstacle presented by the meditator's accessibility to the laity. In particularly well known monasteries, "there are always people coming who want to pay homage to [the meditator] supposing that he is an *arhant,* which inconveniences him" (*Vsm* 120 [N., 124]).

34. The one interesting exception to this pattern of living places is the cremation ground. This place is valued, perhaps, because it represents a kind of place beyond the pale of the social world and hence isolated from it from the viewpoint of conventional mores and psychology.

35. See Olivelle's useful discussion of this topic (1974, 54–64).

36. See also *V*-p 5:193 (H., 6:310–12).

37. Rhys Davids and Stede have noticed that this passage in the *Parivāra* deprecates the *dhutaguṇas* (*PTSD* 342, s.v. *dhuta*). Rhys Davids elsewhere remarks on the relative unimportance of the *dhutaguṇa*s in the monastic way of life: "As a matter of fact the members of the Buddhist Order have not observed them in any completeness. . . . [The] majority of these have undertaken only the second of the thirteen—wearing of three robes; and the others have only been occasionally practised and then usually only one or more at a time, by isolated members" (1890–94, 2:268, n. 1). They were no more than "supplementary or extra vows, conducive, but subsidiary to the ethical self-culture of the Arhant" (ibid.). Elsewhere, he remarks that there is "no evidence that they [the *dhutaguṇa*s] were ever widely adopted" (*PTSD* 342).

38. Interesting in this context is the open attack on *dhutaguṇa* practices by King Milinda, at the beginning of the text. Milinda has approached the forest renunciant Āyupāla

and derides his forest way of life along with its code of *dhutaguṇas*: "It must be in consequence of sins committed in some former birth, that the Buddhist Samaṇas renounce the world, and even subject themselves to the restraints of one or other of the thirteen aids to purity *[dhutaṅga]*. . . . They who live in the open air were, forsooth, in some former birth, dacoits who plundered whole villages. It is in consequence of the *karma* of having destroyed other people's homes, that they now live without a home, and are not allowed the use of huts. It is no virtue on their part, no meritorious abstinence, no righteousness of life. And those who never lie down, they, forsooth, in some former birth, were highwaymen who seized travellers, and bound them, and left them sitting there. It is in consequence of the *karma* of that habit that they have become *nesajjikā* in this life (men who always sit) and get no beds to lie on. It is no virtue on their part, no meritorious abstinence, no righteousness of life" (*Mp* 20 [T.R. 1890–94, 1:32–33]). Āyupāla, thus attacked, makes no reply to the king but sits in silence. The king is unimpressed and after heaping more abuse upon him, heads off to find one who is learned and can debate and discuss with him. He finds this person in Nāgasena, the textually accomplished monk, who is depicted not only as being vastly learned but also as being "in abundant receipt of all the requisites of a member of the Order—robes and bowl and lodging" (22 [1:35]), i.e., one whose way of life and values are quite different from those that provoked Milinda's abuse of Āyupāla. The fact that the attack on the *dhutaguṇas* goes unanswered in this story, and that Milinda so relentlessly belittles and scorns Āyupāla and his way of life, is no doubt another example of the ambivalence of *Mp* (and of Pāli tradition altogether) toward the *dhutaguṇas* and forest Buddhism. The specific content of the attack also raises another question: does this represent what was actually thought by at least some in India at that time, including not only non-Buddhists but also—perhaps mainly—Buddhists, and particularly those aligned with settled monasticism? If the monasteries tended to see a disproportionate number of high-caste members, was the converse true—as tended to be the case in Tantric Buddhism—that those following a forest way of life were disproportionately lower-caste? In such a case, monastic Buddhism could have been easily led to explain what it saw as the inferiority of forest Buddhism by reference to previous negative karma.

39. For a comparison of these two texts, see Bapat 1937b.

40. Buddhaghosa does, in effect, acknowledge this when he comments of the medium and mild grades of this *dhutaguṇa* that "both these last miss the joy of an independent life" (*Vsm* 2.28 [N., 67]).

41. Thus the information provided in Bapat, that *Dhs* omits the practice of accepting whatever place is found and includes the practice of wearing woolen robes, resulting in a thirteenfold list, is incorrect (1964, xxi).

42. The *Mvy* list is presented in this order: 4, 2, 6, 11, 12, 8, 5, 9, 7, 10, 1, 3.

43. Following Norman's translation. The term *ekāsanika* (*PTSD* 159) is, of course, the same term that in the Mahāyāna and Pāli sets of twelve and thirteen *dhutaguṇas* is understood to refer to eating one's food at one sitting. *PTSD* 159 tells us that *ekāsana* also occurs with this meaning. Norman believes that, in this context, *ekāsanin* indicates solitary dwelling. Such is, in fact, a more literal translation, and *PTSD* 159 gives for *ekāsanika* "one who keeps to himself" and for *ekāsana,* "sitting or living alone." It is this meaning of solitude that is most commonly found in Pāli texts, both *suttas* and commentaries (*PTSD* 159). In support of this translation of the term in the context of *Ta,* Norman points out that the term *ekāsana* occurs at *Ta* 239, and that the commentary says that it refers to one who is without companions and who devotes himself to solitude (see Norman's discussion of the term [1969, 245, n. 848, and 170, n. 239]). This meaning of *ekāsanin* in *Ta,* which appears to be early relative to the classical lists, raises the interesting possibility that the practice referred to by this term originally was solitary dwelling but that at a certain time,

the practice was reinterpreted to indicate a convention concerning eating. On dwelling alone, see Ñānananda 1973.

44. Bhaddiya mentions his abandoning of bronze and gold bowls and the taking of the earthenware bowl as his "second coronation," presumably referring to his previous kingly status and his having renounced the world. Then he says that he had been held captive in a fortification by armed guards, for some unspecified reason, "in a city." Then Bhaddiya remarks, "Today fortunate, not fearful, with fear and dread eliminated, Bhaddiya, son of Godhā, meditates having plunged into the wood . . . in due course, I attained the annihilation of all fetters" (*Ta* 862–65).

45. See note 43.

46. In other similar lists in both Nikāya and Mahāyāna Buddhism, exertion is specifically related with meditation. See, e.g., Rahula 1962, 47–49; *Vsm* 3.24 (N., 90); *Bca* 116–35 (Matics 1970, 193).

47. Cf. Norman's notes on verses 843 to 861 (1969, 245–46).

48. I arrive at this enumeration of seventeen *dhutaguṇa*s in the following way. Fourteen of these items are set within the construction *"sacet(d) . . . bhaviṣyati,"* e.g., *sacedāraṇyako bhaviṣyati, sacetpiṇḍapātiko bhaviṣyati,* etc. Three items, *pravivikta, alpeccha,* and *saṃtuṣṭa,* are put together within a fifteenth occurrence of this same construction. In this section, in order to facilitate comparison, I treat them as separate items, as they are treated in *Ta.* At the same time, however, in texts treating of forest renunciation, they frequently occur together and in this section of *Asp,* in contrast to *Ta,* seem to be treated as a set (see note 51).

49. Following Conze's translation of the items (1973b, 231).

50. The standard reference works (*BHSD, SED,* Conze 1973b) interpret this Sanskrit term consistently with this meaning. Inability to document Mahāyāna usage of this term with the meaning of "dwelling in solitude" leads me, with some hesitation, to follow Conze's translation. However, there is a clear need for a full exploration of the meaning and history of this term in both Pāli and Mahāyāna sources.

51. Conze translates this term in a metaphorical way as "detached" (*Asp* 192 [Cz., 231]). However, in this context it makes more sense to take the term literally, as it is often meant (cf. *SED* 692:2), which is certainly allowed by the Tibetan *rab.tu.dben.pa* (1973b, 288; cf. also *TED* 913, s.v. *dben.pa*). According to *PTSD,* the equivalent Pāli term, *pavivitta,* is to be understood as implying this literal meaning, "separated, detached, secluded, singled," and is used "often in the phrase *'appiccha santuṭṭha pavivitta'* referring to an ascetic enjoying the satisfaction of seclusion" (444). It will be recalled that *pavivitta* appears in the *Ta* group, and Norman in fact takes the term in just this literal way, as "secluded" (1969, 82).

52. See Conze 1973a, 48, s.v. *apagata pāda mrakṣaṇa.*

53. *Ekāsanika;* cf. note 33.

54. That such a generally held consensus existed may also be reflected in the fact that textual references to the *dhutaguṇa*s usually do not explain what they are or mention them explicitly, as if they were common knowledge.

55. It will be important to explore the extent to which the Buddhist *dhutaguṇa*s and *dhutaguṇa*-like practices are paralleled by the practices of other, non-Buddhist forest *śramaṇa* schools.

56. Owing to its in some respects evident lateness and dramatic departure from the general consensus of the other *vinaya*s.

57. See Mukherjee's summary and discussion (1966, 74–86).

58. The Mahīśāsakas mention that one should dwell out in the open during eight months and live for four months in grass huts.

59. With slightly different wording.

60. With slightly different wording.

61. Although note that a similar dietary restriction is mentioned in Upatissa's treatment of dwelling in cremation grounds (see Eh., 34).

62. The fourth *niśraya,* which permits only cow's urine as medicine, is in itself interesting. The existence of this alongside the all-important conventions governing food, apparel, and dwelling place suggests that restrictions in relation to "medicine" *(bhaiṣajya;* P., *bhesajja)* were important among early Buddhist forest renunciants. The same is suggested by one of the four *āryavaṃśas* as presented by the *Ugraparipṛcchā* (Schuster 1985, 36–37), "being content with one medicine for illness." But what could have been the importance of this regulation of "medicine"? Let us remember that in the *vinaya,* the category of medicine becomes a vehicle to allow monastics to consume various desirable aliments such as ghee, fresh butter, oil, honey, and molasses, as well as a variety of tallows, roots, astringent decoctions, leaves, fruits, resins, and salts (*V*-p 1:198–201 [H., 4:269–73]). The fourth *niśraya* is, of course, a rule *disallowing* a broad interpretation of medicine. The fact that such a rule exists in this early set of conventions at least suggests that the category of medicine *could be* broadly interpreted from an early time. At face value, this suggests that there was considerable diversity from an early time among renunciants with regard to the issue of rigor versus greater laxity in behavioral conventions. But which might have been the groups behind these two tendencies? It does not seem unreasonable to suppose that the strict group would correspond to forest renunciants, as reflected in the *niśraya*s, and that those who allow greater latitude in the interpretation of medicine, as in other behavioral matters, would correspond to the ancestors of settled monasticism, where such latitude plays a major role, namely, those *śramaṇa*s who were originally town-and-village-renunciants (see Chapter 2). This is further indication of the existence of two parallel but somewhat distinct types of *śramaṇa*s in the sixth century B.C.E., which gave rise to the two major trends of renunciation subsequently found in Indian Buddhism.

63. As mentioned, *Asp*—as a text—contains reflections of an urban environment. However, the material containing the group of *dhutaguṇa*-type practices clearly represents another, quite different environment, probably developmentally earlier than that reflected in the standard Mahāyāna lists found, e.g., in *Mvy.*

64. It is interesting that even today, the standard histories of Indian Buddhism typically give no role whatever to the *dhutaguṇa*s. See, e.g., Warder 1970, Nakamura 1987, and Lamotte 1958.

10

The Buddhist Saints and the Stūpa

In the examination of the Buddha and other Buddhist saints in preceding chapters, attention has been focused upon the living saints, as defined by their hagiographies, ascetic traditions, and cults. However, for most Indian Buddhists, the saints while alive probably provided a less frequent reference point for religious devotion than when they had passed away and were venerated in their stūpas. This is because while they were alive, the saints may often have been relatively inaccessible: they spent much of their time in seclusion in remote places. Moreover, they typically had no fixed abode but wandered from place to place without definite itinerary, and their wandering could carry them to far-flung places. Thus the suppliant's longing to see and venerate the living saints must, by its very nature, have remained to some extent unfulfilled. But when the saints had passed beyond and their relics were enshrined in stūpas, they finally became available to all and could become the objects of an ongoing cult. It is perhaps for this reason that within a few centuries of the Buddha's passing stūpas were to be found throughout the Indian subcontinent, becoming for Buddhism "the religious edifice par excellence" (Foucher 1905–22, 1:59) and even "the chief emblem of the Buddhist faith" (Mitra 1971, 21).

In considering the place of the stūpa within the Indian Buddhist cult of saints, an immediate problem arises. So far in this book, the Buddha and the other Buddhist saints have been treated as belonging to an overarching category, that of the "Buddhist saint." What has been said about the general structure, hagiography, ascetic traditions, and cult of the Buddha has been found to apply, mutatis mutandis, to the other types of Buddhist saint. The stūpa, however, seems at first glance to provide an exception to this general pattern: the great preponderance of available evidence concerns stūpas of the Buddha. Is it not correct, then, to see the stūpa as primarily a reflection of the cult of Buddha Śākyamuni rather than as a typical feature of the cult of the Buddhist saints as such?

A wide range of evidence, some of which will be cited below, suggests that stūpas are as characteristic of the other Indian Buddhist saints as they are of the Buddha. Indeed, in the earlier chapters of this book, frequent reference has been made to the stūpas not only of the Buddha but also of other buddhas as well as of the pratyekabuddhas and arhants. Bareau comments that in our earliest datable evidence of the stūpa cult, deriving from the middle of the third century B.C.E.

(the inscription of Nigālī Sāgar), mention is made of the cults of the stūpas of the former buddhas Konākamuni and Kāśyapa, as well as of Śākyamuni (1975, 187–88). De Visser remarks that the Chinese pilgrims' accounts indicate that, in medieval India, stūpas of the Buddha were outnumbered by stūpas of other saints (1923, 80), and a reading of the pilgrims' accounts gives ample evidence of stūpas to pratyekabuddhas and great arhants. In addition, it was apparently not only widely renowned saints who had stūpas built to them, but saints of more restricted fame as well (Lamotte 1958, 333–34). Schopen has recently drawn our attention to a considerable array of inscriptional evidence of stūpas to local saints, deriving from a variety of archaeological sites (1991c, 306), indicating that stūpas to local saints were numerous and perhaps often considered more important in Buddhist cultic life than stūpas to the great pan-Buddhist saints of textual tradition (301, 308).[1]

Schopen has also suggested that the stūpas of the Buddha and the more famous saints and the stūpas of local saints are specific examples of the same general religious phenomenon. The same beliefs, attitudes, architectural structure, symbolism, and ritual acts found associated with stūpas of the Buddha appear also to be characteristic of the cults of the stūpas of local saints, and this "makes it . . . very difficult to argue that [stūpas to local saints and stūpas to the Buddha] were thought to be, in any essential way, different" (1991c, 300). Schopen believes that the evidence lends weight to the hypothesis that "the relic cult and stūpa of the historical Buddha only represents a special and particularly well known instance" of a general set of beliefs and practices surrounding saints within Indian Buddhism (302). If this has not been fully appreciated before, Schopen argues, it is not because the evidence is wanting, but rather because archaeologists and other scholars have almost exclusively concerned themselves with evidence of stūpas to Buddha Śākyamuni (306–8). The present discussion, reflecting available evidence, will focus upon what is known about the stūpas of the Buddha. However, periodic reference to the stūpas of former buddhas, pratyekabuddhas, the famous arhant-disciples of the Buddha, other pan-Indian saints, and local saints will suggest that the stūpa—in its basic structure, symbolism, and associated ritual acts—is a consistent and central feature of the Indian Buddhist cult of saints as such.

Some Aspects of Stūpa Symbolism

The term *stūpa* designates a mound-shaped structure typically containing the ashes or other remains or representations of a saint. Although known primarily as a Buddhist monument, the stūpa and its cult may be traced to a variety of pre-Buddhist influences, among them the pre-Buddhist Indian practice of erecting mounds over bodily relics,[2] the cult surrounding the death and cremation of the *cakravartin* (P., *cakkavattin*) (universal ruler),[3] and various elements in the worship of deities in India (Bareau 1975, 173).[4] In classical times, the stūpa provided a symbolic and ritual focus of the Buddhist cult of saints.[5] The particular importance of the stūpa in the cult of saints derives from the fact that, once ritually empowered,[6] in an important sense the stūpa *was* the saint, although now the body was composed of mortar and stones, rather than flesh and blood.[7] In reference to the Buddha's stūpas, Bénisti remarks that tradition "directly identifies the *stūpa* with the body of the Master" (1960, 51). In reference to the saints in general, Mus explains, "The sepulchre becomes a substitute for the ephemeral body of the dead person where his mystic being continues to exist . . . we have therefore to do with a *built body* which represents the being of the dead person in such a way as his body did during his lifetime" (cited by Ebert 1980, 219).

This identification of stūpa and body of the saint is reflected in various strands of evidence. The Buddha himself was evidently conceived as a stūpa, a point clearly made in Hsüan-tsang's account of the beginnings of the stūpa tradition. On a certain occasion, the Buddha was worshiped by two merchants and gave them some of his hair and nail parings. When they asked how to worship these, the Buddha, "making a square pile of his saṅghāṭī, or lower robe, laid it on the ground, and did the same with his uttarāsaṅga or outer robe and his Saṃkachchikam *[saṃkakṣikā;* P., *saṃkacchikā],* the robe which goes under the arm pits, in succession. On top of these he placed his bowl inverted, and then set up his mendicant's staff, thus making a tope [stūpa]" (Watters 1904–5, 1:112). The identity of the stūpa with the physical body of the Buddha is also seen in the iconographic tradition, in which the stūpa is seen as the idealized structure of the Buddha's body. Typically, the ground where the stūpa is built is understood as Vajrāsana, the seat of enlightenment. The base of the stūpa is seen as the Buddha's legs and feet, the dome as his torso, the central axis as his spinal column, the *harmika* as his head. Thus, "the identification of the stūpa and the Buddha Body is conveyed in iconography. In Buddhist art the stūpa and the Buddha image are interchangeable" (Snodgrass 1985, 361–63).

Just as the human body of the saints incarnates their enlightened essence while they live, so the stūpa incarnates that essence after they have passed beyond. Harvey observes that the stūpa functions as "a symbol . . . of the enlightened state of a Buddha" (1984, 67), and Pant remarks that "the stūpa . . . symbolized [the *tathāgata*'s] presence" (1973, 472). Hirakawa tells us that "the Buddha's eternal presence is contained in the stūpa, and although enshrining relics, the worshipper sees it as the eternal Buddha" (1963, 88). Harvey comments on the logic of this identification of stūpa with the very essence of the Buddha. When the Buddha passed away at Kuśinagarī, his body was ritually cremated, and the purifying fire of cremation consumed that support of the enlightened wisdom of the Blessed One. Yet not all physical traces vanished, for his bones remained as a kind of distilled essence of his physical person (Harvey 1984, 69). Thus it was that, as Schopen remarks, "the relic in early Buddhist India was thought of as an actual living presence."[8] Like the previously existing mortal body of the Buddha, its remains were thought to be imbued with his enlightenment, compassion, and power (Harvey 1984, 69).[9] The Buddha's ashes, embodying his spiritual charisma and housed in the stūpa, were thus understood as the "life" *(jīvita)* of the stūpa, its quickening agent. The ashes animate the stūpa such that it becomes homologous to the body assumed by the master while he was yet alive (Bénisti 1960, 51). The same pattern of belief is also found associated with stūpas of local saints. Schopen remarks that "the relationship between the *local* dead and the structures that housed their remains was expressed exactly as was the relationship between the 'dead' Buddha and his *stūpa,*'' i.e., that it was the saints themselves rather than their remains that were thought to be housed in the stūpa (1991c, 316). In this connection, Schopen discusses a characteristic inscriptional phrasing that makes it clear that stūpas were not thought to contain the relics of the Buddha so much as to house the Buddha himself. ''He—not his remains—was, apparently, thought to reside inside'' (289). Exactly the same phrasing is used in inscriptions giving evidence of local saints indicating that they, too, in some living form, were thought to reside inside the stūpas (289–91, 300–301).

The stūpa, as the Buddha or other saint, not only embodies the timeless and immovable wisdom but also the various other, more active aspects of the enlightened personality. Like the living saint, the stūpa can be seen ''as radiating a kind of beneficial power'' and as a source of blessings. Thus the *Buddhavaṃsa* remarks, ''The ancients say that the dispersal of the relics of Gotama, the great seer, was out of compassion for living beings'' (Harvey 1984, 69). Schopen tells us that ''the physical relics of Śākyamuni were endowed with more than just 'life' or 'breath.' They were 'informed,' *'parfumée,'* 'saturated,' 'pervaded,' 'imbued' with just those characteristics which defined the living Buddha.'' A Kharoṣṭhī inscription from the first century C.E. thus speaks of the relics as ''infused with morality, infused with concentration, infused with wisdom. . . . That is, the relics themselves were thought to retain—to be infused with, impregnated with—the qualities that animated and defined the living Buddha'' (Schopen 1987a, 205). An inscription of Senavarma, dating to the early first century C.E., says in part, ''I establish these relics which are infused with morality, infused with concentration, wisdom, emancipation and knowledge and vision.'' Schopen remarks, ''The list of faculties and qualities given here looks very much as though it may have been intended for, or is perhaps a haplography of, what the Pāli tradition calls the five *sampadās* or 'attainments' and, of course, normally only a living person can be 'infused' with such 'attainments' '' (1987a, 204–5).

The active compassion of the stūpa is also seen in the magical powers attributed to it. Thus, the stūpa is understood as having a central role in affording protection to kings and their subjects (Fussman 1986, 48). The relics of the stūpa, in fact, seem to have many of the same powers as living saints. Harvey cites the example of King Duṭṭahagāmaṇi, who is shown in the *Mahāvaṃsa* enshrining some relics of Gautama in the great stūpa at Anurādhapura, upon which the relics rise into the air in their casket and emerge to form the shape of the Buddha (1984, 69). The relics, in other words, pass through solid objects (the walls of the stūpa), fly through the air, and assume a certain shape, all reminiscent of the *ṛddhis*.[10]

During their lives, the glory of the saints is restricted by their frail human frames. After their passing, however, in the stūpa the saints may reveal their full splendor, in bodies of vast, multidimensional, and magnificent proportions. A fully developed example of this tendency in the postmortem body of the saint is seen in the discussions of the stūpa in the *Saddharmapuṇḍarīka Sūtra*.[11] Chapter 11 (*Sps* 149–61 [Kn., 227–54]), in particular, describes the central stūpa of the text, which is five hundred *yojana*s high, two hundred and fifty *yojana*s wide, and which appears miraculously out of the earth and comes to rest in midair. This stūpa is made out of the seven precious substances, has five thousand banisters, is filled with innumerable chambers, is adorned with countless jeweled rosaries and banners, and is hung with ten billions of jeweled bells. The scent of sandalwood and Tamāla leaf fills the air. The stūpa thus reveals the unbounded charisma of the Buddha as prototypical Buddhist saint in a way more manifest than could his ordinary human body.

In the center of the stūpa of the *Saddharmapuṇḍarīka Sūtra* is the buddha Prabhūtaratna; this buddha declares that the stūpa is, in fact, the form *(vigraha)* of his own body *(ātmabhāva, =śarīra, BHSD* 92) (*Sps* 150.12 and 14 [Kn., 231]). Many eons ago, Prabhūtaratna took the vow that wherever the *Saddharmapuṇḍarīka Sūtra* would be preached, he would appear and be present, in the body of his miraculous stūpa, so that he could hear the preaching and confirm its truth. Śākyamuni Buddha comes to sit next to him in the center of the stūpa, suggesting that these two buddhas are one in essence (Hirakawa 1963, 88). Here the stūpa is presented as the body of the former saint, in this case Prabhūtaratna, in which he is alive and present. In addition, in the stūpa he is seen to be one with Śākyamuni and closely identified with the preaching of the dharma as the *Saddharmapuṇḍarīka Sūtra.* From the center of the stūpa where the buddha(s) reside, emanations go out to the ten directions for the purpose of teaching the dharma. The idea of a buddha at the center of the stūpa sending out emanations to the ten directions seems to be, from the viewpoint of the text, a standard one, for this phenomenon is repeated twice in chapter 11. First we are told of Prabhūtaratna's emanations. Then, Śākyamuni Buddha sends out emanations filling all of space. It is further made clear that these emanations are integrally part of the central buddhas. For example, if the entire body of Prabhūtaratna is to appear in the stūpa, these emanations must be gathered from the regions where they are preaching the dharma (*Sps* 150.8ff. [Kn., 231ff.]). In the *Saddharmapuṇḍarīka Sūtra,* then, the stūpa as a modality of the saints has, like their human bodies, both quiescent and active dimensions, both wisdom (the buddhas in the center of the stūpa) and compassionate radiation to sentient beings (the buddha emanations).

The jeweled stūpa is also entirely pure, the appropriate residence for Śākyamuni Buddha in his complete body, when all his emanations are gathered to him. For example, the emanations of the Buddha determine to go "to the Saha world system, to the place of Śākyamuni Buddha . . . to the Jeweled stūpa of the Thus Come One Prabhūtaratna." When they come to the stūpa, the world is suddenly transformed, becoming resplendent with jewels, lapis lazuli, and other precious substances. Then Śākyamuni Buddha conjures up for each of the emanations myriads of buddha fields, making them all pure. These are free of beings of the six realms of saṃsāra—including hell, *preta* (ghost), animal, human, *asura* (jealous god), and *deva* worlds—except for those gathered at the assembly. All these realms are a single buddha field, adorned with jewels, banners, and so on (*Sps* 151–52 [Kn., 232–35]). In other words, the stūpa is a circumscribed symbol and, at the same time, the very being of the cosmos itself, in all its purity. This cosmic valence of the Buddha as stūpa is again, of course, the grand manifestation of a meaning that was more hidden in the living saint: as Conze, Lamotte, and others have pointed out, from early times the Buddha was considered a human being who was, at the same time, an enlightened one, inseparable from the ultimate truth and reality of the universe as a totality (Conze 1962b, 168–72; Lamotte 1958, 689).

The Stūpa Cult

The Purpose of the Stūpa and Its Cult

The suppliant of the living saints longs to see them and thereby to participate in their enlightened charisma and receive their blessings. Similarly, the suppliants of the saints-passed-beyond long to see them in their stūpas for the same ends. In this respect, in the *Saddharmapuṇḍarīka Sūtra,* the bodhisattva Mahāpratibhāna asks Buddha Śākyamuni to show the body of the buddha Prabhūtaratna. Śākyamuni's response is to refer to the stūpa, remarking that when Prabhūtaratna made his vow, it included the provision that when his body was to be shown to the four classes of *śrāvakas*, then all his emanations should be gathered to his stūpa and the stūpa should then be opened and his body shown (*Sps* 150.8ff. [Kn., 230–31]). In fact, the stūpa provides the vehicle for the Buddha, passed away, to appear living and present within the world. Thus, the great sage who has attained extinction has come and entered into the stūpa made of precious substances (153.28–31 [238]). This seeing of the Buddha is clearly the longed-for goal of the spiritual life surrounding the stūpa of the *Saddharmapuṇḍarīka Sūtra.* It is a seeing in relation to which the confessions, offerings, praises, and other liturgical acts all make sense. In this respect, it is no doubt a self-sufficient justification of his far-flung journeys when the bodhisattva Gadgadasvara reports in the *Saddharmapuṇḍarīka Sūtra* to the buddha of his realm that he has promoted the welfare of beings, has "seen the stūpa of the relics [*dhātustūpa*] of the arhant, *tathāgata, samyaksaṃbuddha* Prabhūtaratna and venerated it [*vandita*], seen the *tathāgata* Śākyamuni and venerated him, and seen Mañjuśrī, the youthful prince" (149.8–11 [404]). Other texts similarly emphasize the importance of the stūpa as the place where one may come into the presence of the Buddha and see him.[12]

The *Avalokita Sūtra,* a text within the *Mahāvastu* (*Mv* 2:401–536 [Jns., 274–354]),[13] provides insight into various specific goals to which participation in the stūpa might be thought to lead. The text remarks that "when the lights of the world have passed to nirvaṇa, [one should] adore the Buddha's stūpas again and again" (2:501 [2:336]). According to the *Avalokita Sūtra,* there is a twofold goal to the veneration of the stūpa.[14] On the one hand, one may achieve great merit and gain good karmic consequences, including favorable rebirths. On the other, worship of the Buddha at his stūpa leads toward complete and perfect enlightenment. In relation to the first, the *Avalokita Sūtra* has a great deal to say about the relative merit that is gained through participation in the cult of the stūpa. Through seeing the Buddha at the stūpa and making offerings to him, one becomes endowed with well-being, beauty, and wealth (2:490 [2:330]), and one's possessions will not be stolen by robbers or burned in a fire (2:495 [2:333]). In addition, one may expect excellent rebirths, in families of high standing and prosperity, as a great king (2:490–91 [2:330]), as a god, and even as Brahmā himself (2:491–92

[2:331]). The gains won through stūpa worship are not only physical but moral and psychological. Thus, one becomes "mindful, thoughtful, virtuous and assured" (2:489–90 [2:329]). One also becomes "most charitable, brave, freely generous, and not miserly" (2:490 [2:330]), as well as free from misery and oppression (2:495 [2:333]). Through the worship of stūpas, one also wins the respect and honor of beings, both human and superhuman (2:490 [2:330] and 2:496 [2:333]). In summary, it is said in the text that in relation to the benefits to be gained, "one cannot complete the tale, even in hundreds of *koṭis* of *kalpas,* of those who have reverentially saluted a stūpa" (2:492 [2:331]).

The ultimate goal of the stūpa cult as described in the *Avalokita Sūtra* is no less than the attainment of enlightenment (*Mv* 2:489 [Jns., 2:329]). The section of the text concerned with the stūpa cult begins with the remark that one should venerate a stūpa, "having turned his thoughts to enlightenment for the sake of all living things" (2:489 [2:329]). In other words, the stūpa is to be worshiped in the context of the aspiration to enlightenment. Thus, one "shall beget the resolution to become a Buddha in the world" (2:507 [2:339]). Again, it is appropriate to give rise to "a wish for enlightenment into the highest truth" while making an offering of sandalwood powder (2:532 [2:352]). The references to the enlightenment of those who worship stūpas continue. For one who removes withered flowers from a buddha's stūpa, "the noble supreme enlightenment is not far off" (2:532 [2:352]). And, "having enjoyed well-being for thousands of *koṭis* of *kalpas,* for hundreds of *nayutas* of *kalpas,* full of wisdom he awakens to supreme enlightenment" (2:496 [2:333]). "And when he has for a very long time pursued the good in his various lives, he becomes a peerless Buddha in the world" (2:505 [2:338]). "He shall go to the *bodhi* throne at the tree which is the lord of all that grows, and there, without a peer, he shall awaken to the excellent supreme enlightenment" (2:512 [2:341]). "He becomes a Buddha" (2:531 [2:351]). Having attained enlightenment, one becomes invulnerable to injury. "Neither poison nor weapon assails him, nor fire or the blazing brand" (2:531 [2:351]). "He attains the incomparable enlightenment. Having established in the perfect griefless way thousands of *nayutas* of *koṭis* of beings and set rolling in all the world the matchless wheel, he afterwards passes away, his passions quelled and his lusts destroyed" (2:507 [2:339]).

Through this worship, in the context of which one progresses toward enlightenment, one comes to possess the virtues of the path to nirvāṇa such as strength and energy (*Mv* 2:492 [Jns., 2:331]), patience *(kṣānti)* (2:597 [2:334]), mindfulness (2:495 [2:332–33]), understanding of the dharma (2:490 [2:330]), and all good qualities *(guṇa)* (2:497 [2:334]). Moreover, the worshiper of stūpas attains wisdom, for "he has perceived the unsubstantiality *[nairātmya]* and emptiness *[śūnyatā]* of them" (2:490 [2:330]). And through one's worship, one wins that sign of attainment, magical power (2:494 [2:332]), remembering former lives, and so forth (2:494 [2:332]). Thus, one becomes worthy of offerings (2:497 [2:334]). Whoever treats him unkindly or unfairly shall suffer dire consequences (2:499 [2:335]). Thus "he becomes honoured of men as he most nobly fares along in the way of the Conqueror" (2:507 [2:339]).

That stūpa worship was understood to lead toward the goal of enlightenment is seen in other evidence. For example, the existence of "supreme wisdom" *(an-*

uttarajñāna) as a goal of the stūpa cult has been noted by Schopen through his analysis of lithic inscriptions at the site of Indian stūpas (1985, 38). Allusions to the stūpa cult as a vehicle to the goal of enlightenment are also found in *vinaya* texts examined by Bareau. A Mūlasarvāstivdin account, for example, gives the vow that one is to make while standing before the stūpa: "By virtue of the roots of goodness *(kuśalamūla)* existing in the ultimate *(anuttara)* field of merit *(puṇyakṣetra)* of these offerings, may I from birth to birth arrive at the end of existences, at that which is marked by the absence of the growing old of the body."[15] In addition, in the view of the *Saddharmapuṇḍarīka Sūtra,* as Hirakawa points out, "worshiping and making offerings at *stūpas* were practices that led to Buddhahood" (1987, 95). In Śāntideva's reporting, the *Saddharmapuṇḍarīka Sūtra* tells us that those who in the past engaged and in the present engage in such activities either have become or will become "partakers of enlightenment" and "Buddhas in the world." "All these have attained the highest enlightenment" (*Ss* 54:24ff. [BR., 94–95]). According to the *Saddharmapuṇḍarīka Sūtra,* through such acts, the two traditional benefits are achieved. On the one hand, one accrues illimitable merit, thus furthering one's progression to the final goal. On the other hand, participation in the cult leads to the wisdom of liberation. Those who constructed, adorned, and worshiped stūpas "have all of them reached enlightenment; they have become compassionate and, by rousing many *bodhisattvas,* have saved *koṭis* of creatures" (*Sps* 34.19ff. [Kn., 50–51]).[16]

For those who hope to reach this supreme goal, the text suggests as a model for all to emulate one of the Buddha's closest disciples, Mahāmaudgalyāyana. In a prediction made in the text by Buddha Śākyamuni concerning him, the main activity of Mahāmaudgalyāyana on his journey to enlightenment seems to be the worship of buddhas during life and after death in their stūpas, through which he attains enlightenment.

> I announce to you, monks, I make known, that the senior Mahā-Maudgalyāyana here present, my disciple, shall propitiate twenty-eight thousand Buddhas and pay those Lords homage of various kinds; he shall show them respect, &c., and after their expiration build Stūpas consisting of seven precious substances, to wit, gold, silver, lapis lazuli, crystal, red pearl, emerald, and, seventhly, coral; (Stūpas) a thousand yojanas in height and five hundred yojanas in circumference, which Stūpas he shall worship in different ways, with flowers, incense, perfumed wreaths, ointments, powder, robes, umbrellas, banners, flags, and triumphal streamers. Afterwards he shall again pay a similar worship to twenty hundred thousand koṭis of Buddhas; he shall show respect, &c. (*Sps* 102.1–16 [Kn., 149–50])

Most appropriately, Mahāmaudgalyāyana's name as a buddha shall be "Tamālapattracandanagandha," "scent [of] *tamāla* leaves and sandalwood," supreme offerings that should be presented at stūpas.

Conventions of Respect toward the Stūpa

In the preceding discussion, we have seen that the Buddhist saints, by virtue of their realization and holy power, are worthy of deep respect. One should respect the living saints in order to accrue merit and wisdom and also to avoid the results, sometimes calamitous, of inappropriate behavior. The same is true of the saints after death, in their stūpas. Bareau has examined certain sections of the *vinayas* of several Nikāya traditions, which directly pertain to stūpas.[17] In Indian Buddhism, he tells us, the stūpa represents the Buddha and borrows from him a personality; this accounts for the marks of respect that are due to it. Thus, one should treat the stūpa as one would treat the Buddha. For example, the Sarvāstivādins say that just as one should not praise a human being above the Buddha, likewise, one should not praise a person above a stūpa. Just as one would give the Buddha as a guest the best room, likewise one should give a reliquary—a miniature stūpa—the best room. Likewise, one should never stay in an upper room with the reliquary in a lower, but vice versa (Bareau 1962, 252–53).

In a legal perspective, the stūpa—as the Buddha—is viewed as a "person," with legal rights and privileges. Bareau comments, "Like any person, the *stūpa* has the right to possessions . . . and this right must be protected" (1962, 253).[18] Thus, there are prohibitions against anyone's taking and using the goods belonging to the stūpa. Those things belonging to a stūpa must be kept separate from the possessions of the "*saṃgha* of the four directions."[19] Destruction of a stūpa is a very grave offense (1962, 253–57).

An an incarnation of the Buddha, the stūpa, once consecrated, is considered at all times sacred. Thus, the texts of the non-Mahāyāna schools set out a variety of behavioral forms to be observed whether or not any formal liturgical acts are in progress, including some positive conventions and the more numerous prohibitions. Bareau remarks that positive behavioral conventions are very rarely mentioned in the texts and believes that the reason for this is similar to the reason for the lack of information given concerning mental attitude accompanying the making of offerings: the positive conventions were probably in such common usage that they did not need to be spelled out. Nevertheless, some such conventions in the form of marks of respect are mentioned in the documents. Thus, one should circumambulate the stūpa clockwise; one should make prostrations; one should offer praises and vows. Bareau points out that, in spite of only rare mention in the texts, such acts of respect were no doubt a regular and central part of the cult of the stūpa, as shown by the sculptures on and around stūpas, commonly depicting such acts (1962, 250–51).

Much more common in the texts are various kinds of prohibitions. While within the precincts of the stūpa, one must not cover one's head or one's shoulder. When one carries an image from one place to another, one must do so with care and respect. One must not sit down before a stūpa and extend one's legs out toward it. When carrying a reliquary, one should not stick it under one's arm after the fashion of a common parcel. One should not enter the stūpa wearing shoes of leather, nor should one enter the stūpa or make circumambulation wearing shoes or boots that are ornamented. Many other prohibitions regarding shoes are given. One must at all times respect the sanctity of the stūpa and its precincts. One must not make use of the gardens of the stūpa, its flowers and fruits, claiming that this is permissible because the Buddha has transcended passion, aggression, and ignorance. One must likewise not disturb offerings that have been made to the stūpa by others. Activities such as washing, dyeing, or drying clothes must not be carried out within the precincts of a stūpa. One must not wash one's face or hands, nor one's begging bowl, in the ponds of the stūpa grounds. These prohibitions are summarized by, in Bareau's words, "the obligation to not employ possessions of the *stūpa* for profane and personal ends." One should also protect the sacrality of the stūpa from a variety of defilements, including contact with the human body, with animals, and with corpses. The prohibition against contact with the human body explains the interdiction against washing oneself in the stūpa ponds. For the same reasons, one must not spit or yawn within the precincts of the stūpa, and even the breath is considered impure. In addition, the structure of the stūpa itself is subject to a variety of prohibitions. One may not climb upon it, even for the purpose of making offerings (Bareau 1962, 253–54). All these prohibitions mark the stūpa off as a sacred space, an incarnation of the very body of the Buddha, within which one must behave in a particular and ritualized way.

Some Ritual Elements of the Stūpa Cult

In the Buddhist cult of saints, as noted in previous chapters, ritualized behavior plays a central role. Many examples of this fact have already been seen in the hagiographies of the various living saints: the Buddha, Mahākāśyapa, Śāriputra, Piṇḍolabhāradvāja, Upagupta, the pratyekabuddhas, the sixteen great arhants, the cults of the arhants in general, and the bodhisattva saints. In general, one establishes oneself in respectful relation to these saints through the vocabulary of cultic behavior. Specifically, one is to prostrate oneself to the saints and make circumambulation around them. One is to attend them respectfully, making gifts of food, water, and other material items, offer confessions and praises, utter aspirations, follow their instructions, and so on. Typically, of course, the various kinds of behaviors are mentioned in the hagiographies and other texts in passing, with no conscious attempt at systematic listing or explanation. The reason is probably, as Bareau suggests, that such behaviors are so well known that they are taken for granted and not regarded as needing textual confirmation or elaboration. However, textual mentions are not entirely unknown, and in the *Daśabhūmivyākhyāna,*[20] for example, one finds just such an attempt to systematize the range of behaviors appropriate toward saints.[21] The *Daśabhūmivyākhyāna* gives three categories of offering service, or *pūjā,* to be given to those worthy of veneration: material offering *(arthacaryā),* offerings of respect *(satkāracaryā),* and offering through righteous living *(saṃskāracaryā).* The second category is explained by a Chinese commentator[22] as containing the following items:

1. "Utter a salutation."
2. "Bow reverentially."
3. "Spread a cushion."
4. "Take off your sandals."
5. "Expose partially (the right shoulder)."
6. "Prostrate yourself, making five circular impressions with the forehead, two palms, and the two kneecaps."
7. "Touch the feet with the forehead."
8. "Squat, bending the right knee."

9. "Sit with both legs crossed."
10. "Concentrate with palms joined [at the heart]."
11. "Circumambulate sunwise."
12. "Lift head high enough to look about at the level of another's heart" (Nakamura 1951, 347).

Item 12 is the proper posture to be maintained when one sits in front of a revered person ready to receive instruction.[23] This list, of course, constitutes a systematic exposition of the same elements seen piecemeal in previous chapters, as defining the relationship of saints and their suppliants.

It should not be surprising that the same ritual patterns evident in the cult of the living saints also articulate the relation of suppliant to saint in the cult of the stūpas. Thus, for example, one must circumambulate the stūpa (see Nakamura 1951, 345).[24] In the circumambulation *(pradakṣiṇā),* one walks around the stūpa in a clockwise direction, keeping one's right side toward the stūpa. According to the Chinese pilgrim I-ching, "that one should not walk round the holy stūpa with sandals on was taught expressly from the beginning" (Takakusu 1896, 22). Evidently, one might also make circumambulations holding a lamp (Bénisti 1960, 55). In East Asian tradition, one would circumambulate chanting or singing and scattering flowers; this perhaps reflects earlier, Indian practice. One may walk around one, three, or seven times, or many more times. Hsüan-tsang remarks that "circumambulating is done and the number of circlings is usually once or twice, but when one has special requests to make, the number increases according to its importance" (Nakamura 1951, 348).[25] The great merit of circumambulation is expressed in the *Mahāvaṃsa:* "Having turned one's thoughts toward supreme wisdom, for the welfare of all living beings, he who accomplishes the *pradakṣiṇā* around a *stūpa* of the protector of the world becomes skillful, endowed with benefits, wise, possessor of the sacred texts and, in the course of his various births, practices the path to supreme wisdom. He receives the praise of gods, of *yakṣas* and of *rākṣasas;* he is honored thus in various lives when he accomplishes the *pradakṣiṇā* around a *stūpa*" (Bénisti 1960, 55).

Other elements of stūpa worship have been brought to light by Bareau, and these, though sometimes more complex, similarly parallel the veneration carried out to the living saint. According to the Mahāsāṃghikas, for example, it is appropriate to offer flowers, perfumes, music, clothes, drink, and food to the images. Other traditions specify the same and additional offerings: bathing water, flowers, incense, lamps, perfume (unguents, perfumed oil, the scent of flowers), food, and musical instruments. The lamps may be widely placed in the stūpa, and the Sarvāstivādins, in fact, speak of the stūpa as a "place of lamps." Parasols may also be given in offering, these to be real ones and thus distinguished from the more durable figurations of parasols forming a permanent part of the structure of the stūpa at its zenith; banners are also to be offered (Bareau 1962, 244–45). What becomes of the food offered to the stūpa?[26] The Dharmaguptakas comment that the food and the drink offered at the stūpa must be consumed by the monks *(bhikṣu),* by the novices *(śrāmaṇera),* by the faithful laypeople, or by those who planned and constructed the stūpa.[27] Other offerings are sometimes specified in the texts. These include precious stones, generally in the form of necklaces, and bells made of gold or jewels. Also mentioned are elevated platforms that may serve as tables for offerings and as vehicles for transport. These vehicles, or carts, are also mentioned as part of the possessions of the stūpa, and this perhaps indicates that the procession of relics was a regular part of the activities surrounding the stūpa (245–47).

The *Avalokita Sūtra,* as contained in the *Mahāvastu,* presents a picture of the stūpa liturgy in substantial agreement with the picture presented by Bareau. In that text, liturgical acts include circumambulation, offering, the playing of music, the removal of dead flowers, and the cleaning of the stūpa. The offerings themselves include flowers and garlands of flowers, incense, perfume, lights, silk, a flag (to be put on the stūpa), a sunshade, a necklace of gems, and "network coverings" (*Mv* 2:489 [Jns., 2:329ff.]). One should honor the Buddha in his stūpa. One should "reverentially salute a stūpa" (2:592 [2:331]). One should adore the stūpa (2:491 [2:330]). One should render worship to a *tathāgata* (2:494 [2:332]). One should "put adornments on the conqueror's *cetiya*" (2:519 [2:345]). One should make a garland of flowers and place it as an offering on the stūpa (2:493 [2:331]) and offer garlands of flowers (2:492–93 [2:331]). One should place "a festoon of fine silk" as offering on the stūpa (2:494 [2:332]). One should offer "a festoon of fine silk and flowers" (2:495 [2:333]). One should make "a booth of festoons over the relics *[dhātu]*" (2:496 [2:333]). One should "put a flag on *cetiyas* of the Exalted One" (2:507 [2:339]) and give "a flag to the choicest of beings" (2:510 [2:341]). One should hold one light over the stūpa of the Buddha (2:514 [2:343]). Upon seeing the Buddha, one should honor him "with sunshades, flags and banners, incense and garlands" (2:508 [2:340]). One should play "on an instrument of music" at the Buddha's *cetiyas* (2:518 [2:345]). One should cleanse the stūpas of the *tathāgatas* and wash away the dust (2:519 [2:345]). One should anoint the stūpa with perfumes (2:524 [2:348]). One should place a necklace of gems on the *cetiya* of the conqueror (2:525 [2:348]). One should bring "network coverings to the *cetiyas* of the light of the world who is a great field of merit" (2:528 [2:350]). The text also makes it evident that one makes these offerings with particular intentions and vows: in worshiping a stūpa, the suppliant "shall beget the resolution to become a Buddha in the world" (2:507 [2:339]). And through his worship, the suppliant is "turning his thoughts to enlightenment" (2:493 [2:331]).[28] Finally, one is enjoined to act as guardian of the teaching of the Buddha. One is to protect the "sons of the Buddha" (2:501 [2:336]), to "support the true *dharma*" and "guard the teaching of the Master" (2:502 [2:336–37]), and so on.[29]

Certain words are to be uttered in the making of offerings. According to the Mahāsāṃghikas, one states that one has made one's offerings "so that there will be abundance in this world and so that all beings, during the long night [of saṃsāra], may obtain peace and happiness." Also as mentioned, the Mūlasarvāstivādins present this aspiration as appropriate during the act of offering: "By virtue of the roots of goodness existing in the ultimate field of merit of these offerings, may I from birth to birth arrive at the end of existences, at that which is marked by the absence of the growing old of the body." In making offerings, one is also to offer praises. The Mūlasarvāstivādins direct one to advance toward the stūpa and extend offerings, all the while offering praises in abundance. In one version, the suppliant praises the "auspicious mind" *(kuśalacitta)* with which one does homage and makes offerings to the stūpa. This auspicious mind is said to be superior to a gift of a hundred thousand pieces of gold or a hundred thousand cartloads of gold. Prostrations are also part of the liturgy of offerings. The Mūlasarvāstivādins say that one should, in making offerings, prostrate oneself to the object of one's respect, touching knees, elbows, and forehead to the ground (Bareau 1962, 249–51).

It is worth remarking that—although apart from Schopen's study of stūpas of local saints (1991c) there has been no concerted study of this topic—it so far appears that the same general ritual acts carried out in relation to the stūpas of the Buddha were also associated with the stūpas of local saints. For example, Schopen has suggested that the same ritual donations pertinent to the stūpas of the Buddha were also characteristic of stūpas to local saints. Thus the stūpa of a local saint "is presented with 'gifts' exactly like the stūpas of the Buddha himself were" (1991c, 299). Moreover, the same gifts are given (299). In examining stūpa no. 2 at Sāñcī built over the remains of a local saint, Schopen remarks that coping stones, cross-bars, rail-pillars, and pavement slabs, and so on were donated to this stūpa "just as they were to the stūpa of the Buddha at the site" (299). Moreover, "in neither form nor content do the inscriptions associated with *Stūpa* no. 2 differ from those associated with *Stūpa* no. 1 [to the Buddha]. The two sets are virtually indistinguishable" (299).

Bareau remarks upon the general reticence of the texts that he examined vis-à-vis the spiritual value and inner attitude of offerings (1962, 52). In fact, only the Mahāsāṃghika and the Mūlasarvāstivāda make allusion to these dimensions of the act of offering. The other early traditions, Bareau says, pass over the inner, mental aspect of the act of offerings in silence. Bareau further expresses surprise that the texts, so detailed regarding the comportment of monastics and laypeople in relation to the stūpa, should have so little to say in the matter of the internal attitude or disposition of the one who makes the offerings. Bareau then addresses the issue of what conclusions may be drawn from this fact. "Must one conclude that the act of offering is in itself sufficient and has no need to be accompanied by pious thoughts? Such would be quite out of keeping with the very spirit of Indian Buddhism which, almost always in the course of its long history and *a fortiori* to this remote period, remained an interior religion" (249). According to Bareau, interiority remained characteristic of Buddhism throughout its various periods and manifestations. It is thus not to be expected, Bareau concludes, that the worship of the stūpa would be an exception to this fundamental character of the tradition.

In light of this, Bareau suggests another hypothesis.

> May one then not perhaps conclude, to the contrary, that these vows were so well established in usage, were so completely the norm, that the authors of our texts felt themselves able to pass over [their mention]? This would seem quite in contrast with their generally detailed approach, but it is true that the *Vinayapiṭaka*,

> in contrast to the *Sūtrapiṭaka* and the *Abhidharmapiṭaka,* breathes not a word of many spiritual practices, meditations, contemplations, etc. . . . that constitute the very essence of the Buddhist "religion." (249)

Bareau next raises the question concerning another aspect of the "mental attitude" that accompanies offerings made at the stūpa. What acts of recitation or meditation may suppliants have carried out as they stood within the stūpa precincts before a revered image and made offerings? Of this, Bareau says, the texts he consulted say nothing. Again, this silencc docs not tcll us anything about what may or may not have occurred in that context. However, by way of indicating what may well have occurred in those situations, Bareau cites contemporary practice. "Today, in Ceylon where the antiquity of Buddhism is preserved, the cult rendered to the *stūpas* by laypeople as by monks is normally accompanied by meditation and above all by recitation, whether purely mental or in an audible voice, of certain stanzas *(gāthā)*" (249). Such, Bareau thinks, may well have been the case in the ancient stūpa liturgies and accords well with the various expressions of aspirations made in the context of stūpa worship we have seen in the works cited.

Participants in the Stūpa Cult

Three different kinds of Buddhists are depicted in the evidence as participating in the stūpa cult: laypeople, monastics, and forest renunciants. First, of course, are the laypeople. Virtually every text dealing with the stūpa depicts the laity as centrally concerned with stūpa worship. The *Avalokita Sūtra,* for example, mentions many benefits to be derived from stūpa worship. The fact that so many of these would have been of particular interest to the layperson—such as wealth, protection from robbers, rebirth in a high caste, rebirth in a divine realm, and so on—suggests that, in the text, laypeople play and are understood to play a central role in the stūpa cult. (This is, of course, not to say that such layfolk were necessarily uninterested in the ultimate goal of supreme enlightenment, or that renunciants would have been entirely uninterested in many of these relative goals.)

But what of Buddhist renunciants' participation in the stūpa cult? The two-tiered model, of course, would have it that renunciants (monastics) are not to—and do not—participate in stūpa worship. Evidence showing the fallacy of such a belief, at least in relation to the non-Pāli Nikāya traditions, has been provided by Bareau in his article on stūpas (1962). Most important in the present context, the many conventions and rules in these texts concerning appropriate behavior at stūpas are not applied just to laypeople but to monks as well. Bareau: "Neither can one at all say that this cult [of the stūpa] is a matter exclusively for laypeople for, in almost all of our sources, the counsel given on various matters is addressed to monks as much as and even more than to laypeople" (249). In a similar vein, in the same article, Bareau studies a number of different pre-Mahāyāna versions of the story of the building of a stūpa by Buddha Śākyamuni to the former buddha Kāśyapa. The mere fact that Śākyamuni himself, the paradigmatic renunciant, is shown building a stūpa is of course significant, suggesting that the behavior is not only permissible but perhaps normative for renunciants. Beyond this, one of the main points of this story is that the Buddha insists on the importance of the stūpa to his renunciant disciples, telling them of the inestimable merit of constructing a stūpa and of paying homage and making offerings to it (258). Moreover, when they specifically request authorization to assist in the building of the stūpa, he grants them authorization (257ff.). This important story has been noticed by Hirakawa, who offers the obvious conclusion: the fact that this story is found in the *vinayas* of the monastic traditions suggests that the monastic *saṃgha* "must have participated in the worship of stūpas" (1963, 104).[30]

Schopen has produced other evidence that points in the same direction (1985 and 1991c). In inscriptions from the railings of Bhārhut and Sāñcī, dating from 120 to 80 B.C.E., "a considerable portion of the donors" were Buddhist renunciants, as much as 40 percent in the case of Bhārhut. In the Kharoṣṭhī inscriptions edited by Konow, over 40 percent of the donors were renunciants. In donative inscriptions from later periods, the percentage of renunciant donors is even higher. In inscriptions that Schopen judges to be Mahāyānist, over 70 percent of the donors are renunciants. From this evidence, Schopen concludes, "None of this accords very well—if at all—with received views on the matter, with the views that maintain that . . . [the] cult was essentially and overwhelmingly a lay concern in the Indian Buddhist context" (1985, 23–26).

Schopen has also shown that stūpa worship was not only a central concern of Buddhist renunciants from an early time but that stūpas were built at and within monastic compounds on a regular basis. Moreover, such stūpas were not necessarily built by laypeople nor were they even always available for lay worship. Schopen notes cases in which no donative inscriptions exist, implying that the monastery itself may have paid for the construction. And he also points out that some stūpas, particularly those of local saints, were situated in such a way as to suggest a "privatization" of the cult, according to which only the monks of the monastery would have had ready access to the stūpa (1991c, 311–16).

This much may be accepted, but there remains the curious anomaly apparently presented by the Pāli evidence that monastics within Pāli tradition, in contrast to those in other Nikāya schools, were not permitted to and did not actively participate in the stūpa cult. Evidence typically cited in support of this view is, as we have seen, twofold. First, the Pāli *Mahāparinibbāna Sutta* seems to disallow the worship of the stūpa by monastics. Second, in apparent confirmation of a prohibition by the *Mahāparinibbāna Sutta*, the extant Pāli *vinaya* is missing references, found in the other *vinayas*, to behavior at stūpas appropriate to monastics. In two recent articles, Schopen has brought forward good reasons for believing that stūpa worship by monastics was in fact present and accepted in early Pāli tradition just as it was in the other Nikāya schools. In the first article (1991b), Schopen contends that the so-called prohibition in the *Mahāparinirvāṇa Sūtra* (Pāli and other versions) forbidding participation in stūpa worship by monastics in general represents a misreading of the passage in question. In fact, this passage does not concern the worship of stūpas at all and is not addressed to all monastics. In defense of his thesis, Schopen argues that the key technical term in this passage—*śarīra-*

pūjā—does not refer to the worship of the Buddha's relics but rather to the cultic treatment of the Buddha's body after his death, beginning with the wrapping of the body and continuing up to the cremation.[31] The injunction in this passage thus concerns a ritual activity quite different from the cult of relics in stūpa worship. Schopen further believes that the injunction against *śarīrapūjā* is addressed not to monastics in general but specifically to Ānanda, who, as an as-yet-to-be-realized *bhikṣu,* does not have the senior status required of one who performs *śarīrapūjā*. In the Sanskrit version, for example, Mahākāśyapa *does* have this status and *is* shown performing *śarīrapūjā*. For both these reasons, then, it is incorrect to take this passage in the *Mahāparinirvāṇa Sūtra* as forbidding all monastics to engage in the worship of stūpas (Schopen 1991b, 193–95).

In the second article (1989), Schopen puts forward evidence suggesting that the absence of references to stūpa worship in the Pāli *vinaya* may be a later development.[32] In fact, a reading of canonical and extracanonical tradition, viewed in light of the history of the Pāli canon and of the evidence of archaeology, implies that the Pāli *vinaya* originally contained such rules. Therefore, "the fact that they are no longer found in the *Vinaya* known to us could, apparently, only be explained by assuming that either they had inadvertently dropped out of the manuscripts or, perhaps, were intentionally written out" (93). Yet the rules regarding stūpas do not occur in a single block but rather are scattered throughout the *Kṣudrakavastu*s of the various *vinaya*s and are found even in other sections of the *vinaya*s as well (95). Assuming the same type of pattern for the Pāli *vinaya,*

> It would be easy enough to see how some of these scattered rules would have been lost through accidents of transmission, but that all such rules would have been lost in this way seems very unlikely. . . . In light of this the total absence of rules regarding *stūpas* in the Pāli *Vinaya* would seem to make sense only if they had been systematically removed. But acknowledging the possibility—if not the likelihood—of such a systematic removal having actually occurred is one thing; knowing why it might have occurred is something else again. (95)[33]

Schopen's two articles, then, suggest not only that monastics in early Pāli tradition were not disallowed from worshiping at stūpas but that they did in fact participate in the stūpa cult. Thus, as far as stūpa worship by monastics is concerned, the Pāli evidence appears to present a general picture not substantially different from that of the other Nikāya traditions.

One of the difficulties in interpreting evidence of renunciant support for and worship at stūpas, is that it is not always clear what kind of renunciants are meant. Bareau's references, coming as they do from the various classical *vinaya*s, appear specifically to indicate settled monastics who lived in monasteries and followed the *prātimokṣa,* but this is not always clear in the case of the inscriptions cited by Schopen. Thus, for example, some incriptions read *sramaṇa,* and it is unclear whether monastic or forest renunciants are meant. Furthermore, although many inscriptions read *bhikṣu,* this term need not invariably indicate a monastic in the classical sense. Although in Schopen's evidence sometimes these *bhikṣu*s are clearly settled monastics, this cannot be assumed in the case of every such inscription. This raises the issue of the participation of nonmonastic renunciants in the cult of the stūpa. Given that stūpa worship was important for settled monastics following the *vinaya,* is there any evidence that it also played a central role in the religious lives of forest renunciants?

The *Avalokita Sūtra,* in fact, suggests a sometimes close relation between stūpa worship and forest renunciation. This may be seen in one narratively unified section that presents a coherent portrait of the forest renunciant who makes offerings at stūpas (*Mv* 2:516.2–517.4 [Jns., 2:344]). One who worships at stūpas has retired to the forest *(pavana),* is pure in discipline *(viśuddhaśīla),* maintains celibacy *(brahmacarya),* never flags in the practice of the stages of meditation *(dhyāna),* is abundant in (the practice of) these, takes no delight whatever in sensual enjoyment *(kāmabhoga),* and has attained the highest excellence *(suviśeṣaprāpta).* Moreover, the one who worships at stūpas possesses the supernatural powers *(abhijñā)* and does not relinquish the *bodhicitta;* he abides in loving-kindness *(maitrā=maitri),* his mind is uplifted *(hṛṣṭacitta),* and his spiritual enjoyment (*bhoga*) does not decrease. In addition, he possesses a wondrous body, worthy of being seen. Finally, he is venerated by the gods. Closely similar verses in the *Avalokana Sūtra,* preserved in the *Śikṣāsamuccaya,* add that the one who worships stūpas "dwells in the air of the forest, devotes himself to meditation and attains excellence." He is steadfast, devoted to the practice of the meditation stages *(dhyāna),* is noble-minded *(adīnacitta),* and does not abandon wisdom *(jñāna)* (*Ss* 159.9–28 [BR., 273]). From the viewpoint of these verses in the *Avalokita Sūtra* and the corresponding verses in the *Avalokana Sūtra,* the paradigmatic forest renunciant indeed participates in the cult of stūpas.

Hirakawa has presented an argument that specifically links forest saints of the early or proto-Mahāyāna with stūpas and their cult. In an essay translated from the Japanese and published in English in 1963, Hirakawa proposes a theory—novel at the time—of the origins of the Mahāyāna.[34] Hirakawa draws our attention to the figure of the "renunciant *bodhisattva,*" the bodhisattva who is not a layperson, but who has renounced the world. Particularly important in the present context, this renunciant bodhisattva is also not a monastic, has not taken the monastic *pravrajyā* or full ordination *(upasampadā),* and does not follow the monastic *prātimokṣa.* Having no evident connection to the monastery, this bodhisattva lives elsewhere and engages in activities that are very different from those of the monastic. In certain early Mahāyāna texts, Hirakawa tells us, a contrast is continually drawn between the *śrāvakasaṃgha* (the monastic order) and the *bodhisattvagaṇa* (group or community) of bodhisattvas (1963, 70).[35] It is the *bodhisattvagaṇa* to which the Mahāyāna *sūtras* are addressed, and this Mahāyāna community is made up of the sons of good family *(kulaputra)* and the daughters of good family *(kuladuhitṛ),* understood as bodhisattvas.

This conception of community stands in marked contrast to the structure of community implied by the term *saṃgha* that is presented in the pre-Mahāyāna monastic schools. There, the Buddhist community is fourfold and is made up of monks *(bhikṣu)* and nuns *(bhikṣuṇī)* (the monastic *saṃgha*), on the one hand, and laymen *(upāsaka)* and laywomen *(upāsikā),* on the other. Moreover, although both the Mahāyāna community and the Nikāya community contain both laypeople and renunciants, the relation between the two groups is conceived quite differently in each case. In Nikāya Buddhism, the monastic renunciants embody a qualitatively superior spirituality, and the main function of the layfolk is to serve the monastic renunciants. In contrast, in the Mahāyāna conception, the terms *kulaputra* and *kuladuhitṛ* do not specify any fundamental qualitative spiritual distinction between laypeople and renunciants (Hirakawa 1963, 73). These facts suggest to Hirakawa that Mahāyāna Buddhism in its earliest formulation had an entirely different understanding of community and possessed actual communal forms that were different and scparate from the monastically centered forms of Nikāya Buddhism: "The Mahāyāna adherents were composed of an entirely different group of people from the Nikāya Buddhists" (72). The disjunction between the two communities is indicated by the fact that the Nikāya Buddhists do not use the terms *kulaputra* and *kuladuhitṛ,* just as the early Mahāyānists do not use the terminology of the *fourfold saṃgha* (69–73).

In addition, the life rule of the Mahāyāna community of laypeople and renunciants was different from the dominant life rules in Nikāya Buddhism. In the non-Mahāyāna schools, the monastics, on the one hand, passed through the monastic *pravrajyā,* by which in one ceremony they left the world and, in so doing, entered into the status of the *śrāmaṇera* (or *śrāmaṇerikā* [f.]) (novice). Later, they underwent full, *upasampadā* ordination, becoming *bhikṣus* (or *bhikṣuṇīs*), and followed the life rule as defined by the *prātimokṣa.* On the other hand, the layfolk became Buddhists by taking the triple refuge and following ethical conventions appropriate to their status, such as the fivefold *(pañca) śīla.* In early Mahāyāna Buddhism, by contrast, the behavior of both lay bodhisattvas and renunciant bodhisattvas was defined by a different life rule, or *śīla,* namely, that of the *daśakuśalakarmapatha.*[36] Thus, this "*śīla* of the ten virtuous actions" "is an ideal *śīla* to be observed by the priesthood [renunciants] and the laity alike"; "the fact that the early Mahāyānists utilized this leads us to conclude that a distinction was not made between the two" (Hirakawa 1963, 77). This is, of course, the same set of ten virtuous actions that we found recommended in Mahāyāna texts such as the *Ratnaguṇasaṃcayagāthā* and the *Rāṣṭrapālaparipṛcchā Sūtra.*[37] The *Mahāprajñāpāramitā Sūtra,* cited by Hirakawa, mentions the ten actions in the following way: "The *bodhisattvas* teach sentient beings and give them *daśakuśalakarmapathān;* they themselves practice the *daśakuśalakarmapathān* and make others practice them. They themselves practice [the first rule] and make others practice it [rules two through ten similarly mentioned]" (75–76). Indeed, Hirakawa tells us, "the characteristic feature of Mahāyāna Buddhism is expressed in encouraging others, as well as oneself, to practice the *daśakuśala.*" "We can therefore conclude that this was a constant practice since the earliest *Prajñāpāramitā Sūtra*" (76). As noted, according to Hirakawa, both lay bodhisattvas and renunciant bodhisattvas practiced the *śīla* of the ten virtuous actions as their primary and defining life rule. Nevertheless, this life rule seems to have had a slightly different form for the two classes of bodhisattvas. For example, the rule regarding sexual conduct ("to refrain from unethical sexual relationships") is for the lay bodhisattva, whereas for the renunciant bodhisattva, the rule means to refrain from sexual conduct altogether *(brahmacarya)* (77).

The primary *śīla* of the renunciant bodhisattva is thus quite different from the monastic *śīla* of the *bhikṣu* of Nikāya Buddhism. Hirakawa cites a number of other texts in which this distinction is similarly drawn (1963, 78). In addition, the method by which the renunciant bodhisattva "leaves the world" is also different from the monastic *pravrajyā* and *upasampadā*. "There are two Chinese translations of a *bodhisattvaprātimokṣa* and a *bodhisattvakarmavācanā,* which reveal a method of ordination into the *bodhisattva śīla.*" Hirakawa continues, "The ordinations discussed in these works differ vastly from the *upasampadā* method of the *vinayapiṭaka*" (79). Finally, a variety of additional evidence suggests to Hirakawa that, in the early period, the places where the monastics and the renunciant bodhisattvas lived were also entirely separate (80ff.). "The *bhikṣu* and *bodhisattva* [renunciant and lay] must have lived independent of each other" (81); and we are dealing in the early texts with "the fact of two [separate] *saṃghas*" (83). (It will be recalled that our analysis of certain Mahāyāna texts in Chapter 8 tends to confirm that in the early days of the Mahāyāna at least some renunciant bodhisattvas lived independently of Nikāya monasticism.) Thus, Hirakawa tells us, "I have shown through the examination of the relatively older Mahāyāna texts that the *bodhisattva* formed an organization separate from the *śrāvakasaṃgha*" (84).

This raises some important questions: If the renunciant bodhisattvas did not live in a monastic setting, where did they live? And if the monastery was not the institutional center for their Buddhism, does that mean that there was no institutional dimension to their religious life? Or did some other institution fulfill this function? According to Hirakawa, in the earliest Mahāyāna literature, the renunciant bodhisattvas are depicted as having two primary residences. First—and not surprising in light of the Mahāyāna texts we have examined—is the *āraṇyāyatana,* the forest retreat, where they lived in solitude and practiced meditation. In addition, the renunciant bodhisattvas are depicted as living at another place—namely, the stūpa, in order to study and be cared for when ill. In Hirakawa's words, in the early texts, "the living quarters are referred to as *āraṇyāyatana* and *stūpa.* The renunciant *bodhisattva* practices austerities in the *āraṇyāyatana,* but when he becomes ill or when he studies the *sūtras,* he goes to the *stūpa*" (1963, 96). When the renunciant bodhisattvas were fulfilling their vocation of meditation in retreat, they would live in their forest hermitages. But their Buddhism was not without its institutional side, and for this they came to the stūpa. Hirakawa tells us that "it was the *stūpa* which was the religious center for the renunciant *bodhisattva*" (85).[38]

Hirakawa develops his thesis about the nature and functions of the nonmonastic renunciant bodhisattvas living at stūpas in a later article (1987). Stūpas, Hirakawa says, became centers of religious orders, quite distinct from those based on the settled monastery. The bodhisattva renunciants, then, would have served as leaders of orders, teaching lay believers and receiving alms from them.

> However, although these religious specialists led lives similar to those who had abandoned the life of a householder, they still were not monks (*bhikṣus*) [and] . . . had not taken the full set of precepts *(upasampadā)*. . . . Because they felt that certain religious experiences were necessary if they were to teach others, these religious specialists not only taught lay believers but also engaged in strict religious practices. Consequently, they imitated the practices performed by Śākyamuni Buddha and strove to attain an enlightenment identical to that which

Śākyamuni had experienced. Since Śākyamuni had been called a *bodhisattva* before he had realized enlightenment, they too called themselves *bodhisattvas*. (94)

Hirakawa continues that the communities of laypeople and renunciants connected with the stūpas would have been primarily interested in two things: the Buddha's ability to save sentient beings and the types of practices that would enable people to realize buddhahood. These two interests are, of course, the two major trends that characterize the classical Mahāyāna, the notion of the Buddha as a saviour to be worshiped (Pure Land traditions) and the idea of the Buddha as an ideal to be emulated (wisdom traditions *[Ratnaguṇasaṃcayagāthā, Rāṣṭrapālaparipṛcchā Sūtra,* minor *Rāṣṭrapālaparipṛcchā Sūtra, Aṣṭasāhasrikāprajñāpāramitā Sūtra, Saṃdhinirmocana Sūtra,* and *Laṅkāvatāra Sūtra]).* Hirakawa then concludes that "the religious activities of these *bodhisattvas* eventually led to the development of Mahāyāna Buddhism" (1987, 94).

Hirakawa's analyses suggest the following image of renunciant bodhisattvas in the early or proto-Mahāyāna tradition.

1. They were forest renunciants, following forest practices in imitation of the Buddha and striving to attain the Buddha's full enlightenment.
2. They were religious leaders, whose spiritual authority in their own eyes and in the eyes of others was connected with their forest way of life and meditation practiced in retreat.
3. The stūpa played a number of roles in the life of the bodhisattva renunciants and, in an important sense, defined their kind of Buddhism. At the stūpa, they were able to carry out religious functions as leaders of orders and teachers of the laity. At the stūpa, they could also come to receive alms, to study, and to recuperate when sick. And, at the stūpa, their devotion to the Buddha and other saints could find an appropriate focus.

Hirakawa's work, then, parallels some of the major themes of this study. These include the paradigm of the Buddhist saint as a renunciant who emulates the Buddha; the following of a way of life defined by forest asceticism and meditation in seclusion; and the importance of the cult of the stūpa. It may also be added that, on logical grounds alone, the intimate connection between some forest renunciants and the institution of the stūpa should not be surprising. The forest renunciant follows a path in emulation of the Buddhist saints, as defined above, and they epitomize his (or her) kind of Buddhism. The forest renunciant follows the example of the Buddha, belongs to a particular lineage of forest renunciants, and meditates under the guidance of a personal teacher. As the Buddhist saints are the focus of his Buddhism while they live, so are they also after death, for his need of them does not end with their passing. Thus the stūpa is crucial to his enterprise, for there he may continue to find them, experience their compassion, and be guided by them. Moreover, as Hirakawa has suggested, the stūpa provides at least one possible answer to a crucial question: what provided the institutional focus for the individual Buddhist saints of the forest? Although, as we shall see, Hirakawa's account of the origins of Mahāyāna does not provide a complete explanation of this phenomenon, and although his insights need in some cases to be supplemented, his work on the stūpa sheds important light on the Buddhist saints.

Modalities and Parallels of the Stūpa

The stūpa is an important symbol in early and later Indian Buddhism because of its ability to render the Buddha and other departed saints spiritually present. The previous discussion would not be complete without mention of some other Buddhist symbols in and through which the saint is similarly rendered actual. Four examples of such other symbols deserve mention in this context: the sacred text, the image, the Pure Land in Mahāyāna Buddhism, and the maṇḍala in the Vajrayāna.

In the early Mahāyāna, the sacred text may become the symbolic vehicle through which the Buddha becomes present. The following brief depiction of what Schopen calls the cult of the book is given in the *Vajracchedikāprajñāpāramita Sūtra:*[39]

> Moreover, O Subhuti, that spot of earth where one has taken from this discourse on dharma but one stanza of four lines, taught it or illumined it, that spot of earth would be like a shrine *[caityabhūto]* for the whole world with its gods, men and Asuras. What then should we say of those who will bear in mind this discourse on dharma in its entirety, who will recite, study, and illuminate it in full detail for others? Most wonderfully blest, Subhuti, they will be. And on that spot of earth, Subhuti, either the Teacher dwells, or a sage [guru] representing him. (*Vcp* 79.10–15 [Conze 1958a, 50])

Schopen argues that *caitya,* in this context, does not mean "stūpa" but has the more general meaning "shrine" and that *bhūto* does not mean "becomes like" but simply "becomes," thus correcting Conze's translation to read "that spot of earth becomes a *caitya* (shrine)" (1975, 149–52). This passage thus means to say that "the presence (in some form) of a *dharmaparyāya* [dharma teaching] (in this case the *Prajñāpāramitā*) in a particular place has the effect of sacralizing that place in a way which is different from, if not opposed to, the sacralization effected by the presence of a *stūpa*" (152). A second, briefer passage in the *Vajracchedikāprajñāpāramitā Sūtra* adds the additional detail that "that spot of earth will be worthy of being saluted respectfully, worthy of being honoured by circumambulation" (*Vcp* 82.20–22 [Conze 1958a, 56]). In spite of the brevity of the two passages, certain parallelisms to the stūpa and its cult are clear:[40] like the stūpa, the text sacralizes the place on which it is worshiped; the liturgical forms mentioned here are similar to those of the stūpa cult; and the ritual function is the same for both, namely, to render the Buddha spiritually present.

It is significant that the presence of the Buddha seems particularly linked with the act of reciting the *Vajracchedikāprajñāpāramitā Sūtra,* because it, unlike other *Prajñāpāramitā*s such as the *Aṣṭasāhasrikāprajñāpāramitā Sūtra,* reflects oral tradition (Schopen 1975, 155–56). In the *Vajracchedikāprajñāpāramitā Sūtra,* it is through the oral recitation of the text that the presence of the *tathāgata* is effected in the person of the reciter and the sacralization occurs. In contrast to this, in the *Aṣṭasāhasrikāprajñāpāramitā Sūtra,* sacralization of the place is effected simply through the presence of the *dharmaparyāya* as the written text (155), and the presence of the Buddha, as such, is not mentioned. Interestingly enough, passages in other texts that seem to reflect oral tradition reveal a similar trend, that in the person who recites the text the *tathāgata* will be present (158).[41] Schopen remarks,

> Vaj *[Vcp]* 12 says that on that spot which is *caityabhūta* and on which a *gāthā* of four lines from this *dharmaparyāya* is taught, etc., on that spot either the Teacher dwells or a wise *guru (vijñaguru)* representing him. SP [*Sps*] 344, says that where a holy sage *(tādṛśo viduḥ)* teaches a *gāthā* of four lines from this *sūtra,* and where because of this a *stūpa* is to be made, he, the sage, is there "possessed" by the Buddha and there the Buddha himself is. Again, KP [*Kp*] 160 expresses a similar notion: Just as *(tadyathāpi nāma)* one reveres the Tathāgata, so too one is to revere him who takes up, etc., this *dharmaparyāya* on that spot which is *caityabhūta*. . . . In all of these there is an equation of the presence of the *dharmaparyāya* with the presence of the Buddha. . . . [A]ll three passages assert the presence, in some sense, of the Buddha on the spot where the *dharmaparyāya* is or is recited, etc. (174–75)

In the case of passages referring to *caityabhūta* where writing plays an important role, such as the *Aṣṭasāhasrikāprajñāpāramitā Sūtra,* the sacralization of the place is also effected by the spiritual presence of the Buddha. However, here the sacralization is brought about not by the presence of the Buddha in the reciter but rather by the presence of the *prajñāpāramitā* itself. As the text says, to attain enlightenment, *sarvajña* (all-knowing), the Buddha trained himself in the *prajñāpāramitā,* and the "all-knowledge" of the *tathāgata* has therefore come forth from the perfection of wisdom. Thus, "the person who would copy and worship the perfection of wisdom . . . in doing so . . . would worship the cognition of the all-knowing" (*Asp* 28.10–29.27 [Conze 1958a, 104–6]).

In the *Aṣṭasāhasrikāprajñāpāramitā Sūtra* the parallelisms between the stūpa cult and the cult of the book are explicitly spelled out in detail, particularly in a comparison between the participant in the cult of the book and the devotee of the stūpa:

> Suppose that there are two persons. One of the two, a son or daughter of good family, has written down this perfection of wisdom, made a copy of it; he would then put it up, and would honour, revere, worship, and adore it with heavenly flowers, incense, perfumes, wreaths, unguents, aromatic powders, strips of cloth, parasols, banners, bells, flags, with rows of lamps all round, and with manifold kinds of worship. The other would deposit in *stūpa*s the relics of the tathagata who has gone to *parinirvāṇa;* he would take hold of them and preserve them; he would honour, worship and adore them with heavenly flowers, incense, etc. as before. (Schopen 1975, 154)

It is striking here that the liturgical acts performed in the cult of the book are depicted as exactly the same as those in the cult of the stūpa. However, there is an important difference between the two: the merit accrued by the one venerating the sacred text surpasses that accrued by the one venerating the stūpa. This is because, as mentioned, the Buddha attained to all-knowledge through training directly in the *prajñāpāramitā,* while his human body, worshiped in the stūpa, played the lesser role of physically supporting the *prajñāpāramitā* (154).

These kinds of comparisons between the cult of the book and the relic/stūpa cult exist not only in the longer recensions of the *Prajñāpāramitā.* "We find outside this particular body of texts a number of independent texts which also contain arguments against the relic/*stūpa* cult in more or less close conjunction with a proselytism connected with the cult of the book" (Schopen 1975, 157). Schopen believes that these comparisons show the cult of the book in the process of attempting to compete, as a minority movement, with the historically prior and dominant cult of the stūpa of early Buddhism (168): "The compilers of the AsP [*Asp*], etc., were attempting to introduce a radical innovation in the face of an established cult form of central importance" (169). Nevertheless, the close continuities in symbolism of the place, liturgical forms, and ritual function reveal that, to some extent, the cult of the book is seen as replacing and taking over the role previously played by the stūpa.

The other symbols that similarly make the spiritual presence of the Buddha possible may be dealt with more briefly. References to the visualized image of the Buddha as facilitating his presence are found in both early and later tradition. Williams cites an intriguing passage in the *Suttanipāta* in which an old man, although unable physically to go to the Buddha, is nevertheless able to experience his very presence and to engage in his cult through visualizing him (1989, 217). Buddhaghosa similarly remarks that through the meditative visualization of the Buddha the meditator "comes to feel as if he were living in the Master's presence. And his body . . . becomes worthy of veneration as a shrine" (Williams 1989, 218). At some point, perhaps as early as the *Suttanipāta* passage, perhaps much later, physical images of the Buddha came to be fashioned and liturgies were performed in that context, thus becoming vehicles of the Buddha's presence. Paul Mus, as already quoted, has commented upon the essential symbolic identity of the Buddha's physical body, the stūpa, and the image of the Buddha.[42] This equation made it possible for the cult of the image to develop largely in the context of and with the same liturgical forms as stūpa worship and then largely to replace it. As in the cult of the book, the cult of the image exhibits close symbolic and cultic parallelism. The ritual function of making real the presence of the Buddha through the ritual use of the image is, of course, found in both Mahāyāna and even more strongly in Tantric Buddhism (Falk 1987). It is interesting that even in Theravāda Buddhism, which exhibits particular reservations about the worship of the image, the Buddha image may, by liturgical means, become filled with "life and miraculous powers" (Tambiah 1984, 230). Whether or not the image developed directly as a historical transformation of the stūpa, it can be understood to have taken over, to a large extent, the stūpa's role.

The classical notion of the Pure Land in Buddhism represents a place where a buddha is not only present but reigns supreme. Hirakawa believes that at least one Pure Land text found its origin in the stūpa cult, affirming that "there is no doubt that the *sukhāvatī* in the smaller *Sukhāvatīvyūha Sūtra* is modelled after the *stūpa* of the Buddha" (1963, 93). Hirakawa proceeds through a detailed comparison of the "land of bliss" in the smaller *Sukhāvatīvyūha Sūtra* with the symbolism of the stūpa, concluding that "the *sukhāvatī* is the idealized image of a huge Buddha *stūpa*" (92). Hirakawa notes that "the smaller *Sukhāvatīvyūha Sūtra* does not mention the worship of *stūpas.*" However, by consulting older translations of the same text into Chinese, he shows that originally in the smaller *Sukhāvatīvyūha Sūtra* there were references to stūpas. This leads him to conclude that the more recent translation lacks references because "the center of worship is Amitāyus who must have replaced the *stūpa* as the object of devotion" (93). Thus, at least in this one case, the stūpa appears to have become transformed into the Pure Land, and when this transformation became complete, the original associations with the stūpa were forgotten.

A final example of a symbol in which the Buddha becomes spiritually present is the maṇḍala in Vajrayāna Buddhism. The maṇḍala is an image—painted, constructed in sand, or otherwise figured—that plays a central symbolic and liturgical role in the Vajrayāna. The symbolism of the maṇḍala is, of course, closely similar to that of the stūpa. Most important, like the stūpa, the maṇḍala is a constructed "body of the Buddha": in the maṇḍala are present, at specified places, the components of buddhahood—the five wisdoms *(jñāna),* the five purified *skandha*s, the elements of skillful means, and so on. Moreover, maṇḍala and stūpa share the same architectural configuration, being shaped according to a plan of center and four cardinal directions, containing locations for images of the buddhas, having gates at the four cardinal directions, and so on. Because maṇḍala and stūpa are idealized bodies of the Buddha, they are also symbolic representations of the ideal cosmos and of the body of the enlightened saint. In addition, similar ritual patterns apply in liturgies associated with the maṇḍala as apply in liturgies connected with the stūpa: to the maṇḍala one typically offers scented water, flowers, incense, light, perfume, food, music, and so on. Finally, in the Vajrayāna stūpas are themselves identified as maṇḍalas, as in the case of Borobuḍur, and maṇḍalas are identified as stūpas, as in the classical Anuttarayoga Tantra liturgies.

As we have seen, several facts suggest a close relationship between stūpa and these other Buddhist symbols: (1) parallel, sometimes closely related, symbolism of sacred place; (2) closely similar liturgical forms used in each; (3) the same ritual function of making the Buddha present; and sometimes, (4) explicit comparisons. In spite of these similarities, given the present state of our knowledge, it is not possible to ascertain definitively the precise historical relationships between the cults of the book, the image, the Pure Land, and the maṇḍala on the one hand and the stūpa on the other. Did one or more of these four symbols develop as specific historical transformations of the stūpa? Or did they originate independently as different forms that originally had or came to have a similar symbolic structure, associated liturgical acts, and ritual functions? For example, it is possible to conceive of the cult of the book as an offshoot of the stūpa cult. It is equally possible to conceive, as Schopen does, that the cult of the book developed in some independence from the cult of the stūpa, appropriating from it or from other sources many symbolic and cultic forms and competing with it. The cult of the image seems to have a close historical relation with that of the stūpa. The Pure Land tradition, at least in the smaller *Sukhāvatīvyūha Sūtra,* seems likely to have emerged, as Hirakawa argues, as the idealization of the Buddhist stūpa.

And the Vajrayāna maṇḍala and its associated liturgies may well represent a yogic internalization and adaptation of the stūpa and its cult.

Conclusion

The living saint and stūpa are thus two dimensions of the phenomenon of enlightenment, present and embodied: the saint represents its living, human expression, whereas the stūpa represents its expression in mortar and stone after the saint has passed beyond. The essential symbolic and cultic identity of living saint and stūpa is suggested in the *Avalokita Sūtra,* where we are told that "it is all the same if one shall worship the *tathāgata* when he is still living and shall revere him, esteem him and honour him with flowers, perfumes, garlands, sunshades, flags, banners, music, incense, ointments, food, drink, carriages and clothes, or if he shall honour him when he has utterly passed away" (*Mv* 2:489 [Jns., 2:329]). As the *Avalokita Sūtra* says, the difference is chiefly one of sequence, for it is precisely when the saint has attained *parinirvāṇa* that worship of the stūpa becomes appropriate: "And when the Lights of the world have passed to *nirvāṇa,* [the suppliant] adores the Buddha's stūpas again and again whenever he sees them" (2:501 [2:336]). Living saint and stūpa are thus two instances of the same reality, performing different but complementary functions within the larger whole of the Buddhist cult of saints.

The symbolic identity and ritual complementarity of living saint and stūpa may be seen by comparing the paradigm of the Buddhist saints with the stūpa symbolism and cult. In effect, the stūpa replicates and in some ways extends the major features of that part of the paradigm that deals with the saints in their enlightened mode—after realization. The stūpa, like the living saints after realization, reveals enlightenment in the concrete. Like the saints, it possesses great charisma. Like the living saints, the stūpa incarnates an intention to help others and manifests compassionate activity. Like them, it possesses supernatural powers. In these abilities to manifest enlightenment and its activity, the stūpa may even be said to have a kind of communicative function. The stūpa can also have its "disciples," in the sense that it continues the presence of and permits an ongoing relationship with the Buddha or other revered teacher. Like the saints, the stūpa is an object of veneration for both laity and renunciants, who worship with circumambulation, prostrations, offerings, praises, and so on. Like the saints, the stūpa has a kind of supernatural body and, in effect, extends the ability of the saints to remain present among humans.

Living saint and stūpa are each worshiped in different ways by different kinds of suppliants. The laity approach saint and stūpa as holy objects, the worship of which will elicit blessings of all sorts, including those of a material, psychological, and spiritual nature. This is not to deny, of course, that laypeople see in them their ultimate goal, nor that they may themselves at any time become renunciants. The perspective of renunciants is somewhat different from that of ordinary laypeople. For renunciants, the living saint—perhaps their own teacher—and the stūpa represent that condition of liberation that is the object of personal aspiration in this life. As we have seen, this enlightened condition is sometimes described as longevity or immortality, as suggested by the Mūlasarvāstivādin *vinaya* text previously cited, in which the suppliants aspire to "arrive at the end of existences, at that which is marked by the absence of the growing old of the body." In this sense, no less than the saint, the stūpa provides "a model of the enlightened personality" (Harvey 1984, 84) to which renunciant disciples aspire. If Hirakawa is right, in at least some cases, both those who are primarily *devoted* to the saint-stūpa (laypeople) and those who primarily *would emulate* the saint-stūpa (renunciants) follow the pattern of the Buddha and aspire, in the long run, to complete enlightenment. But the perspective of renunciants is more immediate and focused, and they follow a kind of Buddhism that might well be designated—as, in fact, it is in the Vajrayāna—"the short path."

Granted that early Buddhists—including the laity, settled monastics, and forest renunciants—all participated in stūpa worship, let us return again to the question of the contexts in which this cult may have developed. On the one hand, the evidence brought forward by Bareau and, more recently and more fully, by Schopen leaves no doubt that stūpas and their cults were central features of Buddhist settled monastic life in India from the earliest time for which we have datable archaeological remains. On the other hand, as we have seen, Hirakawa argues for the existence of stūpas and stūpa cults that were not aligned with Buddhist monasticism but operated primarily in connection with groups of laity and nonmonastic renunciants. The main value of Hirakawa's hypothesis is not that it provides definitive proof for stūpas in India that were not monastically connected, but rather that it raises a possibility that needs to be seriously entertained.

Hirakawa's argument is circumstantial, based on the assemblage of various bits and pieces of evidence that, at least for Hirakawa, point in a particular direction. Let us set the main trends of Hirakawa's evidence within the context of the present discussion. As we have seen, the earliest renunciant Buddhism—whether that of forest or that of town and village—was characterized by homeless wandering and settling down for, at most, the rains retreat. For at least some, the early traditions of forest renunciation were not definitively abandoned for settled monasticism but continued to provide the norm of Buddhist renunciant life after classical monasticism developed and came to the fore. We have seen many examples of tension and even opposition, in both Nikāya and Mahāyāna evidence, between those who followed the life of forest renunciation and those who were settled monastics. We have also seen—not only in Hirakawa's evidence and argument but in other texts as well—a linkage between forest renunciation and stūpa worship. Also pertinent is the possibility of the origins of certain non-Nikāya traditions in, or in close proximity to, the cult of the stūpa—specifically, the cult of the book, Pure Land, image, and maṇḍala. Given all of this, along with Hirakawa's evidence and argument, it seems too far-fetched to assume that the *only* stūpas existing in India in either the pre- or post-Aśokan eras were under the supervision of settled monasticism. Perhaps this may generally be said of the large, well-endowed stūpas, but to make such a statement about all stūpas would push the argument too far.

Although this conclusion may seem reasonable, there is an important piece of contrary testimony: in the archaeological evidence, stūpas are invariably associated with monastic remains. Does this not rule out the possibility of nonmonastic stūpas as postulated by Hirakawa? Perhaps. But there is another way to read the evidence—namely, that it is unable to show that there were nonmonastic stūpas because stūpas eventually became so thoroughly monasticized. Not only were they built in newly constructed monasteries, but monasteries came to be built in the precincts of already-existing stūpas, such that in archaeologically visible times, stūpas and monasteries are invariably conjoined. This presupposes a process of monasticization of the stūpa that can be viewed from two directions: from the direction of the nonmonastic stūpas that were assimilated to monasticism and from the direction of monasticism as it assimilated the stūpas.

Interestingly enough, there are hints in the evidence of just such a process of the monasticization of stūpas. Hirakawa provides what he believes to be examples in relation to the nonmonastic stūpa traditions hypothesized in his work. By comparing earlier and later Chinese translations of Indian Buddhist texts, Hirakawa believes that he has identified (in the terminology being used here) a pre- and postmonasticized phase of the cult of the stūpa in which the stūpa traditions—originally existing independently of the monastic institutions—subsequently came to be understood as aspects of monasticism. Thus, in the early translation of the *Saddharmapuṇḍarīka Sūtra* from the Sanskrit, the term *stūpa* appears translated by a Chinese term that indicates a relic place. However, in later translations of the same text, this same Chinese term is now understood also to indicate *vihāra,* or monastery. "Such a change must have occurred, because the monks lived on the compounds of a hall enshrining the Buddha" (1963, 89–91). In the earlier translation, the Chinese term for stūpa indicates only a stūpa, whereas a different term is used for *vihāra,* because the original translators understood these as different and separate entities. In the later translations, however, the term originally indicating a stūpa is now used to refer to both stūpa and *vihāra,* suggesting that the later translators understood both stūpa and *vihāra* as parts of the same institutional entity.[43] Hirakawa cites a number of other examples of the same phenomenon.[44]

A glimpse of the same process, this time viewed from the vantage point of Buddhist monasteries, appears in interesting configurations of archaeological evidence summarized by Schopen (1990). Although in these remains stūpas are invariably connected with monasteries,[45] there seems to be a difference in the degree of integration of stūpa and monastery in earlier and later evidence. In the early rock-cut caves of western India, for example, one finds stūpa and monastic complex at the same site, but they are distinct structures and physically separate from one another. The same pattern is observed in other early sites at the Dharmarājika at Taxila and elsewhere, and at Taxila at a somewhat later period. However, in evidence dating from a later time, Schopen finds "some movement towards a different arrangement," which attempts to draw the two structures "into a tighter intimacy." In these cases, the stūpa may be moved into the center of the residential courtyard (200–201). "But these attempts remain tentative, and pale in comparison with a major rearrangement which begins to appear everywhere in the 5th century—at exactly the time that we start to get clear epigraphical references to the Buddha as an actual resident of Indian monasteries." In this new development, a cell within the monastic complex, usually the one in the most honored position, is reserved for the Buddha and in fact contains a Buddha image, at this period a functional equivalent of the stūpa (201). From this time onward, this "shrine-cum-*vihāra*" becomes standard. It is, of course, impossible to say with any certainty what this movement means. But one possible explanation is that it reveals, at least in these times and places, advanced stages in a process of the monasticization of the stūpa. The earliest rock-cut monasteries may testify to a time when the stūpa was considered to be a religiously distinct and separate phenomenon that with time came to be seen as an integral part of the very structure of the monastery itself. The monastic rules, pointed to by Hirakawa, Bareau, and Schopen, in which the property of the stūpa or the Buddha is held to be juristically separate and distinct from that of the monastic *saṃgha,* would then be understood as remnants of just such an original separation between stūpa and monastery.

Although in early Buddhism it appears that all types of Buddhists participated in the stūpa cult, there clearly came a time within Pāli Buddhism at least when stūpa worship was viewed as a specifically lay preoccupation. Although, as has been suggested, the *Mahāparinirvāṇa Sūtra* in the Pāli and other versions appears to provide no direct evidence of this view, the *Milindapañha* does articulate just such a position in its interpretation of the famous *Mahāparinibbāna Sūtta* passage referring to *śarīrapūjā.* According to the *Milindapañha,* as we have seen, this passage means to say that laypeople are to offer worship to stūpas, but monastics are not: "Paying homage is not the work of the sons of the conqueror [the monks], but rather grasping the true nature of all compounded things . . . leaving to others, whether gods or men, the paying of reverence" (*Mp* 177–79 [T.R. 1890–94, 1:246–48]).[46] As Schopen suggests, the *Milindapañha* here evidently represents a revisionist tendency within Pāli commentarial tradition and reflects the growing view that worship of the stūpa is not something in which the ideal monastic should engage (1991b, 195–96). Similarly, it may well be that the same kind of antistūpa tendency evident in the *Milindapañha* is also responsible—if Schopen is correct—for the systematic removal of references to stūpas from the extant version of the Pāli *vinaya.*

Monastic reservation in Pāli tradition about the stūpa and its cult gains momentum in later times. In particular, it is evident in the modern era in certain deeply entrenched tensions, observed by various scholars, that exist in Theravāda Buddhism between pagoda (stūpa) and monastery. One example is provided by Sadler, who explores this phenomenon in a Burmese context (1970). These tensions, Sadler believes, are rooted in Theravāda Buddhism, which displays "so clearly significant [a] dichotomy between two lifestyles (lay and monastic) and the two religious goals (*dathana* and [monastic] discipline)" (284). These tensions are reflected in the insistence by modern elite monks that there are two distinct levels of Buddhism: on the one hand, the Buddhism of the laity, bound up with darśan (seeing) and the stūpa; and, on the other, the Buddhism of the monastic *saṃgha,* based on the *vinaya.*[47] One dimension of the antistūpa trend involves a denial that the elite have any need of stūpas, that stūpas perform any necessary function for the intelligent. Thus, an official of the Saṃgha University in Rangoon commented, "A pagoda ostensibly houses something of the real Buddha. But an image is just symbolic of the Buddha's presence. Intellectual people don't need an image to concentrate their thoughts on. Common people do" (290). Similarly, the modern antistūpa trend also denies the authenticity of stūpa worship outright. When asked if there were not two ways within Buddhism—prayer and devotion (connected with the stūpa), and the more elite way of the monastic—one of Sadler's monastic informants remarked, " 'In Buddhism there is only one way. Prayer is not important. Only morals and meditation.' . . . Q: 'Do you have some Buddhists in Burma who know only prayer?' A: 'Yes! The general public' " (283).[48]

What can be the meaning of this antistūpa trend within Theravādin monasticism, which appears to be reflected in the *Milindapañha,* in the apparently systematic removal of references to rules for the stūpa from the extant Pāli *vinaya* and in the contemporary evidence discussed by Sadler? Such a trend begins to make sense when we recall that the stūpa is an important part of the Buddhist cult of saints and that, as we have seen in several examples in previous chapters, Pāli tradition shows similar negative attitudes to the Buddhist saints of the forest and their cults. This raises the interesting possibility that the Theravādin reservations about the charisma of the stūpa and the charisma of the forest saints may proceed from the same source and be part of the same phenomenon within Theravādin monasticism. This possibility will be considered in the next chapter.[49]

Notes

1. Who are these local saints thus enshrined in stūpas? The evidence suggests that stūpas were built to both male and female saints (Schopen 1991c, 281), though the mention of local female saints seems comparatively rare. A forest lifestyle is sometimes specifically indicated, as when they are termed *āraṇaka* (forest renunciant) or qualified by another of the *dhutaguṇas*: *peṇḍavatika* or *peḍapātika (piṇḍapatika)* (292; 309). These are also people of attainment, indicated by their being called "one possessed of the three knowledges" *(tevija)* (296), "one possessed of the six superknowledges" *(abhijñā)* (310), nonreturner *(anāgāmin)* (296), and arhant (293). They are also called by other terms of respect such as elder *(thera),* reverend *(bhayata)* (293), and reverend *(bhadata)* (296), some of which may have implied spiritual attainment. One saint is called a *vināyaka,* perhaps indicating particular attainment in behavioral purity or mastery of *vinaya* texts (308).

2. Mitra 1971, 21. Also see Barua 1926, 21; Pant 1973, 471–78; and Fussman 1986, 44.

3. Discussed in Bareau 1975.

4. For a discussion of some of the major theories see Bénisti 1960, 42–47.

5. For some general treatments of the symbolism and cult of the stūpa, see Combaz 1932–33; Mus 1935, 1:76ff.; Bénisti 1960; Irwin 1977; and Dallapiccola 1980.

6. On this, see N. Falk 1977.

7. It has often been pointed out that in early Buddhism there are no images of the Buddha and that, in this sense, early Buddhism is aniconic. Mus, in speaking of the early

period, has corrected this view: "There are no sculpted figurations of the Buddha, but there is the *stūpa,* his mystical body" (Bénisti 1960, 53, n. 4). In other words, although there are no early pictorial representations of the Buddha, there is from the earliest times the stūpa itself, understood as a monumental image of the body of the Buddha.

8. Schopen 1987a, 203. In support of this contention, Schopen cites inscriptions written on the outside and inner face of a broken relic lid from Shinkot, according to which the relic is said to be "endowed with life" *(prāṇasameta).* Schopen draws our attention not only to the concept of the relic's life but to the fact that this conception "is the earliest actually attestable conception [of the relic] that we have" (204). The equivalence of Buddha and stūpa is given further definition in some texts cited by Mus, including a Javanese text that states that the body of the Buddha, viewed from the outside, is a stūpa, and the *Lalitavistara,* which remarks that the Buddha is called the *caitya* of the world. According to Bénisti, "Numerous are the plastic representations that attest to this identification of *stūpa* and Buddha" (1960, 51). In particular, she refers to a relief from the great stūpa at Amarāvatī that represents an uninterrupted series of stūpas and seated buddhas as illustration of Mus's phrase "The *stūpa* is the Buddha, the Buddha is the *stūpa*" (51).

9. Harvey remarks, "The relics . . . are thought to contain something of the spiritual force and purity of the person they once formed part of. As they were part of the body of a person whose mind was freed of spiritual faults and possessed of a great energy-for-good, it is believed that they were somehow affected by this" (1984, 69).

10. This reminds us, of course, of the passage cited by Harvey from the *Vibhaṅga Aṭṭhakathā* that remarks that at the end of the five-thousand-year period of the dharma, all the relics in Sri Lanka will come together, in Harvey's words, "travel through the air to the foot of the *bodhi* tree in India, emit rays of light, and then disappear in a flash of light. This is referred to as the *parinibbāna* of the *dhātus*" (1984, 69).

11. *Sps* gives vivid evidence of the cult of the stūpa and affords a view of that cult as it existed in India around the beginning of the common era. Hirakawa comments that *Sps* is "a work based on the institution of the *stūpa*" (1963, 85). Although in later times *Sps* stands quite independent of the stūpa, the contents of the text itself suggest that in its original conception, the text was bound up with the stūpa cult. A number of passages in the text indicate that originally it was only in the sacred precincts of the stūpa that the text was to be recited; see *Sps* 149–50 (Kn., 227–29), where we are told that the stūpa and the text appear together, although, as we shall see, the stūpa in question is not necessarily one of mortar and stone.

12. For example, the *Avalokana Sūtra,* a text on the cult of the stūpa quoted in the *Śikṣāsamuccaya* (*Ss* 156ff. [BR., 270ff.]), and the *Avalokita Sūtra* given in the *Mahāvastu.* See note 13.

13. There are in fact two *sūtra*s in the *Mahāvastu* entitled *Avalokita Sūtra, Mv* 2:357–401 (Jns., 2:242–74) and 2:401–536 (Jns., 274–354). In his translation of *Mv,* Jones refers to these as the "First *Avalokita Sūtra*" and the "Second *Avalokita Sūtra.*" It is the second of these that provides particular insights into the cult of the stūpa. The reader should note that, in what follows, when I refer to the *Avalokita Sūtra,* I mean the second of these two *Avalokita Sūtra*s. Jones (1949–56, 2:242, n. 3) mentions two other versions of this text, the one quoted in the *Śikṣāsamuccaya* and another preserved in Tibetan (reference not given, but perhaps he is thinking of the *Āryāvalokananāmamahāyāna Sūtra;* Tib., *'phags.pa.spyan.ras.gzigs.shes.bya.ba.theg.pa.chen.po'i.mdo,* D., 195).

14. The section of *Als* cited here points to the rewards gained by the worship of stūpas. Most frequently, the text speaks of this veneration employing the term *stūpa* (translated by Jones as "tope"). The text also designates stūpas by the term *cetiya* (translated by Jones as "shrine" or "monument"), and the two terms are used interchangeably (cf., e.g., *Mv*

2:492.2–12 [Jns., 2:331]). Other terms similarly understood in this section of the text as referring to stūpas are *dhātu* (relics) (e.g., *Mv* 2:496 [Jns., 2:333]) and sometimes *buddha* (*Mv* 2:494–95 [Jns., 2:332]). In quoting Jones's translation, I render "tope" as "stūpa."

15. Bareau 1962, 249. This theme of longevity or immortality is important and will be considered further in Chapter 11.

16. As Hirakawa points out, in the chapter on skillful means, a variety of practices leading to buddhahood are discussed, including both the building of stūpas and acts of worship and offering made to stūpas (1963, 95).

17. In this article (Bareau 1962), the author reads various early *vinaya*s for information on stūpas. Although Bareau found no information regarding the cult and construction of stūpas in the Pāli *vinaya,* he uncovered a wealth of information in other extant *vinaya*s, including those of the Mahāsāṃghika, Mūlasarvāstivāda, Mahīśāsaka, Dharmaguptaka, and Sarvāstivāda, suggesting, of course, that the religious life that surrounds the stūpa was of far greater interest to the redactors of these than to those of the Pāli *vinaya,* as we now have it.

18. See also Schopen's article "The Buddha as an Owner of Property and Permanent Resident in Medieval Indian Monasteries" (1990).

19. Bareau 1962, 257. On this, see also Hirakawa 1987, 93–94.

20. Variant title for *Daśabhūmikasūtraśāstra* (Lancaster 1979, 181, entry K., 550).

21. Summarized by Nakamura 1951, 347–48.

22. Tao-hsüan, identified by Nakamura as founder of the Vinaya sect in China (1951, 347).

23. See also Hsüan-tsang's summary of appropriate acts of salutation and reverence (Watters 1904–5, 1:173).

24. On *pradakṣiṇā,* also see I-ching's discussion (Takakusu 1896, 140–46).

25. Bénisti points out that circumambulation of the stūpa had a close connection with the hagiographical depictions at the stūpa of the Buddha's final and previous lives. She remarks, for example, that the rite of *pradakṣiṇā* has ordered, in some sense, the edifying depictions that one finds on the stūpa (1960, 55):

> The balustrade, the base and the dome were ornamented (at Amarāvatī, for example) with bas-reliefs representing scenes drawn from the legend of the Buddha. These episodes unrolled chronologically before the eyes of the worshiper accomplishing the rite of leaving the *stūpa* to his right. The *stūpa* is thus for the devotee a kind of bible: in recounting to him the marvellous history of prince Siddhārtha who, having renounced the things of this world, became Buddha, it incites him to follow the path which leads to the cessation of suffering and to the liberation of all existences. The pathway around the *stūpa* becomes a veritable communion between the edifice and the worshiper: on the one hand, he accomplishes an act of veneration and of respect toward the monument which embodies for him the Buddha and his teaching, and by this act he puts himself on the path first followed by the Buddha; on the other hand, the monument by its symbolic efficacy guides him on that path. Thus it is that the pilgrim, in following with his eyes the grand series of episodes, while he circumambulates the *stūpa,* "on the path of those who have entered into the way . . . finds himself having taken this same route leading to Nirvāṇa." (55–56, quoting Zimmer)

26. For a discussion of the issue of food offerings, see Bareau 1975, 178ff.

27. Another interesting point concerns the offerings of music, which are specifically mentioned in all Bareau's sources. An unidentified Chinese *vinaya* text specifies the use of drum and conch. The Mahāsāṃghika and Mahīśāsaka sources speak of offerings of music as including song and dance. According to the Mahīśāsaka and Dharmaguptaka, monastics may not themselves play the music, nor may they themselves sing or dance; however, monastics may have the laypeople do so.

28. This citation from the *Mahāvastu* reads thus: "He who, directing his mind to enlightenment *[bodhi]*, adores a monument of the Master" (*Mv* 2:492 [Jns., 2:331]).

29. The *Pradakṣiṇā Sūtra,* translated by Bailey (1974), presents a similar picture of the dimensions of stūpa worship.

30. See Schopen's discussion of this material (1985, 7).

31. Or perhaps including the cremation and possibly also the construction of the stūpa (Schopen 1991b, 191–92; 195). Through citation from a number of different texts, Schopen shows that the specific cultic practice of *śarīrapūjā* to the bodies of deceased saints was widespread in early Buddhism.

32. See Schopen's full argument, 1989, 83ff.

33. For some critical responses to Schopen's argument, see Gombrich 1991, Hallisey 1991, and Hinüber 1991. Although not necessarily disputing Schopen's contention—as expressed in this and many other of his articles (see Bibliography)—of tensions between monastic practice as reflected in the Pāli *vinaya* and the actual practice of monastics as evident from other sources (e.g., epigraphy), these responses all express doubts on the specific point that rules regarding stūpas were consciously and systematically removed from the extant version of the *vinaya.*

34. In this article, Hirakawa has attempted to clarify some of the ideas, texts, and institutions of early Mahāyāna Buddhism that shed light on its origins. Hirakawa looks at a wide variety of early Mahāyāna texts and, as part of his methodology, compares early translations of texts into Chinese with ones that have been translated, often in a different way, at a later time (a method now used to advantage by many buddhologists; e.g., see Lancaster 1975 and Harrison 1987). This article has had considerable influence, particularly on Japanese Buddhist scholarship. See, for example, Nakamura's description of Mahāyāna origins (1987a, 457, and 1987b, 151), where the author accepts the main lines of Hirakawa's argument. Certain aspects of Hirakawa's theory have recently been called into question by Schopen (e.g., 1975) and Williams (1989, 20–22); for a discussion, see Chapter 12.

35. See footnote on *gaṇa* in Chapter 8, n. 44.

36. Taught, Hirakawa tells us, in the *āgamas* (1963, 75).

37. For list, see 282n.14. For a discussion of the *karmapatha,* see *BHSD* 170–71, s.v. *karmapatha,* and Lamotte 1958, 45–46. It is well known that the specific path of the bodhisattva at all periods was defined by the six *pāramitās*. The second of these *pāramitās*, *śīla pāramitā,* is the one specifically concerned with discipline or life rule. In the early *Prajnāpāramitā* as translated into Chinese, *śīla pāramitā* is interpreted always as the "the ten virtuous actions" (Hirakawa 1963, 75). Thus, the discipline enjoined upon both lay and renunciant bodhisattvas is this set of ten *kuśalakarmas*. These are not to be confused with another set of *daśaśikṣāpadas*, which are the ten rules followed specifically by novice monastics, more generally in the *prātimokṣa* also by fully ordained monastics. The *prātimokṣa* is, in Lamotte's view, the complex elaboration of this set (1958, 59). The *karmapathas* are not restricted to the Mahāyāna but appear as a set in Pāli, Sarvāstivādin, and Mahāsāṃghika (with some variation) traditions, for examples of which see *BHSD* 170–71, s.v. *karmapatha,* and *PTSD* 194, s.v. *kammapathā.*

38. One may wonder why these patterns of community and institutional life were not previously recognized by scholars. Hirakawa writes of an early time in Mahāyāna history, when the above distinctions were still in force. Somewhat later, of course, the Mahāyāna took on an increasingly monastic form, such that any early nonmonastic origins would have been obscured. But even after the monasticization of the Mahāyāna (see Chapter 12), when Mahāyāna *bhikṣus* along with Nikāya *bhikṣus* are known, the bodhisattva *bhikṣu* is enjoined with—in addition to the *prātimokṣa*—a *śīla* specific to him; this is none other than the *daśakuśaladharma,* which, Hirakawa tells us, needs to be properly understood as a survival

from the earlier period, before the bodhisattva renunciant had anything to do with monastic tradition or its forms (1963, 77–79).

39. This topic has been briefly alluded to in Chapter 8. In a ground-breaking article, Schopen describes the cult of the book as an important cult type in early Mahāyāna (1975). Schopen finds clear evidence of the cult of the book in a very wide range of different kinds of early Mahāyāna texts.

40. See Schopen's comments on this parallelism (1975, 170).

41. This recalls the spiritual presence of the Buddha in the person of the saint, mentioned several times in previous chapters. Schopen makes reference to a number of other passages in nonhagiographic Mahāyāna evidence where this presence is also affirmed (1975, 174–75).

42. There is now some reason to suspect that the image of the Buddha, as a visualized representation and as a physical artifact, may go back to an earlier time than has been supposed. In addition to Williams's mention of a reference in the *Suttanipāta* to the visualization of the Buddha image (1989, 217–18), Huntington points to archaeological finds that suggest a greater than previously believed antiquity of the physical representation (1985, 627).

43. Although these usages reflect the choices of the Chinese translators—Dharmarakṣa for the earlier, Kumārajīva for the later translation—one may suspect that their choices are informed by Indian understandings of their times.

44. For example, earlier and later translations from Sanskrit into Chinese of the *Ugradattaparipṛcchā Sūtra* (Hirakawa 1963, 94–98) and of the *Buddhāvataṃsaka Gocarapariśuddhaparivarta* (94–98). This phenomenon of an important change in Buddhist religious life being evidenced in textual material reflecting different periods is also directly reflected in evidence of Indian Buddhism. In this context, Nakamura mentions that the change from a forest to a communal monastic way of life among the early community is reflected in the discrepancy between terminology of certain earlier *gāthā* portions of early texts and the accompanying, later prose sections: "Ascetics are mentioned as hermits *(ṛṣis* [P., *isis*]) . . . in Gāthās of earlier texts of early Buddhism . . . whereas in prose sections explaining Gāthās, the word *isis* disappears and the world *bhikkhu* is used in its place" (1987c, 58).

45. In order to know precisely how to interpret this evidence, however, we need to know whether all these stūpas were originally parts of monastic complexes or whether in a significant number of cases either monasteries were built in places where stūpas already existed or stūpas were built in places where monasteries already existed.

46. The passage says further, "And if, O king, he had not said so, then would the *bhikkhus* have taken his bowl and his robe, and occupied themselves with paying reverence to the Buddha through them" (*Mp* 177–79 [T.R. 1890–94, 1:246–48]).

47. Sadler further notes the territorial separation of stūpa and monastery, even when they are located within the same religious complex. He thus describes as typical the Kyaik Ka Loke pagoda and monastery where the pagoda complex is separate and built on high ground, whereas the monastic complex is built on low ground. "The separation of *pagoda* grounds from the monastic grounds is very striking here. The *pagoda,* the source of *dathana* (the grace-giving encounter with the holy) and the object of lay (devotional) religion, is placed outside the monastic compound" (1970, 284). Then Sadler continues, "This territorial separation of building complexes is of course not unique to Burmese Buddhism, but points to something fundamental within canonical Theravāda Buddhism and primitive Buddhism, and indeed within modern Buddhism in all its forms, all round the globe" (285).

48. For additional examples of the same kind of antistūpa trend among the monastic elite in other Theravādin countries, cf. Spiro 1982, 204–6.

49. If Hirakawa is right that the stūpa provided an institutional focus of the earliest

Mahāyāna (or at least some aspects of what later comes to be understood as Mahāyāna), then one sees in the history of the stūpa a curious coincidence. In the three or so centuries following Aśoka, the stūpa is undergoing more and more complete monasticization by the Nikāya Buddhist schools. At this same time, in the earliest Mahāyāna texts we find the tradition moving away from close association with the stūpa as a physical monument and toward other symbolic forms. These include the cultivation of *prajñāpāramitā,* image worship, the cult of the book, and the Pure Land traditions. Although these are rightly seen as, to some extent, repudiations of the stūpa, it is also true that texts reflecting these religious preoccupations (e.g., *Rgs, Asp, Sps, Svs* [Hirakawa 1963, 91ff.]) often explicitly mention the stūpa and admit its authenticity, all the while indicating that they themselves are moving on. In addition, as mentioned, these various religious foci often betray much of the same structure, symbolism, and liturgy as those of the stūpa. This suggests that the *prajñāpāramitā,* image worship, the cult of the book, and the Pure Land traditions can be seen as further developments of the cult of the stūpa and its kind of religiosity. If this be deemed reasonable, then one may ask, did the thorough monasticization of the stūpa and the Mahāyāna movement of many early Mahāyāna texts away from the stūpa occur during roughly the same time by chance? Or did the nonmonastic Mahāyāna first begin to move away from the physical stūpa, thus leaving a void of which the monasticization of the stūpa is the result? Or, finally, did the monasticization of the stūpa begin first, encouraging the Mahāyāna to develop other interpretations of the stūpa cult? These questions will be taken up in subsequent chapters.

11

The Cult of Saints and Buddhist Doctrines of Absence and Presence

In the evidence examined in previous chapters, we have seen certain tensions, sometimes oppositions, between two ways of considering the Buddhist saints. On the one hand is the view that the Buddhist saints of the forest are the primary reference point for normative Buddhism. On the other is the view that tends to play down the saints and to find the heart of normative Buddhism elsewhere, in the characteristic values and preoccupations of settled monasticism. This raises the question of whether, at least to some extent, this divergence of views is not an isolated instance, but is rather connected with two distinguishable, sometimes quite different, understandings of what Buddhism is and should be. The present chapter takes up this question by focusing on ways in which these two views tend to express themselves in Buddhist doctrine and, in particular, where they stand in relation to the important question of the extent to which, and the way in which, the Buddhist saint, after death, is immanent within or absent from the deluded world.

A Doctrine of Absence in the *Mahāparinirvāṇa Sūtra*

This section presents an analysis of the *Mahāparinirvāṇa Sūtra* for the light it may shed on early monastic attitudes to questions of the absence and presence of saints. The text will be considered here in its various versions, with primary reference to the Pāli.[1] The *Mahāparinirvāṇa Sūtra* tends toward what may be termed a *doctrine of absence* in relation to the question of the Buddha's status subsequent to his *parinirvāṇa*.[2] This doctrine of absence begins to become clear in the curious position that the text takes with regard to monastic participation in the cult of the Buddha. The *Mahāparinirvāṇa Sūtra* has, in fact, a great deal to say about the cult of the Buddha, both as a living saint and after he has passed away. In addition, the text suggests the role monastics should play in the various dimensions of the Buddha's cult—this is generally a restricted one. In relation to the deceased Buddha, the *Mahāparinirvāṇa Sūtra* mentions two different types of ritual activity, the cultic treatment of the body of the Buddha after his passing and the cult of the stūpa, built over his postcremation remains.

In relation to the cultic treatment of the postmortem body of the Buddha, the previous chapter included a summary of the reasons, brought forward by Schopen, for believing that the *Mahāparinirvāṇa Sūtra* passage addressed to Ānanda concerning the honoring of the remains of the *tathāgata*[3] has been incorrectly taken to indicate a disallowing of stūpa worship by monastics in general. We saw that *śarīrapūjā* does not refer to the worship of the Buddha's relics in the stūpa, and also that the passage seems addressed, not to all monks, but rather specifically to Ānanda. If Ānanda is not to participate in this rite, however, the text mentions others who are, notably *kṣatriyas*, brahmins, and the heads of households (Schopen 1991b, 190–91). This passage, then, suggests a limitation in monastic participation in *śarīrapūjā*. Although the laypeople are to participate in *śarīrapūjā*, the situation for monastics is more mixed: although some may participate in this rite, others (those who are not realized?) may not.[4] This passage thus suggests that whereas *śarīrapūjā* is recommended without reservation as part of the laity's religious life, the same cannot be said in relation to the religious life of the monastic as such.[5]

The second type of cultic behavior toward the deceased Buddha concerns veneration of the stūpa, built over his postcremation remains. As noted in Chapter 1, the *Mahāparinirvāṇa Sūtra* explicitly acknowledges the legitimacy of stūpa worship, saying that it is appropriate to build stūpas to *tathāgatas* and also to two other classes of saints, the pratyekabuddhas and arhants.[6] At the same time, although the *Mahāparinirvāṇa Sūtra* does not prohibit the worship of stūpas by monastics, it is nevertheless true that the text does not portray stūpa worship as standing at the center of their religious life. As we shall presently see, the text advances other activities as particularly characteristic of and incumbent upon monks, activities based on following the *vinaya* and engaging in textual pursuits. In fact, among the many passages in which the specific duties and obligations of monks are outlined, stūpa worship is not mentioned at all, apart from one likely later insertion in some versions of the text (*Mps*-p 5.8).[7] This stands in contrast to the text's advocacy of stūpa worship for the laity, both by implication in the discussion of the building of stūpas and also in the depiction of stūpa worship, which, the text tells us, is to be engaged in by the *bahujana* (the multitudes of people) (5.12).

The *Mahāparinirvāṇa Sūtra* also refers to the cult of the living Buddha. Here, as in relation to the deceased Buddha, the text treats cultic matters with reservation, at least insofar as monastics are concerned. Particularly interesting in this respect are several passages that criticize those who would deeply revere the living Buddha and would engage in his veneration. One such passage occurs in chapter 5 of the Pāli version: the Buddha, having become ill, has entered Kuśinagarī and come to the Sāla Grove of the Mallas; at the place where he is to pass away, he lies down. The text then presents an account of a cosmic veneration of the *tathāgata:*[8]

> Now at that time the twin Sāla trees were all one mass of bloom with flowers out of season; and all over the body of the Tathāgata these dropped and sprinkled and scattered themselves, out of reverence for the successor of the Buddhas of old.

> And heavenly Mandārava flowers, too, and heavenly sandal-wood powder came falling from the sky, and all over the body of the Tathāgata they descended and sprinkled and scattered themselves, out of reverence for the successor of the Buddhas of old. And heavenly music was sounded in the sky, out of reverence for the successor of the Buddhas of old! (5.2)

Then the Blessed One addresses Ānanda and tells him of this cosmic veneration, repeating this paragraph word for word (5.3). These two paragraphs thus contain, twice repeated, an account of certain events,[9] in a cosmic frame of reference, of the veneration the *tathāgata:* the miracle of a tree blooming out of season, and the offering of flowers, sandalwood powder, and music and song. The text of this description is evocative and celebratory. This passage reveals two important things: (1) the veneration of the Buddha takes place in this particular way; and (2) an explicit link is made with preexisting tradition, with "the Buddhas of old." So far, we seem to be told that this is how the Buddha is to be venerated.

Then follows another passage that is jarring by contrast, wherein the Blessed One proceeds to denigrate the deep and universal veneration that has just occurred:

> Now it is not thus, Ānanda, that the Tathāgata is rightly honoured, reverenced, venerated, held sacred or revered. But the brother [*bhikkhu*] or the sister [*bhikkhunī*], the devout man [*upāsaka*] or the devout woman [*upāsikā*], who continually fulfils all the greater and the lesser duties [*dhammānudhamma paṭipanna*],[10] who is correct in life [*samīcipaṭipanna*], walking according to the precepts [*anudhammacārī*]—it is he who rightly honours, reverences, venerates, holds sacred, and reveres the Tathāgata with the worthiest homage. Therefore, O Ānanda, be ye constant in the fulfilment of the greater and of the lesser duties, and be ye correct in life, walking according to the precepts; and thus, Ānanda, should it be taught. (*Mps*-p 5.3)

When compared with the passages that precede it, this passage effects a dramatic change of direction. The first two paragraphs present the positive images of cultic veneration of the *tathāgata,* that in and of themselves suggest normative behavior. The third paragraph, however, tells us that the first two paragraphs actually represent what one should *not* do, and that the person who "rightly honours, reverences, venerates, holds sacred, and reveres the Tathāgata with the worthiest homage" is *not* the one who participates in the cult of the Buddha but is rather the one who follows the *dhamma* in its full extent. As two kinds of behavior are clearly contrasted here, and as *bhikṣu*s and *bhikṣuṇī*s are explicitly mentioned,[11] Rhys Davids is probably right in translating such terms as *dhammānudhamma* in ways that suggest that *vinaya,* moral precepts, and correct behavior in general are meant.[12]

In seeking to explain this sudden shift of direction, let us recall Frauwallner's suggestion that the hypothesized *Old Skandhaka,* of which the earliest core of the *Mahāparinirvāṇa Sūtra* is understood to have originally been a part, was constructed out of preexisting oral material.[13] Frauwallner's remarks are probably valid, mutatis mutandis, not only for the original core of the *Mahāparinirvāṇa Sūtra,* whatever that may actually have been, but also for many of the subsequent additions to the text. In this section of chapter 5 of this text it seems not unlikely that we are dealing with what were originally two distinct and even opposing viewpoints: 5.2 of the Pāli text, repeated in 5.3, represents a preexistent liturgical description presented in positive form; the following material in 5.3 represents the critique of this form by the author/editor of this passage. Just as in relation to the cult of the Buddha after his passing, so here in relation to the cult of the Buddha while yet alive, the cult of the saint occupies a relatively lower position in the hierarchy of spiritual activities of the monastic. The text asserts instead that the highest Buddhism is based on authentic *dhamma,* defined elsewhere in the text as the standard preoccupations of settled monasticism, pure behavior according to the *vinaya* and the preservation and study of texts.[14]

The legitimacy of this interpretation is suggested by the interesting fact that whereas the three versions of the *Mahāparinirvāṇa Sūtra* in which this passage occurs present the same negative evaluation of the veneration of the Buddha, the corresponding section in the *Ekottarāgama,* containing the same description of cultic veneration, reflects, as Bareau has noted, an opposite view (1970–71, 2:14). Thus, Chinese A and D, like the Pāli, each possesses the same structure of cultic forms that are described and then said to be superseded. Bareau believes that these three accounts represent a reaction against the cult (2:17). The *Ekottarāgama* version, however, reflects a very different set of values. Here, the Buddha is in the process of dividing up his three robes. When Ānanda asks him why he is doing this, he replies, "It is for the sake of the patrons *(dānapati)* of the future that I divide up my three robes. I desire to act such that these folk will receive merit" (2:18). Bareau sees this passage in the *Ekottarāgama* as affirming the legitimacy of the cult and promoting its values. In this, he comments, "The spirit of this account is thus directly opposed to that which inspires the three [*Mahāparinirvāṇa Sutra*] texts" (2:18).

That in this passage we are not dealing with a unique phenomenon is suggested by a second, quite similar example of a passage that occurs, with some variation, eight times in the Pāli text and, in varying forms, in the other five versions.[15] This frequent repetition suggests that this passage also reflects material in use at the time of the composition of the sections of the *Mahāparinirvāṇa Sūtra* in which it is found.[16] Let us begin by quoting the Pāli version, 5.21, where Ānanda has arrived among the Mallas and has just told them that the Buddha will pass away in the coming night, in the last watch. "And when they had heard this saying of the Venerable Ānanda, the Mallas, with their young men and their maidens and their wives, were grieved, and sad, and afflicted at heart." Then follows the passage in question:

> And some of them wept, dishevelling their hair, and stretched forth their arms and wept, and fell prostrate on the ground, and rolled to and fro in anquish at the thought: "Too soon will the Exalted One die! Too soon will the Happy One pass away! Full soon will the Light of the world vanish away!"

The passage occurs again in the Pāli text at 6.12; the Buddha has just died, and Ānanda has again arrived among the Mallas, this time to inform them of this fact, announcing, "The Blessed One, O Vāseṭṭhas, is dead; do, then, whatever seemeth to you fit!" What seems fit, no doubt because it was a traditional practice upon such occasions, is given in a repetition, with appropriate changes of verbal tense, of the just quoted passage:

> And some of them wept, dishevelling their hair, and stretched forth their arms and wept, and fell prostrate on the ground, and rolled to and fro in anquish at the thought: "Too soon has the Blessed One died! Too soon has the Happy One passed away! Too soon has the Light of the world vanished!

Three things characterize these two occurrences of the passage: (1) they represent the simplest form of its various occurrences in the Pāli version; (2) the material in these passages is found in all the other occurrences; and (3) unlike the other occurrences, these passages contain no doctrinal commentary or evaluation of the acts that they describe. All of this suggests that these two instances likely represent the earlier form of the passage.

By contrast, the other six occurrences all contain this passage but add a doctrinal commentary to the bare description. For example, the four occurrences in the Pāli recension at 5.6 (two instances) and at 6.11 (two instances) contain a description of various groups of deities who stretch forth their arms and weep, and so on. However, we find added to the passage the phrase *paṭhavisaññiniya* ("of worldly mind"), qualifying the subject—the deities—indicating that their minds are not liberated.[17] At 5.6 of the Pāli, these deities are contrasted with other deities who do not engage in the cultic veneration because they are "free from passion *[vītarāga]*" and are "calm and self-possessed." The same contrast is repeated at 6.11. The passage is repeated again, in yet another context, at 6.10 and 6.19, this time describing the actions of certain *bhikkhu*s. Here, there is similarly added a negative criticism of those *bhikkhu*s who enact the ritual mourning. Thus, we are told that those who engage in these actions are "brethren *[bhikkhu*s] who were not yet free from the passions *[avītarāga]*." At 6.10 of the Pāli, these *bhikkhu*s, as in the passage concerning the deities, are contrasted with their betters, with those who are free from passion *(vītarāga)* and thus do not engage in the ritual mourning. These unenlightened *bhikkhu*s Ānanda must upbraid for unseemly conduct: "Enough my brethren! Weep not, neither lament!" (6.11).[18] The same contrast between the unenlightened and the enlightened *bhikkhu*s is presented at 6.19.[19] The same phenomenon we have already seen may be hypothesized: a preexisting tradition, represented by the passage in its simplest form, which is taken up in the text and subjected to a particular doctrinal interpretation.[20] This phenomenon, considered here in its Pāli manifestation but appearing variously in the other versions of the *Mahāparinirvāṇa Sūtra,* reveals the existence of cultic veneration of the Buddha as a saint but clearly interprets it as a lower form that the elite among the *bhikkhu*s do not engage in.[21]

These two examples of ambivalence in the *Mahāparinirvāṇa Sūtra*—of practices that are accepted on the one hand and rejected on the other—are themselves not isolated examples but, in fact, reflect a basic tension that runs throughout the text in its various recensions. This tension is between, first, a clear recognition of the Buddhist cult of saints as a fact of religious life and, second, an equally clear movement away from that cult toward the specific values of settled monasticism.

The *Mahāparinirvāṇa Sūtra* provides ample testimony of the cult of saints as a presupposition of its own composition. Thus, in the six versions of the text, we find a great number of references to the Buddha and other saints that, taken together, duplicate many of the elements of the paradigm of Buddhist sainthood outlined in earlier chapters.[22] These elements, in the Pāli version, include[23] the life of forest renunciation and meditation of the Buddha (*Mps*-p 1.6),[24] his accomplishments as a meditator (5.26–36),[25] and his full awakening (4.37).[26] The references are often quite specific, as when the Buddha, like the other saints, enters into meditation, he is understood to have attained cessation *(nirodha),* in which he appears as if dead but in fact is not (6.8). Themes of postrealization include the Buddha's great charisma: so bright is the golden hue of his complexion, that a golden robe he wears appears dim by contrast (4.35–37).[27] Compassion is a central trait of his enlightened personality. He has lay devotees as well as close disciples, including men and women and the deities. These latter, in fact, make up half of the eight classes of his listeners: he instructs four classes of humans (*kṣatriya*s, brahmins, worthy householders, and *śramaṇa*s)[28] and four classes of deities (the four divine kings, the gods of the thirty-three, the Māra kings, and the Brahma Kings) (3.21–23).[29]

Miracles surround the Buddha's person (*Mps*-p 3.17)[30] and he is accomplished in magical power.[31] In instructing the eightfold assembly, the Buddha manifests various shapes and forms (3.21–23).[32] The Buddha's attainment brings with it various other magical powers, outlined by the *Mahāparinirvāṇa Sūtra,* such as the *ṛddhi* (3.3).[33] There are also stories of miraculous events, such as the miracle of the clear water (4.21–25)[34] and the story of the cosmic veneration (5.2–3).[35] The text, as noted, also credits the Buddha with the power of longevity, to live to the end of the *kalpa:* "the *tathāgata* . . . could, therefore, should he desire it, live on yet for a *kalpa,* or for that portion of the *kalpa* which has yet to run" (3.3).[36] The Buddha predicts his own death (3.9, 3.37, 3.51)[37] and dies (6.9).[38] His manner of dying is unusual, if not for later saints at least for ordinary humans, for he does so while engaged in meditation. The events of his death are also marked by miracles: an earthquake (predicted at 3.19 and occurring at 6.10) and thunder (6.10).[39] The text's depiction of the events following the Buddha's death, which has been studied in detail by Bareau (1975), gives evidence of the cultic forms connected with the passing of saints (6.15,[40] 6.17–18,[41] 6.22ff.,[42] 6.23ff.,[43] 6.25,[44] and 6.27[45]). The Buddha is associated with many sacred places (lists of which are given at 3.42 and 3.46),[46] with four deserving special reverence (locations of his birth, enlightenment, turning of the wheel of dharma, and passing away) (5.8),[47] which the Buddha recommends that his followers visit, in order to "see" *(dassanīya)* and venerate them. Finally, his relics are of great interest and become the basis of a cult (6.23).

But if the *Mahāparinirvāṇa Sūtra* clearly acknowledges in impressive detail the cult of saints in Buddhism, it does not do so wholeheartedly. In fact, it appears that in the text the cult of saints has been to some extent rendered superfluous, in two respects. First, the Buddha seems to function implicitly as the saint who renders any other saints unnecessary: since he has come, there is now no further need for other saints. Second, owing to the monastic legacy that the Buddha has left behind, even he himself is no longer necessary, and his death can be viewed with equanimity. These points become clear in the famous exchange between the Buddha and Ānanda, when the latter is lamenting the approaching demise of the Blessed One and wondering about the future of the community without its leader. As articulated in the Pāli version, Ānanda seems to put the Buddha in mind of the possibility of appointing a human successor, perhaps one in whom his charisma may live on and continue to be accessible to the community (2.24–25).[48] The Buddha admits that another might come forward to lead the order but repudiates this possibility. He then delivers the famous statement that makes the same point: "Therefore, O Ānanda, be ye lamps unto yourselves. Be ye a refuge to yourselves. Betake yourselves to no external refuge. Hold fast to the Truth [*dhamma*] as a lamp. Hold fast as a refuge to the Truth. Look not for refuge to any one besides yourselves" (2.26).[49]

But if the *tathāgata* is really gone, then what should serve as the basis of the religious life? Here the *Mahāparinirvāṇa Sūtra* is ready with an answer, given on both implicit and explicit levels. Implicit in the text is the presentation of settled monasticism based on the *vinaya* and the authentic dharma as the central reference point for the religious life. The same point is made explicitly in the Pāli recension of the text in terms that are substantially repeated in the other versions:

> The Blessed One addressed the venerable Ānanda, and said, "It may be, Ānanda, that in some of you the thought may arise, 'The word of the Master is ended, we have no teacher [*satthā*] more!' But it is not thus, Ānanda, that you should regard it. The truths [*dhamma*] and the rules of the order [*vinaya*] which I have set forth and laid down for you all, let them, after I am gone, be the Teacher [*satthā*] to you." (6.1)[50]

Although the precise contents of this dharma and *vinaya* are debatable, the basic intention of the *Mahāparinirvāṇa Sūtra* seems clear enough: the point is made that the living saints *(satthā)* and their functions have, to a large extent, been taken over by the authoritative texts, including doctrinal contents (dharma) and the monastic rule *(vinaya)*. In addition, more is implied, for, as we shall presently see, this dharma and *vinaya* must be understood within the context of the community of monks that stands behind the text. In effect, the *Mahāparinirvāṇa Sūtra* has removed the living saint as a primary reference point for its religious life and in his place installed settled monasticism.[51] This is, of course, a theme that we have already seen in the *Old Skandhaka,* discussed in Chapter 1. In this passage in the text, the Buddha has, in effect, been transformed into the values, preoccupations, and institutions of settled monasticism as seen in and as defined by its dharma and *vinaya*. This substitution is reflected in the curious redefinition the *Mahāparinirvāṇa Sūtra* gives to the term *satthā:* formerly it had applied to the Buddha; now it is to be applied to the dharma and *vinaya,* which henceforth will be the only teacher the *saṃgha* will have or need. This is a radical enough transformation, but in some ways it retains the old structure. The *Mahāparinirvāṇa Sūtra* may not look with particular favor upon the monastic who worships—in the sense of doing *pūjā* to—the Buddha either as a living saint or after he has passed away. However, the monastic performs another kind of worship to the Buddha's remains, this time through living according to the *vinaya* and studying the teachings as contained in sacred scripture. These remains are clearly quite different from those typically venerated in the cult of saints, but remains they nevertheless are.

The nature of these remains is defined in some detail in the *Mahāparinirvāṇa Sūtra*. We find the *vinaya* having attained a relatively developed form. For example, in the Pāli version, the *vinaya* has already achieved a definitive shape: the text refers to a group of regulations *that may not be changed* (6.3).[52] In addition, the *vinaya* has achieved a considerable degree of complexity entailing, for example, the need to distinguish between major precepts and minor precepts (6.3). The text also refers to regulations according to which mendicants may enter the order (5.28–29),[53] reflecting a central concern for *vinaya* and a monastic *saṃgha* with relatively complex organization.[54]

The basic meaning of the other part of the Buddha's remains, the dharma, is made clear in the many references in the *Mahāparinirvāṇa Sūtra* to the preoccupation with authoritative texts. For example, all six versions of the text present, as the criteria for discriminating authentic scripture (the word of the Buddha) from that which is inauthentic, the famous "four reliances" or "four references."[55] As articulated in the Pāli version, the criteria of authenticity are divided into two groups: the first concerns the human source of the proposed text and the second its content (4.7–11).

The first criterion lists, in a clearly hierarchical order, the four sources from which a text proffered as authentic may be legitimately alleged to have originated. The proposed text may be claimed, first, to have come from the Buddha himself; second, from a monastic group, in the Pāli from a "company of brethren [*bhikkhus*] with their elders and leaders"; third, from a monastic group "with many elders of the order" who are learned *(bahussuta)*, who have received the correct transmission of the tradition *(āgatāgama)*,[56] and who are textual specialists in the dharma *(dhammadhara)*, of the *vinaya (vinayadhara)*, or of the summaries (P., *mātikā*[Skt., *mātṛkā]dhara*)";[57] fourth, from a solitary *bhikkhu* living alone, but who still has received the correct transmission of the tradition, is very learned, and is a textual specialist in the dharma, *vinaya*, or the summaries. Not considered at all and excluded from this list are, of course, any who are not monks in good standing, presumably as defined by the *vinaya*, and who are not textual specialists in the particular texts considered normative by the authors of this section of the *Mahāparinirvāṇa Sūtra*.

The second major criterion of authenticity is the content of the proposed text, and it is according to this criterion that final judgement is to be rendered. Thus, the proposed text, regardless of the venerability of the human source to which it is attributed, should be compared with the authentic discourses *(sūtra)* and with the rules of the order *(vinaya)*.[58] If the proposed scripture accords with the *sūtra* and *vinaya* already in existence (and considered normative), then it may be accepted as authentic. However, if it does not so accord, then it is to be rejected as inauthentic (*Mps*-p 4.8–11). In other words, even if a proposed text is held to have come from the Buddha or from one of the three other reliances, it is still not to be accepted as authentic unless its content can be shown to accord with already existing canonical tradition.[59]

These criteria reflect the values and preoccupations of settled monasticism in several ways. First, the monastic form of Buddhism, as reflected in the *Mahāparinirvāṇa Sūtra,* sets itself up as the final arbiter of authentic scripture. Second, only fully ordained monastics, the *bhikṣus*, may be considered as legitimate sources of authentic scripture. Third, the virtues of the monks who, collectively or individually, are to act as authorities are monastic virtues: they have received the transmission, they are very learned, and they are textual specialists. Fourth, the collective of the organized monastic *saṃgha* is, apart from the Buddha, the highest authority. Fifth, we find here a particular concern for authentic scripture and the presupposition of the existence of not only an authoritative but a definitive collection of texts. Finally, the reliances reflect an essentially conservative position: only that which accords with received textual tradition can be considered authentic. In fact, even the authority of the Buddha himself is not enough, for texts attributed to him shall be judged by the existing canon. New developments are ruled out, at least on the explicit level.[60]

The *Mahāparinirvāṇa Sūtra* also suggests that monastic life, with its behavioral and textual emphases, was well developed by the time of its completion. In the Pāli text, the principal themes of which are repeated in the other recensions, Māra suggests that the Buddha may now die since *bhikṣus* and *bhikṣuṇīs* and the lay disciples have become true *śrāvakas*, "wise and well-trained, ready and learned, versed in the Scriptures, fulfilling all the greater and the lesser duties, correct in life, walking according to the precepts" (3.7ff.;[61] repeated at 3.35).[62] Moreover, these have "learned the doctrine, [are] able to tell others of it, preach it, make it known, establish it, open it, minutely explain it and make it clear . . . when others start vain doctrine, [they] shall be able by the truth to vanquish and refute it" (3.7;[63] repeated at 3.35).[64] This passage mentions as central to its definition of Buddhism the major preoccupations of settled monasticism: proper fulfillment of behavioral conventions, knowledge of texts, acting in the role of preachers of the dharma, debating with and defeating heretics, and so on. Moreover, we are told, these activities are not incipient but fully developed: the Buddha can now die, because his tradition is "successful, prosperous, widespread, and popular in all its full extent" (3.8;[65] repeated at 3.35).[66] In these passages, the *Mahāparinirvāṇa Sūtra* describes orientations and accomplishments that can only with a stretch of the imagination be attributed to the time period of the Buddha. In this sense, the text is collapsing history, reading its own situation back into the time of the Buddha. But this anachronism is fortuitous because it shows us the conditions that existed when this passage was included in the text.

The *Mahāparinirvāṇa Sūtra,* then, acknowledges the existence and venerability of the Buddhist cult of saints, but, at the same time, it devalues this kind of Buddhism in favor of the specific values and preoccupations of settled monasticism, which it wishes to advocate. It is important for us to avoid reducing this process of advocacy and devaluation merely to a political power struggle between settled monasticism and its Buddhist rivals. More is at stake, and it may not be entirely wrong to see behind the Buddhist cult of saints on the one hand and settled monasticism on the other the tendency toward two characteristic and somewhat divergent interpretations of Buddhism.

The characteristic interpretation of early settled monasticism, as reflected in the *Mahāparinirvāṇa Sūtra,* may be referred to as a doctrine of absence or nonimmanence. The basic shape of this doctrine is given expression in the text in a series of statements that occur in contexts involving discussion of the cult of saints and are explicitly put forth to show that the cult of saints is ultimately an inferior kind of activity. For example, one particularly famous passage, occurring several times in the text (in the Pāli version, e.g., 3.48, 5.6, 5.14, 6.11, 6.20),[67] tells us that when the Buddha dies, he is really gone. This passage, the main themes of which again occur in the other recensions of the *Mahāparinirvāṇa Sūtra,* is found in the Pāli, for example, right after the statement that the Buddha, as a saint, could live to the end of the *kalpa.*

> But now Ānanda, have I not already, on former occasions, told you that it is in the very nature of all things most near and dear unto us that we must divide ourselves from them, leave them, sever ourselves from them? How then, Ānanda, can this be possible—whereas anything whatever born, brought into being, and organised, contains within itself the inherent necessity of dissolution—how, then, can this be possible, that such a being should not be dissolved? No such condition can exist. (3.48)[68]

The Buddha then says, "That the Tathāgata for the sake of living should repent him again [of having relinquished his lifespan]—this can no wise be." This passage occurs again, when the Buddha has just criticized those deities who lament his passing (5.6),[69] and again when Ānanda is rebuked by the Buddha for lamenting his immanent passing (5.14).[70] It occurs once more when Anuruddha exhorts the unenlightened *bhikkhu*s not to weep (6.11).[71] And it occurs still again when Mahākāśyapa similarly calls down the unenlightened *bhikkhus* (6.20).[72] In all these appearances, this passage occurs in contexts where the saint's powers and cult are the main subject of discussion. Moreover, this passage would deliver a coup de grâce to adherents of the cult in articulating the basic reason why the cult is inferior: the *tathāgata* is gone and thus cannot, as a saint, continue to be a reference point for the religious life.[73] The disappearance of the Buddha is also affirmed in other passages. Even the Buddha, he himself says, is subject to impermanence. "Verily, the word has gone forth from the Tathāgata saying, 'The final extinction of the Tathāgata shall take place before long . . . the Tathāgata will die' " (3.48). Similarly, we are told that at the place where the Buddha died, one should say, "Here the Tathāgata passed finally away in that utter passing away which leaves nothing whatever to remain behind *[anupādisesa]*" (5.8).[74]

A Doctrine of Presence or Immanence among the Buddhist Saints

The evidence of the Buddhist saints and their cults suggests, however, that the doctrine of absence or nonimmanence of the *Mahāparinirvāṇa Sūtra* does not represent the only Indian Buddhist position with regard to the saints. There is another, equally logical and consistent position, particularly bound up with the Buddhist cult of saints, which may be termed a *doctrine of presence* or *imma-*

nence. This distinctive position may be identified by reviewing some of the basic doctrinal themes connected with the Buddhist saints. As we have seen, the Buddha, as preeminent Buddhist saint, although passed away, has not, in some readings, entirely disappeared from this world. There are several ways in which he can be found as immanent in the world. First, he appears in his stūpa, vivified by remains of some kind or other.[75] The existence of the saints in their stūpas appears linked to some important doctrines. Hirakawa believes that one of these doctrines, to be explored in more detail, depicts the Buddha himself, after his *parinirvāṇa,* as abiding in the *nirvāṇadhātu,* or realm of nirvāṇa: ''Even after the Buddha died he was not viewed as having completely ceased to exist; rather, he was thought to exist in the realm of *nirvāṇa,''* from whence he could be supplicated (Hirakawa 1987, 93). We saw that the *Mahāparinirvāṇa Sūtra* credits the Buddha with having passed into the realm of nirvāṇa *(nibbānadhātu);* the text is particularly interested in this fact, not because this makes him in any way available, but because it renders him entirely unavailable, because his passing is without remainder. However, it is precisely the immanence of Śākyamuni in his stūpa that enables Aśoka to address him as if he were living there still. What is true of Buddha Śākyamuni is true of the other saints. Mahākāśyapa abides within Mount Kukkuṭapāda in the attainment of cessation, passed beyond, yet in some mysterious way still abiding, and he, according to at least some traditions, will one day rise at the coming of Maitreya. In a closely similar image, in the *Saddharmapuṇḍarīka Sūtra,* when the seven-jeweled stūpa opens, the buddha Prabhūtaratna is seen seated in meditation posture on a lion throne, his body shriveled *(saṃghaṭitakāya)* and dried up *(pariśuṣkagātra),*[76] as one abiding in meditation *(samādhisamāpanna)* (*Sps* 153.5–6 [Kn., 236]).

The Buddha may also become actual, as we have seen, in other symbols such as the book, the Pure Land, the image, and the maṇḍala. Like the stūpa, each of these provides a symbolic vehicle that, liturgically empowered, enables the Buddha to be spiritually alive and present. In addition, as we have seen, the Buddha is also present in his enlightened followers. These saints, on account of their realization, are assimilated to the Buddha, reflected in the title—*buddha*—that may be given to them. The pratyekabuddha is understood as an awakened one, sometimes being called a buddha, sometimes a *tathāgata.* Even more explicit is the identification of the saints with Buddha Śākyamuni in the texts of the Sarvāstivāda. Aśoka affirms that in seeing Piṇḍola, he sees the Buddha: ''By looking at you, I can, even today, see the Tathāgata,'' and he makes a similar remark regarding Upagupta. The bodhisattva, as he travels his path, ever more closely approximates the Buddha in the fullest sense.

It is crucial to realize that, from a certain point of view, the various forms of the Buddha and the different symbols by which he becomes present are finally not separate realities but share an essential and selfsame identity. Śākyamuni attained enlightenment and is therefore Buddha. After his passing, his enlightenment, his very being, appears in his various forms and symbols. The human saints are also no less symbols in this same sense: in them the Buddha becomes spiritually present, and they are thereby consubstantial with him. For this reason, they also participate in the other symbols of the Buddha's presence and exist in their own symbols (relics, stūpas, images, maṇḍalas, and later human saints). Thus, it is that the Buddha and his realization do not disappear but become perpetually present in the world.

Several important themes are connected with the ongoing presence of the Buddha in the world and with the immanence of enlightenment. For one thing, the immanence of the Buddha, in his stūpas and other symbols and in his saints, is typically linked with the theme of compassion. The various symbols exist in order to permit the ongoing presence of the Buddha and most particularly his compassionate activity among human beings. Hirakawa remarks that if nirvāṇa-without-remainder had always been considered a completely quiescent state, then compassionate responses by the Buddha to his suppliants would have been impossible: "Thus the people who worshipped at Buddhist stūpas seem to have believed that the Buddha continued to be active" (Hirakawa 1987, 93).[77] In a similar way, the saints exist, present themselves as recipients of donations, and prolong their lives out of their compassion for suffering beings. Piṇḍola, the others of the sixteen arhants, and the saint Upagupta have agreed to prolong their lives precisely to aid and assist sentient beings. The saints' immanence obviously provides the precondition for a consistent and essential aspect of the cult of saints—namely, that of the "seeing" of the realized ones: one can only see that which is before one to be seen. It is because they are actually present in human form, in stūpas and in other symbols, that one can see the saints and participate in their enlightened charisma.[78]

The preceding discussion contained reference to a number of examples in which the immanence of the Buddha and other saints in the world is connected with the notion of *nirodha,* cessation, or *nirodhasamāpatti,* the attainment of cessation. This is the state of meditation that the pratyekabuddhas prefer above all others (K., 51), and it is in this state that they typically abide on Mount Gandhamādana and from which they arise to go on begging rounds among people. *Nirodhasamāpatti* is the meditative state in which, according to some traditions, Mahākāśyapa abides and from which he will awaken at the coming of Maitreya. Adikaram shows the typical linkage of *nirodhasamāpatti* with the Buddhist saints who are thought to abide in various sacred places in Sri Lanka, presumably reflecting Indian notions (1946, 102–24, et seq.). Not unrelated to these examples is one in which the Buddha, though seeming to be dead and gone, is actually abiding in *nirodhasamāpatti.* In the *Mahāparinirvāṇa Sūtra* passage cited above, the Buddha has progressed through and beyond the eight levels of meditation[79] and appears as if he has passed away. When Ānanda expresses alarm,[80] Anuruddha informs him that the Blessed One is, in fact, not dead but has attained that state in which perceptions (*samjñā;* P., *saññā*) and feelings *(vedayita)* have ceased *(nirodha)* (*Mps*-p 6.8).[81]

In both Pāli and Sanskrit texts, *nirodhasamāpatti* is typically listed as the highest member of each of two frequently mentioned groups. First, *nirodha* is the final and ultimate stage of the nine *anupūrva*(P., *anupubba)vihārasamāpatti*s; this list of stages is composed of the four *dhyāna*s,[82] the four higher *āyatana*s,[83] and *nirodhasamāpatti* (as the ninth stage).[84] Second, *nirodha* is found as the last and highest of the eight *vimokṣas* (P., *vimokkha*), which include three preliminary stages,[85] the four *āyatanas*, and *nirodha* as the final stage of liberation.[86] In both lists—the nine attainments and the eight liberations—as these are found in both Sanskrit and Pāli traditions, *nirodhasamāpatti* is defined in the same terms: *saṃjñāvedayitanirodha* (P., *saññāvedayitanirodha*), the cessation of perceptions and feelings, that is, of the *saṃskāras* (P., *sankhāra*) that compose conditioned existence.[87] The fact that *nirodhasamāpatti* appears as the unsurpassed member in both of these lists and is defined in the same way suggests its secure place as the way in which the culmination of the path of meditation was understood widely in Indian Buddhism.

But *nirodhasamāpatti* is seen as more than the culmination of the meditative path. As La Vallée Poussin notes, as the last and highest spiritual stage, it also represents the attainment of complete realization in this life, explicitly equated with nirvāṇa (see *PTSD* 371).[88] King remarks that *nirodhasamāpatti* is described in canonical works as the *"fullest and most extended realization of Nibbāna possible to human beings in this life"* (1980, 12; emphasis in original). *Nirodhasamāpatti* is not only identified with the attainment of nirvāṇa, it is also sometimes regarded as necessary to that attainment. La Vallée Poussin remarks that "several documents say more or less clearly that *nirodhasamāpatti* is . . . necessary to the acquisition of complete sainthood. The series of the 'nine successive attainments' [*nirodhasamāpatti* is the ninth] . . . was perhaps in certain ascetic milieux, an essential discipline" (1936–37, 217). Although the four *dhyānas* or the eightfold set of the four *dhyānas* and the four formless attainments are acknowledged as pre-Buddhist practices, *nirodhasamāpatti* is understood by its advocates as specifically Buddhist. In the words of La Vallée Poussin,

> The Buddhists recognize an . . . attainment beyond the fourth immaterial attainment which is thus "the ninth of nine successive attainments" (preceded by the four *dhyānas*, the four "immaterials"): but they restrict it to themselves [as Buddhists]. They believe that this ninth was discovered by the Buddha . . . they give [to *nirodhasamāpatti*] a clearly Buddhist character in defining it as actual contact with *nirvāṇa*. (1936–37, 212)

The unexcelled and, for its proponents, orthodox status of *nirodhasamāpatti* is illustrated in a variety of canonical and extracanonical passages. The *Kāśyapaparivarta* says simply, "Enter into the attainment of cessation; for the mendicant who has entered into the attainment of cessation, there is nothing left to do" (*Kp* 144 [La Vallée Poussin 1936–37, 222]). It is remarked in the *Aṅguttaranikāya*,

> What is necessary for there to be nirvāṇa in this life? The ascetic enters into the first *dhyāna* [and so on up to] . . . the fourth immaterial attainment: this is what the Blessed One called, by analogy, nirvāṇa-in-this-life. The ascetic enters into the attainment of *nirodha,* and his vices have been destroyed by the view of *prajñā:* here is what the Blessed One called, without analogy, nirvāṇa-in-this-life. (*An* 4:454 [La Vallée Poussin 1936–37, 216])

Though it transcends experience in the ordinary sense (*samjñā* and *vedanā* have ceased), *nirodhasamāpatti* is clearly not to be understood as an unconscious state. As given in the *Aṅguttaranikāya,*

> Śāriputra said to the monks, "Beatitude nirvāṇa! Beatitude nirvāṇa!" Udāyin asked, "What beatitude [can there be] in nirvāṇa where there is no sensation?" Śāriputra replied, "The beatitude of nirvāṇa is that there is no sensation in nirvāṇa." . . . The monk, passing beyond the fourth immaterial attainment, enters into the attainment of nirodha, and his vices have been destroyed by the experience of prajñā: by this analogy also one can know how nirvāṇa is beatitude. (4:454 [217])

Finally, the *Aṅguttaranikāya* contains a description of the enlightenment of the Buddha in which the Blessed One declares that it was only through the practice of the nine attainments with their culmination in *nirodhasamāpatti* that he finally won through to enlightenment. In this passage, the Buddha describes the first eight attainments and then continues,

> And presently, Ānanda, passing wholly beyond the sphere of neither perception nor non-perception, I entered and abode in the ending of perception and feeling and I saw by wisdom that the cankers were completely destroyed. And so long, Ānanda, as I attained not to, emerged not from these nine attainments of gradual abidings, both forwards and backwards, I realized not completely, as one wholly awakened, the full perfect awakening, unsurpassed in the worlds with its gods, Māras, Brahmās, on earth with its recluses, godly men, devas and men; but when I attained to and emerged from these abidings such wise, then, wholly awakened, I realized completely the full perfect awakening unsurpassed. (*An* 4:438–48 [WH., 4:294–95])

The particular association of *nirodhasamāpatti* with the Buddhist saints is no accident; this term is typically used to characterize the saints' enlightenment in this life.[89] In this sense, it is essentially a yogic attainment and is closely linked with the life of forest renunciation and its meditative way.[90] As we saw in Chapter 6, La Vallée Poussin argues that *nirodhasamāpatti,* as the culminating attainment of the *ubhayatobhāgavimukta,* is a description of enlightenment specifically reserved for saints associated with Buddhist traditions of forest renunciation, asceticism, and meditation. The linkage of *nirodhasamāpatti* with the forest saints is particularly important, for it provides Buddhism with a physical location of nirvāṇa in this world—namely, in the body of the saint, whether it be the body of flesh and blood, stūpa, or another icon. In *nirodhasamāpatti,* the saint remains present and can even be said to have a kind of life, but it is utterly different from the existence of ordinary people. In this sense, it may be mistaken for death by those who are not discerning, as in the passage from the *Mahāparinirvāṇa Sūtra* just cited.[91]

The mistaking of the *nirodhasamāpatti* of the saints for death is a theme found with some frequency in the Nikāya literature. For example, we have seen the story of a pratyekabuddha whose enemies wish to burn him to death and who heap wood around him. However, because of his abiding in *nirodhasamāpatti,* the fire does not touch him, even after seven days, and he arises from his meditation and goes on his way. Buddhaghosa tells a similar story of an elder meditating in the forest, immersed in *nirodhasamāpatti,* who is found by some cowherds and believed to be dead. They build a big fire around him to cremate him, but the elder—owing to his *nirodhasamāpatti*—does not burn and, like the pratyekabuddha in the previous example, proves his invulnerability to fire (*Vsm* 12.32 [N., 16–17]).[92] These examples suggest another element of *nirodhasamāpatti* as immanence: through it, saints may become impervious to death. In other words, because they are not alive in the ordinary sense, they cannot die as ordinary people do. The *Aśokarājāvadāna* illustrates this in a story about the persecutor of the dharma, Puṣyamitra. This evil king wishes to kill a certain arhant but is unable to do so, because the arhant has entered *nirodhasamāpatti.*[93] Buddhaghosa recounts the legend of a saint who goes into a meditation hall and enters into *nirodhasamāpatti.* The hall catches fire, and the elder is engulfed by the inferno. "People brought water and put it out. They removed the ashes, did repairs, scattered flowers, and then stood respectfully waiting. The Elder emerged at the time he had determined. Seeing them, he said 'I am discovered,' and he rose up into the air and went to Piyañgu Island" (*Vsm* 23.36 [N., 829–30]). In a related theme, *nirodhasamāpatti* may also enable saints to extend their lives indefinitely, as evidenced by the example of Mahākāśyapa. *Nirodhasamāpatti* thus represents a state between ordinary life, on the one hand, and *parinirvāṇa,* utter disappearance of the saints, on the other. In this state, the saints abide in complete enlightenment, in this world.[94]

For traditions connected with the Buddhist saints, *nirodhasamāpatti* represents the full and untrammeled attainment of nirvāṇa in this life and is a central theme in the saints' lives and actions. It is interesting, then, that in the developed Nikāya schools *nirodhasamāpatti* has little of this great prestige. In fact, as La Vallée Poussin notes, in the schools as reflected in the various commentarial traditions, *nirodhasamāpatti* is of little interest and is seen as, at most, a by-product and adornment of realization for a few (1936–37, 212–17).[95] As settled monasticism came to dominate the Indian Buddhist landscape, so its characteristic way of understanding enlightenment along the lines of the *dhamma bhikkhu*s, as *prajñāvimukta* alone, also came to prevail (see Chapter 6). In this milieu, *nirodhasamāpatti* was considered unnecessary and even irrelevant to the attainment of nirvāṇa; in La Vallée Poussin's words, it had "no place at all in the economy of salvation" (1936–37, 213).

A revealing view of these themes of the presence and immanence of the Buddha and his saints is provided by the introduction to the *Nandimitrāvadāna.* This text contains a passage closely parallel to one in the *Mahāparinirvāṇa Sūtra* in which the Buddha announces his passing, the hearers respond with expressions of grief, and the Buddha teaches them about impermanence. Most interesting is that, although the components and dramatic structure of the *Nandimitrāvadāna* passage closely resemble that of the similar passage in the *Mahāparinirvāṇa Sūtra,* the interpretive framework is quite different. In the *Nandimitrāvadāna,* it is not the

Buddha who is about to pass away, but rather the saint Nandimitra. Like the Buddha in the *Mahāparinirvāṇa Sūtra,* in the *Nandimitrāvadāna* Nandimitra announces his imminent passing: "From this time forward, I shall not do anything. You will therefore have no support whatever in which to take refuge. You good people should know that, if you have any doubts, you must put them to me" (LC., 7). As in the *Mahāparinirvāṇa Sūtra,* the hearers react with a show of great grief: "When the great assembly heard these words, they raised their voices in lamentation; unable to restrain themselves, they rolled upon the ground." Like the Buddha in the *Mahāparinirvāṇa Sūtra,* Nandimitra is addressed as the sole teacher, the only reference point of enlightenment, the one reliance of sentient beings, whose passing is to be mourned as a cataclysmic event. Using terms of address reminiscent of those used of the Buddha, wherein Nandimitra is assimilated to the Buddha, one among the assembly stands up and says,

> The Buddha Bhagavat entered *nirvāṇa* a long time ago; after him, the five disciples also passed away; the world has been empty for a long time, and there is no authentic leader. Now, there is no one but you, the venerable one, who is the eye of gods and men. How is it that you, in your turn, wish to abandon us? We beg that you will bring down your pity on us and that you will make your life last a while longer. (LC., 7)

Following this, the saint teaches his hearers about impermanence in words that closely resemble those spoken by Śākyamuni in the *Mahāparinirvāṇa Sūtra:*

> Do not weep; good people, know that in this world it is the rule that everything that is born must die. Even the Buddha Tathāgatas, although conquerers of the four Māras and masters of the lengths of their lives, still because they conform to the world, have manifested *nirvāṇa.* How could it possibly be appropriate, then, that I remain permanently? (LC., 8)

Then, like the Buddha in the *Mahāparinirvāṇa Sūtra,* Nandimitra asks his disciples whether they have any questions that they would like to put to him. After further expressing grief at the imminent passing of their teacher, the disciples ask how long the dharma will exist in the world, and Nandimitra replies with the substance of the *Nandimitrāvadāna,* concerning the ongoing existence of the sixteen arhants. When the assembled people hear about these saints, their grief is somewhat assuaged and they find some relief (LC., 8–9).

In spite of the similarity of the *Mahāparinirvāṇa Sūtra* and the *Nandimitrāvadāna* regarding dramatic elements and structure, the doctrinal frames are thus clearly quite different. In the *Mahāparinirvāṇa Sūtra,* the Buddha replies to the consternation of his disciples by referring them to the dharma and *vinaya,* indicating received tradition and not the contemporary, abiding saint. Nandimitra's consolation to his own disciples is, by contrast, that although he himself will pass beyond, the disciples may turn their attention to enlightened saints who will not pass beyond, but who will remain in saṃsāra, available and ready to help sentient beings. Unlike the answer provided by the *Mahāparinirvāṇa Sūtra,* the *Nandimitrāvadāna* presents no fundamental discontinuity in type of religious life, but a continuation of the same kind of devotion to the saint in which Nandimitra's disciples already participate.

Parallel to this doctrinal difference are the different uses to which the section on the announcement of passing, the disciples' grief, and the saint's teaching are put in the two texts. In the *Mahāparinirvāṇa Sūtra,* the grief, shown by certain gods and disciples, is condemned as unworthy. This condemnation is explicit in the section of the text in which the gods and arhants who exhibit such grief are blamed as being, respectively, "worldly" and "not yet free from passion." Certain other arhants and certain deities are said to be above such grief, which is thus implicitly condemned. One should wean oneself away from excessive devotion to and reliance on the saint—here the Buddha—and rely instead on dharma and *vinaya.*

By contrast, in the *Nandimitrāvadāna,* although Nandimitra counsels, "Don't cry and shed tears," in fact, sadness is the norm. There are none who transcend this sadness and no dramatic foils to show that it is unnecessary or inappropriate. Nandimitra, acting in the role of the Buddha,[96] responds to the sadness of the disciples by presenting the tradition of the sixteen arhants, allowing, in effect, for a transference of devotion to those saints who will not pass away. The grief is not blameworthy as in the *Mahāparinirvāṇa Sūtra,* but rather it provides the required basis of a necessary transition.[97] Here, in the *Mahāparinirvāṇa Sūtra* and the *Nandimitrāvadāna,* we have a traditional form put to two different uses. It is interesting that the view of the immanence of the saints espoused in the *Nandimitrāvadāna* closely coincides with the position that the *Mahāparinirvāṇa Sūtra* presupposes and argues against. This suggests that, although the *Nandimitrāvadāna* as a text is obviously much later than the *Mahāparinirvāṇa Sūtra,* its affirmation of the centrality of the saints to Buddhist religious life may possibly represent a developmentally earlier stage when compared with the historically more dominant viewpoint of the *Mahāparinirvāṇa Sūtra.*

Some additional insight into the doctrine of presence or immanence of the saints and its antiquity is provided by Schayer, who, along with his followers, has attempted to identify and summarize the doctrines of the earliest knowable Buddhism. Schayer and his school have explored the early scriptures of Buddhism in the attempt to discern a precanonical level of doctrine.[98] Schayer proposes that in order to find out something about "precanonical Buddhism," it is necessary to develop a method of indentifying the precanonical elements in the early canon. He believes that such a method can be found by looking in the early texts for passages reflecting ideas that contradict the dominant doctrinal positions of the early canon. Where such contradictions can be found, one must ask why these "heterodox" elements were not rejected and cast aside. "There is only one answer: evidently they have been transmitted by a tradition old enough and considered to be authoritative by the compilers of the Canon. The last conclusion follows of itself: these texts representing ideas and doctrines contradictory to the generally admitted canonical viewpoint are survivals of older, precanonical Buddhism" (Schayer 1935, 124). Using this method, Schayer detects evidence of a precanonical cult of saints connected with an immanentalist doctrine.

Régamy (1957), who summarizes some of the major themes of Schayer's work, identifies four points as central to Schayer's reconstruction of precanonical Buddhism. First, the Buddha was considered not so much an ordinary man as an extraordinary being, in whom ultimate reality was embodied and who was an incarnation of the mythical figure of the *tathāgata*. Second, the ties binding the Buddha's disciples and other followers to him were not based on assent to doctrine as much as on attraction to his spiritual charisma and supernatural authority and a commitment of faith emerging from perception of that charisma and authority.[99] Third, the nirvāṇa achieved by the Buddha and other saints was conceived not simply as a "blowing out" in the abhidharmic sense but as the attainment of immortality and the gaining of a deathless sphere from which there would be no falling back. This nirvāṇa, as a transmundane reality or state, is incarnated in the person of the Buddha and makes him who he is. Finally, nirvāṇa is possible because it already dwells as the inmost "consciousness" of the human being, an inmost consciousness that is not subject to birth and death.[100] Using his method, Schayer believes that he has identified precanonical Buddhism, the earliest Buddhism of which we can have knowledge. Whether or not one agrees with the full extent of Schayer's interpretations, there can be no doubt that he has shown, at the very least, a second doctrinal position alongside that of the more dominant tradition, one likely to be of at least equivalent, if not of greater, antiquity.

Schayer's methodology and theses have subsequently been explored in some detail by M. Falk in her *Nāma-rūpa and Dharma-rūpa* (1943). Falk ingeniously uses Schayer's method of looking for ideas that contradict dominant classical tradition to discern various historical layers of development behind the conceptions of the early canon and commentarial literature. This procedure enables her to spell out precanonical Buddhist conceptions of the cosmos, nirvāṇa, the Buddha, the path, and the saint. According to Falk, in precanonical tradition, there is a threefold division of reality (115ff.).[101] At the lowest ontic level is the realm of *rūpadhātu,* the samsaric sphere of name and form *(nāmarūpa)* in which ordinary beings live, die, and are reborn. Above this is the realm of *arūpadhātu,* the sphere of "sheer *nāma,*" produced by *samādhi,* an ethereal realm frequented by *yogin*s but still not entirely liberated. Finally, at the ultimate ontic level and standing "above" or "outside" of the previous realms, is the realm of nirvāṇa, the "*amṛta* sphere," characterized by *prajñā.*[102] This nirvāṇa is seen as an "abode" or "place" that is gained by the enlightened saint (111–13).

Each of these three orders of reality has a "body" and an "eye" appropriate to it. One dwells in the *rūpadhātu* in a *rūpakāya* (body of form or matter) marked by the "eye of flesh" and in the *arūpadhātu* in the *nāmakāya* (nonmaterial body) characterized by the *divyacakṣus,* or divine eye. The saint who has gained the highest "abode" of nirvāṇa dwells in a nirvanic body, a *nirodhakāya* (body of cessation) or a *vidyākāya* (body of knowledge) (Falk 1943, 112). In precanonical tradition, such a one is called a *kāyasākṣin,* one who "had realized and witnessed the *nirvāṇa* bodily, i.e., by means of a body conformable to the transcendent *nirodhadhātu*" (111). The liberated one possesses the eye of *prajñā* (115). Falk sees this scheme reflected in the precanonical conception of the path to salvation. The basis of the Buddhist path in precanonical times is the notion that the nirvanic element, as an ontic "essence" or pure consciousness, is immanent within saṃsāra. In this model, then, the three bodies referred to may be understood as concentric realities: the outer, gross *rūpakāya* is stripped away; then the inner, more subtle *nāmakāya* is abandoned; leaving finally only the *nirodhakāya* of the liberated saint (133–34).[103]

This inmost nirvanic element is gained through a progressive upward ascent—from the *rūpadhātu,* through the *arūpadhātu,* to nirvāṇa—through the agency of the *smṛtyupasthāna*s (P., *satipaṭṭhāna*s, "foundations of mindfulness") and the three trainings *(śīla, samādhi, prajñā).* In a threefold scheme anterior to the classical system of four *smṛtyupasthāna*s, in the first, mindfulness of body *(rūpa),* one abandons identification with the *rūpadhātu* (Falk 1943, 119–24). In the second, mindfulness of mind, one abandons identification with the *arūpadhātu.* In the third, mindfulness of dharmas, one gains liberation: "these *dhammā* were originally only the pure or *anāsravadharmas* constituting *prajñā,* the 'essence' of arhatship, and also the Buddha-body" (120). Similarly, the journey to liberation is defined by the practice of *śīla* in the *rūpadhātu,* then *samādhi* at the level of *arūpadhātu,* and *prajñā* to gain the *nirvāṇadhātu* (115ff.).

The saint, then, is the one who has followed this path to its conclusion and has attained liberation, gaining the *nirodhakāya* and its *prajñācakṣus.* In relation to the attained saint, Falk remarks that "[his] body . . . must have been . . . consubstantial with the Buddha's *amṛtakāya*" (1943, 111). It is this consubstantiation with the Buddha that enables the saint to be given the title of buddha and even *samyaksaṃbuddha.* The titles of the saint in turn reflect the fact that the saint has followed the literal paradigm of the Buddha himself, pursuing his path and gaining the eternal abode of nirvāṇa: "The primitive career of the disciple was a career of imitation: a yogic, dhyānic career like that of Gotama" (111). Falk remarks, "As the Hīnayānic development of Buddhism went the 'negativistic' way, reducing the ideal of perfection to a goal of mere elimination of contingency, it is obvious why no direct mention of the saint's *amṛtakāya* is left in the Canon and why in the exegetic scriptures the *kāyasākṣin* is artificially distinguished from the *arhat*" (111). In these precanonical conceptions, the Buddha is understood to have attained a body with two dimensions: an *amṛtakāya* and a *dharmakāya.* The *amṛtakāya* is utterly transcendent, whereas the *dharmakāya* represents the Buddha's presence within saṃsāra and his ongoing salvific activity of compassion (154). Falk remarks, "This *dharmakāya* of the *buddhas* as leaders, as active within contingency, is by no means the transcendent static *dharmakāya* of the later Trikāya doctrine" (139).

In Falk's view, the notion of the presence of the *dharmakāya* within contingency and the doctrine of the immanence of the nirvanic element within the samsaric consciousness imply one another. As the one dropped out of the early classical canonical doctrine, so did the other. In fact, "only the programmatic reinstauration of a continuity between *saṃsāra* and *nirvāṇa* in the Vijñānavāda creed could again postulate the character of a 'body' for transcendent reality, as the supreme archetype of the immanent and active Doctrine-body [*dharmakāya*]" (Falk 1943, 155). In the orthodox schools behind the "Hīnayāna" canons, then, the immanentalist doctrine is jettisoned, the *amṛtakāya* is rejected, and the *dhar-*

makāya is considerably reduced, such that it is "deprived of its transcendent implications and [comes] to be considered as a mere allegorical formulation of the fact that after the Master's final disappearance, the body of the Sayings [*dharmakāya*] was left to guide the later generations of disciples" (167).[104]

All these notions are, of course, consistent with the major doctrinal themes of presence and immanence that we have found closely linked with the Buddhist saints and their cults. The work of Schayer and Falk is important in the present context for several reasons. First, in the evidence considered earlier we have seen consistent themes of immanence and presence. However, the evidence afforded no more than random glimpses of these ideas, and coherence has been achieved only by piecing together isolated instances. The work of Schayer and his school suggests that a coherent doctrine was, in fact, typically connected with the Buddhist cult of saints. Moreover, they have revealed that doctrine to be one of immanence and presence and have identified some of its major elements, some of the more important of which, such as that of *nirodha,* closely parallel themes developed in this chapter.

Equally important is the clear implication of their work—namely, that the Buddhist cult of saints stands at the center of the earliest knowable Buddhism. Their discovery is striking because Schayer and his school appear not to have set out with any particular interest in the phenomenon of Buddhist saints as such. Their desire was rather simply to apply their method to see if they could identify a precanonical strain of Buddhism. The fact that they were in fact able to make such an identification and that the doctrine they found was primarily concerned with the Buddhist saint as a type would appear strongly to suggest the antiquity of the Buddhist cult of saints. The evidence brought forward in this study suggests that the kind of doctrinal perspectives found by Schayer and his school in precanonical Buddhism provided the characteristic doctrinal expression of the Buddhist cult of saints not only in early but also in later times.

The preceding discussion makes it obvious that the tendency to stress the absence of the Buddha and other saints is most characteristic of the settled monastic evidence (and particularly the conservative settled monastic evidence), whereas the emphasis on the presence of the Buddha and other saints is most typically found among those trends that most strongly reflect the Indian Buddhist cult of saints. At the same time, it has been made clear in the preceding chapters of this study that it is not possible to identify the proponents of these two views simply as "monastic" versus "nonmonastic." To be sure, in the foregoing chapters it is within the conservatism of Pāli monasticism that we have found the greatest hesitation in the face of the charisma of the forest saint. But, as we have seen, within Northern monastic texts the forest saints are much more freely celebrated and identified as progenitors of existing tradition and models who elicit devotion and emulation.[105] This latter example also shows that the two views of the saint are not always opposed to one another, for in the case of the Sarvāstivāda the charisma of the forest saint and the values of settled monasticism are seen as components that are distinctive but that coexist within a harmonious whole. In the

Sarvāstivāda, in other words, it appears that the *Mahāparinirvāṇa Sūtra*'s emphasis on *vinaya,* textual expertise, and settled monasticism is more or less balanced in other evidence by a positive evaluation of the Buddhist saints.

At this point, let us return to the question of the doctrine of the *Mahāparinirvāṇa Sūtra,* the *Old Skandhaka,* the larger *vinaya,* and the early monastic traditions that they reflect, and attempt to summarize the various ways in which their doctrine of absence contrasts with the doctrine of presence associated with the Buddhist cult of saints. It should be kept in mind that although this contrast is presented in terms of a series of oppositions, the distinctions are relative: each orientation has elements of the other, and generally we are dealing with emphases rather than absolute differences. For example, proponents of each orientation can speak on the one hand of a human Buddha who dies or appears to die and, on the other, of a dharma that is undying. The difference between the two orientations comes, then, in the preeminent importance assigned to one or the other side of this polarity and the way in which key terms are defined.

First, for the *Mahāparinirvāṇa Sūtra,* the *Old Skandhaka,* and the *vinaya,* the Buddha, as saint, is departed and gone; their doctrinal viewpoint is inseparable from the notion of his absence. By contrast, for other strains of Buddhist tradition, the Buddha is present, incarnated in various symbols, including the living saints. Second, for the early monastic traditions of the *Mahāparinirvāṇa Sūtra,* because the Buddha is departed and no longer present, among the three jewels (buddha, dharma, *saṃgha*), the *saṃgha* (the monastic community) and the dharma (authoritative textual tradition) provide the natural centers of gravity for tradition. By contrast, for the strands of tradition more oriented to the cult of the saints, religious life would seem to be centered around the jewel of the Buddha, whether in his form as former buddha, as Śākyamuni, as celestial buddha, or as some other saint or symbolic equivalent (stūpa, and so on). Third, these two different doctrinal perspectives give rise to two different attitudes toward the cult of the saints, attitudes that are exemplified in the two ways in which the stūpa is seen. S. Dutt remarks that for the traditions reflected in the *Mahāparinirvāṇa Sūtra,* "the *stūpa* is regarded as only a memorial . . . —a memorial of the noblest kind" (1962, 184). Hirakawa elaborates on this point:

> If one does not believe in the existence of the Buddha, since his human form disappeared at the age of 80, the worship of the *stūpa* is meaningless. . . . Those who believe that the Buddha entered *anupadhiśeṣa-nirvāṇa* at the moment of *parinirvāṇa* do not worship the *stūpa.* Even if such a worship were performed, it would be merely in memory of the Buddha now gone. (1963, 88)

This trend reaches its classical formulation in the Theravāda, where, in Strong's words, "the Buddha is dead and gone: his power has become a thing of the past; he has done all that he needed to do. He is thus incapable of being prayed to, of receiving offerings, or of responding to his devotees" (1987, 99). N. Falk elaborates on the implications of the Theravādin understanding for the interpretation of ritual:

> Conservative Buddhist schools denied such presence, maintaining that the Buddha had totally exited from the world at the time of his final *nirvāṇa*. Performing *pūjās* was of value only as an elementary aspect of self-discipline: venerating the Buddha helped one call to mind the Master's virtues and example, while *pūjā* offerings were a form of *dāna*, the generous giving that shows one's non-attachment to possessions. The Theravāda tradition has been least comfortable with its *pūjās*, officially maintaining that only laity should engage in such actions. (1987, 86)

In contrast, for those who follow a doctrine of presence, for example, "the Buddha's eternal presence is contained in the *stūpa*, and although enshrining relics, the worshipper sees it as the eternal Buddha. . . . [The] faithful who believe that the Buddha is eternal and exists in the ever-present now worship the *stūpa*s as a means of worshipping the Buddha" (Hirakawa 1963, 88). As with the stūpa, so with the other symbols: in the conservative monastic interpretation, the Buddha is not really present; in those traditions more closely aligned with the cult of saints, he does become spiritually alive and present.

These differences are probably not unconnected with the interesting fact that, in Indian Buddhist history, it is precisely the more conservative monastic traditions that tend to view nirvāṇa in terms of absence, taking a more apophatic approach, whereas the nonmonastic traditions tend toward a more kataphatic (i.e., positive) approach. Thus the monastic traditions, and particularly those behind Abhidharma scholasticism and the Madhyamaka, prefer to talk about realization in terms of what it is not. For the Abhidharma schools, it is defined in essentially negative terms. In the Madhyamaka, it is brought to light through an apophatic method wherein the inadequacy of every predicate is realized. By contrast, those traditions that are less strictly monastic and are nonscholastic in origin—such as the early Prajñāpāramitā, the early Yogācāra, the Tathāgatagarbha, and the Vajrayāna—all tend to talk about enlightenment in much more kataphatic ways, in terms of a sacred presence. Thus, the *Aṣṭasāhasrikāprajñāpāramitā*, for all of its well-acknowledged apophasis, mentions the "purity" *(viśuddhi)* of form and the other *skandha*s and refers to *prajñāpāramitā* as the "source of illumination" *(avabhāsakarin)* and "light" *(āloka)* (*Asp* 91 [Cz., 142]); the early Yogācāra talks positively about the content of enlightenment, *paratantra* (Nagao 1978 and 1983); the Tathāgatagarbha tradition speaks of the primordially pure buddha nature within each sentient being (Takasaki 1966, 26–31); and the Vajrayāna refers to enlightenment as attaining to immaculate wisdom (Snellgrove 1987, 2:280).

Probably also connected with the differences enumerated here is another, namely, that the monastic orientation tends to represent the conservative voice within Indian Buddhism, whereas trends more clearly reflective of the Buddhist saints tend to be more progressive. As we have seen, Buddhist monasticism tends to see as fundamental to its task the conservation of the dharma (the words of the Buddha, the *Tripiṭaka*) and the *vinaya* (the rules of the monastic institutions and lifestyles), which it understands to have been specifically entrusted to it by the Blessed One as his essential legacy. By contrast, the orientation more reflective of the Buddhist saints would seem to work against conservatistic trends, because it emphasizes the enlightened (and thus mold-breaking and precedent-setting) charisma of the saint and because it represents a tacit acknowledgment of the primacy of meditation, which by its very nature also tends to counteract rigid conservatisms.

The foregoing suggests a historical observation. In Chapter 10, we saw that the idea that originally stūpa worship was not—either in theory or in practice—engaged in by monks represents an erroneous reading of the evidence. However, as we also saw, it is true that in later Pāli tradition there is indeed an antistūpa strain, found in development in the *Milindapañha* and fully evident somewhat later. According to this more modern Theravādin position, stūpa worship is indeed for the laity and not something in which the ideal Theravādin monk should engage. But all of this leaves us with a puzzling question: if the idea that monks should not worship stūpas is not to be found in early Buddhism, then where does it come from?

The present chapter suggests a possible answer. If the *Mahāparinirvāṇa Sūtra* does not prohibit the cult of the stūpa to monks, and if Schopen's contention is accepted that a recension of the Pāli *vinaya* prior to the one that we now have takes such worship for granted, this still does not necessarily mean that early Buddhist settled monasticism—Pāli or otherwise—was without its own ambivalence with regard to the cult of saints. As we have seen previously, as Weber suspected, and as the hypothesized *Old Skandhaka* suggests, there occurred in some phases of early Buddhism a shift away from a focus on the charismatic saint as primary reference point for the tradition toward the rise of the settled monastery with its monastic *saṃgha* as definitive of normative Buddhism. In this chapter, we have seen the way in which the older parts of the *Mahāparinirvāṇa Sūtra* reflect this process: on the one hand, they acknowledge the existence and venerability of the cult of saints in its various aspects while, on the other, they are clearly in the process of establishing other foundations for their Buddhism. Earlier scholarly interpreters may have been wrong to see an explicit and widespread repudiation of stūpa worship at such an early time. However, at the same time, they have perhaps not entirely missed the truth, having been led on, not only by the more modern Theravādin position, but also—perhaps partly unconsciously—by the kinds of reservations about the Buddhist cult of saints evident in the *vinaya* and the *Mahāparinirvāṇa Sūtra,* in all their extant versions, examples of which have been noted in Chapter 1 and in this chapter.

This suggests that the later negative evaluation within Theravādin tradition of monastic participation in the stūpa cults does not come out of nowhere. Rather, it represents one particular outcome of tendencies that are already evident in the presectarian *Mahāparinirvāṇa Sūtra.* Thus, the Theravāda takes further, rationalizes, and makes consistent the essentially conservative monastic tendency of the *Mahāparinirvāṇa Sūtra,* including its ambivalence toward the cult of the Buddha and the veneration of other Buddhist saints. The other Nikāya traditions, as mentioned, clearly handled the inherent conservatism of the primitive *Mahāparinirvāṇa Sūtra* and its ambivalences in other ways.

Conclusion

This chapter has raised the possibility that the Buddhist cult of saints is as old as Buddhism itself and that it precedes and provides the precondition for the kind of Buddhism expressed in the *Mahāparinirvāṇa Sūtra* and other monastically oriented texts. In reflecting on this same issue of historical anteriority, Bareau argues for different conclusions. In his analysis of the *Mahāparinirvāṇa Sūtra* (1979), he generally holds that the earlier the stratum of the text, the less extensive the references to the cult of Buddhist saints. Conversely, an abundance of references to myth, legend, and cult reflects, in his view, "a relatively late period, wherein the Blessed One was already considered a superhuman being, equal or superior to the most prestigious and most powerful of men, and worthy thereby of a quasi-divine cult" (63). Thus Bareau holds that, in the very earliest core of the *Mahāparinirvāṇa Sūtra,* "the Blessed One appears . . . as a man, a master venerated by his disciples, and not at all as a superman or a god, *if one removes the legendary elements and episodes that were added later to this part*" (emphasis added) (49). This finding leads Bareau to the conclusion that the Buddhist cult of saints is not an essential part of earliest Buddhism but rather something grafted onto the tradition at a later time.[106] As this conclusion is at odds with the clear implications of much of the material examined in the foregoing, it will be worthwhile to review Bareau's argument in some detail.

Bareau does not find the earliest core of the *Mahāparinirvāṇa Sūtra* intact but rather identifies it through comparing the six versions (and parallel texts) according to a three-stage process: first, he finds those *sections* of the text that are earliest; second, within those earliest sections, he finds those *episodes* that are earliest; third, within those earliest episodes, he identifies those *elements* that are earliest, eliminating "the legendary elements and episodes that were added later to this [earliest] part" (1979, 49). The results of this analysis show, Bareau tells us, that the legend, myth, and cult bound up with the Buddhist saints is downplayed in the earliest core of the text; this means, he believes, that the cult of saints was not original to Buddhism.

Bareau discriminates earlier and later episodes in the following way. When an episode is confirmed in all six versions of the text and in parallel canonical passages, this means that it is relatively early, dating from a time before the division of Buddhism into different schools. Episodes that occur less frequently, say in three or four texts, reveal a later time after the first divisions but prior to the division of the schools sharing the episode. Finally, episodes that occur in only one text reveal a relatively late time, when the tradition behind the text had already become separate. By employing such a methodology, Bareau has been able to identify section 8 (recounting the final hours of the Buddha's life at Kuśinagarī; see note 2, this chapter) as the earliest part of the *Mahāparinirvāṇa Sūtra*. Within this section, he locates four episodes as its earliest core: (1) the arrival of the Buddha in Kuśinagarī, where he will pass away; (2) the visit there of Subhadra; (3) the ordination of Subhadra, the last person to be ordained by the Buddha before his death; and (4) the reactions of the faithful immediately after the *parinirvāṇa*.

How does Bareau move further, to eliminate the supposed later elements of these four episodes and to arrive at a definitive "core of the core" that represents the original kernel of the text, virtually devoid, as he claims, of the legendary? He follows the same method as that outlined: he compares the different accounts of the four episodes, retains those details that are shared among the six versions, and rejects those that are not. Those parts of an episode that most or all of the texts share may be considered relatively early, whereas those parts that are found in a few or only one version may be deemed later. It is by this method that Bareau wants to show that the cult of saints is downplayed in the earliest *Mahāparinirvāṇa Sūtra,* that there the Buddha is seen as just a man—a finding, of course, that is a reflection of and supports the two-tiered model of Buddhism.[107]

However, some questions must be raised concerning the adequacy of Bareau's approach. All of these have to do, it may be noted, with the particular nature and dynamics of Indian Buddhist hagiography. To begin with, we may observe that the *Mahāparinirvāṇa Sūtra* in its various versions is a hagiography and exhibits its hagiographical nature in both its formal elements and its specific contents. Bareau himself notes frequently in his analysis of the text that it reflects a variety of characteristic formal elements, including typical themes, idioms, and stereotypes, and that these are structured according to the particular conventions, principles, and logic of Buddhist hagiography (1975, 46, 59, 60, 103). For Bareau, when an episode particularly reflects such formal elements, this suggests that it is imaginary, presumably because it lacks the spontaneity of real life (1975, 59–60). However, it must be questioned whether formality of hagiographic presentation guarantees disjunction from actual events. In this regard, it may be suggested that religious events and experiences do not infrequently unfold—and are not infrequently understood—according to the formal structures expressed in tradition. Such formal elements reflect presuppositions and expectations, and these, in turn, may be—at least in matters religious—intimately connected with the way in which reality is experienced in the first place. Pointing to formal elements in hagiography does not necessarily guarantee that text composition has moved from actuality into fantasy.

As one example, we may cite Bareau's treatment of the Buddha's passing, wherein the Blessed One ascends through the stages of meditation to *nirodhasamāpatti,* descends to the first stage, ascends to the fourth, and expires. Bareau argues that it would have been impossible for the Buddha's followers to have observed these mental phenomena, and the Buddha certainly never reported them, so that these must have been added later, when the Buddha was made into a superhuman, indeed, divine being (1975, 56). Bareau's argument makes sense, provided that the manner of the Buddha's death was *not* part of an accepted tradition, was *not* an expectation of himself and his followers, and did *not* reflect practices of saintly dying current in India in the sixth century B.C.E. However, if the idea and practice of a saint's dying in this prescribed manner *was* an established one, then it cannot be assumed that his death could not have been experienced and understood by those attending his death in just the way reported in the

Mahāparinirvāṇa Sūtra. In fact, as we have seen, the doctrine of *nirodhasamāpatti* certainly suggests the possibility of such a tradition. In modern times, such a method of the dying of Buddhist saints is often assumed both by their followers and by the saints themselves (Trungpa 1977, 68).

A second question must be raised concerning the historical dynamics of Buddhist hagiography. Bareau's method shows that references to the cult of saints occur less frequently in the earliest strata of section 8 of the *Mahāparinirvāṇa Sūtra*. In the gradual evolution of the text from its earliest kernel, Bareau has identified the tendency toward elaboration upon legendary, mythic, and cultic themes. However, it is significant that Bareau has not found an absence of the cult of saints in the earliest stratum, but merely a scaled-down version of it.[108] In the earliest sections of section 8, the Buddha still occupies a place between the human and divine, but the descriptions of the Buddha are less effusive, the praises are simpler, the miracles less extravagant.

The fundamental structure of the Buddha as a paradigmatic saint, as defined in this work, is thus clearly present in the earliest sections of the text. There is, one may argue, between the earlier and later strata, regarding the evidence of the Buddhist saints and their cult, a difference in degree but not in kind. From the materials adduced by Bareau, it is clear that such a difference in degree must be at least partially ascribed to the historical dynamics of Buddhist hagiography itself. When, for example, the earliest core of the *Mahāparinirvāṇa Sūtra* presents one miracle and where later versions present more (for example, in the story of the entry into Kuśinagarī), we are dealing with the typical tendency of Buddhist hagiographers toward effusive elaboration of incidents and details that were originally more simple. Thus, it is to be expected in Buddhist hagiography that the earlier version of a given episode is less elaborate than the later. (In Indian and extra-Indian hagiographical tradition, developments and elaborations of existing tradition provide a prime avenue for hagiographic creativity.) This is, of course, a dynamic well known in the history of religions in general. However, this kind of difference in hagiographical presentation does not necessarily reflect any fundamental difference in religious outlook or understanding.

These differences between the earlier and later parts of the *Mahāparinirvāṇa Sūtra* surely must also be explained by reference to historical developments within Buddhist tradition, but not necessarily the ones adduced by Bareau. For example, it is clear that in the centuries that followed the passing of the Buddha, Buddhism was transformed from a small and limited cult into a pan-Indian religion. This transformation inevitably involved a tremendous increase in the popularity of Buddhism among the Indian population. This increase in popularity, in turn, led to a growth of those dimensions of Buddhism of particular interest to the laity and the culture at large—namely, the cultic. Increased mention of cultic elements in later sections of the text, then, probably also reflects an increased interest in such matters on the part of the hagiographers; and this, in turn, reflects an increased importance of the cult in Buddhism as it was in the process of becoming pan-Indian. However, all of this may well have happened, it can be argued, without any essential or fundamental change in the minds of Buddhists, both renunciant and lay, as regards the basic nature or status of the Buddha or the Buddhist saints.

The difficulty in Bareau's interpretation, in this and the previously mentioned example, is that it fails sufficiently to acknowledge that developments in hagiography may reflect something other than a fundamental change in religious understanding.

A third question must be raised concerning Bareau's method of defining earliness through identifying continuity in his texts, and particularly his application of this method to eliminating the legendary from the four episodes identified as the earliest in section 8. In the course of his analysis, Bareau shows many examples in which details are changed from one version of an episode in the *Mahāparinirvāṇa Sūtra* to another: one of Buddha's disciples may be substituted for another, one town for another, one locale for another, one position in a sequence of events for another, and so on.[109] These all concern specific people, places, and times. If these kinds of concrete details can readily change from one version of an episode to another, how much more changeability may be expected among hagiographical elements with less individuality?

For example, as noted, there is behind Buddhist hagiography a fund of formal elements of design and dramatic structure, as well as stock lists, common themes, and typical motifs. Certain stock items play a major role in Buddhist hagiography, such as the group of miraculous cosmic phenomena that may accompany great events (thunder, earthquake, wind), the ways in which the gods respond to a saint (showering flowers, pouring down water), the magical powers ascribed to saints, the different ways in which people may venerate a saint, and so on. In the stories that compose the *Mahāparinirvāṇa Sūtra,* the magical powers, for example, appear at certain typical moments (that is, climactic ones), are used in certain typical ways (for example, to exhibit the realization of a saint), and lead to certain typical conclusions (for example, conversion). These magical powers may be mentioned individually or in groups.

In Bareau's comparisons of different versions of the same episode, the magical powers attributed to the Buddha appear particularly likely to be substituted for one another or increased in number. Such changes may simply reflect the fact that one stock theme is being replaced by another and that, in the mind of the hagiographer, *which* magical power, cosmic miracle, or cultic offering is mentioned was not as important as the fact *that* a magical power, cosmic miracle, or cultic offering occurred at that point in the story. The *Mahāparinirvāṇa Sūtra* suggests, and other Buddhist hagiography seems to confirm, that such formal elements were especially susceptible to change from one version to another. Such a process would, of course, suggest some limitations to Bareau's method of textual analysis. If stock elements are particularly prone to substitution for one another, then comparison of several versions of the same event will likely show, for example, that different magical powers or even episodes are mentioned or are mentioned in different configurations. If the earliest section of an episode is identified by retaining only those elements that are common, the very changeability of the magical powers or episodes or other formal elements will mean that these will tend to be eliminated. Because the evidence of the Buddhist saints and their cults tends to be portrayed using stock themes of Buddhist hagiography (magic, miracles, offerings), there is the danger that references to them will be eliminated by this method, leaving the impression that the cult of saints is less present in the earliest strata of a legend than was historically the case.

A final question concerns Bareau's use of the evidence that he has found through his methods. Bareau tells us that even in the earliest episodes of the *Mahāparinirvāṇa Sūtra,* we do not see Buddhism as such and as it was "in the beginning" but in a later and more restricted form. In his discussion of the four earliest episodes of the text, Bareau suggests that none reflects actual historical events but is the result of later interpolations. This earliest section of the text, Bareau believes, took shape by the end of the fifth century B.C.E. or by the eighth decade after the passing of the Buddha. Thus, Bareau says, this earliest stratum of the text reflects the intentions of the monastic community nearly a century after the Buddha's passing,[110] roughly the date when, according to scholarly consensus, Buddhist monasticism was taking its classical shape.[111] This means that it is not permissible, strictly speaking, to equate the viewpoint of the earliest *Mahāparinirvāṇa Sūtra* with that of earliest Buddhism.[112] As we have seen, the text *does* exemplify ambivalence in the face of the saints' charisma, particularly in the way it handles preexisting material on the saints. This fact seems implicitly to support Bareau in his view that the cult of saints must be a later addition. However, again, the particular history and dynamics of the *Mahāparinirvāṇa Sūtra,* as demonstrated by Bareau himself, would seem clearly not to allow us to attribute its own ambivalence and hesitation regarding the Buddhist saints to early Buddhism as such.

In fact, one may—as we have seen—use the *Mahāparinirvāṇa Sūtra* fruitfully to work backward, to arrive at something prior, by seeing what it is that the text presupposes and argues against. Thus, if the cult of saints appears downplayed in the earliest core, one reason for this—in addition to those already mentioned—may be precisely that it *did* stand at the heart of earliest Buddhism (rather than that it did not), and the *Mahāparinirvāṇa Sūtra*—as Weber anticipated and Frauwallner has suggested—reflects a movement to shift Buddhism to a different and seemingly more secure foundation. Certainly the rich evidence of the Buddhist saints of the forest and their cults in the *Theragāthā, Therīgāthā, Suttanipāta, Udāna,* and *Itivuttaka,* as well as of Mahāyāna conceptions of its own origins and earliest days (see Chapter 12), is consistent with such a conclusion.

Presumably Bareau does not believe that the Buddhist cult of saints, which he agrees is clearly evidenced in the *Mahāparinirvāṇa Sūtra* (not to speak of other early Buddhist literature), is something invented out of whole cloth by the Buddhists. Presumably, he will grant that, at the least, it was an important and traditional part of the religious context out of which the Buddha and his early disciples emerged. If this much be granted, then, one would think, all the rest must follow. If saints were, in the Buddha's time, typically seen in terms of mythological and legendary categories and if one's relation to them was defined through cultic behavior, then it would seem highly unlikely, perhaps even unimaginable, that the Buddha—who was for close disciples and laity alike the most sacred of saintly beings—would not be understood in such a way. How can it be supposed that such a person could be conceived in a manner harmonious with modern ways of thinking, as a man divested of the timeless and divine?

In the end, by claiming that the Buddhist cult of saints is not original to the Buddha's message and to Buddhism but that it began to creep into and contaminate Buddhism from the earliest times, Bareau and other proponents of the two-tiered model put themselves in an awkward position. This is the position of seeing the entire history of Buddhism, beginning literally within a few years of the Buddha's death and among his most devoted disciples, as an increasing betrayal of the original tradition. Phenomena of betrayal are, of course, part and parcel of the history of religions but, for the reasons suggested in this and previous chapters of this study, it is difficult to believe that a betrayal of this magnitude occurred among the earliest Buddhists.

Notes

1. In the following discussion, *Mps* will be referred to by the Sanskrit title, with indication being given, in the text or notes, as to which version is meant. When supplying terms for quotations in English from the Pāli text, Pāli terminology will be given. Apart from this exception, the general practice will continue to be followed of using the Sanskrit forms of terms. I thank Frank Reynolds for conversations that led me to the theme of this chapter.

2. This discussion draws particularly upon the work of Bareau, who has analyzed the text in several studies, including 1962, 1963, 1970–71, 1974, 1975, and, specifically on *Mps,* 1979. In 1979, Bareau examines the six principal versions of *Mps* (one version each in Pāli [P.] and Sanskrit [Skt.], four in Chinese [Chin. A–D]) and concludes that this text formed gradually over several centuries. The number and order of the episodes vary from one version to the next, and less than half are found in all six versions. Nevertheless, an analysis of the six versions reveals (1) that there is a common plan among them; (2) that the texts share certain principal episodes; and (3) that the principal episodes almost always appear in the same order (1979, 46). The *Mps* in its various versions contains more than eighty episodes, analysis of which allows the construction of a relative chronology that indicates a temporal order in which the episodes were added to the text. (This, of course, does *not* tell us the order in which these individual units originally came into existence, a point presently of importance.) Bareau also hypothesizes an absolute chronology, in which he locates the addition of texts to *Mps* over some four centuries from the death of the Buddha (ca. 480 B.C.E.) to the beginning of the common era. However, he tells us, we should realize that this is "a fragile enough hypothesis" (47). As Bareau sees it, *Mps* may be divided into nine major sections, according to locale of the incidents, and these may be divided into two major groupings, as follows (48):

I. *Mps*-p 1–*Mps*-p 2.20
  1. In the environs of Rājagṛha
  2. From Rājagṛha to Pāṭaligrāma
  3. At Pāṭaligrāma
  4. From Pāṭaligrāma to Vaiśālī
  5. At Vaiśālī

II. *Mps*-p 2.21–*Mps*-p 6.26
  6. In the environs of Vaiśālī
  7. From Vaiśālī to Kuśinagarī
  8. At Kuśinagarī: the final hours of the life of the Buddha
  9. At Kuśinagarī: the last rites of the Buddha

Bareau believes sections 1 to 5 to be the later and sections 6 to 9 to be the earlier parts. "It is precisely these four last sections that contain only episodes intrinsically linked to the context of the Mpns [*Mps*], that is to say, the final months of the life of the Blessed One, his death, and his funeral, while all the stories constituting the first five parts clearly have been artificially attached to this context" (1979, 48). Thus, sections 6 to 9 constitute a kind of proto-*Mahāparinirvāṇa Sūtra* to which parts 1 to 5 were eventually added.

The number of episodes contained by the earlier and later sections varies considerably. The older sections (secs. 6–9) contain between fifteen and nineteen episodes each, whereas the newer sections (secs. 1–5) contain only three to six episodes each. Bareau also points out that, for the earlier parts of *Mps* (secs. 6–9), it appears that some additions continued to be made even after each of the nine parts of the text was added. Thus, each of these nine parts did not originally contain all the episodes present in them today (1979, 49). Within the older part (secs. 6–9), one may make further chronological distinctions. Bareau says that section 8—which recounts the last hours of the Buddha, his final advice to the *saṃgha,* and his passing—represents "the kernel of the work" (1979, 49) and thus the earliest part of the oldest four sections. Following this, section 9 was added, then section 6, then section 7, then the newer sections (1979, 50–51). Having outlined this relative chronology, Bareau then attempts to posit a rough absolute chronology for the different parts of the work. The oldest part of the text, section 8 minus some episodes that Bareau believes were added later, is dated to the second half of the fifth century B.C.E. (1979, 51). The next sections were added from this time onward, with the latest sections (secs. 1–5) being added in the last two centuries before the common era.

The following draws almost entirely upon sections 6 to 9, or those sections of *Mps* judged earliest by Bareau. These sections, Bareau believes, were all composed or at least added to *Mps* within about two centuries following the Buddha's death. Focusing on these sections of *Mps* provides a glimpse of the text in its earlier period. An analysis of those sections deemed later would, in any case, reveal themes closely similar to those discussed here and would not alter this analysis in any major way.

3. *Mps*-p 5.10–11; all six versions: Bareau 1970–71, 2:35–50.

4. The fact that the imperfectly realized monk, Ānanda, is not to engage in *śarīrapūjā,* while Mahākāśyapa is—as are the *kṣatriyas*, brahmins, and the heads of households—is curious. Does this mean that *Mps* understands *śarīrapūjā* as a rite appropriate only for realized monks and the laity? Or does it understand that the senior monk is to preside over this rite, which is attended by the laity but not the other monks? When Mahākāśyapa worships the body of the Buddha just before the cremation, other *bhikṣus* are in attendance.

5. This conclusion is supported by the treatment of this episode in the other five versions of *Mps* (Bareau 1970–71, 2:35–50).

6. P., Chin. A and D (Bareau 1970–71, 2:50–53). This and following references identify the versions where the material in question occurs (P., Skt., Chin. A–D), as well as the part, volume number, and page numbers where Bareau's treatment of this material is found. Note that this and the following references to Bareau 1970–71 identify the section of the study in which Bareau discusses the part of *Mps* in which the cited material is found. In these sections of Bareau 1970–71, Bareau typically makes reference to the cited material but does not always discuss it in detail. Most of Bareau's analysis in this work is, in fact, not particularly interpretive of the material in the various texts. In this study, he is rather primarily concerned to compare the contents of the different texts, showing what they share and where they differ.

7. In this section, monks, nuns, laymen, and laywomen are enjoined to visit the four

pilgrimage sites marking the birth, enlightenment, turning the wheel of dharma, and *parinirvāṇa* of the *tathāgata*.

8. This section occurs in four versions: P., Chin. A, Chin. D, and one parallel *sūtra* (the *Ekottarāgama*) (Bareau 1970–71, 2:14–21).

9. In the Pāli version, these are spontaneous occurrences; in other versions of *Mps*, they are the results of the deities' actions.

10. That is, fulfills the *dhamma* in all its aspects (*PTSD* 37, s.v. *anudhamma*). On this term, see also *PTSD* 337, s.v. *dhammānudhamma*.

11. But interestingly so are the laity.

12. The three *vinaya* versions (P., Chin. A, and Chin. D) are closely similar, whereas the *Ekottarāgama* version presents a sharp contrast to these (Bareau 1970–71, 2:14). Chinese A presents the simplest account—among the various miracles given in the Pāli, mentioning only the trees flowering out of season—suggesting to Bareau that it is the earliest of the three versions. Chinese D adds some material and the Pāli adds even more, suggesting that these represent respectively more developed, later versions of the story. Bareau remarks that the miraculous events summarized in this story undoubtedly reflect cultic acts performed when the texts were composed (1970–71, 2:16).

13. In reference to *Mps* itself, Bareau similarly believes that its compilers drew materials from already existing textual tradition, while imprinting them with their particular viewpoints (1979, 46). He remarks further, "One must also underline the important, even decisive role which the Buddhist community at Vaiśālī played in the formation of our *sūtra*" (1979, 52).

14. Bareau sees such a pattern in this last quoted passage, remarking that "it is necessary to see there a reaction against the excesses of the material forms of the cult" (1970–71, 2:17). The reason for this reaction is, of course, another matter; see discussion at the end of this section. This kind of historical "layering" evident in Buddhist texts is, of course, the rule. One may suspect such layering when, in a particular section of a text, divergent, incongruent, or opposed values appear side by side attributed to the same person. Among many possible examples is the opening section of the *Milindapañha*, already discussed earlier in another context, in which Nāgasena is represented as one who lives in the forest, meditates, and has achieved enlightenment; at the same time, he is fully trained not only in the entirety of Buddhist textual tradition but in the *Vedas* as well and with infinite ease and accomplishment can debate and discuss, and refute opponents. In this first section, in fact, Nāgasena's textual expertise represents the main theme, whereas his forest credentials are given only nodding acknowledgment (further, elsewhere in this section, forest values and renunciants are criticized) (*Mp* 24 [T.R. 1890–94, 1:39]). If, in fact, such layering is at work here, the interesting question is raised of whether Nāgasena was originally a forest saint who came to be associated with textual Buddhism or whether he was originally a renowned textual specialist, who by virtue of his repute in the course of time attracted forest values to his person. Of course, one would not want to rule out at least the theoretical possibility of occasional exceptions to the mutual exclusivity of preeminence in textual matters, on the one hand, and meditational matters, on the other. However, such exceptions, if they occurred, must have been rare and can certainly not be assumed to be the reason for the frequent depictions of such dual achievement in the texts.

15. The passages are: (1) and (2) *Mps*-p 5.6 (two instances); (3) 5.21; (4) 6.9; (5) and (6) 6.11 (two instances); (7) 6.12; and (8) 6.19.

16. These passages are treated in the following sections of Bareau 1970–71: (1) all six versions (2:21–29); (2) all six versions (2:21–29); (3) all six versions (2:76–92); (4) all six versions (2:171–74); (5) and (6) all six versions (2:171–74); (7) all six versions (2:175–78); and (8) all six versions (2:215–22).

17. Rhys Davids admits some uncertainty regarding this phrase (see his justification, 1881, 119, n. 2). Of particular importance, these deities are contrasted at *Mps*-p 6.11 with deities "who are free from passion" and do not engage in this kind of behavior. One of these occurrences contains the same kind of dramatic shift of direction noted in the previously cited example. In the episode of their coming to see the Buddha for the last time and of their lamenting his passing, we are told that the heavenly and earthly spirits, having come from afar, *fervently desire to see the tathāgata* one last time before he passes away (*Mps*-p 5.4ff.) (all six versions, Bareau 1970–71, 2:21–29; among these, P., Skt., Chin. A, and Chin. D show particularly close filiation). Yet the disciple Upavana, to whom these deities are invisible, is standing in front of the *tathāgata* fanning him and blocking their vision. And how does the *tathāgata* respond to the desire of the deities to see him? He responds with tenderness and compassion, with no hint of criticism. He speaks sharply to Upavana, bidding him move so that the spirits can fulfill their hearts' desire and see him once more before he dies. Thus, the Buddha condones their seeing of him, and it is here that they engage in their lamentations. Dramatically speaking, the account of the (ritualized?) mourning of the *tathāgata* is so far gripping and convincing. Somewhat jarring, then, is the critical doctrinal commentary, already referred to, interspersed with this account and found at its end. The spirits who thus mourn are, we are told, "of worldly mind." At the end of this account of mourning (*Mps*-p 5.6), we are told that such mourning is inappropriate for those who have real understanding. "The spirits who are free from passion bear it, calm and self-possessed, mindful of the saying which begins, 'Impermanent indeed are all component things. How then is it possible?' " (*Mps*-p 5.6). These enlightened spirits do not engage in the cult of the saints. As noted, Bareau sees in this type of shift of direction a commentary made to establish a particular doctrinal point.

18. In these instances, the negative interpretation in the Pāli given those who engage in lamentation is not invariantly found in the other *vinaya*s, nor, when it does occur, is it necessarily expressed in the same terms. For example, the contrast between deities "of worldly mind" and those "free from passion" in instance 1 are found only in the Pāli and Chinese D. In instances 5 and 6, precisely the same contrast is found only in the Pāli, Sanskrit, and Chinese C. Other of the negative evaluations found in the Pāli, however, are substantially repeated in all six *vinaya*s, e.g., instance 4. Thus, this negative evaluation does appear in all six *vinaya*s, although in different configurations.

19. In variance from the previously cited passage, it is now not Ānanda who upbraids the unenlightened *bhikkhu*s but Subhadda, and he does so not because he represents normative tradition but *because he does not respect the Buddha!* Thus he remarks, "Enough, brethren! Weep not, neither lament! We are well rid of the great Samaṇa. We used to be annoyed by being told, 'This beseems you, this beseems you not.' But now we shall be able to do whatever we like" (*Mps*-p 6.20). This passage, then, suggests different reasons for nonparticipation in the lamentation from those evident in the passages just discussed. There, the enlightenment of the *bhikkhu*s led them to refrain from the actions of lamentation. Here, however, nonparticipation is ascribed to a disrespect of the Buddha. This passage, then, appears to articulate precisely the same doctrinal point against which *Mps* argues—namely, that participation in the actions of lamentation represents a higher respect of the Buddha.

20. Bareau appears to agree with this interpretation when he remarks that the criticism of the monks represents "probably just an invention based on doctrinal themes" (1979, 63) and "doctrinal considerations" (65).

21. It is interesting that we find the passage in its simplest form in the cases of the laity. Perhaps there is no mention of laity who are free from passion and nonparticipants

in the lamentation because laity were believed at this time and by this group to be unable to attain enlightenment. It should be noted that *Mps* sometimes explicitly advocates the validity of the cult for monks (see *Mps*-p 5.8), found in four versions of *Mps* (P., Skt., Chin. A, Chin. D) (Bareau 1970–71, 2:29–32).

22. See Bareau's discussion of the superhuman personality of the Buddha as depicted in the Dharmaguptaka version of *Mps* (Bareau 1969).

23. In the Pāli version, but equally abundant in the other five *vinaya*s.

24. In five versions of *Mps* (Bareau 1970–71, 1:26–39). In the different versions of *Mps,* different forest habitations are mentioned, including forest hermitages, wooded plateaus, mountains, mountain caves, mountain peaks, the foot of trees, the edges of lakes, and so on (1970–71, 1:30). These are mentioned alongside other items that reflect the settled monastic way of life.

25. All six versions (Bareau 1970–71, 1:282–95). The meditative ideal is affirmed at Bareau 1970–71, 2:12–15.

26. All six versions (Bareau 1970–71, 1:296–99).

27. All six versions (Bareau 1970–71, 1:296–99).

28. Interestingly enough, this set of the four classes of humans contrasts with the classical list of monks, nuns, laymen, and laywomen.

29. All six versions (Bareau 1970–71, 1:177–81). See also *Mps*-p 4.42 (all six versions [Bareau 1970–71, 1:301–10]); *Mps*-p 5.5–6 (all six versions [1970–71, 2:21–29]); *Mps*-p 5.23–30 (all six versions [1970–71, 2:92–131]).

30. All six versions (Bareau 1970–71, 2:172–74).

31. Such miracles and magical powers are, in the *vinaya*, abundantly associated with the Buddha; for an example see Kloppenborg 1973, 50–68.

32. All six versions (Bareau 1970–71, 1:177–81).

33. All six versions (Bareau 1970–71, 1:147–56). Another of the classical set of *abhijñā*s is described at *Mps*-p 2.6–7, where the Buddha demonstrates his ability to know the former births of various people; five versions (1970–71, 1:85–89).

34. All six versions (Bareau 1970–71, 1:276–81).

35. In three versions (P., Chin. A, Chin. D) and one parallel *sūtra* (contained in the *Ekottarāgama*) (Bareau 1970–71, 2:14–21). *Mps*-p 1.33–34 contains the well-known miracle of the Buddha's crossing of the Ganges, which, we are told, is marked as a sacred place. In five versions (1970–71, 1:72–77).

36. All six versions (Bareau 1970–71, 1:147–56). Repeated at *Mps*-p 3.40; all six versions (1970–71, 1:172–81). Repeated several times at *Mps*-p 5.41–47; in *Mps*-p only and occurring, according to Bareau, as a kind of appendix to *Mps*-p 3.40 (1970–71, 1:194–96). It is quite interesting that in the *Milindapañha* (140–41 [T.R. 1890–94, 1:198–201]), the king expresses some confusion over the issue of the Buddha's length of life, as discussed in *Mps*. Milinda remarks, on the one hand, that it is said that the Buddha can live to the end of a *kalpa* but, on the other, that he will expire in three months' time. The king desires that Nāgasena resolve this apparent contradiction. Nāgasena responds by redefining the word *kalpa,* an ingenious if not entirely convincing maneuver: *kalpa* should be understood to mean, he says, not the cosmic period but the usual length of an ordinary person's life. Thus, he seems to say, the Buddha here claims nothing other than the power to live a normal life. Nāgasena's response is not convincing because (1) the Buddha has already lived a normal life; (2) Nāgasena must invoke a definition of the term *kalpa* that is unusual (Nyanatiloka 1980, 90, s.v. *kappa*); (3) the longevity of the Buddhist saints is, as has been mentioned and as I have shown elsewhere, an important theme during all periods; and (4) in the remainder of Nāgasena's reply to Milinda's query, the monk seems to accept the power of buddhas to live for periods far longer than normal (Ray 1990). In spite of the

forced nature of Nāgasena's explanation, it is interesting that this logic has been cited in attempts to prove the non-Buddhist nature of the cult of saints; see, e.g., Maung Kin 1903, 227–28.

37. *Mps*-p 3.9, all six versions (Bareau 1970–71, 1:156–71); *Mps*-p 3.37, all six versions (1970–71, 1:182–94); *Mps*-p 3.51, all six versions (1970–71, 1:196–207).

38. All six versions (Bareau 1970–71, 2:150–56).

39. *Mps*-p 3.19, all six versions (Bareau 1970–71, 1:172–74); *Mps*-p 6.10, all six versions (1970–71, 2:157–71).

40. All six versions (Bareau 1970–71, 2:193–209).

41. All six versions (Bareau 1970–71, 2:209–14).

42. All six versions (Bareau 1970–71, 2:240–65).

43. All six versions (Bareau 1970–71, 2:265–88).

44. Partially found in all six versions (Bareau 1970–71, 2:288–308).

45. All six versions (Bareau 1970–71, 2:308–23).

46. Only in P. (Bareau 1970–71, 1:194–96).

47. Four versions, P., Skt., Chin. A, Chin. D (Bareau 1970–71, 2:29–32).

48. Five versions (Bareau 1970–71, 1:137–47).

49. Five versions (Bareau 1970–71, 1:137–47).

50. All six versions (Bareau 1970–71, 2:131–44).

51. Mus has noticed this pattern (1935, 56ff.).

52. Four versions (Bareau 1970–71, 2:137–38). Lesser and minor precepts *(khuddānukhuddakāni sikkhāpadāni)* that may be abolished imply, of course, precepts that are not lesser and minor and that may not be abolished.

53. All six versions (Bareau 1970–71, 2:114–31).

54. The sections of *Mps* identified by Bareau as later also strongly reflect, as might be expected, the values and preoccupations of settled monasticism. Thus we hear of the service hall of *bhikkhus* living in a particular neighborhood to which the Buddha goes (*Mps*-p 1.6; all six versions [Bareau 1970–1971, 1:26–39]). Here the Buddha outlines seven conditions for the welfare of a community, including "full and frequent assemblies," meeting together in concord, actions according to the duties of the order, adherence to a tradition understood as fixed (they should establish nothing that has not already been prescribed and abrogate nothing that has already been established), and respect for the elders of the order (ibid.).

55. All six versions (Bareau 1970–71, 1:222–39).

56. Bareau 1970–71, 1:227.

57. Bareau (1970–71, 1:227) comments that this threefold set (dharma, *vinaya, mātṛkā),* which is found in the Pāli and Sanskrit versions of *Mps* and also in the *vinaya*s, "clearly reflects, in the Pāli, the Sanskrit and the Vinaya, awareness of a certain phase in the constitution of the Buddhist canon, one in which it was divided into three recensions forming the triple basket *(Tripiṭaka).*"

58. See T.R. 1881, 67, n. 1.

59. "This necessarily presupposes the existence of a canon in the time period when this primitive version was composed, a canon made up of a certain number of sermons and of disciplinary rules of which the authenticity was recognized, of which the text was determined at least in its essential parts, but of which the order and the classification were probably not fixed" (Bareau 1970–71, 1:229–30).

60. At *Mps*-p 2.25, the Buddha says, "I have preached the truth without making a distinction between exoteric and esoteric doctrine." Applying the principle that what a text such as *Mps* argues against may well reflect existing Buddhist practice that it opposes, one arrives at the interesting possibility that *Mps* is here pointing to the existence of other

Buddhists who hold the contrary position; that in addition to more exoteric doctrine, there also existed esoteric doctrine of the few (of forest traditions?).

61. All six versions (Bareau 1970–71, 1:156–71).

62. Bareau 1970–71, 1:156–71, esp. 162–63.

63. All six versions (Bareau 1970–71, 1:156–71).

64. Bareau 1970–71, 1:156–71, esp. 162–63.

65. All six versions (Bareau 1970–71, 1:156–71).

66. Bareau 1970–71, 1:156–71, esp. 162–63.

67. *Mps*-p 3.48, Pāli version only (Bareau 1970–71, 1:194–96); *Mps*-p 5.6, all six versions (1970–71, 2:21–29); *Mps*-p 5.14, all six versions (1970–71, 2:54–65); *Mps*-p 6.11, all six versions (1970–71, 2:171–74); *Mps*-p 6.20, all six versions (1970–71, 2:223–30, esp. 227–28).

68. Pāli version only (Bareau 1970–71, 1:194–96).

69. All six versions (Bareau 1970–71, 2:21–29).

70. All six versions (Bareau 1970–71, 2:54–65).

71. All six versions (Bareau 1970–71, 2:171–74).

72. All six versions (Bareau 1970–71, 2:223–30, esp. 227–28).

73. Bareau suggests the likelihood of this interpretation when, in commenting on the occurrence at *Mps*-p 3.48, he points to a contradiction between this passage and the theme of the potential longevity of the Buddha (1970–71, 1:195–96). If the imminent disappearance of the Buddha is really inevitable, as we seem to be told here, then why did the Buddha just blame Ānanda for his failure to request that the Buddha continue to live, even for a *kalpa?* One obvious explanation is that this contradiction reflects two different doctrinal viewpoints that uneasily coexist within this story.

74. All six versions (Bareau 1970–71, 2:29–32).

75. It is interesting that the ongoing presence of the Buddha at his sacred places, among which the stūpas are preeminent, is clearly affirmed in *Mps*. Schopen, after citing the Sanskrit version of *Mps,* where explicit reference is made to the ongoing presence of the Buddha at his pilgrimage sites, similarly remarks that "the redactor of the Sanskrit version seems clearly to have thought that the Buddha, though dead, was somehow actually present at the places where he was formerly known to have been" (1987a, 203).

76. Edgerton remarks on the connection of this term with meditation (*BHSD* 549, s.v. *pariśuṣkagātra*).

77. We have seen some examples of such "activity" in Chapter 10.

78. *Mps,* which clearly has other aims besides advocating the cult of the saints, cannot refrain from acknowledging the possibility and virtue of seeing the saints. In the Pāli version we read that one—whether monastic or layperson—should come to the four chief places sanctified by the Buddha's life (where he was born, attained enlightenment, etc.), and one should see these places. In Schopen's translation, "Ānanda, there are these four places that a devout son of good family must do *darśan* of, and powerfully experience" (1987a, 195). Schopen remarks, "The final sections of the Pāli version of the *Mahāparinibbāna Sutta* are clearly marked with the notion and importance of *darśan,* and *darśan* is about direct, intimate contact with a living presence" (1987a, 195).

79. The first four are called *dhyāna;* the second four are merely listed by name.

80. It is not insignificant that it is precisely the unattained disciple, Ānanda, who fails to comprehend the true nature of the cessation in which the Buddha abides.

81. Referred to by *Mp* (176 [T.R. 1890–94, 245]). This is, of course, the classical definition of *nirodhasamāpatti*. See the similar passage, *Mn* 1:245 (Hn., 1:299).

82. *PTSD* defines these as follows:

> 1) The mystic, with his mind free from sensuous and worldly ideas, concentrates his throughts on some special subject (for instance, the impermanence of all things). This he thinks out

> by attention to the facts, and by reasoning. 2) Then uplifted above attention and reasoning, he experiences joy and ease both of body and mind. 3) Then the bliss passes away, and he becomes suffused with a sense of ease, and 4) he becomes aware of pure lucidity of mind and equanimity of heart. (286, s.v. *jhāna*)

PTSD makes the important point that "the whole really forms one series of mental states, and the stages might have been fixed at other points in the series" (ibid.). For other formulations of the *jhāna*s, cf. *PTSD* (ibid.).

83. The four are (1) infinity of space *(ākāśānantyāyatana;* P., *ākāsānañcāyatana),* (2) infinity of consciousness *(vijñānānantyāyatana;* P., *viññāṇānañcāy-),* (3) nothing at all *(ākiṃcanyāyatana;* P., *ākiñcaññāy-),* and (4) neither consciousness nor unconsciousness *(naivasaṃjñānāsaṃjñāyatana;* P., *nevasaññānāsaññāy-).* These are *arūpya* (P., *āruppa*), "formless," in contrast to the four *dhyāna*s, which become known as the *"rūpadhyānas"* (P., *rūpajjhānas*) (*PTSD,* 286).

84. For discussion of terms and textual references in Sanskrit and Pāli, see *BHSD* 30, s.v. *anupūrvavihāra,* and *PTSD* 39, s.v. *anupubbavihāra.* The first eight of these are, of course, the practices that, prior to his enlightenment, Gautama is held to have studied under his two *śramaṇa* gurus, practices with which he was not satisfied (King 1980, 10–13).

85. *PTSD* defines these three as *"rūpī, arūpasaññī,* recognition of *subha"* (632); i.e., as "having form," "perceiving the formless," and recognition of the "resplendent." Corresponding Sanskrit definitions are given in *Mvy* 1511–13.

86. For the eight *vimokṣa*s in Sanskrit tradition, see *Mvy* 1510–18. For textual references, see *BHSD* 497, s.v. *vimokṣa.* For a discussion of this group in Pāli tradition and for textual references, see *PTSD* 632, s.v. *vimokkha.*

87. See references to *anupūrvavihāra, anupubbavihāra, vimokṣa,* and *vimokkha* above.

88. *PTSD* remarks further that in relation to *nibbāna* and *parinibbāna, nirodha* "may be said to be even a stronger expression as far as the *active* destruction of the causes of life is concerned" *(PTSD* 371, s.v. *nirodha).* See also King 1980, 104.

89. Buddhaghosa expresses the classical view when he equates *nirodhasamāpatti* with enlightenment attained in this life (*Vsm* 322 [N., 402]).

90. Kloppenborg remarks,

> The *nirodhasamāpatti,* in which *nibbāna* is experienced in this body, is the *yogin*'s way of meditation. It is of minor importance in the Theravāda tradition of meditation of the four noble truths which leads to insight. This connection with ancient ascetic practices could be the reason that the *nirodhasamāpatti* is mentioned often as the *paccekabuddha*'s favourite state of meditation. (1974, 51).

91. In this regard, King remarks that in *nirodhasamāpatti* all bodily functions cease, including breathing, and mental and verbal functions are inoperative as well.

92. Sung Yun tells us that in a certain temple "there formerly dwelt a Shami *[śrāmaṇera]* . . . who, being constantly occupied in sifting ashes (belonging to the convent), fell into a state of fixed composure *[samādhi]*. . . . The Karmadana of the convent had his funeral obsequies performed, thinking he was dead, and not observing that his skin continued unchanged" (Beal 1869, 196–97). This person was subsequently recognized as a saint, and "the king of the country founded a chapel to the Rishi, and placed in it a figure of him as he appeared, and ornamented with much gold leaf" (ibid.).

93. Przyluski 1923, 301–3. Cf. also Lamotte 1958, 426.

94. Interesting in light of the foregoing themes are certain doctrines attributed to some of the northern Mahāsāṃghikas, in which the Buddha is explicitly identified with a personhood that is not subject to birth and death, that is *lokottara* (transcendent of conditioning). As the Buddha never really entered the world, so he never really left it, thus providing the doctrinal ground for the appearance of the Buddha at any time. We are told that buddhas

are supermundane *(lokottara)* (Bareau 1955, 57); their bodies are entirely free from impurity and conditionality *(laukikadharma)* and are perfect, unlimited, and of the nature of the *dharmadhātu.* The material body *(rūpakāya)* of the *tathāgata* is unlimited (Bareau 1955, 58); Paramārtha mentions three aspects: it is unlimited in measure, meaning that it can appear great or small, as circumstances require; it is unlimited in number such that the Buddha can manifest as many bodies as are necessary to teaching beings; and it is unlimited in the good causes that have given birth to it (59). The buddhas always abide in meditation *(samādhi)* (76); they neither sleep nor dream; their lifespan is unlimited, goes on without end, and is not subject to destruction (59). The Buddha's life is unlimited so that he can help the innumerable kinds of beings, and his wisdom is such that he comprehends all things in a single instant (59–60). The Buddha's compassion is unlimited. The Buddha's powers are unlimited and are such that he can manifest them in all directions and in all universes, without conscious intention (59). And so the list continues. Taken together, these doctrines imply that the Buddha, though transcendent of samsāric conditioning is, nevertheless, immanent within the world. He exists always and everywhere, he is undying, he is immersed in meditation but acting compassionately at all times, and so on. For the Mahāsāṃghikas behind these doctrines, what seems to ordinary beings to be the death of the Buddha is, from a level of deeper understanding, just an artifice created in order to teach beings. For the Mahāsāṃghikas, the doctrine of nonimmanence represents an incipient level of understanding, whereas the doctrine of the perpetual presence of the Buddha represents the deeper truth. The similarity of these themes with those of the transcendent presence of the saint, beyond apparent death, raises the interesting question of what kind of historical connection may exist between these themes and those examined in this chapter.

95. For a summary of commentarial interpretations of *nirodhasamāpatti,* including those of the Theravāda, Vaibhāṣika, and Yogācāra, see Griffiths 1986.

96. It may be noted that in *Na,* Nandimitra clearly performs the same function for his own era and *saṃgha* that the Buddha performed for his, seen here in the fact that the parallel passages of *Mps* and *Na* put the Buddha and Nandimitra in equivalent dramatic positions.

97. The similarity of dramatic components and structure between *Mps* and *Na,* yet the difference in interpretation, reinforce the impression that this announcement of impending death, expressions of grief, imploring to remain, and teaching of impermanence that we have in *Mps* are less expressions of a single historical instance and more expressions of a traditional form, which may have been quite widespread in early Buddhism.

98. For a statement of Schayer's position, see Schayer 1935, 121–32. A useful summary of Schayer's work is provided by Constantin Régamy 1957, 37–58.

99. These are, of course, the same points made by Max Weber in his own reconstruction of "original Buddhism," summarized in Chapter 1.

100. In retrospect, perhaps unfortunately, Schayer chose to use the word "theism" in reference to precanonical Buddhism. This, along with his specific reconstruction of precanonical Buddhism, led critics to charge Schayer with propounding a "Buddhist theism" similar to Hindu theism (Régamy 1957, 57). Régamy responds to this by remarking that "Schayer . . . never wanted to affirm that the Buddha was considered in the pre-canonical period as a personal deity, a creator and judge of the world, nor even as a Hindu *iśvara* and, in speaking of theism in pre-canonical Buddhism, he wanted to insist above all on the religious character of Buddhism, possessing its myth, its cult and based on faith in the supernatural authority of the founder" (57).

101. The following is a brief résumé of Falk's long, detailed, and complex analysis.

102. This scheme contrasts, of course, with the later classical enumeration of saṃsāra as composed of three realms, in order of descent, the *arūpadhātu,* the *rūpadhātu,* and, at

the lowest end, the *kāmadhātu*. Falk, following Przyluski, judges the *kāmadhātu* to be a later addition to the original twofold division of saṃsāra (Falk 1943, 98, 116).

103. Falk finds traces of this precanonical "immanentalist" position in the Pudgalavādin theory of the *pudgala* and the Sautrāntika notion of *ekarasaskandha*. This position becomes prominent again in the theories of Yogācāra and Tathāgatagarbha (Falk 1943, 133–34).

104. See Harvey's suggestive article (1983).

105. A tendency that continues in various schools of extra-Indian Buddhism, e.g., in Tibet.

106. See his discussion of the exchange between Ānanda and the Buddha concerning the treatment of the *tathāgata*'s body after death (*Mps*-p 5.10–11 [discussed by Bareau 1970–71, 2:35–50]).

107. Bareau concludes his article by remarking that "the analysis of this text . . . allows us to understand quite well how and why the simple method of salvation, as a kind of lived philosophy, which Buddhism was in 'essence,' quickly became and remained a religion in the full sense of the term" (1979, 103).

108. This is explicitly admitted, e.g., Bareau 1970–71, 1:179.

109. E.g., Bareau 1970–71, 2:171.

110. Bareau himself tells us that the material of *Mps* reflects the specific concerns and doctrinal viewpoints of a particular group of monks in the period following the Buddha's death (e.g., 1979, 52 and 61). He also tells us that these monks took preexisting material, drew on it selectively in order to compile *Mps* and added their own particular interpretations (ibid). This insight surely shows that an examination of the entry of materials into *Mps* reveals something about the authors of *Mps* but not necessarily about Indian Buddhism as such and as a whole.

111. Thus, Bareau seems to have discovered some historical movement within the monastic community behind *Mps*. In the beginning, the initial inspiration of *Mps* lay in establishing the normativity of settled monasticism. This initial inspiration is reflected in the earliest core and later. At a later stage, the text actively and explicitly engages the Buddhist cult of saints, allowing it some status but subordinating it to the values of settled monasticism.

112. Presumably, we are then to believe that within this very early period represented by section 8 of *Mps*, two different kinds of episodes were invented: historically first were those that presented the Buddha as a man; historically second were those that see him as more than a man, as a superhuman or divine being. This means that the difference between the less legendary and more legendary material does not necessarily reflect a difference between the Buddha as he actually was and the Buddha as he was later conceived. Rather, it more likely reflects the Buddha as he was seen by the earlier compilers of *Mps* (for Bareau, pre-Mauryan times [1979, 63–64]) and the Buddha as he was seen by later compilers (post-Mauryan). At this point, then, again, one is talking about tendencies in the ways the Buddha was conceived by the communities behind *Mps*.

12

The Buddhist Saints and the Process of Monasticization

The preceding chapters have several times referred to the "process of monasticization," whereby phenomena that were originally connected with the Buddhist saints of the forest were translocated and transplanted into a settled monastic context. In some cases, this process involved the appropriation of one or another individual element of the forest saints' traditions by settled monasticism. For example, the forest saint Mahākāśyapa was adopted by settled monasticism to serve its need for a charismatic leader. Upagupta, Piṇḍolabhāradvāja, Devadatta, and perhaps also Śāriputra, originally essentially forest saints, similarly came to have—through different means and in varying degrees—relations with settled monasticism. The initially nonmonastic ideals of Buddha (and bodhisattva), arhant, and pratyekabuddha came, again in various ways, to be understood in relationship to settled monasticism. And ideals and practices such as the magical powers, the *dhutaguṇa*s, and the stūpa also came to be increasingly integrated into the monastic context. In addition to describing individual forest elements undergoing the process of monasticization, the foregoing has made reference to this process on a grand scale, by which traditions that were entirely or primarily ones of forest renunciation became converted into those of settled monasticism. Such has been discussed in relation to the original form of Buddhism itself and mentioned briefly in connection with the Mahāyāna.

The present chapter contains three sections: first, an exploration of the original monasticization, whereby settled monasticism first developed out of the earliest Buddhist community of peripatetic renunciants; second, an examination of the transition of the early or proto-Mahāyāna from an entirely or largely forest tradition, such as that reflected in the texts examined in Chapter 8, into what became the conventional, monastic Mahāyāna; and third, a review of some reactions of forest traditions, both non-Mahāyānist and proto-Mahāyānist, to the process of monasticization, as these traditions see it occurring in their day.

The Origins of Buddhist Monasticism Reconsidered

According to Buddhist tradition, as enshrined in the *vinaya,* it was the Buddha himself who instituted the classical monastic tradition both in general and in its specifics. As we have seen, however, the matter was considerably more complex. In fact, earliest Buddhist tradition consisted of a bipolar structure wherein settled monasticism does not figure. On the one hand were the renunciants, who followed the peripatetic lifestyle of the *śramaṇas*. On the other were the laity who made donations to and revered the realized among these wandering folk. The Buddha was himself a forest renunciant. It may well be that originally all his *śramaṇa* disciples were also forest renunciants, emulating the ideal he embodied and following the forest way he preached, perhaps in agreement with the picture presented in texts such as the *Suttanipāta,* other forest texts of the *Khuddakanikāya,* and additional forest texts reviewed in previous chapters. At the same time, the possibility must be admitted that the Buddha, during his lifetime, accepted town-and-village renunciants as legitimate members of the renunciant *saṃgha.*[1] But even if this was the case, there can be no doubt that the forest ideal was earliest (the Buddha himself followed it), was seen as superior (it led directly to realization), and was considered normative for earliest Buddhism (it represented direct emulation of the Buddha's example, and, furthermore, those who followed it practiced what the Buddhist town-and-village renunciants would have preached).

Whether or not town-and-village renunciation is "original" to Buddhism or developed in Buddhism only after the Buddha's passing, its significance for later tradition can hardly be overestimated. It was from this form of renunciation that settled monasticism initially took its lead, eventually developing its classical form. But to say this does not solve the perplexing problem of why and how town-and-village renunciation was transformed into classical monasticism. After all, other *śramaṇa* groups contemporary with early Buddhism exhibited the same town-and-village renunciant mode that was at some point taken on by Buddhism. Why and how was it that Buddhism, originally alone—as is believed—developed the innovation represented by settled monasticism?

S. Dutt, in his *Buddhist Monks and Monasteries of India* (1962), makes the intriguing but undeveloped observation that the rise of Buddhist monasticism is connected with the "universalism" of the Buddhist faith from its earliest days. Such a universalism is amply reflected in the accounts of the Buddha's own aspirations on his journey to enlightenment, his decision to teach, his some forty-five years of teaching, and the injunction he is said to have given to his disciples "to go forth and wander about for the good of the many *(bahujana),* the happiness of the many—in compassion for the world—for the good, the welfare and happiness of gods and men" (Dutt 1962, 35, quoting the *Mahāvagga*). In relation to this theme of universalism, Dutt remarks that the Buddha was known not only as teacher (P., *satthā*) of his disciples but also as a universal teacher *(samyaksaṃbuddha;* P., *sammāsaṃbuddha),* who taught not only individual salvation but also "welfare and happiness of the many" (50–51). This suggests that the challenge presented by the Buddha to his disciples, and thence to the first generations of followers after his passing, was twofold: they were to maintain the integrity of the path to liberation preached by the master, and they were to carry his message of liberation to the world. The development of the classical Buddhist monastic system was originally, it may be argued, a response to the second part of this challenge.

In order to understand this point, let us consider Buddhism strictly in terms of its earliest and ultimate ideal, seen in the Buddha himself, that of forest renunciation. The forest renunciants performed a function within Indian society that was strictly circumscribed. If we may believe the evidence of the early and later forest texts that we have examined, the tradition maintained by these renunciants was an austere and demanding one, attractive only to the few. In addition, these renunciants' relations with the various laypeople they met were not conducive to regularization. In particular, their availability to the laity was necessarily restricted. As mendicants with no home base, they could be given donations when they appeared at one's door, but only so much as they could carry could be given. As individuals, they had little organized institutional power vis-à-vis the social, political, and religious institutions of Brahmanical orthodoxy of their day. Their way of forest renunciation, in and of itself, was limited in its ability to respond to the Buddha's universalistic imperative.

The situation would have been different for Buddhist renunciants of town and village, who are depicted as wandering about in groups, as settling down in groups during the rainy season, and as accepting in groups the generosity of the laity of food, robes, and lodging.[2] And the situation would have been more different still for their monastic successors. For one thing, monasticism provided a relatively broad gate for those desiring to renounce the world. The way of the forest renunciant has always been regarded in Buddhism as extremely arduous, and with good reason. Only a relatively few are able to make its commitments and sacrifices, to accept its material privation, and to endure its insecure, uncomfortable, and demanding way of life. The classical Buddhist monastic system in effect provided a far less forbidding, much more accessible mode of Buddhist renunciant life, one that encouraged a great many more people to renounce the world than would have been possible under the more arduous and restrictive ideal. Moreover, even for those desirous of the meditative life of the retreatant, monastic life could and often did represent an important stage of training, one that could in due course be left behind for the more "direct path."

In addition, the monastery provided a uniquely effective vehicle for bringing the Buddhist dharma to society at large. The early forest renunciants are depicted as living and wandering alone or in tiny groups. The development of the monastic system provided a very different way of communicating with the larger society. In particular, the monastery acted as a kind of institutionalized middle ground and meeting point between the ultimate Buddhist norm of forest renunciation and the laity. This role of the monastery in Buddhism is pointed out by Dutt, who contrasts Buddhist monasticism with its Christian counterpart:

> Isolation from society was never the cue of Buddhist monachism. . . . [The] Buddhist *saṃgha* set out on its historic career from a completely divergent start-

> ing point [from Christian monasticism]. It was toward the Bahujana [the multitudes] that its eyes were turned. By their very *raison d'être,* the monasteries had to function differently, and isolation from society was no object of monastic life. (1962, 25–26)

The precise role of the monastery as a middle ground between the ideal of forest renunciation and the larger social, political, and religious world of greater India is made clear when we consider the two central preoccupations of Buddhist monastic tradition: the concern for behavioral purity and the preservation and study of texts. One may well ask how—as neither of these concerns appears to have been nearly as important to earliest Buddhism as they later became—these came to be so central within later tradition. To be sure, the more communal *śramaṇa* form, in which regularized relations with society were more important and discussion and debate were prominent, provided the seeds from which these two central monastic preoccupations could spring. But, again, a considerable distance separates these seeds from the fully matured monastic manifestations. How and why did these evolve in the way and to the extent that they did?

Part of the answer may be found by considering an intriguing series of congruities, already alluded to, between the major concerns, emphases, and interpretations of Buddhist monasticism and those of orthodox Brahmanical culture within which Buddhism was trying to make its way. In orthodox tradition, as defined and exemplified by the priestly Brahmanical elite, one finds two central preoccupations—the same two preoccupations, significantly enough, that characterize monastic Buddhism: a concern for behavioral purity and a preoccupation with the mastery of authoritative religious texts.

First, for orthodox Brahmanical tradition, behavioral and ritual purity is a central concern, such that spiritual well-being and status are defined largely in terms of this purity.[3] As is well known, the position of the priestly Brahmanical elite in relation to Indian society as a whole has traditionally been regulated through observance of behavioral purity, and the maintenance of such purity has been a primary concern of social life in India.[4] In the monastic tradition, one finds Buddhism taking account of the presupposition in Indian, and particularly Brahmanical, society that links behavioral purity with spiritual authenticity, reliability, and power. In fulfilling the many rules of the *prātimokṣa,* the Buddhist monastics are, in effect, guaranteeing their own spiritual status in the eyes of those for whom purity is central—not only those outside but those within the *saṃgha* as well.

Second, for orthodox Brahmanism, the sacred text, specifically the revealed *(śruti) Vedas*—but also commentarial literature—provide a central reference point for religious authority and for the religious life. The religious power of the brahmin priest is inseparably bound up with his possession and mastery of the texts. By "knowing" the revealed texts through memorizing them, the priest is able to control their spiritual power and channel it to others. Through mastering the content of the commentarial literature, he can make available their life-giving normative paradigms. Buddhist monastic tradition, to a large extent, took on the scholastic values of its orthodox context. As observed in Chapter 1, in monastic life, great importance is attached to the preservation and mastery of the sacred texts. In some interpretations, as we have seen, the integrity of the dharma is virtually identified with textual learning, and a monk's spiritual accomplishment defined in terms of scholastic ability.

Buddhist monasticism's emulation of Brahmanical patterns goes further. As mentioned in Chapter 1, Frauwallner believes that, in assembling its canon, the early monastic *saṃgha* attempted to construct lineages for its texts and that this effort was specifically modeled on the Brahmanical pattern. The monastic Buddhists, according to Frauwallner, developed their own lineage lists to try to establish a culturally acceptable authenticity for the Buddhist texts that was equivalent to the authenticity of the Brahmanical texts. In effect, the Buddhists were addressing their audience with the kind of argument for spiritual authenticity to which such people could, given their tradition and their values, respond positively.[5] In addition, Przyluski has suggested yet another side of monastic Buddhism's emulation of Brahmanical patterns, namely, its adoption of a similar structure of community.

> At this period of its development, the Buddhist community was exactly fashioned on the model of Brahmanical society. The post-vedic *sūtra*s reveal, in effect, that there are four orders: those of householder, student, *bhikṣu* or *sannyāsin,* and forest hermit *(āraṇyaka).* These four orders correspond to the four categories of the faithful in ancient Buddhism: householder, disciple [novice], master [fully ordained monastic], and *āraṇyaka* [forest renunciant]. It would be impossible to exaggerate the importance of this modeling of the Buddhist community on Brahmanical society. (1926–28, 293).

Przyluski's observation may be taken a step further: in Brahmanical tradition, although the forest renunciant is tolerated, it is the ideal of the learned and behaviorally pure priest that provides the center of gravity. It would seem that classical Buddhist monasticism has replicated this pattern: in classical monasticism the forest renunciant, if admitted, tends to be downplayed, whereas the learned and behaviorally pure *bhikṣu* defines the normative renunciant ideal of Buddhism.[6]

It is also worth noting that—claims of universal accessibility notwithstanding—Buddhist monastic tradition, like orthodox Brahmanism, tends in fact to be exclusivistic in its conception of religious privilege. Just as the brahmins alone are at the top of the orthodox religious hierarchy, so are the monks in the Buddhist context. The brahmin is the quintessentially learned one in Brahmanism, just as the monk is in Buddhism. Just as the brahmin alone has direct access to the sacred texts and their power, so has the Buddhist monk, by virtue not of his social but of his religious "caste"—through the training, values, and preoccupations of his monastic lifestyle. Just as the brahmin alone may enjoy the spiritual prerogatives of his position, so may the Buddhist monk. Just as the brahmin has attained his position through merit accumulated in past lifetimes, so has the Buddhist monk. Just as others of the Brahmanical faith may hope to gain such a good rebirth in a future life, so may all those Buddhists who are not monks in the present life. Just as respect for and appropriate behavior toward brahmins is an important part of accruing merit in Brahmanism, the same is true of behavior directed toward Buddhist monks.

In addition, just as those who are not (male) brahmins have a decidedly lower status on the social scale, so those who are not (male) monastics—namely, laypeople and women—similarly are accorded, as we have seen, a dramatically lower status within classical monasticism.[7] It appears, in fact, that laypeople and women are for Buddhist monasticism what the lower castes are for Indian culture in general: they are there to serve the higher castes but are inherently debarred from the full privileges of those above them in the hierarchy; their primary hope is, through devoted service to those above them, to attain in some future birth an elevated status. As we have seen, it would appear that such values are not found, at least certainly not to this degree, in the nonmonastic renunciant traditions of earliest Buddhism. In this respect, Przyluski, among others, points to this "profound inequality between the religious and the laity" in classical monasticism and remarks further that "the sharp opposition between clerics and laity, between monastics and those of the world, is foreign to primitive Buddhism" (1926–28, 293).[8]

Acknowledging this emulation of rival Brahmanical tradition helps us perhaps to come to a deeper understanding of the particular monastic emphasis on doctrines of absence and nonimmanence, explored in the previous chapter. We have seen the identity crisis faced by the newly emerging monastic tradition. On the one hand, it wanted to secure itself as not only a legitimate but also an authoritative—perhaps even definitive—form of Buddhism, as over and against the originally more prestigious tradition of forest renunciation. On the other hand, Buddhist monasticism needed to establish itself as an effective rival to Brahmanical tradition. The fact that the monastic tradition, in its essential form, so closely emulated many of the attitudes, values, and structures of its surrounding Brahmanical context can only have deepened the anxiety of the identity crisis that it faced. How could a tradition that so deeply modeled itself on its non-Buddhist environment establish itself as normatively Buddhist?

The answer was perhaps to compensate for its Brahmanization by attempting to doubly reaffirm its identity in the doctrinal sphere. This may be one reason why, in the scholastic literature of Buddhist monasticism, there is a shift in the definition of Buddhist identity away from behavior and realization (from a forest lifestyle, meditation, and the attainment of enlightenment) toward "correct doctrine." In this shift, Buddhist monasticism chose the distinctively Buddhist teaching of *anātman* and developed it in a systematically apophatic way, asserting this teaching through the methodology of the vocation of texts and scholarship. The irony, of course, is that the very method and arena chosen to establish authentic Buddhist identity shows so much more affinity with Brahmanism than it does with the earliest normative Buddhism of the forest.

In contrast to these developments within Buddhist monasticism, the saints of the forest retained the ancient normative Buddhist forms and continued to affirm their Buddhist identity through the traditional criteria of lifestyle, meditation, and realization. They seem to have felt no particular need to depart from the earlier rich and varied usage of language, evident in forest texts such as the *Theragāthā* and *Therīgāthā,* which describes enlightenment with a wide range of terms and images, both apophatic and kataphatic. They certainly felt, as we have seen, no need to rigorously weed out essentialist, immanentalist language. Nor did they avoid, as we have also seen, apophatic language. For them, evidently, the doctrinal sphere was definitive not in and of itself but rather in its subserviance to meditation and realization.[9]

In the beginning, the divergence from earliest peripatetic Buddhism into what we now call classical monasticism must have been gradual and must have initially involved no more than a small body of renunciants. Frauwallner makes an intriguing argument for a single geographical center from which this unique Buddhist innovation spread out in waves of missionary activity to far-flung places (1956, 12, 18–19). It was largely these early missionary schools, Frauwallner argues, that eventually became what we now understand to be the major early sects of Buddhism and that have become identified, in conventional wisdom, with early Buddhism itself. The remarkable identities of the early *vinaya*s strongly suggest the pattern of a single early source and subsequent diffusion proposed by Frauwallner.

The rise of classical Buddhist monasticism appears to have resulted from a complex situation in which both creative and degenerative factors were operative. The universalism of the Buddha's teaching led to an interest within the early *saṃgha* in spreading his message far and wide. This, in turn, necessitated developing forms through which this aim might be realized. Within the context of a Brahmanical society, it is not surprising that such forms, coalescing in the institution of the Buddhist monastery, would be compatible with Brahmanical socioreligious structures and values and, indeed, as we have seen, in large measure reflective of them.

The inspiration to actualize the universalism and compassion of the Buddhist message must have led gifted individuals initially to develop what became classical Buddhist monastic life.[10] This may surely be interpreted, at least partially, as an act of generosity on the part of some early Buddhist renunciants toward their society, such that they were willing to depart in such a major and sustained way from the free and wandering patterns that characterized earliest Buddhism.[11] These renunciants accommodated the values and presuppositions of their social context to a remarkable degree and redirected Buddhism into new and unprecedented directions. According to Buddhism, both Nikāya and Mahāyāna, communication of realized ones to humanity at large is made possible by the extent to which they are willing provisionally to accept the personal and cultural vocabulary of the other.[12] Although perhaps not explicitly or even consciously, early settled monasticism seems at least to some extent to have been engaged in such a process.

However, what was in part a creative inspiration also opened the way to certain abuses and degenerations. The wider the Buddha's message was spread, the more people of different sorts and backgrounds would have sought to become renunciants. The success Buddhism enjoyed among the laity, the development of the institution of the monastery, and the increase in donations and endowments disseminated even more widely the attraction of renouncing the world. In greater numbers, there were among renunciants people who were not interested in a meditative life in seclusion at all, or even in the more modified wandering of the town-and-village renunciants, but who wanted to live the settled, relatively economically secure and socially prestigious life of the monastic in the monastery. Indeed, those primarily with certain quasi-worldly or worldly ambitions, including a career of scholarship or bureaucracy, with fruitions of renown, power, and some material well-being, might find in the monastery an ideal setting for realizing their aims. The *Milindapañha* mentions a variety of questionable motives among some who entered monastic life, including greed, being a slave to one's stomach, seeking material gain, and desiring worldly fame and glory (6.16 [T.R. 1890–94, 2:261]). The *Milindapañha* in the same place also mentions the evil cravings in the hearts of some monks, as well as their hypocrisy. Ironically, the willingness of the tradition to make room (some, but not too much!) for such "human" traits helped make Buddhism the successful tradition that it became. But it is equally true that from the viewpoint of the meditative way—which Buddhism in theory has more or less consistently acknowledged as the highest pursuit of the renunciant life—such accommodations were not without danger. And when, as sometimes happened, institutional Buddhism (always less or more obliged to social, political, and economic concerns) set itself up—as it sometimes did—as the norm by which all forms of Buddhism were to be judged, we may rightly speak, to use Jensen's useful concept, of a degenerative "phase of application"[13] of Buddhism. Here the Weberian analysis has its place.

There is another important factor in the early development of settled monasticism that, in addition to factors already mentioned, helps explain the very rapid success of the settled monastic form of Buddhism. As suggested in its earliest *vinaya,* monastic Buddhism developed an institutional cohesion, direction, and strength unprecedented in earliest Buddhism or, as far as is known, any other early *śramaṇa* school. This institution, like other institutions, could not avoid a tendency to self-perpetuation and self-aggrandizement. It had the religious prestige that attached to renunciant traditions, but unlike other renunciant traditions, its form enabled it to accommodate much larger numbers of renunciants and make contact with relatively much larger numbers of laity—and it could effectively organize all this potential power. In settled monasticism, the notion of donations and merit-making connected with renunciant traditions had an unprecedented focus, one that was ever available and could accommodate virtually any amount of wealth and any degree of desire on the part of the laity, not only to make merit, but to have a visible and ongoing demonstration to their neighbors of their munificence. Historians have linked the early success of Buddhist monasticism with the new and growing availability of a wealth that could be transferred to the monastery (Thapar 1966, 67–69; 1975; 1978, 70–78). This "new money" is obviously crucial to the equation, but what has perhaps not been seen is the role played by the development of the very idea of the monastic institution in the first place. Wealth means little unless there are things to spend it on: what matters is what things exist and are valued in a cultural environment upon which wealth may be spent. In effect, Buddhism created a commodity that seems not to have existed before: the monastic institution, as such, formed a ready, attractive, and all-accommodating recipient of wealth. As far as we know, no other renunciant tradition matched in this respect the early brilliance and opportunism of Buddhism.[14]

It was, then, a complex of mixed motives that enabled Buddhism to grow as rapidly and surely as it did: to develop a broad appeal to Indian society, to become the recipient of increasingly expanding donations, to begin to attract more and more applicants, to acquire increasingly substantial properties, to become a powerful and respected institution within Indian society, and eventually to create premier centers of learning and culture within India. And it is precisely these accomplishments that allowed Buddhist monastic tradition to play a major role in the spread of Buddhism to new areas and particularly to new cultures, magnetizing political power and wealth and attracting the elites of the cultures to which it was attempting to travel.

In this study (in Chapter 2 and at the beginning of the present section), the question has been raised of the form(s) of the earliest Buddhist community. It will be recalled that two alternatives have been proposed, the available evidence being insufficient to enable a clear choice between them. On the one hand, it may be that town-and-village renunciation was itself admitted by the Buddha as a legitimate renunciant option for his disciples. On the other, it may be that town-and-village renunciation was not so admitted. But if this latter is the case, as has been argued in this chapter, this renunciant style and its classical monastic descendent may be understood as developing at least partially as a response to the imperative of compassion within the early Buddhist teachings. On the question of the shape of the earliest Buddhist community, most scholars have tended to take one or the other of two contrasting views. Predominant in modern interpretation is, as we have seen, the position of those holding some version of the two-tiered model: that the Buddha himself established settled monasticism or at least that the renunciant ideal he favored was one concordant in values and preoccupations with town-and-village renunciation, as defined in this study, and that this developed quickly and without incident into settled monasticism. A few scholars, of whom Weber is a good example, favor the opposite position, that the Buddha taught a renunciant ideal concordant with forest renunciation and that settled monasticism represented a radical departure from and betrayal of earlier Buddhism. The two alternatives proposed in this study depart from both of these received interpretations. In response to the first interpretation, I would propose that forest Buddhism provided the highest ideal of earliest Buddhism, with town-and-village renunciation—even if admitted by the Buddha—in a subordinate position. In response to the second interpretation, I would propose that the development of town-and-village renunciation and its descendent, settled monasticism, are not adequately understood if they are seen as repudiations and betrayals of the Buddha's teachings. Even if they did not exist as accepted Buddhist alternatives in the days of the Buddha, they are best understood—at least, in part—as responses to seeds already at the heart of the early Buddhist teachings.

The Origins of the Mahāyāna and the Process of Monasticization

At the forefront of the many puzzles presented by the Indian Mahāyāna is that of the time and place of its origins. Some evidence suggests a southeastern origin in about the first century B.C.E., whereas other evidence implies a somewhat later northwestern origin. The following represent some of the evidence that scholars typically bring forward in support of southeastern origins. (1) A passage in the various *Prajñāpāramitā*s says that the Mahāyāna teaching will originate in the south, will proceed to the east, and will finally travel to the north.[15] (2) Tibetan tradition holds that there existed a *Prajñāpāramitā* in the Prakrit dialect belonging to the Śaila sect whose center was in the south. (3) The *Mañjuśrīmūlakalpa* identifies Nāgārjunikoṇḍa, Amarāvatī, and other southeastern sites as important centers of the Mahāyāna; and the *Gaṇḍavyūha* points to the south as a place of special Mahāyāna creativity (Dutt 1930, 40–43). (4) The birthplace of the "founder of the Mahāyāna," Nāgārjuna, is depicted as in the south, and the saint is particularly connected with Śrīparvata in southeastern India, as are Āryadeva and other members of his school (Conze 1959, 124). (5) A Sri Lankan tradition ascribes the *Ratnakūṭa,* an important collection containing early Mahāyāna *sūtra*s, to the Andhras (Warder 1970, 354, n. 1). (6) A number of important Mahāyāna doctrines show close similarities with doctrines of the Mahāsāṃghikas, who had centers in the southeast. Evidence such as this leads some scholars to conclude that the Mahāyāna arose in the southeast, among the Mahāsāṃghika schools in that area. Conze, a representative example of those advocating a southeastern origin, locates the origins of the Prajñāpāramitā in south India between the Godāvarī River and the Kṛṣṇā River, near Amarāvatī and Nāgārjunikoṇḍa (1951, 124) at about 100 B.C.E. (1973b, x).[16]

Lamotte and others have pointed to various difficulties with the evidence usually cited in defense of a southeastern origin for the Mahāyāna (1954, 386–87). For one thing, of the above six points, all but number 6 represent Buddhist legends of one sort or another that cannot necessarily be taken at face value. Lamotte has specifically questioned the reliability of the traditions reporting the origination of the Prajñāpāramitā in the south (1980, 25, n. 1). In addition, the close linkage of Mahāsāṃghika and Mahāyāna doctrines does not necessarily lead to the conclusion of a southeastern origin, for two reasons. First, the Lokottaravāda, with doctrines closest to the Mahāyāna, is known to have flourished in the northwest, whereas the Andhaka schools, which were prominent in the southeast, are doctrinally much more removed. Second, although the Northwestern schools were in existence during a relatively early period, the Southeastern schools are not documented in inscriptional evidence until the middle of the third century C.E. The *Mañjuśrīmūlakalpa*'s identification of Nāgārjunikoṇḍa, Amarāvatī, and other southeastern sites as important centers of the Mahāyāna is also problematic in view of the evidence: in spite of the existence of many inscriptions in these places dating from the third century, none mentions the Mahāyāna; and, in fact, the first solid evidence for Mahāyāna centers in these areas does not occur until the seventh century, in Chinese pilgrim reports. The association of Nāgārjuna with Nāgārjunikoṇḍa is also of uncertain value, because no inscriptions containing Nāgārjuna's name have turned up at this location (although one does survive from Amarāvatī), because there are legends that also link him with the northwest, and because the most important works attributed to him betray a northwestern origin. These points do not necessarily disprove a southeastern origin for the Mahāyāna, but they make such an origin uncertain at best.

Lamotte, along with some other scholars,[17] favors a later, northwestern locale as most likely for the origins of the Mahāyāna. Hirakawa summarizes some of the evidence typically cited by scholars favoring this alternative. For example, Nāgārjuna utilized a number of Sarvāstivādin doctrines. In particular, the notion of the *Tripiṭaka* that he uses is Sarvāstivādin (Hirakawa 1963, 59). The *vinaya* system included in the *Mahāprajñāpāramitā Śāstra* coincides with the Sarvāstivādin *vinaya* (59). The text also cites Sarvāstivādin *abhidharma* works and, although Nāgārjuna was familiar with a variety of *abhidharmas*, the doctrines utilized by the *Mahāprajñāpāramitā Śāstra* are drawn primarily from the Sarvāstivāda (60). Finally, the text also contains a number of specifically Sarvāstivādin doctrines (60). Lamotte, in his "Sur la formation du Mahāyāna" (1954), puts forward additional evidence in favor of northwestern origins.[18] The *Mañjuśrīmūlakalpa,* for example, tells us that it was under Kaniṣka that the Prajñāpāramitā became established in the northwest. We also read that under the son of Kaniṣka, both laypeople and renunciants taught the Mahāyāna in the northwest. However the historicity of these legends may be evaluated, they show the Mahāyāna's own view of the importance of the northwest in its own development. Also at this time, various texts appeared in the northwest, including the *Ratnakūṭa,* the *Avataṃsaka,* the *Laṅkāvatāra,* and the *Dharmasaṃgīti.* A text translated into Chinese in the sixth century mentions eleven centers of the Mahāyāna, and, Lamotte says, it is remarkable that seven are situated in the northwest, in Kuṣāṇa territory (1954, 390).

In addition, Lamotte points out that although certain legends connect Nāgārjuna with the southeast, the texts actually attributed to him "betray on every page their northern origin." According to Demiéville, for example, the *Upadeśa (Mahāprajñāpāramitā Śāstra)* was certainly redacted in the northwest and most likely by authors nourished by Sarvāstivādin or Mūlasarvāstivādin tradition. This work is well acquainted with the great Kuṣāṇa empire and gives geographical and ethnologic information that links it with the northwest. It refers to scriptures exclusively of the Sarvāstivāda-Vaibhāṣika of the northwest: the Sanskrit version of the *āgamas*, the *vinayas* of the Sarvāstivādins and Mūlasarvāstivādins, the *Jñānaprasthāna* of Kātyāyana, and the *Vibhāṣā* of the Kashmiri arhants. The *Jātaka* and *Avadāna* to which it makes reference similarly show a northwestern venue. "Finally and above all, all the doctrinal analyses of the *Upadeśa* unfold within the framework of Sarvāstivādin categories and terms, and it is always in direct opposition to the system of Kātyāyana that it wants to insist on the superiority of its own position." Lamotte also cites the assessments of Buddhist monasteries in the northwest made by Fa-hsien in the fifth century and Hsüan-tsang in the seventh century, which show the Mahāyāna monasteries to be flourishing there as nowhere else in India. This can leave little doubt, Lamotte tells us, about the important role played by the Kuṣāṇa states in the formation of the Mahāyāna (1954, 390–92). Let us consider the seemingly conflicting evidence just reviewed in light of the perspectives being developed in this study and particularly in terms of the Mahāyāna *sūtras* we have examined.

First Mahāyāna Origins: The Mahāyāna of the Forest

The Mahāyāna *sūtra*s examined in Chapter 8 state that the Mahāyāna from the beginning was primarily a forest tradition, entirely nonmonastic in character. The *Ugraparipṛcchā Sūtra* remarks that "the *bodhisattva* who has left the world must reflect that the forest life was ordained by the Buddha" and that in following the forest life "there is fulfillment of the Pure Law" (*Ss* 110.17–19 [BR., 193]). The *Ratnaguṇasaṃcayagāthā* takes a similar view, mentioning that the Buddha wandered freely without a home; advocating this as the highest life of the renunciant bodhisattva; and saying that in this way complete buddhahood should be sought. The *Rāṣṭrapālaparipṛcchā Sūtra* similarly presents the forest life as normative for the bodhisattva, who is to live in the forest practicing the *dhutaguṇa*s and meditating. The *Saṃdhinirmocana Sūtra* also understands the forest life to have been ordained by the Buddha and sees the bodhisattva renunciant as the one who most purely fulfills this ideal. These "Mahāyāna" forest texts do not present their kind Buddhism as anything new. Instead, they see it as simply a continuation of the normative forest ideal established by the Buddha in the beginning, which they understand as his highest teaching. For them, this is the original bodhisattva Buddhism, and they understand it as nothing other than original Buddhism in its most quintessential form.

Let us take the viewpoint expressed in these *sūtra*s as the basis of a hypothesis: that the Mahāyāna originated as a tradition of forest renunciation, as defined in these texts. Let us then ask how well or badly such a hypothesis explains some of the evidence connected with Mahāyāna origins. It is obvious that this hypothesis provides an interesting perspective on the question of an earlier southeastern versus a later northwestern origin. The evidence of a northwestern origin shows the Mahāyāna to be a monastic movement, whereas the same cannot be said of the evidence for a southeastern origin. The evidence suggests that both of these could be authentic origins of the Mahāyāna, but in different senses: the Mahāyāna could have initially developed in the southeast as a nonmonastic tradition; later, it could have undergone a process of monasticization and emerged as a monastic movement in the northwest, as reflected in the evidence brought forward by Lamotte.

The originally nonmonastic character of the Mahāyāna, as it developed in the southeast, is consistent with the absence of archaeological remains of the Mahāyāna in that area.[19] As noted, even as late as the third century C.E., one finds no Mahāyānist schools represented in the monastic communities at Nāgārjunikoṇḍa. Nor is there any other external evidence of the Mahāyāna as a movement in the south until a relatively late date, in the seventh century in Hsüan-tsang's report of Amarāvatī as a Mahāyāna center. A forest tradition of *yogin*s and their lay devotees would not necessarily have any fixed centers that could attract substantial donations, buildings, and inscriptions. A nonmonastic origin of the Mahāyāna is also consistent with the curious fact, noted by Bareau, that the *Vibhāṣā* (Sarvāstivāda, northwest India) and the *Kathāvatthu* (Theravāda, Sri Lanka), both dating from the third century and both citing and refuting the doctrinal tenets of a great variety of Buddhist and non-Buddhist schools, make no mention of any specifically Mahāyānist doctrine. In Buddhism, polemical discussions most often occur between peers: one monastic tradition will debate another or a well-established Brahmanical school. One would not expect such scholars to debate the views of isolated *yogin*s and their disciples living in the jungle and meditating.

If the forest origins of the Mahāyāna, as put forward by the *sūtra*s we examined, are accepted, this means that the Mahāyāna did not originate at a monastic center, such as Nāgārjunikoṇḍa seems to have been from an early time. But if it did not originate there, then what other southeastern locale may be suggested? Bareau makes the interesting suggestion that the Mahāyāna initially developed north of Nāgārjunikoṇḍa, between the Godāvarī River (which lies some distance to the north of the Kṛṣṇā River in Andhra, the site of Nāgārjunikoṇḍa) and the Ganges Basin, that is, in the area of Koṅkana, Orissa, and Mahākosala. Bareau notes that Hsüan-tsang, in the seventh century, found in this locale the most important Mahāyāna center in India. Bareau's thesis is of special interest for the possible forest beginnings of the Mahāyāna, because this area is "a relatively wild area, located far from the great centers of civilization, the great pilgrimage places, and the main routes frequented by pilgrims." This locale, far from centers of civilization and of established Buddhism, is in fact just the kind of place favored by forest renunciants, who prefer, in the *Rāṣṭrapālaparipṛcchā Sūtra*'s terms, "border areas." Bareau also suggests how the Mahāyāna, developing in this region, could have adopted Mahāsāṃghika ideas. This Deccan region is in fact encircled by the great Mahāsāṃghika centers of old. In addition, a link with the schools of the north is provided by the Bahuśrutīyas, who were not only important in the north but also had an important center in the southeast (Bareau 1955, 300–305).[20]

Some further insight into the possible forest origins of the Mahāyāna is provided by Hirakawa in the two articles discussed above (1963 and 1987). In these articles, Hirakawa argues, as we saw, that the Mahāyāna originated in a nonmonastic context. Hirakawa also believes he has established the Buddhist stūpa as the institution in connection with which the Mahāyāna first arose. Further, Hirakawa sees the earliest Mahāyāna as composed of two prime actors: the lay bodhisattva, for whom the stūpa provides the prime Buddhist center; and the renunciant bodhisattva, who lives sometimes in the forest practicing meditation and sometimes at the stūpa, coming there when sick or wanting to study or obtain material support. In addition, renunciant bodhisattvas might live semipermanently at the stūpa, for it was from the ranks of these, Hirakawa believes, that the priesthood of the stūpa was drawn.

Hirakawa's discussion is important for two reasons. First, it suggests, from an entirely different angle and in terms of different evidence, the possible role of the forest renunciant in the inception of the Mahāyāna. Second, it shows in a plausible way how the forest-renunciant bodhisattva may be seen as intimately involved with the stūpa and therefore with the kinds of symbolic and liturgical Buddhism that become so important in later Mahāyāna Buddhism. Although Hirakawa believes that the stūpa provides *the* single point of origin of the Mahāyāna, it is more likely that he has identified one element in the early history of the Mahāyāna. For example, taking Hirakawa's thesis as stated, one would expect to find stūpas implicated one way or another in all early evidence of the Mahāyāna, but such, as Schopen points out, is not the case.[21] In Hirakawa's evidence, the forest-renunciant bodhisattva is connected with the stūpa, but in the *Ratnaguṇasaṃcayagāthā,* the *Rāṣṭrapālaparipṛcchā Sūtra,* and the *Saṃdhinirmocana Sūtra,* this figure is shown living a religious life in which stūpas play little or no role. In addition, in those traditions discussed in Chapter 10 oriented to the cult of the book, the stūpa is likewise not prominent.

The idea that what eventually came to be understood as the Mahāyāna originated as a tradition of forest saints and their devotees helps lead us to a fresh appreciation of some of the evidence of the early Mahāyāna. For example, Harrison notes the fact that early Mahāyāna *sūtra*s do not show a strong sense of self-conscious identity as over and against the "Hīnayāna" (1987, 73). Such a lack of self-conscious identity is what one would expect from groups of forest renunciants who have no strong institutional focus, are spread out in remote areas, and spend their time in meditation. It may well not have been until the Mahāyāna became significantly monasticized and thereby developed cohesion and centripetalism, that its identity as a particular vehicle took definitive shape. Harrison also mentions that the Mahāyāna remained a minority movement in India for a long time, as seen in the reports of the Chinese pilgrims, and "in its infancy was probably even more insignificant numerically" (80). This is, again, what one would expect of a tradition of forest saints and their devotees that became monasticized only relatively late in its developmental history. It is likely that the Mahāyāna began to become numerically significant only when the process of monasticization had gained some momentum.

The hypothesis of a forest origin of the Mahāyāna also makes sense in terms of the locale frequently mentioned for the preaching of Mahāyāna *sūtras*—Gṛdhrakūṭaparvata, "Vulture Peak Mountain," near Rājagṛha. Conze wryly notes that among the various theories of the place of origin of the Mahāyāna, no one has looked to Vulture Peak Mountain.[22] It may be that this frequent reference locates the origins of the Mahāyāna not geographically (although this can perhaps not be automatically ruled out) but rather in terms of religious context, in this case that of the forest Buddhism associated with this locale. For Vulture Peak Mountain is, Conze tells us, "a particularly desolate district, all stones and empty air" (1973b, xiv). Watters remarks similarly that the image of Vulture Peak Mountain in the literature is one of "natural caves, large and small" and that from the earliest days of Buddhism it was particularly known as a retreat for meditating renunciants (1904–5, 2:151–52). We are told in the *Mahāprajñāpāramitā Śāstra* that it is particularly on Vulture Peak Mountain that the realized saints *(ārya)* and the meditators *(dhyāyin)* dwell. In Hsüan-tsang's time, the place still retained this character and continued to be known for the various great saints who meditated there, including the Buddha and his major disciples. Also on the mountain is the cave identified by Hsüan-tsang as the place where the Buddha preached the *Saddharmapuṇḍarīka Sūtra* and by Fa-hsien as the site where the *Śūraṅgamasamādhi Sūtra* was delivered (Lamotte 1980, 190ff.). In light of the previous discussion, it may be suggested that the statements that certain important Mahāyāna *sūtra*s were preached by the Buddha on Vulture Peak Mountain are a further indication of the original, esoteric, forest-renunciant context of the earliest Mahāyāna.

The hypothesis of the Mahāyāna's forest origins, furthermore, sheds some interesting light upon the general configuration of the tradition's own accounts of its inception. Lamotte summarizes some of the major themes of the traditional accounts, all of which revolve around the central ideas of the advanced and secret nature of the early teachings: their original preaching on Vulture Peak Mountain during the lifetime of the Buddha; the more advanced nature of the early Mahāyāna teaching compared with that being given to the greater multitudes ("Hīnayāna"); the presentation of this teaching to a privileged circle of disciples; the transmission of certain important texts to great bodhisattvas; the keeping secret of these teachings for many centuries, in Lamotte's words, "in mysterious and inaccessible regions"; and, finally, the spreading abroad of these doctrines at a later time, eventuating in the historically visible Mahāyāna (1954, 381–86).

In contrast to Lamotte's interpretation, which would see these legends as fanciful and created entirely after the fact,[23] another possibility may be admitted in the context of the present discussion. Let us recall that the motif of secrecy is one frequently found, explicitly or by implication, in the materials that surround the Buddhist saints of the forest. The Indian Vajrayāna in its early forest days is called *guhyamantra*[24] (secret mantra), and this expression reflects an important characteristic of this tradition: the core teachings are given by masters only to qualified and properly prepared disciples. This general pattern is one we find implicit in the very structure of the Buddhist saintly tradition: the inner circle of close disciples clearly receives a different sort of instruction from the larger penumbra of followers and devotees. The pratyekabuddhas are known for not teaching widely but restricting their teaching to chosen disciples. The transmission of the teaching of the early forest saints clearly has a privileged element. The later saints are shown teaching one disciple or a small group of disciples and generally maintaining a certain distance from the laity (Tambiah 1984, 81–110).

The preceding discussion raises the possibility that the theme of secrecy that stands at the heart of the Mahāyāna story of origins simply reflects the actual situation of the earliest tradition. These texts certainly suggest that the Mahāyāna, for some indeterminate period of time, was a tradition in which the central teachings were confined to restricted circles, chiefly those of forest meditators.[25] Only later, when the Mahāyāna became monasticized, was it spread widely abroad and able to become available to much larger groups.[26]

Secondary Origins: The Monasticization of the Mahāyāna

In contrast with the evidence for a southeastern Mahāyāna origin, which is consistent with a forest type of Buddhism, the evidence for a northwestern origin is, as mentioned, primarily monastic in nature and shows the Mahāyāna as an institutionalized, monastic movement. The *Mañjuśrīmūlakalpa* mentions that Kaniṣka presided over the establishment of the Prajñāpāramitā in the northwest, and Tāranātha tells us that under Kaniṣka, five hundred bodhisattvas attended the council at Jālandhara monastery, suggesting some institutional strength (*Tcj* 31b [Chattopadhyaya 1970, 92–93]). Although the literal accuracy of these legends may be doubted, they reflect the Mahāyāna belief—perhaps memory—that the institutionalization of the Mahāyāna took place first in the northwest. The specific mention of significant royal patronage may also represent memories of actual events. It stands to reason that kings most typically become patrons of Buddhist schools when those schools already possess institutional form and strength. It seems likely that the stories about Kaniṣka really tell us not about the absolute origins of the Mahāyāna as such but about the successes of the Mahāyāna as an institutionalized, monastic tradition.[27]

Similarly, the fact that important Mahāyāna *sūtras* come to light in the northwest is not necessarily evidence of their original composition, but may rather reflect their propagation and popularization. The widespread writing down and translation of texts in the northwest after Kaniṣka suggests that at that time there was a strong Mahāyāna monastic tradition in that region able to support such activity.[28] Along the same lines, the scholastic works of the Madhyamaka cited by Lamotte and others as betraying a northwestern locale presuppose settled monastic life, with its availability of written texts, ability to train monastic scholars, context of textual study and debate, and general priority of textual scholarship. The formulation of the Mahāyāna canon in Northwestern categories points in the same direction, as the collection and codification of texts implies the influence of settled monasticism. Finally, the Chinese pilgrims' affirmations that the greatest strength of Mahāyāna monasticism was in the northwest similarly seem to confirm the hypothesis that this region provided the early hub of Mahāyāna monasticism, as does Lamotte's citation of the statement that seven of the eleven main centers of the Mahāyāna were in the northwest.

When might this northwestern monasticization of the Mahāyāna have taken place? As we have seen, legend connects this process with the rule of King Kaniṣka, in the late first or early second century C.E. However, although we may perhaps trust the bare report of significant northwestern royal patronage as a key factor in the development of Mahāyāna monasticism, the traditional association of the flourishing of the Mahāyāna with Kaniṣka is questionable. To begin with, this notion must be evaluated in light of the fact that Buddhist legendary tradition tends to assimilate historical figures to certain paradigmatic types and personalities, whether saintly, scholarly, or royal. The association of the consolidation and popularization of the Mahāyāna with Kaniṣka may reflect such an assimilation rather than literal historical fact. A first-century date for Mahāyāna monasticization is doubtful on several specific grounds. First, as noted, the third-century *Vibhāṣā* makes no reference to the Mahāyāna, and this at least suggests that at that time the Mahāyāna was not seen by at least one important Nikāya school as a significant monastic rival.[29] In addition, archaeological remains tend to go along with institutional Buddhism,[30] and apart from one image of Amitābha, the significance of which is unclear,[31] there are no archaeological finds in the northwest that even suggest the existence of an institutionalized Mahāyāna during the Kuṣāṇa period (?78–320 C.E.). Summarizing the testimony of the epigraphical evidence, Schopen remarks that the Mahāyāna "attracted absolutely no *documented* public or popular support [prior to the fourth century]. . . . It is again a demonstrable fact that anything even approaching popular support for the Mahāyāna cannot be documented until the 4th/5th century AD''[32] (1987c, 124–25) (emphasis in original).

However, in and after the fourth century, we see a dramatic shift in the evidence. (1) As noted, in Lamotte's report, a sixth-century Chinese text specifies a number of Mahāyānist centers, suggesting that by this time Mahāyāna monasticism was a fact of Indian Buddhist life. (2) Hirakawa mentions a reference in the *Yogācārabhūmiśāstra,* dating from the fourth century, specifically identifying the bodhisattva as a monastic: ''The *bodhisattva* is to be ordained by the rules of the *vinaya,* receiving *upasampadā* and observing *prātimokṣa* (250 *śikṣāpada*) together with the *śrāvakayāna bhikṣu*'' (1963, 73). (3) Schopen draws our attention to inscriptional evidence confirming the fourth century as a time when there are monasteries known as Mahāyānist. Thus, in the fourth century and after, we find the terms *śākyabhikṣu* and *śākyabhikṣuṇī* in wide use specifically referring to Mahāyānist monastics. In addition, a set of Mahāyānist inscriptions dating from this same period mentions *vihārasvāmin* and *vihārasvāminī,* reflecting monasteries associated with the Mahāyāna movement.[33] (4) With the Gupta period (320–500 C.E.), archaeological evidence of the Mahāyāna begins to appear (Nakamura 1987c, 146). (5) Fa-hsien's fifth-century report makes several references to Mahāyāna Buddhism as a monastic movement in the northwest,[34] and Hsüan-tsang's[35] and I-ching's seventh-century reports reveal more substantial evidence of Mahāyāna monasticism (Dutt 1962, 175),[36] although even at this time, Nikāya monasteries outnumbered those of the Mahāyāna (169). These scattered pieces of evidence converge and indicate that, by the fourth century, the Mahāyāna was developing or had developed a significant monastic side.[37]

We have previously seen that the forest Mahāyāna sometimes defines its own ''way'' in contrast to that of the *śrāvaka*s by emphasizing differences in lifestyle and preoccupation. The thoroughness of the monasticization eventually undergone by the Mahāyāna is perhaps reflected in the seventh century by I-ching, who, wishing to contrast the ''Hīnayāna'' and Mahāyāna, does not mention lifestyle or preoccupations as important features: ''Those who worship the *bodhisattva* and read the Mahāyāna *sūtras* are called Mahāyānists, while those who do not perform these are called Hīnayānists. There are two kinds of the so-called Mahāyāna: first, the Mādhyamika; second, the Yoga'' (Takakusu 1896, 15). In this observation, ''Hīnayānists'' and Mahāyānists are to be distinguished not by lifestyle, but only by preferred texts and objects of worship. This seems to reflect a time when the Mahāyāna has become monasticized and is identified, at least in the mind of the Chinese pilgrim, as an essentially settled monastic tradition.

The preceding evidence suggests a two-stage development in the evolution of Indian Mahāyāna Buddhism. In the first stage, the Mahāyāna arose as a forest movement. This early Mahāyāna cannot be dated with any precision, although Conze's date of the second or first century B.C.E. seems not unreasonable. In the second stage, which occurred some centuries later, perhaps in the late third and fourth centuries, we find the Mahāyāna developing a monastic side, which is reflected in the evidence from the northwest.[38] By the seventh century, Mahāyāna monasticism is well established, particularly in the northwest.[39]

The preceding evidence also enables us to hypothesize some of the processes by which the Mahāyāna became monasticized. At first, perhaps there were monks living in Nikāya monasteries and following their *vinaya*s who began to take an interest in the Mahāyāna. It may also be that some forest renunciants, who belonged to what became the Mahāyāna, desired to live the less arduous renunciant life of the monastery. Sickness, old age, or simply the desire for a more secure and comfortable life could have been motivating factors. Because at first there were no Mahāyānist monasteries, becoming monks for these people would have required undergoing Nikāya ordination and living by Nikāya *prātimokṣa*s. Thus, they would have brought their Mahāyāna orientation and affiliation with them into the originally non-Mahāyāna monastic system. That Nikāya monasticism provides the point of origin for Mahāyāna monasticism is demonstrated, of course, in the fact that the Indian Mahāyāna did not initially develop its own *vinaya* but adopted the *vinaya* of Nikāya Buddhism and used that in subsequent history. Thus, the first step in the monasticization of the Mahāyāna would likely have been the presence within Nikāya monasteries of those with allegiance to the emerging Mahāyāna. Such monks would have lived in Nikāya monasteries, following their rule, but being understood as followers of the Mahāyāna teaching. This situation may not be so different from that reflected subsequently in the Chinese pilgrims' accounts of Nikāya and Mahāyānist monks living together in the same monastery (Dutt 1962, 177).

A more advanced stage in the monasticization of the Mahāyāna would have occurred when the movement had become sufficiently public and popular that the majority of monks in a given monastery identified themselves as Mahāyānists. This is the stage perhaps reflected in the mention of *śākyabhikṣu*s and *śākyabhikṣuṇī*s in Buddhist epigraphy. In a somewhat later stage, the emerging Mahāyāna movement would have begun to see itself as possessing a separate and specific identity; in inscriptions dating from the sixth century, the term *Mahāyāna* begins to be used for the first time in relation to such *bhikṣu*s and *upāsaka*s.[40] At a later stage still, as in the case of I-ching in the seventh century, the Mahāyāna would have come to be understood as a major monastic tradition in India alongside Nikāya Buddhism. It is interesting and ironic that, eventually, the Mahāyāna came to be understood primarily if not entirely as a monastic movement against which the forest-renunciant Tantric Buddhist *yogin*s, as reflected in Vajrayāna hagiography of the eleventh century and after, felt compelled to mount a critique—very similar in nature to the critiques found in the *Ratnaguṇasaṃcayagāthā,* the *Rāṣṭrapālaparipṛcchā Sūtra,* the *Saṃdhinirmocana Sūtra,* and other Mahāyāna texts we have examined.[41]

In general, the process of Mahāyāna monasticization shows the flexibility of the early forest Mahāyāna and, in particular, its adaptability not only to lay contexts (in the admission of lay bodhisattvas) but also to those of conventional Nikāya monasticism. But, no less, it also reveals the flexibility of settled monasticism in its willingness to engage in potentially creative appropriation of a non-Nikāya forest tradition. Buddhist monastic institutions and Buddhist monks, as representing the Buddhist establishment, always need to avoid rigidity and stultifying conservatism and to remain relevant and religiously attractive. Thus, it is not surprising to find the Buddhist monastery and its monks willing and able to appropriate and assimilate forms of Buddhist religious life that originally have reflected a different environment. In this instance, Nikāya monasticism showed an ability to incorporate and assimilate the traditions of the originally nonmonastic Mahāyāna, including the forest Mahāyāna. The efficacy of this strategy is shown in the great success that Mahāyāna monasticism eventually came to have in India and beyond. Most interesting in such cases of monastic assimilation is the mutual transformation that occurs in both assimilator and that which is assimilated. It may be argued that the identity of the monastic traditions into which the Mahāyāna entered was markedly changed by the process. It may equally be argued that the Mahāyāna was also dramatically transformed by being converted from a forest tradition to one predominantly of settled monasticism.

This discussion has so far treated the early, premonastic phase of the Mahāyāna as if it were coterminous with the forest Mahāyāna. However, it may be recalled that the lay devotee is necessarily implied by the type of the forest renunciant (Chapter 2); and, in fact, we have noticed lay Mahāyānists standing in the background of the Mahāyāna forest texts examined above (Chapter 8). Several of the Mahāyāna texts explicitly admit the existence of two legitimate bodhisattva ideals, that of the forest renunciant and that of the layperson. It will also be recalled that, among the forest Mahāyāna texts, there is considerable diversity in both perspective and terminology. There is a variety of additional evidence suggesting that the situation of the premonastic Mahāyāna may have been even more complex. In some Mahāyāna literature reflecting a nonmonastic and perhaps premonastic context, we find the lay bodhisattva ideal presented not in close dependence on the forest renunciant but as a more freestanding ideal. This does not necessarily mean that individuals following such traditions did not have forest gurus, but it does show that the lay ideal was sometimes understood as being a relatively independent and in some cases even unsurpassed option for the bodhisattva. For example, it is mentioned in the prose *Aṣṭasāhasrikāprajñāpāramitā Sūtra* (as we saw in Chapter 8) that birth in Madhyadeśa, in large towns where civilized values predominate, is appropriate for the high-level bodhisattva; this seems to suggest that some trends of the early Mahāyāna occurred in urban settings. Perhaps not unrelated, another type of nonmonastic but also nonforest context is implied by a text such as the *Vimalakīrtinirdeśa Sūtra,* in which a lay bodhisattva ideal is advanced as preferable. Another important dimension of the early Mahāyāna, the cult of the book, similarly appears in at least some manifestations to exist independent of classical monasticism but not necessarily to imply a forest context.[42] Yet another setting already mentioned is that of the stūpa. In spite of the forest connections that can be found in some evidence of the stūpa, it is reasonable to assume that, as many have argued, there were stūpa traditions managed primarily by and for laypersons.[43] Such, perhaps, lies behind texts like the *Saddharmapuṇḍarīka Sūtra* and, if Hirakawa is right, the smaller *Sukhāvatī Sūtra* and possibly also, following Wayman, the *Śrīmālādevīsiṃhanāda Sūtra.*[44] This kind of evidence suggests that in addition to the two main kinds of origins of the Mahāyāna (nonmonastic and monastic), the early nonmonastic Mahāyāna must itself be understood as exhibiting some diversity of type.

Such diversity would have been encouraged by the very structure of the early tradition, as reflected in the Mahāyāna *sūtras*.[45] Schopen, in his study of the cult of the book in the Mahāyāna, suggests a plausible picture of the early Mahāyāna, remarking that,

> since each text placed itself at the center of its own cult, early Mahāyāna (from a sociological point of view), rather than being an identifiable single group, was in the beginning a loose federation of a number of distinct though related cults, all of the same pattern, but each associated with its specific text. (1975, 181)

More recently, Nakamura has suggested a similar scenario: that individual Mahāyāna traditions often possessed a central text, seen as a complete and self-sufficient expression of the dharma:

> Unlike the various recensions of the Hīnayāna canon, which were virtually closed by the early centuries of the common era and which shared, at least ideally, a common structure . . . , the Mahāyāna scriptures were composed in a variety of disparate social and religious environments over the course of several centuries, diverge widely from each other in content and outlook, and were in many cases meant to stand as individual works representing (it has been conjectured) rivals to the entire Hīnayāna corpus. (1987b, 461)

These texts, when taken together, would give evidence of what Harrison terms the "astonishingly prolific literary creativity" of the early Mahāyāna (1987, 80), in spite of the fact that it was a minority movement and, as we have seen, archaeologically undocumented until a relatively advanced stage in its Indian history.

This leads to the question of how the various forest-renunciant and other trends may have come to understand themselves as belonging to the orientation later designated as Mahāyāna. It is significant that these trends all represent manifestations of a widespread resurgence of the cult (including both emulation and adoration)[46] of the Buddha. Let us recall that the ideal of the bodhisattva—always understood, of course, as leading to and thus inseparable from that of the buddha—figured importantly in all trends later identified as Mahāyānist. This leads to the hypothesis that the cult of the bodhisattva-buddha provided the common reference point in terms of which the various trends now identified as Mahāyānist were able eventually to fashion a coherent sense of Mahāyāna self-identity.[47] As we have seen, the bodhisattva notion appears with two rather distinct meanings among those traditions later identified as Mahāyānist. On the one hand, in texts such as the *Ratnaguṇasaṃcayagāthā,* the *Aṣṭasāhasrikāprajñāpāramitā Sūtra,* the *Saṃdhinirmocana Sūtra,* and the *Laṅkāvatāra Sūtra,* the bodhisattva is presented as an ideal to be emulated: salvation is obtained by becoming a bodhisattva and following the bodhisattva path to full buddhahood. On the other hand, in the *Saddharmapuṇḍarīka Sūtra* and Pure Land texts, the bodhisattva-buddha is an object of devotion: one advances toward salvation primarily by recollecting and adoring the great celestial bodhisattvas and buddhas. The development of a self-conscious Mahāyāna identity built around the bodhisattva-buddha ideal, then, perhaps included two (at least conceptually) identifiable phases, one in which a sense of close kinship developed among the members of each of these two great families and one in which these two great families recognized in one another a common orientation, although in each the bodhisattva ideal performed somewhat different functions. In sum, then, the Mahāyāna can be seen as the recoalescence under a single rubric (Mahāyāna) of trends, each of which had its origins in the cult of the buddha.

The fact that a self-conscious Mahāyāna identity arose relatively late in the history of the traditions that the term eventually came to designate raises the questions of why this identity did not appear earlier and why it developed when it did. As is well known, many Mahāyāna *sūtras*—and not just those reflecting a forest Mahāyāna—exhibit a defensiveness toward the Śrāvakayāna (sometimes also the Pratyekabuddhayāna) or the "Hīnayāna"; in the texts the Mahāyāna is evidently being criticized by these non-Mahāyānists. Moreover, as we have seen, those making these critiques are frequently depicted as settled monastics. This raises the interesting possibility that such attacks against the trends later identified as Mahāyānist became common and, in fact, helped to galvanize those trends into a sense of collective identity. This development would have been facilitated by two facts: these proto-Mahāyāna trends already shared common ground as developments of the cult of the bodhisattva-buddha; and Buddhist monasticism possessed a distinct and unique institutional form, something that the proto-Mahāyāna trends were all alike in *not* possessing. There is also something ironic in the formulation of a coherent Mahāyāna identity, for, as suggested above, it seems to have come about at roughly the time that the Mahāyāna itself became monasticized. But this is not entirely surprising, as self-conscious religious identity, particularly of a doctrinal nature, is facilitated by institutionalization and scholasticism—characteristics of Buddhist monasticism.

In support of the hypothesis that the trends now identified as Mahāyānist owe their origins to the cult of the bodhisattva-buddha, it may be observed that the various trends, diverse as they may now appear, can be seen to represent one or another development of this cultic type. Thus, the early traditions of forest renunciation are retained in the Mahāyāna in the person and cult of the bodhisattva of the forest. The trends manifest in traditions that evince a particular connection with the stūpa cult—such as the *Saddharmapuṇḍarīka Sūtra,* the smaller *Sukhāvatīvyūha Sūtra,* and perhaps also the *Śrīmālādevīsiṃhanāda Sūtra*—and that derive from the worship of the Buddha's body, and thus his essence, in its passed-beyond condition thus represent different transformations of the cult of the bodhisattva-buddha. Other trends, such as the cult of the image, can equally be seen as developments of the stūpa cult. If the cult of the book is not a transformation of the stūpa cult, it functions like a stūpa in making the saint present. Still other trends, as evidenced in the *Aṣṭasāhasrikāprajñāpāramitā Sūtra,* represent a focus on the pure wisdom of the saints. This way of looking at the evidence suggests that of the various forms of the early Mahāyāna, the forest saint in classical configuration is structurally the simplest and probably historically the oldest. At the same time, it may be noted that this priority is only a historical one, for each of the other forms represents an integral symbolic and cultic transformation by which it is able to retain and transmit the full charisma of the original form.

Some scholars would like to see the Mahāyāna as, in Migot's words, "a heresy, a deformation, a degeneration of Buddhism,'' whereas others would hold that it ''has its inception in the very origins of Buddhism itself'' and represents ''a return to [Buddhist] beginnings rather than an innovative movement'' (1983, 229).[48] The present argument suggests what may be true and what may be false in each of these positions. Certainly the historical Mahāyāna—that is, that which is revealed in extant evidence—is a later development. However, the division of the Mahāyāna into monastic and nonmonastic, the identification of this latter type as earlier, and the attempt to provide a developmental sequence for the nonmonastic forms suggest a way in which the original seeds of the Mahāyāna can easily be imagined to have lain within earliest Buddhism itself. This presupposes, of course, the existence at the time of the Buddha not only of those who aspired to be arhants and pratyekabuddhas but also those, however few, who sought to emulate Śākyamuni more exactly, by becoming bodhisattvas, more specifically bodhisattvas of the forest. That such an ideal was in the environment of early Buddhism is suggested, of course, by Śākyamuni himself. What needs to be added is only that he was not the only one inspired by this ideal and that his life did not cut off the possibility of others making the same vow that he had made. If this is the case, then the fundamental ideal and inspiration of the Mahāyāna may indeed be said to derive from the earliest and most authentic Buddhism, just as the Mahāyāna has always claimed.

A Forest Response to the Process of Monasticization

As we have seen in the preceding pages, the Buddhist monastery, once established, tended to move more and more to center stage, appropriating elements of forest Buddhism and even sometimes supplanting forest Buddhism itself. This process of monasticization did not, of course, go unnoticed by the forest renunciant traditions, and in some of the texts we have observed an apprehension at what the forest traditions regard as certain ominous effects of the decline of the forest life in favor of the settled, communal renunciant life of Buddhist monasticism. Devadatta's schism, of course, provides an early expression of this sentiment, which reaches such an extreme that—if the sources are accurate—it led at least one renunciant tradition to separate from developing Buddhism altogether. For those forest traditions that remained within the Buddhist fold, however, this apprehension took the shape of a particular interpretation of history found in both Nikāya and Mahāyānist evidence in references to the *paścimakāla* (P., *pacchimakāla*) (the final or latter times), in which the dharma of the Buddha will be eroded and even disappear from the earth. Texts such as the *Theragāthā,* the *Rāṣṭrapālaparipṛcchā Sūtra,* and the minor *Rāṣṭrapālaparipṛcchā Sūtra* refer to these evil days; the mention in the *Ratnaguṇasaṃcayagāthā* is more indirect.[49] In general, these texts provide a coherent and consistent explanation that attributes the demise of the dharma to the disappearance of the way of life of the forest renunciant and the rise to dominance of the values and preoccupations associated with settled monasticism.

As we have seen, in the song of Phussa, the saint describes the decay of the dharma in the future, in the latter times *(pacchimakāla)* (*Ta* 977). In the future, there will be *bhikṣus* who, finding life in the forest too difficult, will take up their residence in villages. They will be lazy, self-indulgent, and garrulous. They will be conceited and arrogant. They will have no respect for their teachers. They will argue with one another. These will not deserve the yellow robe of the Buddhist renunciant. This will be a very fearful time. Such will be the latter days of the dharma. It seems clear, as noted, that this description of the latter days is a projection into the future of a process that was well under way at the time of the composition of this song. This interpretation is corroborated, as noted, by the song of Pārāpariya, which is found next to that of Phussa and echoes the very same themes, also explicitly mentioning *pacchimakāla* (*Ta* 947), with the important difference that Pārāpariya is not describing future events but ones occurring in his own day. In this song, Pārāpariya laments the change that is occurring among Buddhist renunciants as the forest-renunciant life is being overshadowed and gradually eclipsed by settled monasticism. For Pārāpariya, "this is the time of evil characteristics and defilements." He says, moreover, "because of the complete annihilation of good characteristics and wisdom, the conqueror's teaching, endowed with all excellent qualities, is destroyed" (*Ta* 929). For Pārāpariya, the latter days have clearly already arrived. Nevertheless, even in these final times, the authentic dharma (*saddharma)* may be practiced by the remnant, for "those who are ready for seclusion possess the remainder of the true doctrine" (*Ta* 930).

We noted the same themes of the decay and destruction of the genuine dharma in the *Rāṣṭrapālaparipṛcchā Sūtra*. There, *bhikṣus* are described who live in groups and whose practices and values are undermining the genuine dharma. These *bhikṣus* preoccupy themselves with the appearance of behavioral purity, but they are inwardly filled with greed, aggression, and confusion. These *bhikṣus* moreover strive after knowledge, but the knowledge they seek is impure and they are without wisdom. Not only is the dharma practiced by the *bhikṣus* a mere imitation of the real thing, but the *bhikṣus* show no respect for the real dharma. They neither meditate nor possess the traits of one who is accomplished in meditation. They have no respect for the gurus or other holy persons, they despise the *gaṇa* of bodhisattvas, and they have no use for the bodhisattva's codes of morality and lifestyle, including the *dhutaguṇas*. Far from making progress toward liberation, these *bhikṣus* will be reborn in the lower realms, among animals, as hungry ghosts, and in the hells. It is these *bhikṣus* and their defiled behavior that will in a future time lead to the destruction of the dharma and its disappearance from the earth.

The *Theragāthā* and the *Rāṣṭrapālaparipṛcchā Sūtra,* as we saw, do not agree about exactly who will bring about the downfall of the dharma. As might be expected from Nikāya texts, the songs of the *Theragāthā* implicitly recognize two sorts of *bhikṣus*: one upholds the genuine dharma by living in the forest, the other departs from this way and will eventually bring about the ruin of the dharma. For the *Rāṣṭrapālaparipṛcchā Sūtra,* the forest ideal of the text is called a bodhisattva, and the text presents what seems to be a blanket condemnation of *bhikṣus*, implying that the *bhikṣus* as such will lead to the destruction of the dharma. As the Mahāyāna as reflected in the *Rāṣṭrapālaparipṛcchā Sūtra* is a nonmonastic tradition, in identifying *bhikṣus* as responsible for the ruin of the dharma, the text comes very close to condemning the Nikāya traditions as such.

The minor *Rāṣṭrapālaparipṛcchā Sūtra,* in its final form, as we saw in the Appendix to Chapter 8, also talks about the latter times and the destruction of the dharma—in fact, this issue is given as the pretext for the Buddha's preaching the *sūtra* in the first place. The interlocutor asks the Buddha, "Exalted One, of what character are the beings that bring the teaching of the *tathāgata* to ruin?" As we saw, the minor *Rāṣṭrapālaparipṛcchā Sūtra* replies in a way quite different from the kind of blanket condemnation found in the *Rāṣṭrapālaparipṛcchā Sūtra.* Making explicit what is implicit in the longer text, it defines *bhikṣus* as those renunciants who belong to the Śrāvakayāna and who follow the *prātimokṣa.* The shorter text continues that it is not the Śrāvakayāna as such that will lead to the ruin of the dharma, but those *bhikṣus* of the Śrāvakayāna who have abandoned the way of forest renunciation and its pursuit of solitary meditation. Those *bhikṣus* who follow the normative way of forest renunciation are very close to the bodhisattva of the forest, differing only in discipline (the *bhikṣus* follow the *prātimokṣa*), aspiration (they seek their own liberation), and attainment (they attain to one of the four classes of holy persons).[50] On the other hand, those who will destroy the dharma are *bhikṣus* who have abandoned the life of forest renunciation and follow a way concordant with settled monasticism. Although the shorter *Rāṣṭrapāla Sūtra* disagrees with the longer on the precise historical identity of the person who will bring about the destruction of the dharma, it entirely agrees as to the type: it is the renunciant who has rejected the normative life of forest renunciation, given up the meditative life, and is following other pursuits.[51] In sum, the texts cited here, deriving from different traditions but all reflecting an ideal of forest renunciation, provide a simple, coherent, and consistent explanation of the reasons for the destruction of the dharma. This tragic event will occur as a result of the abandonment of the forest life on the part of Buddhist renunciants, a process that is already under way.

These texts share a common understanding of Buddhist history, which they see as following a particular temporal progression: first, the dharma is practiced in a pure form by forest renunciants, following the model of the Buddha and taught by him, including life in the forest, the practice of meditation, and the attainment of realization. Second, the dharma enters into decline, during which the forest life and meditation are replaced by other lifestyles and preoccupations, including an emphasis on pure behavior, the scholarly study of texts, and worldly involvements. Finally, as a result of this decline, the authentic dharma will eventually suffer destruction.

The theme of the decline of the dharma is, of course, an important one in Indian Buddhism from, according to Conze, 200 B.C.E. onward (1951, 114).[52] Indeed, the passages on this theme in the *Theragāthā* suggest that this concern may be older. In any case, the texts cited represent only a small portion of the corpus of texts dealing with *paścimakāla,* most of which postdate these texts. However, it is interesting that in many of these other texts, there are substantial thematic continuities with the discussion in the forest-oriented texts just examined.[53] For example, the *Milindapañha* (130–34 [T.R. 1890–94, 1:186–90]) tells us that as the dharma declines, the first to disappear will be the degrees of holiness (*adhigama,* attainment), followed by practice *(paṭipatti),*[54] and finally by even the external signs of Buddhism *(liṅga).* The *Manorathapūraṇī* (*Mrp* 1.87 [Lamotte 1958, 216]) describes the dharma's decline in a slightly more elaborate but similar scheme: first holiness will disappear *(adhigama),* followed progressively by the disappearance of practice *(paṭipatti),* study *(pariyatti),* the external signs *(nimitta)* of the religious, and finally the relics *(dhātu).* The *Mātṛkā* of the Haimavata holds that the dharma will disappear after five hundred years according to yet another, but similar set of stages. It attributes to each of the five centuries of the dharma's life a predominant concern, in order: (1) liberation *(vimokṣa);* (2) meditation *(samādhi);* (3) behavioral purity *(śīladhara);* (4) textual learning *(bahuśruta);* and (5) material offerings *(dāna)* (Lamotte 1958, 212). In a similar vein, the *Mahāsaṃnipāta Sūtra,* which predicts the end of the dharma after twenty-five hundred years, divides the decline of the dharma into five five-hundred-year periods, during which the faithful are strong in (1) direct realization of the truth *(satyābhisamaya);* (2) meditation *(samādhi, dhyāna);* (3) textual learning *(śruta);* (4) building monasteries; and (5) quarrels and blame, at which time the pure dharma becomes invisible (Lamotte 1958, 214–15).[55] Finally, a short *Mahāparinirvāṇa Sūtra* in Chinese holds that the dharma will disappear in one thousand years, with each century in the decline being characterized by a particular feature: (1) the holy dharma *(āryadharma);* (2) the practice of meditation *(śamatha);* (3) correct behavior *(samyakcarita);* (4) renunciation *(vairāgya);* (5) interpretation of the dharma *(dharmārtha);*[56] (6) teaching of the dharma *(dharmadeśanā);* (7) honor and gain *(lābhasatkāra);* (8) disputation *(vivāda);* (9) agitation *(auddhatya);*[57] and (10) wrong conceptualization *(prapañca).*

These different traditions agree on some basic points: the dharma was initially presented in its integrity and, soon after, began to undergo a progressive degeneration. In its integrity, the dharma was marked by realization and practice of meditation, but as it gradually declined, other progressively grosser motivations began to take over. Thus, the initial period of realization is followed by one of meditation, and this is followed either by a decline into behavioral purity thence to scholarship or directly into scholarship. Following this, the dharma declines into its complete submergence in mundane motivations and degraded behavior.

These later, not specifically forest-oriented texts, then, generally agree with the patterns seen in the forest-oriented texts. The dharma is in decline and will disappear, owing to the movement among renunciants away from concern for the original tradition of meditation and realization. Renunciants will turn toward other, less holy preoccupations, among which concern for behavioral purity, scholarship, teaching, and the building of monasteries are mentioned. These certainly are consistent with a movement away from the life of forest renunciation to that of settled monasticism. This movement, in turn, provides the ground for more worldly manifestations of defilement, greed for material gain, the seeking of honor, and delight in disputation and blame—a pattern and themes found less systematically in the songs of Phussa and Pārāpariya in the *Theragāthā* and in the *Rāṣṭrapālaparipṛcchā Sūtra* and the minor *Rāṣṭrapālaparipṛcchā Sūtra.*

The later texts appear not explicitly to equate the decline and destruction of the dharma with the abandonment of the forest life and the rise to dominance of settled monasticism. However, they detail the very same themes described in the *sūtra*s in which such an interpretation is explicitly given. This raises the fascinating question of the relation of the unsystematized discussions of the disappearance of the dharma in the forest-oriented texts with the later, more systematic accounts. Did the Buddhist idea of the disappearance of the dharma originally develop among traditions of forest renunciation as their response to the rise to dominance of settled monasticism? Texts such as the *Theragāthā,* the *Rāṣṭrapālaparipṛcchā Sūtra,* and the minor *Rāṣṭrapālaparipṛcchā Sūtra* certainly suggest such a possibility.

Appendix: Some Limitations of Weber's Model of Early Buddhism

At this point, it will be useful to consider some limitations in Weber's model of the development of early Buddhism. As noted, the particular contribution of Weber's analysis to the present discussion has been to suggest certain fallacies of the two-tiered model. First, Weber makes a revealing analysis of the contrast between the early wandering form of Buddhism and that of classical monasticism and shows how the later, developed classical monastic form became normative. Then he points to social, political, and economic conditioning, suggesting that a correct interpretation of monastic Buddhism necessitates taking these factors into account. By pointing to certain patterns of self-interest in the origin, development, and operation of settled monasticism, Weber raises the very good question of the extent to which, in its application, monastic Buddhism represents a redirection of earlier Buddhism. In clarifying the innovative and socially and economically influenced nature of the Buddhist monastic institution, Weber's analysis in effect calls into question the two-tiered model as an adequate descriptive model of Indian Buddhism as such.

However, in so doing, Weber also puts forward a variety of interpretations of early Buddhism that require further comment. In Weber's reading, the development of the monastic institution as such, in and of itself, is seen as a betrayal of the Buddha's teaching. For Weber, the development of the monastery heralds the routinization of the Buddha's charisma and the loss of the openness, dynamism, spontaneity, freedom, and vitality of the golden age of the founder. Weber appears to see in the monastery the capitulation of Buddhism to concerns for material security, official status, bureaucracy, and political power. He makes his views explicit in his *Religion of India,* in which he comments on the "contradiction" he finds between the wandering ideal of the Buddha and the settled "church" of the monastery. "Actually it appears even as a contradiction that the Buddha, who was quite aloof from forming a 'church' or even a 'parish' and who expressly rejected the possibility and pretension of being able to 'lead' an order, has founded an order after all. The contradiction remains unless the institution here, in contrast to Christendom, was rather the mere creation of his students" (1958, 213–14). Elsewhere in the same work he remarks, "It looks as if even the few, finally created elements of organization and discipline, hence the establishment of an order, and likewise the fixing of the teaching, occurred only after the death of the founder and against his own intentions'' (223). But, one must ask, to what extent is such a conclusion justified by the evidence of Buddhism itself?

For Weber, charisma is an antiorganizational, antieconomic, and, finally, asocial force. In reference to this latter, Weber tells us that in Buddhism ''salvation is an absolutely personal performance of the self-reliant individual. No one, and particularly no social community can help him. The specific asocial character of all genuine mysticism is here carried to its maximum'' (1958, 213). For Weber, given this understanding of charisma in Buddhism, when social, institutional, economic, and political considerations obtrude, such charisma is routinized, that is, changed into something else. Here Weber makes a number of judgments that are unproved assumptions. He assumes, for example, that the charismatic Buddha and his earliest disciples were unconcerned with social approbation, economic survival, communal organization and hierarchy, political relations, and so on. Is this assumption justifiable?

We are told by unanimous tradition that the Buddha taught precisely so that his teachings might reach ''the many.'' We may judge the absolutism of the two-tiered model of Buddhism to be unacceptable; but it would seem to be an unwarranted further assumption that the Buddha totally rejected any notion of community, hierarchy of disciples, or stabilized relations to society and state as having a legitimate role in the spread of his teachings. Although in later Buddhist history, charismatic Buddhist saints characteristically showed less or at least a different kind of concern for such matters from that shown by monastic personnel, it cannot be said that they were universally indifferent to issues of this kind. To take Weber's position is to assume that the Buddha and those among his disciples who carried on his type were necessarily indifferent to the survival of Buddhism, and nothing in Buddhist tradition warrants such an assumption.

Further, Weber assumes that the charismatic nature of early Buddhism—indeed, of ''all genuine mysticisms''—is necessarily inimical to communal forms. He further assumes that communal structures can have nothing but a negative relation to charismatic saints. Nowhere does he allow for the possibility of a positive relationship between monastic life and the development of the saint or charismatic leader. Weber is surely right that the kinds of structures that occur in Buddhist monastic tradition *can* militate against charisma, but is it correct to say that they do so necessarily in every case?

Third, in a similar way, Weber takes for granted the incompatibility of spiritual motivations and social, political, and economic motivations among the disciples of the Buddha, and he assumes that a concern among the disciples for the continuation and stability of the tradition must have been anticharismatic. Again, one must ask, must genuinely spiritual and other motivations be deemed necessarily incompatible? In the end, in rejecting the substantialism of the two-tiered model of Buddhism, Weber has reintroduced a substantialism that is its mirror opposite. Weber assumes that the monastery, under any and all conditions, runs counter to the charismatic teaching of the Buddha and that the kinds of concerns that characterize monastic Buddhism are inherently contradictory to spiritual charisma in all applications. In effect, Weber attempts to set up one particular form—here, his model of the particular shape of the early community—and to identify it with normative Buddhism.

Weber's notion of charisma is substantialistic at least partly because it is also one-sidedly externalistic. Perhaps because he has the model of Western Christianity in mind, Weber tends to see charisma as residing exclusively in an exterior situation: in the Buddha or in certain early masters or in the external form of the early community. Weber seems to neglect the fact that, at least in Buddhism, the charisma or spiritual power of the Buddha is ultimately not external to the ordinary human being. In fact, it is potentially available to everyone, and it is seen as the task of each Buddhist to develop that inner charisma. To the extent to which the inner charisma is developed, it will be manifested as outer charisma. Moreover, it is the ultimate purpose of the renunciant life in Buddhism to develop that inner charisma (wisdom) together with its outer expression (compassion). It is precisely this that makes possible an ongoing cult of saints in Buddhist history.

Because Weber does not see the inner as well as the outer expression of charisma in the tradition, he tends to identify the charismatic element of Buddhism with its founder and with its early form of organization. When the finally interior and readily available nature of charisma is appreciated, one will see that "genuine Buddhism" cannot be identified exclusively with any particular form or situation. At the same time, obviously some forms and situations are more conducive to the development of charisma than others, but to say this is very different from attempting to identify a particular lifestyle as invariably genuine and to reject others as invariably ingenuine. A study of Buddhist history would seem to indicate that, in the case of the settled monastery, this kind of Buddhism, like any other, must be judged according to whether, in application, it does or does not lead, in the standard Buddhist formulation, "to the abatement of passion, aggression, and delusion." The rejection of the validity of the two-tiered model of Buddhism and of its antithesis in the Weberian critique invites the question of what model of Buddhism may be more appropriate to the actual history of the tradition, a question to be addressed in the conclusion to this work.

Notes

1. Those few scholars who have seen forest renunciation as a significant factor in earliest Buddhism have tended to prefer the first alternative, that town-and-village renunciation formed no part of the original teaching of the Buddha. See, e.g., Nakamura 1987c, 58–59.

2. The Nikāya Buddhist texts that depict the Buddha preaching to large crowds, having the ears of regional potentates, and accepting donations for large monasteries appear to reflect the situation of Indian Buddhism at some historical remove from the time of the Buddha. In any case, as mentioned in Chapter 2, it cannot simply be assumed that these images reflect the time period of the Buddha, or even the generations immediately following his death.

3. Well established in the time of the Buddha (Thapar 1975, 123).

4. These two concerns were, of course, deeply rooted in orthodox tradition since the Vedic period. The sacrificial ritual depended for its efficacy upon both the knowledge and

the purity of the officiating priests. On the one hand, the priest was expected to have a thorough and accurate knowledge of the texts wherein were detailed the facets of the preparation and celebration of the sacrifice; on the other, he had to maintain himself in a condition of ritual purity. The patron, on whose behalf the sacrifice was performed, was dependent, of course, on the brahmin priest's efficacious performance of the sacrifice, not only to attain the desired ends for which the rite was being performed, but also to avoid disastrous consequences to himself should mistakes be made. Thus, for the lay patron, full confidence in the learning and purity of the priest was crucial to the priest's prestige.

5. In two recent articles, Gombrich has agreed with the general drift of Frauwallner's reasoning: "It would never have occurred to the Buddhists that such a feat of preservation [of texts] was even possible had they not had before them the example of the brahmins" (1990b, 23); and, "The Buddhists had to emulate the brahmins by preserving a large body of texts" (1990a, 6).

6. Przyluski comes to different conclusions, for which see 1923, 292–93.

7. Although in theory the Mahāyāna admits the spiritual capacities of women, Mahāyāna monasticism would seem to reproduce many of the attitudes and beliefs in relation to women found in non-Mahāyāna monastic tradition. Such is clearly exemplified in Śāntideva's *Bodhicaryāvatāra,* especially chapter 8 (*Bca* 136–66 [Matics 1970, 194–210; Batchelor 1979, 99–130]), and in the fact that the great Mahāyānist scholastic authors are all men. This, of course, contrasts with the sometimes positive role of women in Mahāyāna *sūtra*s (Williams 1989, 21) and, more dramatically, with the appearance of women as enlightened saints in Tantric Buddhism (Ray 1980).

8. It was not only at the beginning of Buddhist history that Buddhist monasticism emulated patterns and methods of its non-Buddhist environment. For this same phenomenon in the development of Madhyamaka, see Robinson 1967, 50.

9. It is, of course, a great irony of Buddhist history that the scholastic traditions of the Abhidharma and Madhyamaka, for all the pains they took to develop Buddhist nonsubstantialism in the doctrinal sphere, found themselves criticized by the more contemplative traditions for being substantialistic. Thus the Abhidharma is criticized by the *Prajñāpāramitā Sūtra* for its substantialism (Conze 1954a). And the Madhyamaka emphasis on *śūnyatā* is criticized for its substantialism (making *śūnyatā* into a "thing" or reference point), sometimes explicitly, sometimes implicitly, by the *Saṃdhinirmocana Sūtra,* by the classical Yogācāra, and by the Vajrayāna allied with the *gzhan.stong* ("emptiness of other") tradition in Tibet (Ray 1988).

10. The fact that the development of the town-and-village monastery was at least partially a result of altruistic motives is suggested by the set of five rules that are attributed to Devadatta in the Mūlasarvāstivādin *vinaya.* These rules, it will be recalled, have to do with acting in a compassionate manner to sentient beings, both humans and animals. The first four rules involve: (1) the avoidance of taking milk and curds because to do so would harm calves; (2) the avoidance of eating meat because to do so would implicate one in the injury of sentient beings; (3) the avoidance of salt because it is produced by sweat; and (4) the avoidance of wearing a certain kind of robe so as not to disrupt the weavers' trade. The fifth rule is very interesting in the present context: "The *śramaṇa* Gautama lives in the wilds; but we will live in villages because by his practice men cannot perform works of charity" (*V*-t, D., *'dul.ba,* nga, 289a–b [R., 87–88]). In other words, this rule explicitly gives as the motivation for living not in the forest but in villages the benefiting of the laity.

11. This "free and wandering" characterization would have applied to both forest renunciation and town-and-village renunciation.

12. In the *Mahāparinibbāna Sutta,* for example, the Buddha is quoted as saying, "When I used to enter into an assembly of many hundred nobles, before I had seated myself there

or talked to them or started a conversation with them, I used to become in colour like unto their colour, and in voice like unto their voice'' (*Mps*-p 3.21–23). In the *Bodhisattvabhūmi* of Asaṅga we read that the bodhisattva, when he enters into an assembly, assumes the character of those in the assembly, adopting their physical appearance, speaking in their manner, and taking up the subjects that they deem important (*Bbh* 12–13). The phrasing in the two texts is very similar.

13. Jensen 1963, 4, 6, 43, and passim. Jensen pertinently comments, ''Every human usage arose at some moment of history . . . at the time of its origination it was an 'expression' of a very specific attitude toward the environment. . . . Like all other cultural phenomena, customs relentlessly move from the 'expressive' stage into that of 'application.' It is therefore necessary to examine any cultural configuration to see the extent to which it has maintained contact with its original and proper meaning. According to an inescapable law, anything that culture has created must grow more distant from the content of the creative idea; finally, it will be only a pale reflection of its original 'expression' and may even be transformed into its exact mirror image'' (193–94).

14. See the remarks of Gombrich on this point (1990a, 6). Tatia informs us that during the early period of Jain history renunciants were strictly prohibited from living in permanent residences. Subsequently, these were built for Jain renunciants by their laity, under the influence, Tatia believes, of Buddhist monasticism (1980, 327).

15. N. Dutt cites *Asp*. The passage in question reads, ''Moreover, these *sūtras* associated with the six perfections will, after the passing away of the *tathāgata*, appear in the South. From the South they will spread to the East, and from there to the North'' (*Asp* 112.1–3 [Cz., 159]).

16. The evidence for a southeastern origin is given more fully and systematically by Conze (1960, 9–11). In most discussions of Mahāyāna origins, Conze acknowledges the debate between those preferring a southeastern and those favoring a northwestern locale (for example, 1959, 297; 1960, 12; 1973b, xiv–xv; and 1980, 44). However, although acknowledging both sides of the debate, Conze himself clearly prefers the southeast as the place where the Mahāyāna first arose (see, for example, 1960, 9–12).

17. E.g., Basham 1981, 27–38; conclusions, 37–38.

18. Prior to taking this position, Lamotte favored a southern origin for the Mahāyāna. In 1944–76, he remarks, ''On a de bonnes raisons pour croire que les Mahāyāna *sūtra* en général, et les Prajñā en particulier, proviennent du Sud (pays d'Andhra)'' (25, n. 1). The passage in question is found in vol. 1 (1944). The article under discussion was published in 1954.

19. As Nakamura has suggested, a lack of archaeological evidence would be expected from a tradition that was noninstitutional in character (1987c, 146).

20. It is a well-known fact that the earlier Northwestern schools (Lokottaravādin, Gokulika, Ekavyavahārika, Bahuśrutīya, Prajñaptivādin) held doctrines most closely associated with the Mahāyāna, whereas the later Southeastern schools (Buddhaghosa's ''Andhakas'' [Caitika, Andhaka, Pūrvaśaila . . .]) claimed derivation from the Sthavira and were doctrinally much more dissimilar to the Mahāyāna. However, the Bahuśrutīya had an important center in southeast India and, in Bareau's view, acted as a connecting link joining northwest and southeast. Bareau believes that although the Northwestern schools show the closest doctrinal affinities to the Mahāyāna, their influence could have been felt in the southeast. In addition, as Williams observes, ''some form of supramundane teaching appears to have been common to all Mahāsāṃghika schools, since it is found strongly stated in the Pūrvaśaila *Lokānuvartana Sūtra* as well'' (1989, 18).

In defense of his hypothesis, Bareau offers a strong critique of the theory of northwestern origins. It is true, Bareau says, that there is some significant evidence apparently suggesting a northwestern origin. For example, one may point to the existence of Chinese translations dating from the second century by Parthian, Sogdien, and Khotanese monks. This tells us of the existence of a Buddhist community at this time outside of India, in the northwest and north, but such is hardly proof of northwestern origins for the Mahāyāna. This area existed on the trade route that would in any case be followed by missionary monks going north from anywhere in India. Mahāyānist missionaries from the Deccan could easily have passed through northwest India, unnoticed by the Sarvāstivāda. Again, Bareau says, it has often been argued that although the Sarvāstivāda does not show significant affinities in the matter of buddhology with the Mahāyāna, still there are important ontological continuities: the Sautrāntika, it is typically argued, had a notion of the emptiness of dharmas that became fundamental for the Mahāyāna. This commonly held opinion Bareau strenuously rejects: "I declare that for my part I have never encountered . . . any thesis like this attributed to the Sautrāntika. I have the impression that this idea is born from an incorrect interpretation and faulty generalization of a group of theses propounded by the Sautrāntika and the Dārṣṭāntika." Bareau also points to another misconception often brought forward to bolster up this position, namely, that the Sautrāntika and the Prajñaptivādin are to be identified as a single school. Then, he asks, can one find Mahāyāna ontology prefigured in any of the Hīnayāna schools? His answer is that one can among the sects of the Mahāsāṃghika group, and he offers an array of evidence in support of this contention. Finally, Bareau makes brief allusion to, but does not really discuss, perhaps the strongest evidence for northwestern origins, particularly stressed by Lamotte—namely, the whole range of affinities between certain Madhyamaka texts attributed to Nāgārjuna and Sarvāstivādin texts, textual categories, and doctrines. Bareau concludes, then, that it appears that the Mahāyāna originated in the region north of the Deccan, in Koṅkana, Orissa, and Mahākosala, among the subsects of the Mahāsāṃghika, and perhaps particularly among the Prajñaptivāda and Bahuśrutīya, who seem to have formed a link between the older northern Mahāsāṃghika and the later southeastern Mahāsāṃghika. Bareau also mentions that, according to Hsüan-tsang and I-ching, by the seventh century the southern Mahāsāṃghikas had disappeared, seeming to have been replaced by the Mahāyāna. Bareau feels that what must have occurred is that the Mahāyāna grew out of the Mahāsāṃghika sects, and then the Mahāsāṃghika sects gradually themselves became Mahāyānist. Thus, by the seventh century, the region proposed for Mahāyāna origins had ceased to be a stronghold for the Mahāsāṃghika and became instead an important Indian center of the Mahāyāna. To identify this as the area of Mahāyāna origins is not, of course, to deny the importance of other centers at various stages in the evolution of the Mahāyāna. But these other centers, such as Magadha, the northwest, and the area south of the Deccan, were strictly later and secondary (Bareau 1955, 301–5). Conze would agree with Bareau's rebuttal of northwestern origins. He takes note of the argument for northwestern origins put forward by Lamotte and then remarks, "I believe that [Lamotte] has shown no more than that the Prajñāpāramitā had a great success in the North-West at the Kuṣāṇa period, and that, to use his own words (p. 392), that region may well be the 'fortress and hearth,' though not necessarily the cradle of the Mahāyānistic movement. The *Mañjuśrīmūlakalpa* (L. III v. 574) says that under Kaniṣka the Prajñāpāramitā was 'established' . . . in the North-West, but not that it originated there" (1960, 12).

21. Schopen 1975, 179–81. See also Kajiyama 1985.

22. Conze 1973b, xiv. See, however, Lamotte (1981, 25, n. 1), who takes the geographical specification of this statement quite seriously. See also Lamotte 1944–80, 190–97.

23. Lamotte finds the traditional accounts "fables without value" (1954, 382). For

him, the real meaning behind the legend of the secrecy of the original Mahāyāna and its public dissemination centuries later is simply that these teachings did not exist in the early period and arose only later (381). Lamotte believes the traditional accounts were invented by Mahāyānists in an attempt to lend credibility to their tradition (381).

24. Tib., *gsang.sngags.*

25. It is significant that Buddhist historians sometimes explicitly connect Mahāyāna ideas, prior to the tradition's actual propagation, with forest renunciation. Paramārtha, for example, tells us that Mahāyāna-type ideas entered the Mahāsāṃghika through a certain forest saint. This individual lived during the time of the Buddha and, after becoming an arhant, always followed him everywhere, even into the heavens, to hear the dharma. Prior to the *parinirvāṇa* of the Buddha, this arhant retired into the Himalayas to meditate, and he remained there, seated in meditation, for two hundred years. At the end of this time, he emerged from his solitary retreat to find that the Mahāsāṃghika tradition preserved only the superficial sense of the *Tripiṭaka.* He then preached the profound meaning of the *Tripiṭaka,* which Paramārtha identifies as the essential meaning of the Mahāyāna (Demiéville 1932, 47). This preaching led to the formation of the Bahuśrutīya subsect of the Mahāsāṃghika (47–49; cf. also Bareau 1955, 81). The notion that a Nikāya forest saint understood the meaning of the Mahāyāna is of course reflective of a theme developed in Chapter 8.

26. Gombrich remarks that forms of Buddhism standing apart from those of Nikāya Buddhism "may have arisen earlier, but we shall never know, for they were doomed to be ephemeral because they did not have the institutional wherewithall, as did monastic Buddhism, to maintain a continuous textual tradition" (1990b, 30). Nevertheless, there is some evidence, within the monastically preserved canons, that texts could be transmitted and preserved outside of the monastic context. Norman, for example, draws our attention to a reference in the *vinaya* (*V*-p 1:140–41 [H., 3:188]) to the preservation of a text by a layperson (although concern is expressed that the text will be lost) (Norman 1989, 30). Forest Buddhism, as seen in texts such as *Sn, Ta,* and *Ti,* obviously provides another context in which texts could be preserved. In relation to the composition and preservation of Mahāyāna texts outside of monastic contexts, Gombrich is surely right that any such composition and preservation could not have occurred after the fashion of the monastery, with its focused and extensive resources for maintaining textual tradition. On the other hand, it seems quite plausible that certain Mahāyāna *sūtra*s emerged as more or less self-sufficient expositions of the dharma. In relation to texts giving evidence of forest renunciation, some might have been connected with stūpa worship, and here stūpas could have provided an institutional apparatus to maintain textual continuity. At the same time, small communities or even lineages of individuals without any particular institutional focus could also have developed certain texts and passed them on from generation to generation. The example of the Indian Vajrayāna is instructive here, for many of the tremendous number of Indian Tantric Buddhist texts surviving in the Tibetan and Chinese canons reflect just such a process. See Schopen's discussion of the cult of the book in the Mahāyāna (1975), much of which is congruent with the perspectives being developed here.

27. In *Tcj,* Tāranātha, whom Lamotte cites, typically makes a distinction between the absolute origins of a tradition and the establishment of a tradition as a socially accepted and supported entity. Tāranātha's account in his *chos.'byung* indicates the latter process, not the former (e.g., *Tcj* 136aff. [Chattopadhyaya 1970, 343ff.]).

28. The fact of early Mahāyāna translations into Chinese does not reflect the same thing. See Bareau's comment that Mahāyāna missionaries from the southeast could have participated in making these translations. Along the same lines, Schopen remarks that "although there was—as we know from Chinese translations—a large and early Mahāyāna

literature, there was no early organized, independent, publicly supported movement that it could have belonged to'' (1987b, 124–25).

29. Interestingly enough, Tāranātha tells us that this was the case. During the time of Kaniṣka, the *śrāvaka* traditions were entirely dominant. However, beginning at this time, ''some of the Mahāyāna scriptures reached the human world. A few monks who attained the *anutpattikadharma-kṣānti* stage [acceptance of dharmas that fail to be produced] preached these a little. However, since this did not become very extensive, the *śrāvaka*-s did not contest it'' (*Tcj* 32a [Chattopadhyaya 1970, 95]).

30. Nakamura comments, ''The number of hitherto discovered inscriptions may be an index of the influence and prestige of the Buddhist orders in the society of that time'' (1987c, 146).

31. In 1987b, Schopen draws our attention to the first epigraphic evidence of the Mahāyāna, an inscription on a Kuṣāṇa image of Amitābha dating from the early second century C.E. (99).

32. Schopen 1987b, 124–25. Schopen remarks that ''at Mathurā at least the movement we now call 'the Mahāyāna' had not yet achieved complete independence even as late as the second quarter of the 5th century A.D.'' (1987b, 123).

33. Schopen has provided a useful summary of these remains, particularly in 1979, 1–19 and 1987b, 99–134. In 1987b, he makes reference to the second-century Amitābha image. In 1979, he analyzes two sets of inscriptions giving evidence of the Mahāyāna. The first is a set of about eighty inscriptions dating from the fourth century and after, not mentioning Mahāyāna by name but nevertheless, Schopen's analysis shows, giving evidence of the existence of the Mahāyāna. The second set contains a group of fourteen inscriptions dating from the sixth to the twelfth century that mention the Mahāyāna by name. Many of the fourth-century and later inscriptions use terminology that reflects the Mahāyāna as a monastic movement, and one finds references both to Mahāyāna *bhikṣu*s (*śākyabhikṣu* and *śākyabhikṣuṇī*, which Schopen shows refer specifically to Mahāyānists) and to *upāsaka*s and *upāsikā*s. One also finds some reference to monasteries (in the terms *vihārasvāmin* and *vihārasvāminī*). This suggests that, at least by the fourth century C.E., the Mahāyāna had begun to become a monastic movement. An interesting peculiarity of the archaeological evidence is that it tends to stand in some tension with the literary remains. The literary remains suggest, as noted, that Mahāyāna monasticism originally developed in the northwest among the Sarvāstivādins, leading Lamotte to his hypothesis of northwestern origins. The epigraphical remains that give evidence of the monastic Mahāyāna derive from a wide-ranging territory, from Ajaṇṭā in the southwest to Bihār and Bengal in the northeast. In surveying the evidence, Schopen remarks that ''it is a little surprising to note that almost the only places in which our formula and its associated titles do not occur in inscriptions is in the south of India, Nāgārjunikoṇḍā, etc. and in the North-West, the two areas most often connected with the origin and development of Mahāyāna'' (1979b, 15). In light of the argument being presented here, the absence of archaeological evidence at least from the southeast is what one might expect.

34. Beal 1869, 8–9, 10, 13, 51, etc. See also Hazra 1983, 2–5.

35. See Lamotte's summary of information provided by Hsüan-tsang (1958, 597–600).

36. Schopen remarks that a statistical analysis of epigraphical data shows that ''the Mahāyāna was a monk dominated movement'' (1985, 26). Two comments need to be made concerning the evidence put forward by Schopen. First, his evidence indicates that in so far as it is revealed by the epigraphical data, the Mahāyāna is a movement dominated by *bhikṣus*. Because archaeological remains tend to reflect institutionalization, this is not surprising. Second—and this is a more difficult problem—it must be recognized that, as we have amply seen in this study, when we find the term *bhikṣu,* without additional qualifica-

tion, we cannot be certain what kind of renunciant is meant, whether of settled monastery or of the forest. Moreover, *bhikṣus* of the forest are mentioned in the texts, not only early but later in Indian Buddhism in both Mahāyāna (e.g., the minor *Rāṣṭrapālaparipṛcchā Sūtra,* cf. Chapter 8, Appendix) and Vajrayāna (*Caturaśītisiddhapravṛtti* 172–82 [Rb., 174–79]). This raises interesting questions concerning the interpretation of Schopen's data. At the same time, it is also clear that in Schopen's inscriptions, in a considerable number of cases, "these individuals were not just ordinary [*bhikṣus*], but doctrinal specialists . . . and the acknowledged transmitters of Buddhist teaching" (1985, 26), suggesting that they were in fact monks in the conventional sense.

37. Interesting in this context is the second-century or third-century date usually given for the Buddhist master Nāgārjuna (Walleser 1922; Robinson 1967, 25; Yün-hua 1970, 148), revealed in his hagiography as a great saint and in his compositions (e.g., the *Mūlamadhyamakakārikā*) as the paradigmatic Mahāyāna monastic scholar. The date usually given for Nāgārjuna must be measured against the fact that institutional Mahāyāna is not visible for at least a century after the time usually given for him. The second- or third-century date is not inconsistent with one dimension of Nāgārjuna's personality, i.e., as the great forest saint who is a Mahāyānist innovator and propagator, as revealed in the earliest biography of this figure by Kumārajīva, dating to the early fifth century, and in subsequent "lives" (Ray 1990 contains an enumeration of hagiographical evidence bearing on Nāgārjuna). In Kumārajīva's work, we are told that in Nāgārjuna's time, the Mahāyāna lacked a tradition of scholarly reasoning and exposition, i.e., that it was not yet monasticized. On the other hand, the scholastic texts attributed to Nāgārjuna, e.g., the *Mūlamadhyamakakārikā* and similar works (cf. the list of twelve additional texts proposed as authentic by Lindtner 1982, 11), reveal a tradition of Mahāyāna textual learning and scholastic commentary and a Madhyamaka tradition that has reached a mature and confident level of self-definition. This, of course, suggests a background of substantial settled monastic development. This discrepancy raises the question of whether the saintly Mahāyāna innovator, who is identified as a forest saint living prior to the time of Mahāyāna monasticism, can on formal grounds alone be thought to have been the author of the texts most often attributed to him. And this question raises the issue of the complex development of Buddhist hagiography and hagiographic figures, frequently alluded to in this study, and of what must have been the even more complex relationship between any given figure, at one or another stage of the development of his hagiography and cult, and the works that eventually come to be attributed to him.

38. Schopen remarks that "between the end of the Kuṣān Period and the middle of the Gupta Period, the people involved in the Mathurān Buddhist community and the patterns of patronage changed—as they did in almost all Buddhist communities in India—in some profound ways. The changes at Mathurā were manifested—as they were elsewhere—by the appearance of Avalokiteśvara as a cult figure, by a decided drop in the number of lay donors—particularly women—and a corresponding rise in monk donors" (1987b, 120).

39. These two phases are reflected, for example, in two of the most important types of Mahāyāna literature, namely, the Prajñāpāramitā and the Madhyamaka works attributed to Nāgārjuna. It is common knowledge that there is a close filiation between these two kinds of texts (Robinson 1967, 61). Robinson, however, has shown the marked differences in style, format, and content between the earlier Prajñāpāramitā (e.g., *Asp*) and Nāgārjuna's most important work, the *Mūlamadhyamakakārikā*. Such differences are not at all surprising once one recognizes that these two bodies of literature are indicative of very different times, places, and, most important, religious contexts (1967, 61–65)—*Asp* reflecting a primarily nonmonastic context, the Madhyamaka works a monastic one.

40. Schopen 1979, 1 and 1987b, 99. Schopen, after remarking that at Mathurā the

Mahāyāna had not achieved complete independence as late as the second quarter of the fifth century C.E., continues,

> That a new "movement" should look like this in the beginning is not very surprising. What is a little more surprising is the fact that—epigraphically—the "beginning" of the Mahāyāna in India is not documentable until the 2nd century AD, and that even as "late" as that it was still an extremely limited minority movement that left almost no mark on Buddhist epigraphy or art. . . . What is even more surprising still is the additional fact that even after its initial appearance in the public domain in the 2nd century it appears to have remained an extremely limited minority movement—if it remained at all—that attracted absolutely no *documented* public or popular support for at least two more centuries. It is again a demonstrable fact that anything even approaching popular support for the Mahāyāna cannot be documented until the 4th/5th century AD, and even then the support is overwhelmingly by monastic, not lay donors. In fact, prior to our inscription from Govindnagar there was simply no epigraphic evidence for the "early" Mahāyāna at all. This, in the end, is the real significance of the Govindnagar inscription when seen in its proper context: it establishes the presence of the very beginnings of "the Mahāyāna" as a public movement in the 2nd century AD and indicates, by its total isolation and lack of influence, the tenuous, hesitant, and faltering character of those "beginnings." . . . [This] suggests that, although there was—as we know from Chinese translations—a large and early Mahāyāna literature, there was no early organized, independent, publically supported movement that it could have belonged to. (1987b, 124–25)

Schopen's comments, as he notes, apply to the Mahāyāna as a exoteric, public, and popular movement.

41. Cf. *Csp* 8–17 (Rb., 27–32).

42. These various trends are not, of course, necessarily mutually exclusive.

43. Cf., e.g., Hirakawa 1963 and Wayman 1978, 1ff.

44. Wayman and Wayman believe that the *tathāgatagarbha* theory and stūpa worship may be the theoretical and practical dimensions, respectively, of the same religious orientation. In this regard, the Waymans have formulated the interesting hypothesis that the *Śrīmālādevīsiṃhanāda Sūtra,* with its emphasis on *tathāgatagarbha,* was first composed by a group engaging in the cult of the stūpa out of the felt need to provide theological justifications for what they were doing (1974, 8; see also Wayman 1978, 42). The Waymans further argue that, although the text itself may be quite late relative to the Nikāya texts, the Buddhism practiced by the group behind the *Śrīmālādevīsiṃhanāda Sūtra* may have been much earlier (1974, 8). The Waymans do not connect the need for such theological justifications with criticisms made by Nikāya sects, but the sharp polemics of the *Sds* make this more than a little likely. The Waymans' logic, that certain Mahāyāna texts appear much later than the origins of the Buddhism they reflect, may very well apply, mutatis mutandis, to the appearance of other seminal Mahāyāna *sūtras*.

45. See the suggestive remarks of Schuster 1985, 50–52.

46. The reader is reminded that here, as elsewhere in this study, the term *cult* refers not to the purely popular phenomenon of worship of an external object of devotion but rather to that grouping of religious beliefs and activities that includes *both* emulation and adoration, both yogic assimilation to the person of the saint and worship of him or her as external to oneself, as two generally inseparable components of a larger religious complex.

47. As Mus saw half a century ago in his *Borobuḍur* (1:252ff.). See also Williams 1989, 25.

48. This latter quotation represents Migot's preferred position. Migot awkwardly and unconvincingly attempts to locate this "original Buddhism" within the monastic sects: "Within each sect, certain of the faithful retained the ancient spirit of Buddhism" (1983, 229). Other scholars similarly believe that the original ideas of the Mahāyāna reach back

to earliest Buddhism. Conze, for example, mentions the occurrence of the term *śūnyatā* in the scriptures of the Sthaviras and then remarks, "There was, in fact, in these circles some resistance to just those utterances of the Tathāgata which were . . . 'connected with the Void' and it is not impossible that the Mahāyāna in this respect preserved the original teaching more faithfully than the Sthaviras" (1962b, 59). Rahula similarly expresses the view that the Mahāyāna developed out of ideas that are already in evidence in the Pāli canon (1962, 40). Neither scholar, however, suggests the precise mechanism by which such ideas could have been preserved and transmitted.

49. This summary epitomizes what the forest-oriented texts discussed in this study have to say on this subject. For a survey of other texts also addressing this issue, see Lamotte 1958, 211–22.

50. The fact that certain *bhikṣus* who belong to the Śrāvakayāna approximate the ideal of the forest renunciant and yet follow the *prātimokṣa* is quite interesting. It will be recalled that the *prātimokṣa*—in its content, its ritual usage, and its context of the *vinaya*—is linked with the development of the settled monastery. Yet these individuals are sometimes shown in the texts considered above (the minor *Rāṣṭrapāla Sūtra* is an example) without any evident monastic ties. The fact that such forest renunciants follow this code suggests the possibility that they, or at least the forest traditions they follow, were at some point under the aegis of settled monasticism. This further implies the possibility of a process the reverse of monasticization by which monastics move from a monastic way of life to that of the forest, yet retain certain features of their previous monastic identities.

51. *Rgs,* it will be recalled, also talks about a future time when the dharma will be under attack and will suffer diminution. Its explanations for the reason for this decline are less explicit than those given in *Ta, Rps,* and *Rps*-m, but *Rgs* nevertheless echoes many themes present in those texts. Thus, we learn in chapter 11 of a future time when, as a result of Māra's evil activities, the genuine dharma will decline. The *prajñāpāramitā* is the ultimate dharma of the buddhas and, in this latter time, will be under attack from Māra. In that time renunciants will desire honor *(satkāra)* and gain *(lābha)* and will be dependent *(sāpekṣa)* upon close ties with high-caste families (*kulasaṃstava*) (11.6). They will reject the genuine dharma and will act in an antidharmic *(adharma)* way (11.6). At this time of many obstacles, many *bhikṣus* will be confused and will not preserve *(na dhārayanti)* the *prajñāpāramitā* (11.8). In this time, people will reject the genuine dharma and will settle for an inferior version. Like one who turns away from the root of a tree, preferring the branches, like one who has the entire elephant but prefers the foot, they will reject the true dharma of the *prajñāpāramitā* and will turn to the *sūtras* (of the disciples) (11.4). Thus, bodhisattvas will seek for the enlightenment of arhants, just as one who has got the best food would seek for inferior food (11.5). Inspiration will arise but will then disappear without benefiting the world (11.2). Doubts as to one's own spiritual lineage will arise and cause beings to turn away from the teachings (11.3). People will at first produce faith in the excellent dharma and wish to hear it, but when preaching is not forthcoming, they will go away devoid of joy and very sad (11.7). However, this will not necessarily be a time of complete despair, for although Māra will cause obstacles, the buddhas of the ten directions will be there to help (11.10).

52. Lamotte 1958, 210–22; Conze 1951, 114–16; Chappell 1980; Nattier 1988.

53. See, e.g., *Vcp* 76–77 (Conze 1958a, 30–31); *Asp* 57 (Conze 1973b, 121–22). Also see Nattier's useful résumé of references in the *Saddharmapuṇḍarīka Sūtra* (1988, 340–47).

54. In these schemes, *paṭipatti* means "practice," seeming to include both the practice of meditation and that of behavioral purity. The following quotation from the *Anāgatavaṃsa,* e.g., shows what is understood to fall within *paṭipatti:* "Being unable to practise

jhāna, insight, the Ways and the fruits, they will guard no more the four entire purities of moral habit'' (Conze 1954b, 47). As seen in this quotation, and in the schemes where meditation and behavioral purity are separate items, meditation has priority.

55. In the original French edition, Lamotte does not give the Sanskrit for these final two categories.

56. Perhaps here one of the *pratisaṃvid* (*BHSD* 370).

57. Lamotte, in the French original, fails to provide the Sanskrit of this member of the list but gives only ''l'agitation'' (1958, 213). In the English translation, however, the term is given (Lamotte 1988, 195).

Conclusion: Toward a Threefold Model of Buddhism

This study has involved the identification and interpretation of various strands of evidence bearing upon the Buddhist saints. It has been noted that, when taken individually and considered from the viewpoints of texts and canons espousing different ideals, these strands may seem neither particularly coherent nor significant. However, when set alongside one another and considered within their own frames of reference, they exhibit a striking coherence and begin to tell an engrossing story, one with implications for the understanding of Indian Buddhist history at every level. It is hoped that the foregoing has, at the least, pointed to the importance of the Buddhist saints as specific objects of research. The saints represent a still largely unexplored field of evidence; this study will have been worthwhile if, in both what it has been able to accomplish and what it has not, it stimulates others to carry out further research into this area. As the process of bringing forward and interpreting the evidence of the Buddhist saints goes on, one may anticipate that it will increasingly challenge, energize, and revitalize our understanding of Indian Buddhism.

One particularly important area of needed research that I would like to single out concerns the question of the continuity of forest Buddhism from early to modern times. The evidence cited in this study reveals the existence of forest Buddhism in the formative history of both Nikāya and Mahāyāna traditions. It is also clear that forest Buddhism has existed and played a significant role in Buddhism in subsequent history right down to the present day, in both the Theravāda and Mahāyāna. This certainly raises the likelihood of a continuity of this genre of Buddhism from the early to the recent period, but of such an intervening history we know practically nothing. The filling in of this vast, trackless expanse of Indian and extra-Indian Buddhist history is surely one of the primary desiderata of contemporary and future Buddhist scholarship.

The preceding has made it clear that the two-tiered model is not adequate as an objective, scholarly model of Indian Buddhism as a whole. Strictly speaking, its validity does not extend beyond its ability to reflect certain dominant monastic ways of conceiving Buddhism within the Theravāda, both in some key classical texts and in the subsequent history of the Theravādin school, particularly after the victory of the Dhammakathika party in the first century B.C.E. At the same time, however, as we have also seen, tendencies toward the two-tiered model are already evident in the presectarian *Mahāparinirvāṇa Sūtra* and turn up in other Nikāya and Mahāyāna evidence. Another important future project for buddhological research will be to determine the precise extent to which the two-tiered model is a particular model of the Theravāda and the extent to which it is characteristic of Buddhist monasticism as such.

The particular inadequacy of the two-tiered model may be brought into focus by noting the interesting fact that, in ignoring the strains of Buddhism that crystallize around the forest renunciant, this hermeneutic asks monastic Buddhism to take on a variety of functions that it can perform only with difficulty. The monastic type of Buddhism is asked to be custodian of the elite practices of meditation and to bear responsibility for the actualization of the highest ideal of enlightenment, as well as to be the repository of Buddhist textual tradition and scholarship, the seat of morally pure (construed in terms of conventionally acceptable) behavior, and the chief renunciant actor in the worlds of economic, social, and political power, all at the same time. These meditative, active, individual, and institutional functions are essential elements of Indian Buddhism. However, in asking Buddhist monasticism to perform them all, the two-tiered model does not succeed in glorifying the Buddhist monastery and its inhabitants, but rather suggests the sheer implausibility of the ideal. This makes clear the need for another kind of model to describe the prime actors within Indian Buddhism and more accurately reflect the evidence as we have it.

Three Kinds of Actors in Buddhist History

This study has given priority to evidence of the Buddhist saints of the forest, which has led to an impression of Indian Buddhism that is shaped by the Buddhist saints and their understanding of the Buddha's dharma. Although the amplification of the forest voice has been the primary goal of this study, obviously the forest perspective, like that of the settled monastic, is only part of the picture that is Indian Buddhism. An accurate and satisfying understanding of Indian Buddhism must, in fact, be based not on any one voice or norm but rather on a balanced appreciation of the various centers of meaning within the tradition.

Such a model must differ from the two-tiered model by giving proper due to each of the three types of Buddhists discussed in this study: forest renunciant, settled monastic renunciant, and layperson. In addition, this model needs to differ from the two-tiered model in relying less on the conservative monastic evidence; instead, it must seek a description of these three types in a broad selection of texts and other evidence, including not only that which reflects a monastic viewpoint but also that which reflects yogic and lay contexts. Further, such a model must be less absolutistic and more descriptive. It should attempt not so much to evaluate as to describe the nature and functions of these three types of Buddhists and the Buddhism they practice, asking what may have been the particular role of each type within the overall structural and historical economy of the tradition as a whole. Such a description will lead to a more interactional picture of Buddhism: the tradition will then be seen to consist of a series of relationships of different individuals and communities, representing different and nonstatic views and methodologies, rather than as a unilinear tradition defined by a fixed and monolithic norm. Instead of a two-tiered model, a threefold model of Buddhism would provide a useful tool to illuminate not only the Buddhist past but also its present.[1]

Settled monasticism constitutes the face that renunciant Buddhism most often shows to society at large. It is clear from the image of the monastic style—not only in the *Mahāparinirvāṇa Sūtra,* the larger *vinaya,* and the *Milindapañha* but also in less monastically oriented texts such as the *Divyāvadāna*—that in the monastery Indian Buddhism provides laypeople with an ongoing, stable, reliable, conventionally respected institution with which they may enter into regularized relations. Donations may be given and merit reliably earned. Families may see their offspring take up the life of the monastic and have some confidence in their material well-being and respectability. The laity may additionally look to the monastery for the fulfillment of various other socially important functions such as education, counseling, and caring for the sick. Through all of this, the laity have a dependable recipient of their generosity through which they may earn merit, address their spiritual longings, and allay their anxieties about the future in this life and those to come. Through the *prātimokṣa,* Buddhism expresses its willingness to support the concerns of society at large for socially esteemed behavior. Moreover, this willingness does not lack integrity, for—as noted—behavioral purity and its expression in the *prātimokṣa* are understood by settled monastics as central to their spiritual lives. This meeting between Buddhist monasticism and its socioreligious context, then, enables monastics to demonstrate, in language that can be understood by society, the reliability and worthiness of their tradition.

Similarly, through textual scholarship, monastics assure the laity of the legitimacy of their spiritual understanding, preserve the traditional texts, and make important contributions to the doctrinal integrity and public articulation of Buddhism. Monastics teach the laity and defend Buddhism against ''heretics.'' In addition, they make alliances with the powers that be, ensuring the institutional continuation of Buddhism. And they provide a training ground for the next generation not only of Buddhist monastics but also, in many contexts, of forest renunciants, many of whom come from the ranks of monastics.

However—as seen in the images of monastic life presented in the *Theragāthā* and *Therīgāthā,* the *Vimuttimagga,* the *Divyāvadāna,* some of the early Mahāyāna *sūtra*s, and more strictly monastically oriented works such as the *Visuddhimagga,* but also in anthropological data on the function of monasteries in modern times—monastics, as such and within their settled monastic lifestyle, are not normally engaged in the retreatant way of the forest renunciant; they are thus not normally in a position either to practice intensive meditation or, through that, to actualize the highest goal of the tradition, enlightenment. For this actualization, monastics must rely on the forest renunciant. It is this latter who, as we have seen, through meditation and realization, makes the ultimate goal of Buddhism actual. The forest renunciant is free from the degree and kind of obligations to convention that bind the monastic but is under another kind of perhaps more rigorous obligation, namely, to follow the Buddhist path to its final conclusion. This function, though far more limited in scope than the functions of the monastic, is ultimately what maintains the integrity of Buddhism as a tradition.[2] Without people who are understood to strive directly for and actually attain the goal of enlightenment, the entire Buddhist enterprise must become suspect. The monastic also relies on the forest renunciant in a way that is more individual and personal. As we have seen, monastics may look to the forest renunciants as teachers because monastics, although with access to textual learning, may feel the need to develop meditational understanding. Some monastics will desire to attain full realization and take the further step of leaving the monastery and entering the forest way of life under a competent master.

The laity are in constant interaction with both monastic and forest renunciant, and their interactions are different in each case. The laity make donations to the town-and-village monastic and stand to receive much in return, not only in terms of generosity demonstrated, honor won, and merit earned, but also in the way of counsel, guidance, and instruction for living. The donations are sometimes to individual monastics but are also often to monastics as a group or to the monastic institution. Individual monastics may have specific patrons; monastics may have certain laypeople to whom they consistently go for donations or who may regularly bring food to the monastery or provide other assistance; and the monastery also has its wealthy donors, who may be counted on for donations against the upkeep and improvement of the monastery and in support of large festivals and celebrations. In all these interactions, as Weber and others have pointed out, regularization is the key. The laity know who the monastics are, where they live, and how they will behave, and the monastics are valued and relatively predictable components of the rationalized social and political framework within which the laity live and operate. In the monastics, the laity experience charisma, but in a more or less predictable and measured fashion.

The relation between the laity and the forest renunciants is in some ways quite different. The laity make donations to the forest renunciants also, but usually on the whole, these are more minimal. The giving of food, robes, or money on a grand scale is not typical. Besides material donations, the laity provide veneration in high degree. King Aśoka's example in the *Divyāvadāna* is instructive. Aśoka reveres the monastic Yaśas, to be sure, but he sees him also as a trusted friend and reliable ally. Of a different order is Aśoka's veneration of Piṇḍolabhāradvāja and Upagupta, whom the great king regards as virtual buddhas in the flesh.

What do the laity receive in return for their veneration of and donations to the saints? Of course, they receive merit; considering that in Buddhism exactly how much merit is gained by a donation depends at least partially on the sanctity of the recipient, in giving to the forest renunciants, the laity may hope to gain considerable merit indeed. As the hagiographic images we examined make clear, they also receive teachings and, for those desirous and deemed worthy, meditation instructions. Not fully separable from these benefits, the laity gain something else: in the forest saint, they may hope to meet an enlightened one face to face and to participate in the intensity of his or her enlightened charisma. As noted, gains won may include a glimpse of liberation or even, for the fortunate, some stage of liberation itself, as was true for early disciples who met the Buddha and heard but a few words from his mouth. No less is in question for Bimbisāra upon seeing the Buddha or for Aśoka in reference to Piṇḍola. The laity's access to the unbounded charisma of the saints is symbolized by the importance of blessings given by them and by the veneration of objects (stūpa, text, image, relics) that embody their charisma.

There are some things that the laity may *not* expect from the forest renunciants, and for this they are prepared by a fundamental assumption within Indian society—namely, that the greatest of saints are not bound by the wishes, conventions, or rules of the world. Because the renunciants wander about and reside in out-of-the-way places—from the laity's viewpoint—they are often remote and not easy to find. But in a sense, this retreatant mode only guarantees their authenticity and power and, hence, their value. Similarly, the laity may not expect from such people easy and regularized interactions. As we have seen, their relationship to convention, either social or religious, is uncertain, and they are quite ready to offer critiques of the foibles of both institutionalized religion and society. Such teachers are often depicted as powerful and unpredictable, and therefore as dangerous. However, these very characteristics testify that the forest saints embody the independence and numinous power of ultimate reality itself, and this in turn further enhances their charisma. It is ironic that the very features in which forest renunciants differ most markedly from settled monastics, and which make the laity wary, are those that attract laypeople and doubtless monastics as well.

We have already seen how monastics and laypeople are involved in a complex web of interdependence: monastics rely on laypeople and forest renunciants, while laypeople similarly rely on monastics and forest renunciants. Although in the *Vimuttimagga* the independence and "freedom from ties" of the forest renunciant is a central theme, it is no less true that, in their own way, forest renunciants rely in some crucial ways upon laypeople and monastics. Forest renunciants typically depend upon the laity for material sustenance. They may beg food from door to door, neither avoiding some families nor cultivating others, with the aim that independence from any given family be retained. Nevertheless, the forest renunciants remain in a kind of general debt to the laity as such, a debt that is defined from one side by the laity's suffering, generosity, and spiritual need and, from the other, by the buddhas and other saints, whose examples and explicit teachings make mandatory the service of others, however that may be conceived. What is important is that the situation of the laity's donation, a source of the forest renunciants' indebtedness, also provides the occasion for their discharging of it through the transmission of their charisma to the laity and through teaching and counseling them at the time of receiving alms.

The forest renunciants are also dependent upon the monastics in some interesting ways. For example, in the "forest" chapter of the *Śikṣāsamuccaya,* it is remarked that the bodhisattva of the forest may come to the town or village in order to listen to the recitation of texts and their exposition. This implies that forest-renunciant traditions could view the textual preoccupations of town-and-village monastics not only as legitimately Buddhist from the monastic viewpoint, but also as contributing in a positive way to their own spiritual path.

The forest renunciant is dependent upon the monastic in another way. The early Buddhist texts make clear that, from the beginning of Buddhism, the laity have desired and have even demanded a certain regularity in their relations with renunciant Buddhism. It is primarily the monastic community that has responded to this demand for regularization. Without this particular kind of regularization, instead of spreading far and wide for the good of the many, Buddhism might have suffered an early demise from the Indian scene, like most of the other *śramaṇa* sects of the sixth century B.C.E. Buddhism could not then have gained success in greater Asia. Be this as it may, because monastic Buddhism broadly responds to this need for regularization, the forest renunciants are free to follow their own paths of relative solitude and independence.

It is worth underlining the point that the model of Buddhism described here is better termed a *threefold* rather than a *three-tiered* model, because the first term has fewer hierarchical connotations. It is true that, from one point of view, the forest renunciants do indeed stand at the top of a hierarchy of three types, both in their approximation of the original normative Buddhist ideal, exemplified in the Buddha himself, and subsequently in the degree of their fidelity to the ultimate value of enlightenment. However, an appreciation of this ascendency must be balanced by a recognition that in individual cases either a monastic or a lay lifestyle may be more conducive to enlightenment. Upagupta's training of his own disciples gives ample expression to this view. Other lines of interpretation we have not explored, particularly those preserved in East Asian Pure Land Buddhism and the Vajrayāna, sometimes find in lay life unequaled possibilities for enlightenment. In addition, even an affirmation of the generally superior spiritual efficacy of the forest life is quite different from saying that individuals who pursue the way of forest renunciation are necessarily more realized than those following the monastic or lay forms of Buddhism. As has been suggested, forest saints may "return to the world" in various ways. Conversely, although the *type* of the forest renunciant may generally occupy the ascendant position, *individuals* who attempt to adhere to that type may not. Not only may saints be found in monasteries and lay life, but—obviously—rogues may be found in the forest. A three-tiered model, with forest renunciants at the top, might suggest that individuals attain value based on their place within the scheme rather than that the scheme attains its value based on what individuals reflecting one or another place in the scheme actually accomplish. It is realized people who are of supreme value rather than the particular lifestyles by which they become realized or in which, once realized, they are found. Any model of Buddhist types must remain to some extent relative and open, for no one can ever know how much, from a spiritual viewpoint, any individual can or will attain in one situation as opposed to another.

Some Dynamics of the Threefold Model

Thus, within the overall economy of Buddhism, each of the three types of Buddhist actors performs characteristic functions for the tradition as a whole. For example, in the institution of the monastery, with its loyal laity, Buddhism fulfills its needs for conservative trends. The monastery, because of its particular variety of Buddhism and its characteristic preoccupations, tends to retain those forms that have been received and tends to be slow to change. Similarly, owing to its proximity to and dependence on the social, economic, and political establishments in its culture, the monastery—although assuredly providing an alternative and a challenge—has often also tended to accept and reinforce the status quo of its context.

By contrast, forest renunciants, with their faithful laity, owing to their relatively lesser institutionalization and their meditative focus, can better tolerate and even encourage innovation and nonconformity. When new developments occur within Buddhism, they often come from the solitary and remote locales of forest renunciants. This certainly seems to have been the case with many of the grand developments within Indian Buddhism (the rise of Buddhism itself, the early Mahāyāna, the Vajrayāna). Forest renunciants live on the periphery of the Buddhist establishment, but it is precisely this position that enables them to see the shortcomings of the establishment, to mount critiques, to have the spiritual authority to make those critiques stick, and to give birth to new developments. In economic, social, and political matters, the forest renunciant often tends—and in earlier times, as we noted, and more recently, as Tambiah points out—to look with a sympathetic eye on the neglected, the poor, and the downtrodden and to become a rallying point for their aspirations (Tambiah 1984, 72–77, 293–320).

Identification of the type of the forest saint also provides a reference point for viewing some large patterns of Indian Buddhist history. Conze, in a modern rendering of the "decline of the dharma" theory (1980, 11–16), suggests that Indian Buddhist history—not only in Buddhist theory but in historiographic fact—seems to unfold according to a pattern of five-hundred-year cycles. According to Conze, each cycle, starting with the birth of Indian Buddhism itself, begins with genuine spirituality and ends in institutionalization, intellectualization, and rigidification, a decline that calls for a new beginning. In the present context, it may be suggested that the cycles identified by Conze most often attest to a movement initially from the forest into the world and then subsequently back again into the forest. The Buddha himself was a forest meditator who strove for realization. Once he attained realization, so we are told, he wavered between withdrawing permanently into the forest and returning to the world to teach others. Moved by compassion, he chose the latter course and so set the standard for the tradition. Similarly, earliest Buddhism was, at its core, a tradition of forest renunciation. Yet, drawing on the inspiration provided by the Buddha's example, it could increasingly develop a town-and-village wing, which eventually became classical monasticism.

Thus, in Buddhism, the realization of the forest saints expresses itself in compassionate action, and this expression leads to renewed contact and interaction between the saint and the world. Worldly people recognize the saint's wisdom, compassion, and power and would benefit from them. And the saint is moved by compassion to benefit others with what he or she has found. From the worldly viewpoint, the results of this energetic movement back in the direction of the world are seen as positive and beneficial, including as it does the creation of institutions to contain and mediate the Buddha's charisma; the presence of monastics, who provide accessible and reliable if tempered embodiments of the Buddha's charisma; the scholastic refinement and articulation of Buddhist doctrine; and so on. But from another viewpoint, that of the primacy of realization itself, this development is ambiguous and fraught with danger, for it opens the way to a deterioration of Buddhist values, wherein the traditions of the saints fall prey to worldly concerns. When the return to the world leads to positive results, the saints must view their work in the world in a positive light. When this ceases to be the case—and the texts analyzed in this study express the view that this has not infrequently occurred—then a return to the forest, in its deepest meanings, is called for.

In the preceding pages, this kind of return to the forest has been mentioned several times. Buddhism itself first developed, at least partially, as a response to the predominance of external values in Brahmanism and a perceived lack of genuine realization. In time, Buddhism became monasticized, provoking a reaction from within Nikāya Buddhism of saints such as Pārāpariya and Phussa, as well as those behind the *Aṭṭhakavagga* of the *Suttanipāta* and other forest texts, who see the values of the forest as the only answer to this degradation. The rise of the early Mahāyāna as seen in the *Rāṣṭrapālaparipṛcchā Sūtra,* represents another response to this decline. Other texts, such as the *Saṃdhinirmocana Sūtra* and the *Laṅkāvatāra Sūtra,* similarly see the forest and its contemplative life as a corrective for the pretension and scholasticism of more worldly Buddhist renunciants. When, in time, the Mahāyāna became predominantly a conventional monastic tradition, another reaction occurred with the historical appearance of the Vajrayāna, particularly of the eighty-four siddhas. In time, certain Vajrayāna traditions also became monasticized, leading to yet other returns to the forest. Conze's notion that Indian Buddhism unfolds according to five-hundred-year cycles may be oversimplified, but it has the virtue of pointing to some important dynamics in the history of the Indian dharma.

It may also be pointed out that within the overall economy of Buddhism, each of the three types of Buddhism to some important extent relies upon the existence of the others and needs the others to maintain its full integrity. This fact can be highlighted if we try to imagine Buddhism without one of these three types. Without the layperson, renunciant Buddhism of both monastic and *yogin* would have neither a basis for the donations needed for support in the present nor a source of new recruits to the Buddhist renunciant life needed to carry on in the future. Fresh recruits also possess immediate psychological connection to the cultural world within which the renunciants live, with all its problems, developments, and concerns. Without this grounding, the renunciant life would quickly become inarticulate and irrelevant. Without the monastery, Buddhism would lack an institutional side, with all that this has historically provided to the tradition. It would lack a middle ground between the laity and the arduous forest life, and it would not have the institutional foundation necessary to an ongoing textual tradition. Lacking a strong textual tradition, it would tend toward doctrinal diffusion and loss of identity and would lose much of its basis for engaging the larger culture in its many facets. Without the forest renunciant, Buddhism would not have those who carry through and validate its highest ideals and who are in a position to carry out reformations in the tradition based on the unquestionable authority of that attainment.

Each of these types makes its characteristic contribution to the economy of the whole, and each also has its characteristic limitations and weaknesses. Thus, in certain situations, monastic Buddhism can veer in the direction of a dry and rigid scholasticism, a concern for decorous behavior for its own sake, or social, political, or economic opportunism. The forest-renunciant tradition can retreat into the jungle and remain the concern of a tiny, esoteric group of initiates, without immediate benefit to the larger world. Lay Buddhism can become an uninformed affirmation of the status quo rather than a religion that is willing to put the status quo in question. It is interesting that these characteristic weaknesses of each type of Buddhism appear to emerge historially precisely when one or another of the types becomes disconnected from one or both of the other two. It appears to be the monastery and the laity that pull the *yogin*s out of the forest and enable their realizations to become available for the larger good. The existence of the forest tradition and the monastery reveal the limitations of lay life and the need for genuine renunciation. And the forest tradition reveals to settled monasticism that monastic life is in fact a middle ground between lay life and the radical renunciation of the forest—rather than the be-all and end-all of Buddhism, in and of itself.

Buddhist history may be said to put forward a norm for itself: namely, that of an organism that encompasses all three of these ideals, including the characteristic contributions of each to the development and identity of the tradition as a whole. Measured by this norm, each type of Buddhism tends to go wrong when it gets into a situation of isolation and loses sight of itself within a three-way conversation in which the other two are integral partners. Such isolation tends to lead to the solidification and absolutization of the isolated tradition. The threefold model emphasizes both the unique contributions of each type as well as its interdependence with the others. There is a subtle chemistry here, and no type of Buddhism—whatever tensions it may feel with the others—would be the same without them. Seen from this viewpoint, the threefold model defines Buddhism in terms of a series of relationships, and it is the integrity of these *relationships,* rather than one or another of the individual types of Buddhism, that—it may be suggested—becomes normative for Buddhism.

In judging the extent to which each of these three foci of Buddhist life, and the traditions deriving from them, remained faithful to the teachings of the founder (the Buddha, earliest Buddhism, pre-canonical Buddhism, as one may prefer), the question is not whether each fulfilled, in a self-sufficient way, the entire challenge of early Buddhism. As we have seen, given the historical nature of Buddhism, such an expectation would be unreasonable. The question becomes, rather, whether each fulfilled a particular role within the economy of the whole. Did it see itself as coparticipant in the larger enterprise, an enterprise that included forest renunciants, monastic renunciants, and the laity? Did each realistically assess its own inherent strengths and limitations within this largest context? Did each continue to acknowledge the value of the role played by the other two ideals? And did it continue to admit its own dependence on the inspiration and activities of the other two? These questions—which also articulate unreasonable expections—may be rephrased into one simple and revealing question: how did each type of Buddhism understand itself and view the other types? The answers that different historical traditions give to this question become a useful litmus paper for disclosing some of the subtle dynamics of Buddhist history.

In this study a model has been proposed defining the major type and subtypes of the Buddhist saint, each with a particular lifestyle and religious context, and each with characteristic roles and functions within the whole. This is, of course, more or less of an abstraction, for the history of a religion such as Buddhism is immeasurably subtle and complex. This means that the ideal paradigm can function as no more than a starting point in understanding a concrete example of a type of saint or individual saint, as revealed in the evidence. Given the specificity and uniqueness of each historical situation, the model will always need to be corrected for each one. It will be rare to find in any given case the "pure type" as defined here. In this section, by way of summary, let us review the issue of the application of the model to historical situations and some of the more important issues involved in that application.

The paradigm, with its major type and subtypes, purports to shed light on the appearance of Buddhist saints in the documents. However, concrete examples are typically complex and not infrequently appear to run counter to type. In examining the various types of saints—particularly those of arhant, pratyekabuddha, and bodhisattva—we have seen that the evidence presents various contradictions. For example, arhants are defined in the different texts in various ways, some of which appear to accord with the basic paradigm, others of which do not: sometimes arhants live in the forest, sometimes in the monastery; sometimes they are textually learned, other times they are altogether ignorant in such matters; even more, sometimes they are realized saints, sometimes they are not; and so on. The same kinds of contradictions are evident among various documents depicting both the pratyekabuddhas and the bodhisattvas. Such complexities, it was argued, can often be best understood as reflecting something other than that Indian Buddhists have no coherent idea of the nature of the saint. Rather, the kinds of ambiguities found in the texts with regard to saintly types attest to the fact that Indian Buddhism retains certain basic preconceptions concerning Buddhist saints; that these in turn provoke various kinds of responses and reactions as Indian Buddhism develops; and that these affect the evidence in various ways, causing various discrepancies.

The same kinds of dynamics as are found among the *types* of Buddhist saints are also operative in the cases of the individual saints Mahākāśyapa, Upagupta, Śāriputra, Piṇḍolabhāradvāja, and Devadatta. There appeared to be certain kinds of ambiguities and contradictions in the textual evidence of each of these saints: although some elements clearly approximate the model of the Buddhist saint, others are far more complex. For example, Mahākāśyapa is both creator and guarantor of the establishment as well as the outsider and implicit critic; Upagupta and Piṇḍolabhāradvāja are depicted as great saints and also receive blame and censure for manifesting their sainthood; Śāriputra is the prototype of the ideal monastic yet possesses forest credentials; and Devadatta is at once saint and criminal. As with the saintly types, so with the individual saints, the ambiguities, tensions, and contradictions are often best explained as functions of history: the personalities of these saints develop, typically reflecting in their hagiographies the course of the temporal unfolding of Buddhism. The ambiguities, discrepancies, and contradictions found in most of the examples of both types and individual examples of Buddhist saints begin to show how complex Indian Buddhist history can be, and how an accurate understanding of each saintly type and each individual saint requires that full account be taken of historical individuality. In these instances, there seems to be a typical pattern, wherein an originally relatively clear manifestation of a forest-saintly type or individual forest saint becomes increasingly complex and ambiguous in the course of Buddhist history, particularly when the values and orientations of settled monasticism become part of the picture.

This study has generally referred to forest Buddhism and settled monasticism as relatively fixed categories, with Buddhist saints assigned to the forest and monastics and settled monasticism acting as their foils. At the same time, we have seen that the categories of forest and monastery can take on different connotations in different contexts. In relation to the notion of the forest, some texts identify the literal forest with normative Buddhism—for example, in the interpretations of Pārāpariya and Phussa and the two *Rāṣṭrapāla Sūtra*s. Other texts, particularly those in the Mahāyāna, such as the *Ratnaguṇa,* while accepting the forest venue of the saint, argue for a more subtle understanding of this locale, seeing it as most fundamentally a state of mind rather than a specific geographical place. This interpretation allows for the notion of a saint who does not live in the forest at all—namely, the lay bodhisattva. This tendency becomes pronounced in the siddhas of the Vajrayāna: some siddhas accomplish their renunciation and their meditative practice strictly in the context of lay life.

The abstract notion of monasticism also invariably needs to be adjusted to capture accurately its different connotations in specific contexts. Of particular importance, as we have seen, is the fact that monastic attitudes toward and relations with forest renunciants may vary considerably from one tradition to another. The Theravādin monastic evidence, developing further certain attitudes and interpretations already evident in the presectarian *vinaya,* exhibits a relatively consistent downplaying of the Buddhist saints and of phenomena connected with them. Examples of this tendency discussed above include the emphasis on the urban personality of the Buddha in the Pāli sources; the diminution in the Theravādin *vinaya* of the saintly charisma of Mahākāśyapa; the *Lokapaññatti*'s criticism of Upagupta for his failure to fulfill monastic ideals; the ascendency to paradigmatic status in the Theravāda of Śāriputra as the embodiment of monastic values; the particular criticisms leveled at Piṇḍolabhāradvāja in the Pāli *vinaya* and commentaries; the special vilification of the forest saint Devadatta in the Theravāda and other early Sthavira-derived schools; and the particular limitations placed by the Theravāda on the magical power and cult of the pratyekabuddha. This same tendency to downplay the forest saints is also reflected in the Theravādin reservations about magical power in general, its lack of interest in and clear ambivalence toward the *dhutaguṇa*s, and the absence of rules for monastic stūpa worship in its *vinaya.* The fact that this interpretive line is a characteristic of mainline Theravādin monasticism but not of the Theravāda in general is revealed, as we have seen, in the positive images of forest Buddhism and its saints found in the *Suttanipāta, Theragāthā,* and other forest texts of the *Khuddakanikāya,* images that seem to be carried forward into the forest Buddhism of the modern Theravāda. The particular character of the Pāli monastic evidence is thrown into bold relief when considered in relation to that of another tradition deriving from the Sthavira branch—namely, the Sarvāstivāda, which shows, in relation to many of the examples just cited, a more positive if still sometimes ambivalent evaluation of forest Buddhism and its saints.

As noted, the Pāli evidence, taken as a whole, reveals a state of considerable polarization and even alienation in the relations of forest Buddhism and settled monasticism. This is seen from the monastic side in the examples just cited. It is also clear in the Pāli forest evidence. The same kind of polarization is found in the *Rāṣṭrapāla Sūtra*s. The *Laṅkāvatāra Sūtra* takes a less extreme view, admitting that although scholastic Buddhism is a markedly lower path than that of meditation, it was still taught by the Buddha, thereby lending it a certain legitimacy. The Northern traditions surrounding Mahākāśyapa and Upagupta present an even more conciliatory view of the attitudes of settled monasticism toward the forest and its saints. It will be recalled that, for the Sarvāstivāda, the Buddha's lineage holder and founder of the church is the forest saint par excellence, Mahākāśyapa, whereas the later forest saint Upagupta is presented as having cooperative and amicable relations with settled monasteries and with monastics. These examples reveal some of the limitations of the threefold model but, at the same time, reveal its utility: it is the model itself that has enabled us to see more clearly and with more subtlety dynamics such as these that are operative in the various traditions.

Further study of the evidence of Indian Buddhism would, in addition, reveal that there are frequent exceptions to the types as defined above. In illustration, it may be mentioned that in Buddhist history one finds forest-renunciant traditions that share many features of the monastery, as a type defined here, as well as settled monastic traditions that contain features more typical of forest renunciation. One also finds individuals within the different types of institutions who depart from their type: forest renunciants who spend time in monasteries, monastics who are unconventional, forest renunciants or laypeople who are learned, laypeople or monastics who meditate, and so on. And finally, of course, room must always be made for the exceptional individual in each context: in addition to forest renunciants who are enlightened, realized saints may also be found in the monastery or among the laity.[3] Such exceptions reveal the care that needs to be exercised in the definition and understanding of the Buddhist saints. At the same time, these exceptions also show the way in which the threefold model of Buddhism can throw into relief nonconforming patterns and sensitize us to their dynamics.

It is also worth noting that even the basic types of *yogin,* monastic, and layperson do not remain entirely stable. In general, the later the time period, the more complexity involved in the Buddhist situation and the more subtlety required in its interpretation. In particular, the fact that all three kinds of Buddhism have interacted in some way with one another throughout most of Indian Buddhist history has meant that each has influenced and changed the others. What is Buddhist monasticism in early Buddhism is not Buddhist monasticism in its most successful Nikāya manifestations, and this in turn differs from what it is in Mahāyāna Buddhism or in the Vajrayāna. When the Mahāyāna became monasticized, for example, it retained the particular early Mahāyāna flavor of the forest in its doctrinal emphasis on the nonsubstantiality of language (Prajñāpāramitā and Madhyamaka), its valorization of the spiritual potential of lay life and of women (in the bodhisattva ideal), and its ethics based on universal compassion. Similarly, the forest renunciants in Theravāda Buddhism manifest particular and distinctive types that emerge from the peculiarities of Theravādin history. For example, in contemporary times, Theravādin saints of the forest are known as those who fulfill the monastic *vinaya* (Tambiah 1984, 101).

The historical interactions of the three principal actors on the stage of Buddhist history have also given rise to various hybrid types. For example, at least after the Indian Vajrayāna underwent some limited monasticization, in the eighth century and after, settled monasticism as a type tended to develop forms that approximate all three types of Buddhism in the threefold model. Among many examples, there is evidence in India of established forest monasteries where forest renunciants lived (for example, Marpa's hermitage at Phullahari)[4] and of monasteries of married monastics. In reference to these latter, Tāranātha tells us that this tradition developed in India, where a monastic might be married and work the fields to make a living, yet be considered a *bhikṣu* at the same time (*Kbdd,*438).

These Indian prototypes have considerable importance for forms developed in extra-Indian Buddhism. Tibetan Buddhism may be taken as an apt example. Indian usages undoubtedly stand in the background of Tibetan tradition, where one finds, in effect and in spite of many overlappings, three distinguishable types of monastic tradition. The first are those that tend to approximate the values and orientations of the classical Indian Buddhist monastic model. It has been the special genius of the Gelugpa sect to train monastic scholars in the scholastic traditions of Buddhism. Also, in keeping with the emphasis of the Indian master Atīśa and the Kadampa tradition out of which they arise, the Gelugpas take special pride in the *prātimokṣa* and its proper fulfillment. The second are the monastic traditions that, in some real sense, act as a kind of frame for earlier forest traditions. The Kagyupa, for example, define their own tradition as a merging of the forest tradition of the Tantric siddhas with the classical Indian monastic model.

This merging is symbolically depicted in the well-known story of the meeting of Milarepa, the great saint who embodies the traditions of the Indian siddhas, and the Kadampa monastic Gampopa (*Mgb,* 618–58 [Cg., 2:463–97]). In this story, it is significant that Milarepa, the forest *yogin,* is the guru, whereas Gampopa becomes the disciple. Gampopa meets Milarepa, who in his inimitable Tantric style offers him a cup of wine, which the *vinaya*-abiding monastic is tempted to refuse. Feeling he is at a crossroads, the monk drinks, breaks the *vinaya,* and eventually becomes a chosen disciple of the saint and a lineage holder. Yet he does not renounce his monastic training or identity. From then on, the Kagyupas become a monastic order, but one in which meditation in caves and other retreat sites is the keynote. Although the Kagyus have their scholastic traditions, there is among them relatively less emphasis on scholarship. The ascetic codes have special prominence here, and the Kagyu saints are often known for their fulfillment of *dhutaguṇa*-like vows (Trungpa 1977, 59–68).

Other factors of forest Buddhism remain extremely important among the Kagyu, including the personal guru and the guru-disciple relationship, oral and secret teachings, and so on. Finally, in Tibet, among the Nyingmapa, or old school, one finds traditions of married monastics—in other words, monastics who may be attached to a monastery yet follow the lifestyle of the layperson, live outside the monastery, are married, and support themselves by their own labor. It must be added that within each tradition, dominant trends are balanced by countertrends. The Gelugpas have their charismatic forest saints, the Kagyupas their great scholars; and in the different traditions one may adopt a settled monastic or a forest lifestyle at different phases of one's career.

In both later Indian Buddhism and the Buddhism of Tibet, the layperson as a type also shows considerable variation. Thus, texts such as the *Vimalakīrtinirdeśa Sūtra* and traditions such as Pure Land and the Indian Vajrayāna provide examples of the laity as a kind of elite. In the latter case, one finds a hybrid type, the householder-*yogin,* who is a layperson but is privy to and practices the elite teachings of the Vajrayāna, sometimes in retreat but also sometimes within a specific lay context. Within Tibetan Buddhism, Marpa, "the translator," is one of the better-known examples of this phenomenon (Nālandā and Trungpa 1982). All of this suggests how complex the Buddhist picture becomes historically, but again a threefold model of Buddhism, such as the one proposed here, allows us to appreciate that complexity, even long after traditions representing the pure type have become rare.

These various forms are possible because, although it is the forest that typically produces saints, it cannot contain them. The bankruptcy of ordinary life in the world and in the monastery may lead certain individuals to the drastic step of withdrawing into the forest. But the dynamic of realization, with its imperative of compassion, compels an opposite movement in which the realized renunciant leaves the forest and returns to the arena of conventional life and activity. In Buddhism, saints can be found anywhere, and, ideally, their own freedom enables them to transform the institutions and situations with which they come into contact.

The threefold model of Buddhism suggested here, with its strengths and limitations as an explanatory device, represents a distinct improvement over the two-tiered model in helping us to understand not only forest renunciation and forest saints in India but Indian Buddhism itself. The advance marked by the threefold model may be thrown into relief by noting a striking irony in the interpretation of Indian Buddhism. Let us recall that according to the two-tiered model, authentic Buddhism is defined by the conservative monastic norm, with its emphasis on pure behavior, its preoccupation with textual learning, its preference for apophatic doctrine, its tendency to formal and explicit separation from its non-Buddhist environment, and so on. But in this study, it has been suggested that although Buddhism superficially seems to make the most radical departure from its non-Buddhist context in its monastic form, when seen at a deeper level, monasticization reflects just as much or more so a Brahmanization of earliest Buddhism. At the same time, according to the two-tiered model, the Buddhist saints embody a deviation from the authenticity of the monastic norm, a falling back to the type of the non-Buddhist renunciant. The argument as typically made runs that the forest renunciants have little or nothing to do with the monastery, are not most typically concerned with purity of behavior or with textual learning, do not tend toward the most extreme separation from their non-Buddhist environment, and are comfortable with kataphatic modes of expression, the adoration of the laity, cultic activities, and so on—that is, with "Hindu" forms. Yet in this study, it has been argued that this interpretation is overly superficial and that we must pay more attention to the deep structures and intentions of the Buddhist forest saints themselves, as reflected in the texts. In fact, as we have seen, the very evidence that is adduced as incriminating by the proponents of the two-tiered model of Buddhism may, when seen from a different angle, equally—perhaps even more forcefully and convincingly—make a case for just the opposite conclusion: that the forest saints embody the highest ideals of Indian Buddhism and represent a unique kind of Buddhist creativity, without an appreciation of which the origin and much of the dynamics of Buddhism in India cannot be adequately understood.

Notes

1. The works of contemporary anthropologists cited in this study, including Tambiah, Bunnag, Carrithers, Schober, and others, have all provided food for thought. Particularly helpful has been Tambiah, who, in his study of Buddhist forest saints in Thailand (1984), has already suggested, if not fully explicated, the kind of model proposed here. Thus in a section entitled "Paradigms," Tambiah presents two "schematic maps," identifying the major sources of institutionalized power, authority, and action within the Thai Buddhist context (1984, 72–77). In the first map, Tambiah describes a structure of triadic relations including political ruler, village/town-dwelling monastic *saṃgha,* and forest-dwelling monks (sects/fraternities). In the second, he describes a structure of pentadic relations including central political authority, town-and-village monk communities, forest-monk communities, and town-and-village laity. The present threefold model differs from Tambiah's in three respects: (1) its emphasis is on groups as embodiments of ideal types and on their interactions; (2) it identifies the primary types as forest renunciant, monastic, and layperson (with royalty as a subcategory of the laity); and (3) in Tambiah's model, the forest monk is an ordained monastic living in some communal setting, whereas for the threefold model the forest renunciant is not necessarily an ordained monastic and does not necessarily live in a community.

2. Maquet makes this point in relation to contemporary forest Buddhism in Sri Lanka (1980, 146).

3. See Keyes 1982 for an example.

4. Nālandā and Trungpa 1982.

BIBLIOGRAPHY

Texts

Abhidharmakośabhāṣyam of Vasubandhu. Ed. by Prahlad Pradhan. Tibetan-Sanskrit Works Series 8. Patna, 1975.

Amitāyurdhyāna Sūtra. See *Kuan wu liang shou fo ching*.

Aṅguttaranikāya. Ed. by R. Morris and E. Hardy (vols. 1–5) and M. Hunt (vol. 6, indexes). 6 vols. Rev. and ed. by C.A.F. Rhys Davids. London, 1885–1910.

The Apadāna of the Khuddaka Nikāya. Ed. by Mary E. Lilley. 2 vols. London, 1925–1927.

Aśokarāja Sūtra. Chin., *A yü wang ching*. T. 2043, 50:131b–170a.

Aśokarājāvadāna. Chin., *A yü wang chuan*. T. 2042, 50:99a–131a.

Aśokāvadāna. Ed. by Sujitkumar Mukhopadhyaya. New Delhi, 1963.

Aṣṭasāhasrikāprajñāpāramitā Sūtra, with Haribhadra's Commentary Called Āloka. Ed. by P. L. Vaidya. Buddhist Sanskrit Texts 4. Darbhanga, India, 1960.

Avadānaśataka. Ed. by J. S. Speyer. Bibliotheca Buddhica 3. 2 vols. Saint Petersburg, 1902–1909. Reprinted Indo-Iranian Reprints 3, The Hague, 1958; and P. L. Vaidya, ed., Buddhist Sanskrit Texts 19, Darbhanga, India, 1958. References are to the Indo-Iranian Reprints edition.

Avalokana Sūtra. As quoted in the *Sikṣāsamuccaya*.

Avalokita Sūtra. *Mahāvastu* 2:401–536.

Bodhicaryāvatāra. Ed. by P. L. Vaidya. Buddhist Sanskrit Texts 12. Darbhanga, India, 1960.

Bodhisattvabhūmi. Ed. by Nalinaksha Dutt. 2d ed. Patna, 1978.

Buddhacarita (partial). Ed. by E. H. Johnston. In Johnston (1936): 1–161.

Buddhacarita. Chin., *Fo so hsing tsan ching*. T. 192.

Buddhacarita (in Tib.). Ed. by Friedrich Weller. In Weller (1926–1928).

Buddhacarita. Tib., *sangs.rgyas.kyi.spyod.pa.shes.bya.ba'i.snyan.dngags.chen.po*. Pk., mdo. 'grel (skyes.rabs) (nge), 1–124b.

Caturaśītisiddhapravṛtti. Tib., *grub.thob.brgyad.cu.rtsa.bzhi'i.lo.rgyus*. Ed. by Sempa Dorje. In *The Biography of Eighty-Four Saints*. Sarnath, 1979, pp. 1–172.

Cūḷasuññata Sutta. *Majjhimanikāya* 3:104–9.

Cullaniddesa, Niddesa II. Ed. by W. Stede. London, 1918.

Cullavagga. Pāli *vinaya* 2:1–308.

Daśabhūmika Sūtra. Ed. by P. L. Vaidya (based on the edition of J. Rahder, Paris, 1926). Buddhist Sanskrit Texts 7. Darbhanga, India, 1967.

Daśabhūmivyākhyāna (Daśabhūmikasūtra Śāstra). See *Shih ti ching lun*.

Dhammapada. Ed. by S. Sumangala. London, 1914.

Dhammapada-aṭṭhakathā (*Dhammapada* commentary). Ed. by H. Smith and H. C. Norman (L. S. Tailang, indexes). 5 vols. London, 1905–1915.

Dharmasaṃgraha. Ed. by Kenjiu Kasawara, F. Max Müller, and H. Wenzel. Oxford, 1885. Reprint Amsterdam, 1972.
Dhutaguṇanirdeśa. Tib., *rnam.par.grol.ba'i.lam.las.sbyangs.pa'i.yon.tan.bstan.pa*. In Bapat (1964): 2–87.
Dīghanikāya. Ed. by T. W. Rhys Davids and J. E. Carpenter. 3 vols. London, 1890–1911.
Divyāvadāna. Ed. by E. B. Cowell and R. A. Neil. Cambridge, 1886.
Gilgit Buddhist Manuscripts. Ed. by R. Vira and L. Chandra. Satapiṭaka Series 10. New Delhi, 1966–1970.
Gilgit Manuscripts. Ed. by Nalinaksha Dutt. 9 vols. Srinagar and Calcutta, 1939–1959.
Isigili Sutta. *Majjhimanikāya* 3:68–71.
Itivuttaka. Ed. by Ernst Windisch. London, 1889.
Jātaka Together with Its Commentary. Ed. by V. Fausböll. 6 vols. London, 1877–1896.
Jātakamālā by Ārya-śūra. Ed. by H. Kern. Cambridge, 1891.
bKa'.babs.bdun.ldan. In Tseten Dorji, *Five Historical Works of Tāranātha*. Arunachal Pradesh, India, 1974, pp. 361–499.
Kāśyapaparivarta. Ed. by Baron A. von Staël-holstein. Shanghai, 1926.
Khaggavisāṇa Sutta. *Suttanipāta*, vs. 35–75.
Kuan wu liang shou fo ching (Amitāyurdhyāna Sūtra). T. 365.
Lalitavistara. Ed. by P. L. Vaidya. Buddhist Sanskrit Texts 1. Darbhanga, India, 1958.
Laṅkāvatāra Sūtra. Ed. by P. L. Vaidya. Buddhist Sanskrit Texts 3. Darbhanga, India, 1963.
Lokapaññatti. Ed. by Eugene Denis. In Denis (1977): 1:1–227.
Mahāpadāna Sutta. *Dīghanikāya* 2:1–54.
Mahāparinibbāna Sutta. *Dīghanikāya* 2:71–168.
Mahāparinirvāṇa Sūtra. Ed. by E. Waldschmidt. In Waldschmidt (1950–1951).
Mahāprajñāpāramitā Śāstra. Chin., *Ta chih tu lun*. T. 1509.
Mahāsuññata Sutta. *Majjhimanikāya* 3:109–18.
Mahāvagga. Pāli *vinaya* 1:1–360.
Mahāvastu. Ed. by Radhagovinda Basak. Calcutta Sanskrit College Research Series 21, 30, 43. 3 vols. Calcutta, 1963–1968.
Mahāvyutpatti. Ed. by R. Sakaki. 2 vols. Kyoto, 1916; indexes added 1925 and 1936.
Majjhimanikāya. Ed. by V. Trenckner, R. Chalmers, and C.A.F. Rhys Davids. 4 vols. London, 1888–1925.
Mañjuśrīmūlakalpa. Ed. by T. Ganapati Sastri. Trivandrum Sanskrit Series 70, 76, 84. 3 vols. Trivandrum, India, 1920–1925.
Manorathapūraṇī. Ed. by M. Walleser and H. Kopp. 5 vols. London, 1924–1956.
Mi.la'i.mgur.'bum. Ed. by gTsang.smyon he.ru.ka. Reprinted from the 1980 Kokonor edition. Gangtok, 1983.
Milindapañha. Ed. by V. Trenckner. London, 1880.
Nandimitrāvadāna. Chin., *Ta a lo han nan t'i mi to lo so shuo fa chu chi*. T. 2030.
Nandimitrāvadāna. Tib., *dga'.ba'i.bshes gnyen.gyi.rtogs.[pa].brjod.[pa]*. Pk., mdo.'grel ('dul.ba)(U), 299b–306b.
Nidānakathā. In *Jātaka* 1:2–94.
Pañcaviṃśatisāhasrikāprajñāpāramitā Sūtra (Skt., partial). In *Gilgit Buddhist Manuscripts*, Satapiṭaka Series 10, parts 3–5.
Pañcaviṃśatisāhasrikāprajñāpāramitā Sūtra (Chin.). T. 221, 222, 223.
Paramatthadīpanī (Theragāthā-aṭṭhakathā) (*Theragāthā* commentary). Ed. by F. L. Woodward. 2 vols. London, 1940–1952.

Paramatthadīpanī (Therīgāthā-vaṇṇanā) (*Therīgāthā* commentary). Ed. by E. Muller. London, 1893.

Paramattha–jotikā, II (*Suttanipāta* commentary). Ed. by H. Smith. 3 vols. London, 1916–1918.

Parivāra. Pāli *vinaya* 5:1–226.

Pratyekabuddhabhūmi. Ed. by A. Wayman. In "The Sacittikā and Acittikā Bhūmi and the *Pratyekabuddhabhūmi* (Sanskrit texts)." *Indogaku Bukky ogaku kenky u.* (*Journal of Indian and Buddhist Studies*) 7, no. 1 (Jan. 1960): 374–79.

Rāṣṭrapālaparipṛcchā Sūtra. Ed. by Louis Finot. Bibliotheca Buddhica 2. Saint Petersburg, 1901. Reprinted Indo-Iranian Reprints, The Hague, 1957; and P. L. Vaidya, ed., Buddhist Sanskrit Texts 17, Darbhanga, India, 1961, pp. 120–64.

Rāṣṭrapālaparipṛcchā Sūtra. Tib., *'phags.pa.yul.'khor.skyong.gis.zhus.pa.* Ed. by J. Ensink. In Ensink (1952): 60–125.

Rāṣṭrapālaparipṛcchā Sūtra (in Tib., *Rps*-m). Ed. by J. Ensink. In Ensink (1952): 126–32.

Rāṣṭrapālaparipṛcchā Sūtra (in Tib.). Pk., dkon.brtsegs (shi), 192a–226b.

Rāṣṭrapālaparipṛcchā Sūtra (in Tib., *Rps*-m). Pk., dkon.brtsegs (phu), 181a–184b.

Ratnaguṇasaṃcayagāthā. Ed. by Akira Yuyama. Cambridge, 1976.

Saddharmapuṇḍarīka Sūtra. Ed. by P. L. Vaidya. Buddhist Sanskrit Texts 6. Darbhanga, India, 1960.

Samādhirāja Sūtra. Ed. by P. L. Vaidya. Buddhist Sanskrit Texts 2. Darbhanga, India, 1961.

Saṃdhinirmocana Sūtra. Tib., *dgongs.pa.nges.par.'grel.pa.* Ed. by E. Lamotte. In Lamotte (1935): 31–166.

Saṃyuktāgama Sūtra. T. 99.

Saṃyuttanikāya. Ed. by L. Feer (vols. 1–5) and C.A.F. Rhys Davids (vol. 6, index). 6 vols. London, 1884–1904.

Sāratthappakāsinī. Ed. by F. L. Woodward. 3 vols. London, 1929–1937.

Shih ti ching lun (Daśabhūmivyākhyāna). T. 1522.

Śikṣāsamuccaya. Ed. by P. L. Vaidya. Buddhist Sanskrit Texts 11. Darbhanga, India, 1961.

Śrīmālādevīsiṃhanāda Sūtra (in Chin.). T. 353 and 310.

*Sthavirāvadāna** (Skt., partial). In *Gilgit Manuscripts,* vol. 3, part 1, pp. 162–218.

Sukhāvatī(amṛta)vyūha Sūtra. Ed. by F. M. Müller and B. Nanjio. Anecdota Oxoniensia Aryan Series 1. London, 1883. Reprinted in P. L. Vaidya, ed., Buddhist Sanskrit Texts 17, Darbhanga, India, pp. 254–57.

Sukhāvatīvyūha Sūtra. Ed. by F. M. Müller and B. Nanjio. Anecdota Oxoniensia Aryan Series 1. London, 1883. Reprinted in P. L. Vaidya, ed., Buddhist Sanskrit Texts 17, Darbhanga, India, 1961, pp. 221–53.

Suttanipāta. Ed. by D. Anderson and H. Smith. London, 1913; 2d ed., 1948.

Tā.ra.nā.tha'i.rgya.gar.chos.'byung. Lhasa (Potala), 1946.

Theragāthā. Ed. by H. Oldenberg. In H. Oldenberg and R. Pischel, eds., *The Thera- and Therīgāthā.* London, 1883. 2d ed. with appendices, K. R. Norman and L. Alsdorf, eds., London, 1966, pp. 1–115.

Therīgāthā. Ed. by R. Pischel. In H. Oldenberg and R. Pischel, eds., *The Thera- and Therīgāthā.* London, 1883. 2d ed. with appendices, K. R. Norman and L. Alsdorf, eds., London, 1966, pp. 123–74.

*Title for this body of material suggested by Hofinger (1954, 8).

Tsa a han ching (Saṃyuktāgama). T. 99.
Tseng i a han ching (Ekottarāgama). T. 125.
Udāna. Ed. by P. Steinthal. London, 1885.
Vajracchedikāprajñāpāramitā Sūtra. Ed. by F. M. Müller. London, 1881. Reprinted with emendations in P. L. Vaidya, ed., Buddhist Sanskrit Texts 17, Darbhanga, India, 1961, pp. 75–89.
Vimalakīrtinirdeśa Sūtra. Tib., *dri.ma.med.par.grags.pas.bstan.pa*. Pk., mdo.sna.tshogs (bu), 180a–250b.
Vimuttimagga. Chin., *Chieh t'o tao lun*. T. 1648.
Vinaya (Mūlasarvāstivādin, partial). In *Gilgit Manuscripts,* vol. 3, parts 1–4.
Vinaya. Tib., *D. 'dul.ba.*
Vinaya Piṭaka. Ed. by H. Oldenburg. Vol. 1, *Mahāvagga;* vol. 2, *Cullavagga;* vol. 3, *Suttavibhaṅga* (first part); vol. 4, *Suttavibhaṅga* (second part); vol. 5, *Parivāra*. London, 1879–1883.
Visuddhimagga (*The Visuddhi-magga of Buddhaghosa*). Ed. by C.A.F. Rhys Davids. 2 vols. London, 1920–1921. Reprint, 1975.

Translations and Secondary Sources

Adikaram, E. W. (1946). *Early History of Buddhism in Ceylon*. Colombo, Sri Lanka.
Bailey, H. W. (1974). "The *Pradakṣinā Sūtra* of Chang Tsiang-Kuin." In Cousins et al. (1974): 15–18.
Balasooriya, Somaratna, et al., eds. (1980). *Buddhist Studies in Honour of Walpola Rahula*. London.
Bapat, P. V. (1937a). *"Dhutaṅgas* (or The Ascetic Practices of Purification in Buddhism)." *Indian Historical Quarterly* 13:44–51.
——— (1937b). *Vimuttimagga and Visuddhimagga: A Comparative Study*. Poona, India.
———, ed. and trans. (1964). *Vimuktimārga Dhutaguṇanirdeśa*. New York.
Bareau, André (1955). *Les sectes bouddhiques du petit véhicule*. Publications de l'École Française d'Extrême-Orient 38. Saigon.
——— (1957). "Les controverses relative à la nature de l'Arhant dans le bouddhisme ancien." *Indo-Iranian Journal* 1:241–50.
——— (1958). *Les premiers conciles bouddhiques. Annales du Musée Guimet* 60. Paris.
——— (1959). "Les disciples." *France-Asie* 16, nos. 153, 157 *(Présence du Bouddhisme):* 351–68.
——— (1962). "La construction et le culte des stūpa d'aprés les *vinayapiṭaka.*" *Bulletin de l'École Française d'Extrême-Orient* 50:229–74.
——— (1963). *Recherches sur la biographie du Buddha dans les Sūtrapiṭaka et les Vinayapiṭaka anciens.* 1: *De la quête de l'eveil à la conversion de Śāriputra et de Maudgalyāyana*. Paris.
——— (1969). "The Superhuman Personality of the Buddha and Its Symbolism in the *Mahāparinirvāṇa Sūtra* of the Dharmaguptaka." In *Myths and Symbols: Studies in Honor of Mircea Eliade,* ed. by Joseph M. Kitagawa and Charles H. Long. Chicago, pp. 9–21.
——— (1970–1971). *Recherches sur la biographie du Buddha dans les Sūtrapiṭaka et les Vinayapiṭaka anciens.* 2: *Les derniers mois, le parinirvāṇa et les funérailles*. 2 vols. Paris.

——— (1972–1973). "La communauté bouddhique, de l'origine au lendemain du parinirvāṇa du Buddha." *Annuaire du Collège de France,* pp. 460–69.

——— (1973–1974). "La communauté primitive et la naissance de la religion bouddhique." *Annuaire du Collège de France,* pp. 415–30.

——— (1974). "Le *parinirvāṇa* du Buddha et la naissance de la religion bouddhique." *Bulletin de l'École Française d'Extrême-Orient* 61:275–99.

——— (1975). "Les récits canoniques des funérailles du Buddha et leurs anomalies: Nouvel essai d'interprétation." *Bulletin de l'École Française d'Extrême-Orient* 62:151–89.

——— (1979). "La composition et les étapes de la formation progressive du *Mahāparinirvāṇasūtra* ancien." *Bulletin de l'École Française d'Extrême-Orient* 66:45–103.

——— (1980). "The Place of the Buddha Gautama in the Buddhist Religion during the Reign of King Aśoka." In Balasooriya et al. (1980): 1–9.

——— (1982). "Un personnage bien mystérieux: L'épouse du Buddha." In Hercus et al. (1982): 31–59.

——— (1985). "Sainteté—Le bouddhisme." In *Encyclopaedia Universalis* 14:605–6. Paris.

——— (1988–1989). "Étude du bouddhisme." *Annuaire du Collège de France,* pp. 533–47.

Barnes, Michael (1981). "The Buddhist Way of Deliverance." *Studia Missionalia* 30:223–77.

Barua, B. M. (1926). "Stupa and Tomb." *Indian Historical Quarterly* 2:2–27.

Barua, Dipak Kumar (1966). "Buddhism and Lay Worshippers." *The Maha Bodhi* 74, nos. 3–4:38–44.

Basham, A. L. (1981). "The Evolution of the Concept of the Bodhisattva." In Kawamura (1981): 19–59.

Batchelor, Stephan, trans. (1979). *A Guide to the Bodhisattva's Way of Life.* Dharamsala, India.

Beal, Samuel, trans. (1869). *The Travels of Fah-hian and Sung yun.* London.

———, trans. (1883). *The Fo-sho-hing-tsan-king: A Life of the Buddha by Aśvaghoṣa Bodhisattva.* Sacred Books of the East 19. Oxford.

———, trans. (1884). *Si-yu-ki: Buddhist Records of the Western World.* 2 vols. London.

Bechert, Heinz (1973). "Remarks on the Textual History of *Saddharmapuṇḍarīka.*" In *Studies in Indo-Asian Art and Culture, Acharya Raghu Vira Commemoration Volume,* ed. by Perala Ratnam. Śata-piṭaka Series 96, no. 2:21–27. New Delhi.

——— (1989a). "Vimuttimagga and Amatākaravaṇṇanā." In Samtani and Prasad (1989): 11–14.

——— (1989b). "Aspects of Theravāda Buddhism in Sri Lanka and Southeast Asia." In Skorupski (1989): 19–28.

Bechert, Heinz, and Richard Gombrich (1984). *The World of Buddhism: Buddhist Monks and Nuns in Society and Culture.* London.

Bendall, Cecil, and W.H.D. Rouse, trans. (1922). *Śikshāsamuccaya: A Compendium of Buddhist Doctrine.* London. Reprint Delhi, 1971.

Bénisti, Mireille (1960). "Étude sur le *stūpa* dans l'Inde ancienne." *Bulletin de l'École Française d'Extrême-Orient* 50:37–116.

Beyer, Stephan V. (1975a). "Buddhism in Tibet." In Prebish (1975): 239–47.

——— (1975b). "Doctrine of Meditation in the Mahāyāna." In Prebish (1975):148–58.

——— (1977). "Notes on the Vision Quest in Early Mahāyāna." In Lancaster (1977): 329–40.

Bollée, W. B. (1974). "Buddhists and Buddhism in the Earlier Literature of the Śvetāmbhara Jains." In Cousins et al. (1974): 27–39.

Bond, George D. (1984). "The Development and Elaboration of the Arahant Ideal in the Theravāda Buddhist Tradition." *Journal of the American Academy of Religion* 52, no. 2:227–42.

——— (1988). "The Arahant: Sainthood in Theravāda Buddhism." In Kieckhefer and Bond (1988): 140–71.

Bronkhorst, Johannes (1986). *Two Traditions of Meditation in Ancient India.* Stuttgart.

Brown, Peter (1981). *The Cult of Saints: Its Rise and Function in Latin Christianity.* Chicago.

Bunnag, Jane (1973). *Buddhist Monk, Buddhist Layman: A Study of Urban Monastic Organization in Central Thailand.* Cambridge.

——— (1984). "The Way of the Monk and the Way of the World: Buddhism in Thailand, Laos, and Cambodia." In Bechert and Gombrich (1984): 159–70.

Burlingame, E. W., trans. (1921). *Buddhist Legends.* London. Reprint London, 1979.

Burnouf, E. (1876). *Introduction à l'histoire du bouddhisme indien.* 2d ed. Paris.

Caillat, Colette (1987). "Jainism." In *ER* 7:507–14.

Carrithers, Michael (1983). *The Forest Monks of Sri Lanka.* Delhi.

Chakraborty, Haripada (1973). *Asceticism in Ancient India in Brahmanical, Buddhist, Jaina and Ajivika Societies.* Calcutta.

Chandra, Lokesh (1986). *Tibetan-Sanskrit Dictionary.* 2 vols. Delhi.

Chang, Garma C. C., trans. (1962). *The Hundred Thousand Songs of Milarepa.* 2 vols. New Hyde Park, N.Y.

Chappell, David Wellington (1980). "Early Forebodings of the Death of Buddhism." *Numen* 27, no. 1:122–54.

Charpentier, Jarl (1908). *Paccekabuddhageschichten, Studien zur Indischen Erzählungsliteratur.* Upsala.

Chattopadhyaya, Alaka, trans. (1970). *Tāranātha's History of Buddhism in India.* Simla, India.

Chavannes, Edouard, trans. (1910–1935). *Cinq cents contes et apologues, extraits du Tripiṭaka chinois.* 4 vols. Paris.

Chen, Kenneth S. (1947). "A Study of the Svāgata Sthavira in the *Divya Avadāna.*" *Harvard Journal of Oriental Studies* 9, nos. 3–4:207–314.

Collins, Steven (1982). *Selfless Persons: Imagery and Thought in Theravāda Buddhism.* Cambridge.

———(1988). "Monasticism, Utopias and Comparative Social Theory." *Religion* 18:101–35.

Combaz, Gisbert (1932–1936). "L'evolution du stūpa en Asie." *Mélanges Chinois et Bouddhiques* 2 (1932–1933): 163–305; 3 (1933–1934): 93–143; 4 (1935–1936): 1–125.

Conze, Edward (1951). *Buddhism: Essence and Development.* London.

——— (1954a). "Ontology of the Prajñāpāramitā." *Philosophy East and West* 3:117–29.

——— (1954b). *Buddhist Texts through the Ages.* Oxford.

——— (1958a). *Buddhist Wisdom Books.* London.

——— (1958b). "The Oldest Prajñāpāramitā." *Middle Way* 32:136–41.

——— (1959). "Mahāyāna Buddhism." In *The Concise Encyclopedia of Living Faiths,* ed. by R. C. Zaehner. Boston, pp. 296–320.

——— (1960). *The Prajñāpāramitā Literature.* The Hague.

———, trans. (1962a). *The Accumulation of Precious Qualities (Prajñāpāramitāratnaguṇasaṃcayagāthā).* In *Indo-Asian Studies,* ed. by Ragu Vira. Part 1. New Delhi, pp. 126–78.

——— (1962b). *Buddhist Thought in India.* London.

——— (1967). *Thirty Years of Buddhist Studies.* Oxford.

——— (1967a). "Recent Progress in Buddhist Studies." In Conze (1967): 1–10.

——— (1967b). "The Development of Prajñāpāramitā Thought." In Conze (1967): 123–47.

——— (1973a). *Materials for a Dictionary of the Prajñāpāramitā Literature*. Tokyo.

———, trans. (1973b). *The Perfection of Wisdom in Eight Thousand Lines and Its Verse Summary*. Bolinas, Calif.

———, trans. (1975). *The Large Sūtra on Perfect Wisdom with the Divisions of the Abhisamayālaṅkāra*. Berkeley.

——— (1980). *A Short History of Indian Buddhism*. London.

——— (1982). *Buddhist Scriptures: A Bibliography*. Ed. and rev. by Lewis Lancaster. New York.

Cousins, L. S. (1984). "Samatha-yāna and Vipassanā-yāna." In Dhammapala et al. (1984): 56–68.

Cousins, L. S., et al., eds. (1974). *Buddhist Studies in Honour of I. B. Horner*. Dordrecht, The Netherlands.

Couture, André (1988). "Revue de la littérature française concernant l'hagiographie du Bouddhisme indien ancien." In *Monks and Magicians: Religious Biographies in Asia*, ed. by Phyllis Granoff and Koici Shinohara. New York, pp. 9–31.

Cowell, E. B., trans. (1895–1931). *The Jātaka: Or, Stories of the Buddha's Former Births*. UNESCO Collection of Representative Works. 6 vols. and index. London. Reprint London, 1969.

Dallapiccola, Anna Libera, ed. (1980); in collaboration with Stephanie Zingel-Avé Lallemant. *The Stūpa: Its Religious, Historical, and Architectural Significance*. Wiesbaden.

Das, S. C. (1970). *Tibetan-English Dictionary*. Delhi. Originally published 1902.

Dayal, Har (1932). *The Bodhisattva Doctrine in Buddhist Sanskrit Literature*. London. Reprint Delhi, 1970.

de Jong, J. W. (1953). Review of Ensink (1952). *Journal Asiatique* 241:545–49. Reprinted in de Jong (1979): 407–11.

——— (1957). Appendix to the Indo-Iranian Reprints edition of L. Finot, ed., *Rāṣṭrapālaparipṛcchā*. Reprinted in de Jong (1979): 421–27.

——— (1968). "Remarks on the Text of the *Rāṣṭrapālaparipṛcchā*." *Adyar Library Bulletin* 31–32:1–7. Reprinted in de Jong (1979): 413–19.

——— (1976). Review of Kloppenborg (1974). *Indo-Iranian Journal* 17:322–24. Reprinted in de Jong (1979): 223–25.

——— (1977). Review of Hurvitz (1976). *The Eastern Buddhist*, n.s. 10, no. 2:169–74.

——— (1979). *Buddhist Studies*. Ed. by Gregory Schopen. Berkeley.

Demiéville, Paul (1932). "L'origins des sectes bouddhiques d'aprés Paramārtha." *Mélanges Chinois et Bouddhiques* 1 (1931–1932): 15–64.

———, trans. (1954). "La Yogācārabhūmi de Saṅgharakṣa." *Bulletin de l'École Française d'Extrême-Orient* 44:339–436.

Denis, Eugene, trans. (1977). *La Lokapaññatti et les idées cosmologiques du bouddhisme ancien*. 3 vols. Lille.

Denwood, Philip, and Alexander Piatagorsky (1983). *Buddhist Studies: Ancient and Modern*. London.

De Visser, M. W. (1922–1923). *The Arhants in China and Japan*. Berlin.

Dhammapala, Gatare, et al., eds. (1984). *Buddhist Studies in Honour of Hammalawa Saddhātissa*. Nugegoda, Sri Lanka.

Dhammaratana, U. (1964). *Guide through the Visuddhimagga*. Varanasi.

Dharma Publishing (1980). *Guide to the Nyingma Edition of the sde.dge.bka'.'gyur and bstan'gyur (Derge Tripiṭaka)*. 2 vols. Oakland, Calif.

Doré, Henri (1914–1938). *Researches into Chinese Superstitions.* Trans. by Kennelly et al. 13 vols. Shanghai.

Dumoulin, Heinrich (1988). *Zen Buddhism: A History.* 1: *India and China.* New York.

Duroiselle, M. C. (1904). "Upagutta et Māra." *Bulletin de l'École Française d'Extrême-Orient* 4:414–28.

Durt, Hubert (1980). "Mahalla/Mahallaka et la crise de la communauté après le *parinirvāṇa* du Buddha." In *Indianisme et bouddhisme* (1980): 79–99.

Dutt, Nalinaksha (1930). *Aspects of Mahāyāna Buddhism and Its Relation to Hīnayāna.* London.

——— (1960). *Early Monastic Buddhism.* Calcutta.

——— (1970). *Buddhist Sects in India.* Calcutta.

Dutt, Sukumar (1957). *The Buddha and Five after Centuries.* London.

——— (1962). *Buddhist Monks and Monasteries of India.* London.

——— (1984). *Early Buddhist Monachism.* 2d ed. New Delhi. Originally published London, 1924.

Ebert, Jorinde (1980). "Parinirvāṇa and Stūpa: Was the Stūpa Only a 'Symbolical' Depiction of Parinirvāṇa?" In Dallapiccola (1980): 219–25.

Eck, Diana L. (1981). *Darśan: Seeing the Divine Image in India.* 2d ed. Chambersburg, Pa.

Edgerton, Franklin (1970). *Buddhist Hybrid Sanskrit Dictionary.* Delhi.

Ehara, N.R.M.; Soma Thera; and Kheminda Thera (1961). *The Path of Freedom by the Arahant Upatissa.* Colombo, Śrī Laṅka.

Eliade, Mircea (1969). *Yoga: Immortality and Freedom.* 2d ed. Princeton. First English edition Princeton, 1958; first French edition Paris, 1954.

———, ed. (1987). *Encyclopedia of Religion.* 16 vols. New York.

Eliot, Charles (1921). *Hinduism and Buddhism.* 3 vols. London.

Ensink, Jacob, trans. (1952). *The Question of Rāṣṭrapāla.* Zwolle, The Netherlands.

Falk, Maryla (1943). *Nāma-rūpa and Dharma-rūpa: Origin and Aspects of an Ancient Indian Conception.* Calcutta.

Falk, Nancy (1977). "To Gaze on the Sacred Traces." *History of Religions* 16, no. 4:281–93.

——— (1987). "Buddhist Pūjā." In *ER* 12:85–86.

Faure, Bernard (1986). "Bodhidharma as Textual and Religious Paradigm." *History of Religions* 25, no. 3:187–98.

Fausböll, V., trans. (1881). "The Sutta-nipāta." Part 2 of *The Dhammapada and the Sutta-nipāta.* Sacred Books of the East 10. Oxford. Reprint Delhi, 1965.

Feer, Léon, trans. (1891). *L'Avadānaśataka, cent légendes bouddhiques. Annales du Musée Guimet* 18. Paris.

Filliozat, Jean (1963). "La mort voluntaire par le feu et la tradition bouddhique indienne." *Journal Asiatique* 251:21–51.

Finot, Louis (1901). "Introduction." In *Rāṣṭrapālaparipṛcchā Sūtra,* ed. by Louis Finot. Saint Petersburg.

Foucaux, Philippe Edouard (1884–1892). *Dévelopment des jeux (Lalita Vistara).* 2 vols. Paris.

Foucher, Alfred (1905–1922). *L'art greco-bouddhique du Gandhara.* 2 vols. Paris.

——— (1949). *La vie du Bouddha.* Paris.

——— (1963). *The Life of the Buddha According to the Ancient Texts and Monuments of India.* Abridged trans. of Foucher (1949) by Simone Brangier Boas. Middletown, Conn.

Frauwallner, Erich (1956). *The Earliest Vinaya and the Beginnings of Buddhist Literature.* Rome.

——— (1969). *Die Philosophie des Buddhismus.* Berlin.

Fujita, Kotatsu (1975). "One Vehicle or Three." *Journal of Indian Philosophy* 3:79–166.

——— (1980). "Pure Land Buddhism and the Lotus Sutra." In *Indianisme et bouddhisme* (1980): 117–30.

Fussman, Gerard (1986). "Symbolism of the Buddhist Stūpa." *Journal of the International Association of Buddhist Studies* 9, no. 2:37–53.

Galloway, Brian (1981). "Sudden Enlightenment in Indian Buddhism." *Weiner Zeitschrift für die Kunde Südasiens und Archive für Indische Philosophie* 25:205–11.

——— (1985). "Once Again on the Indian Sudden Enlightenment Doctrine." *Weiner Zeitschrift für die Kunde Südasiens und Archive für Indische Philosophie* 29:207–10.

Gangoly, O. C. (1938). "The Antiquity of the Buddha Image: The Cult of the Buddha." *Ostasiatische Zeitschrift* 14:41–59.

Gernet, Jacques (1960). "Les suicides par le feu chez les bouddhistes chinois du Ve an X^{e} siécle." In *Mélanges Publiés par l'Institut des Hautes Études Chinoises* 2:527–58.

Gokhale, B. G. (1980). "Bhakti and Early Buddhism." *Journal of Asian and African Studies* 15:1–28.

——— (1965). "The Early Buddhist Elite." *Journal of Indian History* 43, no. 2:391–402.

——— (1976). "The Image-World of the Thera-Therīgāthās." In Wijesekera (1976): 96–110.

——— (1989). "Āloko Udapādi: The Imagery of Illumination in Early Buddhist Literature." In Samtani and Prasad (1989): 1–10.

Gombrich, R. F. (1971). *Precept and Practice: Traditional Buddhism in the Rural Highlands of Ceylon.* Oxford.

——— (1979). Review of Kloppenborg (1974). *Orientalistische Literaturzeitung* 74:78–80.

——— (1980). "The Significance of Former Buddhas in the Theravāda Tradition." In Balasooriya et al. (1980): 62–72.

——— (1984a). "Buddhism in Ancient India." In Bechert (1984): 77–89.

——— (1984b). "Notes on the Brahminical Background to Buddhist Ethics." In Dhammapala et al. (1984): 91–101.

——— (1986). Review of original French version of Wijayaratna (1990). *Religion* 16:387–89.

——— (1988). *Theravāda Buddhism: A Social History from Ancient Benares to Modern Columbo.* London.

——— (1990a). "Recovering the Buddha's Message." In Skorupski (1991): 5–20.

——— (1990b). "How the Mahāyāna Began." In Skorupski (1991): 21–30.

——— (1991). "Making Mountains Without Molehills: The Case of the Missing Stūpa." *Journal of the Pāli Text Society* 15:141–43.

Gomez, Luis O. (1976). "Proto-Mādhyamika in the Pāli Canon." *Philosophy East and West* 26, no. 2:137–65.

——— (1977). "The Bodhisattva as Wonder-worker." In Lancaster (1977): 221–61.

Gonda, J. (1969). *Eye and Gaze in the Veda.* Amsterdam.

Govinda, Lama Anagarika (1976). *The Psycho-cosmic Symbolism of the Buddhist Stūpa.* Emeryville, Calif.

Granoff, Phyllis (1984). "Holy Warriors: A Preliminary Study of Some Biographies of Saints and Kings in the Classical Indian Tradition." *Journal of Indian Philosophy* 12, no. 3:291–303.

Griffiths, Paul J. (1981). "Concentration or Insight: The Problematic of Theravāda Buddhist Meditation Theory." *Journal of the American Academy of Religion* 49:606–24.
——— (1986). *On Being Mindless: Buddhist Meditation and the Mind-Body Problem*. La Salle, Ill.
Griffiths, Paul J., et al. (1989). *The Realm of Awakening: Chapter Ten of Asaṅga's Mahāyānasaṅgraha*. New York.
Guenther, H. V. (1963). *Life and Teaching of Nāropa*. Oxford.
Gunawardana, R.A.L.H. (1979). *Robe and Plough: Monasticism and Economic Interest in Early Medieval Sri Lanka*. Tucson, Ariz.
Gyatso, Geshe Kelsang (1980). *Meaningful to Behold*. Cumbria, England.
Hallisey, Charles (1991). "Apropos the Pāli Vinaya as a Historical Document: A Reply to Gregory Schopen." *Journal of the Pāli Text Society* 15:197–208.
Hara, Minoru (1980). "A Note on the Buddha's Birth Story." In *Indianisme et bouddhisme* (1980): 143–57.
Harrison, Paul (1987). "Who Gets to Ride in the Great Vehicle? Self-Image and Identity Among the Followers of the Early Mahāyāna." *Journal of the International Association of Buddhist Studies* 10, no. 1:67–89.
Harvey, Peter (1983). "The Nature of the *Tathāgata*." In Denwood and Piatigorsky (1983): 35–52.
——— (1984). "Symbolism of the Early Stūpa." *Journal of the International Association of Buddhist Studies* 7, no. 2:67–93.
Hastings, James, ed. (1908–1926). *Encyclopedia of Religion and Ethics*. 13 vols. Edinburgh.
Hazra, Kanai Lal (1983). *Buddhism in India as Described by the Chinese Pilgrims: A.D. 399–689*. New Delhi.
Hercus, L. A., et al., eds. (1982). *Indological and Buddhist Studies: Volume in Honour of Professor J. W. de Jong on His Sixtieth Birthday*. Canberra.
Hinüber, O. v. (1991). "Khandhakavatta: Loss of Text in the Pāli Vinayapiṭaka?" *Journal of the Pāli Text Society* 15:127–38.
Hirakawa, Akira (1963). "The Rise of Mahāyāna Buddhism and Its Relationship to the Worship of Stūpas." *Memoires of the Research Department of the Toyo Bunkyo* 22:57–106.
——— (1966). "The Twofold Structure of the Buddhist Saṅgha." *Journal of the Oriental Institute* 16, no. 3:131–37.
——— (1987). "Stupa Worship." In *ER* 14:92–96.
Hocart, A. M. (1923). "Buddha and Devadatta." *Indian Antiquary* 52:267–72.
Hofinger, Marcel, trans. (1954). *Le congrès du Lac Anavatapta (Vies de saints bouddhiques)*. Louvain.
Holt, John (1981). *Discipline: The Canonical Buddhism of the Vinayapiṭaka*. Delhi.
Homans, Peter (1985). "C. G. Jung: Christian or Post Christian Psychologist." In *Essays on Jung and the Study of Religion*, ed. by Luther H. Martin and James Goss. New York, pp. 26–44.
Honda, Megumu, trans. (1968). *Annotated Translation of the Daśabhūmika Sūtra*. In *Studies in South, East, and Central Asia*, ed. by Denis Sinor. New Delhi.
Horner, I. B. (1930). *Women Under Primitive Buddhism*. London.
——— (1936). *The Early Buddhist Theory of Man Perfected*. London.
———, trans. (1938–1966). *The Book of Discipline*. Sacred Books of the Buddhists 10, 11, 13, 14, 20, 25. 6 vols. 1: *Suttavibhaṅga;* 2: *Suttavibhaṅga;* 3: *Suttavibhaṅga;* 4: *Mahāvagga;* 5: *Cullavagga;* 6: *Parivāra*. London.

———, trans. (1954–1959). *The Middle Length Sayings*. Pali Text Society Translation Series 29–31. 3 vols. London.

Huntington, Susan L. (1985). *The Art of Ancient India*. New York.

Hurvitz, Leon (1976). *Scripture of the Lotus Blossom of the Fine Dharma (Lotus Sūtra)*. New York.

I-liang, Chou (1945). "Tantrism in China." *Harvard Journal of Asiatic Studies* 8 (Mar.): 241–332.

Indianisme et bouddhisme: Mélanges offerts à Mgr. Étienne Lamotte (n.a.) (1980). Louvain-la-Neuve.

Irwin, J. (1977). "The Stūpa and the Cosmic Axis: the Archaeological Evidence." In *South Asian Archaeology*, ed. by M. Taddei, vol. 2. Naples, pp. 799–845.

Jaini, Padmanabh S. (1958). "Buddha's Prolongation of Life." *Bulletin of the School of Oriental and African Studies* 21:546–52.

——— (1970). "Śramaṇas of Pre-Buddhist India." In *Chapters in Indian Civilization*, ed. by Joseph W. Elder. Dubuque, Iowa, pp. 40–81.

——— (1976). "The Jina as Tathāgata: Amṛtacandra's Critique of Buddhist Doctrine." In Wijesekera (1976): 148–56.

Jan, Yün-hua (1970). "Nāgārjuna, One or More? A New Interpretation of Buddhist Hagiography." *History of Religions* 10, no. 2:139–55.

——— (1987). "Fa-hsien." *ER* 5:245–46.

Jayatilleke, K. N. (1963). *Early Buddhist Theory of Knowledge*. London.

Jensen, Adolf E. (1963). *Myth and Cult Among Primitive Peoples*. Trans. by Marianna Tax Choldin and Wolfgang Weissleder. Chicago.

Johnston, Edward Hamilton, trans. (1936). *The Buddhacarita or Acts of the Buddha*. 2 vols. Calcutta. Reprint Delhi, 1972 and 1978.

———, trans. (1937). "The Buddha's Mission and Last Journey." *Acta Orientalia* 15:1–128.

———, trans. (1984). *Aśvaghoṣa's Buddhacarita or Acts of the Buddha: Sanskrit Text of Cantos I-XIV with English Translation of Cantos I-XXVII*. New enlarged edition (Johnston 1936 and 1937 bound together). Delhi.

Jones, J. J., trans. (1949–1956). *The Mahāvastu*. Sacred Books of the Buddhists 16, 18, 19. 3 vols. London.

Kajiyama, Y. (1982). "On the Meanings of the Words Bodhisattva and Mahāsattva in Prajñāpāramitā Literature." In Hercus et al. (1982): 253–70.

——— (1985). "Stūpas, the Mother of the Buddhas, and Dharma Body." In Warder (1985): 9–16.

Katz, Nathan (1982). *Buddhist Images of Human Perfection*. Delhi.

Kawamura, Leslie S. (1981). *The Bodhisattva Doctrine in Buddhism*. Waterloo, Ontario.

Keith, A. B. (1923). *Buddhist Philosophy in India and Ceylon*. London.

Kern, H., trans. (1884). *The Saddharmapuṇḍarīka or The Lotus of the True Law*. Oxford. Reprint Delhi, 1965.

——— (1886). *Manual of Indian Buddhism*. Strasbourg.

——— (1901–1903). *Histoire du Bouddhisme dans l'Inde*. 2 vols. Trans. by J. Huet. Paris.

Keyes, Charles F. (1982). "Death of Two Buddhist Saints in Thailand." In *Charisma and Sacred Biography*, ed. by Michael A. Williams. Journal of the American Academy of Religions Thematic Studies 48, nos. 3 and 4:149–80.

Khantipalo, Bhikkhu (1965). "With Robes and Bowls: Glimpses of the Thudon Bhikkhu Life." *Wheel* 83–84:1–76.

——— (1976). *The Splendour of Enlightenment: A Life of the Buddha*. Bangkok.

——— (1979). *Banner of the Arahants.* Kandy, Śrī Laṅka.

Kieckhefer, Richard, and George Bond, eds. (1988). *Sainthood: Its Manifestations in World Religions.* Berkeley.

King, Winston L. (1980). *Theravada Meditation: The Buddhist Transformation of Yoga.* University Park, Pa.

Kiyota, M. (1978). *Mahāyāna Buddhist Meditation.* Honolulu.

Kloetzli, W. Randolph (1987). "Buddhist Cosmology." *ER* 4:113–19.

Kloppenborg, Ria, trans. (1973). *The Sūtra on the Foundation of the Buddhist Order (Catuṣpariṣatsūtra).* Leiden.

——— (1974). *The Paccekabuddha, A Buddhist Ascetic.* Leiden.

Ku, Cheng-mei (1984). "The Mahāyānic View of Women: A Doctrinal Study." Ph.D. diss., University of Wisconsin, Madison.

Kumagusu, Minakata (1899). "The Wandering Jew." *Notes and Queries* (9th ser.) 4:121–24.

Kunst, Arnold (1980). "Some of the Polemics in the *Laṅkāvatārasūtra.*" In Balasooriya et al. (1980): 103–12.

Lamotte, Étienne, trans. (1935). *Saṃdhinirmocana Sūtra: l'explication des mystères.* Louvain.

———, trans. (1944–1980). *Le traité de la grande vertu de sagesse (Mahāprajñāpāramitā Śāstra).* 5 vols. Louvain.

——— (1947). "La critique d'authenticité dans le bouddhisme." In *India Antiqua, Published in Honour of J. Ph. Vogel.* Leyden, pp. 213–22.

——— (1947–1948). "La légende du Buddha." *Revue de l'Histoire des Religions* 134:37–71.

——— (1949). "La critique d'interprétation dans le bouddhisme." *Annuaire de l'Institut de Philologie et d'Histoire Orientales et Slaves* 9:341–61.

——— (1954). "Sur la formation du Mahāyāna." In *Asiatica: Festschrift Friedrich Weller.* Leipzig, pp. 377–96.

——— (1955a). "La personnalité et l'esprit de Śākyamuni." *Bulletin de la Classe des Lettres et des Sciences . . . de l'Académie Royale de Belgique* 41:198–218.

——— (1955b). "Le bouddhisme de laïcs." *Studies in Indology and Buddhology Presented in Honour of Professor S. Yamaguchi.* Kyoto, pp. 73–89.

——— (1956). "Problèmes concernant les textes canoniques 'Mineurs.' " *Journal Asiatique,* pp. 249–64.

——— (1957). "*Khuddakanikāya* and *Kṣudrakapiṭaka.*" *East and West* 7:341–48.

——— (1958). *Histoire du Bouddhisme indien.* Louvain.

———, trans. (1962). *L'enseignement de Vimalakīrti.* Bibliothèque du Muséon 51. Louvain.

——— (1965). "Le suicide religieux dans le bouddhisme." *Bulletin de la Classe des Lettres et des Sciences . . . de l'Académie Royale de Belgique* 51:156–68.

——— (1970). "Le Buddha insulta-t-il Devadatta?" *Bulletin of the School of Oriental and African Studies* 33:107–15.

——— (1973). "Trois sūtra du *Saṃyukta* sur la vacuité." *Bulletin of the School of Oriental and African Studies* 36, part 2:312–23.

——— (1980). "Conditioned Co-production and Supreme Enlightenment." In Balasooriya et al. (1980): 118–32.

——— (1981). Reprint of Lamotte (1944–1980).

——— (1984a). "The Buddha, His Teachings and His Saṃgha." In Bechert and Gombrich (1984): 41–58.

——— (1984b). "Mahāyāna Buddhism." In Bechert and Gombrich (1984): 90–93.

——— (1988). *History of Indian Buddhism.* English translation of Lamotte (1958). Trans. by Sara Webb-Boin. Louvain-la-Neuve.

Lancaster, Lewis (1975). "The Oldest Mahāyāna Sūtra: Its Significance for the Study of Buddhist Development." *Eastern Buddhist* 8, no. 1:30–41.

——— (1976). "Samādhi Names in Buddhist Texts." In Wijesekera (1976): 196–202.

———, ed. (1977). *The Prajñāpāramitā and Related Systems.* Berkeley Buddhist Studies Series. Berkeley.

——— (1979). *The Korean Buddhist Canon: A Descriptive Catalogue.* Berkeley.

——— (1984). "Elite and Folk: Comments on the Two-Tiered Theory." In *Religion and the Family in East Asia,* ed. by George A. De Vos and Takao Sofue. Berkeley, pp. 87–95.

——— (1987). "Maitreya." *ER* 9:136–41.

La Vallée Poussin, Louis de (1898). *Bouddhisme: Études et matériaux.* London.

——— (1908–1927a). "Bodhisattvas." *ERE* 2:739–52.

——— (1908–1927b). "Magic (Buddhist)." *ERE* 8:255–57.

——— (1908–1927c). "The Pratyekabuddha." *ERE* 10:152–54.

——— (1927). *La morale bouddhique.* Paris.

——— (1929). "Le chemin du *nirvāṇa:* Extase et spéculation (Dhyāna et Prajñā)." In *Indian Studies in Honour of Charles Rockwell Lanman.* Cambridge, Mass., pp. 135–36.

——— (1936–1937). "Musīla et Nārada." *Mélanges Chinois et Bouddhiques* 5:189–222.

———, trans. (1971). *L'Abhidharmakośa de Vasubandhu.* Ed. by Etienne Lamotte. *Mélanges Chinois et Bouddhiques* 16. 6 vols. Brussels. Original edition Paris, 1923–1931.

———, trans. (1988–1990). *The Abhidharmakośabhāṣyam by Louis de La Vallée Poussin.* Trans. from the French by Leo Pruden. 4 vols. Berkeley.

Legge, James, trans. (1886). *A Record of Buddhistic Kingdoms.* Oxford.

Lester, Robert C. (1973). *Theravāda Buddhism in Southeast Asia.* Ann Arbor.

Lethcoe, Nancy (1977). "The Bodhisattva Ideal in the Aṣṭa and Pañca Prajñāpāramitā Sūtras." In Lancaster (1977): 263–80.

Lévi, Sylvain, and Édouard Chavannes (1916). "Les seize *arhat* protecteurs de la loi." *Journal Asiatique* 8:1–166 (in offprint).

Lévi, Sylvain, and J. Takakusu, dirs., and Paul Demiéville, ed. (1930–). *Hôbôgirin: Dictionnaire encyclopédique du Bouddhisme d'après les sources chinoises et japonaises.* Tokyo.

Lévy, Paul (1957). *Buddhism: A Mystery Religion?* London.

Lindtner, C. (1982). *Nagarjuniana: Studies in the Writings and Philosophy of Nāgārjuna.* Delhi.

Ling, Trevor O. (1972). *A Dictionary of Buddhism.* New York.

Lingat, R. (1937). "Vinaya et droit laïque." *Bulletin de l'École Française d'Extrême-Orient* 37:415–77.

Long, Charles H. (1986). *Significations.* Philadelphia.

Lopez, Donald S., Jr. (1988). "Sanctification on the Bodhisattva Path." In Kieckhefer and Bond (1984): 172–217.

Lüders, Heinrich (1926). *Bruchstücke der Kalpanāmaṇḍitikā des Kumāralāta. Kleinere Sanskrit-texte aus den Turfanfunden,* no. 2. Leipzig.

MacQueen, G. (1981–1982). "Inspired Speech in Early Mahāyāna Buddhism." *Religion* 11 (1981): 303–19; 12 (1982): 49–65.

McRae, John R. (1986). *The Northern School and the Formation of Early Ch'an Buddhism.* Honolulu.

Malalasekera, G. P., ed. (1961–). *Encyclopedia of Buddhism*. Colombo, Sri Lanka.
Malavaniya, Dalsukh D. (1989). "A Note on the Word Pratyekabuddha in Jainism." In Samtani and Prasad (1989): 232–33.
Maquet, Jacques (1980). "Bhāvanā in Contemporary Sri Lanka: The Idea and the Practice." In Balasooriya et al. (1980): 1–9.
Masefield, Peter (1986). *Divine Revelation in Pali Buddhism*. London.
Matics, Marion L., trans. (1970). *Entering the Path of Enlightenment*. New York.
Maung Kin (1903). "The Legend of Upagutta." *Buddhism* (Rangoon) 1:219–42.
Migot, André (1954). "Un grand disciple du Buddha: Śāriputra." *Bulletin de l'École Française d'Extrême-Orient* 46, no. 2:405–554.
——— (1983). *Le Bouddha*. Brussels.
Mitra, Debala (1971). *Buddhist Monuments*. Calcutta.
Monier-Williams, Sir Monier (1899). *A Sanskrit-English Dictionary*. Oxford.
Mukherjee, Biswadeb (1966). *Die Überlieferung von Devadatta, dem Widersacher des Buddha, in den kanonischen Schriften*. Munich.
Murti, T.V.R. (1960). *The Central Philosophy of Buddhism*. 2d ed. London.
Mus, Paul (1928). "Le Buddha paré, son origin indienne. Śākyamuni dans le mahāyānisme moyen." *Bulletin de l'École Française d'Extrême-Orient* 28:153–278.
——— (1935). *Borobuḍur: esquisse d'une histoire du bouddhisme fondée sur la critique archéologique des textes*. 2 vols. Hanoi. Reprint New York, 1978.
Nagao, Gadjin M. (1978). "What Remains in Śūnyatā: A Yogācāra Interpretation of Emptiness." In Kiyota (1978). Reprinted in Nagao (1991): 51–60.
——— (1981). "The Bodhisattva Returns to this World." In Kawamura (1981): 61–79. Reprinted in Nagao (1991): 23–34.
——— (1983). "The Buddhist World-View as Elucidated in the Three-Nature Theory and Its Simile." *Eastern Buddhist* 16, no. 1:1–18. Reprinted in Nagao (1991): 61–74.
——— (1991). *Mādhyamika and Yogācāra: A Study of Mahāyāna Philosophies*. Albany, N.Y.
Nakamura, Hajime (1980). "The *Aṣṭamahāsthānacaityastotra* and the Chinese and Tibetan Versions of a Text Similar to It." In *Indianisme et bouddhisme* (1980): 259–65.
——— (1987a). "Bodhisattva Path." *ER* 2:265–69.
——— (1987b). "Mahāyāna Buddhism." *ER* 2:457–72.
——— (1987c). *Indian Buddhism: A Survey with Bibiliographical Notes*. Delhi. First published Hirakaṭa City, Japan, 1980.
Nakamura, Susumu W. (1951). "Pradakṣinā, A Buddhist Form of Obeisance." In *Semitic and Oriental Studies: A Volume Presented to William Popper*. Berkeley, pp. 345–54.
Nālandā and Chögyam Trungpa, trans. (1982). *The Life of Marpa the Translator*. Boulder, Colo.
Ñāṇananada, Bhikkhu (1973). *Ideal Solitude: An Exposition of the Bhaddekaratta Sutta*. Wheel Publication 188. Kandy, Sri Lanka.
Narain, A. K. (1980). *Studies in the History of Buddhism*. Delhi.
Narasimhan, Chakravarthi (1965). *The Mahābhārata*. New York.
Nattier, Jan (1988). " 'The Candragarbha-Sūtra' in Central and East Asia: Studies in a Buddhist Prophecy of Decline." Ph.D. diss., Harvard University.
Norman, K. R., trans. (1969). *The Elders' Verses I, Theragāthā*. Pali Text Society Translation Series 38. London.
———, trans. (1971). *The Elders' Verses II, Therīgāthā*. Pali Text Society Translation Series 40. London.
——— (1983). *Pāli Literature: Including the Canonical Literature of Prakrit and Sanskrit*

of all Hīnayāna Schools of Buddhism. In J. Gonda, *A History of Indian Literature* (vol. VII, fasc. 2). Wiesbaden.

——— (1983). "The Pratyeka-buddha in Buddhism and Jainism." In *Buddhist Studies: Ancient and Modern*, ed. by Philip Denwood and Alexander Piatigorsky. London and Dublin, pp. 92–106.

———, trans. (1985). *The Rhinoceros Horn and Other Early Buddhist Poems (Sutta-nipāta)*. London.

——— (1989). "The Pāli Language and Scriptures." In Skorupski (1989): 29–54.

Nyāṇamoli, Bhikkhu, trans. (1976). *The Path of Purification*. 2 vols. 2d ed. Berkeley. Original edition Colombo, Śrī Lañka, 1954.

Nyanaponika (1962). *The Heart of Buddhist Meditation*. New York.

——— (1966). *The Life of Sāriputta*. Wheel Series. Kandy, Śrī Lañka.

Nyanatiloka (1980). *Buddhist Dictionary: Manual of Buddhist Terms and Doctrines*. 4th rev. ed. Kandy, Śrī Lañka.

Obermiller, E. (1931). *History of Buddhism (chos.'byung) by Bu.ston*. Heidelberg.

Oldenberg, Herman (1881). *Buddha, sein Leben, seine Lehre, seine Gemeinde*. Berlin.

Olivelle, Patrick (1974). *The Origin and Early Development of Buddhist Monachism*. Colombo, Śrī Lañka.

Pachow, W. (1955). *A Comparative Study of the Prātimoksa*. Santiniketan, India.

——— (1976). "Gautama Buddha: Man or Superman." In Wijesekera (1976): 257–69.

Pant, Sushila (1973). "The Origin and Development of the Stūpa Architecture in India." *Journal of Indian History* (Dec.): 472–78.

Prebish, Charles S. (1973). "Theories Concerning the Skandhaka: An Appraisal." *Journal of Asian Studies* 32, no. 4:669–78.

——— (1975a). *Buddhism: A Modern Perspective*. University Park, Pa.

——— (1975b). *Buddhist Monastic Discipline*. University Park, Pa.

——— (1979a). "Recent Progress in Vinaya Studies." In Narain (1980): 297–306.

——— (1979b). "Vinaya and Prātimokṣa: The Foundation of Buddhist Ethics." In Narain (1980): 223–64.

Prebish, Charles S., and Janice J. Nattier (1977). "Mahāsāṃghika Origins: The Beginning of Buddhist Sectarianism." *History of Religions* 16:237–72.

Pruden, Leo (1988–1990). See Louis de La Vallée Poussin (1988–1990).

Przyluski, J. (1914)."Le Nord-ouest de l'inde dans le Vinaya des Mūlasarvāstivādin et les textes apparentés." *Journal Asiatique* 4:493–568.

——— (1923). *La légende de l'empereur Aśoka dans les textes indiens et chinois (Aśoka avadāna)*. Paris.

——— (1926–1928). *Le concile de Rājagṛha*. Paris.

Radhakrishnan, S., trans. (1950). *The Dhammapada*. Madras.

Rahula, Bhikkhu Telwatte (1978). *A Critical Study of the Mahāvastu*. Delhi.

Rahula, Walpola (1962). *What the Buddha Taught*. New York.

——— (1966). *History of Buddhism in Ceylon*. 2d ed. Colombo, Śrī Lañka.

——— (1971). "L'idéal du bodhisattva dans le Theravāda et le Mahāyāna." *Journal Asiatique* 259:63–70.

Rawlinson, Andrew (1977). "The Position of the Aṣṭasāhasrikā Prajñāpāramitā in the Development of Early Mahāyāna." In Lancaster (1977): 3–34.

Ray, Reginald A. (1980). "Accomplished Women in Tantric Buddhism of Medieval India and Tibet." In *Unspoken Worlds: Women's Religious Lives in Non-Western Cultures*, ed. by Nancy A. Falk and Rita M. Gross. New York, pp. 227–42.

——— (1987). "Mahāsiddhas." *ER* 9:122–26.

——— (1988). "Response to Cobb." *Buddhist Christian Studies* 8:83–101.

——— (1990). "The Longevity of Nāgārjuna." Buddhism Workshop, University of Chicago.

——— (1993). Review of Strong (1991). *History of Religions* 33:204–6.

Régamy, Constantin (1957). "Le problem du bouddhisme primitif et les derniers travaux de Stanislaw Schayer." *Rocznik Orjentalistyczny Kraków-Lwów* 21:37–58.

Reynolds, Frank E. (1976). "The Many Lives of the Buddha: A Study of Sacred Biography and Theravāda Tradition." In Reynolds and Capps (1976): 37–61.

——— (1977). "The Several Bodies of the Buddha: Reflections on a Neglected Aspect of Theravāda Tradition." *History of Religions* 16, no. 4:374–406.

——— (1981). *Guide to the Buddhist Religion.* Boston.

Reynolds, Frank E., and Donald Capps, eds. (1976). *The Biographical Process.* Religion and Reason Series 11. The Hague, pp. 37–61.

Reynolds, Frank E., and Charles Hallisey (1987). "Buddha." *ER* 2:319–33.

——— (1987a). "Buddhism: An Overview." *ER* 2:334–51.

Rhys Davids, C.A.F., trans. (1909). *Psalms of the Sisters.* Pali Text Translation Series 1. London. Reprinted and bound together with *Psalms of the Brethren* in C.A.F. Rhys Davids (1980).

———, trans. (1913). *Psalms of the Brethren.* Pali Text Translation Series 4. Reprinted and bound together with *Psalms of the Sisters* in C.A.F. Rhys Davids (1980).

——— (1931). *Sākya or Buddhist Origins.* London.

———, trans. (1980). *Psalms of the Early Buddhists.* London.

Rhys Davids, C.A.F., and F. Woodward, trans. (1917–1930). *Kindred Sayings (Saṃyuttanikāya).* 5 vols. London.

Rhys Davids, T. W. (1877). "On *Nirvāṇa,* and on the Buddhist Doctrines of the 'Groups,' the *Samskāras, Karma* and the 'Paths.' " *The Contemporary Review,* pp. 249–70.

———, trans. (1880). *Buddhist Birth Stories.* Translation of *Nidānakathā.* London. New edition by C.A.F. Rhys Davids, 1926.

———, trans. (1881). *Buddhist Suttas.* Sacred Books of the East 11. Oxford. Reprint Delhi, 1965.

———, trans. (1890–1894). *The Questions of King Milinda.* 2 vols. Oxford. Reprint Delhi, 1965.

Rhys Davids, T. W., and C.A.F. Rhys Davids (1899–1921). *Dialogues of the Buddha.* 3 vols. London.

Rhys Davids, T. W., and William Stede (1921–1925). *The Pali Text Society's Pali-English Dictionary.* London.

Robinson, James B., trans. (1979). *Buddha's Lions.* Berkeley.

Robinson, Richard (1967). *Early Mādhyamika in India and China.* Madison.

Robinson, Richard H., and Willard L. Johnson (1982). *The Buddhist Religion: An Introduction.* 3d ed. Belmont, Calif.

Rockhill, William Woodville (1884). *The Life of the Buddha and the Early History of His Order.* London.

Ruegg, David S. (1969). *La théorie du Tathāgatagarbha et du Gotra.* Paris.

Sadatissa, H. (1970). *Buddhist Ethics.* New York.

———, trans. (1985). *The Sutta-nipāta.* London.

Sadler, A. W. (1970). "Pagoda and Monastery: Reflections on the Social Morphology of Burmese Buddhism." *Journal of Asian and African Studies* 5, no. 1:282–93.

Samtani, N. H. (1989). "On Vagarcārin Pratyekabuddha(s)." In Samtani and Prasad (1989): 165–70.

Samtani, N. H., and H. S. Prasad, eds. (1989). *Amalā Prajñā: Aspects of Buddhist Studies: Professor P. V. Bapat Felicitation Volume*. Bibliotheca Indo Buddhica 63. Delhi.

Sangharakshita, Bhikshu (1980). *A Survey of Buddhism*. Boulder, Colo.

Sankalia, Hasmukh D. (1934). *The University of Nalanda*. Madras.

Sarkar, Himansu Bhusan, ed. (1970). *R. C. Majumdar Felicitation Volume*. Calcutta.

Schayer, Stanislaw (1935). "Pre-canonical Buddhism." *Acta Orientalia* 7:121–32.

Schiefner, A., and W. Ralston, trans. (1906). *Tibetan Tales Derived from Indian Sources*. London.

Schmidt, Kurt (1947). *Buddhistishche Heileige: Charakterbilder*. Konstanz, Germany.

Schmithausen, Lambert (1987). *Ālayavijñāna: On the Origin and the Early Development of Yogācāra Philosophy*. 2 vols. Tokyo.

Schober, Juliane Sybille (1989). "Paths to Enlightenment: Theravada Buddhism in Upper Burma." Ph.D. diss., University of Illinois at Urbana-Champaign.

Schopen, Gregory (1975). "The Phrase *'sa pṛthivīpradeśaś caityabhūto bhavet,'* in the *Vajraccedikā:* Notes on the Cult of the Book in the Mahāyāna." *Indo-Iranian Journal* 17:147–81.

——— (1977). Review of Conze (1975). *Indo-Iranian Journal* 19:135–52.

——— (1978). Review of Yuyama (1976). *Indo-Iranian Journal* 20:110–24.

——— (1979a). See de Jong (1979).

——— (1979b). "The Mahāyāna in Indian Inscriptions." *Indo-Iranian Journal* 21:1–19.

——— (1985). "Two Problems in the History of Indian Buddhism: The Layman/Monk Distinction and the Doctrines of the Transference of Merit." *Studien zur Indologie und Iranistik* 10:9–47.

——— (1987a). "Burial 'Ad Sanctos' and the Physical Presence of the Buddha in Early Indian Buddhism: A Study in the Archaeology of Religions." *Religion* 17:193–225.

——— (1987b). "The Inscription on the Kuṣān Image of Amitābha and the Character of the Early Mahāyāna in India." *Journal of the International Association of Buddhist Studies* 10, no. 2:99–134.

——— (1988). "On Monks, Nuns, and 'Vulgar' Practices: The Introduction of the Image Cult into Indian Buddhism." *Artibus Asiae* 49, nos. 1/2:153–68.

——— (1989). "The Stūpa Cult and the Extant Pāli Vinaya." *Journal of the Pāli Text Society* 13:83–100.

——— (1990). "The Buddha as an Owner of Property and Permanent Resident in Medieval Indian Monasteries." *Journal of Indian Philosophy* 18:181–217.

——— (1991a). "Archaeology and Protestant Presuppositions in the Study of Indian Buddhism." *History of Religions* 31, no. 1:1–23.

——— (1991b). "Monks and the Relic Cult in the Mahāparinibbāna Sutta: An Old Misunderstanding in Regard to Monastic Buddhism." In *From Benaras to Beijing: Essays on Buddhism and Chinese Religion in Honour of Jan Yün-Hua*, ed. by G. Schopen and K. Shinohara. Oakville, Ontario, pp. 187–201.

——— (1991c). "An Old Inscription from Amarāvatī and the Cult of the Local Monastic Dead in Indian Buddhist Monasteries." *Journal of the International Association of Buddhist Studies* 14, no. 2:281–329.

——— (1992a). "The Ritual Obligations and Donor Roles of Monks in the Pāli Vinaya." *Journal of the Pāli Text Society* 16:87–107.

——— (1992b). "On Avoiding Ghosts and Social Censure: Monastic Funerals in the Mūlasarvāstivāda-Vinaya." *Journal of Indian Philosophy* 20:1–39.

Schuster, Nancy J. (1985). "The *Bodhisattva* Figure in the *Ugraparipṛcchā*." In Warder (1985): 26–56.

Senart, Émile (1882). *Essai sur la légende du Bouddha*. 2d ed. Paris.

Shan Shih (1961). *The Sixteen Arhants and the Eighteen Arhants*. Peking.

Shastri, A. M. (1965). *An Outline of Early Buddhism*. Varanasi, India.

Shorto, H. L. (1970). "The Gavāmpati Tradition in Burma." In Sarkar (1970): 15–30.

Singh, Jaideva, trans. (1988). *Paratrisika Vivarana: The Secret of Tantric Mysticism*. Delhi.

Skorupski, Tadeusz (1989). *The Buddhist Heritage*. Tring, U.K.

——— (1990). *The Buddhist Forum*. 1: *Seminar Papers 1987–88*. London.

Slater, R. L. (1951). *Paradox and Nirvāṇa*. Chicago.

Snellgrove, David L. (1969). "Cosmological Patterns in Buddhist Tradition." *Studia Missionalia* 87:109.

——— (1970). "Sanctified Man in Buddhism." *Studia Missionalia* 88:55–85.

——— (1973). "Śākyamuni's Final Nirvāṇa." *Bulletin of the School of Oriental and African Studies* 36:399–411.

——— (1987). *Indo-Tibetan Buddhism: Indian Buddhists and Their Tibetan Successors*. 2 vols. Boston.

——— (1989). "Multiple Features of Buddhist Heritage." In Skorupski (1989): 7–18.

Snodgrass, Adrian (1985). *The Symbolism of the Stūpa*. Ithaca, N.Y.

Spae, Joseph (1979). "Modèles de sainteté dans le bouddhisme." *Concilum* 149:95–105.

Speyer, J. S., trans. (1895). *The Jātakamālā, Garland of Birth Stories of Āryaśūra*. London. Reprint Delhi, 1971.

Spiro, Melford E. (1982). *Buddhism and Society*. 2d ed. Berkeley.

Sponberg, Alan (1987). "Hsüan-tsang." *ER* 6:480–82.

Stcherbatsky, T. (1923). *The Central Conception of Buddhism and the Meaning of the Word "Dharma."* London. Reprint Delhi, 1970.

Strong, John (1975). Review of Kloppenborg (1974). *History of Religions* 15:104–5.

——— (1977). "Gandhakuṭī: The Perfumed Chamber of the Buddha." *History of Religions* 16:390–406.

——— (1979). "The Legend of the Lion-Roarer: A Study of the Buddhist Arhat Piṇḍola Bhāradvāja." *Numen* 26:50–88.

——— (1983). *The Legend of King Aśoka: A Study and Translation of the Aśokāvadāna*. Princeton.

——— (1985). "The Buddhist Avadānists and the Elder Upagupta." In *Tantric and Taoist Studies in Honor of R. A. Stein,* ed. by Michel Strickmann. *Mélanges Chinois et Bouddhiques* 22, no. 3:862–81.

——— (1987). "Images: Veneration of Images." *ER* 7:97–104.

——— (1992). *Legend and Cult of Upagupta*. Princeton.

Sugimoto, T. (1982). "A Re-evaluation of Devadatta: the Salvation of Evil Men in Buddhism." *Ronshu: Studies in Religions East and West* 9:360–76.

Sutton, Florin Giripescu (1991). *Existence and Enlightenment in the Laṅkāvatāra Sūtra*. Albany, N.Y.

Suzuki, D. T. (1930). *Studies in the Laṅkāvatāra Sūtra*. London.

———, trans. (1932). *The Laṅkāvatāra Sūtra*. London.

Swearer, Donald K. (1987). *"Arhat." ER* 1:403–5.

Takakusu, Junjiro, trans. (1894). "The *Amitāyurdhyāna Sūtra*." In *Buddhist Mahāyāna Texts,* ed. by E. B. Cowell. Sacred Books of the East 49, part 2. Oxford. Reprint Delhi, 1972, pp. 161–201.

———, trans. (1896). *A Record of the Buddhist Religion, by I-Tsing*. Oxford.

——— (1904). "The Life of Vasubandhu by Paramārtha (A.D. 499–569)." *T'oung-pao* 5:269–96.

Takasaki, Jikido (1966). *A Study on the Ratnagotravibhāga (Uttara Tantra): Being a Treatise on the Tathāgatagarbha Theory of Mahāyāna Buddhism*. Rome.

——— (1980). "Analysis of the Laṅkāvatāra Sūtra: In Search of Its Original Form." In *Indianisme et bouddhisme* (1980): 339–52.
——— (1982). "Sources of the *Laṅkāvatāra* and Its Position in Mahāyāna Buddhism." In Hercus et al. (1982): 545–68.
Tambiah, Stanley (1973). "Buddhism and This-Worldly Activity." *Modern Asian Studies* 7, no. 1:1–20.
——— (1984). *The Buddhist Saints of the Forest and the Cult of Amulets*. Cambridge.
Tate, John (1989). "The Sixteen Arhats in Tibetan Painting." *Oriental Art* 4:196–206.
Tatia, N. (1980). "The Interaction of Jainism and Buddhism and Its Impact on the History of Buddhist Monasticism." In Narian (1980): 321–38.
Thapar, Romila (1966). *A History of India*. Middlesex, England.
——— (1975). "Ethics, Religion, and Social Protest in the First Millennium B.C. in Northern India." *Daedalus* (Spring): 119–32.
——— (1978). "Renunciation: The Making of a Counter-Culture?" In Romila Thapar, *Ancient Indian Social History: Some Interpretations*. New Delhi, pp. 63–104.
Thomas, Edward J. (1927). See Thomas (1949).
——— (1941). "Epithets of an Arhat in the *Divyāvadāna*." *Indian Historical Quarterly* 17:104–7.
——— (1949). *The Life of Buddha as Legend and History*. 3d ed. London. First ed. London, 1927.
Trungpa, Chögyam, Rinpoche (1977). *Born in Tibet*. 3d ed. Boulder, Colo.
Tucci, Giuseppe (1949). *Tibetan Painted Scrolls*. 3 vols. Rome.
——— (1988). *Stūpa: Art, Architectonics, and Symbolism*. Trans. by U. M. Vesci. New Delhi. First published in Italian, Rome, 1932.
Turner, Victor (1969). *The Ritual Process*. Chicago.
Urubshurow, Victoria (1988). "Transformation of Religious Symbol in Indian Buddhism: Reflections on Method from a Reading of Mus's *Borobuḍur*." *Numen* 35, no. 2:260–79.
Vasu, Nagendra Nath (1911). *The Modern Buddhism and Its Followers in Orissa*. Calcutta. Reprint Delhi, 1986.
Vogel, J. P. (1954). "The Past Buddhas and Kāśyapa in Indian Art and Epigraphy." In *Asiatica: Festschrift Friedrich Weller*. Leipzig, pp. 808–16.
Wach, Joachim (1951). "The Concept of the 'Classical' in the Study of Religions." In Joachim Wach, *Types of Religious Experience*. Chicago, pp. 48–57.
Waddell, L. A. (1897). "Upagupta, the Fourth Buddhist Patriarch and High Priest of Aśoka." *Journal of the Asiatic Society of Bengal* 66:76–84.
Wagle, Narendra K. (1966). *Society at the Time of the Buddha*. Bombay.
——— (1985). "The Gods in Early Buddhism." In Warder (1985): 57–80.
Waldschmidt, Ernst (1950–1951). *Das Mahāparinirvāṇasūtra*. 2 vols. Berlin.
——— (1964). "Reste von Devadatta-Episoden aus dem Vinaya der Sarvāstivādins." *Zeitschrift der Deutschen Morgenländischen Gesellschaft* 113, no. 3:552–58.
——— (1980). "The Rāṣṭrapālasūtra in Sanskrit Remnants from Central Asia." In *Indianisme et bouddhisme* (1980): 359–74.
Walleser, Max (1922). "The Life of Nāgārjuna from Tibetan and Chinese Sources." In *Hirth Anniversary Volume*. London, pp. 421–55.
Warder, A. K. (1970). *Indian Buddhism*. Delhi.
——— (1985). *New Paths in Buddhist Research*. Durham, N.C.
Warren, Henry Clarke (1886). *Buddhism in Translations*. Cambridge, Mass.
Watters, Thomas (1898). "The Eighteen Lohan of Chinese Buddhist Temples." *Journal of the Royal Asiatic Society*, pp. 329–47.

——— (1904–1905). *On Yuan Chwang's Travels in India, 629–645 A.D.* 2 vols. Ed. by T. W. Rhys Davids and S. W. Bushell. London. Reprint Delhi, 1973.

Wayman, Alex, (1961). *Analysis of the Śrāvakabhūmi Manuscript.* University of California Publications in Classical Philology 17. Berkeley.

——— (1978). "The Mahāsāṃghika and the Tathāgatagarbha (Buddhist Doctrinal History, Study 1)." *Journal of the International Association of Buddhist Studies* 1, no. 1:35–50.

Wayman, Alex, and Hideko Wayman (1974). *The Lion's Roar of Queen Śrīmālā.* New York.

Weber, Max (1958). *The Religion of India: The Sociology of Hinduism and Buddhism.* Ed. and trans. by Hans H. Gerth and Don Martindale. New York.

——— (1968). *On Charisma and Institution Building: Selected Papers.* Ed. by S. N. Eisenstadt. Chicago.

——— (1968a). "The Pure Types of Legitimate Authority." Trans. by A. R. Henderson and Talcott Parsons. In Weber (1968): 46–47.

——— (1968b). "The Nature of Charismatic Authority and Its Routinization." Trans. by A. R. Henderson and Talcott Parsons. In Weber (1968): 48–65.

——— (1968c). "Bureaucracy." Trans. by H. H. Gerth and C. Wright Mills. In Weber (1968): 66–77.

Weeraratne, W. G., et al. (1961). "Arahant." In Malalasekera (1961–) 2:41–54.

Weinstein, Stanley (1958). "The Ālaya-vijñāna in Early Yogācāra Buddhism—A Comparison of Its Meaning in the Saṃdhinirmocana Sūtra and the Vijñaptimātratā-siddhi of Dharmapāla." In *Transactions of the International Conference of Orientalists in Japan,* no. 3:46–58.

Welbon, Guy (1968). *The Buddhist Nirvāṇa and Its Western Interpreters.* Chicago.

Weller, F., trans. (1926–1928). *Das Leben des Buddha von Aśvaghoṣa.* Parts 1 (1926) and 2 (1928). Leipzig.

Werner, Karel (1983). "Bodhi and Arattaphala." In Denwood and Piatagorsky (1983): 167–81.

Wijayaratna, Mohan (1990). *Buddhist Monastic Life.* Trans. by Claude Grangier and Steven Collins. New York.

Wijesekera, O. H. De A., ed. (1976). *Malalasekera Commemoration Volume.* Colombo, Śrī Lañka.

Williams, Paul (1989). *Mahāyāna Buddhism: The Doctrinal Foundation.* London.

Wiltshire, Martin G. (1990). *Ascetic Figures Before and in Early Buddhism: The Emergence of Gautama as the Buddha.* Berlin.

Winternitz, Maurice (1933). *A History of Indian Literature.* 3 vols. English translation by S. Ketkar. Calcutta.

Witanachchi, C. (1976). "Upagupta and Indagutta." In Wijesekera (1976): 353–62.

Woodward, F. L., trans. (1935). *The Minor Anthologies of the Pāli Canon.* 2: *Udāna—Verses of Uplift* and *Itivuttaka—As It Was Said.* London.

Woodward, F. L., and E. M. Hare, trans. (1932–1936). *The Book of Gradual Sayings (Añguttara Nikāya) or More Numbered Suttas.* 5 vols. London.

Yamamoto, Kosho (1973). *The Mahāyāna Mahāparinirvāṇa Sūtra.* 3 vols. Ube City, Japan.

Yuyama, Akira, trans. (1977). "The First Two Chapters of the Prajñā-pāramitā-ratna-guṇa-saṃcaya-gāthā." In Lancaster (1977): 203–18.

——— (1989). "The Tathāgata Prabhūtaratna in the Stūpa." In Samtani and Prasad (1989): 181–85.

INDEX

Foucher, Alfred, 13n.14, 42n.54, 73n.31
Frauwallner, Erich, 25–26, 31, 36, 40n.44, 41n.46, 148n.69, 294–95, 360, 400
  on early Buddhism, 25–29
Funeral lament, 143n.20

Gadgadasvara (the bodhisattva), 329
Gain. *See lābha*
Gampopa, 445
Gaṇa (group, community), 285n.44, 340
Gaṇḍavyūha, 405
Gandhamādana, Mt., 152, 180, 216, 220, 221, 222, 225, 226, 245n.44, 369
  description of, 216–17
Ganges, 58
Ganges Basin, 408
Ganthadhura (P.) (vocation of texts and scholarship), 16, 201. *See also* Textual study; Vocation of texts and scholarship
Garments of felt or wool, one who wears. See *Nāma(n)tika*
Gavāṃpati, 11n.7, 74n.41, 103n.41, 205n.2, 206n.10
Gavāmpati (P.). *See* Gavāṃpati
Gelugpa, 445, 446
Generosity as a lay virtue, 19
Godāvarī River, 405, 408
Gokulika. *See* Mahāsāṃghika: Northwestern schools
Gombrich, Richard, 16, 31, 36n.8, 40n.43, 42n.55, 43nn.60,64, 424n.5, 425n.14, 427n.26
Govindnagar, 429n.40
Gṛdhrakūṭa *(parvata)* (Vulture Peak Mountain), 180, 188, 409–10
Griffiths, Paul, 202
Guhyamantra (secret mantra), 410
Gupta, 412, 429n.38
Guru, 445–46
  and disciple, 313
  seeking and finding of teacher or (theme 5), 49, 85–86, 105–6, 115, 128–29, 134, 151, 216, 262
Gzhan.stong (emptiness of other), 424

Hagiographer, Buddhist, 6, 10n.4, 14n.17, 382–83
Hagiography, Buddhist, 11n.7, 13n.14, 14n.17, 41n.51, 57, 100n.7, 411. *See also* Buddha, the: hagiography of
  dynamics of, 59, 79, 382–86, 388n.14, 411, 429n.37
  as evidence, 8, 13nn.14,16
  historical layering in, 388n.14
  of saints, 44
  and stūpas, 228–29
Haimavata, 420
Harrison, Paul, 409
Harvey, Peter, 326, 353n.9
Hells *(naraka),* 107
Hemavata Sutta, 75n.50
Himalaya, 152, 427n.25
"Hīnayāna," 10n.2, 175n.17, 212n.61, 213, 315, 316, 376, 409, 410, 412, 415, 416
Hirakawa, Akira, 42n.54, 326, 331, 338, 340–43, 346–47, 349, 350, 351, 355nn.34,36, 368, 369, 378, 379, 406, 408–9, 412, 414
History
  of individuals, 14n.17
  of traditions, movements, trends, 14n.17
History of religions, 7–10, 45
Hofinger, Marcel, 99n.2
Honor. See *Satkāra*
Householder-*yogin,* 446
Household life, the symbolic meaning of, 54
Hsüan-tsang, 17, 172, 177nn.38,45, 191–97, 205, 206n.4, 208n.29, 234, 314, 326, 334, 406, 407, 408, 409, 412, 425n.20
Human nature, perfectibility of, viii, 57

I-ching, 208n.29, 334, 412, 425n.20
Iddhi (P.). See *Ṛddhi*
Ideal type, 10n.4
  process of identifying, 10n.4
Image worship, 357n.49
Inda. *See* Indra
Independence of renunciant, 29
Indra, 89, 110, 111, 117, 144n.34,36
Iñgada, 179, 205n.2
Inheritance, Indian notion of, 61

Monasticization (*continued*)
and early Buddhism, 397–404
forest response to, 417–21
as seen in
the Mahāyāna, 410–17
the *Theragāthā*, 96–99
Monastic rules. *See also* Monastic *saṃgha; Vinaya*
for monks, 37n.9
for nuns, 37n.9
Monastic saṃgha, 16, 19, 20, 21, 27, 28, 37n.13, 41n.46, 47, 43nn.60,63,64, 64, 65, 94, 96, 103n.49, 104n.50, 107, 108, 109, 117, 118, 142n.18, 145n.44, 157, 158, 159, 160, 161, 162, 166, 175nn.20,24, 184–85, 192, 193, 201, 246n.56, 285n.44, 319nn.23,31, 332, 338, 340–42, 351–52, 356n.38, 365, 366, 378, 380, 386n.2, 400
Monk, viii, 15, 16, 17, 18, 19, 20, 21, 22, 23, 26, 27, 28, 29, 30, 31, 36nn.3,8, 37n.14, 38nn.21,22, 39n.42, 42n.55, 43n.60, 45, 64–65, 68, 96, 98–99, 110, 111, 122–23, 125, 126, 130, 131, 158, 159–60, 160–61, 171, 184, 187, 190, 192, 194, 195, 196, 209nn.33,35,42, 210, 229, 231, 244n.31, 247n.61, 252, 255, 257, 259, 266, 268, 285nn.43,44, 304, 305, 306, 307, 319n.23, 320n.38, 334, 337, 340, 341, 342, 350, 351, 352, 354n.27, 359, 364, 366, 380, 387nn.4,7, 389nn.20,21, 390nn.28,36, 392n.78, 395n.110, 400, 401, 403, 413, 414, 425n.20, 428nn.29,36, 429n.39, 445, 446, 447n.1. See also *Bhikṣu;* Monastic *saṃgha*
behavioral purity of, 15–17, 27, 31, 104n.55, 158, 187, 195, 209n.43, 264, 266, 313, 352n.1, 399, 418, 420, 431n.54, 435, 441, 446. See also *Śīla*
and brahmin priest compared, 400–401
and the Buddha compared, 64–65
characteristic preoccupations of, 15–18, 31–36
conventionality of, 16–17, 65
Mahāyāna, 65
Nikāya, 65
as a term, 39n.42
textual preoccupations and, 31–36, 187
as worthy recipients of lay donations, 15–22
Mourning, ritualized, 58, 373–74, 361–62, 389nn.17,18,19,21. See also *Śarīrapūjā*
Mṛdubhāṣin (being of soft or gentle speech), 311
Mukherjee, Biswadeb, 160–62, 163–69
Mūlamadhyamakakārikā, 429nn.37,39
Mūlasarvāstivāda, 313, 331, 335–36, 406. *See also* Northern Buddhism
Muni (silent one), 77n.64, 100n.4, 237
Mus, Paul, 8, 13nn.11,12,14,15, 61, 326, 346, 352n.7, 353n.8, 430n.47
Musīla, 199–201
Myth, 7, 12n.9, 79

Nāga, 74n.41, 192
Nāgārjuna, 11n.7, 197, 405, 406, 425n.20, 429nn.37,39
Nāgārjunikoṇḍa, 405, 407, 408, 428n.33
Nāgasena, 19, 30, 37n.14, 205n.2, 209n.42, 320n.38, 388n.14, 390n.36
one of the sixteen arhants, 179
Naiṣadika (practice of not lying down), 87, 296, 297–98, 302, 309, 311, 320n.32
Nakamura, Hajime, 355n.34, 415, 428n.30
Nakula. *See* Vakula
Nālāgiri, 148n.74
Nālaka Sutta, 75n.50
Nālandā, 192
Nāmakāya (nonmaterial body), 375, 376
Nāma(n)tika (one who wears garments of felt or wool), 297, 308, 311
Nāmarūpa (name and form), 375
Nanda, 205n.2
Nandamāṇavapucchā Sutta, 77n.64
Nandamūlaka cave, 216

Nandimitra, 179, 183, 373–74, 394n.96, 206n.3
Nandimitrāvadāna, 155, 157, 179, 197, 205n.2, 206n.4, 372–74, 394n.97. *See also* Piṇḍolabhāradvāja: in the *Nandimitrāvadāna;* Sixteen arhants, the: in the *Nandimitrāvadāna*
  context of, 183–85
  cult of the Buddha in, 183–84
  cult of the dharma in, 184
  cult of the *saṃgha* in, 184
Nārada, 199–201
Naṭabhaṭa (the forest), 122, 123
Naṭabhaṭika (the hermitage), 121
Nattier, Jan, 431n.53
Nemiṃdhara, Mt., 180, 206n.9
Nesajjika (P.). See *Naiṣadika*
Nettipakaraṇa, 246n.55
Nibbāna (P.). *See* Nirvāṇa
Nidānakathā, 70n.8
Nigalī Sāgar, 325
Nikāya
  forest saints, 427n.25
  literature, 17, 371
  monasticism, 17, 412, 413–14, 445
  schools, 18, 26, 205, 251, 372, 380, 411
  texts, 75n.48, 162, 418, 423, 427n.26, 430n.44
Nikāya (collection of texts), 43n.64
  as a designation for the early Buddhist sects, 10n.2
Nikāya Buddhism, 5, 65, 235, 236, 251, 314, 315, 316, 340–41, 403, 413, 417, 433, 440
  community in, 340–42
Nikāya commentaries, 18, 35, 37n.13, 211n.50, 235, 240–41, 243n.21, 248n.71, 249n.73, 250n.74, 372, 375, 394n.95. *See also* Pāli commentaries
Nimitta (external signs), 420
Nirgrantha Jñātiputra, 174n.9
Nirodha (cessation), 369, 377, 393n.88
Nirodhadhātu (sphere of cessation), 375
Nirodhakāya (body of cessation), 375, 376
Nirodhasamāpatti (attainment of cessation), 144n.38, 146n.50, 198, 199, 201, 203, 218, 222, 226, 368, 369–72, 382–83, 392n.81, 393nn.89,90,91, 394n.95
  the Buddha as a practicioner of, 369, 371
  equated with nirvāṇa, 370
  as highest of the *anupūrva*s, 369–70, 371
  as highest of the *vimokṣa*s, 370
  linkage with forest saints, 371
  as necessary to enlightenment, 370, 371
  in Pāli texts, 369, 370
  in Sanskrit texts, 369, 370
  similarity to death, 371–72
Nirvāṇa, 15, 16, 18, 20, 21, 22, 42n.55, 43n.63, 63, 65, 102n.39, 108, 109, 115, 122, 127, 128, 144nn.32,33,35,36, 152, 182, 183, 184, 188, 189, 198, 199, 201, 202, 208n.26, 213, 217, 219, 220, 225, 226, 227, 241n.13, 247n.62, 275, 277, 330, 348, 369, 370, 371, 372, 373, 375, 376, 378, 375–77, 379
  as a "blank," 13n.10
  as a goal for monastics, 15, 16
  not for the laity, 42n.55
Nirvāṇadhātu (realm of nirvāṇa), 375
Niścaya, 72n.14
*Niśraya*s (ascetic requisites), 26–27, 41n.48, 101n.16, 111, 112, 294, 299, 301, 303, 315, 316, 317
  exceptions to, 27, 41n.48
Nissaya (P.). See *Niśraya*s
Nonreturner. See *Anāgāmin*
Norman, K. R., 79, 99n.1, 237, 427n.26
Northern Buddhism, 119, 377
  evaluation of saints within, 377–78
  images of forest Buddhism in, 131, 136–40
  Mahākāśyapa in. *See* (Mahā)kāśyapa: in Northern Buddhism
  role in Mahāyāna origins, 405–6, 410–12
  texts of, 75n.50
  treatment of supernatural powers in, 224